Lecture Notes in Computer Science 14772

The series Lecture Notes in Computer Science (LNCS), including its subseries Lecture Notes in Artificial Intelligence (LNAI) and Lecture Notes in Bioinformatics (LNBI), has established itself as a medium for the publication of new developments in computer science and information technology research, teaching, and education.

LNCS enjoys close cooperation with the computer science R & D community, the series counts many renowned academics among its volume editors and paper authors, and collaborates with prestigious societies. Its mission is to serve this international community by providing an invaluable service, mainly focused on the publication of conference and workshop proceedings and postproceedings. LNCS commenced publication in 1973.

Markku-Juhani Saarinen · Daniel Smith-Tone
Editors

Post-Quantum Cryptography

15th International Workshop, PQCrypto 2024 Oxford, UK, June 12–14, 2024 Proceedings, Part II

Springer

Editors
Markku-Juhani Saarinen
Tampere University
Tampere, Finland

Daniel Smith-Tone
University of Louisville
Louisville, KY, USA

National Institute of Standards
and Technology
Gaithersburg, MD, USA

ISSN 0302-9743 ISSN 1611-3349 (electronic)
Lecture Notes in Computer Science
ISBN 978-3-031-62745-3 ISBN 978-3-031-62746-0 (eBook)
https://doi.org/10.1007/978-3-031-62746-0

This Springer imprint is published by the registered company Springer Nature Switzerland AG
The registered company address is: Gewerbestrasse 11, 6330 Cham, Switzerland

Preface

PQCrypto 2024, the 15th International Conference on Post-Quantum Cryptography, was held at the Mathematical Institute, University of Oxford, United Kingdom on June 12–14, 2024. The PQCrypto conference series provides a venue for the communication of research results on cryptography under the assumption that large-scale quantum computers are available to adversaries. Since its inception, the conference focus has grown to serve not only academic and theoretical work in post-quantum cryptography but also applied and technical work, further developing the science and advancing the practical aspects of implementation and deployment of post-quantum cryptographic schemes.

PQCrypto 2024 utilized a double-blind review model. Submissions were required to be anonymized for review. 76 papers by 225 authors from 23 countries fulfilled the technical criteria and were accepted for peer review. Each one of these papers was reviewed by at least three members of the program committee. The PQCrypto 2024 program committee consisted of 44 members and additionally 28 subreviewers conducted 31 reviews. The committee then engaged in an intensive discussion phase, conducted online. Through this process, the Program Committee selected a total of 28 papers for inclusion in the technical program and for publication in these proceedings.

The diverse array of accepted articles found in these proceedings discuss multiple research arenas within the scope of the conference, including code-based cryptography, group-action-based cryptography, isogeny-based cryptography, lattice-based cryptography, multivariate cryptography, quantum algorithms, and applications.

The success of this iteration of PQCrypto was due to the efforts of many individuals and organizations. We are indebted to everyone who contributed to making PQCrypto 2024 a success. We owe thanks to the many scientists, engineers, and authors who submitted their work (of notably high average quality) to our conference. We would like to thank all members of the Program Committee and the external reviewers whose commitment and labor-intensive efforts in evaluating and discussing the submissions allowed us to compile a technical program of such high quality.

We thank our hosts, the Mathematical Institute, University of Oxford for excellent conference facilities and support. Our General Chairs Federico Pintore and Ali El Kaafarani created the event, and additionally we would like to thank Elvira Carasol and others at PQShield for local organization. We also wish to express our gratitude to Springer for handling the publication of these conference proceedings.

June 2024

Markku-Juhani Saarinen
Daniel Smith-Tone

Preface

Organization

General Chairs

Ali El Kaafarani	PQShield and University of Oxford, UK
Federico Pintore	University of Trento, Italy

Program Committee Chairs

Markku-Juhani O. Saarinen	Tampere University, Finland and PQShield, UK
Daniel Smith-Tone	National Institute of Standards and Technology, USA and University of Louisville, USA

Program Committee

Magali Bardet	University of Rouen Normandie, France
Daniel J. Bernstein	UIC, USA/RUB, Germany/Academia Sinica, Taiwan
Ward Beullens	IBM, Switzerland
Olivier Blazy	École Polytechnique, France
Katharina Boudgoust	CNRS, Univ Montpellier, LIRMM, France
Daniel Cabarcas	Universidad Nacional de Colombia sede Medellín, Colombia
Ryann Cartor	Clemson University, USA
Sanjit Chatterjee	Indian Institute of Science, India
Anupam Chattopadhyay	Nanyang Technological University, Singapore
Chen-Mou Cheng	BTQ Technologies Corp, Japan
Jung Hee Cheon	Seoul National University, Republic of Korea
Thomas Decru	Université libre de Bruxelles, Belgium
Martin Ekerå	KTH Royal Institute of Technology and Swedish NCSA, Sweden
Thibauld Feneuil	CryptoExperts, France
Scott Fluhrer	Cisco Systems, USA
Philippe Gaborit	University of Limoges, France
Tommaso Gagliardoni	Kudelski Security, Switzerland
Qian Guo	Lund University, Sweden
Michael Hamburg	Rambus Cryptography Research, USA

David Jao	University of Waterloo, Canada
Thomas Johansson	Lund University, Canada
Shuichi Katsumata	PQShield and AIST, Japan
John Kelsey	NIST, USA and KU Leuven, Belgium
Jon-Lark Kim	Sogang University, Republic of Korea
Elena Kirshanova	Technology Innovation Institute, UAE
Dustin Moody	NIST, USA
Ray Perlner	NIST, USA
Edoardo Persichetti	FAU, USA and Sapienza University, Italy
Thomas Pöppelmann	Infineon, Germany
Thomas Prest	PQShield, France
Angela Robinson	NIST, USA
Mélissa Rossi	ANSSI, France
Palash Sarkar	Indian Statistical Institute, India
Nicolas Sendrier	Inria, France
Benjamin Smith	Inria, France
Damien Stehlé	ENS Lyon, France
Rainer Steinwandt	University of Alabama in Huntsville, USA
Tsuyoshi Takagi	University of Tokyo, Japan
Atsushi Takayasu	University of Tokyo, Japan
Jean-Pierre Tillich	Inria, France
Yang Yu	Tsinghua University, China
Yu Yu	Shanghai Jiao Tong University, China
Aaram Yun	Ewha Womans University, Republic of Korea
Rina Zeitoun	IDEMIA, France

Additional Reviewers

Abel Laval
Adrien Vinçotte
Alexander Karenin
Andre Esser
Changmin Lee
Charles Meyer-Hilfiger
Denis Nabokov
Erik Mårtensson
Giulia Gaggero
Huiwen Jia
Hyeongmin Choe
Jesse Elliott
Joel Gärtner
Johan Håstad
Jonas Meers
Karan Khathuria
Keewoo Lee
Matthieu Rivain
Minki Hhan
Minsik Kang
Nicolas Aragon
Olivier Ruatta
Peter Pessl
Takanori Yasuda
Thom Wiggers
Yasuhiko Ikematsu
Youcef Mokrani
Yu Sasaki

Contents – Part II

Quantum Algorithms

Transforms and Proofs

Contents – Part I

Lattice-Based Cryptography

Isogeny-Based Cryptography

Adaptive Attacks Against FESTA Without Input Validation or Constant-Time Implementation

Tomoki Moriya[1], Hiroshi Onuki[2], Maozhi Xu[3(✉)], and Guoqing Zhou[3(✉)]

[1] School of Computer Science, University of Birmingham, Birmingham, UK
t.moriya@bham.ac.uk

[2] Department of Mathematical Informatics, The University of Tokyo, Tokyo, Japan
onuki@mist.i.u-tokyo.ac.jp

[3] School of Mathematical Sciences, Peking University, Beijing, China
{mzxu,zgqsms}@pku.edu.cn

Abstract. A FESTA trapdoor function is an isogeny-based trapdoor function based on an attempt to apply Kani's theorem to cryptography. This paper claims that there are adaptive attacks for a FESTA-based scheme if this scheme does not check the correctness of the input matrix or is not implemented in constant time. Our attacks do not apply to the constant-time implementation of the IND-CCA PKE scheme named FESTA proposed in the FESTA original paper. In this paper, we provide adaptive attacks for a FESTA trapdoor function using auxiliary oracles, which reveals the secret key of the function. These oracles may be constructed if the FESTA trapdoor function is used without validating the input matrix or implemented in non-constant time.

Keywords: Isogeny-based cryptography · FESTA · Kani's theorem · adaptive attack · side-channel attack

1 Introduction

Public key cryptography is an important technology for securing information in present-day society. Currently we rely on RSA [18] and Elliptic Curve Cryptography [12,14] to prevent leakage of our information on the internet. However, Shor showed that quantum computers may be able to break these cryptosystems in polynomial time [20]. Therefore, we need to construct novel cryptosystems to resist the attacks via quantum computers. We refer to such cryptosystems as post-quantum cryptography (PQC).

Isogeny-based cryptography is one of the approaches used for post-quantum cryptography. Cryptosystems based on isogenies have attracted interest from cryptographers due to the compactness of their keys and the elegance of their mathematical structures. Indeed, SIKE [1], which is an isogeny-based key encapsulation scheme based on SIDH [10], survived as an alternative candidate into the 4th round of the NIST PQC standardization process [17]. However, in 2022,

M.-J. Saarinen and D. Smith-Tone (Eds.): PQCrypto 2024, LNCS 14772, pp. 3–19, 2024.
https://doi.org/10.1007/978-3-031-62746-0_1

new results were obtained which break SIDH and cryptosystems related to SIDH [3,13,19]. These studies use Kani's theorem [11], which describes the relationship between an isogeny diagram of elliptic curves and an isogeny of abelian varieties of dimension 2. Although other isogeny-based schemes such as CSIDH (an isogeny-based key exchange scheme) [4] and SQISign (an isogeny-based digital signature scheme) [6] are not directly affected by these attacks, the findings have caused some loss of confidence in isogeny-based cryptography.

On the other hand, Kani's theorem also leads to some novel constructions of isogeny-based schemes. In 2023, Dartois, Leroux, Robert, and Wesolowski proposed a novel isogeny-based digital signature SQISignHD [5], which is based on Kani's theorem and is more compact than SQISign. Subsequently, Basso, Maino, and Pope proposed a novel isogeny-based trapdoor function and a public key encryption (PKE) scheme based on this trapdoor function called FESTA (Fast Encryption from Supersingular Torsion Attacks) [2], which also uses Kani's theorem in a constructive way. Understanding the applications of these new schemes and analyzing their security remains important for the future development of isogeny-based cryptography.

1.1 Contribution

In this paper, we show that there are adaptive attacks if a FESTA trapdoor function is used in the wrong way or implemented in non-constant time. There are several studies of adaptive attacks for SIDH (*e.g.*, [7,8]). We construct a similar attack for a FESTA trapdoor function and related schemes.

As a part of the input of a FESTA trapdoor function, the original FESTA paper proposed a 2×2 diagonal matrix but also mentioned circulant matrices as a possible alternative. In computing the inverse map of the trapdoor function, we usually check whether this 2×2 matrix satisfies the appropriate property: circulant or diagonal. We show that we can construct a specific oracle O for a possible FESTA variant in which the property is not checked, or not checked in constant time, and an adversary can reveal the secret key of the FESTA trapdoor functions by using this oracle.

Note that the constant-time implementation of FESTA is not threatened by our attacks directly because we check the correctness of the ciphertexts in its decryption process.

2 Preliminaries

In this section, we introduce some mathematical concepts and facts.

2.1 Abelian Varieties and Isogenies

This subsection provides some knowledge about abelian varieties and isogenies. Refer to [16] and [21] for more detail.

Let k be a field. We denote the characteristic of k by $\mathrm{ch}(k)$. Let A be an abelian variety over k with an isomorphism $\varphi\colon A \to \hat{A}$, where $\hat{A}$ is the dual abelian variety of A. We call the pair (A, φ) a principally polarised abelian variety over k. In this paper, we often omit the polarisation φ and represent (A, φ) by A. An elliptic curve is a principally polarised abelian variety of dimension 1. Let d be a non-negative integer. The d-torsion subgroup of A is a subgroup of A defined as $\{P \in A \mid dP = 0\}$ over an algebraic closure of k. We denote this group by $A[d]$. If d is coprime to $\mathrm{ch}(k)$, then it holds that

$$A[d] \cong (\mathbb{Z}/d\mathbb{Z})^{2\dim A}.$$

Suppose that $\mathrm{ch}(k) = p$ for a prime number p. Let E be an elliptic curve. If it holds that $E[p] = \{0\}$, we call E a supersingular elliptic curve. If a principally polarised abelian variety A satisfies, as an abelian variety, $A \cong \prod_{i=1}^{\dim A} E_i$ for supersingular elliptic curves $E_1, \ldots, E_{\dim A}$, we call A a superspecial principally polarised abelian variety.

Let A and B be principally polarised abelian varieties. An isogeny $\phi\colon A \to B$ is a morphism between A and B such that ϕ is surjective, ϕ is a group morphism, and the kernel of ϕ is a finite subgroup of A. Let G be a finite subgroup of A. There is a separable isogeny $\phi\colon A \to B$ with $\ker\phi = G$. Moreover, the image variety B is unique up to isomorphism. We denote by A/G a representative of the isomorphism class of a principally polarized abelian variety B. If A is of dimension 1 or 2, there are well-known algorithms to compute an isogeny $A \to A/G$ from given principally polarised abelian variety A and its finite subgroup G (*e.g.*, [23] and [22]). Let ϕ be an isogeny between principally polarised abelian varieties $\phi\colon (A, \varphi_A) \to (B, \varphi_B)$. By the functorial description of $\hat{A}$, we have the isogeny $\tilde{\phi}\colon \hat{B} \to \hat{A}$. The dual isogeny $\hat{\phi}$ of ϕ is the isogeny from B to A defined by $\hat{\phi} = \varphi_A^{-1} \circ \tilde{\phi} \circ \varphi_B$.

2.2 Kani's Theorem

In this subsection, we introduce Kani's theorem provided in [11]. Kani's theorem describes the relationship between an isogeny of products of two elliptic curves and an isogeny diamond of elliptic curves.

Definition 1 (Isogeny diamond). *Let E_0 be an elliptic curve. Let G_1 and G_2 be finite subgroups of E_0 such that $\gcd(\#G_1, \#G_2) = 1$. Then, there is the following commutative diagram:*

$$\begin{array}{ccc} E_0 & \xrightarrow{\phi_1} & E_0/G_1 \\ {\scriptstyle \phi_2}\downarrow & & \downarrow{\scriptstyle [\phi_1]_*\phi_2} \\ E_0/G_2 & \xrightarrow{[\phi_2]_*\phi_1} & E_0/\langle G_1, G_2\rangle \end{array}$$

Here, an isogeny ϕ_1 (resp. an isogeny ϕ_2) is a separable isogeny with $\ker\phi_1 = G_1$ (resp. $\ker\phi_2 = G_2$), and an isogeny $[\phi_2]_*\phi_1$ (resp. an isogeny $[\phi_1]_*\phi_2$) is a separable isogeny with $\ker[\phi_2]_*\phi_1 = \phi_2(G_1)$ (resp. $\ker[\phi_1]_*\phi_2 = \phi_1(G_2)$) satisfying $([\phi_2]_*\phi_1) \circ \phi_2 = ([\phi_1]_*\phi_2) \circ \phi_1$. We call this diagram an isogeny diamond.

Theorem 1 (Kani's theorem [11]). *Suppose that there is an isogeny diamond:*

$$
\begin{array}{ccc}
E_0 & \xrightarrow{\phi_1} & E_1 \\
\phi_2 \downarrow & & \downarrow [\phi_1]_*\phi_2 \\
E_2 & \xrightarrow{[\phi_2]_*\phi_1} & E_3
\end{array}
$$

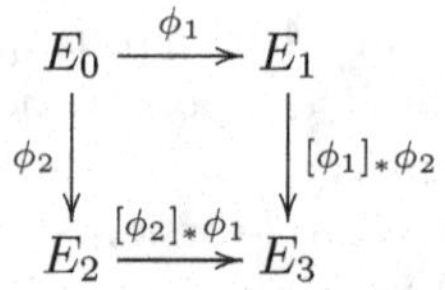

Then, there is an isogeny $\Phi\colon E_2 \times E_1 \to E_0 \times E_3$ *defined as*

$$
\Phi = \begin{pmatrix} \hat{\phi}_2 & -\hat{\phi}_1 \\ [\phi_2]_*\phi_1 & [\phi_1]_*\phi_2 \end{pmatrix}
$$

with $\ker \Phi = \langle (\deg \phi_1 P, \phi_1 \circ \hat{\phi}_2(P)) \mid P \in E_2[\deg \phi_1 + \deg \phi_2] \rangle.$

From Kani's theorem, Robert's attack [19] against SIDH can be abstracted as a generic algorithm that recovers an isogeny $\phi : E_0 \to E_1$ of degree d when it receives the curve E_0, E_1, the degree d, a basis $\{P_0, Q_0\}$ of $E_0[n]$ where $n \geqslant d$, and points $\{P_1 = \phi(P_0), P_2 = \phi(Q_0)\}$. We denote this algorithm as

$$
\mathsf{TorAtk}(E_0, (P_0, Q_0), E_1, (P_1, Q_1), d).
$$

3 FESTA Trapdoor Function

This section introduces an overview of a FESTA trapdoor function [2].

3.1 Construction

The following diagram shows the outline of a FESTA trapdoor function. The public parameter is E_0 and (P_b, Q_b), where E_0 is a supersingular elliptic curve and (P_b, Q_b) is a basis of $E_0[2^b]$. The symbols **A** and **B** represent 2×2 matrices belonging to a set \mathcal{M}_b that is defined as a commutative subgroup of the general linear group $\mathrm{GL}_2(\mathbb{Z}/2^b\mathbb{Z})$. We can use the set of regular circulant matrices or that of regular diagonal matrices for \mathcal{M}_b.

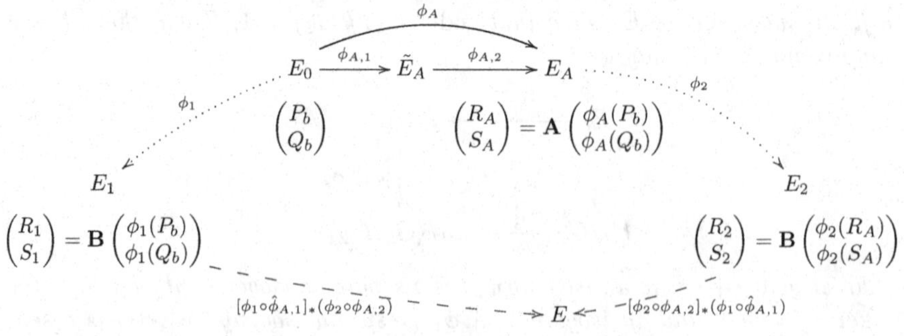

We explain more details of a FESTA trapdoor function:

Public parameter: Let λ be a security parameter. Let $d_1, d_2, d_{A,1}, d_{A,2}, m_1, m_2$ be odd integers such that they are pairwise coprime, $d_1, d_2, (d_{A,1}d_{A,2}) > 2^{2\lambda}$, and there is an integer b with $b > 3\lambda$ satisfying

$$m_1^2 d_{A,1} d_1 + m_2^2 d_{A,2} d_2 = 2^b.$$

Define a prime p as $p = 2^b d_1 d_2 (d_{A,1}d_{A,2})_{\mathsf{sf}} f - 1$, where f is a small positive integer and $(d_{A,1}d_{A,2})_{\mathsf{sf}}$ is the square-free part of $d_{A,1}d_{A,2}$. Let E_0 be a supersingular elliptic curve over $\mathbb{F}_{p^2}$ whose j-invariant is not 1728 or 0. Let (P_b, Q_b) be a basis of $E_0[2^b]$. Define $\mathcal{M}_b$ as a commutative subgroup of $\mathrm{GL}_2(\mathbb{Z}/2^b\mathbb{Z})$.

Public key: We compute a $d_{A,1}$-isogeny $\phi_{A,1}\colon E_0 \to \tilde{E}_A$ and a $d_{A,2}$-isogeny $\phi_{A,2}\colon \tilde{E}_A \to E_A$. Denote $\phi_{A,2} \circ \phi_{A,1}$ by ϕ_A. Take a random matrix $\mathbf{A}$ in $\mathcal{M}_b$. We compute

$$\begin{pmatrix} R_A \\ S_A \end{pmatrix} = \mathbf{A} \cdot \phi_A \begin{pmatrix} P_b \\ Q_b \end{pmatrix}.$$

Here, we denote $(\phi_A(P_b), \phi_A(Q_b))$ by $\phi_A(P_b, Q_b)$ by abuse of notation. Finally, publish (E_A, R_A, S_A) as a public key, and keep $(\mathbf{A}, \phi_{A,1}, \phi_{A,2})$ as a secret.

FESTA trapdoor function: Let ϕ_1 be a d_1-isogeny mapping from E_0 to E_1, and ϕ_2 be a d_2-isogeny mapping from E_A to E_2. Let $\mathbf{B}$ be a matrix in $\mathcal{M}_b$. Compute (R_1, S_1) and (R_2, S_2) such that

$$\begin{pmatrix} R_1 \\ S_1 \end{pmatrix} = \mathbf{B} \cdot \phi_1 \begin{pmatrix} P_b \\ Q_b \end{pmatrix}, \quad \begin{pmatrix} R_2 \\ S_2 \end{pmatrix} = \mathbf{B} \cdot \phi_2 \begin{pmatrix} R_A \\ S_A \end{pmatrix}.$$

Output $(E_1, (R_1, S_1), E_2, (R_2, S_2))$.

Inverse map: We first compute ${}^t(R_2', S_2') = \mathbf{A}^{-1} \cdot {}^t(R_2, S_2)$. Since $\mathbf{AB} = \mathbf{BA}$, it holds that

$$\begin{pmatrix} R_2' \\ S_2' \end{pmatrix} = \mathbf{B} \cdot \phi_2 \circ \phi_A \begin{pmatrix} P_b \\ Q_b \end{pmatrix}.$$

Therefore, from Kani's theorem, the group

$$\langle (m_2 d_{A,2} d_2 R_1, m_1 d_1 R_2'), (m_2 d_{A,2} d_2 S_1, m_1 d_1 S_2') \rangle$$

is the kernel of the $(2^b, 2^b)$-isogeny $\Phi\colon E_1 \times E_2 \to \tilde{E}_A \times E$ defined as

$$\Phi = \begin{pmatrix} m_1 \phi_{A,1} \circ \hat{\phi}_1 & -m_2 \hat{\phi}_{A,2} \circ \hat{\phi}_2 \\ m_2 [\phi_1 \circ \hat{\phi}_{A,1}]_*(\phi_2 \circ \phi_{A,2}) & m_1 [\phi_2 \circ \phi_{A,2}]_*(\phi_1 \circ \hat{\phi}_{A,1}) \end{pmatrix}.$$

Since, the integers $m_1 d_{A,1}$ and $m_2 d_{A,2}$ are coprime to d_1 and d_2 respectively, we have

$$\ker \phi_1 = \hat{\phi}_{A,1} \circ (m_1 \phi_{A,1} \circ \hat{\phi}_1)(E_1[d_1]), \ \ker \phi_2 = \phi_{A,2} \circ (-m_1 \hat{\phi}_{A,2} \circ \hat{\phi}_2)(E_2[d_2]).$$

Hence, we can get ϕ_1 and ϕ_2 by computing the images of $E_1[d_1] \times \{0\}$ and $\{0\} \times E_2[d_2]$ under Φ. If the image of Φ is not a product of two elliptic curves, we output $\perp$. Finally, we compute $(\hat{\phi}_1(R_1), \hat{\phi}_1(S_1))$ and find a matrix $\mathbf{B}$ such that

$$\begin{pmatrix} \hat{\phi}_1(R_1) \\ \hat{\phi}_1(S_1) \end{pmatrix} = d_1 \mathbf{B} \begin{pmatrix} P_b \\ Q_b \end{pmatrix}$$

by the Pohlig-Hellman algorithm. If $\mathbf{B} \notin \mathcal{M}_b$, we output $\perp$. If $\mathbf{B} \in \mathcal{M}_b$, we output $(\mathbf{B}, \phi_1, \phi_2)$.

4 Attack Model

In this section, we explain the attack model that we consider. We use the FESTA notation (the same notation in Sect. 3).

The goal of the adversary is to reveal the secret key of the FESTA trapdoor function f_{E_A,R_A,S_A} (*i.e.*, $\phi_{A,1}$, $\phi_{A,2}$, and $\mathbf{A}$).

4.1 Oracles for the Attack

Let (P_1, Q_1) be a basis of $E_1[2^b]$, and (P_2, Q_2) be a basis of $E_2[2^b]$. We assume that the adversary can access the following oracle O':

$$O'(E_1, (P_1, Q_1), E_2, (P_2, Q_2)) = \begin{cases} 1 & (\text{if } (E_1 \times E_2)/G \cong \tilde{E}_A \times E) \\ 0 & (\text{otherwise}) \end{cases},$$

where

$$G = \langle (m_2 d_{A,2} d_2 P_1, m_1 d_1 P_2'), (m_2 d_{A,2} d_2 Q_1, m_1 d_1 Q_2') \rangle$$

for ${}^t(P_2', Q_2') = \mathbf{A}^{-1} \cdot {}^t(P_2, Q_2)$.

We now provide the context for possible attacks related to this assumption. For example, we can consider an attack for a public key encryption scheme based on FESTA trapdoor function under the following setting:

1. The recipient does not compute $\mathbf{B}$ in the decryption process.
2. The adversary has access to a decryption oracle.

The adversary takes a ciphertext corresponding to $(E_1, (P_1, Q_1), E_2, (P_2, Q_2))$ and sends it to the decryption oracle. If the decryption oracle returns a plaintext μ, the adversary knows $(E_1 \times E_2)/G \cong \tilde{E}_A \times E$, and if it fails to output the correct plaintext μ or refuses the encryption, it knows the ciphertext is incorrect. Therefore, we can construct the oracle O' from the decryption oracle.

From the Kani's theorem, the kernel of the $(2^b, 2^b)$-isogeny $E_1 \times E_2 \to \tilde{E}_A \times E$ is $\langle (m_2 d_{A,2} d_2 P, m_1 \phi_2 \circ \phi_A \circ \hat{\phi}_1(P)) \mid P \in E_1[2^b] \rangle$. Since the number of isomorphism classes of superspecial abelian varieties is $\approx p^3$ if $p \geqslant 7$ (see [9, Theorem 3.3]), we can define an oracle O'' that is heuristically equivalent to O' as follows:

$$O''(E_1, (P_1, Q_1), E_2, (P_2, Q_2)) = \begin{cases} 1 & \left(\text{if } \begin{pmatrix} P_2' \\ Q_2' \end{pmatrix} = \frac{1}{d_1} \phi_2 \circ \phi_A \circ \hat{\phi}_1 \begin{pmatrix} P_1 \\ Q_1 \end{pmatrix}\right) \\ 0 & (\text{otherwise}) \end{cases},$$

where ${}^t(P_2', Q_2') = \mathbf{A}^{-1} \cdot {}^t(P_2, Q_2)$.

Furthermore, we can make the oracle O'' simpler by the following proposition.

Proposition 1. *Let O'' be the oracle defined above, and $\phi_1 : E_0 \to E_1$ and $\phi_2 : E_A \to E_2$ be isogenies of degree d_1 and d_2, respectively. Define $P_1 = \phi_1(P_b)$, $Q_1 = \phi_1(Q_b)$, $P_2 = \phi_2(P_A)$, and $Q_2 = \phi_2(Q_A)$. Then for any matrices $\mathbf{B}', \mathbf{B}'' \in \mathrm{GL}_2(\mathbb{Z}/2^b\mathbb{Z})$,*

$$O''(E_1, (P_1, Q_1)^t\mathbf{B}', E_2, (P_2, Q_2)^t\mathbf{B}'') = 1$$

if and only if $\mathbf{AB}' = \mathbf{B}''\mathbf{A}$.

Proof. By the definition, $O''(E_1, (P_1, Q_1)^t\mathbf{B}', E_2, (P_2, Q_2)^t\mathbf{B}'') = 1$ if and only if

$$\mathbf{A}^{-1}\mathbf{B}'' \begin{pmatrix} P_2 \\ Q_2 \end{pmatrix} = \frac{1}{d_1}\phi_2 \circ \phi_A \circ \hat{\phi}_1 \mathbf{B}' \begin{pmatrix} P_1 \\ Q_1 \end{pmatrix}.$$

The latter equation is equivalent to

$$\mathbf{A}^{-1}\mathbf{B}''\mathbf{A}\phi_2 \circ \phi_A \begin{pmatrix} P_b \\ Q_b \end{pmatrix} = \mathbf{B}'\phi_2 \circ \phi_A \begin{pmatrix} P_b \\ Q_b \end{pmatrix}.$$

Since $(\phi_2 \circ \phi_A(P_b), \phi_2 \circ \phi_A(Q_b))$ is a basis of $E_2[2^b]$, the last equation is equivalent to $\mathbf{AB}' = \mathbf{B}''\mathbf{A}$. □

By the above proposition, we obtain an oracle that returns whether $\mathbf{AB}' = \mathbf{B}''\mathbf{A}$ or not. We denote this by $O(\mathbf{B}', \mathbf{B}'')$.

Remark 1. One may think that we can prevent this attack by using the Weil pairing. Note that we have

$$e_{2^b}(\mathbf{B}' \cdot {}^t(\phi_1(P_b), \phi_1(Q_b))) = e_{2^b}(P_b, Q_b)^{d_1 \det \mathbf{B}'},$$
$$e_{2^b}(\mathbf{B}'' \cdot {}^t(\phi_2(R_A), \phi_2(S_A)) = e_{2^b}(P_b, Q_b)^{d_2 d_{A,1} d_{A,2} \det \mathbf{A} \det \mathbf{B}''}$$

for the Weil pairing e_{2^b}. Therefore, a simple strategy of the countermeasure is to check whether

$$e_{2^b}(P_1, Q_1)^{d_2 d_{A,1} d_{A,2} \det \mathbf{A}} = e_{2^b}(P_2, Q_2)^{d_1},$$

and stop the process if the above equation does not hold. This strategy, however, does not work to prevent our attack, because if $\mathbf{AB}' = \mathbf{B}''\mathbf{A}$, then it holds that $\det \mathbf{B}' = \det \mathbf{B}''$. Therefore, the process always proceeds if the adversary takes $(\mathbf{B}', \mathbf{B}'')$ satisfying $\mathbf{AB}' = \mathbf{B}''\mathbf{A}$, and the adversary can know $\mathbf{AB}' \neq \mathbf{B}''\mathbf{A}$ if the process stops.

4.2 Situations in Which One Can Construct the Oracle

In the previous subsection, we do not have any restriction on the input matrix to the oracle O. However, as mentioned in Sect. 3, the users of a FESTA trapdoor function check whether the matrix $\mathbf{B}$ belongs to $\mathcal{M}_b$ or not after computing the inverse map. This is a problem because our strategies provided in Sect. 5 use matrices not belonging to $\mathcal{M}_b$.

In this subsection, we explain practical situations in which an adversary can construct the oracle in the previous subsection. In this paper, we introduce two situations: the first one is that the user of the function forgets the checking process of the inclusion of the matrix $\mathbf{B}$ in $\mathcal{M}_b$ (thereby failing to validate the matrix), and the second one is that the function is not implemented in constant time.

No Input Validation. The first situation is that the user does not check whether the matrix $\mathbf{B}$ belongs to $\mathcal{M}_b$ or not.

This situation does not occur in the usual use of a FESTA trapdoor function. However, we can provide an easy public key encryption scheme based on a FESTA trapdoor function in which the user does not check the existence of the matrix $\mathbf{B}$ in $\mathcal{M}_b$. The following scheme is one example of such a PKE scheme.

All notations are the same as in the previous sections. Bob (sender) tries to send a message to Alice (recipient).

Public parameters: Take the same parameters as those of the FESTA trapdoor function. In addition, take one basis (P, Q) of $E_0[d_1]$.

Public key: Alice computes ϕ_A and (R_A, S_A), and publishes (E_A, R_A, S_A). She keeps $(\mathbf{A}, \phi_{A,1}, \phi_{A,2})$ as a secret.

Encryption: Bob takes a plaintext μ from $\mathbb{Z}/d_1\mathbb{Z}$. He computes an isogeny ϕ_1 with $\ker\phi_1 = \langle P + \mu Q\rangle$. He takes ϕ_2 and $\mathbf{B}$ at random. He computes $f_{E_A,R_A,S_A}(\mathbf{B}, \phi_1, \phi_2)$ and sends it to Alice as a ciphertext.

Decryption: Alice detects ϕ_1 by computing the inverse map of f_{E_A,R_A,S_A}. It provides a plaintext μ.

Non-constant Time Implementation. The second situation is that a FESTA trapdoor function is not implemented in constant time. In this case, the FESTA trapdoor function is vulnerable to side-channel attacks, which will assist the adversary again in accessing the oracle O.

In the proof-of-concept implementation of FESTA, there are two possible exceptions, with different return values.

Exception 1: the decryption algorithm will throw a 'ValueError' if

$$\mathbf{B}'' \begin{pmatrix} P_2 \\ Q_2 \end{pmatrix} \neq \mathbf{A} \cdot \frac{1}{d_1} \phi_2 \circ \phi_A \circ \widehat{\phi_1}\, \mathbf{B}' \begin{pmatrix} P_1 \\ Q_1 \end{pmatrix},$$

Exception 2: the decryption algorithm will return 'False' if

$$\mathbf{B}'' \begin{pmatrix} P_2 \\ Q_2 \end{pmatrix} = \mathbf{A} \cdot \frac{1}{d_1} \phi_2 \circ \phi_A \circ \widehat{\phi_1}\, \mathbf{B}' \begin{pmatrix} P_1 \\ Q_1 \end{pmatrix}, \text{ but } \mathbf{B}' \notin \mathcal{M}_b.$$

Hence, given a FESTA decryption machine, we can distinguish between these two exceptions by catching 'ValueError'. The two exceptions correspond to two different outputs of oracle O, so anyone who can distinguish between these two exceptions has access to the oracle O.

Note that the difference is quite large between when Exception 1 occurs and when Exception 2 occurs in the number of steps in the decryption algorithm [2, Algorithm 7]. Even though the decryption algorithm returns the same symbol in the above two exceptions, we can still infer the output of the oracle through the running time in the decryption process.

For example, the inputs given in the following proposition lead to different exceptions.

Proposition 2. *Suppose that there is an honest ciphertext of FESTA* $(E_1, (P_1, Q_1), E_2, (P_2, Q_2))$. *The outputs of*

$$\begin{cases} O''(E_1, (P_1 + [2^{b-1}]Q_1, Q_1), E_2, (P_2 + [2^{b-1}]Q_2, Q_2)), \\ O''(E_1, (P_1, Q_1 + [2^{b-1}]P_1), E_2, (P_2 + [2^{b-1}]Q_2, Q_2)) \end{cases}$$

must be different.

Proof. From Proposition 1, it is sufficient to show that only one of the matrices $\begin{pmatrix} 1 & 2^{b-1} \\ 0 & 1 \end{pmatrix} \mathbf{A} \begin{pmatrix} 1 & 2^{b-1} \\ 0 & 1 \end{pmatrix}$ and $\begin{pmatrix} 1 & 2^{b-1} \\ 0 & 1 \end{pmatrix} \mathbf{A} \begin{pmatrix} 1 & 0 \\ 2^{b-1} & 1 \end{pmatrix}$ equals to the secret matrix $\mathbf{A}$ in $\mathrm{GL}_2(\mathbb{Z}/2^b\mathbb{Z})$.

If FESTA uses secret circulant matrices, i.e., $\mathbf{A} = \begin{pmatrix} \gamma & \delta \\ \delta & \gamma \end{pmatrix}$, then

$$\begin{pmatrix} 1 & 2^{b-1} \\ 0 & 1 \end{pmatrix} \mathbf{A} \begin{pmatrix} 1 & 2^{b-1} \\ 0 & 1 \end{pmatrix} = \begin{pmatrix} \gamma + 2^{b-1}\delta & \delta \\ \delta & \gamma + 2^{b-1}\delta \end{pmatrix},$$

$$\text{and } \begin{pmatrix} 1 & 2^{b-1} \\ 0 & 1 \end{pmatrix} \mathbf{A} \begin{pmatrix} 1 & 0 \\ 2^{b-1} & 1 \end{pmatrix} = \begin{pmatrix} \gamma & \delta + 2^{b-1}\gamma \\ \delta + 2^{b-1}\gamma & \gamma \end{pmatrix}.$$

It is known that $\det \boldsymbol{A} = \gamma^2 - \delta^2 \in (\mathbb{Z}/2^b\mathbb{Z})^\times$. It follows that the parity of γ and δ is opposite. Thus only one of the matrices above equals $\mathbf{A}$.

If FESTA uses secret diagonal matrices, i.e., $\mathbf{A} = \begin{pmatrix} \gamma & 0 \\ 0 & \delta \end{pmatrix}$, then

$$\begin{pmatrix} 1 & 2^{b-1} \\ 0 & 1 \end{pmatrix} \mathbf{A} \begin{pmatrix} 1 & 2^{b-1} \\ 0 & 1 \end{pmatrix} = \begin{pmatrix} \gamma & 2^{b-1}(\gamma + \delta) \\ 0 & \delta \end{pmatrix} \xlongequal{\gamma,\delta \in (\mathbb{Z}/2^b\mathbb{Z})^\times} \mathbf{A},$$

$$\text{and } \begin{pmatrix} 1 & 2^{b-1} \\ 0 & 1 \end{pmatrix} \mathbf{A} \begin{pmatrix} 1 & 0 \\ 2^{b-1} & 1 \end{pmatrix} = \begin{pmatrix} \gamma & 2^{b-1}\delta \\ 2^{b-1}\delta & \delta \end{pmatrix} \neq \mathbf{A}.$$

□

The two inputs in the above proposition lead to different outputs of oracle O'', thereby, different exceptions in decryption process. The adversary who records the running time in the decryption process with above two inputs can distinguish between two exceptions. On a single performance core of an AMD Ryzen 7 7840H CPU, the average running time in the decryption process when Exception 1 occurs is 6.682 s, while that when Exception 2 occurs is 10.474 s. It is feasible to distinguish between these two exceptions.

Therefore, if FESTA is not implemented in constant time, then the adversary has the ability to distinguish between two exceptions, which means he can access the oracle O.

4.3 Settings

We use the same notation as in Sect. 3. We assume that $b > 3$.

We consider the two cases for $\mathcal{M}_b$. The first one is that $\mathcal{M}_b$ is the group of regular circulant matrices over $\mathbb{Z}/2^b\mathbb{Z}$. I.e.,

$$\mathcal{M}_b = \left\{ \begin{pmatrix} \alpha & \beta \\ \beta & \alpha \end{pmatrix} \;\middle|\; \alpha, \beta \in \mathbb{Z}/2^b\mathbb{Z},\ \alpha^2 - \beta^2 \in (\mathbb{Z}/2^b\mathbb{Z})^\times \right\}.$$

The second one is that $\mathcal{M}_b$ is the group of regular diagonal matrices over $\mathbb{Z}/2^b\mathbb{Z}$. I.e.,

$$\mathcal{M}_b = \left\{ \begin{pmatrix} \alpha & 0 \\ 0 & \beta \end{pmatrix} \;\middle|\; \alpha, \beta \in (\mathbb{Z}/2^b\mathbb{Z})^\times \right\}.$$

Put $\mathbf{A}$ as

$$\mathbf{A} = \begin{pmatrix} \gamma & \delta \\ \delta & \gamma \end{pmatrix} \quad \text{or} \quad \mathbf{A} = \begin{pmatrix} \gamma & 0 \\ 0 & \delta \end{pmatrix}.$$

By using the Weil pairing for (P_b, Q_b) and (P_A, Q_A), we can detect $\det \mathbf{A}$. If $\mathbf{C}$ is a matrix in $\mathcal{M}_b$ with $\det \mathbf{C} = \det \mathbf{A}^{-1}$, then $O(\mathbf{CB}', \mathbf{B}''\mathbf{C}) = 1$ if and only if $(\mathbf{AC})\mathbf{B}' = \mathbf{B}''(\mathbf{AC})$. Therefore, we can assume that $\det \mathbf{A} = 1$ since $\det \mathbf{AC} = 1$.

Let $\gamma_0, \ldots, \gamma_{b-1}, \delta_0, \ldots, \delta_{b-1}$ be values in $\{0, 1\}$ such that

$$\gamma = \gamma_0 2^0 + \gamma_1 2^1 + \cdots + \gamma_{b-1} 2^{b-1},$$
$$\delta = \delta_0 2^0 + \delta_1 2^1 + \cdots + \delta_{b-1} 2^{b-1}.$$

By Robert's attack [19], detecting $\mathbf{A}$ or $-\mathbf{A}$ reveals the secret key of the FESTA trapdoor function.

Remark 2. If we know $\mathbf{A}$, we obtain the secret key by generating a random ciphertext and decrypting it. Therefore, in the FESTA setting, we do not need Robert's attack. The reason why we adopt Robert's attack is that we may need it in more general cases (*e.g.*, IS-CUBE [15]).

Note that not all bits of secret matrix $\mathbf{A}$ need to be recovered since the degree d_A of secret isogeny ϕ_A is much smaller than the order 2^b of the torsion points in FESTA. The concrete parameters proposed by [2] are as shown in the following Table 1. If we use the 2-dimensional attack TorAtk then it suffices to recover $\lceil \log_2 d_A \rceil$ bits of $\mathbf{A}$ since we know the endomorphism ring of E_0 in FESTA. In addition, if we use Robert's 8-dimensional attack [19] then we can reduce the number of bits recovered to $\lceil (\log_2 d_A)/2 \rceil$. We let b' be $\lceil \log_2 d_A \rceil$ or $\lceil (\log_2 d_A)/2 \rceil$ depending on the dimension of the attack we use. Note that it always holds that $b' < \frac{b}{2}$.

Recalling that the key-generation process of FESTA, points R_A and S_A in the public key satisfy $\begin{pmatrix} R_A \\ S_A \end{pmatrix} = \mathbf{A} \begin{pmatrix} \phi_A(P_b) \\ \phi_A(Q_b) \end{pmatrix}$. Thus, for a matrix $\mathbf{A}_1 \equiv \mathbf{A} \bmod 2^{b'}$,

$$\begin{pmatrix} [2^{b-b'}]R_A \\ [2^{b-b'}]S_A \end{pmatrix} = \mathbf{A} \begin{pmatrix} \phi_A([2^{b-b'}]P_b) \\ \phi_A([2^{b-b'}]Q_b) \end{pmatrix} = \mathbf{A}_1 \begin{pmatrix} \phi_A([2^{b-b'}]P_b) \\ \phi_A([2^{b-b'}]Q_b) \end{pmatrix}.$$

Table 1. FESTA parameters

Security	$\log_2 d_A \in$	$b =$
FESTA-128	$(272, 273)$	632
FESTA-192	$(386, 387)$	992
FESTA-256	$(525, 526)$	1472

If we recover matrix $\mathbf{A}_1$, then we can get the secret isogeny ϕ_A from TorAtk or Robert's 8-dimensional attack. Therefore, the matrix A_1 is sufficient for the attack. It means that it suffices to detect values

$$\gamma_0, \ldots, \gamma_{b'-1}, \delta_0, \ldots, \delta_{b'-1}$$

to attack the FESTA trapdoor functions. Thus, we assume that the adversary tries to detect these values instead of the secret key.

5 Strategies

In this section, we provide our adaptive attacks for a FESTA trapdoor function. We consider two types of adversaries $\mathcal{A}_1$ and $\mathcal{A}_2$. They both have access to the oracle O. The adversary $\mathcal{A}_1$ has the ability to generate ciphertexts himself, while $\mathcal{A}_2$ only has knowledge of some given ciphertexts.

5.1 Circulant Matrices

We first explain the case that we use circulant matrices. I.e.,

$$\mathbf{A} = \begin{pmatrix} \gamma & \delta \\ \delta & \gamma \end{pmatrix} \in \mathrm{GL}_2(\mathbb{Z}/2^b\mathbb{Z}), \ \gamma^2 - \delta^2 = 1.$$

From the analysis in Sect. 4.3, it suffices to find $\gamma \pmod{2^{b'}}$ and $\delta \pmod{2^{b'}}$ for detecting $\mathbf{A}_1 \equiv \mathbf{A} \pmod{2^{b'}}$.

For the Adversary $\mathcal{A}_1$. Let $\varepsilon_1, \varepsilon_2$ be elements in $\mathbb{Z}/2^b\mathbb{Z}$ such that $\mathbf{B} + \begin{pmatrix} \varepsilon_1 & 0 \\ \varepsilon_2 & 0 \end{pmatrix}$ is regular for some $\mathbf{B} \in \mathcal{M}_b$ (*i.e.*, at least one of ε_1 and ε_2 is even). Then we have

$$\mathbf{A}\left(\mathbf{B} + \begin{pmatrix} \varepsilon_1 & 0 \\ \varepsilon_2 & 0 \end{pmatrix}\right) = \left(\mathbf{B} + \begin{pmatrix} 0 & 0 \\ \varepsilon_2 & \varepsilon_1 \end{pmatrix}\right)\mathbf{A} \quad \text{if and only if } \varepsilon_1\gamma + \varepsilon_2\delta = 0.$$

Therefore, by our oracle O, we can determine whether $\varepsilon_1\gamma + \varepsilon_2\delta = 0$ for any $\varepsilon_1, \varepsilon_2 \in \mathbb{Z}/2^b\mathbb{Z}$ such that at least one of ε_1 and ε_2 is even. We denote an oracle checking $\varepsilon_1\gamma + \varepsilon_2\delta = 0$ by $O_{\mathsf{coeff}}(\varepsilon_1, \varepsilon_2)$.

At first, the adversary determines (γ_0, δ_0). Note that $\gamma_0 \neq \delta_0$ since $\gamma^2 - \delta^2 = 1$. Since $2^{b-1}\gamma = 2^{b-1}\gamma_0$, the adversary obtains γ_0 by checking $O_{\mathsf{coeff}}(2^{b-1}, 0)$.

Without loss of generality, we can assume $\gamma_0 = 1$ because we can swap γ and δ by multiplying $\begin{pmatrix} 0 & 1 \\ 1 & 0 \end{pmatrix}$ to $\mathbf{B}'$ and $\mathbf{B}''$ from left and right, respectively.

We next discuss how to determine (γ_1, δ_1). In fact, we do not need to find the "correct" value of γ_1. Robert's attack also works if the adversary detects $(-\gamma, -\delta)$ instead of (γ, δ). Therefore, we can assume $\gamma_1 = 0$ since $\gamma_0 = 1$. Note that we assume that $b > 3$. We have $(\gamma^{(1)})^2 - (\delta^{(1)})^2 \equiv 1 \pmod{2^3}$ since $\gamma^2 - \delta^2 = 1$. Therefore, it holds that $\delta_1 = 0$.

We denote $\sum_{i=0}^{k} \gamma_i 2^i$ by $\gamma^{(k)}$ and use the same notation for δ. For detecting $\mathbf{A}_1$, we define the following two procedures:

1. $\mathsf{GetDelta}_k$: Require $\gamma^{(k-1)}$ and $\delta^{(k-1)}$ with $k \in [2, b'-1]$, and ensure δ_k,
2. $\mathsf{GetGamma}_k$: Require $\gamma^{(k-1)}$ and $\delta^{(k-1)}$ with $k \in [2, b'-1]$, and ensure γ_k.

The details of these procedures for the adversary $\mathcal{A}_1$ are as follows:

GetDelta$_k$: Note that $\delta^{(k-1)} \equiv 0 \pmod 2$. Therefore, it holds that

$$\begin{aligned} U_k &= -2^{b-k-1}\delta^{(k-1)} \cdot \gamma + 2^{b-k-1}\gamma^{(k-1)} \cdot \delta \\ &= 2^{b-k-1}(-\delta^{(k-1)}(\gamma^{(k-1)} + \gamma_k 2^k) + \gamma^{(k-1)}(\delta^{(k-1)} + \delta_k 2^k)) \\ &= \delta_k 2^{b-1}. \end{aligned} \tag{1}$$

Hence, the output of $O_{\text{coeff}}(-2^{b-k-1}\delta^{(k-1)}, 2^{b-k-1}\gamma^{(k-1)})$ returns TRUE if and only if $\delta_k = 0$.

GetGamma$_k$: Note that $\delta + \delta^{(k-1)} \equiv 0 \pmod{2^2}$ and $k \leqslant b-2$. We have

$$\begin{aligned} \gamma^2 - (\delta^{(k-1)})^2 &= 1 + \delta^2 - (\delta^{(k-1)})^2 \\ &= 1 + (\delta + \delta^{(k-1)}) \sum_{i=k}^{b-1} \delta_i 2^i \equiv 1 \pmod{2^{k+2}}. \end{aligned}$$

Therefore, the adversary knows $\gamma^2 \bmod 2^{k+2}$ by computing $1 + (\delta^{(k-1)})^2 \bmod 2^{k+2}$. This value is determined by $\gamma^{(k-1)}$ and γ_k. In particular, it holds that

$$\gamma^2 = \left(\gamma^{(k-1)} + 2^k \sum_{i=k}^{b-1} \gamma_i 2^{i-k-1}\right)^2 \equiv (\gamma^{(k-1)})^2 + \gamma_k 2^{k+1} \pmod{2^{k+2}}$$

since $k \geqslant 2$. Hence, the adversary can find γ_k.

Remark 3. As noted in Sect. 4, we need to assume that the recipient does not compute $\mathbf{B}$ in the decryption process. Indeed, the incorrect input

$$\mathbf{B} + 2^{b-k-1}\begin{pmatrix} -\delta^{(k-1)} & 0 \\ \gamma^{(k-1)} & 0 \end{pmatrix},$$

which appears in $\mathsf{GetDelta_k}$, does not belong to $\mathcal{M}_b$.

For the Adversary $\mathcal{A}_2$. Given an honest ciphertext $(E_1, (P_1, Q_1), E_2, (P_2, Q_2))$, the adversary recovers the secret matrix as follows.

To recover first bits (γ_0, δ_0), we select malicious matrices $\mathbf{B}'_0 = \mathbf{B}''_0 = \begin{pmatrix} 1 & 2^{b-1} \\ 0 & 1 \end{pmatrix}$, then from the proof of Proposition 2, we have $\mathbf{B}''^{-1}_0 \mathbf{A} \mathbf{B}'_0 = \mathbf{A}$ if and only if $\delta_0 = 0$. Exploiting the fact that only one of γ and δ is even, after querying oracle once, we can recover (γ_0, δ_0).

As in the case of the adversary $\mathcal{A}_1$, we can assume γ is odd without loss of generality. Since the (γ, δ) and $(-\gamma, -\delta)$ both work in the attack, we can also assume that $\gamma_1 = 0$ and $\delta_1 = 0$.

To recover other bits, we also construct procedures $\mathsf{GetDelta}_k$ and $\mathsf{GetGamma}_k$ for the adversary $\mathcal{A}_2$.

$\mathsf{GetDelta}_k$: We select malicious matrices

$$\mathbf{B}'_k = \begin{pmatrix} 1 + 2^{b-k-2}\delta^{(k-1)} & 2^{b-k-1}\gamma^{(k-1)} \\ 0 & 1 - 2^{b-k-2}\delta^{(k-1)} \end{pmatrix},$$

$$\mathbf{B}''_k = \begin{pmatrix} 1 - 2^{b-k-2}\delta^{(k-1)} & 2^{b-k-1}\gamma^{(k-1)} \\ 0 & 1 + 2^{b-k-2}\delta^{(k-1)} \end{pmatrix}.$$

Then $k \leqslant b' - 1 < \frac{b}{2} - 1$, $2(b - k - 1) \geqslant b$ and it can be computed that in $\mathrm{GL}_2(\mathbb{Z}/2^b\mathbb{Z})$,

$$\mathbf{B}''^{-1}_k \mathbf{A} \mathbf{B}'_k = \begin{pmatrix} \gamma + U_k & \delta \\ \delta & \gamma - U_k \end{pmatrix},$$

where U_k is defined in equation (1). Hence,

$$O(\mathbf{B}'_k, \mathbf{B}''_k) = 1 \Longleftrightarrow \mathbf{B}''^{-1}_k \mathbf{A} \mathbf{B}'_k = \mathbf{A} \Longleftrightarrow \delta_k = 0.$$

$\mathsf{GetGamma}_k$: Use the same **$\mathsf{GetGamma}_k$** as for the adversary $\mathcal{A}_1$.

By using the above two procedures, two types of adversaries can both detect $\mathbf{A}_1$. The following is the outline of our strategies for determining $\mathbf{A}_1$.

1. The adversary $\mathcal{A}_1$ finds γ_0 from checking $O_{\text{coeff}}(2^{b-1}, 0)$, and the adversary $\mathcal{A}_2$ finds γ_0 from the output of $O(\mathbf{B}'_0, \mathbf{B}''_0)$. We can assume $\gamma_0 = 1$ and $\delta_0 = 0$ by swapping γ and δ.
2. Set $\gamma_1 = \delta_1 = 0$.
3. For $k = 2, \ldots, b' - 1$:
   a) Determine δ_k by $\mathsf{GetDelta}_k$.
   b) Determine γ_k by $\mathsf{GetGamma}_k$.
4. Output the matrix $\mathbf{A}_1 = \begin{pmatrix} \gamma^{(b'-1)} & \delta^{(b'-1)} \\ \delta^{(b'-1)} & \gamma^{(b'-1)} \end{pmatrix}$.

From the above steps, two types of adversaries can know the matrix $\mathbf{A}_1$ in $b' - 1$ queries to the oracle O.

5.2 Diagonal Matrices

We now explain the case that we use diagonal matrices. I.e.,

$$\mathbf{A} = \begin{pmatrix} \gamma & 0 \\ 0 & \delta \end{pmatrix} \in \mathrm{GL}_2(\mathbb{Z}/2^b\mathbb{Z}),\ \gamma\delta = 1.$$

From the analysis in Sect. 4.3, it suffices to find $\gamma \pmod{2^{b'}}$ for detecting $\mathbf{A}_1 \equiv \mathbf{A} \pmod{2^{b'}}$.

For the Adversary $\mathcal{A}_1$. Let $\varepsilon_1, \varepsilon_2$ be elements in $\mathbb{Z}/2^b\mathbb{Z}$. Then, for any diagonal matrix $\mathbf{B}$, we have

$$\mathbf{A}\left(\mathbf{B} + \begin{pmatrix} 0 & 0 \\ \varepsilon_2 & 0 \end{pmatrix}\right) = \left(\mathbf{B} + \begin{pmatrix} 0 & 0 \\ \varepsilon_1 & 0 \end{pmatrix}\right)\mathbf{A} \quad \text{if and only if } \varepsilon_1\gamma = \varepsilon_2\delta.$$

Therefore, by our oracle O, we can determine whether $\varepsilon_1\gamma^2 - \varepsilon_2 = 0$ for any $\varepsilon_1, \varepsilon_2 \in \mathbb{Z}/2^b\mathbb{Z}$. We denote an oracle checking $\varepsilon_1\gamma^2 - \varepsilon_2 = 0$ by $O_{\mathrm{coeff}}(\varepsilon_1, \varepsilon_2)$.

It is clear that $\gamma_0 = 1$. Since Robert's attack also works if the adversary detects $-\gamma$ instead of γ, we can assume $\gamma_1 = 0$ without loss of generality.

We denote $\sum_{i=0}^{k} \gamma_i 2^i$ by $\gamma^{(k)}$. For detecting $\mathbf{A}_1$, we define the following procedure for the adversary $\mathcal{A}_1$:

- $\mathsf{GetGamma}_k$: Require $\gamma^{(k-1)}$ with $k \in [2, b'-1]$, and ensure γ_k.

$\mathsf{GetGamma}_k$: Since $\gamma + \gamma^{(k-1)} \equiv 2 \pmod{2^2}$, we have

$$\begin{aligned} 2^{b-k-2}\gamma^2 - 2^{b-k-2}(\gamma^{(k-1)})^2 &= 2^{b-2}(\gamma_k + \gamma_{k+1}2)(\gamma + \gamma^{(k-1)}) \\ &= \gamma_k 2^{b-1}. \end{aligned} \tag{2}$$

Therefore, the output of $O_{\mathrm{coeff}}(2^{b-k-2}, 2^{b-k-2}(\gamma^{(k-1)})^2)$ is TRUE if and only if $\gamma_k = 0$. Hence, the adversary can obtain γ_k.

For the Adversary $\mathcal{A}_2$. Given an honest ciphertext $(E_1, (P_1, Q_1), E_2, (P_2, Q_2))$, he recovers the secret matrix as follows.

It is known that the first bits $\gamma_0 = 1$. We can also assume that $\gamma_1 = 0$ since the (γ, δ) and $(-\gamma, -\delta)$ both work in the attack.

To recover the other bits, we also construct the procedure $\mathsf{GetGamma}_k$ for the adversary $\mathcal{A}_2$.

$\mathsf{GetGamma}_k$: Since $\gamma\delta \equiv 1 \pmod{2^2}$, we have $\gamma - \delta \equiv 0 \pmod{2^2}$. For $2 \leqslant k \leqslant b' - 1$, we select malicious matrices

$$\mathbf{B}'_k = \begin{pmatrix} 1 + (\gamma^{(k-1)})^2 2^{b-k-2} & 2^{b-k-2} \\ -(\gamma^{(k-1)})^2 2^{b-k-2} & 1 - 2^{b-k-2} \end{pmatrix},$$

$$\mathbf{B}''_k = \begin{pmatrix} 1 + 2^{b-k-2} & (\gamma^{(k-1)})^2 2^{b-k-2} \\ -2^{b-k-2} & 1 - (\gamma^{(k-1)})^2 2^{b-k-2} \end{pmatrix}.$$

Then $(2^{b-k-2})^2(\gamma-\delta)=0$ and it can be computed that in $\mathrm{GL}_2(\mathbb{Z}/2^b\mathbb{Z})$,

$$\mathbf{B}_k''^{-1}\mathbf{A}\mathbf{B}_k' = \begin{pmatrix} \gamma & V_k \\ V_k & \delta \end{pmatrix},$$

where

$$\begin{aligned} V_k &= 2^{b-k-2}\cdot\gamma - (\gamma^{(k-1)})^2 2^{b-k-2}\cdot\delta && \text{(by equation (2))} \\ &= \gamma^{-1}2^{b-k-2}\cdot(\gamma^2-(\gamma^{(k-1)})^2) \\ &= \gamma^{-1}\gamma_k 2^{b-1} \\ &= \gamma_k 2^{b-1}. \end{aligned}$$

It means that

$$O(\mathbf{B}_k', \mathbf{B}_k'') = 1 \iff \mathbf{B}_k''^{-1}\mathbf{A}\mathbf{B}_k' = \mathbf{A} \iff \gamma_k = 0.$$

Hence, the adversary can obtain γ_k.

By using the above two procedures, two types of adversaries can both detect $\mathbf{A}_1$. The following is the outline of our strategies to determine $\mathbf{A}_1$.

1. Set $\gamma_0 = 1$ and $\gamma_1 = 0$.
2. For $k = 2, \ldots, b'-1$, determine γ_k by $\mathsf{GetGamma}_k$.
3. Output the matrix $\mathbf{A}_1 = \begin{pmatrix} \gamma^{(b'-1)} & 0 \\ 0 & (\gamma^{(b'-1)})^{-1} \bmod 2^{b'} \end{pmatrix}$.

From the above steps, two types of adversaries can both know the matrix $\mathbf{A}_1$ in $b'-2$ queries to the oracle O.

6 Conclusion

We showed that adaptive attacks might be viable if a FESTA trapdoor function is used in the wrong way or implemented in non-constant time. These attacks reveal its secret key.

For our attacks, we need an oracle that judges whether a correct $(2^b, 2^b)$-isogeny can be calculated in the process of computing the inverse map of the FESTA trapdoor function from a given input. We showed that this oracle could be constructed if the FESTA trapdoor function is used without input validation (*i.e.*, the recipient does not check in the decryption process whether the sender's matrix $\mathbf{B}$ belongs to the fixed group $\mathcal{M}_b$) or is not implemented in constant time.

The constant-time implementation of IND-CCA secure PKE scheme named FESTA proposed in [2] is not affected by our adaptive attacks.

Acknowledgements. The authors would like to thank Andrea Basso, Luciano Maino, Giacomo Pope, and the anonymous referees for helpful comments on an earlier raft of this paper. This work was supported by the National Key R&D Program of China under Grant No. 2022YFB2703000, the National Natural Science Foundation of China under Grants Nos. 62072011 and 61672059, EPSRC through grant EP/V011324/1 and in part conducted under a contract of "Research and development on new generation cryptography for secure wireless communication services" among "Research and Development for Expansion of Radio Wave Resources (JPJ000254)", which was supported by the Ministry of Internal Affairs and Communications, Japan.

References

1. Azarderakhsh, R., et al.: Supersingular isogeny key encapsulation. In: Submission to the NIST Post-Quantum Standardization project (2017)
2. Basso, A., Maino, L., Pope, G.: FESTA: fast encryption from supersingular torsion attacks. In: Guo, J., Steinfeld, R. (eds.) ASIACRYPT 2023. LNCS, vol. 14444, pp. 98–126. Springer, Singapore (2023). https://doi.org/10.1007/978-981-99-8739-9_4
3. Castryck, W., Decru, T.: An efficient key recovery attack on SIDH. In: Hazay, C., Stam, M. (eds.) EUROCRYPT 2023. LNCS, vol. 14008, pp. 423–447. Springer, Cham (2023). https://doi.org/10.1007/978-3-031-30589-4_15
4. Castryck, W., Lange, T., Martindale, C., Panny, L., Renes, J.: CSIDH: an efficient post-quantum commutative group action. In: Peyrin, T., Galbraith, S. (eds.) ASIACRYPT 2018. LNCS, vol. 11274, pp. 395–427. Springer, Cham (2018). https://doi.org/10.1007/978-3-030-03332-3_15
5. Dartois, P., Leroux, A., Robert, D., Wesolowski, B.: SQIsignHD: new dimensions in cryptography. In: Joye, M., Leander, G. (eds.) EUROCRYPT 2024. LNCS, vol. 14651, pp. 3–32. Springer, Cham (2023). https://doi.org/10.1007/978-3-031-58716-0_1, https://ia.cr/2023/436
6. De Feo, L., Kohel, D., Leroux, A., Petit, C., Wesolowski, B.: SQISign: compact post-quantum signatures from quaternions and isogenies. In: Moriai, S., Wang, H. (eds.) ASIACRYPT 2020. LNCS, vol. 12491, pp. 64–93. Springer, Cham (2020). https://doi.org/10.1007/978-3-030-64837-4_3
7. Fouotsa, T.B., Petit, C.: A new adaptive attack on SIDH. In: Galbraith, S.D. (ed.) CT-RSA 2022. LNCS, vol. 13161, pp. 322–344. Springer, Cham (2022). https://doi.org/10.1007/978-3-030-95312-6_14
8. Galbraith, S.D., Petit, C., Shani, B., Ti, Y.B.: On the security of supersingular isogeny cryptosystems. In: Cheon, J.H., Takagi, T. (eds.) ASIACRYPT 2016. LNCS, vol. 10031, pp. 63–91. Springer, Heidelberg (2016). https://doi.org/10.1007/978-3-662-53887-6_3
9. Ibukiyama, T., Katsura, T., Oort, F.: Supersingular curves of genus two and class numbers. Compos. Math. **57**(2), 127–152 (1986)
10. Jao, D., De Feo, L.: Towards quantum-resistant cryptosystems from supersingular elliptic curve isogenies. In: Yang, B.-Y. (ed.) PQCrypto 2011. LNCS, vol. 7071, pp. 19–34. Springer, Heidelberg (2011). https://doi.org/10.1007/978-3-642-25405-5_2
11. Kani, E.: The number of curves of genus two with elliptic differentials (1997)
12. Koblitz, N.: Elliptic curve cryptosystems. Math. Comput. **48**, 203–209 (1987)
13. Maino, L., Martindale, C., Panny, L., Pope, G., Wesolowski, B.: A direct key recovery attack on SIDH. In: Hazay, C., Stam, M. (eds.) EUROCRYPT 2023.

LNCS, vol. 14008, pp. 448–471. Springer, Cham (2023). https://doi.org/10.1007/978-3-031-30589-4_16
14. Miller, V.S.: Use of elliptic curves in cryptography. In: Williams, H.C. (ed.) CRYPTO 1985. LNCS, vol. 218, pp. 417–426. Springer, Heidelberg (1986). https://doi.org/10.1007/3-540-39799-X_31
15. Moriya, T.: IS-CUBE: An isogeny-based compact KEM using a boxed SIDH diagram (2023). https://eprint.iacr.org/2023/1516
16. Mumford, D., Ramanujam, C.P., Manin, J.I.: Abelian Varieties, vol. 5. Oxford University Press, Oxford (1974)
17. National Institute of Standards and Technology. Post–quantum cryptography standardization. https://csrc.nist.gov/Projects/post-quantum-cryptography/round-4-submissions
18. Rivest, R.L., Shamir, A., Adleman, L.: A method for obtaining digital signatures and public-key cryptosystems. Commun. ACM **21**, 120–126 (1978)
19. Robert, D.: Breaking SIDH in polynomial time. In: Hazay, C., Stam, M. (eds.) EUROCRYPT 2023. LNCS, vol. 14008, pp. 472–503. Springer, Cham (2023). https://doi.org/10.1007/978-3-031-30589-4_17
20. Shor, P.W.: Algorithms for quantum computation: Discrete logarithms and factoring. In: Proceedings 35th Annual Symposium on Foundations of Computer Science - FOCS 1994, pp. 124–134. IEEE (1994)
21. Silverman, J.H.: The Arithmetic of Elliptic Curves, vol. 106. Springer, New York (2009). https://doi.org/10.1007/978-0-387-09494-6
22. Smith, B.: Explicit endomorphisms and correspondences. PhD thesis, University of Sydney (2005)
23. Vélu, J.: Isogénies entre courbes elliptiques. CR Acad. Sci. Paris Sér. A **273**(5), 238–241 (1971)

Updatable Encryption from Group Actions

Antonin Leroux[1,2] and Maxime Roméas[3(✉)]

[1] DGA-MI, Bruz, France
[2] IRMAR, UMR 6625, Université de Rennes, Rennes, France
antonin.leroux@polytechnique.org
[3] ANSSI, Paris, France
maxime.romeas@ssi.gouv.fr

Abstract. Updatable Encryption (UE) allows to rotate the encryption key in the outsourced storage setting while minimizing the bandwith used. The server can update ciphertexts to the new key using a token provided by the client. UE schemes should provide strong confidentiality guarantees against an adversary that can corrupt keys and tokens.

This paper studies the problem of building UE in the group action framework. We introduce a new notion of Mappable Effective Group Action (MEGA) and show that we can build CCA secure UE from a MEGA by generalizing the SHINE construction of Boyd *et al.* at Crypto 2020. Unfortunately, we do not know how to instantiate this new construction in the post-quantum setting. Doing so would solve the open problem of building a CCA secure post-quantum UE scheme.

Isogeny-based group actions are the most studied post-quantum group actions. Unfortunately, the resulting group actions are not mappable. We show that we can still build UE from isogenies by introducing a new algebraic structure called Effective Triple Orbital Group Action (ETOGA). We prove that UE can be built from an ETOGA and show how to instantiate this abstract structure from isogeny-based group actions. This new construction solves two open problems in ciphertext-independent post-quantum UE. First, this is the first post-quantum UE scheme that supports an unbounded number of updates. Second, our isogeny-based UE scheme is the first post-quantum UE scheme not based on lattices. The security of this new scheme holds under an extended version of the weak pseudorandomness of the standard isogeny group action.

Keywords: Updatable Encryption · Group Actions · Isogenies · Post-Quantum Cryptography

1 Introduction

Updatable Encryption (UE), introduced by Boneh *et al.* in 2013 [6], is a variant of symmetric encryption that is useful for storing encrypted data on an untrusted cloud server. To fight against risks of seeing the secret key compromised, the client can always download its data, decrypt it, encrypt it under a new key and upload it back on the server. However, this solution uses too much bandwith to

M.-J. Saarinen and D. Smith-Tone (Eds.): PQCrypto 2024, LNCS 14772, pp. 20–53, 2024.
https://doi.org/10.1007/978-3-031-62746-0_2

be considered practical. Dealing with key rotation while minimizing bandwith usage is the goal of UE. This work focuses on the *ciphertext-independent* variant of UE, where the client generates a single value, called a *token*, when rotating its key. This token can then be used by the server to update all of the client's ciphertexts under the latest key. Unlike symmetric encryption, UE schemes aim at preserving the confidentiality of the data in a setting where secret keys and update tokens can leak. The huge real-life applications of UE explains the recent renewed interest on the subject [8, 23–25, 30].

Related Work on UE. Security notions for UE have evolved a lot since the original proposal of [6]. Lehmann and Tackmann [25] proposed two CPA security notions where the adversary can adaptively corrupt keys and tokens. Their IND-ENC notion requires fresh encryptions to be indistinguishable and their IND-UPD notion asks the same for updated ciphertexts. Klooß *et al.* [24] augmented the previous notions with CCA security and integrity protection. Boyd *et al.* [8] introduced the IND-UE notion which is stronger than previous ones and requires fresh encryptions to be indistinguishable from updated ciphertexts. They also show that a CPA UE scheme with ciphertext integrity (CTXT) is CCA-secure.

As for UE constructions in the classical setting, RISE of [25], is an updatable variant of ElGamal where the public key is used in the token. [24] introduced two generic constructions based on encrypt-and-MAC (secure under DDH) and on the Naor-Yung transform (secure under SXDH). Boyd *et al.* [8] proposed the permutation-based SHINE schemes, that achieve their stronger detIND-UE-CCA security notion in the ideal cipher model (under DDH).

In the post-quantum setting, Jiang [23] presented the first post-quantum UE scheme LWEUE (secure under LWE). In [30], Nishimaki introduced RtR, another LWE-based UE scheme, which is the first ciphertext-independent UE scheme that prevents the adversary from obtaining the new key from the knowledge of the update token and the old key. Nishimaki showed that UE schemes with this property, called *unidirectional* UE schemes, have stronger security than those without. Unlike RtR, the UE schemes introduced in this work are not unidirectional. Such schemes have been obtained from the DDH assumption [27]. However, it is not clear how to achieve unidirectional UE with post-quantum group actions. Finally, the LWE-based UE schemes LWEUE and RtR use homomorphic operations to re-randomize updated ciphertexts which has two main drawbacks. On one hand, ciphertext noise grows with each key update, which means that these schemes only support a bounded number of updates. On the other hand, using the homomorphic property and the knowledge of the update token, an adversary can craft ciphertexts of related messages which means that these schemes are not CCA secure (only randIND-UE-CPA).

Related Work on Group Actions. We try to overcome these issues by using group actions to build UE. The first efficient post-quantum group action was introduced by Castryck *et al.* using isogenies [10]. It is called CSIDH and it uses the group action of the class group of the quadratic order $\mathbb{Z}[\sqrt{-p}]$ on the supersingular curves defined over $\mathbb{F}_p$. Other proposals following the same idea but for different families of quadratic orders have been introduced such as SCALLOP [19] and its recent variant SCALLOP-HD [12]. The resulting group actions are believed to be post-quantum one-way, i.e., hard to invert, and this has motivated to study the protocols that can be built generically upon a cryptographic group action. This is what is done for instance in the work of Alamati *et al.* [2]. Since then, other proposals of post-quantum group actions have been introduced such as the work of Tang *et al.* [36] or of Ji *et al.* [22], both based on multivariate problems. To our knowledge, there does not exists any UE scheme in the group action framework, even if we will show that the SHINE construction fits into that framework.

Overview of the Contributions. We present two new generic constructions of UE from abstract algebraic frameworks. The first construction is called GAINE for Group-Action Ideal-cipher Nonce-based Encryption. GAINE generalizes the SHINE [8] construction and builds UE from a weak pseudorandom group action as defined in [2]. In fact, SHINE is a concrete instantiation of GAINE for the group action of $\mathbb{Z}_q^*$ on any cyclic group H of order q by exponentiation. The hardness of the DDH problem over this group implies that the resulting group action is weak pseudorandom. For SHINE, and GAINE, to work, we need one other thing: that the set H is mappable, i.e., that there exists an invertible and efficient map π going from the space of messages to the set of the group action. The authors of SHINE showed how to build this map when H is the group of points of an elliptic curve. The idea is to use this map to translate messages as elements of H before encrypting them with a group action (exponentiation in SHINE), using secret keys as group elements. In that setting, if $(G, H, \star)$ is a group action, an encryption of $m \in H$ under a key $k \in G$ is $k \star m$, the token used for updating ciphertexts from an old key k_{old} to a new key k_{new} is the group element $k_{\mathsf{new}}(k_{\mathsf{old}}^{-1})$ and an update is just another group action computation.

Overall, we show that SHINE adapts naturally to the setting of cryptographic group actions. If the group action is abelian and transitive, a straightforward generalization of SHINE's security proof shows that we can instantiate GAINE with a group action that satisfies the analog of the classical DDH assumption for group actions. Moreover, we show that it is still possible to instantiate GAINE with a nonabelian group action. Only this time, we need the group action to be weak pseudorandom, i.e., an adversary cannot distinguish between many samples that are either of the form $(s_i, g \star s_i)$, where g is a random group element and the elements s_i are random set elements, or samples of the form (s_i, t_i) where s_i and t_i are random set elements. Finally, we show that we can apply the transform used in SHINE to make our GAINE UE scheme CCA secure.

Unfortunately, we do not know how to instantiate GAINE in the post-quantum setting. Indeed, there are currently two cryptographic group actions that are mappable and believed to be post-quantum. The first one was introduced by Tang *et al.* [36] and uses alternating trilinear forms, while the second one from Ji *et al.* [22] is based on tensors. These two group actions are not abelian and they are conjectured to be weak pseudorandom but only over a very small number of samples. However, when working with nonabelian group actions, our security proof for GAINE needs one sample per ciphertext. Thus, we are not currently able to give a practical post-quantum instantiation for GAINE. Finding one would solve the problem left open by Jiang [23] at Asiacrypt2020 to build a CCA secure post-quantum UE scheme.

Isogeny-based cryptography provides another source of post-quantum weak pseudorandom group actions. However, it is notoriously hard to sample elements in the set of the known group actions based on isogenies (see [7]), and it is the case for CSIDH [10] and SCALLOP(-HD) [12,19], the two most promising group actions based on isogenies. Thus, we cannot really hope to instantiate GAINE from isogenies. However, these group actions remain credible post-quantum candidates since they are not affected by the recent attacks against SIDH [11,26,33].

This is why we show how to build UE from the CSIDH and SCALLOP(-HD) group actions. We circumvent the mappable requirement by using an idea of Moriya *et al.* for their SIGAMAL encryption scheme [28]. Intuitively, their idea is to see messages as scalars that are mapped to points of an elliptic curve using the scalar multiplication but this time in a group where discrete logarithm is easy so that we can decrypt efficiently. The points obtained in this manner are encrypted using isogenies. We obtain an analog of the standard isogeny group action by considering a set made of elements constituted by a curve and a point (and not just a curve). We will require that this extended group action is weak pseudorandom, which is a much less standard assumption than the pseudorandomness of the usual isogeny group action. Nonetheless, this problem has been studied in the context of SIGAMAL and it is still believed to be hard. In particular the recent paper [9] explored to no-effect an avenue of attacks based on self-pairings. We refine the idea of Moriya *et al.* to get a scheme that is updatable.

The way we circumvent the issue that CSIDH is not mappable could be of independent interest as there are several examples of protocols where this proves to be a big obstacle [1,4]. We extracted an abstract framework of this idea to identify the algebraic structure required by our new UE scheme. This gave us what we call a TOGA for Triple Orbital Group Action. As the name suggests, there are three group actions involved in this scheme, each with a specific role, and we require the three different operations to interact in a very specific way that we summarized in Fig. 6. We introduce TOGA-UE, a generic UE protocol based on a TOGA family. Unfortunately, deriving a CCA encryption scheme from TOGA-UE seems hard and we leave that to future work.

Finally, we show how to build a TOGA from the isogeny group actions CSIDH and SCALLOP(-HD). This gives an instantiation of post-quantum UE based on another family of assumptions. In particular, it is the first post-quantum UE scheme that does not suffer any limitations regarding the number of updates, contrary to the solutions based on lattices. The known instantiations of these group actions reach a fixed level of security due to the sub-exponential complexity of some of the algorithms. We leave the problem of overcoming this obstacle to future work.

Outline of the Paper. In Sect. 2 we introduce the necessary notions and backgrounds. Section 3 is dedicated to our first construction GAINE of UE from a MEGA. Our second UE scheme TOGA-UE is introduced in Sect. 4, where we present our new algebraic structure of TOGA before showing how to build UE from it. Finally, in Sect. 5, we show how to instantiate TOGA-UE.

2 Preliminaries

Notations. For a finite set S, we use $s \xleftarrow{\$} S$ to sample uniformly from S. For a probability distribution $\mathcal{D}$ on a finite set S, we use $s \leftarrow \mathcal{D}$ to sample from $\mathcal{D}$. We use $\mathfrak{S}(S)$ to denote the set of permutations of a finite set S. For an algorithm $\mathcal{A}$ and an oracle $\mathcal{O}$, $\mathcal{A}$ having access to $\mathcal{O}$ is denoted by $\mathcal{A}^{\mathcal{O}}$.

2.1 Cryptographic Group Actions

In this section, we give a few reminders about group actions and how they can be endowed with hardness properties for cryptographic use. We use the framework of cryptographic group actions of Alamati *et al.* [2].

Definition 1 (Group Action). *Let G be a group for a law written multiplicatively and let S be a set. A group action of G on S is an operation $\star : G \times S \rightarrow S$ such that*

1. *If 1_G is the identity element of G, then for any $s \in S$, we have $1_G \star s = s$.*
2. *For any $g, h \in G$ and any $s \in S$, we have $(gh) \star s = g \star (h \star s)$.*

We may use the notation $(G, S, \star)$ to denote a group action. We stress that the group actions used in this work do not need to be abelian. A group action $(G, S, \star)$ partitions the set S into a disjoint union of *orbits* where the orbit of $s \in S$ is the set $\mathrm{Orb}(s) := \{g \star s \mid g \in G\} \subseteq S$.

Properties of Group Actions. Our group actions $(G, S, \star)$ can be:

1. Transitive: A group action is *transitive* if it has a single orbit, i.e., if for any $(s_1, s_2) \in S$, there exists $g \in G$ such that $g \star s_1 = s_2$. We can always obtain a transitive group action from any group action. Indeed, take $s \in S$, one can easily verify that $(G, \mathrm{Orb}(s), \star)$ is a transitive group action.
2. Free: A group action is *free* if for all $g \in G$, $g = 1_G$ if and only if there exists $s \in S$ such that $g \star s = s$.

Since we need to define computational assumptions related to group actions, we need a notion of efficiency. We say that a group action $(G, S, \star)$ is *effective* (EGA) if G and S can be efficiently represented, the operations and sampling in G as well as $\star$ are efficient. A formal definition is given in Definition 2.

Definition 2 (Effective Group Action [2]). *$(G, S, \star)$ is an effective group action (EGA), with respect to a parameter λ, if the following properties are satisfied:*

1. *The group G is finite and there exist PPT algorithms for:*
   (a) Membership testing, i.e., to decide if a given bit string represents a valid element in G.
   (b) Equality testing, i.e., to decide if two bit strings represent the same group element in G.
   (c) Sampling, i.e., to sample an element g from a distribution $\mathcal{D}_G$ on G.

   (d) Operation, i.e., to compute gh for any $g, h \in G$.
   (e) Inversion, i.e., to compute g^{-1} for any $g \in G$.
2. *The set S is finite and there exist efficient PPT algorithms for:*
   (a) Membership testing.
   (b) Unique representation, i.e., given any arbitrary set element $s \in S$, compute a string $\hat{s}$ that canonically represents s.
3. *There exists a distinguished element $s_0 \in S$, called the origin, such that its bit-string representation is known.*
4. *There exists a PPT algorithm that given (some bit-string representations of) any $g \in G$ and any $s \in S$, outputs $g \star s$.*

Definition 3 (Group Action Family). *We say that $\mathcal{GA}$ is a group action family if, for a security parameter λ, $\mathcal{GA}(\lambda)$ consists of a group action $(G, S, \star)$ where $|G|, |S| = \mathsf{poly}(\lambda)$.*

In the following, let $\mathcal{GA}$ be a group action family. We define weak pseudorandom group actions:

Definition 4 (Weak Pseudorandom Group Action [2]). *Let $(G, S, \star)$ be $\mathcal{GA}(\lambda)$ for some security parameter λ. Let $\mathcal{D}_G$ and $\mathcal{D}_S$ be distributions on G and S respectively. For $g \in G$, let $\pi_g : S \to S$ be the permutation defined by $\pi_g : s \mapsto g \star s$. For a permutation $f \in \mathfrak{S}(S)$, we use $f^{\$}$ to denote the randomized oracle that, when queried, samples $s \leftarrow \mathcal{D}_S$ and outputs $(s, f(s))$. We say that $(G, S, \star)$ is $(\mathcal{D}_G, \mathcal{D}_S)$-weakly pseudorandom if, for all PPT adversaries $\mathcal{A}$, we have:*

$$\mathbf{Adv}^{\text{wk-PR}}_{\mathcal{GA},\mathcal{A}}(\lambda) := \left|\Pr[\mathbf{Exp}^{\text{wk-PR-0}}_{\mathcal{GA},\mathcal{A}}(\lambda) = 1] - \Pr[\mathbf{Exp}^{\text{wk-PR-1}}_{\mathcal{GA},\mathcal{A}}(\lambda) = 1]\right| \leq \mathsf{negl}(\lambda)$$

where $\mathbf{Exp}^{\text{wk-PR-}b}_{\mathcal{GA},\mathcal{A}}(\lambda)$ is the experiment described in Fig. 1.

Informally, a group action $(G, S, \star)$ is $(\mathcal{D}_G, \mathcal{D}_S)$-weakly pseudorandom if there is no PPT adversary that can distinguish tuples of the form $(s_i, g \star s_i)$ from (s_i, u_i) where $g \leftarrow \mathcal{D}_G$ and each $s_i, u_i \leftarrow \mathcal{D}_S$. If both distributions are uniform, we omit them and we say that the group action is weakly pseudorandom.

2.2 Updatable Encryption

In this section, we describe the syntax and security definitions of UE, we follow the presentations of [8,23,25,30]. An UE scheme operates in *epochs*, where an epoch e is an index incremented with each key update. Let $n+1$ be the maximum number of epochs (this is only for proof purposes).

Definition 5. *An updatable encryption scheme* UE *for message space $\mathcal{M}$ consists of a tuple of PPT algorithms* ($\mathsf{UE.Setup}$, $\mathsf{UE.KeyGen}$, $\mathsf{UE.TokenGen}$, $\mathsf{UE.Enc}$, $\mathsf{UE.Dec}$, $\mathsf{UE.Upd}$) *where:*

$\mathbf{Exp}^{\text{wk-PR-}b}_{\mathcal{GA},\mathcal{A}}(\lambda)$:

1. $(G, S, \star) \leftarrow \mathcal{GA}(\lambda)$
2. **if** $b = 0$
3. $\quad g \leftarrow \mathcal{D}_G$
4. $\quad \mathcal{O}.\mathsf{Sample} \leftarrow \pi_g^{\$}$
5. **else** $(b = 1)$
6. $\quad \pi \xleftarrow{\$} \mathfrak{S}(S)$
7. $\quad \mathcal{O}.\mathsf{Sample} \leftarrow \pi^{\$}$
8. $b' \leftarrow \mathcal{A}^{\mathcal{O}.\mathsf{Sample}}(1^\lambda, (G, S, \star))$
9. **if** $b' = b$
10. $\quad$ **return** 1
11. **else**
12. $\quad$ **return** 0

Fig. 1. Weak pseudorandom group action experiment. Recall that $\mathcal{D}_G$ and $\mathcal{D}_S$ are distributions on G and S respectively. For a permutation $f \in \mathfrak{S}(S)$, we use $f^{\$}$ to denote the randomized oracle that samples $s \leftarrow \mathcal{D}_S$ and outputs $(s, f(s))$.

- $\mathsf{UE.Setup}(1^\lambda) \rightarrow \mathsf{pp}$: *The setup algorithm takes as input the security parameter and outputs a public parameter* pp.
- $\mathsf{UE.KeyGen}(\mathsf{pp}) \rightarrow k_{\mathsf{e}}$: *The key generation algorithm takes as input the public parameter* pp *and outputs an epoch key* k_{e}.
- $\mathsf{UE.Enc}(k, m) \rightarrow c$: *The encryption algorithm takes as input an epoch key* k *and a message* m *and outputs a ciphertext* c.
- $\mathsf{UE.Dec}(k, c) \rightarrow m$: *The encryption algorithm takes as input an epoch key* k *and a ciphertext* c *and outputs a message* m *or* $\perp$.
- $\mathsf{UE.TokenGen}(k_{\mathsf{e}}, k_{\mathsf{e}+1}) \rightarrow \Delta_{\mathsf{e}+1}$: *The token generation algorithm takes as input two keys of consecutive epochs* e *and* $\mathsf{e}+1$ *and outputs a token* $\Delta_{\mathsf{e}+1}$.
- $\mathsf{UE.Upd}(\Delta_{\mathsf{e}+1}, c_{\mathsf{e}}) \rightarrow c_{\mathsf{e}+1}$: *The update algorithm takes as input a token* $\Delta_{\mathsf{e}+1}$ *and a ciphertext* c_{e} *and outputs a ciphertext* $c_{\mathsf{e}+1}$.

Definition 6 (Correctness). *For any* $m \in \mathcal{M}$, *for* $0 \leq \mathsf{e}_1 \leq \mathsf{e}_2 \leq n+1$, *it holds that* $\Pr[\mathsf{UE.Dec}(k_{\mathsf{e}_2}, c_{\mathsf{e}_2}) \neq m] \leq \mathsf{negl}(\lambda)$, *where* $\mathsf{pp} \leftarrow \mathsf{UE.Setup}(1^\lambda)$, $k_{\mathsf{e}_1}, \ldots, k_{\mathsf{e}_2} \leftarrow \mathsf{UE.KeyGen}(\mathsf{pp})$, $c_{\mathsf{e}_1} \leftarrow \mathsf{UE.Enc}(k_{\mathsf{e}_1}, m)$, *and* $\Delta_{i+1} \leftarrow \mathsf{UE.TokenGen}(k_i, k_{i+1})$, $c_{i+1} \leftarrow \mathsf{UE.Upd}(\Delta_{i+1}, c_i)$ *for* $i \in [\mathsf{e}_1, \mathsf{e}_2 - 1]$.

Security Definitions. In all of our UE schemes, the Upd algorithm is *deterministic.* Thus, we only consider security definitions in the deterministic update setting. An adaptation of the usual indistinguishability security notions in the context of UE is given in Definition 7. We briefly explain the oracles used in this definition, they are described precisely in Fig. 3. Enc and Dec are the usual encryption and decryption oracles. The Next oracle increments the epoch counter, samples a new secret key and its associated update token. If a challenge ciphertext has been issued, Next updates it. On input key (resp. token) and an epoch, the oracle Corr returns the key (resp. token) of that epoch. The Chall oracle samples a bit b uniformly and returns either an encryption of the message or an update of the ciphertext given as inputs, the returned ciphertext is the challenge and the goal of the adversary is to guess the bit b. The $\mathsf{Upd}\tilde{\mathsf{C}}$ oracle returns the updated version of the challenge ciphertext. All of these oracles keep track of the values returned to, or computable by the adversary. These values are stored in the sets written in calligraphic font (see Sect. 2.2 for a description of these sets).

Definition 7 (detIND-UE-atk [8]). *Let* UE = (UE.Setup, UE.KeyGen, UE.TokenGen, UE.Enc, UE.Dec, UE.Upd) *be an updatable encryption scheme. The* detIND-UE-atk *advantage, for* atk ∈ {CPA, CCA} *of an adversary* $\mathcal{A}$ *against* UE *is given by*

$$\mathbf{Adv}^{\mathsf{detIND\text{-}UE\text{-}atk}}_{\mathsf{UE},\mathcal{A}}(\lambda) := \left|\Pr[\mathbf{Exp}^{\mathsf{detIND\text{-}UE\text{-}atk\text{-}0}}_{\mathsf{UE},\mathcal{A}} = 1] - \Pr[\mathbf{Exp}^{\mathsf{detIND\text{-}UE\text{-}atk\text{-}1}}_{\mathsf{UE},\mathcal{A}} = 1]\right|$$

where the confidentiality experiment $\mathbf{Exp}^{\mathsf{detIND\text{-}UE\text{-}atk\text{-}}b}_{\mathsf{UE},\mathcal{A}}$ *is given in Fig. 2.*

$\mathbf{Exp}^{\mathsf{detIND\text{-}UE\text{-}atk\text{-}}b}_{\mathsf{UE},\mathcal{A}}(\lambda)$

1. **do** $\mathsf{UE.Setup}(1^\lambda)$
2. **ors** $\leftarrow \mathcal{O}.\{\mathsf{Enc}, \mathsf{Upd}, \mathsf{Next}, \mathsf{Corr}\}$ //the set of oracles available to the adversary.
3. **if** atk = CCA
4.   **ors** ← **ors** $\cup \{\mathcal{O}.\mathsf{Dec}\}$ //add a decryption oracle in the CCA case.
5. $(\bar{M}, \bar{C}) \leftarrow \mathcal{A}^{\mathbf{ors}}(1^\lambda)$
6. phase ← 1, $\tilde{\mathsf{e}} \leftarrow \mathsf{e}$ //the challenge has been issued in epoch $\tilde{\mathsf{e}}$.
7. $\tilde{C}_{\mathsf{e}} \leftarrow \mathcal{O}.\mathsf{Chall}(\bar{M}, \bar{C})$
8. $b' \leftarrow \mathcal{A}^{\mathbf{ors}, \mathcal{O}.\mathsf{Upd}\tilde{\mathsf{C}}}(\tilde{C}_{\mathsf{e}})$
9. **if** $\mathcal{K}^* \cap \mathcal{C}^* \neq \emptyset$ **or** $\mathcal{I}^* \cap \mathcal{C}^* \neq \emptyset$ //check for trivial wins.
10.   twf ← 1 //a trivial win condition has been triggered.
11. **if** twf = 1
12. $b' \xleftarrow{\$} \{0, 1\}$
13. **return** b'

Fig. 2. Description of the confidentiality experiment $\mathbf{Exp}^{\mathsf{detIND\text{-}UE\text{-}atk\text{-}}b}_{\mathsf{UE},\mathcal{A}}$ for scheme UE (with deterministic updates) and adversary $\mathcal{A}$, for atk ∈ {CPA, CCA}. The oracles are given in Fig. 3. Trivial win conditions, i.e., deciding the value of twf and computing $\mathcal{K}^*$, $\mathcal{C}^*$, $\mathcal{I}^*$ are discussed in Sect. 2.2 and 2.2

Leakage Sets. We follow the bookkeeping technique [8,25] to maintain the epoch leakage sets.

- $\mathcal{C}$: List of epochs in which the adversary learned an updated version of the challenge ciphertext (from $\mathcal{O}$.Chall or $\mathcal{O}.\mathsf{Upd}\tilde{\mathsf{C}}$).
- $\mathcal{K}$: List of epochs in which the adversary corrupted the encryption key.
- $\mathcal{T}$: List of epochs in which the adversary corrupted the update token.

The adversary can also learn the values of ciphertexts and their updates.

Setup(1^λ)

1. $\mathsf{pp} \leftarrow \mathsf{UE.Setup}(1^\lambda)$
2. $k_0 \leftarrow \mathsf{UE.KeyGen}(\mathsf{pp})$
3. $\Delta_0 \leftarrow \perp$
4. $\mathsf{e}, \mathsf{c} \leftarrow 0$
5. $\mathsf{phase}, \mathsf{twf} \leftarrow 0$
6. $\mathcal{L}, \tilde{\mathcal{L}}, \mathcal{C}, \mathcal{K}, \mathcal{T} \leftarrow \emptyset$

$\mathcal{O}.\mathsf{Enc}(M)$

1. $C \leftarrow \mathsf{UE.Enc}(k_\mathsf{e}, M)$
2. $\mathsf{c} \leftarrow \mathsf{c} + 1$
3. $\mathcal{L} \leftarrow \mathcal{L} \cup \{(\mathsf{c}, C, \mathsf{e})\}$
4. **return** C

$\mathcal{O}.\mathsf{Dec}(C)$

1. **if** $\mathsf{phase} = 1$ **and** $C \in \tilde{\mathcal{L}}$
2. $\quad \mathsf{twf} \leftarrow 1$
3. M **or** $\perp \leftarrow \mathsf{UE.Dec}(k_\mathsf{e}, C)$
4. **return** M **or** $\perp$

$\mathcal{O}.\mathsf{Next}$

1. $\mathsf{e} \leftarrow \mathsf{e} + 1$
2. $k_\mathsf{e} \leftarrow \mathsf{UE.KeyGen}(\mathsf{pp})$
3. $\Delta_\mathsf{e} \leftarrow \mathsf{UE.TokenGen}(k_{\mathsf{e}-1}, k_\mathsf{e})$
4. **if** $\mathsf{phase} = 1$
5. $\quad \tilde{C}_\mathsf{e} \leftarrow \mathsf{UE.Upd}(\Delta_\mathsf{e}, \tilde{C}_{\mathsf{e}-1})$

$\mathcal{O}.\mathsf{Upd}(C_{\mathsf{e}-1})$

1. **if** $(j, C_{\mathsf{e}-1}, \mathsf{e}-1) \notin \mathcal{L}$
2. $\quad$ **return** $\perp$
3. $C_\mathsf{e} \leftarrow \mathsf{UE.Upd}(\Delta_\mathsf{e}, C_{\mathsf{e}-1})$
4. $\mathcal{L} \leftarrow \mathcal{L} \cup \{(j, C_\mathsf{e}, \mathsf{e})\}$
5. **return** C_e

$\mathcal{O}.\mathsf{Corr}(\mathsf{inp}, \hat{\mathsf{e}})$

1. **if** $\hat{\mathsf{e}} > \mathsf{e}$
2. $\quad$ **return** $\perp$
3. **if** $\mathsf{inp} = \mathsf{key}$
4. $\quad \mathcal{K} \leftarrow \mathcal{K} \cup \{\hat{\mathsf{e}}\}$
5. $\quad$ **return** $k_{\hat{\mathsf{e}}}$
6. **if** $\mathsf{inp} = \mathsf{token}$
7. $\quad \mathcal{T} \leftarrow \mathcal{T} \cup \{\hat{\mathsf{e}}\}$
8. $\quad$ **return** $\Delta_{\hat{\mathsf{e}}}$

$\mathcal{O}.\mathsf{Chall}(\bar{M}, \bar{C})$

1. **if** $\mathsf{phase} \neq 1$
2. $\quad$ **return** $\perp$
3. **if** $(\cdot, \bar{C}, \mathsf{e}-1) \notin \mathcal{L}$
4. $\quad$ **return** $\perp$
5. **if** $b = 0$
6. $\quad \tilde{C}_\mathsf{e} \leftarrow \mathsf{UE.Enc}(k_\mathsf{e}, \bar{M})$
7. **else** $(b = 1)$
8. $\quad \tilde{C}_\mathsf{e} \leftarrow \mathsf{UE.Upd}(\Delta_\mathsf{e}, \bar{C})$
9. $\mathcal{C} \leftarrow \mathcal{C} \cup \{\mathsf{e}\}$
10. $\tilde{\mathcal{L}} \leftarrow \tilde{\mathcal{L}} \cup \{(\tilde{C}_\mathsf{e}, \mathsf{e})\}$
11. **return** $\tilde{C}_\mathsf{e}$

$\mathcal{O}.\mathsf{Upd}\tilde{\mathsf{C}}$

1. **if** $\mathsf{phase} \neq 1$
2. $\quad$ **return** $\perp$
3. $\mathcal{C} \leftarrow \mathcal{C} \cup \{\mathsf{e}\}$
4. $\tilde{\mathcal{L}} \leftarrow \tilde{\mathcal{L}} \cup \{(\tilde{C}_\mathsf{e}, \mathsf{e})\}$
5. **return** $\tilde{C}_\mathsf{e}$

Fig. 3. Oracles in security games for UE with deterministic updates. Computing the leakage sets is discussed in Sect. 2.2

- $\mathcal{L}$: List of non-challenge ciphertexts (from $\mathcal{O}.\mathsf{Enc}$ or $\mathcal{O}.\mathsf{Upd}$) with entries of the form $(\mathsf{c}, C, \mathsf{e})$, where c is a counter incremented with each $\mathcal{O}.\mathsf{Enc}$ query.
- $\tilde{\mathcal{L}}$: List of updated versions of challenge ciphertext (created by $\mathcal{O}.\mathsf{Next}$ and returned by $\mathcal{O}.\mathsf{Upd}\tilde{\mathsf{C}}$), with entries of the form $(\tilde{C}, \mathsf{e})$.

Trivial Wins via Keys and Ciphertexts. We consider the extended epoch leakage sets $\mathcal{C}^*$, $\mathcal{K}^*$ and $\mathcal{T}^*$ inferred from $\mathcal{C}$, $\mathcal{K}$ and $\mathcal{T}$. These extended sets are used to identify trivial wins, i.e., if $\mathcal{C}^* \cap \mathcal{K}^* \neq \emptyset$, then there exists an epoch in which the adversary knows the epoch key and a valid update of the challenge ciphertext. The challenger computes these sets once the adversary has finished running. We give their precise descriptions in Appendix A.

Trivial Wins via Direct Updates. Define $\mathcal{I}$ as the set of epochs in which the adversary learned an updated version of the ciphertext given as challenge input ($\bar{C}$). Furthermore, define $\mathcal{I}^*$ to be the extended set in which the adversary has inferred information via token corruption. Since, in our case, the algorithm Upd is deterministic, an updated ciphertext is uniquely determined by a token and a ciphertext. Thus, the adversary trivially wins if $\mathcal{I}^* \cap \mathcal{C}^* \neq \emptyset$. Indeed, there exists an epoch in which the adversary knows the updated ciphertext of the challenge input $\bar{C}$ and a valid challenge-equal ciphertext. Comparing them allows the adversary to win the game.

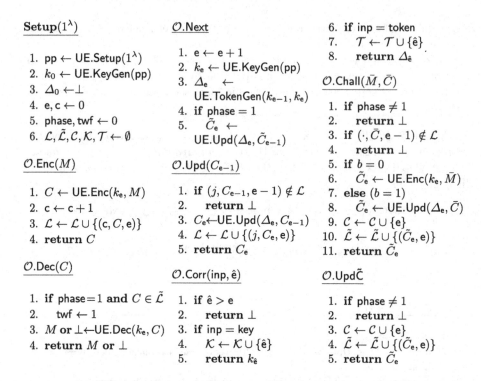

In [8], $\mathcal{I}$ is computed by finding an entry in $\mathcal{L}$ that contains the challenge input $\bar{C}$. Then, note the query identifier c for that entry and scan $\mathcal{L}$ for other entries with this identifier $\mathcal{I} := \{\mathsf{e} \in \{0, \ldots, n\} \mid (\mathsf{c}, \cdot, \mathsf{e}) \in \mathcal{L}\}$. We show how to extend $\mathcal{I}$ into $\mathcal{I}^*$ in Appendix A.

2.3 Elliptic Curves and Isogenies

Let K be a field. An elliptic curve over K is a smooth projective curve of genus 1 with a distinguished base point defined over K. For our purpose, it is enough to consider elliptic curves as curves defined by an equation of the form $E : y^2 = x^3 + ax + b$. The set of points $E(K)$ is made of the solutions (x, y) to the equation of the curve. A good generic reference on elliptic curves is the book from Silverman [35]. The set of points is a group for a law that we write $\oplus$. The scalar multiplication $[n] : E(K) \to E(K)$ is the operation $\oplus$ iterated n times. We write $E[n]$ for the kernel of the morphism $[n]$.

An isogeny $\varphi : E_1 \to E_2$ is a non-constant morphism sending the identity of E_1 to that of E_2. The degree of an isogeny is its degree as a rational map. When the degree $\deg(\varphi) = d$ is coprime to p, the isogeny is necessarily *separable*. An isogeny induces a homomorphism of groups $E_1(K) \to E_2(K)$ and, if separable, the kernel of φ is a group of order d. Such an isogeny is entirely described by its kernel, meaning that there is a one-to-one correspondence between separable isogenies (up to an isomorphism of the target curve) and finite subgroups of $E(\overline{K})$. An isogeny can be computed from its kernel G using Vélu's formula [37], in this case we write $\varphi : E \to E/G$. The degree of $\varphi \circ \psi$ is equal to $\deg(\varphi) \deg(\psi)$. For any isogeny $\varphi : E_1 \to E_2$, there exists a unique dual isogeny $\hat{\varphi} : E_2 \to E_1$, satisfying $\varphi \circ \hat{\varphi} = [\deg(\varphi)]$, the multiplication-by-$\deg(\varphi)$ map on E_2. Similarly $\hat{\varphi} \circ \varphi$ is the multiplication-by-$\deg(\varphi)$ map on E_1. An endomorphism of E is an isogeny $\theta : E \to E$. The set of endomorphisms is a ring with addition and composition that we write $\mathrm{End}(E)$.

Let us take K, a finite field of characteristic $p \neq 2, 3$. Over K, a curve is said to be *supersingular* when $\mathrm{End}(E)$ is a maximal order inside the quaternion algebra ramified at p and ∞. The Frobenius morphism is defined as $\pi : (x, y) \to (x^p, y^p)$, it sends any curve $E : y^2 = x^3 + ax + b$ to $E^{(p)} : y^2 = x^3 + a^p x + b^p$. π is the only isogeny of degree p between any two supersingular curves.

3 UE from Group Action

We generalize the SHINE scheme of Boyd *et al.* [8] using the framework of cryptographic group actions of Alamati *et al.* [2].

3.1 Generalizing SHINE to Group Actions

First, we introduce the novel *mappable* EGA (MEGA) definition.

Definition 8 (Mappable EGA). *Let $(G, S, \star)$ be an EGA. We say that $(G, S, \star)$ is a mappable EGA if there exists an efficient bijection $\pi : \{0,1\}^N \to S$.*

Let $\mathcal{GA}$ be a MEGA family and let $(G, S, \star)$ be $\mathcal{GA}(\lambda)$: a MEGA with bijection $\pi : \{0,1\}^{m+v} \to S$, for integers m and v. Let $\mathcal{M} := \{0,1\}^m$ be the message space and $\mathcal{N} := \{0,1\}^v$ be the nonce space.

We present our generalization of the SHINE scheme [8] to group actions, which we call GAINE for Group Action Ideal-cipher Nonce-based Encryption, in Fig. 4. We use group elements as keys and set elements as messages. Encryption, decryption and updates boil down to a group action computation. Ciphertexts are randomized by adding a random nonce as input to π. The group action used in the original proposal of Boyd *et al.* [8] is the action of the group $\mathbb{Z}_q^*$ on S by exponentiation, where S is a cyclic group of prime order q in which the discrete logarithm problem is hard. GAINE is correct, even for non-abelian group actions.

$\mathsf{Setup}(1^\lambda)$:

1. $(G, S, \star) \leftarrow \mathcal{GA}(\lambda)$
2. Choose π, m, v as above
3. $\mathsf{pp} \leftarrow (G, S, \star), \pi, m, v$
4. **return** pp

$\mathsf{KeyGen}(\mathsf{pp})$:

1. $k \xleftarrow{\$} G$
2. **return** k

$\mathsf{TokenGen}(k_\mathsf{e}, k_{\mathsf{e}+1})$:

1. $\Delta_{\mathsf{e}+1} \leftarrow k_{\mathsf{e}+1} k_\mathsf{e}^{-1}$
2. **return** $\Delta_{\mathsf{e}+1}$

$\mathsf{Upd}(\Delta_{\mathsf{e}+1}, C_\mathsf{e})$:

1. $C_{\mathsf{e}+1} \leftarrow \Delta_{\mathsf{e}+1} \star C_\mathsf{e}$
2. **return** $C_{\mathsf{e}+1}$

$\mathsf{Enc}(k_\mathsf{e}, M)$:

1. $N \xleftarrow{\$} \mathcal{N}$
2. $C_\mathsf{e} \leftarrow k_\mathsf{e} \star \pi(N \| M)$
3. **return** C_e

$\mathsf{Dec}(k_\mathsf{e}, C_\mathsf{e})$:

1. $s \leftarrow \pi^{-1}(k_\mathsf{e}^{-1} \star C_\mathsf{e})$
2. Parse s as $N' \| M'$
3. **return** M'

Fig. 4. GAINE: our generalization of the SHINE scheme using group actions.

Proposition 1 (Correctness of updates). *Let $k_\mathsf{e}, k_{\mathsf{e}+1} \in G$ be two keys and $C_\mathsf{e} := k_\mathsf{e} \star s$ for some $s \in S$. If $\Delta_{\mathsf{e}+1} :=$ TokenGen$(k_\mathsf{e}, k_{\mathsf{e}+1})$, then* Upd$(\Delta_{\mathsf{e}+1}, C_\mathsf{e}) = k_{\mathsf{e}+1} \star s$.

Proof By definition of TokenGen, we have $\Delta_{\mathsf{e}+1} := k_{\mathsf{e}+1} k_\mathsf{e}^{-1}$. By definition of Upd, we have $\mathsf{Upd}(\Delta_{\mathsf{e}+1}, C_\mathsf{e}) = \Delta_{\mathsf{e}+1} \star C_\mathsf{e} = (k_{\mathsf{e}+1} k_\mathsf{e}^{-1}) \star (k_\mathsf{e} \star s) = k_{\mathsf{e}+1} \star s$, where the last equality holds because of the *compatibility* of the group action (see Item 2 of Definition 1) and because k_e^{-1} is the inverse of k_e in the group G.

Proposition 2 (Correctness). *The* GAINE *scheme is correct.*

Proof Let $0 \leq \mathsf{e}_1 \leq \mathsf{e}_2 \leq n+1$ be two epochs and let us consider a ciphertext C_{e_2} updated through the successive tokens Δ_{i+1} for $i \in [\mathsf{e}_1, \mathsf{e}_2 - 1]$ from an initial ciphertext C_{e_1} that is the encryption of a message m under the key $k_{\mathsf{e}-1}$ as in Definition 6. By definition of $C_{\mathsf{e}_1} := \mathsf{Enc}(k_{\mathsf{e}_1}, M)$, we have $C_{\mathsf{e}_1} = k_{\mathsf{e}_1} \star \pi(N \| M)$

for some random nonce N. By applying Proposition 1 on the updates of C_{e_1}, we have that $C_{\mathsf{e}_2} = k_{\mathsf{e}_2} \star \pi(N\|M)$. Then, we get

$$k_{\mathsf{e}_2}^{-1} \star C_{\mathsf{e}_2} = k_{\mathsf{e}_2}^{-1} \star (k_{\mathsf{e}_2} \star \pi(N\|M)) = 1_G \star \pi(N\|M) = \pi(N\|M)$$

where the penultimate equality holds because of the *compatibility* of the group action (see Item 2 of Definition 1) and the last equality holds because of the *identity* property of the group action (see Item 1 of Definition 1). Finally, we have $\pi^{-1}(k_{\mathsf{e}_2}^{-1} \star C_{\mathsf{e}_2}) = N\|M$ and $\mathsf{Dec}(k_{\mathsf{e}_2}, C_{\mathsf{e}_2})$ returns M.

3.2 Security - GAINE is detIND-UE-CPA Secure

In Theorem 1, we show that GAINE is detIND-UE-CPA in the ideal cipher model, if the group action is a weakly pseudorandom MEGA. The ideal cipher model, introduced by Shannon [34] and shown to be equivalent to the random oracle model [14,21], gives all parties access to a permutation chosen randomly from all possible key permutations of appropriate length. The GAINE scheme acts on the outputs of the permutation with the epoch key to encrypt, so our reduction can "program" the transformation from permutation outputs to set elements.

Theorem 1 (GAINE is detIND-UE-CPA). *Let* GAINE *be the UE scheme described in Fig. 4 for a MEGA family $\mathcal{GA}$. For any ideal cipher model adversary $\mathcal{A}$, there exists a reduction $\mathcal{B}$ such that*

$$\mathbf{Adv}^{\mathsf{detIND\text{-}UE\text{-}CPA}}_{\mathsf{GAINE},\mathcal{A}}(\lambda) \leq 2(n+1)^3 \cdot \mathbf{Adv}^{\mathsf{wk\text{-}PR}}_{\mathcal{GA},\mathcal{B}}(\lambda)$$

We follow the proof strategy of [8] and use their hybrid argument across insulated regions. In each hybrid, we can embed at one firewall of the insulated region and simulate all tokens within that insulated region to answer queries to both $\mathcal{O}.\mathsf{Upd}$ and $\mathcal{O}.\mathsf{Upd}\tilde{\mathsf{C}}$. In GAINE, we update a ciphertext from epoch e to epoch $\mathsf{e}+1$ by computing the action of the group element $k_{\mathsf{e}+1}k_{\mathsf{e}}^{-1}$. Fresh ciphertexts are randomized using a nonce N but updates are deterministic, thus our reduction will need to provide consistent ciphertexts to the adversary, i.e., the N value must be consistent.

We give a reduction $\mathcal{B}$ which receives a group action $(G, S, \star)$ and an oracle $\mathcal{O}.\mathsf{Sample}$ that returns either tuples of the form $(s_i, g \star s_i)$ or (s_i, u_i) where $g \xleftarrow{\$} G$ and $s_i, u_i \xleftarrow{\$} S$. $\mathcal{B}$ will use the tuples of $\mathcal{O}.\mathsf{Sample}$ to perfectly simulate the detIND-UE-CPA experiment for GAINE when those tuples are of the form $(s_i, g \star s_i)$ (and a random experiment otherwise). The idea is to embed g to a well chosen epoch key by using s_i as randomness and $g \star s_i$ as ciphertext value. Thus, if we know an efficient adversary $\mathcal{A}$ against the detIND-UE-CPA security of GAINE, using the hybrid argument of [8], $\mathcal{B}$ can use $\mathcal{A}$ to break the weak pseudorandomness of $(G, S, \star)$.

Proof. Play hybrid games. We partition the non corrupted key space as follows: $\{0, \ldots, n\} \setminus \mathcal{K}^* = \cup_{(j,\mathsf{fwl}_j,\mathsf{fwr}_j)\in\mathcal{FW}}\{\mathsf{fwl}_j \ldots \mathsf{fwr}_j\}$, where fwl_i and fwr_i are firewalls of the i-th insulated region. For $b \in \{0,1\}$, define game $\mathcal{G}_i^b$ as $\mathbf{Exp}^{\mathsf{detIND\text{-}UE\text{-}CPA}\text{-}b}_{\mathsf{GAINE},\mathcal{A}}$ except for:

1. The game randomly picks $\mathsf{fwl}_i, \mathsf{fwr}_i \xleftarrow{\$} \{0, \ldots, n\}$ and if they are not the i-th firewalls, it aborts and returns a random bit b'. This loss is upper-bounded by $(n+1)^2$.
2. For the challenge (made in epoch $\tilde{\mathsf{e}}$ on input $(\bar{M}, \bar{C})$), the game returns an updated version of $\bar{C}$ if $\tilde{\mathsf{e}} < \mathsf{fwl}_i$ and it returns an encryption of $\bar{M}$ if $\tilde{\mathsf{e}} > \mathsf{fwr}_i$. Finally, if $\mathsf{fwl}_i \leq \tilde{\mathsf{e}} \leq \mathsf{fwr}_i$, the game returns an encryption of $\bar{M}$ if $b = 0$ and an updated version of $\bar{C}$ if $b = 1$.
3. After $\mathcal{A}$ outputs b', the game returns b' if $\mathsf{twf} \neq 1$ or some additional trivial win condition triggers.

If fwl_i, fwr_i are the desired values, then $\mathcal{G}_1^0$ is $\mathbf{Exp}_{\mathsf{GAINE},\mathcal{A}}^{\mathsf{detIND\text{-}UE\text{-}CPA\text{-}0}}$, i.e., all challenges are encryptions of $\bar{M}$. Let ℓ be the total number of insulated regions (bounded by $n+1$), such that $\mathcal{G}_\ell^1$ is $\mathbf{Exp}_{\mathsf{GAINE},\mathcal{A}}^{\mathsf{detIND\text{-}UE\text{-}CPA\text{-}1}}$, i.e., all challenges are updates of $\bar{C}$. Let E be the event that fwl_i and fwr_i are the desired values. By definition, for any $1 \leq i \leq n+1$ and $b \in \{0,1\}$, we have $\Pr[\mathcal{G}_i^b = 1 \mid \neg E] = 1/2$. Then

$$\begin{aligned}\Pr[\mathcal{G}_\ell^1 = 1] &= \Pr[\mathcal{G}_\ell^1 = 1 \mid E] \cdot \Pr[E] + \Pr[\mathcal{G}_\ell^1 = 1 \mid \neg E] \cdot \Pr[\neg E] \\ &= \Pr[\mathbf{Exp}_{\mathsf{GAINE},\mathcal{A}}^{\mathsf{detIND\text{-}UE\text{-}CPA\text{-}1}} = 1] \cdot \frac{1}{(n+1)^2} + \frac{1}{2} \cdot (1 - \frac{1}{(n+1)^2}), \text{ and} \\ \Pr[\mathcal{G}_1^0 = 1] &= \Pr[\mathbf{Exp}_{\mathsf{GAINE},\mathcal{A}}^{\mathsf{detIND\text{-}UE\text{-}CPA\text{-}0}} = 1] \cdot \frac{1}{(n+1)^2} + \frac{1}{2} \cdot (1 - \frac{1}{(n+1)^2})\end{aligned}$$

Thus, we have $|\Pr[\mathcal{G}_\ell^1 = 1] - \Pr[\mathcal{G}_1^0 = 1]| = \frac{1}{(n+1)^2} \cdot \mathbf{Adv}_{\mathsf{GAINE},\mathcal{A}}^{\mathsf{detIND\text{-}UE\text{-}CPA}}(\lambda)$.

Notice that the games $\mathcal{G}_{i-1}^1$ and $\mathcal{G}_i^0$ behave in the same way: for the challenge query and $\mathcal{O}.\mathsf{Upd}\tilde{\mathsf{C}}$, in an epoch in the first $i-1$ insulated regions, the reduction returns an update of $\bar{C}$, otherwise it returns an encryption of $\bar{M}$. Thus, for any $\ell \leq n+1$, $|\Pr[\mathcal{G}_\ell^1 = 1] - \Pr[\mathcal{G}_1^0 = 1]| \leq \sum_{i=1}^{\ell} |\Pr[\mathcal{G}_i^1 = 1] - \Pr[\mathcal{G}_i^0 = 1]|$. In the following, we prove that for any $1 \leq i \leq \ell$, $|\Pr[\mathcal{G}_i^1 = 1] - \Pr[\mathcal{G}_i^0 = 1]| \leq 2\mathbf{Adv}_{\mathcal{GA},\mathcal{B}}^{\mathsf{wk\text{-}PR}}(\lambda)$ for a reduction $\mathcal{B}$.

In Hybrid i. Let $\mathcal{A}_i$ be an adversary trying to distinguish $\mathcal{G}_i^0$ from $\mathcal{G}_i^1$. For all queries concerning epochs outside of the i-th insulated region, the responses of both games are the same. Thus, we assume that $\mathcal{A}_i$ asks for at least one challenge ciphertext in an epoch within the i-th insulated region. This is where we will embed the weak pseudorandom group action samples in our reduction.

We construct a reduction $\mathcal{B}$, presented in Fig. 5, that is playing the weak pseudorandom group action game (Definition 4) and will simulate the responses of queries made by adversary $\mathcal{A}_i$. Since we do not assume the group action $(G, S, \star)$ to be abelian, we define $(\prod_{i=0}^n g_i) \star s := (g_0 g_1 \cdots g_n) \star s$ for $s \in S$ and $g_0, \ldots, g_n \in G$.

Recall that $\mathcal{A}_i$ is an adversary attempting to distinguish $\mathcal{G}_i^0$ from $\mathcal{G}_i^1$. $\mathcal{B}$ will use $\mathcal{A}$ to break the weak pseudorandomness of the group action $(G, S, \star)$. In $\mathbf{Exp}_{\mathcal{GA},\mathcal{B}}^{\mathsf{wk\text{-}PR}}(\lambda)$, when $\mathcal{O}.\mathsf{Sample}$ returns pairs of the form $(s_j, g \star s_j)$ for $g \xleftarrow{\$} G$ and $s_j \xleftarrow{\$} S$, $\mathcal{B}$ will perfectly simulate the environment of $\mathcal{A}_i$ in $\mathcal{G}_i^b$. When $\mathcal{O}.\mathsf{Sample}$

Reduction $\mathcal{B}$ playing $\mathbf{Exp}^{\mathsf{wk\text{-}PR\text{-}}b^*}_{\mathcal{GA},\mathcal{B}}(\lambda)$

1. **receive** $(G, S, \star)$ and $\mathcal{O}.\mathsf{Sample}$
2. **do** $\mathbf{Setup}(1^\lambda)$
3. $\bar{M}, \bar{C} \leftarrow \mathcal{A}^{\mathtt{ors}}(\lambda)$
4. $\mathsf{phase} \leftarrow 1$
5. $\tilde{C}_{\tilde{\mathsf{e}}} \leftarrow \mathcal{O}.\mathsf{Chall}(\bar{M}, \bar{C})$
6. $b' \leftarrow \mathcal{A}^{\mathtt{ors}, \mathcal{O}.\mathsf{Upd}\tilde{\mathsf{C}}}(\tilde{C}_{\tilde{\mathsf{e}}})$
7. **if** $\mathcal{C}^* \cap \mathcal{K}^* \neq \emptyset$ **or** $\mathcal{I}^* \cap \mathcal{C}^* \neq \emptyset$
8. $\mathsf{twf} \leftarrow 1$
9. **if** `ABORT` occurred **or** $\mathsf{twf} = 1$
10. $\quad b' \xleftarrow{\$} \{0, 1\}$
11. $\quad$ **return** b'
12. **if** $(i, \mathsf{fwl}_i, \mathsf{fwr}_i) \notin \mathcal{FW}$
13. $\quad b' \xleftarrow{\$} \{0, 1\}$
14. $\quad$ **return** b'
15. **if** $b' = b$
16. $\quad$ **return** 0
17. **else**
18. $\quad$ **return** 1

$\underline{\mathbf{Setup}(1^\lambda)}$

1. $b \xleftarrow{\$} \{0, 1\}$
2. $\mathsf{pp} \leftarrow \mathsf{GAINE.Setup}(1^\lambda)$
3. $k_0 \leftarrow \mathsf{GAINE.KeyGen}(\mathsf{pp})$
4. $\Delta_0 \leftarrow \perp$
5. $\mathsf{e}, \mathsf{c}, \mathsf{phase}, \mathsf{twf} \leftarrow 0$
6. $\mathcal{L}, \tilde{\mathcal{L}}, \mathcal{C}, \mathcal{K}, \mathcal{T} \leftarrow \emptyset$
7. $\mathsf{fwl}_i, \mathsf{fwr}_i \xleftarrow{\$} \{0, \ldots, n\}$
8. **for** $j \in \{0, \ldots, \mathsf{fwl}_i - 1\}$ **do**
9. $\quad k_j \xleftarrow{\$} G; \Delta_j \leftarrow k_j k_{j-1}^{-1}\ \bowtie$
10. **for** $j \in \{\mathsf{fwr}_i + 1, \ldots, n\}$ **do**
11. $\quad k_j \xleftarrow{\$} G; \Delta_j \leftarrow k_j k_{j-1}^{-1}\ \bowtie$
12. **for** $j \in \{\mathsf{fwl}_i + 1, \ldots, \mathsf{fwr}_i\}$ **do**
13. $\quad \Delta_j \xleftarrow{\$} G$

$\underline{\mathcal{O}.\mathsf{Enc}(M)}$

1. $\mathsf{c} \leftarrow \mathsf{c} + 1$
2. $(\mathsf{inf}_1, \mathsf{inf}_2) \leftarrow \mathcal{O}.\mathsf{Sample}$
3. $\pi(N \| M) \leftarrow \mathsf{inf}_1$
4. **if** $\mathsf{e} \in \{0, \mathsf{fwl}_i - 1\} \cup \{\mathsf{fwr}_i + 1, \ldots, n\}$
5. $\quad C_{\mathsf{e}} \leftarrow k_{\mathsf{e}} \star \mathsf{inf}_1$
6. **else**
7. $\quad C_{\mathsf{fwl}_i} \leftarrow \mathsf{inf}_2$
8. $\quad$ **for** $j \in \{\mathsf{fwl}_i + 1, \ldots, \mathsf{e}\}$ **do**
9. $\quad\quad C_j \leftarrow \Delta_j \star C_{j-1}$
10. $\mathsf{inf} \leftarrow (\mathsf{inf}_1, \mathsf{inf}_2)$
11. $\mathcal{L} \leftarrow \mathcal{L} \cup \{(\mathsf{c}, C_{\mathsf{e}}, \mathsf{e}; \mathsf{inf})\}$
12. **return** C_{e}

$\underline{\mathcal{O}.\mathsf{Upd}(C_{\mathsf{e}-1})}$

1. **if** $(\mathsf{c}, C_{\mathsf{e}-1}, \mathsf{e} - 1; \mathsf{inf}) \notin \mathcal{L}$
2. $\quad$ **return** $\perp$
3. **if** $\mathsf{e} \in \{1, \ldots, \mathsf{fwl}_i - 1\} \cup \{\mathsf{fwr}_i + 1, \ldots, n\}$
4. $\quad (\mathsf{inf}_1, \mathsf{inf}_2) \leftarrow \mathsf{inf}$
5. $\quad C_{\mathsf{e}} \leftarrow k_{\mathsf{e}} \star \mathsf{inf}_1$
6. **else**
7. $\quad (\mathsf{inf}_1, \mathsf{inf}_2) \leftarrow \mathsf{inf}$
8. $\quad C_{\mathsf{fwl}_i} \leftarrow \mathsf{inf}_2$
9. $\quad$ **for** $j \in \{\mathsf{fwl}_i + 1, \ldots, \mathsf{e}\}$ **do**
10. $\quad\quad C_j \leftarrow \Delta_j \star C_{j-1}$
11. $\mathcal{L} \leftarrow \mathcal{L} \cup \{(\mathsf{c}, C_{\mathsf{e}}, \mathsf{e}; \mathsf{inf})\}$
12. **return** C_{e}

$\underline{\mathcal{O}.\mathsf{Corr}(\mathsf{inp}, \hat{\mathsf{e}})}$

1. $\mathsf{Check}(\mathsf{inp}, \hat{\mathsf{e}}; \mathsf{e}; \mathsf{fwl}_i, \mathsf{fwr}_i)$
2. **if** $\mathsf{inp} = \mathsf{key}$
3. $\quad \mathcal{K} \leftarrow \mathcal{K} \cup \{\hat{\mathsf{e}}\}$
4. $\quad$ **return** $k_{\hat{\mathsf{e}}}$
5. **if** $\mathsf{inp} = \mathsf{token}$
6. $\quad \mathcal{T} \leftarrow \mathcal{T} \cup \{\hat{\mathsf{e}}\}$
7. $\quad$ **return** $\Delta_{\hat{\mathsf{e}}}$

$\underline{\mathcal{O}.\mathsf{Next}}$

1. $\mathsf{e} \leftarrow \mathsf{e} + 1$

$\underline{\mathcal{O}.\mathsf{Chall}(\bar{M}, \bar{C})}$

1. **if** $(\mathsf{c}, \bar{C}, \tilde{\mathsf{e}} - 1; \mathsf{inf}) \notin \mathcal{L}$
2. $\quad$ **return** `ABORT`
3. **if** $b = 0$
4. $\quad (s, t) \leftarrow \mathcal{O}.\mathsf{Sample}()$
5. $\quad \pi(N \| \bar{M}) \leftarrow s$
6. $\quad \tilde{C}_{\mathsf{fwl}_i} \leftarrow t$
7. **else**
8. $\quad (\mathsf{inf}_1, \mathsf{inf}_2) \leftarrow \mathsf{inf}$
9. $\quad \pi(N \| \bar{M}) \xleftarrow{\$} S$
10. $\quad \tilde{C}_{\mathsf{fwl}_i} \leftarrow \mathsf{inf}_2$
11. **for** $j \in \{0, \ldots, \mathsf{fwl}_i - 1\}$ **do**
12. $\quad \tilde{C}_j \leftarrow (\prod_{k=j}^{1} \Delta_k)(\prod_{k=1}^{\tilde{\mathsf{e}}-1} \Delta_k^{-1}) \star \bar{C}$ `//left`
13. **for** $j \in \{\mathsf{fwl}_i + 1, \ldots, \mathsf{fwr}_i\}$ **do**
14. $\quad \tilde{C}_j \leftarrow \Delta_j \star \tilde{C}_{j-1}$ `//embed`
15. **for** $j \in \{\mathsf{fwr}_i + 1, \ldots, n\}$ **do**
16. $\quad \tilde{C}_j \leftarrow k_j \star \pi(N \| \bar{M})$ `//right`
17. $\tilde{\mathcal{L}} \leftarrow \cup_{j=0}^{n} \{(\tilde{C}_j, j)\}$
18. **return** $\tilde{C}_{\mathsf{e}}$

$\underline{\mathcal{O}.\mathsf{Upd}\tilde{\mathsf{C}}}$

1. $\mathcal{C} \leftarrow \mathcal{C} \cup \{\mathsf{e}\}$
2. **find** $(\tilde{C}_{\mathsf{e}}, \mathsf{e}) \in \tilde{\mathcal{L}}$
3. **return** $\tilde{C}_{\mathsf{e}}$

Fig. 5. Our reduction $\mathcal{B}$ for proof of th. 1 in hybrid i. inf encodes fixed programming information: it marks two set elements $(\mathsf{inf}_1, \mathsf{inf}_2)$ sampled with $\mathcal{O}.\mathsf{Sample}$. inf_1 is the randomness used during encryption and inf_2 is the ciphertext value in epoch fwl_i. `ors` refers to the set $\{\mathcal{O}.\mathsf{Enc}, \mathcal{O}.\mathsf{Next}, \mathcal{O}.\mathsf{Upd}, \mathcal{O}.\mathsf{Corr}\}$. $\bowtie$ indicates that Δ_0 and $\Delta_{\mathsf{fwr}_i+1}$ are skipped in the computation.

returns pairs of the form (s_j, t_j) for $s_j, t_j \xleftarrow{\$} S$, $\mathcal{B}$ will give random inputs to $\mathcal{A}_i$ such that $\mathcal{A}_i$ distinguishes $\mathcal{G}_i^0$ from $\mathcal{G}_i^1$ with advantage 0. We explain how our reduction $\mathcal{B}$ does this without knowing which $\mathcal{O}.\mathsf{Sample}$ oracle was provided to it.

The reduction $\mathcal{B}$ receives the oracle $\mathcal{O}.\mathsf{Sample}$, takes $b \xleftarrow{\$} \{0,1\}$ and simulates $\mathcal{G}_i^b$. Whenever the reduction needs to provide an output of $\pi(\cdot)$ to $\mathcal{A}_i$, it chooses some set value $s \in S$ such that $\pi(\cdot) = s$. In this setting, computing π^{-1} is simply a lookup to this mapping of the ideal cipher π. We explain our simulation:

Initially,

1. $\mathcal{B}$ guesses the values of fwl_i and fwr_i.
2. $\mathcal{B}$ generates all keys and tokens except for $k_{\mathsf{fwl}_i}, \ldots, k_{\mathsf{fwr}_i}, \Delta_{\mathsf{fwl}_i}, \Delta_{\mathsf{fwr}_i+1}$. If $\mathcal{A}_i$ corrupts these keys and tokens, this means that the firewall guess is wrong and the reduction aborts the game using the Check algorithm of Appendix B.

$\mathcal{B}$ will operate so as to embed the value g used by $\mathcal{O}.\mathsf{Sample}$ to the key k_{fwl_i} and the value $gk_{\mathsf{fwl}_i-1}^{-1}$ to the token Δ_{fwl_i}. If $\mathcal{O}.\mathsf{Sample}$ returns uniformly distributed pairs of set elements instead, all the ciphertexts inside insulated region i will be random set elements (no key or token could possibly explain these ciphertexts).

To simulate a non-challenge ciphertext that is:

- An $\mathcal{O}.\mathsf{Enc}$ query in epoch $\mathsf{e} \in \{0, \ldots \mathsf{fwl}_i - 1\} \cup \{\mathsf{fwr}_i + 1, \ldots, n\}$: $\mathcal{B}$ queries $\mathcal{O}.\mathsf{Sample}$ to get a pair $(s,t) \in S^2$. $\mathcal{B}$ uses s as a random value by programming $\pi(\cdot) \leftarrow s$ (so the randomness will be consistent with calls that $\mathcal{A}_i$ makes to $\mathcal{O}.\mathsf{Upd}$), computes the ciphertext $C_\mathsf{e} = k_\mathsf{e} \star s$ (the value of k_e is known to $\mathcal{B}$ in these epochs) and stores (s,t) in its memory for later use. To respond to $\mathcal{O}.\mathsf{Upd}$ queries in these epochs, $\mathcal{B}$ computes $C_\mathsf{e} = k_\mathsf{e} \star s$ using the randomness s generated during the first encryption of the input ciphertext.
- An $\mathcal{O}.\mathsf{Enc}$ query in epoch $\mathsf{e} \in \{\mathsf{fwl}_i, \ldots, \mathsf{fwr}_i\}$: $\mathcal{B}$ queries $\mathcal{O}.\mathsf{Sample}$ to get a pair $(s,t) \in S^2$ and programs $\pi(\cdot) \leftarrow s$. It sets $C_{\mathsf{fwl}_i} = t$ (so that all ciphertexts will be encrypted under the key g in epoch fwl_i if $\mathcal{O}.\mathsf{Sample}$ returns pairs of the form $(s_j, g \star s_j)$) and updates C_{fwl_i} to the right epoch e using its simulated tokens (remember that $\mathcal{B}$ does not know the keys inside the i-th insulated region). To respond to $\mathcal{O}.\mathsf{Upd}$ queries in these epochs, $\mathcal{B}$ uses the value t (if $t = g \star s$ then the randomness will still be consistent) generated during the first encryption of the input ciphertext as ciphertext value in epoch fwl_i and updates t to the right epoch e using its simulated tokens.

During the challenge call, the adversary will provide a ciphertext $\bar{C}$ which was created during the c-th call to $\mathcal{O}.\mathsf{Enc}$. The adversary cannot ask for an update of the c-th encryption in an epoch $\mathsf{e} \geq \mathsf{fwl}_i$, as this would trigger the trivial win condition $[\mathsf{fwl}_i, \mathsf{fwr}_i] \subseteq \mathcal{I}^* \cap \mathcal{C}^* \neq \emptyset$.

To simulate challenge-equal ciphertext in an epoch that is:

- To the left of the i-th insulated region: $\mathcal{B}$ simulates $\mathsf{GAINE.Upd}(\bar{C})$ using tokens that it created itself.

- Within the i-th insulated region: $\mathcal{B}$ simulates $\mathsf{GAINE.Upd}(\bar{C})$ if $b = 1$, and simulates $\mathsf{GAINE.Enc}(\bar{M})$ if $b = 0$. More precisely, if $\mathcal{O}.\mathsf{Sample}$ returns pairs of the form $(s_j, g \star s_j)$, $\mathcal{B}$ embeds g to k_{fwl_i} and $gk^{-1}_{\mathsf{fwl}_i-1}$ to Δ_{fwl_i}. If $b = 0$, the reduction samples $(s, t) \leftarrow \mathcal{O}.\mathsf{Sample}()$, gives value s to $\pi(N\|\bar{M})$ and t to $\tilde{C}_{\mathsf{fwl}_i}$ (we want $k_{\mathsf{fwl}_i} = g$) since
$$\tilde{C}_{\mathsf{fwl}_i} = \mathsf{GAINE.Enc}(\bar{M}) = k_{\mathsf{fwl}_i} \star \pi(N\|\bar{M})$$
If $b = 1$, assume that $\bar{C}$ is an update of $\bar{C}_{\mathsf{e_c}}$, the output of the c-th $\mathcal{O}.\mathsf{Enc}$ query. $\mathcal{B}$ sampled $(s, t) \leftarrow \mathcal{O}.\mathsf{Sample}()$ and used s as randomness to create $\bar{C}_{\mathsf{e_c}}$ and to update it in epochs $\mathsf{e} < \mathsf{fwl}_i$. The reduction gives value t to $\tilde{C}_{\mathsf{fwl}_i}$ (we want $\Delta_{\mathsf{fwl}_i} = gk^{-1}_{\mathsf{fwl}_i-1}$) since
$$\tilde{C}_{\mathsf{fwl}_i} = \mathsf{GAINE.Upd}(\bar{C}) = \Delta_{\mathsf{fwl}_i} \star (k_{\mathsf{fwl}_i-1} \star s)$$
Furthermore, the reduction uses tokens $\Delta_{\mathsf{fwl}_i+1}, \ldots, \Delta_{\mathsf{fwr}_i}$ to update $\tilde{C}_{\mathsf{fwl}_i}$ to simulate all challenge ciphertexts in epochs within the insulated region.
- To the right of the i-th insulated region: $\mathcal{B}$ simulates $\mathsf{GAINE.Enc}(\bar{M})$ using the keys that it created itself.

Eventually, $\mathcal{B}$ receives the output bit b' from $\mathcal{A}_i$. If $b' = b$, then $\mathcal{B}$ guesses that $\mathcal{O}.\mathsf{Sample}$ returned pairs of the form $(s_j, g \star s_j)$ (returns 0 to the wk-PR challenger), otherwise, $\mathcal{B}$ guesses that it has seen uniformly chosen pairs of set elements (returns 1). If $\mathcal{B}$ receives an oracle $\mathcal{O}.\mathsf{Sample}$ that samples pairs of the form $(s_j, g \star s_j)$, then $\mathcal{B}$ perfectly simulates the environment of $\mathcal{A}_i$ in $\mathcal{G}_i^b$. If $\mathcal{B}$ receives an oracle $\mathcal{O}.\mathsf{Sample}$ that samples pairs uniformly at random, then $\mathcal{B}$ wins with probability 1/2. A standard advantage computation yields $\mathbf{Adv}^{\mathsf{detIND\text{-}UE\text{-}CPA}}_{\mathsf{GAINE},\mathcal{A}}(\lambda) \leq 2(n+1)^3 \mathbf{Adv}^{\mathsf{wk\text{-}PR}}_{\mathcal{GA},\mathcal{B}}(\lambda)$.

In [8, sec. 5.1.1], a variant of SHINE with added ciphertext integrity, called SHINE0, is given by using $N\|M\|0^t$, for some t, as input of the permutation π during encryption and by checking that the 0 string is still present during decryption. This version of SHINE is shown to be detIND-UE-CCA secure under CDH [8, th. 5]. It is possible to define GAINE0 similarly to SHINE0 and prove that it is detIND-UE-CCA secure if the group action is *weakly unpredictable*. Informally, $(G, S, \star)$ is $(\mathcal{D}_G, \mathcal{D}_S)$-weakly unpredictable if, given polynomially many tuples of the form $(s_i, g \star s_i)$ where $g \leftarrow \mathcal{D}_G$ and each $s_i \leftarrow \mathcal{D}_S$, there is no PPT adversary that can compute $g \star s^*$ for a given challenge $s^* \leftarrow \mathcal{D}_S$. A full proof and precise definitions are given in the full version of the paper.

3.3 Post-quantum Instantiations of GAINE

Potential candidates for instantiating GAINE include the non-abelian group actions of the general linear group on the set of alternating trilinear forms introduced by Tang *et al.* [36] and on the set of k-tensors, for $k \geq 3$, by Ji *et al.* [22]. These two actions act on a finite vector space $V \simeq \mathbb{F}^n$ where $\mathbb{F}$ is a finite field and n an integer. This implies that these two actions are mappable. Unfortunately, these two actions are also linear, meaning that the map $f_g : s \mapsto g \star s$ is a linear transformation of V. Given enough samples of the form $(s_i, g \star s_i)$ for a fixed g, one can compute $g \star s$ for any $s \in V$. This means that this action is not weak pseudorandom if the adversary gains access to too many samples of the weak pseudorandom experiment of Fig. 1. Since our security proof for GAINE uses one such sample per ciphertext, we can only use these two group actions to instantiate GAINE when there are few ciphertexts, which is unpractical.

4 UE from Triple Orbital Group Action

Below, we present a new abstract algebraic structure that we call Triple Orbital Group Action (TOGA). The formulation of this framework is in fact motivated by the fact that we cannot instantiate GAINE with the most-studied post-quantum group action based on isogenies because it is notoriously hard [7] to hash into the set of supersingular elliptic curves.

Let us start with a quick overview. A TOGA is made of three group actions, each with a distinct role. The main group action, that we write $(A, S, \star_A)$, is our starting point. The main ingredient to get a TOGA from the simple group action $\star_A$ is a congruence relation $\sim_A$. This relation allows us to derive a second group action $(A/\sim_A, S/\sim_S, \star_G)$, called the induced group action, of the quotient group on the quotient set (see Definition 9 for $\sim_S$). Of course, this induced group action is not mappable as we would not need a TOGA to build UE in this case. This time, we consider plaintexts as group elements of a third group action $(H, S, \star_H)$. For decryption to be possible, we assume that this action is efficiently invertible. We want $\star_H$ to commute with $\star_A$ but also that the orbits of $\star_H$ are exactly the classes of equivalences of $S/\sim_S$, which is what we call to be *orbital*. For a visualization of the interaction between the three group actions of a TOGA, see Fig. 6. The algebraic structure TOGA is explained in Sect. 4.1, while the computational model is given in Sect. 4.2. In Sect. 4.3, we show how to build UE from a TOGA.

4.1 The Algebraic Structure

Let us assume that we have a group action $(A, S, \star_A)$ for an abelian multiplicative group A and a set S. We write 1_A for the identity element of A. If there exists a congruence relation $\sim_A$ on A (we recall that a *congruence* on a set with an intern law is an equivalence relation compatible with the law, i.e., such that if $a_1 \sim_A a_2$ and $b_1 \sim_A b_2$ we have $a_1 b_1 \sim_A a_2 b_2$), then we get that $G = A/\sim_A$ is an abelian group for the law naturally derived from the multiplication in A.

Definition 9. *Let A be an abelian group and let $\sim_A$ be a congruence relation on A. Let S be a set and let $\star_A$ be a group action of A on S. The relation $\sim_S$ induced by $\sim_A$ and $\star_A$ is*

$$s_1 \sim_S s_2 \iff \exists a_1, a_2 \in A \text{ with } a_1 \sim_A a_2 \text{ such that } a_1 \star_A s_1 = a_2 \star_A s_2$$

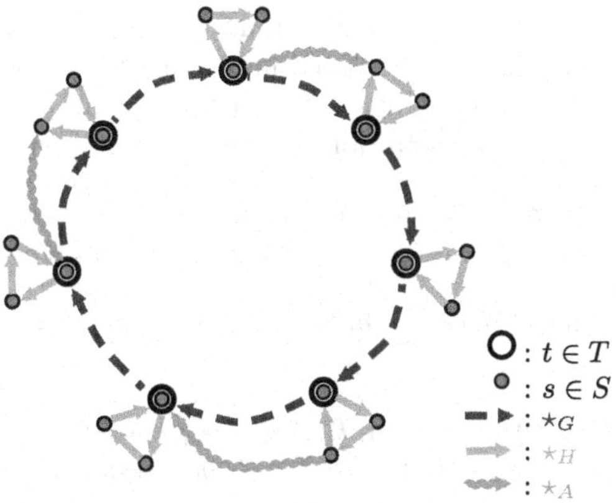

Fig. 6. Diagram for a TOGA $A, H, S, \star_A, \sim_A, \star_H$.

Proposition 3. *Keeping the notations of Definition 9, we have that* $\sim_S$ *is an equivalence relation and* $\star_A$ *induces a group action* $\star_G$ *of* $G := A/\sim_A$ *on* $T := S/\sim_S$.

Proof. The relation $\sim_S$ is clearly reflexive and symmetric. For transitivity let us take $s_1, s_2, s_3 \in S$ with $s_1 \sim_S s_2$ and $s_2 \sim_S s_3$, we have $a_1 \star_A s_1 = a_2 \star_A s_2$ and $b_2 \star_A s_2 = b_3 \star_A s_3$, thus $a_1 b_2 \star_A s_1 = a_2 b_3 \star_A s_3$ and $a_1 b_2 \sim_A a_2 b_3$ since $\sim_A$ is a congruence. Let us write $G = A/\sim_A$ and $T = S/\sim_S$. First, we need to verify that the operation $\star_A$ is well-defined on the quotients. To see that, we need to verify that $a_1 \star_A s_1 \sim_S a_2 \star_A s_2$ when $a_1 \sim_A a_2$ and $s_1 \sim_S s_2$. This is true because we have $b_1 \sim_A b_2$ such that $b_1 \star_A s_1 = b_2 \star_A s_2$, and so $(a_2 b_1) \star_A (a_1 \star_A s_1) = (a_1 b_2) \star_A (a_2 \star_A s_2)$ with $a_2 b_1 \sim_A a_1 b_2$ because $\sim_A$ is a congruence. Then, we need to show that $\star_A : G \times T \to T$ verifies the usual group action properties from Defintion 1. First, let us take $a \sim_A 1_A$. We must have $a \star_A s \sim_S s$ for any $s \in S$, which is clearly the case. Then, for any $a_1, a_2 \in A$, $s \in S$, we have the equality $(a_1 a_2) \star_A s = a_1 \star_A (a_2 \star_A s)$ and this equality remains true when considering the quotients G, T.

Definition 10. *Given* $A, S, \star_A, \sim_A$ *as in Proposition 3, the group action* $\star_G$ *of* $A/\sim_A$ *on* $S/\sim_S$ *is called the group action induced by* $A, \star_A, \sim_A$ *(or induced by* A *when it is clear from the context) and* $(A, S, \star_A)$ *is called the main group action.*

We obtain a third group action (hence the name of triple group action) by looking at the classes of equivalence of S. We want to consider these classes as the orbits of a third group action $\star_H : H \times S \to S$ for another abelian group H. By that we mean that, for any $s \in S$ and $h \in H$, we have $s \sim_S h \star_H s$ and that, for all $s' \sim_S s$, there exists $h \in H$ with $s' = h \star_H s$. Additionally, we need the group action $(H, S, \star_H)$ to be *free* because we will need to invert $\star_H$. When these constraints are respected we qualify the group action $(H, S, \star_H)$ to be *orbital.*

Finally, we want that $\star_A$ and $\star_H$ commute and that for any $a_1, a_2 \in A$ such that $a_1a_2 \sim_A 1_A$, there exists a unique element $h(a_1, a_2) \in H$ such that $(a_1a_2) \star_A s = h(a_1, a_2) \star_H s$ for any $s \in S$. With Proposition 4, we give a useful reformulation that will prove useful for the correctness of our scheme.

Proposition 4. *For any $a, b \in A$ with $a \sim_A b$, we have $a \star_A s = (h(a, c)h(b, c)^{-1}) \star_H (b \star_A s)$ for any $c \in A$ with $ac \sim_A 1_A$ and $s \in S$.*

Proof. We have $h(a, c) \star_H (b \star_A s) = (ac) \star_A (b \star_A s) = (abc) \star_A s = (bc) \star_A (a \star_A s) = h(b, c) \star_H (a \star_A s)$.

Definition 11 (TOGA). *When $A, H, S, \star_A, \sim_A, \star_H$ satisfy all the above properties we say that we have a Triple Orbital Group Action (TOGA).*

Remark 1. Note that A being a group is not really necessary for the UE scheme that we will introduce below. In fact, we only need that A is a monoid and that the quotient $A/\sim_A$ is a group. We only assumed that A is a group for simplicity.

4.2 Computational Model

As for group actions, we define an ETOGA as an Effective TOGA:

Definition 12 (ETOGA). *A TOGA $A, H, S, \star_A, \sim_A, \star_H$ is effective if:*

1. *$(H, S, \star_H)$ is an Effective and Easy Group Action (EEGA), meaning:*
   (a) *The group action $(H, S, \star_H)$ is a free EGA.*
   (b) *There is a PPT inversion algorithm $\mathsf{Invert}_H : S^2 \to \{\perp\} \cup H$ taking two elements s_1, s_2 and that outputs either $\perp$ when $s_1 \not\sim_S s_2$ or the element $h \in H$ such that $s_1 = h \star_H s_2$.*
2. *There exists a finite subset $A' \subset A$ such that:*
   (a) *The class of equivalence of A' forms a generating set of G, i.e., $G = A'/\sim_A$.*
   (b) *There is a PPT algorithm to compute $a' \star_A s$ for any $s \in S$ and $a' \in A'$.*
   (c) *There exists a PPT algorithm $\mathsf{Reduce}_A : A \to A'$ that takes an element $a \in A$ and outputs $a' \sim_A a$.*
   (d) *There exists a PPT algorithm to sample from A' in a distribution statistically close to the uniform distribution, we write $a' \xleftarrow{\$} A'$ for elements sampled in that manner.*
   (e) *The distribution $\mathcal{D}_G$ that samples $a' \xleftarrow{\$} A'$ and returns the class of $\mathsf{Reduce}_A(a')$ in G is statistically close to the uniform distribution.*
3. *There exists a deterministic PPT algorithm Reduce_S to compute a canonical representative for equivalence classes in $S/\sim_S$.*

Remark 2. Note that the Reduce_A algorithm may or may not be deterministic. For efficiency, it is interesting to try to select the element a' in the class of a that minimizes the computation cost of $a' \star_A s$ for any $s \in S$.

Note that when $a_1 a_2 \sim 1_A$, we have $h(a_1, a_2) = \mathsf{Invert}_H((a_1 a_2) \star_A s, s)$ for any $s \in S$. Thus, we can define a PPT algorithm to compute $h(a_1, a_2)$ from Invert_H. We abuse notations and write h for this algorithm.

Since the function Reduce_S is deterministic, we can abuse notations and assimilate $T = S/\sim_S$ and $\mathsf{Reduce}_S(S)$ by identifying the elements of T to their canonical representative in S through Reduce_S. Using this, we sometimes apply the action $\star_A$ on the elements of T (it suffices to compose $\star_A$ with Reduce_S to obtain the canonical representative afterward).

4.3 The Updatable Encryption Scheme

Let $\mathcal{TOGA}$ be an ETOGA family and let $(A, H, S, \star_A, \sim_A, \star_H)$ be $\mathcal{TOGA}(1^\lambda)$ for some λ. We fix a starting element $s_0 \in S$, and we also assume the existence of an invertible map $\psi : \mathcal{M} \to H$ where $\mathcal{M}$ is the space of the messages. We will use the function ψ to send the messages in the group H before encrypting them with $\star_H$. Then, decryption will rely on Invert_H. This operation is efficient by definition of an ETOGA. This principle basically solves the problem of needing our group action $\star_A$ to be mappable. The rest of our scheme follows the framework of GAINE with keys being elements of $A \times H$ and updates being obtained by applying $\star_A$ and $\star_H$. The security relies on the fact that the main group action $(A, S, \star_A)$ is weakly pseudorandom. Our UE scheme TOGA-UE is given in Fig. 7.

$\mathsf{Setup}(1^\lambda)$:

1. $(A, H, S, \star_A, \sim_A, \star_H) \leftarrow \mathcal{TOGA}(\lambda)$
2. Choose ψ, s_0 as above
3. $\mathsf{pp} \leftarrow (A, H, S, \star_A, \sim_A, \star_H, \psi, s_0)$
4. **return** pp

$\mathsf{KeyGen}(\mathsf{pp})$:

1. $a' \xleftarrow{\$} A'$
2. $h \xleftarrow{\$} H$
3. **return** $\mathsf{Reduce}_A(a'), h$

$\mathsf{TokenGen}(k_e, k_{e+1})$:

1. $(a_e, h_e) \leftarrow k_e$
2. $(a_{e+1}, h_{e+1}) \leftarrow k_{e+1}$
3. $c_e \leftarrow \mathsf{Reduce}_A(a_e^{-1} a_{e+1})$
4. Compute $h = h(a_e^{-1} a_{e+1}, c_e^{-1})$
5. **return** $c_e, h h_{e+1} h_e^{-1}$

$\mathsf{Upd}(\Delta_{e+1}, C_e)$:

1. $a, h \leftarrow \Delta_{e+1}$
2. **return** $h \star_H (a \star_A C_e)$

$\mathsf{Enc}(k_e, M)$:

1. $r' \xleftarrow{\$} A'$
2. $r \leftarrow \mathsf{Reduce}_A(r')$
3. $s = \mathsf{Reduce}_S(r \star_A s_0)$
4. $(a_e, h_e) \leftarrow k_e$
5. **return** $(\psi(M) h_e) \star_H (a_e \star_A s)$

$\mathsf{Dec}(k_e, C_e)$:

1. $(a_e, h_e) \leftarrow k_e$
2. $b_e \leftarrow \mathsf{Reduce}_A(a_e^{-1})$
3. $h' \leftarrow h(a_e, b_e)$
4. $s' \leftarrow (h_e h')^{-1} \star_H (b_e \star_A C_e)$
5. $s \leftarrow \mathsf{Reduce}_S(s')$
6. $M' \leftarrow \psi^{-1}(\mathsf{Invert}_H(s', s))$
7. **return** M'

Fig. 7. TOGA-UE: UE from ETOGA. The key and token space is $A \times H$, the plaintext space is $\{0,1\}^n$ for some integer n and the ciphertext space is S.

Proposition 5 (Correctness of updates). *Let* $k_e, k_{e+1} = (a_e, h_e), (a_{e+1}, h_{e+1})$ *be two keys and* $C_e = h_e \star_H (a_e \star_A s)$ *for some* $s \in S$. *If* $\Delta_{e+1} = \mathsf{TokenGen}(k_e, k_{e+1})$, *then* $\mathsf{Upd}(\Delta_{e+1}, C_e) = h_{e+1} \star_H (a_{e+1} \star_A s)$.

Proof. We reuse the notation of TokenGen, we have for $c_e = \mathsf{Reduce}_A(a_e^{-1} a_{e+1})$. Since $c_e \sim_A a_{e+1} a_e^{-1}$, we have that $c_e \star_A (a_e \star_A s') = (h(c_e, c_e^{-1}) h(a_{e+1} a_e^{-1}, c_e^{-1})^{-1}) \star_H ((a_{e+1} a_e^{-1} a_e) \star_A s')$ by Proposition 4. The proof is completed by the fact that $(a_{e+1} a_e^{-1} a_e) \star_A s' = a_{e+1} \star_A s'$ and $h(c_e, c_e^{-1}) = 1_H$.

Proposition 6 (Correctness). *The* TOGA-UE *scheme is correct.*

Proposition 6 follows from Proposition 5.

Proof. Let $e_1 \leq e_2 \leq n+1$ be two epochs and let us consider a ciphertext c_{e_2} updated through the successive tokens Δ_{i+1} for $i \in [e_1, e_2 - 1]$ from an initial ciphertext c_{e_1} that is the encryption of a message m under the key k_{e-1} as in Definition 6. Each key k_i can be decomposed as $a_i, h_i \in A \times H$. By definition of $c_{e_1} = \mathsf{Enc}(k_{e_1}, m)$, we have $c_{e_1} = (h_{e_1} \psi(m)) \star_H a_{e_1} \star_A \mathsf{Reduce}_S(s_1)$ for some $s_1 \in S$. By applying Proposition 5 on $s = \psi(m) \star_H \mathsf{Reduce}_S(s_1)$, we have that $c_{e_2} = h_{e_2} \psi(m) \star_A a_{e_2} \star_A \mathsf{Reduce}_S(s_1)$ since $\star_A$ and $\star_H$ commute. Then, let us take any $b_{e_2} \in A'$ such that $a_{e_2} b_{e_2} \sim_A 1_A$. By definition of h we know that $(b_{e_2} a_{e_2}) \star_A x = h(b_{e_2}, a_{e_2}) \star_H x$ for any $x \in S$. Thus, $s' = (h_{e_2} h(b_{e_2}, a_{e_2}))^{-1} \star_H b_{e_2} \star_A c_{e_2} = \psi(M) \star_H \mathsf{Reduce}_S(s_1)$. Then, since the orbits of $\star_H$ are exactly the equivalence classes of S, we have $s' \sim_S s_1$ and so $\mathsf{Reduce}_S(s') = \mathsf{Reduce}_S(s_1)$. Thus, when we compute $\mathsf{Invert}_H(s', \mathsf{Reduce}_S(s'))$ we obtain $\psi(m)$ and the message is recovered by applying ψ^{-1}.

4.4 Security - TOGA-UE is detIND-UE-CPA Secure

Let $A, H, S, \star_A, \sim_A, \star_H$ be an ETOGA, fix $s_0 \in S$ and let $(A, S, \star_A)$ be the main group action of A on S. In Theorem 2, we show that our UE scheme TOGA-UE (described in Fig. 7) is detIND-UE-CPA secure if the group action $(A, S, \star_A)$ is $(\mathcal{D}_A, \mathcal{D}_S)$-weakly pseudorandom where $\mathcal{D}_S$ is the distribution that samples $a \xleftarrow{\$} A'$ and returns $s := \mathsf{Reduce}_S(a \star_A s_0)$ and $\mathcal{D}_A$ is the distribution that samples $a \xleftarrow{\$} A'$ and returns $\mathsf{Reduce}_A(a)$.

Theorem 2 (TOGA-UE **is** detIND-UE-CPA)**.** *Let* TOGA-UE *be the UE scheme described in Fig. 7 for an ETOGA family* $\mathcal{TOGA}$. *We define a group action family* $\mathcal{GA}$, *where* $\mathcal{GA}(1^\lambda)$ *is* $(A, S, \star_A)$, *the main group action of* $\mathcal{TOGA}(1^\lambda)$ *(as in Definition 10). For any adversary* $\mathcal{A}$, *there exists a reduction* $\mathcal{B}$ *such that*

$$\mathbf{Adv}_{\mathsf{TOGA\text{-}UE},\mathcal{A}}^{\mathsf{detIND\text{-}UE\text{-}CPA}}(\lambda) \leq \mathcal{O}(1)(n+1)^3 \cdot \mathbf{Adv}_{\mathcal{GA},\mathcal{B}}^{\mathsf{wk\text{-}PR}}(\lambda)$$

Proof. The proof uses the same hybrid argument as the one of Theorem 1, thus we only point out the differences between both proofs. Contrary to the proof of Theorem 1, we do not need to use the ideal cipher model. Indeed, in TOGA-UE, randomization of ciphertexts is not done through the permutation ψ. Thus, we do not need to "program" ψ to get consistent randomness throughout our reduction. Our reduction $\mathcal{B}$ is given in Fig. 8. It uses the following notations. Given a ciphertext C_{e} and a token Δ_{e}, we can downgrade C_{e} to epoch $\mathsf{e}-1$ like so:

1. $(c, h) \leftarrow \Delta_{\mathsf{e}}$
2. $b \leftarrow \mathsf{Reduce}_A(c^{-1})$
3. $h' \leftarrow h(b, c)$
4. $C_{\mathsf{e}-1} \leftarrow (hh')^{-1} \star_H (b \star_A C_{\mathsf{e}})$
5. **return** $C_{\mathsf{e}-1}$

For readability, we will use the (abuse of) notation $\Delta_{\mathsf{e}}^{-1} \star C_{\mathsf{e}}$ to denote this downgrade. Similarly, if $\Delta_{\mathsf{e}} = (c, h)$, we will use the notation $\Delta_{\mathsf{e}} \star C_{\mathsf{e}-1}$ to denote the update $h \star_H (c \star_A C_{\mathsf{e}-1})$.

The reduction $\mathcal{B}$ starts by receiving a group action $(A, S, \star_A)$ and an oracle $\mathcal{O}.\mathsf{Sample}$ that returns either tuples of the form $(s_i, a \star_A s_i)$ or (s_i, t_i) where $a \leftarrow \mathcal{D}_A$ and $s_i, t_i \leftarrow \mathcal{D}_S$. We use the same hybrid argument over insulated regions as in Theorem 1. $\mathcal{B}$ will use the tuples of $\mathcal{O}.\mathsf{Sample}$ to perfectly simulate the detIND-UE-CPA experiment for TOGA-UE when those tuples are of the form $(s_i, a \star_A s_i)$. Thus, if we know an efficient adversary $\mathcal{A}$ against the detIND-UE-CPA security of TOGA-UE, using the hybrid argument of Theorem 1, $\mathcal{B}$ can use $\mathcal{A}$ to break the weak pseudorandomness of $(A, S, \star_A)$.

In TOGA-UE, a ciphertext is of the form $C_{\mathsf{e}} := h_{\mathsf{e}} \star_H (a_{\mathsf{e}} \star_A r)$ with $k_{\mathsf{e}} := (a_{\mathsf{e}}, h_{\mathsf{e}})$, where $a_{\mathsf{e}} \leftarrow \mathcal{D}_A$, $h_{\mathsf{e}} \xleftarrow{\$} H$ and $r \leftarrow \mathcal{D}_S$ is the randomness used during the first encryption. Reduction $\mathcal{B}$ will try to embed the $\mathcal{O}.\mathsf{Sample}$ tuples in the i-th insulated region $[\mathsf{fwl}_i, \mathsf{fwr}_i]$. If $(r, s) \leftarrow \mathcal{O}.\mathsf{Sample}()$, $\mathcal{B}$ uses r as randomness for new ciphertexts. When updating ciphertext $C_{\mathsf{fwl}_i-1} := h_{\mathsf{fwl}_i-1} \star_H (a_{\mathsf{fwl}_i-1} \star_A r)$ to epoch fwl_i, $\mathcal{B}$ sets $C_{\mathsf{fwl}_i} := h_{\mathsf{fwl}_i} \star_H s$ where h_{fwl_i} is simulated by $\mathcal{B}$. If (r, s) is of the form $(r, a \star_A r)$, $\mathcal{B}$ has embedded a into $k_{\mathsf{fwl}_i} := (a, h_{\mathsf{fwl}_i})$ and the randomness of the ciphertext stays consistent because of Proposition 5. Else, if (r, s) is a tuple of random elements of S, the ciphertexts inside the i-th insulated region are all random (there is no consistent key or randomness linking them).

Recall that a token $\Delta_{\mathsf{e}+1} := (c_{\mathsf{e}}, h h_{\mathsf{e}+1} h_{\mathsf{e}}^{-1})$ where $h_{\mathsf{e}}, h_{\mathsf{e}+1}$ are part of the epoch keys k_{e} and $k_{\mathsf{e}+1}$ and c_{e}, h are computed by Upd using those keys. When both keys are unknown (like in the i-th insulated region), c_{e} is uniformly distributed in G by Definition 12 item 2e. Recall that $h \in H$ is useful for the correction of updates (see Proposition 5) and that it is not independent of c_{e}. However, h_{e} and $h_{\mathsf{e}+1}$ are sampled uniformly in H and are not used in the computations of c_{e} and h. Since h_{e} and $h_{\mathsf{e}+1}$ are unknown to the adversary in the i-th insulated region, $h h_{\mathsf{e}+1} h_{\mathsf{e}}^{-1}$ is uniformly distributed in H and reduction $\mathcal{B}$ can perfectly simulate tokens inside the i-th insulated region.

Because of the correctness of updates in TOGA-UE (see Proposition 5) and of the observations above, when $\mathcal{O}.\mathsf{Sample}$ returns tuples of the form $(s_i, a \star_A s_i)$, the reduction $\mathcal{B}$ perfectly simulates the environment of the adversary $\mathcal{A}$ and we get a similar result as the one of Theorem 1.

Reduction $\mathcal{B}$ playing $\mathbf{Exp}^{\text{wk-PR-b*}}_{\mathcal{GA},\mathcal{B}}(\lambda)$

1. **receive** $(A, S, \star_A)$ and $\mathcal{O}.\mathsf{Sample}$
2. **do Setup**(1^λ)
3. $\bar{M}, \bar{C} \leftarrow \mathcal{A}^{\mathtt{ors}}(\lambda)$
4. $\mathsf{phase} \leftarrow 1$
5. $\tilde{C}_{\tilde{\mathsf{e}}} \leftarrow \mathcal{O}.\mathsf{Chall}(\bar{M}, \bar{C})$
6. $b' \leftarrow \mathcal{A}^{\mathtt{ors}, \mathcal{O}.\mathsf{Upd}\tilde{\mathsf{C}}}(\tilde{C}_{\tilde{\mathsf{e}}})$
7. **if** $\mathcal{C}^* \cap \mathcal{K}^* \neq \emptyset$ **or** $\mathcal{I}^* \cap \mathcal{C}^* \neq \emptyset$
8. $\quad \mathsf{twf} \leftarrow 1$
9. **if** ABORT occurred **or** $\mathsf{twf} = 1$
10. $\quad b' \xleftarrow{\$} \{0, 1\}$
11. $\quad$ **return** b'
12. **if** $(i, \mathsf{fwl}_i, \mathsf{fwr}_i) \notin \mathcal{FW}$
13. $\quad b' \xleftarrow{\$} \{0, 1\}$
14. $\quad$ **return** b'
15. **if** $b' = b$
16. $\quad$ **return** 0
17. **else**
18. $\quad$ **return** 1

Setup(1^λ)

1. $b \xleftarrow{\$} \{0, 1\}$
2. $\mathsf{pp} \leftarrow \mathsf{TOGA\text{-}UE.Setup}(1^\lambda)$
3. $k_0 \leftarrow \mathsf{TOGA\text{-}UE.KeyGen}(\mathsf{pp})$
4. $\Delta_0 \leftarrow \perp$
5. $\mathsf{e}, \mathsf{c}, \mathsf{phase}, \mathsf{twf} \leftarrow 0$
6. $\mathcal{L}, \tilde{\mathcal{L}}, \mathcal{C}, \mathcal{K}, \mathcal{T} \leftarrow \emptyset$
7. $\mathsf{fwl}_i, \mathsf{fwr}_i \xleftarrow{\$} \{0, \ldots, n\}$
8. **for** $j \in \{0, \ldots, \mathsf{fwl}_i - 1\} \cup \{\mathsf{fwr}_i + 1, \ldots, n\}$ **do**
9. $\quad a_j \leftarrow \mathcal{D}_A, h_j \xleftarrow{\$} H$
10. $\quad k_j \leftarrow (a_j, h_j)$
11. $\quad \Delta_j \leftarrow \mathsf{TOGA\text{-}UE.TokenGen}(k_j, k_{j+1})^{\bowtie}$
12. **for** $j \in \{\mathsf{fwl}_i + 1, \ldots, \mathsf{fwr}_i\}$ **do**
13. $\quad c_j \leftarrow \mathcal{D}_A, h_j \xleftarrow{\$} H$
14. $\quad \Delta_j \leftarrow (c_j, h_j)$
15. $h_{\mathsf{fwl}_i} \xleftarrow{\$} H$

$\mathcal{O}.\mathsf{Enc}(M)$

1. $\mathsf{c} \leftarrow \mathsf{c} + 1$
2. $(\mathsf{inf}_1, \mathsf{inf}_2) \leftarrow \mathcal{O}.\mathsf{Sample}()$
3. **if** $\mathsf{e} \in \{0, \mathsf{fwl}_i - 1\} \cup \{\mathsf{fwr}_i + 1, \ldots, n\}$
4. $\quad (a_{\mathsf{e}}, h_{\mathsf{e}}) \leftarrow k_{\mathsf{e}}$
5. $\quad C_{\mathsf{e}} \leftarrow (\psi(M) h_{\mathsf{e}}) \star_H (a_{\mathsf{e}} \star_A \mathsf{inf}_1)$
6. **else**
7. $\quad C_{\mathsf{fwl}_i} \leftarrow (\psi(M) h_{\mathsf{fwl}_i}) \star_H \mathsf{inf}_2$
8. $\quad$ **for** $j \in \{\mathsf{fwl}_i + 1, \ldots, \mathsf{e}\}$ **do**
9. $\quad\quad C_j \leftarrow \Delta_j \star C_{j-1}$
10. $\mathsf{inf} \leftarrow (\mathsf{inf}_1, \mathsf{inf}_2, M)$
11. $\mathcal{L} \leftarrow \mathcal{L} \cup \{(\mathsf{c}, C_{\mathsf{e}}, \mathsf{e}; \mathsf{inf})\}$
12. **return** C_{e}

$\mathcal{O}.\mathsf{Next}$

1. $\mathsf{e} \leftarrow \mathsf{e} + 1$

$\mathcal{O}.\mathsf{Upd}(C_{\mathsf{e}-1})$

1. **if** $(\mathsf{c}, C_{\mathsf{e}-1}, \mathsf{e} - 1; \mathsf{inf}) \notin \mathcal{L}$
2. $\quad$ **return** $\perp$
3. **if** $\mathsf{e} \in \{1, \ldots, \mathsf{fwl}_i - 1\} \cup \{\mathsf{fwr}_i + 1, \ldots, n\}$
4. $\quad (\mathsf{inf}_1, \mathsf{inf}_2, M) \leftarrow \mathsf{inf}$
5. $\quad (a_{\mathsf{e}}, h_{\mathsf{e}}) \leftarrow k_{\mathsf{e}}$
6. $\quad C_{\mathsf{e}} \leftarrow (\psi(M) h_{\mathsf{e}}) \star_H (a_{\mathsf{e}} \star_A \mathsf{inf}_1)$
7. **else**
8. $\quad (\mathsf{inf}_1, \mathsf{inf}_2, M) \leftarrow \mathsf{inf}$
9. $\quad C_{\mathsf{fwl}_i} \leftarrow (\psi(M) h_{\mathsf{fwl}_i}) \star_H \mathsf{inf}_2$
10. $\quad$ **for** $j \in \{\mathsf{fwl}_i + 1, \ldots, \mathsf{e}\}$ **do**
11. $\quad\quad C_j \leftarrow \Delta_j \star C_{j-1}$
12. $\mathcal{L} \leftarrow \mathcal{L} \cup \{(\mathsf{c}, C_{\mathsf{e}}, \mathsf{e}; \mathsf{inf})\}$
13. **return** C_{e}

$\mathcal{O}.\mathsf{Corr}(\mathsf{inp}, \hat{\mathsf{e}})$

1. **do** $\mathsf{Check}(\mathsf{inp}, \hat{\mathsf{e}}; \mathsf{e}; \mathsf{fwl}_i, \mathsf{fwr}_i)$
2. **if** $\mathsf{inp} = \mathsf{key}$
3. $\quad \mathcal{K} \leftarrow \mathcal{K} \cup \{\hat{\mathsf{e}}\}$
4. $\quad$ **return** $k_{\hat{\mathsf{e}}}$
5. **if** $\mathsf{inp} = \mathsf{token}$
6. $\quad \mathcal{T} \leftarrow \mathcal{T} \cup \{\hat{\mathsf{e}}\}$
7. $\quad$ **return** $\Delta_{\hat{\mathsf{e}}}$

$\mathcal{O}.\mathsf{Chall}(\bar{M}, \bar{C})$

1. **if** $(\mathsf{c}, \bar{C}, \tilde{\mathsf{e}} - 1; \mathsf{inf}) \notin \mathcal{L}$
2. $\quad$ **return** ABORT
3. **if** $b = 0$
4. $\quad (s, t) \leftarrow \mathcal{O}.\mathsf{Sample}()$
5. $\quad r \leftarrow s$
6. $\quad \tilde{C}_{\mathsf{fwl}_i} \leftarrow (\psi(\bar{M}) h_{\mathsf{fwl}_i}) \star_H t$
7. **else**
8. $\quad (\mathsf{inf}_1, \mathsf{inf}_2, M) \leftarrow \mathsf{inf}$
9. $\quad r \leftarrow \mathcal{D}_S$
10. $\quad \tilde{C}_{\mathsf{fwl}_i} \leftarrow (\psi(M) h_{\mathsf{fwl}_i}) \star_H \mathsf{inf}_2$
11. **for** $j \in \{0, \ldots, \mathsf{fwl}_i - 1\}$ **do**
12. $\quad \tilde{C}_j \leftarrow (\prod_{k=j}^{1} \Delta_k)(\prod_{k=1}^{\tilde{\mathsf{e}}-1} \Delta_k^{-1}) \star \bar{C}$ //left
13. **for** $j \in \{\mathsf{fwl}_i + 1, \ldots, \mathsf{fwr}_i\}$ **do**
14. $\quad \tilde{C}_j \leftarrow \Delta_j \star \tilde{C}_{j-1}$ //embed
15. **for** $j \in \{\mathsf{fwr}_i + 1, \ldots, n\}$ **do**
16. $\quad (a_j, h_j) \leftarrow k_j$
17. $\quad \tilde{C}_j \leftarrow (\psi(\bar{M}) h_j) \star_H (a_j \star_A r)$ //right
18. $\tilde{\mathcal{L}} \leftarrow \cup_{j=0}^{n} \{(\tilde{C}_j, j)\}$
19. **return** $\tilde{C}_{\mathsf{e}}$

$\mathcal{O}.\mathsf{Upd}\tilde{\mathsf{C}}$

1. $\mathcal{C} \leftarrow \mathcal{C} \cup \{\mathsf{e}\}$
2. **find** $(\tilde{C}_{\mathsf{e}}, \mathsf{e}) \in \tilde{\mathcal{L}}$
3. **return** $\tilde{C}_{\mathsf{e}}$

Fig. 8. Our reduction $\mathcal{B}$ for proof of th. 2 in hybrid i. $\mathtt{ors}$ refers to the set $\{\mathcal{O}.\mathsf{Enc}, \mathcal{O}.\mathsf{Next}, \mathcal{O}.\mathsf{Upd}, \mathcal{O}.\mathsf{Corr}\}$. $\bowtie$ indicates that Δ_0 and $\Delta_{\mathsf{fwr}_i+1}$ are skipped in the computation.

On the CCA Security of TOGA-UE. Unlike GAINE, making TOGA-UE CCA secure appears to be hard. Indeed, our construction has a pretty clear malleability property: let M, M' be two distinct messages, under the ψ map we get two elements $h := \psi(M), h' := \psi(M')$. Then, for any encryption c of the message M, we compute $h'h^{-1} \star_H c$ to obtain a valid encryption of M'. We leave the problem of making TOGA-UE CCA secure open for future work.

5 Instantiation from Isogenies

The GAINE construction introduced in Sect. 3 requires a MEGA, i.e., that the underlying group action is mappable (which we showed was implying the group action to be hashable). Isogeny-based cryptography is one of the main providers of post-quantum cryptographic group action so it is natural to ask if we can instantiate GAINE from them. Unfortunately, it is notoriously hard to hash into the set of supersingular curves [7] and this implies that building a MEGA from isogenies is probably very hard. This fact is what motivated the introduction of our new TOGA framework to build UE. In fact, our UE scheme is inspired by the SIGAMAL encryption scheme from Moriya, Onuki and Takagi [28]. Instead of encrypting messages as curves (wich would require to hash into the set of supersingular curves), we propose to encrypt messages as scalars similarly to what is done in SIGAMAL. In that sense, the instantiation of our UE scheme with isogenies can be considered as an updatable version of SIGAMAL. More precisely, our main group action $\star_A$ will be the one of fractional ideals of quadratic orders on orientations of supersingular curves. Under the usual equivalence relation on ideals, the group action $\star_G$ induced by this group action is the standard group action of the class group on oriented supersingular curves used in isogeny-based cryptography [10,13,17]. To obtain the richer structure of TOGA as in Definition 11, we consider orientations on curves with a level N-structure, i.e., curves that are enriched with a point of order N. In that setting, the group H is simply $\mathbb{Z}/N\mathbb{Z}^*$ and the action $\star_H$ is the scalar multiplication on the points of order N. For everything to be well-defined and behave as expected by our computational model, we must take N as a smooth number split in the quadratic order.

5.1 A TOGA from Isogenies

We fix a prime p and consider the supersingular elliptic curves in characteristic p. In practice, they can always be defined over $\mathbb{F}_{p^2}$. We take a quadratic order $\mathfrak{O}$ of discriminant Δ and write $\mathfrak{K}$ for the quadratic imaginary field $\mathbb{Q} \otimes \mathfrak{O}$.

Definition 13. *For any elliptic curve E, a $\mathfrak{K}$-orientation is a ring homomorphism $\iota : \mathfrak{K} \hookrightarrow \mathrm{End}(E) \otimes \mathbb{Q}$. A $\mathfrak{K}$-orientation induces an $\mathfrak{O}$-orientation if $\iota(\mathfrak{O}) = \mathrm{End}(E) \cap \iota(\mathfrak{K})$. In that case, the couple (E, ι) is called an $\mathfrak{O}$-oriented curve and E is an $\mathfrak{O}$-orientable curve.*

In what follows, we consider the elements of $\mathcal{S}(p)/\pi$ rather than $\mathcal{S}(p)$ because the Frobenius π creates two orientations (one in E and one in $E^{(p)}$) from each optimal embedding of $\mathfrak{O}$ in a quaternion maximal order of $B_{p,\infty}$. Note that this is not the convention taken in [31,38] where orientations are not considered up to Galois conjugacy.

Definition 14. *$\mathcal{S}_{\mathfrak{O}}(p)$ is the set of $\mathfrak{O}$-oriented curves E, ι up to isomorphisms and Galois conjugacy.*

More concretely, we obtain an orientation E, ι by an endomorphism $\theta \in \text{End}(E)$ such that $\iota(\mathfrak{O}) = \mathbb{Z}[\theta]$. Note that $\mathcal{S}_{\mathfrak{O}}(p)$ may be empty for some quadratic orders $\mathfrak{O}$ but it is also non-empty for an infinite number of order $\mathfrak{O}$ given any prime p.

The Group Action of Fractional Ideals. When we consider fractional $\mathfrak{O}$-ideal, we get an abelian group (for the multiplication operation). This group acts on the elements of $\mathcal{S}_{\mathfrak{O}}(p)$ by an operation that we write $\star_A$. This action is computed concretely using isogenies. Given an integral ideal $\mathfrak{a}$ and $E, \iota \in \mathcal{S}_{\mathfrak{O}}(p)$, we define the kernel of $\mathfrak{a}$ as $E[\mathfrak{a}] := \{P \in E[n(\mathfrak{a})] \mid \iota(\alpha)(P) = 0, \ \forall \alpha \in \mathfrak{a}\}$. The isogeny $\varphi_{\mathfrak{a}}^E : E \to E_{\mathfrak{a}}$ is simply the isogeny of kernel $E[\mathfrak{a}]$. Thus, we have $E_{\mathfrak{a}} = E/E[\mathfrak{a}]$ and $\iota_{\mathfrak{a}}(x) = \frac{1}{n(\mathfrak{a})} \varphi_{\mathfrak{a}}^E \circ \iota(x) \circ \hat{\varphi}_{\mathfrak{a}}^E$.

Fractional ideals can always be expressed as the multiplication of an integral ideal and a scalar in $\mathbb{Q}$. Thus, we will decompose the action of fractional ideals by applying first the action of the integral part as defined above, then by doing a scalar multiplication. We will explain how we propose to do this exactly a bit later when we introduce the set S.

Since our goal, in the end, is to get an ETOGA as defined in Sect. 4.2, we define the concrete group A that we will use as a subgroup of the group of $\mathfrak{O}$-ideals. This restriction is motivated by efficiency of the computation of $\star_A$. Indeed, the cost of computing an isogeny of degree D is in $O(\sqrt{D'})$ where D' is the biggest factor of D (see [16]). Thus, it is pointless to consider ideals that are multiples of prime ideals of big prime norm. This is why we fix an effective factor base of the $\mathfrak{O}$-ideals as a collection of ideals $\mathfrak{l}_1, \dots, \mathfrak{l}_n$ where each $\mathfrak{l}_i$ is an ideal of norm ℓ_i for a small prime ℓ_i that is split in $\mathfrak{O}$ (here, small is to be considered with respect to some complexity parameter λ). We stress that the need for small factors is standard across isogenies. Note that any such ideal $\mathfrak{l}_i$ has a *dual* ideal, usually denoted by $\overline{\mathfrak{l}_i}$, such that $\mathfrak{O}\ell_i = \mathfrak{l}_i\overline{\mathfrak{l}_i}$. Then, we can define the inverse of $\mathfrak{l}_i$ as $\mathfrak{l}_i^{-1} := \overline{\mathfrak{l}_i}/\ell_i$. Thus, $\mathfrak{l}_i^e$ is defined for any $e \in \mathbb{Z}$. With these definitions, we set our group A as $\langle \mathfrak{l}_1, \dots, \mathfrak{l}_n \rangle_{\mathbb{Z}} := \{\prod_{i=1}^n \mathfrak{l}_i^{e_i} \ell_i^{f_i} \mid (e_1, \dots, e_n) \in \mathbb{Z}^n, (f_1 \dots, f_n) \in \mathbb{Z}^n\}$, the subgroup generated by our collection of prime ideals and their inverse. The implicit bijection between A and $\mathbb{Z}^{2n}$ given in our definition provides a way of representing the elements of A.

The standard cryptographic group action used in isogeny-based cryptography is obtained from our main group action of ideals by considering the equivalence relation $\sim_A$ defined as $\mathfrak{a} \sim_A \mathfrak{b}$ iff there exist non zero-elements $a, b \in \mathfrak{O}$ with $(a)\mathfrak{a} = (b)\mathfrak{b}$. It can be verified that $\sim_A$ is a congruence relation and so $A/\sim_A$ is an abelian group. If n is big enough A contains all equivalence classes of $\mathfrak{O}$-ideals. In that case, the group $A/\sim_A$ is called the *class group* of $\mathfrak{O}$ and written $\text{Cl}(\mathfrak{O})$.

By definition of $\mathcal{S}_{\mathfrak{O}}(p)$ (up to isomorphisms and Galois conjugacy), equivalent ideals act identically on the elements of $\mathcal{S}_{\mathfrak{O}}(p)$. Thus, the group action induced by $\star_A$ on $\mathcal{S}_{\mathfrak{O}}(p)$ as in Definition 10 is the usual isogeny-based group action. Since we clearly have $\ell\mathfrak{a} \sim_A \mathfrak{a}$ for any $\ell \in \mathbb{Q}^*$ and $\mathfrak{a} \in A$, we see that any ideal class of $A/\sim_A$ admits a representative of the form $\prod_{i=1}^n \mathfrak{l}_i^{e_i}$ where $(e_1,\ldots,e_n) \in \mathbb{Z}^n$. Thus, we can use elements of $\mathbb{Z}^n$ to represent the elements of G. More concretely, $\Phi : (e_1,\ldots,e_n) \mapsto \prod_{i=1}^n \mathfrak{l}_i^{e_i}$ yields an isomorphism between $A/\sim_A$ and $\mathbb{Z}^n/\mathcal{L}$ where $\mathcal{L}$ is the lattice generated by the $\mathbf{e} \in \mathbb{Z}^n$ such that $\Phi(\mathbf{e}) \sim_A 1_A$. The lattice $\mathcal{L}$ is usually called the *lattice of relations* of $\mathrm{Cl}(\mathfrak{O})$ for the factor basis $\mathfrak{l}_1,\ldots,\mathfrak{l}_n$.

The Orbital Group Action. We now introduce our third group action (written $\star_H$ in Definition 11). To get this orbital group action, our idea is to use the group of points of the orientable elliptic curves. Let us take N a split integer in $\mathfrak{O}$ coprime with all the ℓ_i for $1 \leq i \leq n$. We can consider elements of the form E,ι,P where $P \in E[N]$ has order N. The group of fractional ideals of norm coprime with N acts on this set in the following manner: let us consider the fractional ideal $(a/b)\mathfrak{a}$ where $\mathfrak{a}$ is an integral ideal, we have the action $(a/b)\mathfrak{a} \star (E,\iota,P) = E_{\mathfrak{a}},\iota_{\mathfrak{a}},[ac]\varphi_{\mathfrak{a}}^E(P)$ where $c = b^{-1} \mod N$. However, in this setting, it seems hard to get a group action $\star_H$ as we desire. Indeed, equivalent ideals will send E,ι,P on E_1,ι_1,P_1 and E_2,ι_2,P_2 where we have $E_1,\iota_1 = E_2,\iota_2$ but we cannot tell anything about the points P_1,P_2 apart from the fact that they are two points of order N. Fortunately, if we restrict the set of points of order N we consider, the situation becomes a lot simpler. For that, if we have $\mathfrak{O} = \mathbb{Z}[\theta]$, it suffices to consider one eigenvalue of θ, i.e., one value ν such that $\ker(\iota(\theta)-\nu) \cap E[N]$ is a cyclic subgroup of order N. Since N is split, we know there exists one such eigenvalue ν and if $P \in \ker(\iota(\theta)-\nu) \cap E[N]$, we get that $\varphi^E\mathfrak{a}(P) \in \ker(\iota_{\mathfrak{a}}(\theta)-\nu) \cap E_{\mathfrak{a}}[N]$. Let us take

$$S = \{(E,\iota,P) \mid (E,\iota) \in \mathcal{S}_{\mathfrak{O}}(p) \text{ and } \langle P\rangle = E[N] \cap \ker(\iota(\theta)-\nu\}. \quad (1)$$

With that choice of S, the image under the group action of two equivalent fractional ideals $\mathfrak{a}_1,\mathfrak{a}_2$ on $E,\iota,P \in S$ will give E_1,ι_1,P_1 and E_2,ι_2,P_2 with P_1 and P_2 in the same subgroup, i.e., there exists $\mu \in H = \mathbb{Z}/N\mathbb{Z}^*$ such that $P_1 = \mu P_2$. Moreover, it is easily verified that the scalar μ depends only on two ideals $\mathfrak{a}_1,\mathfrak{a}_2$ (and not on E,ι and P) as it corresponds to the action of the endomorphism corresponding to $\mathfrak{a}_1\overline{\mathfrak{a}_2}$ on the eigen-space of ν. This scalar μ is what we call $h(\mathfrak{a}_1,\mathfrak{a}_2)$ in our definition of a TOGA.

In that setting, for any scalar $h \in H$, we define $h \star_H (E,\iota,P)$ as $(E,\iota,[h]P)$ and it can be verified that $(A,H,S,\star_A,\sim_A,\star_H)$ is a TOGA.

5.2 Making the Isogeny TOGA Effective

To instantiate our protocol, we not only need a TOGA but an ETOGA as in Sect. 4.2. Below, we address the efficiency requirements. We try to stay generic in our approach and a more detailed example can be found in Sect. 5.3.

In fact, we are going to see that our proposed solution from isogeny is not exactly an ETOGA, but we can assume every operations to be practical assuming some (possibly-heavy) precomputation. In what follows, we discuss these limitations to understand what are the main obstacles.

The Elements of S and the Canonical Representation of Equivalence Classes. We need to verify that the set S satisfies several properties. First, it needs to be finite which is our case (the cardinal is equal to $\varphi(N)h(\mathfrak{O})$ where φ is Euler's totient function). Regarding the existence of an origin s_0, it suffices to fix an element $s_0 \in \mathrm{S}$ as the origin. There may be different ways of finding one, depending on the concrete $\mathfrak{O}$ and p, but a generic algorithm to compute one is given in [17] (in the context of generating backdoor curves for the Séta encryption scheme).

Regarding the unique representation of the elements of S, it suffices to use a canonical representation of a class of isomorphic curves (using the j-invariant for instance). Once the curve E is fixed, we can deterministically derive a representation of the orientation ι and of any point P. The naive way of representing the point P would be by giving its coordinates x, y but we propose to use another way that is more compact in most cases. The idea is that given a basis P_1, P_2 of $E[N]$, any points $P \in E[N]$ is equal to $[a]P_1 + [b]P_2$ for some $a, b \in \mathbb{Z}/N\mathbb{Z}$. If the basis P_1, P_2 can be computed deterministically from E, the coefficients a, b are enough to recover the point P from the knowledge of E. This representation has size $2\log(N)$ which is usually a lot better than what we can expect with the naive method (that can be in $O(N\log(p))$ in the worst case). A deterministic algorithm to compute a basis of $E[N]$ from N can be easily derived from a deterministic algorithm $\mathsf{Point}(E, N, i)$ that takes an elliptic curve E and two integers i, N and outputs a point $P(i)$ of order N in E (the role of i is simply to index the points). There are numerous examples of such algorithms in the literature (see [3,15,29,32,39] for instance) so we do not describe one in detail. This algorithm will be useful for Reduce_S as well.

Membership testing for a given element E, ι, P in S consists in: veriyfing that E is supersingular, that ι is a correct orientation and that P is in $\ker(\iota(\theta) - \nu)$ and has order N. The first check can always be performed in polynomial time if p is in $\mathsf{poly}(\lambda)$, because supersingular curves have a known order. The second check will really depend on the choice of $\mathfrak{O}$ so it cannot be described generically but the idea is that we need to be able to verify the norm and trace of $\iota(\theta)$. For the third check, we simply need to be able to perform efficient operations on the N-torsion, so we need $E[N]$ to be defined over a field extension of degree polynomial in p. For the examples of CSIDH and SCALLOP given in Sect. 5.3 all these operations are efficient.

The last ingredient we need for S is the Reduce_S algorithm. Its goal is to determine a unique representative of the classes of S for the equivalence relation $\sim_S$. We recall that these classes correspond to the orbits of the group action of H. Thus, what we need concretely is an efficient way to compute a canonical point P_E of order N in $E[N] \cap \ker(\iota(\theta) - \nu)$ from E, ι. We will use the Point algorithm for that. Let us write ν', the second eigenvalues of $\iota(\theta)$.

$\mathsf{Reduce}_S(E, \iota, \cdot)$:

1. Compute $U = E[N] \cap \ker(\iota(\theta) - \nu)$ and $V = E[N] \cap \ker(\iota(\theta) - \nu')$.
2. Let $i = 0$, Repeat the following:
   (a) $P = \mathsf{Point}(E, N, i)$.
   (b) Compute the unique decomposition $P = P_U + P_V$ where $P_U \in U$ and $P_V \in V$.
   (c) $i = i + 1$.
3. Until P_V has order N.
4. Return E, ι, P_V.

The unique decomposition $P = P_U + P_V$ can be computed efficiently because the discrete logarithm problem is easy in $E[N]$.

Making $(H, S, \star_H)$ *into an EEGA.* First, note that it is easily verified that the group $H = \mathbb{Z}/N\mathbb{Z}^*$ is meeting all the requirements in terms of membership and equality testing, sampling and operations. Finally, the group action $\star_H$ being the scalar multiplication, it is clear that it can be performed in polynomial time when all the other operations can be done in PPT. For $(H, S, \star_H)$ to be an EEGA, we need to be able to invert efficiently $\star_H$. It is easily seen that Invert_H is simply a DLP in a cyclic subgroup of $E[N]$. For this operation to be efficient with the Pohlig-Hellman algorithm, we need N to be smooth (with smoothness bound polynomial in λ). Fortunately, this condition is rather agreeable with the other constraint regarding the field of definition of $E[N]$. Indeed, for any prime p, we know that $E[N]$ has a field of definition whose degree is polynomial (in the powersmoothness bound of N) for any p. In practice, we can even choose the prime p to ensure that $E[N]$ is defined over $\mathbb{F}_p$ or $\mathbb{F}_{p^2}$. This allows us to consider smooth values of N as well (for instance a power of 2).

The Subset A'. The main requirement for A' is efficiency of $\star_A$. The complexity of this computation mainly depends on $n(\mathfrak{a})$ (because $\star_A$ consists in the computation of an isogeny of degree $n(\mathfrak{a})$). More concretely, the computation of an isogeny of degree $\prod_{i=1}^n \ell_i^{e_i}$ is in $O(n \max_{1\le i \le n} e_i \max_{1 \le i \le n} \sqrt{\ell_i})$. Thus, we need that $n, \max_{1 \le i \le n} \ell_i$ and $\max_{1\le i\le n} e_i$ are all polynomial in λ. We have already assumed that it was the case for n and the ℓ_i, so we only need to put a bound m on the exponent. Unfortunately, having an asymptotic polynomial bound on m will not be possible due to the Reduce_A algorithm that we will detail below. However, the value of m will remain reasonably small in practice as was demonstrated for CSIDH in [5] and SCALLOP [19]. This motivates to set A' as $\{\prod_{i=1}^n \mathfrak{l}_i^{e_i} \mid \mathbf{e} = (e_1, \ldots, e_n) \in \mathbb{Z}^n \text{ and } \|\mathbf{e}\|_\infty \le m\}$ for some value m. Under the map Φ that we introduced in Sect. 5.1, we can sample elements of A' as image under Φ of random vectors in the ball $\mathcal{B}_\infty(m) = \{\mathbf{e} \in \mathbb{Z}^n \mid \|\mathbf{e}\|_\infty \le m\}$ inside $\mathbb{Z}^n$ and it is clear that we can sample uniform vectors in that set. In the definition of an ETOGA, we also need that A' covers all equivalence classes of $A/\sim_A$ and that sampling in A' gives classes that are statistically distributed uniformly in G. We see that the cardinal of A' is $(2m+1)^n$. Thus, even when $\#A/\sim_A$ is exponential in λ, we can take small values of m, n such that A' is big enough to hope that all equivalence classes are covered and that sampling in A' provide a good distribution in $\mathrm{Cl}(\mathfrak{O})$. In practice, this is what we observe for the example given in Sect. 5.3.

Regarding the Reduce_A function, we use Φ again. Let us take an element $\mathfrak{a} \in A$. We know that this corresponds to an element of $\mathbb{Z}^{2n}$. Once again, since scalars are in the class of 1_A, we can simply ignore them and consider the equivalent ideal of the form $\prod_{i=1}^{n} \mathfrak{l}_i^{e_i}$ that corresponds to the vector $(e_1, \ldots, e_n) \in \mathbb{Z}^n$ under the map Φ. The ideal that we look for is $\Phi(\mathbf{e}')$ where $\mathbf{e}' \in \mathcal{B}_\infty(m)$ and $\mathbf{e}' \in \mathcal{L}$. If m is big enough, a correct solution e' is given by solving a Closest Vector Problem (CVP). Hence, we define a parameter $\gamma \geq 1$ and look for a solution of the γ-CVP. Of course, the parameter γ and m need to be compatible in the sense that we want the solutions of our γ-CVP to be contained in $\mathcal{B}_\infty(m)$.

More concretely, the Reduce_A algorithms consists in the following steps given an ideal $\mathfrak{a}$ as input: divide $\mathfrak{a}$ by its scalar factor to get another ideal $\mathfrak{a}'$, compute $\mathbf{e} = \Phi^{-1}(\mathfrak{a}')$, compute $\mathbf{e}'$ a solution for the γ-CVP for $\mathbf{e}$ and $\mathcal{L}$, output $\Phi(\mathbf{e}')$. The complexity of Reduce_A mainly depends on the complexity of solving the γ-CVP problem. The best known algorithm are sub-exponential in the dimension of the lattice $\mathcal{L}$ (here it is n) but the cost can be greatly reduced if the lattice $\mathcal{L}$ comes with a small basis of $\mathcal{L}$ (see [18]). This shifts the computational cost to the precomputation of a nice basis of $\mathcal{L}$. The cost of this precomputation is why we cannot have m polynomial in λ. Indeed, having a polynomial m would require to make a precomputation of exponential complexity (which would be greater than the complexity of attacks) to compute a good basis of the lattice $\mathcal{L}$. Thus, asymptotically, it is only possible to have m sub-exponential in λ so that the basis reduction remains feasible. However, in the practical examples of the literature, the dimension of the lattice remains small enough that it is possible to obtain a reasonable value of m (see [5,19] and our discussion in Sect. 5.3) The choice of γ might also offer interesting tradeoffs between the cost of $\star_A$ and the cost of Reduce_A.

5.3 Concrete Instantiation for Isogeny TOGA and TOGA-UE

There are currently two candidates to instantiate our ETOGA from isogenies. The most standard one is the CSIDH group action [10], but there is also the recent SCALLOP construction [19] and its improved variant SCALLOP-HD [12]. Below we will briefly explain the limitations and advantages of these two family of schemes. Then, we will discuss their security.

In CSIDH, the quadratic order $\mathfrak{O}$ is $\mathbb{Z}[\sqrt{-p}]$. This particular choice allows us to compute the group action quite efficiently when the prime p is chosen carefully. Indeed, the orientation of $\mathfrak{O}$ is induced by the Frobenius endomorphism which is always very easy to compute. A very nice side effect is that all the curves considered are defined over $\mathbb{F}_p$ (and not $\mathbb{F}_{p^2}$ as is the case for all the other supersingular curves). The common example in the literature is the CSIDH-512 prime given in [10] for which the computation of the group action is particularly efficient for ideals of norm $\prod_{i=1}^{n} \ell_i^{e_i}$ with $\{\ell_i\}_{1 \leq i \leq n}$ the set of the 74 small primes that divide $p+1$. All the necessary precomputations related to this prime were performed in [5]. The authors of [5] implemented the full group action and obtained reasonable performances. However, the problem with CSIDH is that there is no control over the structure of the class group $\mathrm{Cl}(\mathfrak{O})$. Computing this structure is the bottleneck of the precomputation, and it seems currently infeasible to scale the precomputations made in [5] to higher level of security. This is a big obstacle given the lack of consensus in the community regarding the exact security level of CSIDH-512 (see the security paragraph below).

The recent SCALLOP construction [19] was introduced to overcome some of the limitations of CSIDH. In particular, the authors of SCALLOP propose to use $\mathfrak{O} = \mathbb{Z}[f\sqrt{-1}]$ for a well-chosen prime number f. In that case, the exact structure of the class group $\mathrm{Cl}(\mathfrak{O})$ is given freely by a mathematical theorem. This, in turn, gives some freedom to choose the value of f in a way that greatly simplifies the rest of the required precomputations. However, the concrete orientation is not realized by a simple endomorphism like the Frobenius, and so the group action in itself is generally much slower than the one of CSIDH for the same level of security. Nonetheless, SCALLOP appears more promising than CSIDH to reach a high level of security. The authors managed to perform the necessary precomputation for a level of security equivalent to CSIDH-1024 (essentially doubling the level of security of CSIDH-512) without any extensive computational resources. However, the performances they obtained are not very practical (one group action takes several minutes to compute). Recently, a variant of SCALLOP based on high dimensional isogenies was introduced in [12]. The main improvement of the resulting group action called SCALLOP-HD is a faster precomputation, but there is also some room to improve the efficiency of the group action computation in itself. Unfortunately, these improvements do not increase radically the performances of SCALLOP.

The Security. First, we want to stress that establishing the exact level of security reached by a specific instance of CSIDH and SCALLOP in the post-quantum setting is out of the scope of this paper so we do not claim any particular security level.

The standard group action used in isogeny-based cryptography corresponds to the induced one $\star_G$ in our ETOGA. In the case of CSIDH, it is a quite standard assumption that this group action is weak-PR. Given how recent the scheme is, the weak pseudorandomness of $\star_G$ in SCALLOP has been a lot less studied, but there is currently no reason to believe that it might not hold. However, our scheme requires that the main group action $\star_A$ is also weak pseudorandom. In the case of CSIDH, this was studied in the context of SIGAMAL [28]. The same cannot be said for $\star_A$ in SCALLOP, even though, once again, there are currently no reason to believe that it might be easier than its CSIDH counterpart.

As of yet, both constructions are not affected by the recent attacks against SIDH [11,26,33]. This has already been stated several times in the literature for the main group action of CSIDH, and the analysis of SCALLOP in [19] also concludes that the scheme remains safe for now. Similarly, the recent attacks against SIDH do not appear to affect the weak pseudorandomness of $\star_A$. Indeed, the fact that the image of a point under the secret isogeny is revealed does not seem problematic when the degree is unknown (and there does not seem to be a way to use the point to obtain some information on the degree either). In particular, we see that some of the attacks developed in [20] do not apply in our case because the image of only one point is given and so the Weil pairing (which is self-trivial) does not help in recovering information on the degree. The lack of existence of such a self-pairing in the case that interests us was recently demonstrated in [9]. Some recent techniques presented by Castryck and Vercauteren were showed to be ineffective to attack SCALLOP(-HD) in [12]. Nonetheless, further analysis of these problems is required in order to gain confidence in their hardness and to estimate concretely the size of the parameters required to get the weak pseudorandomness of $\star_A$.

In conclusion, even though CSIDH and SCALLOP(-HD) are not perfect candidates, they are currently the best solution we have. We hope that our construction will motivate further research in that topic and that our ETOGA construction can help building more advanced protocols from isogenies.

Acknowledgements. The authors are very thankful to Jonas Lehmann and Sabrina Kunzweiler for pointing out a mistake in an earlier version of the paper.

Appendix A Computing Leakage Sets

Following [25], extended epoch leakage sets $\mathcal{C}^*$, $\mathcal{K}^*$ and $\mathcal{T}^*$ are computed as follows:

$$\begin{aligned}
&\mathcal{K}^* \leftarrow \{\mathsf{e} \in \{0,\dots,n\} \mid \mathsf{CorrK(e)} = \mathsf{true}\}\\
&\quad \mathsf{true} \leftarrow \mathsf{CorrK(e)} \Leftrightarrow (\mathsf{e} \in \mathcal{K}) \vee (\mathsf{CorrK(e}-1) \wedge \mathsf{e} \in \mathcal{T}) \vee (\mathsf{CorrK(e}+1) \wedge \mathsf{e}+1 \in \mathcal{T})\\
&\mathcal{T}^* \leftarrow \{\mathsf{e} \in \{0,\dots,n\} \mid (\mathsf{e} \in \mathcal{T}) \vee (\mathsf{e} \in \mathcal{K}^* \wedge \mathsf{e}-1 \in \mathcal{K}^*)\}\\
&\mathcal{C}^* \leftarrow \{\mathsf{e} \in \{0,\dots,n\} \mid \mathsf{ChallEq(e)} = \mathsf{true}\}\\
&\quad \mathsf{true} \leftarrow \mathsf{ChallEq(e)} \Leftrightarrow (\mathsf{e} = \tilde{\mathsf{e}}) \vee (\mathsf{e} \in \mathcal{C}) \vee (\mathsf{ChallEq(e}-1) \wedge \mathsf{e} \in \mathcal{T}^*) \vee\\
&\qquad\qquad (\mathsf{ChallEq(e}+1) \wedge \mathsf{e}+1 \in \mathcal{T}^*)
\end{aligned}$$

Likewise, we extend $\mathcal{I}$ into $\mathcal{I}^*$:

$$\begin{aligned}
&\mathcal{I}^* \leftarrow \{\mathsf{e} \in \{0,\dots,n\} \mid \mathsf{ChallInpEq(e)} = \mathsf{true}\}\\
&\quad \mathsf{true} \leftarrow \mathsf{ChallInpEq(e)} \Leftrightarrow (\mathsf{e} \in \mathcal{I}) \vee (\mathsf{ChallInpEq(e}-1) \wedge \mathsf{e} \in \mathcal{T}^*) \vee\\
&\qquad\qquad (\mathsf{ChallInpEq(e}+1) \wedge \mathsf{e}+1 \in \mathcal{T}^*)
\end{aligned}$$

Appendix B The Check Algorithm

In our proofs, reductions play hybrid games and guess the location of the i-th insulated region. If the adversary sends a corrupt query inside this insulated region, the guess is wrong and reductions have to abort. We use the algorithm Check of [8], described in Fig. 9, to check if this event happens.

Check(inp, ê; e; fwl, fwr)

1. **if** ê > e
2. **return** ⊥
3. **if** inp = key **and** ê ∈ {fwl, ..., fwr}
4. **return** ABORT
5. **if** inp = token **and** ê ∈ {fwl, ..., fwr + 1}
6. **return** ABORT

Fig. 9. Algorithm Check of [8] used in our proofs. ê is the epoch in the adversary's request and e is the current epoch.

References

1. Abdalla, M., Eisenhofer, T., Kiltz, E., Kunzweiler, S., Riepel, D.: Password-authenticated key exchange from group actions. In: Dodis, Y., Shrimpton, T. (eds.) CRYPTO 2022, Part II. LNCS, vol. 13508, pp. 699–728. Springer, Cham (2022). https://doi.org/10.1007/978-3-031-15979-4_24
2. Alamati, N., De Feo, L., Montgomery, H., Patranabis, S.: Cryptographic group actions and applications. In: Moriai, S., Wang, H. (eds.) ASIACRYPT 2020, Part II. LNCS, vol. 12492, pp. 411–439. Springer, Cham (2020). https://doi.org/10.1007/978-3-030-64834-3_14
3. Azarderakhsh, R., Jao, D., Kalach, K., Koziel, B., Leonardi, C.: Key compression for isogeny-based cryptosystems. In: Proceedings of the 3rd ACM International Workshop on ASIA Public-Key Cryptography. ACM (2016)
4. Basso, A.: A post-quantum round-optimal oblivious PRF from isogenies. Cryptology ePrint Archive (2023)
5. Beullens, W., Kleinjung, T., Vercauteren, F.: CSI-FiSh: efficient isogeny based signatures through class group computations. In: Galbraith, S.D., Moriai, S. (eds.) ASIACRYPT 2019. LNCS, vol. 11921, pp. 227–247. Springer, Cham (2019). https://doi.org/10.1007/978-3-030-34578-5_9
6. Boneh, D., Lewi, K., Montgomery, H., Raghunathan, A.: Key homomorphic PRFs and their applications. In: Canetti, R., Garay, J.A. (eds.) CRYPTO 2013. LNCS, vol. 8042, pp. 410–428. Springer, Heidelberg (2013). https://doi.org/10.1007/978-3-642-40041-4_23
7. Booher, J., et al.: Failing to hash into supersingular isogeny graphs. arXiv preprint arXiv:2205.00135 (2022)
8. Boyd, C., Davies, G.T., Gjøsteen, K., Jiang, Y.: Fast and secure updatable encryption. In: Micciancio, D., Ristenpart, T. (eds.) CRYPTO 2020, Part I. LNCS, vol. 12170, pp. 464–493. Springer, Cham (2020). https://doi.org/10.1007/978-3-030-56784-2_16
9. Castryck, W., Houben, M., Merz, S.P., Mula, M., Buuren, S.V., Vercauteren, F.: Weak instances of class group action based cryptography via self-pairings. In: Handschuh, H., Lysyanskaya, A. (eds.) CRYPTO 2023. LNCS, vol. 14083, pp. 762–792. Springer, Cham (2023)
10. Castryck, W., Lange, T., Martindale, C., Panny, L., Renes, J.: CSIDH: an efficient post-quantum commutative group action. In: Peyrin, T., Galbraith, S. (eds.) ASIACRYPT 2018. LNCS, vol. 11274, pp. 395–427. Springer, Cham (2018). https://doi.org/10.1007/978-3-030-03332-3_15

11. Castryck, W., Sotáková, J., Vercauteren, F.: Breaking the decisional Diffie-Hellman problem for class group actions using genus theory. In: Micciancio, D., Ristenpart, T. (eds.) CRYPTO 2020. LNCS, vol. 12171, pp. 92–120. Springer, Cham (2020). https://doi.org/10.1007/978-3-030-56880-1_4
12. Chen, M., Leroux, A.: Scallop-HD: group action from 2-dimensional isogenies., Cryptology ePrint Archive (2023)
13. Colò, L., Kohel, D.: Orienting supersingular isogeny graphs. J. Math. Cryptol. **14**, 414–437 (2020)
14. Coron, J.-S., Patarin, J., Seurin, Y.: The random oracle model and the ideal cipher model are equivalent. In: Wagner, D. (ed.) CRYPTO 2008. LNCS, vol. 5157, pp. 1–20. Springer, Heidelberg (2008). https://doi.org/10.1007/978-3-540-85174-5_1
15. Costello, C., Jao, D., Longa, P., Naehrig, M., Renes, J., Urbanik, D.: Efficient compression of SIDH public keys. In: Coron, J.-S., Nielsen, J.B. (eds.) EUROCRYPT 2017. LNCS, vol. 10210, pp. 679–706. Springer, Cham (2017). https://doi.org/10.1007/978-3-319-56620-7_24
16. Bernstein, D.J., De Feo, L., Leroux, A., Smith, B.: Faster computation of isogenies of large prime degree. ANTS XIV **4**(1), 39–55 (2020)
17. De Feo, L., et al.: Séta: supersingular encryption from torsion attacks. In: Tibouchi, M., Wang, H. (eds.) ASIACRYPT 2021. LNCS, vol. 13093, pp. 249–278. Springer, Cham (2021). https://doi.org/10.1007/978-3-030-92068-5_9
18. Espitau, T., Kirchner, P.: The nearest-colattice algorithm: time-approximation tradeoff for approx-CVP. Open Book Series **4**(1), 251–266 (2020)
19. Feo, L.D., et al.: SCALLOP: scaling the CSI-FiSh. In: Boldyreva, A., Kolesnikov, V. (eds.) PKC 2023. LNCS, vol. 13940, pp. 345–375. Springer, Cham (2023). https://doi.org/10.1007/978-3-031-31368-4_13
20. Fouotsa, T.B., Moriya, T., Petit, C.: M-SIDH and MD-SIDH: countering SIDH attacks by masking information. In: Hazay, C., Stam, M. (eds.) EUROCRYPT 2023. LNCS, vol. 14008, pp. 282–309. Springer, Cham (2023). https://doi.org/10.1007/978-3-031-30589-4_10
21. Holenstein, T., Künzler, R., Tessaro, S.: The equivalence of the random oracle model and the ideal cipher model, revisited. In: Proceedings of the Forty-Third Annual ACM Symposium on Theory of Computing, STOC 2011, pp. 89-98. Association for Computing Machinery, New York (2011)
22. Ji, Z., Qiao, Y., Song, F., Yun, A.: General linear group action on tensors: a candidate for post-quantum cryptography. In: Hofheinz, D., Rosen, A. (eds.) TCC 2019. LNCS, vol. 11891, pp. 251–281. Springer, Cham (2019). https://doi.org/10.1007/978-3-030-36030-6_11
23. Jiang, Y.: The direction of updatable encryption does not matter much. In: Moriai, S., Wang, H. (eds.) ASIACRYPT 2020. LNCS, vol. 12493, pp. 529–558. Springer, Cham (2020). https://doi.org/10.1007/978-3-030-64840-4_18
24. Klooß, M., Lehmann, A., Rupp, A.: (R)CCA secure updatable encryption with integrity protection. In: Ishai, Y., Rijmen, V. (eds.) EUROCRYPT 2019. LNCS, vol. 11476, pp. 68–99. Springer, Cham (2019). https://doi.org/10.1007/978-3-030-17653-2_3
25. Lehmann, A., Tackmann, B.: Updatable encryption with post-compromise security. In: Nielsen, J.B., Rijmen, V. (eds.) EUROCRYPT 2018. LNCS, vol. 10822, pp. 685–716. Springer, Cham (2018). https://doi.org/10.1007/978-3-319-78372-7_22
26. Maino, L., Martindale, C., Panny, L., Pope, G., Wesolowski, B.: A direct key recovery attack on SIDH. In: Hazay, C., Stam, M. (eds.) EUROCRYPT 2023. LNCS, vol. 14008, pp. 448–471. Springer, Cham (2023). https://doi.org/10.1007/978-3-031-30589-4_16

27. Miao, P., Patranabis, S., Watson, G.: Unidirectional updatable encryption and proxy re-encryption from DDH. In: Boldyreva, A., Kolesnikov, V. (eds.) PKC 2023. LNCS, vol. 13941, pp. 368–398. Springer, Cham (2023). https://doi.org/10.1007/978-3-031-31371-4_13
28. Moriya, T., Onuki, H., Takagi, T.: SiGamal: a supersingular isogeny-based PKE and its application to a PRF. In: Moriai, S., Wang, H. (eds.) ASIACRYPT 2020. LNCS, vol. 12492, pp. 551–580. Springer, Cham (2020). https://doi.org/10.1007/978-3-030-64834-3_19
29. Naehrig, M., Renes, J.: Dual isogenies and their application to public-key compression for isogeny-based cryptography. In: Galbraith, S.D., Moriai, S. (eds.) ASIACRYPT 2019. LNCS, vol. 11922, pp. 243–272. Springer, Cham (2019). https://doi.org/10.1007/978-3-030-34621-8_9
30. Nishimaki, R.: The direction of updatable encryption does matter. In: Hanaoka, G., Shikata, J., Watanabe, Y. (eds.) PKC 2022, Part II. LNCS, vol. 13178, pp. 194–224. Springer, Cham (2022). https://doi.org/10.1007/978-3-030-97131-1_7
31. Onuki, H.: On oriented supersingular elliptic curves. Finite Fields Appl. **69**, 101777 (2021)
32. Pereira, G., Doliskani, J., Jao, D.: X-only point addition formula and faster compressed SIKE. J. Cryptogr. Eng. **11**, 1–13 (2021)
33. Robert, D.: Breaking SIDH in polynomial time. In: Hazay, C., Stam, M. (eds.) EUROCRYPT 2023. LNCS, vol. 14008, pp. 472–503. Springer, Cham (2023). https://doi.org/10.1007/978-3-031-30589-4_17
34. Shannon, C.E.: Communication theory of secrecy systems. Bell Syst. Tech. J. **28**(4), 656–715 (1949)
35. Shor, P.W.: Algorithms for quantum computation: discrete logarithms and factoring. In: Proceedings 35th Annual Symposium on Foundations of Computer Science, pp. 124–134 (1994)
36. Tang, G., Duong, D.H., Joux, A., Plantard, T., Qiao, Y., Susilo, W.: Practical post-quantum signature schemes from isomorphism problems of trilinear forms. In: Dunkelman, O., Dziembowski, S. (eds.) EUROCRYPT 2022. LNCS, vol. 13277, pp. 582–612. Springer, Cham (2022). https://doi.org/10.1007/978-3-031-07082-2_21
37. Vélu, J.: Isogénies entre courbes elliptiques. Compt.-Rendus l'Acad. Sci. Série I **273**, 238–241 (1971)
38. Wesolowski, B.: Orientations and the supersingular endomorphism ring problem. In: Dunkelman, O., Dziembowski, S. (eds.) EUROCRYPT 2022. LNCS, vol. 13277, pp. 345–371. Springer, Cham (2022). https://doi.org/10.1007/978-3-031-07082-2_13
39. Zanon, G.H.M., Simplicio, M.A., Pereira, G.C.C.F., Doliskani, J., Barreto, P.S.L.M.: Faster isogeny-based compressed key agreement. In: Lange, T., Steinwandt, R. (eds.) PQCrypto 2018. LNCS, vol. 10786, pp. 248–268. Springer, Cham (2018). https://doi.org/10.1007/978-3-319-79063-3_12

Fault Attack on SQIsign

Jeonghwan Lee[1], Donghoe Heo[1], Hyeonhak Kim[1], Gyusang Kim[1], Suhri Kim[3], Heeseok Kim[2], and Seokhie Hong[1(✉)]

[1] School of Cybersecurity, Korea University, Seoul 02841, South Korea
shhong@korea.ac.kr

[2] Department of AI Cyber Security, College of Science and Technology, Korea University, Sejong 30019, South Korea

[3] School of Mathematics, Statistics and Data Science, Sungshin Women's University, Seoul 02844, South Korea

Abstract. In this paper, we introduce the first fault attack on SQIsign. By injecting a fault into the ideal generator during the commitment phase, we demonstrate a meaningful probability of inducing the generation of order $\mathcal{O}_0$. The probability is bounded by one parameter, the degree of commitment isogeny. We also show that the probability can be reasonably estimated by assuming uniform randomness of a random variable, and provide empirical evidence supporting the validity of this approximation. In addition, we identify a loop-abort vulnerability due to the iterative structure of the isogeny operation. Exploiting these vulnerabilities, we present key recovery fault attack scenarios for two versions of SQIsign—one deterministic and the other randomized. We then analyze the time complexity and the number of queries required for each attack. Finally, we discuss straightforward countermeasures that can be implemented against the attack.

Keywords: Isogeny · Quaternion Algebra · Post-Quantum Cryptography · Fault Attack

1 Introduction

National Institute of Standards and Technology (NIST) initiated the Post Quantum Cryptography (PQC) standardization process in 2016, responding to the significant threat to widely used public-key encryption systems due to quantum computers. After several rounds of evaluation, CRYSTALS-Kyber in Key Encapsulation Mechanism (KEM) category, and CRYSTALS-Dilithium, FALCON, and SPHINCS+ in digital signature category were selected as schemes for standardization on July 5th, 2022. Subsequently, in August 2023, NIST announced the first drafts for CRYSTALS-Kyber, CRYSTALS-Dilithium, and SPHINCS+ as FIPS 203, 204, and 205, respectively (standardization for Falcon is still in progress). However, because three of the four standardization schemes were lattice-based, NIST began an additional standardization process for digital

M.-J. Saarinen and D. Smith-Tone (Eds.): PQCrypto 2024, LNCS 14772, pp. 54–76, 2024.
https://doi.org/10.1007/978-3-031-62746-0_3

signatures based on various mathematical problems. As of June 2023, 40 additional submissions have been published, and security analyses are ongoing for each algorithm.

SQIsign[1] is the only isogeny-based digital signature among the candidates in the additional round 1. In particular, it is currently recognized as the most compact post-quantum signature scheme with efficient verification. SQIsign effectively exploits the Deuring correspondence, which establishes a mathematical equivalence between the domain of supersingular elliptic curves and that of maximal orders in a quaternion algebra. Unlike many isogeny-based schemes similar to SIDH that are vulnerable to Castryck-Decru-Maino-Martindale-Robert attacks [7,17,18], SQIsign remains secure, as its public information does not disclose torsion point information.

In addition to ensuring the mathematical security of cryptographic algorithms, it is necessary to consider aspects such as memory usage, key size, ciphertext or signature size, and optimized implementation to meet the needs of various cryptographic infrastructures. Equally important is the need to address the resilience of these schemes against physical attacks, namely, side-channel and fault attacks. Substantial research has been done on physical attacks on isogeny-based cryptography, especially fault attacks. Notable examples include the introduction of loop-abort faults during isogeny computation in the SIDH cryptosystem [15], resulting in the exposure of secret keys. A similar vulnerability for CSIDH is presented in a related paper [5]. Safe-error key recovery attacks on both SIKE and CSIDH have been demonstrated by [6], which perturbs memory locations on the computation of isogeny. Furthermore, the fault attack introduced by [2] manipulates the computation related to the *orientation* of a point in CSIDH, causing the secret-dependent faulty curve from which the attack can recover the secret key. Vulnerabilities have also been discovered outside of isogeny computation. The authors of [20] and [19] have shown that they can inject faults into torsion points in SIDH and exchange them for vulnerable torsion points, enabling an attacker to retrieve a secret key. Injecting faults into intermediate curves in SIDH [1] have been introduced, which can leak information about certain aspects of secret isogeny over the $\mathbb{F}_p$ curve.

However, to the best of our knowledge, there have been no reported fault attacks on SQIsign, especially in the context of quaternion algebra operations. In this paper, we present the first fault attack on SQIsign. First, we prove that by injecting a fault into the ideal generator, we can, with a significant probability, generate the order $\mathcal{O}_0$ instead of the expected commitment ideal during the commitment phase. The probability is bounded by a single factor: the degree of a commitment isogeny. We show that the probability can be roughly estimated by assuming the uniform randomness of a random variable. The validity of this approximation is further supported by empirical estimation. We also reveal the existence of a loop-abort vulnerability caused by the iterative structure of the isogeny operation, as similarly described in [15]. Using the identified vulnerabil-

[1] Throughout the paper, the term "SQIsign" and its implementation refer to version 1.0 released as a NIST Round 1 addition signature candidate on June 1, 2023.

ities, we present key recovery attack scenarios for two versions of SQIsign[2], one deterministic, and the other randomized. Then, we analyze the time complexity and the number of queries required for each attack. Finally, we discuss simple countermeasures that can be taken against the attack.

The rest sections of the paper are structured as follows: Sect. 2 provides the mathematical background necessary for understanding the SQIsign signing process, along with an introduction to fault injection. In Sect. 3, the paper analyzes two vulnerabilities induced by fault injection in the commitment phase. Section 4 presents key recovery attack scenarios for deterministic and randomized SQIsign based on the earlier vulnerability analyses. Finally, Sect. 5 discusses countermeasures and concludes the paper.

2 Preliminaries

In this paper, we consider a prime number p that satisfies $p \equiv 3 \pmod 4$, and $\mathbb{F}_{p^2}$ denotes a finite field of size p^2. The mathematical aspects of SQIsign are outlined in Sect. 2.1. The signing process of SQIsign, which is the focus of the attack, is explained in Sect. 2.2. And Sect. 2.3 introduces two types of fault vulnerabilities in SQIsign. More details can be found in [8,10,11].

2.1 Mathematical Background

Elliptic Curves and Isogenies. SQIsign makes use of supersingular elliptic curves over $\mathbb{F}_{p^2}$ with an endomorphism ring defined over the same field. It uses a *separable* isogeny, completely described by its kernel. Using formulas such as Vélu [21] or $\sqrt{\text{e}}$lu [4], the separable isogeny ϕ can be computed from its kernel G, denoted as $\phi : E \to E/G$. The degree of the composite isogeny $\phi \circ \psi$ is equal to $deg(\phi) \cdot deg(\psi)$. It can be factored into the composition of e_i isogenies of degree p_i for $i = 1$ to n for any *separable* isogeny ϕ of degree $d = \prod_{i=1}^{n} p_i^{e_i}$, satisfying $\phi \circ \hat{\phi} = [deg(\phi)]$, the multiplication-by-$[deg(\phi)]$ map on E_1, vice versa.

All operations in SQIsign are conducted in Montgomery form using only the x-coordinate for efficiency, and higher extension fields than $\mathbb{F}_{p^2}$ are not used. However, computing isogenies with large degrees using (p^2-1)-torsion points is infeasible over $\mathbb{F}_{p^2}$. To address this, SQIsign utilizes two curves: an elliptic curve E with $(p+1)$-torsion and its twist E^t with $(p-1)$-torsion. Isogenies are computed by forming two kernels from these curves. Despite the use of two kernels, the computations in E and E^t are the same in Montgomery form. Therefore, in this paper, we express them under a single elliptic curve E. For instance, when representing the set of torsion points, the set of $(p+1)$-torsion points on E is denoted as $E[p+1]$, and the set of $(p-1)$-torsion set on E^t is also denoted as $E[p-1]$.

2 While SQIsign [8] does not explicitly mention deterministic and randomized versions, it is noted that Fiat-Shamir heuristic-based digital signatures such as CRYSTALS-Dilithium [12] and HAETAE [9] (one of the candidates on NIST round 1 additional signatures) included or now include deterministic algorithms. Thus, it is reasonable to consider the attack on the two versions of SQIsign.

Quaternion Algebras. SQIsign uses the quaternion algebra over $\mathbb{Q}$, denoted as $B_{p,\infty}$. This algebra is based on $1, i, j, k$, where $i^2 = -1$, $j^2 = -p$, and $k = ij = -ji$. A canonical involution in $B_{p,\infty}$ maps an element $\alpha = a_1 + a_2 i + a_3 j + a_4 k$ to its conjugate $\overline{\alpha} = a_1 - a_2 i - a_3 j - a_4 k$. The *reduced trace* and *reduced norm* are defined as $tr(\alpha) = \alpha + \overline{\alpha}$ and $nrd(\alpha) = \alpha\overline{\alpha}$, respectively. An element α in $B_{p,\infty}$ is called integral if both its *reduced trace* and *reduced norm* belong to $\mathbb{Z}$.

A full-rank $\mathbb{Z}$-lattice in $B_{p,\infty}$ is termed a fractional ideal I, and can be expressed as $I = \alpha_1\mathbb{Z} + \alpha_2\mathbb{Z} + \alpha_3\mathbb{Z} + \alpha_4\mathbb{Z}$. An order $\mathcal{O}$ is a subring of $B_{p,\infty}$ that also qualifies as a fractional ideal. Elements of order $\mathcal{O}$ are integral as they have *reduced trace* and *reduced norm* in $\mathbb{Z}$. An element $\alpha \in \mathcal{O}$ can be denoted as $[\alpha]_B$, which is a 4-dimensional coordinate of α with respect to the basis B of $\mathcal{O}$. A maximal order is not encompassed by any larger order. The left order of a fractional ideal I is denoted as $\mathcal{O}_L(I) = \{\alpha \in B_{p,\infty} \mid \alpha I \subset I\}$, and the right order is represented as $\mathcal{O}_R(I)$. An order $\mathcal{O}$ can define a left fractional $\mathcal{O}$-ideal if the set I is closed under left-multiplication by elements of $\mathcal{O}$, which implies $\mathcal{O} \subseteq \mathcal{O}_L(I)$. A right fractional $\mathcal{O}'$-ideal is formed when I is closed under right-multiplication by elements of $\mathcal{O}'$. An I that qualifies as both a left fractional $\mathcal{O}$-ideal and a right fractional $\mathcal{O}'$-ideal is called a connecting $(\mathcal{O}, \mathcal{O}')$-ideal.

A fractional ideal that is contained in both its left and right orders is called an integral ideal, or simply an ideal. The norm of an ideal I, represented as $nrd(I)$, is defined as $\gcd(\{nrd(\alpha) \mid \alpha \in I\})$. A left $\mathcal{O}$-ideal I can be generated as $I = \mathcal{O} \cdot \alpha + \mathcal{O} \cdot nrd(I)$, provided $\alpha \in \mathcal{O}$ and $\gcd(nrd(\alpha), nrd(I)^2) = nrd(I)$, and similarly for a right $\mathcal{O}'$-ideal. In short, this notation can be written as $\mathcal{O} \cdot \alpha + \mathcal{O} \cdot N = \mathcal{O}\langle \alpha, N\rangle$, applicable to any order $\mathcal{O}$ and integer N, simplifying the expression. The product IJ of ideals, where $\mathcal{O}_R(I) = \mathcal{O}_L(J)$, is the ideal generated by the products of pairs in $I \times J$. This product is also an integral ideal, and its left order is $\mathcal{O}_L(IJ) = \mathcal{O}_L(I)$, while its right order is $\mathcal{O}_R(IJ) = \mathcal{O}_R(J)$. The conjugate of an ideal $\overline{I}$ is the set of conjugates of elements of I, which is an ideal satisfying $I\overline{I} = nrd(I)\mathcal{O}_L(I)$ and $\overline{I}I = nrd(I)\mathcal{O}_R(I)$ when I is invertible. SQIsign uses only *locally principal* ideals, which are always invertible.

The Deuring Correspondence. In the domain of quaternion algebra and elliptic curves, a bijective correspondence is established. An isogeny, denoted as $\phi : E \rightarrow E'$, is linked with an ideal I_ϕ. This ideal has a left order $\mathcal{O}$, which is isomorphic to the endomorphism ring of E, denoted as $End(E)$, and a right order $\mathcal{O}'$, which is isomorphic to the endomorphism ring of E', denoted as $End(E')$. Moreover, the degree of the isogeny ϕ is the same as the norm of the ideal I_ϕ. The dual isogeny, denoted as $\widehat{\phi}$, corresponds to the conjugate of the ideal I_ϕ, denoted as $\overline{I_\phi}$, which is equal to the ideal of the dual isogeny, denoted as $I_{\widehat{\phi}}$. The composition of two isogenies, denoted as $\phi \circ \psi$, corresponds to the multiplication of two ideals $I_\psi \cdot I_\phi$. Lastly, when two ideals, I and J, are equivalent, their right orders are isomorphic. Therefore, the isogenies associated with these ideals, ϕ_I and ϕ_J, have isomorphic codomains.

The KLPT Algorithm. The KLPT algorithm [16] is a method that can be used to find an equivalent ideal J with a prescribed norm, given an initial ideal I. This algorithm can be used to efficiently determine the isogeny between elliptic curves with known endomorphism rings. However, the original formulation of the KLPT algorithm is only applicable to $\mathcal{O}_0$-ideals, where $\mathcal{O}_0$ represents a conditioned maximal order. The authors of [10] later generalized the algorithm to accommodate arbitrary order $\mathcal{O}$. This generalization expands the applicability of the KLPT algorithm, but requires a connecting $(\mathcal{O}_0, \mathcal{O})$-ideal and a 1.5 times larger norm bound for the output than the previous one.

Computational Problems. The foundation of SQIsign is based on two computational problems: the *isogeny path problem* and the *endomorphism ring problem.* The *isogeny path problem* is about finding an isogeny $E_1 \rightarrow E_2$ given two elliptic curves E_1 and E_2. The *endomorphism ring problem* is about computing $End(E)$ given an elliptic curve E. For supersingular case, these problems are equal under polynomial time reductions [13,22].

Table 1. SQIsign parameters

NIST-I
$p =$ 0x34e29e286b95d98c33a6a86587407437252c9e49355147ffffffffffffffff
$f = 75$
$T = 3^{36} \cdot 7^4 \cdot 11 \cdot 13 \cdot 23^2 \cdot 37 \cdot 59^2 \cdot 89 \cdot 97 \cdot 101^2 \cdot 107 \cdot 109^2 \cdot 131 \cdot 137 \cdot 197^2 \cdot 223 \cdot 239$ $\cdot 383 \cdot 389 \cdot 491^2 \cdot 499 \cdot 607 \cdot 743^2 \cdot 1033 \cdot 1049 \cdot 1193 \cdot 1913^2 \cdot 1973$
NIST-III
$p =$ 0x3df6eeeab0871a2c6ae604a45d10ad665bc2e0a90aeb751c722f669356ea4684c6174 c1ffffffffffffffffffff
$f = 97$
$T = 3^{68} \cdot 5 \cdot 7^{12} \cdot 11^4 \cdot 13 \cdot 47^4 \cdot 89 \cdot 113 \cdot 157^4 \cdot 173 \cdot 233 \cdot 239 \cdot 241 \cdot 443 \cdot 509^4 \cdot 569$ $\cdot 761^4 \cdot 1229 \cdot 2393 \cdot 3371 \cdot 4517 \cdot 5147 \cdot 5693 \cdot 5813 \cdot 9397 \cdot 26777 \cdot 39679 \cdot 47441$
NIST-V
$p =$ 0x255946a8869bc68c15b0036936e79202bdbe6326507d01fe3ac5904a0dea65faf0a29 a781974ce994c68ada6e1ffffffffffffffffffffffffffffffffff
$f = 145$
$T = 3^{72} \cdot 5 \cdot 7 \cdot 13^6 \cdot 17 \cdot 37 \cdot 41^6 \cdot 53 \cdot 67^6 \cdot 73 \cdot 103^6 \cdot 127 \cdot 151 \cdot 461^6 \cdot 643 \cdot 733 \cdot 739$ $\cdot 827^6 \cdot 1009 \cdot 2539 \cdot 4153 \cdot 5059 \cdot 7127 \cdot 10597 \cdot 13591 \cdot 14923 \cdot 15541 \cdot 15991 \cdot 18583$ $\cdot 23227 \cdot 48187 \cdot 63247 \cdot 65521 \cdot 318233$

2.2 SQIsign

We now describe the parameters of SQIsign, and then explain SQIsign signing process, the targeted algorithm in the paper.

Parameters of SQIsign. In SQIsign, a value denoted as T is carefully chosen to balance security and computational efficiency. This value determines the available torsion and subsequently influences the degree of the isogenies used in the scheme. Specifically, T is an odd, smooth integer larger than $p^{5/4}$ and satisfies $T|(p^2-1)$. Let g be the largest integer that is a power of 3 and a divisor of T. The degree of the commitment isogeny, denoted as D_{com}, is then given by $T/3^g$, and the degree of the challenge isogeny, denoted as D_{chall}, is given by $2^f 3^g$. The parameter values corresponding to NIST levels are outlined in Table 1.

Algorithm 1. SQISign signing protocol(simplified)

Input: A Message M
Input: A secret key sk
Output: A signature σ

Commitment process

Sample a_0, b_0 randomly from interval $[1, D_{com}]$ until $gcd(a_0, b_0, D_{com}) = 1$.
$I_{com} := \mathcal{O}_0\langle \gamma \cdot (a_0 + b_0\bar{\theta}), D_{com}\rangle$
$K_{com} := a_0 P_0 + b_0\theta(P_0)$, where $P_0 \in B_{0,D_{com}}$
Compute an isogeny $\phi_{com} : E_0 \to E_1$ with the kernel $\langle K_{com}\rangle$.
$P_{1,chall} := \phi_{com}(P_{0,chall}), Q_{1,chall} := \phi_{com}(P_{0,chall})$

Challenge process

$a_1, b_1 := H(M, E_1)$
Find a D_{chall}-torsion basis (P_{E_1}, Q_{E_1}) on E_1 deterministically.
$K_{chall} := a_1 P_{E_1} + b_1 Q_{E_1}$
Compute an isogeny $\phi_{chall} : E_1 \to E_2$ with the kernel $\langle K_{chall}\rangle$.
Find integers α, β such that $[\alpha]P_{1,chall} + [\beta]Q_{1,chall} = K_{chall}$.
Compute a left $\mathcal{O}_0$-ideal I'_{chall} corresponding to the isogeny with the kernel $\langle[\alpha]P_{0,chall} + [\beta]Q_{0,chall}\rangle$.
$I_{chall} := [I_{com}]_* I'_{chall}$
Given K_{chall}, deterministically find another D_{chall}-torsion point L_{chall} such that a pair (K_{chall}, L_{chall}) is the basis of $E_1[D_{chall}]$.
$L'_{chall} := \phi_{chall}(L_{chall})$
Find a D_{chall}-torsion basis (P_{E_2}, Q_{E_2}) on E_2 deterministically.
Find integers s_1, s_2 such that $[s_1]P_{E_2} + [s_2]Q_{E_2} = L'_{chall}$.
Given (L'_{chall}, s_1, s_2), deterministically find another D_{chall}-torsion point M'_{chall} such that a pair (L'_{chall}, M'_{chall}) is the basis of $E_2[D_{chall}]$.
Compute an isogeny $\widehat{\phi_{chall}} : E_2 \to E_1$ with the kernel $\langle L'_{chall}\rangle$.
$M_{chall} := \widehat{\phi_{chall}}(M'_{chall})$
Find r such that $K_{chall} = [r]M_{chall}$.

Response process

$J_{res} := \overline{I_{secret}} \cdot I_{com} \cdot I_{chall}$
Find an ideal J'_{res} of norm 2^e which is equivalent to J_{res} such that $J\overline{I_{chall}}$ is cyclic using *SigningKLPT*.
Convert the ideal J'_{res} into the isogeny σ of degree 2^e using sk.
return σ, r, s_1, s_2

The SQIsign Signing Process. The SQIsign signing process consists of three stages: the commitment phase, the challenge phase, and the response phase. Details that are not crucial to the overall understanding of the attack, such as the Montgomery normalized process, are omitted. For a more in-depth algorithmic explanation, refer to [8].

In the commitment phase of SQIsign, the signing oracle initiates by choosing a_0 and b_0 at random such that $\gcd(a_0, b_0, D_{com}) = 1$. This selection is used to form a commitment ideal I_{com} with a norm of D_{com}. Subsequently, the isogeny $\phi_{com} : E_0 \rightarrow E_1$, which corresponds to I_{com}, is computed. The phase concludes with the evaluation of $P_{0,chall}$ and $Q_{0,chall}$, the basis of $E_0[D_{chall}]$, through ϕ_{com} to yield $P_{1,chall}$ and $Q_{1,chall}$. Moving to the challenge phase, the oracle computes the challenge isogeny $\phi_{chall} : E_1 \rightarrow E_2$, with a kernel $\langle K_{chall} \rangle$ that is derived by hashing the message M and the elliptic curve E_1. The K_{chall} is then decomposed along the basis P_1 and Q_1, which was obtained during the commitment phase. SQIsign then computes (s_1, s_2), compression of the dual of the challenge isogeny, by computing the kernel generator L'_{chall} of $\widehat{\phi_{chall}}$ and decomposing it along a deterministically computed D_{chall}-torsion basis on the curve E_2. At the end of the challenge phase, computations are carried out to determine a generator M_{chall} of ϕ_{chall}, which is obtained by evaluating M'_{chall} through the dual of ϕ_{chall}. Subsequently, a scalar r is computed, which fulfills the condition $K_{chall} = [r]Q$. In the response phase, the oracle computes $\overline{I_{secret}} \cdot I_{com} \cdot I_{chall}$ and identifies an equivalent ideal J with a norm of 2^e using *SigningKLPT*. This process of finding J is repeated until $J\overline{I_{secret}}$ becomes cyclic. SQIsign finally returns (σ, r, s_1, s_2) as the completed signature.

Throughout the paper, SQIsign is referred to as deterministic when the initial step of selecting a_0, b_0 is performed deterministically. As a result, the protocol will always yield the same output for the same message and key. Conversely, when we mention randomized SQIsign, it implies that these values are determined based on a random number generator, leading to different outputs for each query, even when the same message and key are used.

2.3 Fault Attacks

Fault attacks are a category of side-channel attacks in which an attacker gains access to a cryptographic device and injects faults, such as power, electromagnetic waves, or laser-induced faults, at specific points. The attacker then analyzes the output to extract sensitive information. Several types of vulnerabilities can be induced by fault attacks, including variable randomization and loop-abort, which we will use in this paper. Variable randomization is random changes induced by faults in the values of variables used in cryptographic computations, resulting in faulty output values. The attacker can extract confidential information by analyzing the values themselves or by comparing them to normal output values [2,19,20]. When it comes to loop abort, it can be done in one of two ways. The first is through variable randomization, as explained earlier. In this approach, the attacker uses fault injection to randomize the loop index, causing the loop to abort at the desired point. The second is instruction skipping. With this, the attacker injects a fault during the execution of a jump instruction that causes the loop to abort. In the field of isogeny-based cryptography, the occurrence of loops as a result of isogeny operations has led to studies of loop-abort fault attacks [3,15]. A similar vulnerability can also be found in SQIsign. We will discuss it in Sect. 3.

Consider a scenario where the attacker can introduce n number of faults into a cryptographic system while it is in operation. This scenario is known as an n-th order fault attack. In Sect. 4, we will examine a first-order fault attack on the deterministic SQIsign algorithm and a second-order fault attack on the randomized SQIsign algorithm.

3 Fault Vulnerabilities in SQIsign

In this section, we examine the implementation of SQIsign and analyze its vulnerabilities. First, we look at the vulnerabilities that arise during an ideal generation and the associated operations. After that, we will discuss the characteristics of the isogeny operations and the vulnerabilities that arise from them.

3.1 Randomization While Generating Commitment Ideal

Algorithm 2. Making primitive then generating an ideal I_{com}

Input: A special p-extremal maximal order $\mathcal{O}_0$
Input: A generator coordinates $[g]_B$ w.r.t. the standard basis
Input: The norm D_{com}
Output: A commitment ideal I_{com}

1: Let $B := \{1, i, j, ij\}$ be a set of the standard basis in quaternion algebra.
2: Let $B_{\mathcal{O}_0} := \{\beta_1, \beta_2, \beta_3, \beta_4\}$ be a set of the basis of order $\mathcal{O}_0$
3: Convert $[g]_B$ into $[g]_{B_{\mathcal{O}_0}}$ using gaussian ellimination.
4: $content := gcd([g]_{B_{\mathcal{O}_0}})$
5: $[g']_{B_{\mathcal{O}_0}} := [g]_{B_{\mathcal{O}_0}} / content$
6: $[g']_B := [g']_{B_{\mathcal{O}_0}} * B_{\mathcal{O}_0}$
7: $D'_{com} := D_{com} / gcd(content, D_{com})$
8: $I_{com} := \mathcal{O}_0\langle g', D'_{com}\rangle$
9: **return** I_{com}

In the SQIsign protocol, the generation of the commitment ideal involves first sampling a_0 and b_0 in a way that satisfies $\gcd(a_0, b_0, D_{com}) = 1$, as shown in line 1 of Algorithm 1. These values are then used to generate the ideal I_{com}. During this process, the generator γ of an ideal of norm D_{com} is multiplied by $a_0 + b_0\overline{\theta}$ to produce the kernel generator $g = \gamma(a_0 + b_0\overline{\theta})$. However, since g may not be primitive, it is essential to convert the input generator to a primitive element

```
int quat_lattice_contains_without_alg(quat_alg_coord_t *coord,
    const quat_lattice_t *lat, const quat_alg_elem_t *x){
    // Test if rank 4 lattice under HNF ...
    // Convert the basis by using gaussian elimination
    // Final test
    // Copy result
    if(res && (coord != NULL)){
        for(int i = 0; i < 4;i++){
            ibz_copy(&((*coord)[i]),&(work_coord[i]));
        }
    }
    // Finalize
}
```

Fig. 1. Reference C source code for line 3 in Algorithm 2

before generating the ideal. This conversion is described in Algorithm 2, lines 1 to 8.

First, the input generator, represented on the standard basis $B = \{1, i, j, k\}$, is transformed by Gaussian elimination into the basis $B_{\mathcal{O}_0} = \{1, i, \frac{i+j}{2}, \frac{1+k}{2}\}$ of $\mathcal{O}_0$, resulting in $[g]_{B_{\mathcal{O}_0}}$. Then, the gcd of each coordinate of $[g]_{B_{\mathcal{O}_0}}$, called *content*, is computed. This *content* is then used to compute the primitive generator g' by dividing $[g]_{B_{\mathcal{O}_0}}$. D'_{com} is computed as D_{com} divided by $\gcd(content, D_{com})$. Finally, I_{com} is generated by the generator g' and D'_{com} (Algorithm 2).

It is important to note that in the C implementation corresponding to line 3 of Algorithm 2, a copy function is used during the return of the transformed coordinates $[g]_{B_{\mathcal{O}_0}}$. Injecting a fault into the copy process could cause one of the four returned coordinates to be randomized. Assume that a fault is injected during the first iteration of the for-loop, and let us denote the faulty copy as g^f. Since the fault only causes the coordinates to be randomized with respect to the basis of order $\mathcal{O}_0$, g^f is still an element of $\mathcal{O}_0$. According to Algorithm 2, g^f is then transformed into a primitive element, which leads to the generation of the fault-induced ideal I^f_{com}. This process can lead to a vulnerability that can be exploited in a key-recovery-attack scenario in Sect. 4.

To elaborate further, as described in Sect. 2, for a $\mathcal{O}_0$-ideal, the generator $\alpha \in \mathcal{O}_0$ must meet the condition $gcd(nrd(\alpha), nrd(I)^2) = nrd(I)$. However, by Theorem 1, the result of the ideal generation process will be $\mathcal{O}_0$ if α is subjected to fault injection to satisfy a certain condition.

Theorem 1. *Let $\mathcal{O}_0$ be a maximal order given the basis $(1, i, \frac{i+j}{2}, \frac{1+k}{2})$. For $N \in \mathbb{Z}^+$, $\alpha \in \mathcal{O}_0$, if $\gcd(nrd(\alpha), N) = 1$, then $\mathcal{O}_0 \cdot \alpha + \mathcal{O}_0 \cdot N = \mathcal{O}_0$*

Proof. The element $\mathcal{O}_0$ represents an order, and therefore, a ring. Additionally, both $\mathcal{O}_0 \cdot \alpha$ and $\mathcal{O}_0.N$ are principal ideals on the ring $\mathcal{O}_0$. For any arbitrary $\alpha \in \mathcal{O}_0$ expressed as $\alpha = \alpha_1 + \alpha_2 \cdot i + \alpha_3 \cdot \frac{i+j}{2} + \alpha_4 \cdot \frac{1+k}{2}$, the conjugate is given by $\overline{\alpha} = \alpha_1 - \alpha_2 \cdot i - \alpha_3 \cdot \frac{i+j}{2} + \alpha_4 \cdot \frac{1-k}{2}$.

Now, consider $\alpha' = \alpha_1 - \alpha_2 \cdot i - \alpha_3 \cdot \frac{i+j}{2} - \alpha_4 \cdot \frac{1+k}{2} \in \mathcal{O}_0$. Since $\alpha_4 \in \mathbb{Z}$, it follows that $\overline{\alpha} = \alpha' + \alpha_4 \in \mathcal{O}_0$. Consequently, the conjugate $\overline{\alpha}$ of any element α in $\mathcal{O}_0$ is also an element of $\mathcal{O}_0$.

This implies that $nrd(\alpha) = \overline{\alpha} \cdot \alpha \in (\mathcal{O}_0 \cdot \alpha + \mathcal{O}_0 \cdot N)$. Meanwhile, as $\gcd(nrd(\alpha), N) = 1$, there exist integers a and b such that $a \cdot nrd(\alpha) + b \cdot N = 1$. Hence, $\mathcal{O}_0 \cdot \alpha$ and $\mathcal{O}_0 \cdot N$ are relatively prime ideals, and their sum is the entire ring $\mathcal{O}_0$, that is, $\mathcal{O}_0 \cdot \alpha + \mathcal{O}_0 \cdot N = \mathcal{O}_0$.

□

In addition, using Lemma 1, Lemma 2, and Theorem 2, we can compute upper and lower bounds, as well as an approximation, for the probability that the result of the ideal generation process becomes $\mathcal{O}_0$ due to fault injection, based solely on the parameter D_{com}. In the following Lemmas and Theorem, φ denotes Euler's totient function.

Lemma 1 (Upper Bound). *Consider an input g for Algorithm 2, and let g^f be the version of g after fault injection. Suppose that the fault is injected during the first iteration of for-loop, the parameter D_{com} is not divided by 2, and the amount of change Δ due to fault injection is uniformly random in $\mathbb{Z}$. Then, the probability that $nrd(g^f)$ and D_{com} are coprime has an upper bound:*

$$P(\gcd((nrd(g^f), D_{com})) = 1) < \frac{\varphi(D_{com})}{D_{com}}$$

Proof. According to line 2 of Algorithm 1, g is computed as $\gamma \cdot (a_0 + b_0\overline{\theta})$ where a_0 and b_0 are sampled integers, and γ and $\overline{\theta}$ are fixed parameters. Here, when expressing the parameters γ and $\overline{\theta}$ in terms of the standard basis of quaternion algebra, each coordinate is represented by an integer value. To be more specific, $\gamma = 1 + \gamma_2 \cdot i + \gamma_3 \cdot j + \gamma_4 \cdot k$, where $\gamma_2, \gamma_3, \gamma_4 \in \mathbb{Z}$, and $\overline{\theta} = \overline{\theta}_1 + \overline{\theta}_2 \cdot i + \overline{\theta}_3 \cdot j + \overline{\theta}_4 \cdot k$, where $\overline{\theta}_1, \overline{\theta}_2, \overline{\theta}_3, \overline{\theta}_4 \in \mathbb{Z}$. Hence, g is represented as $g = g_1 + g_2 \cdot i + g_3 \cdot j + g_4 \cdot k$ where $g_1, g_2, g_3, g_4 \in \mathbb{Z}$. Then, the fault-injected version g^f can be represented as $(g_1 + \Delta) + g_2 \cdot i + g_3 \cdot j + g_4 \cdot k$. According to the properties of the greatest common divisor, we can express $\gcd(nrd(g^f), D_{com})$ as:

$$\gcd(nrd(g^f) - D_{com} \cdot h, D_{com}) = \gcd(nrd(g^f) - nrd(g), D_{com})$$

where $nrd(g) = D_{com} \cdot h$ for some integer h. By calculating this in terms of Δ, we get:

$$\begin{aligned}
&\gcd(nrd(g^f) - nrd(g), D_{com}) \\
&= \gcd\left(((g_1 + \Delta)^2 + g_2^2 + g_3^2 \cdot p + g_4^2 \cdot p) - (g_1^2 + g_2^2 + g_3^2 \cdot p + g_4^2 \cdot p), D_{com}\right) \\
&= \gcd\left(\Delta \cdot (\Delta + 2 \cdot g_1), D_{com}\right)
\end{aligned}$$

If $\gcd(\Delta \cdot (\Delta + 2 \cdot g_1), D_{com}) = 1$, then it implies $\gcd(\Delta, D_{com}) = 1$. Therefore, we can conclude that

$$P(\gcd(\Delta \cdot (\Delta + 2 \cdot g_1), D_{com}) = 1) < P(\gcd(\Delta, D_{com}) = 1) = \frac{\varphi(D_{com})}{D_{com}}$$

□

Lemma 2 (Lower Bound). *Under the same conditions as in Lemma 1, the probability that $nrd(g^f)$ and D_{com} are coprime has a lower bound:*

$$(\frac{\varphi(D_{com})}{D_{com}})^3 < P(\gcd((nrd(g^f), D_{com})) = 1)$$

Proof. Let us maintain the notations as defined in Lemma 1. To prove the lower bound, we first decompose $P(\gcd(\Delta \cdot (\Delta + 2 \cdot g_1), D_{com}) = 1)$ as follows:

$$\begin{aligned} &P(\gcd(\Delta \cdot (\Delta + 2 \cdot g_1), D_{com}) = 1) \\ &= P(\gcd(\Delta, D_{com}) = 1 \wedge \gcd(\Delta + 2 \cdot g_1, D_{com}) = 1) \\ &= \sum_{\substack{\Delta \equiv k \pmod{D_{com}} \\ k \in \mathbb{Z}^*_{D_{com}}}} P(\Delta \equiv k \pmod{D_{com}}) \cdot P(gcd(k + 2 \cdot g_1, D_{com}) = 1) \\ &= \frac{1}{D_{com}} \cdot \sum_{\substack{\Delta \equiv k \pmod{D_{com}} \\ k \in \mathbb{Z}^*_{D_{com}}}} P(gcd(k + 2 \cdot g_1, D_{com}) = 1) \end{aligned}$$

In this context, the probability $P(\gcd(k + 2 \cdot g_1, D_{com}) = 1)$ is equivalent to the probability that $k + 2 \cdot g_1 \pmod{D_{com}} \in \mathbb{Z}^*_{Dcom}$ for the random variables g_1. Note that since g is determined by the product of γ and $a_0 + b_0\overline{\theta}$, g_1 is not uniformly random. Consequently, the distribution of $k + 2 \cdot g_1$ on $\mathbb{Z}_{Dcom}$ is not uniformly random.

In order to examine this distribution, we express g_1 in terms of a_0 and b_0 as $a_0 + m \cdot b_0$ for some $m \in \mathbb{Z}$. By Algorithm 1, a_0 and b_0 are randomly selected with uniform probability within the specified range: $1 \leq a_0 \leq D_{com}$ and $1 \leq b_0 \leq D_{com}$. Subsequently, they are verified if the selected a_0 and b_0 satisfy the condition $\gcd(a_0, b_0, D_{com}) = 1$. Only pairs that meet this condition are retained and considered sample values.

Let S denote the set of valid pairs (a_0, b_0) defined as follows.

$$S = \{(a_0, b_0) | 1 \leq a_0 \leq D_{com}, 1 \leq b_0 \leq D_{com}, \gcd(a_0, b_0, D_{com}) = 1\}$$

Then, the probability $P(\gcd(k + 2 \cdot g_1, D_{com}) = 1)$ can be expressed as:

$$\begin{aligned} &P(\gcd(k + 2 \cdot g_1, D_{com}) = 1) \\ &= \frac{|\{(a_0, b_0) | k + 2 \cdot (a_0 + mb_0) \pmod{D_{com}} \in \mathbb{Z}^*_{D_{com}}\}|}{|S|} \end{aligned}$$

The set $\{(a_0, b_0) | k + 2 \cdot (a_0 + mb_0) \pmod{D_{com}} \in \mathbb{Z}^*_{D_{com}}\}$ can be partitioned into subsets $\{(a_0, b_0) | k + 2 \cdot (a_0 + mb_0) = t \pmod{D_{com}}\}$ for $t \in \mathbb{Z}^*_{D_{com}}$. Moreover, each subset can be further divided into two partitions:

$$\begin{aligned} S_{k,t,1} = \{(a_0, b_0) | 1 \leq a_0, b_0 \leq D_{com}, gcd(b_0, D_{com}) = 1, \\ k + 2 \cdot (a_0 + mb_0) = t \pmod{D_{com}}\}, \end{aligned}$$

$$S_{k,t,2} = \{(a_0, b_0)|1 \le a_0, b_0 \le D_{com}, gcd(b_0, D_{com}) \ne 1,$$
$$\gcd(a_0, b_0, D_{com}) = 1, k + 2 \cdot (a_0 + mb_0) = t \pmod{D_{com}}\}$$

For every b_0 satisfies $1 \le b_0 \le D_{com}$ and $\gcd(b_0, D_{com}) = 1$, there is a unique value for a_0 since $1 \le a_0 \le D_{com}$ and D_{com} is coprime to 2. We can deduce that $S_{k,t,1} = \varphi(D_{com})$. Thus,

$$\begin{aligned}
&|\{(a_0, b_0)|k + 2 \cdot (a_0 + mb_0) \pmod{D_{com}} \in \mathbb{Z}^*_{D_{com}}\}| \\
&= \sum_{t \in \mathbb{Z}^*_{D_{com}}} |\{(a_0, b_0)|k + 2 \cdot (a_0 + mb_0) = t \pmod{D_{com}}\}| \\
&= \sum_{t \in \mathbb{Z}^*_{D_{com}}} (S_{k,t,1} + S_{k,t,2}) > \sum_{t \in \mathbb{Z}^*_{D_{com}}} S_{k,t,1} \\
&= \sum_{t \in \mathbb{Z}^*_{D_{com}}} \varphi(D_{com}) = (\varphi(D_{com}))^2
\end{aligned}$$

Since $D^2_{com} > |S|$,

$$\begin{aligned}
&P(\gcd(\Delta \cdot (\Delta + 2 \cdot g_1), D_{com}) = 1) \\
&= \frac{1}{D_{com}} \cdot \sum_{\substack{\Delta \equiv k \pmod{D_{com}} \\ k \in \mathbb{Z}^*_{D_{com}}}} P(gcd(k + 2 \cdot g_1, D_{com}) = 1) \\
&= \frac{1}{D_{com}} \cdot \sum_{\substack{\Delta \equiv k \pmod{D_{com}} \\ k \in \mathbb{Z}^*_{D_{com}}}} \frac{|\{(a_0, b_0)|k + 2 \cdot (a_0 + mb_0) \pmod{D_{com}} \in \mathbb{Z}^*_{D_{com}}\}|}{|S|} \\
&> \frac{1}{D_{com}} \cdot \sum_{\substack{\Delta \equiv k \pmod{D_{com}} \\ k \in \mathbb{Z}^*_{D_{com}}}} \frac{\varphi(D_{com})^2}{D^2_{com}} = (\frac{\varphi(D_{com})}{D_{com}})^3
\end{aligned}$$

Therefore, the following inequality holds:

$$(\frac{\varphi(D_{com})}{D_{com}})^3 < P(\gcd((nrd(g^f), D_{com})) = 1)$$

□

Theorem 2 (Estimation). *With the same notations in Lemma 1 and Lemma 2, if we assume g_1 is uniformly random in $\mathbb{Z}_{D_{com}}$, an estimate for the probability that $nrd(g^f)$ and D_{com} are coprime can be expressed as:*

$$P(\gcd(nrd(g^f), D_{com}) = 1) \approx (\frac{\varphi(D_{com})}{D_{com}})^2$$

.

Proof. Since g_1 is uniformly random in $\mathbb{Z}_{D_{com}}$, we can approximate as follows:

$$P(\gcd(k + 2g_1, D_{com}) = 1) \approx \frac{\varphi(D_{com})}{D_{com}},$$

where $\Delta \equiv k \pmod{D_{com}}$. As a result,

$$P(\gcd(\Delta \cdot (\Delta + 2g_1), D_{com}) = 1)$$

$$= \frac{1}{D_{com}} \cdot \sum_{\substack{\Delta \equiv k \pmod{D_{com}} \\ k \in \mathbb{Z}^*_{D_{com}}}} P(gcd(k + 2g_1, D_{com}) = 1) \approx (\frac{\varphi(D_{com})}{D_{com}})^2$$

□

Table 2. The probability of generating order $\mathcal{O}_0$ through fault injection.

NIST level	Upper bound $\frac{\varphi(D_{com})}{D_{com}}$	Lower bound $(\frac{\varphi(D_{com})}{D_{com}})^3$	Approximation $(\frac{\varphi(D_{com})}{D_{com}})^2$	Simulation (×100,000)
NIST-I	0.59843	0.21430	0.35811	0.35782
NIST-III	0.53314	0.15154	0.28424	0.27910
NIST-V	0.52081	0.14126	0.27124	0.26797

Table 2 shows the theoretical upper bound, lower bound, approximation of the probability that the faulty ideal I^f_{com} generated by the above fault injection becomes $\mathcal{O}_0$ for each NIST security level parameter of SQIsign, and the statistical probability values when simulated 100,000 times with the actual reference code. We can see that the probabilities are all significant for NIST-I, III, V.

3.2 Loop-Aborts While Computing Isogeny

As mentioned in Sect. 2.1, SQIsign uses the Montgomery curve, and consequently, during the computation of the commitment isogeny ϕ, it separates the operations into two kernels: $E[p+1] \cap ker(\phi)$ and $E[p-1] \cap ker(\phi)$. Thus, in the implementation of the commitment isogeny, the process is divided into two parts, one for computing the isogeny with a kernel corresponding to $E[p+1] \cap ker(\phi)$ (refer to lines 4 to 5 of Algorithm 2), and the other for computing the isogeny with a kernel corresponding to $E[p-1] \cap ker(\phi)$ (refer to lines 13 to 20 of Algorithm 2).

The operations for each kernel involve two nested for-loops. The outer loop sequentially selects distinct prime factors from a table, and the inner loop computes the isogeny for each prime factor's power. The factors and their powers are pre-stored in a table. (Therefore we assume the attacker knows the table's order).

Algorithm 3. Odd-degree isogeny computation and the basis evaluation in lines 4 to 5 of Algorithm 1

Input: A domain curve E
Input: A generator $K^{\pm}$ of $E[p \pm 1] \cap ker(\phi)$, respectively
Input: A basis (P, Q) of $E[D]$ such that $gcd(D, deg(\phi)) = 1$
Output: An image curve E_c
Output: An evaluated basis $(\phi(P), \phi(Q))$

Let $deg(\phi) = p_1^{e_1} \cdot p_2^{e_2} \cdots p_n^{e_n}$ for $n \in \mathbb{Z}^+$ such that $p_i | (p+1)$ for $1 \leq i \leq h$ and $p_i | (p-1)$ for $h < i \leq n$.
$E_{1,0} := E$
$P_{1,0}, Q_{1,0} := P, Q$
  Evaluate isogenies with kernel in $E[p+1]$
for $i \in \{1, ..., h\}$ **do**
    $K_i^+ := [p_{i+1}^{e_{i+1}} \cdot p_{i+2}^{e_{i+2}} \cdots p_h^{e_h}]K^+$
    for $j \in \{1, ..., e_i\}$ **do**
        $K_{i,j}^+ := [p_i^{e_i - j}]K_i^+$
        Compute isogeny $\phi_{i,j}$ of $deg(\phi_{i,j}) = p_i$ corresponding to the kernel $K_{i,j}^+$
        $E_{i,j} := \phi_{i,j}(E_{i,j-1})$, $K^+ := \phi_{i,j}(K^+)$, $K^- := \phi_{i,j}(K^-)$
        $P_{i,j}, Q_{i,j} := \phi_{i,j}(P_{i,j-1}), \phi_{i,j}(Q_{i,j-1})$
    end for
end for
  Evaluate isogenies with kernel in $E[p-1]$
for $i \in \{h+1, ..., n\}$ **do**
    $K_i^- := [p_{i+1}^{e_{i+1}} \cdot p_{i+2}^{e_{i+2}} \cdots p_n^{e_n}]K^-$
    for $j \in \{1, ..., e_i\}$ **do**
        $K_{i,j}^- := [p_i^{e_i - j}]K_i^-$
        Compute isogeny $\phi_{i,j}$ of $deg(\phi_{i,j}) = p_i$ corresponding to the kernel $K_{i,j}^-$
        $E_{i,j} := \phi_{i,j}(E_{i,j-1})$, $K^- := \phi_{i,j}(K^-)$
        $P_{i,j}, Q_{i,j} := \phi_{i,j}(P_{i,j-1}), \phi_{i,j}(Q_{i,j-1})$
    end for
end for
$E_c := E_{n,e^n}$
$\phi(P), \phi(Q) := P_{n,e^n}, Q_{n,e^n}$
return $E_c, (\phi(P), \phi(Q))$

However, a notable issue arises in the outer for-loop concerning the index value i used for the $E[p+1] \cap ker(\phi)$ kernel. The index i is not reset after the first for-loop; instead, it continues to be used in the second for-loop. In other words, if the first for-loop concludes with $i = h$, the second for-loop begins with $i = h + 1$. From an attacker's perspective, this operation can be seen as a single for-loop, exhibiting a loop-aborts vulnerability in the isogeny computation process proposed in [15].

An attacker can inject faults at the point where index i is computed, randomizing i and inducing loop-aborts at the desired moment. For example, injecting a fault immediately after the computation of $i = h'$ would prevent $i = h' + 1$ from proceeding, leading to termination of the for-loop and outputting an isogeny of degree $p_1^{e_1} \cdot p_2^{e_2} \cdot \cdots \cdot p_{h'}^{e_{h'}}$.

4 Fault Attack on SQIsign

The vulnerabilities discussed in the previous section can be exploited to inject faults into the commitment phase of SQIsign to reduce the degree of commitment isogeny or to make the commitment ideal $\mathcal{O}_0$, i.e., the norm is 1. If the attacker can recover the isogeny between the starting curve E_0 and the public key curve E_A from the faulty signature and public information, the attacker can use the isogeny as a secret key. In this section, we introduce the attacker model for deterministic SQIsign and randomized SQIsign, and present a scenario of key recovery fault attack in each situation, i.e., recovering the isogeny between E_A and E_0, and analyze the time complexity and number of queries required for the attack.

4.1 Key Recovery Fault Attack for Deterministic SQIsign

The key recovery fault attack on deterministic SQIsign is performed under the following assumptions. First, the attacker is allowed to make multiple queries to SQIsign signing oracle using the same key and messages. Second, the oracle generates a signature for each query and the attacker receives these signatures. Third, the attack assumes a first-order fault situation, which allows the attacker to inject a fault once during the oracle's operation.

To illustrate the attack scenario, we explore the data flow of the SQIsign signing protocol when a first-order fault is injected as described in Sect. 3.2. Initially, a faulty commitment isogeny ϕ^f_{com} is generated due to the fault injection in the commitment phase. This affects the computation of the basis points $P_{0,chall}$ and $Q_{0,chall}$ for $E_0[D_{chall}]$, yielding $P^f_{1,chall}$ and $Q^f_{1,chall}$. Consequently, a faulty curve E^f_1 and a faulty kernel K^f_{chall} are generated, leading to the computation of the faulty challenge isogeny ϕ^f_{chall}. The faulty challenge isogeny leads to the generation of I^f_{chall} after decomposing K_{chall} along the basis $P^f_{1,chall}$ and $Q^f_{1,chall}$. The oracle continues to generate r^f, s^f_1, s^f_2, components of the signature, using E^f_1 and E^f_2. Detailed steps are omitted as r^f, s^f_1, s^f_2 are not utilized in the attack. Refer to Algorithm 4 for detailed steps. In the response phase, the oracle computes $\overline{I_{secret}} \cdot I_{com} \cdot I^f_{chall}$ to obtain J^f_{res} and uses *signingKLPT* to generate an equivalent ideal $(J'_{res})^f$ with a norm of 2^e. Finally, the oracle converts the isogeny σ^f corresponding to $(J'_{res})^f$ and yields $(\sigma^f, r^f, s^f_1, s^f_2)$ as the signature. Note that the codomain of σ^f is not E^f_2. Since the domain of ϕ^f_{chall} is E^f_1, and the left order of I^f_{chall} is $\mathcal{O}_1$ instead of $\mathcal{O}^f_1$, the curve corresponding to the right order of I^f_{chall} is not E^f_2. For the attacker, this implies that E^f_2 can be obtained from the signature of the fault-injected SQIsign, but neither E_{1^f} nor E_1 can be recovered through this.

Algorithm 4. First-order fault injected SQISign signing protocol (simplified)

Input: A Message M
Input: A secret key sk
Output: A faulty signature $(\sigma^f, r^f, s_1^f, s_2^f)$

Commitment process

Sample a_0, b_0 randomly from interval $[1, D_{com}]$ until $gcd(a_0, b_0, D_{com}) = 1$.
$I_{com} := \mathcal{O}_0\langle \gamma \cdot (a_0 + b_0\bar{\theta}), D_{com}\rangle$
$K_{com} := a_0 P_0 + b_0\theta(P_0)$, where $P_0 \in B_{0,D_{com}}$
Compute a faulty isogeny $\phi_{com}^f : E_0 \rightarrow E_1^f$.
$P_{1,chall}^f := \phi_{com}^f(P_{0,chall}), Q_{1,chall}^f := \phi_{com}^f(P_{0,chall})$

Challenge process

$a_1^f, b_1^f := H(M, E_1^f)$
Find a D_{chall}-torsion basis $(P_{E_1}^f, Q_{E_1}^f)$ on E_1^f deterministically.
$K_{chall}^f := a_1^f P_{E_1}^f + b_1^f Q_{E_1}^f$
Compute a faulty isogeny $\phi_{chall}^f : E_1^f \rightarrow E_2^f$ with the kernel $\langle K_{chall}^f\rangle$.
Find integers α^f, β^f such that $[\alpha^f]P_{1,chall}^f + [\beta^f]Q_{1,chall}^f = K_{chall}^f$.
Compute a left $\mathcal{O}_0$-ideal $(I'_{chall})^f$ corresponding to the isogeny with the kernel $\langle[\alpha^f]P_{0,chall} + [\beta^f]Q_{0,chall}\rangle$.
$I_{chall}^f := [I_{com}]_*(I'_{chall})^f$
Given K_{chall}^f, deterministically find another D_{chall}-torsion point L_{chall}^f such that a pair $(K_{chall}^f, L_{chall}^f)$ is the basis of $E_1^f[D_{chall}]$.
$(L'_{chall})^f := \phi_{chall}^f(L_{chall}^f)$
Find a D_{chall}-torsion basis $(P_{E_2}^f, Q_{E_2}^f)$ on E_2^f deterministically.
Find integers s_1^f, s_2^f such that $[s_1^f]P_{E_2}^f + [s_2^f]Q_{E_2}^f = (L'_{chall})^f$.
Given $((L'_{chall})^f, s_1^f, s_2^f)$, deterministically find another D_{chall}-torsion point $(M'_{chall})^f$ such that a pair $((L'_{chall})^f, (M'_{chall})^f)$ is the basis of $E_2^f[D_{chall}]$.
Compute an isogeny $\widehat{\phi_{chall}^f} : E_2^f \rightarrow E_1^f$ with the kernel $\langle(L'_{chall})^f\rangle$.
$M_{chall}^f := \widehat{\phi_{chall}^f}((M'_{chall})^f)$
Find r^f such that $K_{chall}^f = [r^f]M_{chall}^f$.

Response process

$J_{res}^f := \overline{I_{secret}} \cdot I_{com} \cdot I_{chall}^f$
Find an ideal $(J'_{res})^f$ of norm 2^e which is equivalent to J_{res}^f such that $(J'_{res})^f \cdot \overline{I_{chall}^f}$ is cyclic using *SigningKLPT*.
Convert the ideal $(J'_{res})^f$ into the isogeny σ^f of degree 2^e using sk.
return $(\sigma^f, r^f, s_1^f, s_2^f)$

The key recovery scenario of the first-order fault attack is as follows. The attacker first interacts with the SQIsign signing oracle, querying the same message $n+1$ times. The final query is processed normally to obtain a valid signature, while the preceding n queries are faulted during the oracle's operation, leading to loop aborts as described in Sect. 3.2 and resulting in faulty signatures. If we denote the loop index in Algorithm 3 corresponding to the fault injection point of the j-th query as i_j, the faults are injected such that $i_1 > i_2 > ... > i_n$.

The attacker can exploit these faulty signatures to reconstruct the isogeny between E_0 and E_1. Consider a scenario in which the attacker tries to recover a

Algorithm 5. Recovery of (E_0, E_1)-isogeny by divide-and-conquer

Input: A public key E_A
Input: A message M
Input: A valid signature σ, faulty signatures $(\sigma_1, ..., \sigma_n)$
Input: $deg(\phi_{com}) = p_1^{e_1} \cdot p_2^{e_2} \cdots p_n^{e_n}$
Input: Fault-injected indices $i_1, i_2, ..., i_n$
Output: A recovered commitment isogeny $\psi : E_0 \to E_1$
Output: $success$

1: $i_0 := n$
2: $(E_1)_0 := E_1$
3: **for** $j \in \{1, ..., n\}$ **do**
4: Compute the codomain of σ_j, denoted as $(E_2)_j$.
5: $\widetilde{p_{i_j}} := \displaystyle\prod_{k=i_j}^{i_{j-1}} p_k^{e_k}$
6: **for** $k \in \{1, ..., \widetilde{p_{i_j}} + 1\}$ **do**
7: Compute a candidate isogeny $\psi_{j,k} : (E_1)_{j,k} \to (E_1)_{j-1}$
8: $(a_1)_{j,k}, (b_1)_{j,k} := H(M, (E_1)_{j,k})$
9: Find a D_{chall}-torsion basis $(P_{(E_1)_{j,k}}, Q_{(E_1)_{j,k}})$ on $(E_1)_{j,k}$ deterministically.
10: $(K_{chall})_{j,k} := (a_1)_{j,k} \cdot P_{(E_1)_{j,k}} + (b_1)_{j,k} \cdot Q_{(E_1)_{j,k}}$
11: Compute an isogeny $(\phi_-)_{j,k} : (E_1)_{j,k} \to (E_-)_{j,k}$ with the kernel $(K_{chall})_{j,k}$.
12: $\psi_k := \psi \circ \psi_{j,k}$
13: $(\phi_{chall})_{j,k} := [\psi_k]_* \phi_{-,j,k}$
14: Compute the codomain of $(\phi_{chall})_{j,k}$, denoted as $(E_2)_{j,k}$.
15: **if** $j((E_2)_j) = j((E_2)_{j,k})$ **then**
16: $\psi_j := \psi_{j,k}$
17: $\psi := \psi \circ \psi_j$
18: **else**
19: $\psi_j := \bot$
20: **end if**
21: **end for**
22: **if** $\psi_j = \bot$ **then**
23: $\psi := \bot$
24: $sccess := False$
25: **return** $\psi, sccess$
26: **end if**
27: **end for**
28: $sccess := True$
29: **return** $\psi, sccess$

component of the commitment isogeny from the j-th faulty signature. Now we denote by $\psi : (E_1)_{j-1} \to E_1$ the isogeny that the attacker has recovered using $j-1$ faulty signatures, and by $\psi_j : (E_1)_j \to (E_1)_{j-1}$ the isogeny to be recovered at the j-th stage. If the degree of the commitment isogeny ϕ_{com} is $p_1^{e_1} \cdot p_2^{e_2} \cdots \cdot p_n^{e_n}$, then the degree of ψ_j is given by $\prod_{k=i_j}^{i_{j-1}} p_k^{e_k}$, denoted as $\widetilde{p_{i_j}}$. We also denote the faulty commitment isogeny ϕ_{com}^f from the j-th fault-injected SQIsign signing oracle operation as $(\phi_{com})_j$ (refer to line 4 of Algorithm 4). Similarly, $(I'_{chall})^f$

and its corresponding isogeny are represented as $(I'_{chall})_j$ and $(\phi'_{chall})_j$(refer to line 12 of Algorithm 4), respectively. The outcome of $[I_{com}]_*(I'_{com})_j$ is represented as $(I_{chall})_j$, and its corresponding isogeny is denoted as $(\phi_{chall})_j$.

In this context, the commitment isogeny ϕ_{com} can be expressed as $\psi \circ \psi_j \circ (\phi_{com})_j$. Given that D_{com} and D_{chall} are coprime, the following holds:

$$[\phi_{com}]_*(\phi'_{chall})_j = [\psi \circ \psi_j \circ (\phi_{com})_j]_*(\phi'_{chall})_j = [\psi]_*[\psi_j]_*[(\phi_{com})_j]_*(\phi'_{chall})_j.$$

The attacker can brute force all isogenies of degree $\widetilde{p_{i_j}}$ whose codomain is the domain of ψ, denoted as $\psi_{j,k} : (E_1)_{j,k} \to (E_1)_{j-1}$ for $k \in \{1, \ldots, \widetilde{p_{i_j}} + 1\}$ and operate on $[\psi]_*[\psi_{j,k}]_*[(\phi_{com})_j]_*(\phi'_{chall})_j$ for each $\psi_{j,k}$. If $\psi_{j,k}$ is indeed a component of the commitment isogeny, then the j-invariant of the codomain of $[\psi]_*[\psi_{j,k}]_*[(\phi_{com})_j]_*(\phi'_{chall})_j$ should coincide with the j-invariant of the j-th faulty signature σ_j. Otherwise, it should differ. Repeating this procedure n times allows the isogeny between E_0 and E_1 to be recovered using a divide-and-conquer strategy, as described in Algorithm 5. The attacker can then compute the isogeny between E_0 and E_A and use it as a secret key.

Analysis of the Attack. The number of queries required for the attack, assuming that fault injection always succeeds, is $n+1$. However, in a real fault injection environment, not all fault injections are always successful. Therefore, the success probability of fault injection must be considered. If we denote the probability as μ, the number of queries required for the attack scenario by the attacker can be seen to be $O(\frac{n}{\mu})$.

The time complexity of the attack needs to consider two factors. First, the time complexity of recovering the isogeny through brute force. In the proposed attack scenario, a meet-in-the-middle attack cannot be performed during isogeny recovery, so the brute-force time complexity of each isogeny can be seen to be $O(\widetilde{p_{i_j}})$. Second, the number of isogenies that need to be recovered by brute force. This is the same as the number of queries, n, by the attacker. If we denote the largest value among $\widetilde{p_{i_j}}$ where $j \in \{1, \cdots, n\}$ as $\widetilde{p_{max}}$, then considering both time complexities together, the overall time complexity of the proposed attack can be seen to be $O(\widetilde{p_{max}} \cdot n)$.

4.2 Key Recovery Fault Attack for Randomized SQIsign

The fault attack on the randomized SQIsign for key recovery is performed under different assumptions than those of the deterministic one. Firstly, the attacker is allowed to query the SQIsign signing oracle multiple times using their messages. Note that this attack does not require the oracle to operate with the same key, as the attacker can recover the secret key with just one successful fault injection. Secondly, the oracle generates a signature for each query, which are received by the attacker. Lastly, the attack assumes a second-order fault scenario, allowing the attacker to inject a fault twice during the oracle's operation.

We now examine the data flow of the SQIsign signing protocol when two faults are injected as detailed in Sects. 3.1 and 3.2. The primary difference from

Algorithm 6. Second-order fault injected SQISign signing protocol (simplified)

Input: A Message M
Input: A secret key sk
Output: A faulty signature $(\sigma^f, r^f, s_1^f, s_2^f)$

Commitment process

1: Sample a_0, b_0 randomly from interval $[1, D_{com}]$ until $gcd(a_0, b_0, D_{com}) = 1$.
2: $I_{com}^f := \mathcal{O}_0\langle(\gamma \cdot (a_0 + b_0\bar{\theta}))^f, D_{com}\rangle$
3: $K_{com} := a_0 P_0 + b_0\theta(P_0)$, where $P_0 \in B_{0,D_{com}}$
4: Compute a faulty isogeny $\phi_{com}^f : E_0 \rightarrow E_1^f$.
5: $P_{1,chall}^f := \phi_{com}^f(P_{0,chall})$, $Q_{1,chall}^f := \phi_{com}^f(P_{0,chall})$

Challenge process

6: $a_1^f, b_1^f := H(M, E_1^f)$
7: Find a D_{chall}-torsion basis $(P_{E_1}^f, Q_{E_1}^f)$ on E_1^f deterministically.
8: $K_{chall}^f := a_1^f P_{E_1}^f + b_1^f Q_{E_1}^f$
9: Compute a faulty isogeny $\phi_{chall} : E_1^f \rightarrow E_2^f$ with the kernel $\langle K_{chall}^f \rangle$.
10: Find integers α^f, β^f such that $[\alpha^f]P_{1,chall}^f + [\beta^f]Q_{1,chall}^f = K_{chall}^f$.
11: Compute a left $\mathcal{O}_0$-ideal $(I'_{chall})^f$ corresponding to the isogeny with the kernel $\langle[\alpha^f]P_{0,chall} + [\beta^f]Q_{0,chall}\rangle$.
12: $I_{chall}^f := [I_{com}^f]_*(I'_{chall})^f$
13: Given K_{chall}^f, deterministically find another D_{chall}-torsion point L_{chall}^f such that a pair $(K_{chall}^f, L_{chall}^f)$ is the basis of $E_1^f[D_{chall}]$.
14: $(L'_{chall})^f := \phi_{chall}^f(L_{chall}^f)$
15: Find a D_{chall}-torsion basis $(P_{E_2}^f, Q_{E_2}^f)$ on E_2^f deterministically.
16: Find integers s_1^f, s_2^f such that $[s_1^f]P_{E_2}^f + [s_2^f]Q_{E_2}^f = (L'_{chall})^f$.
17: Given $((L'_{chall})^f, s_1^f, s_2^f)$, deterministically find another D_{chall}-torsion point $(M'_{chall})^f$ such that a pair $((L'_{chall})^f, (M'_{chall})^f)$ is the basis of $E_2^f[D_{chall}]$.
18: Compute an isogeny $\widehat{\phi_{chall}^f} : E_2^f \rightarrow E_1^f$ with the kernel $\langle (L'_{chall})^f \rangle$.
19: $M_{chall}^f := \widehat{\phi_{chall}^f}((M'_{chall})^f)$
20: Find r^f such that $K_{chall}^f = [r^f]M_{chall}^f$.

Response process

21: $J_{res}^f := \overline{I_{secret}} \cdot I_{com}^f \cdot I_{chall}^f$
22: Find an ideal $(J'_{res})^f$ of norm 2^e which is equivalent to J_{res}^f such that $(J'_{res})^f \cdot \overline{I_{chall}^f}$ is cyclic using *SigningKLPT*.
23: Convert the ideal $(J'_{res})^f$ into the isogeny σ^f of degree 2^e using sk.
24: **return** $(\sigma^f, r^f, s_1^f, s_2^f)$

the first-order fault-injected SQIsign signing protocol is that in the commitment phase, an additional fault injection creates a faulty commitment ideal I_{com}^f, in addition to ϕ_{com}^f. This influences the computation of $[I_{com}^f]_*(I'_{chall})^f$, yielding a different I_{chall}^f from the first-order scenario in line 12 of Algorithm 6. In the response phase, the ideal operation $\overline{I_{secret}} \cdot I_{com}^f \cdot I_{chall}^f$ computes J_{res}^f, which affects σ^f. However, as mentioned in Sect. 3.1, we only consider when $I_{com}^f = \mathcal{O}_0$, so I_{chall}^f becomes $(I'_{chall})^f$ and J_{res}^f becomes $\overline{I_{secret}} \cdot \mathcal{O}_0 \cdot I_{chall}^f = \overline{I_{secret}} \cdot I_{chall}^f$.

Algorithm 7. Recovery of (E_0, E_{σ^f})-isogeny

Input: A message M
Input: A faulty signature σ^f
Input: $deg(\phi_{com}) = p_1^{e_1} \cdot p_2^{e_2} \cdots p_n^{e_n}$
Input: A fault-injected index i
Output: A recovered isogeny $\psi : E_0 \to E_{\sigma^f}$
Output: *success*

1: Compute the codomain of σ^f, denoted as E_{σ^f}.

2: $\widetilde{p} := \prod\limits_{k=1}^{i} p_k^{e_k}$

3: **for** $j \in \{1, ..., \widetilde{p}+1\}$ **do**
4: Compute a candidate isogeny $\psi_j : E_0 \to (E_1)_j$
5: $(a_1)_j, (b_1)_j := H(M, (E_1)_j)$
6: Find a D_{chall}-torsion basis $(P_{(E_1)_j}, Q_{(E_1)_j})$ on $(E_1)_j$ deterministically.
7: $(K_{chall})_j := (a_1)_j \cdot P_{(E_1)_j} + (b_1)_j \cdot Q_{(E_1)_j}$
8: Compute an isogeny $(\phi_-)_j : (E_1)_j \to (E_-)_j$ with the kernel $\langle (K_{chall})_j \rangle$.
9: $(\phi_{chall})_j := [\psi_j]^* \phi_{-,j}$
10: Compute the codomain of $(\phi_{chall})_j$, denoted as $(E_2)_j$.
11: **if** $j(E_{\sigma^f}) = j((E_2)_j)$ **then**
12: $\psi := \psi_j$
13: $sccess := True$
14: **return** $\psi, sccess$
15: **end if**
16: **end for**
17: $\psi := \bot$
18: $sccess := False$
19: **return** $\psi, sccess$

The key recovery scenario of the second-order fault attack is as follows. The attacker first interacts with the SQIsign signing oracle, querying one time. The oracle are faulted during operation, leading to randomization as described in Sect. 3.1 and loop abort as described in Sect. 3.2, resulting in a faulty signature. The attacker can exploit the faulty signature to reconstruct the isogeny between E_0 and E_{σ^f}, the codomain of σ^f.

We now denote the loop index in Algorithm 3 corresponding to the fault injection point as i, and the isogeny that the attacker aims to recover using the faulty signature as $\psi : (E_0) \to E_{\sigma^f}$. If the degree of the commitment isogeny ϕ_{com} is $p_1^{e_1} \cdot p_2^{e_2} \cdot \cdots \cdot p_n^{e_n}$, then the degree of ψ is given by $\prod_{k=1}^{i} p_k^{e_k}$, denoted as \widetilde{p}. The isogeny corresponding to $(I'_{chall})^f$ is represented as $(\phi'_{chall})^f$.

Referring to line 11 of Algorithm 6, the kernel generator of $(\phi'_{chall})^f$ is $[\alpha^f]P_{0,chall} + [\beta^f]P_{0,chall}$, hence $(\phi'_{chall})^f = [\phi_{com}^f]^* \phi_{chall}^f$. Since $I_{chall}^f = (I'_{chall})^f$, the isogeny corresponding to I_{chall}^f is $[\phi_{com}^f]^* \phi_{chall}^f$. Meanwhile, the codomain of σ^f corresponds to the right order of J_{res}^f, which is also the right order of I_{chall}^f. Furthermore, the right order of I_{chall}^f corresponds to the codomain of

$[\phi^f_{com}]^*\phi^f_{chall}$, hence the j-invariant of the codomain of σ^f and $[\phi^f_{com}]^*\phi^f_{chall}$ must be identical.

In this context, the attacker can brute force all isogenies of degree $\widetilde{p}$ that have E_0 as their domain. These isogenies are denoted as $\psi_j : E_0 \to (E_1)_j$. If the isogeny ψ_j, which is guessed by the attacker, matches the actual computed faulty commitment isogeny ϕ^f_{com}, then the j-invariant of the codomain of $[\psi_j]^*(\phi_{\_})_j$ will be the same as the j-invariant of E_{σ^f}. If it does not match, then it will be different. Here, $(\phi_{\_})_j$ is an isogeny of the kernel $\langle (K_{chall})_j \rangle$, which is computed by the codomain $(E_1)_j$ of the guessed isogeny ψ_j(refer to lines 4 to 10 of Algorithm 7). Using this, the attacker can recover the isogeny between E_0 and E_{σ^f} from the given faulty curve. By composing this with σ^f, they can compute the isogeny between E_0 and E_A. This computed isogeny can then be used as a secret key.

Analysis of the Attack. Assuming that every attempt at fault injection is successful, the only factor we need to consider is the probability that a successful fault injection leads to the generation of $\mathcal{O}_0$ as I^f_{com}. This probability, denoted as λ, is discussed in Table 2 of Sect. 3.1. In addition to this, we also need to consider the success rate of fault injection, which we denote as μ. Therefore, the number of queries required for the attack can be approximated as $O(\frac{1}{\lambda \cdot \mu})$.

When considering the time complexity of the attack, the only factor we need to consider is the recovery of the isogeny through brute-force. Therefore, the time complexity is solely determined by the brute-force recovery of the isogeny, which can be approximated as $O(\widetilde{p})$.

5 Conclusion and Countermeasures

In this paper, we identify and discuss two vulnerabilities in SQIsign that can be exploited by fault attacks. The first vulnerability relates to the computational process of generating an ideal during the commitment phase of SQIsign. If an fault is injected into the generator during the process, it can cause the ideal to be of order $\mathcal{O}_0$, which acts as a multiplication-by-[1] map on E_0 by the Deuring correspondence. We have performed an analysis to determine the range and estimation of the probability of this vulnerability occurring. The second vulnerability lies in the isogeny computation in SQIsign, where the entire operation is performed using a single counter during the commitment phase, making it vulnerable to loop abort. Exploiting these vulnerabilities, we outline attack scenarios for cryptographic key recovery in both deterministic and randomized versions of SQIsign. The former scenario assumes a first-order fault attack scenario, while the latter considers a second-order fault attack environment. In addition, we provide analyses of the number of queries and time complexity associated with each attack strategy.

Both vulnerabilities can be countered using intuitive methods. First, for the loop-abort vulnerability related to isogeny operations, it is possible to address it by checking whether the counter of the for-loop has been filled with the correct number of iterations when the for-loop is functioning normally. This was discussed similarly in [14,15]. If the environment allows for high-order fault attacks, checking the counter in parallel using multiple checkers can increase the security against fault attacks. Likewise, a countermeasure against the fault attack on the computation while generating an ideal can be realized by checking the norm of a commitment ideal. In the high-order fault attack situation, it can also be countered by adding additional checkers and ensuring that all checkers have the expected norm of the commitment ideal.

Acknowledgement. We thank the anonymous reviewers for their helpful comments on this work. This work was supported by the National Research Foundation of Korea (NRF) Grant funded by the Korean Government (MSIT) under Grant NRF-2020R1A2C1011769.

References

1. Adj, G., Chi-Domínguez, J.J., Mateu, V., Rodríguez-Henríquez, F.: Faulty isogenies: a new kind of leakage. arXiv preprint arXiv:2202.04896 (2022)
2. Banegas, G., et al.: Disorientation faults in CSIDH. In: Hazay, C., Stam, M. (eds.) EUROCRYPT 2023. LNCS, vol. 14008, pp. 310–342. Springer, Cham (2023). https://doi.org/10.1007/978-3-031-30589-4_11
3. Beegala, P., Roy, D.B., Ravi, P., Bhasin, S., Chattopadhyay, A., Mukhopadhyay, D.: Efficient loop abort fault attacks on Supersingular Isogeny based Key Exchange (SIKE). In: 2022 IEEE International Symposium on Defect and Fault Tolerance in VLSI and Nanotechnology Systems (DFT), pp. 1–6. IEEE (2022)
4. Bernstein, D.J., De Feo, L., Leroux, A., Smith, B.: Faster computation of isogenies of large prime degree. Open Book Series **4**(1), 39–55 (2020)
5. Campos, F., Kannwischer, M.J., Meyer, M., Onuki, H., Stöttinger, M.: Trouble at the CSIDH: protecting CSIDH with dummy-operations against fault injection attacks. In: 2020 Workshop on Fault Detection and Tolerance in Cryptography (FDTC), pp. 57–65. IEEE (2020)
6. Campos, F., Krämer, J., Müller, M.: Safe-error attacks on SIKE and CSIDH. In: Batina, L., Picek, S., Mondal, M. (eds.) SPACE 2021. LNCS, vol. 13162, pp. 104–125. Springer, Cham (2022). https://doi.org/10.1007/978-3-030-95085-9_6
7. Castryck, W., Decru, T.: An efficient key recovery attack on SIDH. In: Hazay, C., Stam, M. (eds.) EUROCRYPT 2023. LNCS, vol. 14008, pp. 423–447. Springer, Cham (2023). https://doi.org/10.1007/978-3-031-30589-4_15
8. Chavez-Saab, J., et al.: SQIsign: algorithm specifications and supporting documentation (2023). https://csrc.nist.gov/csrc/media/Projects/pqc-dig-sig/documents/round-1/spec-files/sqisign-spec-web.pdf
9. Cheon, J.H., et al.: HAETAE: shorter lattice-based Fiat-Shamir signatures. Cryptology ePrint Archive (2023)
10. De Feo, L., Kohel, D., Leroux, A., Petit, C., Wesolowski, B.: SQISign: compact post-quantum signatures from quaternions and isogenies. In: Moriai, S., Wang, H. (eds.) ASIACRYPT 2020. LNCS, vol. 12491, pp. 64–93. Springer, Cham (2020). https://doi.org/10.1007/978-3-030-64837-4_3
11. De Feo, L., Leroux, A., Longa, P., Wesolowski, B.: New algorithms for the Deuring correspondence: towards practical and secure SQISign signatures. In: Hazay, C.,

Stam, M. (eds.) EUROCRYPT 2023. LNCS, vol. 14008, pp. 659–690. Springer, Cham (2023). https://doi.org/10.1007/978-3-031-30589-4_23
12. Ducas, L., et al.: CRYSTALS-Dilithium: a lattice-based digital signature scheme. IACR Trans. Cryptographic Hardware Embed. Syst. 238–268 (2018)
13. Eisenträger, K., Hallgren, S., Lauter, K., Morrison, T., Petit, C.: Supersingular isogeny graphs and endomorphism rings: reductions and solutions. In: Nielsen, J.B., Rijmen, V. (eds.) EUROCRYPT 2018. LNCS, vol. 10822, pp. 329–368. Springer, Cham (2018). https://doi.org/10.1007/978-3-319-78372-7_11
14. Espitau, T., Fouque, P.-A., Gérard, B., Tibouchi, M.: Loop-abort faults on lattice-based Fiat-Shamir and hash-and-sign signatures. In: Avanzi, R., Heys, H. (eds.) SAC 2016. LNCS, vol. 10532, pp. 140–158. Springer, Cham (2017). https://doi.org/10.1007/978-3-319-69453-5_8
15. Gélin, A., Wesolowski, B.: Loop-abort faults on supersingular isogeny cryptosystems. In: Lange, T., Takagi, T. (eds.) PQCrypto 2017. LNCS, vol. 10346, pp. 93–106. Springer, Cham (2017). https://doi.org/10.1007/978-3-319-59879-6_6
16. Kohel, D., Lauter, K., Petit, C., Tignol, J.P.: On the quaternion-isogeny path problem. LMS J. Comput. Math. **17**(A), 418–432 (2014)
17. Maino, L., Martindale, C., Panny, L., Pope, G., Wesolowski, B.: A direct key recovery attack on SIDH. In: Hazay, C., Stam, M. (eds.) EUROCRYPT 2023. LNCS, vol. 14008, pp. 448–471. Springer, Cham (2023). https://doi.org/10.1007/978-3-031-30589-4_16
18. Robert, D.: Breaking SIDH in polynomial time. In: Hazay, C., Stam, M. (eds.) EUROCRYPT 2023. LNCS, vol. 14008, pp. 472–503. Springer, Cham (2023). https://doi.org/10.1007/978-3-031-30589-4_17
19. Tasso, É., De Feo, L., El Mrabet, N., Pontié, S.: Resistance of isogeny-based cryptographic implementations to a fault attack. In: Bhasin, S., De Santis, F. (eds.) COSADE 2021. LNCS, vol. 12910, pp. 255–276. Springer, Cham (2021). https://doi.org/10.1007/978-3-030-89915-8_12
20. Ti, Y.B.: Fault attack on supersingular isogeny cryptosystems. In: Lange, T., Takagi, T. (eds.) PQCrypto 2017. LNCS, vol. 10346, pp. 107–122. Springer, Cham (2017). https://doi.org/10.1007/978-3-319-59879-6_7
21. Vélu, J.: Isogénies entre courbes elliptiques. Comptes-Rendus de l'Académie des Sciences **273**, 238–241 (1971)
22. Wesolowski, B.: The supersingular isogeny path and endomorphism ring problems are equivalent. In: 2021 IEEE 62nd Annual Symposium on Foundations of Computer Science (FOCS), pp. 1100–1111. IEEE (2022)

Multivariate Cryptography

Cryptanalysis of the SNOVA Signature Scheme

Peigen Li[1,2(✉)] and Jintai Ding[1,2]

[1] Beijing Institute of Mathematical Sciences and Applications, Beijing, China
lpg22@bimsa.cn
[2] Yau Mathematical Sciences Center, Tsinghua University, Beijing, China

Abstract. SNOVA is a variant of a UOV-type signature scheme over a noncommutative ring. In this article, we demonstrate that certain parameters provided by authors in SNOVA fail to meet the NIST security level, and the complexities are lower than those claimed by SNOVA.

Keywords: multivariate public key cryptography · UOV · SNOVA

1 Introduction

Public key cryptosystems currently used such as RSA and ECC can be broken by a quantum computer executing Shor's algorithm [24] in polynomial time. Therefore, cryptosystems resistant to quantum computers are gaining increasing importance. There are many post-quantum cryptosystems based on different theory such as lattice theory, algebraic geometry, coding theory, and the isogeny theory of elliptic curves.

In 2022, the U.S. National Institute for Standards and Technology (NIST) on post-quantum cryptography (PQC) posted a call for additional digital signature proposals to be considered in the PQC standardization process. In 2023, 50 different signature schemes were submitted, including code-based signatures, isogeny signatures, lattice-based signatures, multivariate signatures, and others.

A multivariate public key cryptosystem (MPKC) has a set of quadratic polynomials over a finite field as its public key. Its security based on the difficulty of solving a system of multivariate quadratic polynomial equations over a finite field (MQ problem). See [9]. Garey and Johnson proved [17] that MQ problem is NP-complete in general.

The oil and vinegar and later derived unbalanced oil and vinegar signature schemes(UOV) [20,22], are well-known signature schemes known for their efficiency and short signature. The UOV scheme has withstood attacks for more than 20 years and is still regarded as a secure signature scheme. It is worth mentioning that the HFE scheme [21] also withstood long-term attacks, but was attacked by Tao et al. in [26]. Notably, the Rainbow signature scheme proposed by Ding and Schmidt [10], a multilayer UOV variant, was selected as a third-round finalist in the NIST PQC project. Although some parameters of Rainbow

M.-J. Saarinen and D. Smith-Tone (Eds.): PQCrypto 2024, LNCS 14772, pp. 79–91, 2024.
https://doi.org/10.1007/978-3-031-62746-0_4

schemes are broken by Beullens, see [4], the structure of UOV is still safe by now. However, both UOV and Rainbow suffer from the disadvantage of having large public key size compared to other PQC candidates, for example, lattice-based signature schemes.

For multivariate signature schemes, the size of public key mainly depends on the number of variables, the number of equations, and the size of the finite field. Depending on different influencing factors, there are different research approaches to develop UOV variants. The first approach does not change the original design of UOV scheme, but only changes the way of key generation. The compression technique [23] developed by Petzoldt et al., which is based on the fact that a part of public key can be arbitrarily chosen before generating the secret key. This implies that a part of public key can be generated using a seed of pseudo-random number generator and the size of public key mainly depends on the dimension of the oil space, the number of equations and the size of the finite field. Note that this technique can be applied to various UOV variants. The second approach is to use polynomials defined over small field as the public key, while the signature and message spaces are defined over the extension field, see LUOV in [5]. But several of its parameters were broken by Ding et al. [12]. The third approach is to reduce the dimension of oil space in the **KeyGen** step. In the **Sign** step, they use different methods to induce a new oil space from the original oil space such that the dimension of the new oil space is greater or equal to the number of equations, for example, QR-UOV [15], MAYO [3], SNOVA [28]. The authors of QR-UOV [15] construct oil space over the extension field then mapping it into the vector space over base field by trace function or tensor product, see also [18]. The signature and message spaces are defined over the base field. BAC-UOV [25] is similar with QR-UOV but it is broken by Furue et al. [16]. For MAYO [3], they increase the dimension of oil space by whipping up the oil and vinegar map $\mathcal{P} : \mathbb{F}_q^n \to \mathbb{F}_q^m$ into a larger map $\mathcal{P}^* : \mathbb{F}_q^{kn} \to \mathbb{F}_q^m$. The authors of SNOVA [28] choose the noncommutative matrix $\mathcal{R}$ of $l \times l$ matrices over $\mathbb{F}_q$ to be the coefficient ring and they construct a UOV-like scheme with coefficients in $\mathcal{R}$. Actually, we can construct oil space in the space $\mathbb{F}_q^{nl}$ and make Kronecker product with $\mathbb{F}_q^l$ to map such oil space into a new oil space of $\mathcal{R}^n$.

Our Contribution. In this paper, our focus is on the multivariate signature SNOVA scheme [28]. We observe that an SNOVA(v, o, q, l) scheme over $\mathcal{R}$ can be viewed as a UOV(lv, lo, q) scheme with l^2o equations over $\mathbb{F}_q$, rather than a UOV(l^2v, l^2o, q) scheme over $\mathbb{F}_q$ as claimed by the authors in [28]. See Sect. 2.2. Consequently, we demonstrate that some parameters provided by the authors in SNOVA can't meet the NIST security level, and the complexities are lower than they claimed, see Table 1. Additionally, the coefficient matrices of these l^2o equations induced by the SNOVA(v, o, q, l) scheme exhibit special forms and are not randomly generated. In most cases, we observe that the l^2o equations induced by SNOVA have more solutions than l^2o random equations from a UOV scheme. Therefore, the actual complexity of SNOVA may be lower than theoretically estimated. Applying the same method, we find that NOVA [27] also has lower complexities claimed by the authors in their article.

2 SNOVA Scheme

2.1 Description of SNOVA Scheme

In [28], the authors introduce a UOV-type signature scheme over a noncommutative ring, which is called SNOVA.

Let v, o, l be positive integers with $v > o$ and $\mathbb{F}_q$ a finite field with q elements. Let $\mathcal{R}$ be the ring of $l \times l$ matrices over the finite field $\mathbb{F}_q$. Set $n = v + o$ and $m = o$, $\mathbf{x} = (x_1, \cdots, x_n)^t, \mathbf{u} = (u_1, \cdots, u_n)^t \in \mathcal{R}^n$, $[P], [F]$ denote some $n \times n$ matrices whose entries are elements of $\mathcal{R}$. For each $Q \in \mathcal{R}$, $[\Lambda_Q]$ denote the $n \times n$ matrix in $\mathbf{M}_{n\times n}(\mathcal{R})$ whose diagonal elements are Q.

The Space $\mathbb{F}_q[s]$. We first randomly choose an $l \times l$ symmetric matrix s such that the characteristic polynomial of s is irreducible. Set

$$\mathbb{F}_q[s] = \left\{a_0 + \cdots + a_{l-1}s^{l-1} : \ a_0, \cdots, a_{l-1} \in \mathbb{F}_q\right\}.$$

Note that $\dim_{\mathbb{F}_q} \mathbb{F}_q[s] = l$ and each nonzero element in $\mathbb{F}_q[s]$ is invertible and symmetric. In particular, $\mathbb{F}_q[s]$ is a subfield of $\mathcal{R}$.

Central Map. The central map of SNOVA scheme is $F = (F_1, \cdots, F_m) : \mathcal{R}^n \to \mathcal{R}^m$. Set $\Omega = \{(j,k) : \ 1 \le j,k \le n\} - \{(j,k) : \ m+1 \le j,k \le n\}$. For each i, F_i is the form of

$$\begin{aligned} F_i(x_1, \cdots, x_n) &= \sum_{\alpha=1}^{l^2} A_\alpha \cdot \Big(\sum_{(j,k)\in\Omega} x_j^t (Q_{\alpha 1} F_{i,jk} Q_{\alpha 2}) x_k \Big) \cdot B_\alpha \\ &= \sum_{\alpha=1}^{l^2} A_\alpha \cdot \mathbf{x}^t([\Lambda_{Q_{\alpha 1}}][F_i][\Lambda_{Q_{\alpha 2}}])\mathbf{x} \cdot B_\alpha \end{aligned}$$

where $F_{i,jk}$ are randomly chosen from $\mathcal{R}$, A_α and B_α are invertible elements randomly chosen from $\mathcal{R}$, and $Q_{\alpha 1}, Q_{\alpha 2}$ are invertible elements randomly chosen from $\mathbb{F}_q[s]$. Indeed, $[F_i] = (F_{i,jk})$ is the form of

$$[F_i] = \begin{pmatrix} F_{11} & F_{12} \\ F_{21} & 0_{o\times o} \end{pmatrix} \in \mathbf{M}_{n\times n}(\mathcal{R}),$$

with $F_{11} \in \mathbf{M}_{v\times v}(\mathcal{R})$, $F_{12} \in \mathbf{M}_{v\times o}(\mathcal{R})$ and $F_{21} \in \mathbf{M}_{o\times v}(\mathcal{R})$.

Public Key and Private Key. Let $T : \mathcal{R}^n \to \mathcal{R}^n$ be the map corresponding to the matrix

$$[T] = \begin{pmatrix} I_{v\times v} & T_{v\times o} \\ 0 & I_{o\times o} \end{pmatrix},$$

where $T_{v\times o}$ is a $v \times o$ matrix whose entries are chosen randomly from $\mathbb{F}_q[s]$. $I_{v\times v}$ and $I_{o\times o}$ are the diagonal matrices with all entries being the identity matrix in $\mathcal{R}$.

Let $P = F \circ T$. Set $\mathbf{x} = [T] \cdot \mathbf{u}$ and $P_i = F_i \circ T$. We get

$$\begin{aligned} P_i(\mathbf{u}) &= \sum_{\alpha=1}^{l^2} \sum_{d_j=1}^{n} \sum_{d_k=1}^{n} A_\alpha \cdot u_{d_j}^t (Q_{\alpha 1} P_{i,d_j d_k} Q_{\alpha 2}) u_{d_k} \cdot B_\alpha \\ &= \sum_{\alpha=1}^{l^2} A_\alpha \cdot \mathbf{u}^t([\Lambda_{Q_{\alpha 1}}][P_i][\Lambda_{Q_{\alpha 2}}])\mathbf{u} \cdot B_\alpha \end{aligned}$$

where $P_{i,d_j d_k} = \sum_{(j,k)\in\Omega} t_{j,d_j} \cdot F_{i,jk} \cdot t_{k,d_k}$. Note that

$$[P_i] = [P_{i,d_j d_k}] = [T]^t [F_i][T], \ i = 1, \cdots, m.$$

The public key of SNOVA consists of the map $P : \mathcal{R}^n \to \mathcal{R}^m$, i.e., the corresponding matrices $[P_i]$ for $i = 1, \cdots, m$, and matrices $A_\alpha, B_\alpha, Q_{\alpha k}$ for $\alpha = 1, \cdots, l^2$ and $k = 1, 2$. The private key of SNOVA is (F, T), i.e., the matrix $[T]$ and the matrices $[F_i]$ for $i = 1, \cdots, m$.

Signature. Let **Message** be the message to be signed. Set $Hash(\mathbf{Message}) = \mathbf{y} = (y_1, \cdots, y_m)^t \in \mathcal{R}^m$. We first choose random values $a_1, \cdots, a_v \in \mathcal{R}$ as the vinegar variables. Then, the following equation $F(\mathbf{a}, \mathbf{x}_o) = \mathbf{y}$ is a linear system of $\mathbf{x}_o \in \mathcal{R}^o$, and we can obtain a solution $\mathbf{x}_o = (a_{v+1}, \cdots, a_n)$ for the equation

$$F(a_1, \cdots, a_v, x_{v+1}, \cdots, x_n) = \mathbf{y}.$$

If there is no solution to the equation, we choose new random values $a_1', \cdots, a_v' \in \mathcal{R}$ and repeat the procedure. Set $\mathbf{x} = (a_1, \cdots, a_v, a_{v+1}, \cdots, a_n)^t$. Secondly, the signature is $\mathbf{sign} = T^{-1}(\mathbf{x})$.

Verification. Let $\mathbf{sign} = (s_1, \cdots, s_n)$ be the signature to be verified. If $Hash(\mathbf{Message}) = P(\mathbf{sign})$, then the signature is accepted, otherwise rejected.

2.2 Structure of SNOVA

The authors assert in [28] that an SNOVA(v, o, q, l) scheme over $\mathcal{R}$ can be considered as a UOV$(l^2 v, l^2 o, q)$ scheme over $\mathbb{F}_q$. However, we argue that it should only be regarded as a UOV(lv, lo, q) scheme with $l^2 o$ equations over $\mathbb{F}_q$. In the second part of this section, we claim that an SNOVA(v, o, q, l) can induce a standard UOV(v, o, q^l) scheme. Here standard means that the dimension of oil space equals to the number of equations.

Claim 1. An SNOVA(v, o, q, l) scheme can be regarded as a UOV(lv, lo, q) scheme with $l^2 o$ equations over $\mathbb{F}_q$.

In fact, all the matrices $[F_i]$, $[T]$, and $[P_i]$ in the SNOVA scheme can be viewed as $ln \times ln$ matrices in $\mathbf{M}_{ln\times ln}(\mathbb{F}_q)$ with

$$[P_i] = [T]^t \cdot [F_i] \cdot [T] \in \mathbf{M}_{ln\times ln}(\mathbb{F}_q), \quad i = 1, \cdots, m.$$

Based on the design of the central map F, the lower-right $lo \times lo$ block is zero block for each $[F_i]$. Therefore there exists a common oil space of $[P_i]$ over $\mathbb{F}_q$ with dimension lo for all i. Set

$$\mathcal{O}_1 = \{(0, \cdots, 0, a_{lv+1}, \cdots, a_{ln})^t \in \mathbb{F}_q^{ln} : a_i \in \mathbb{F}_q\} \text{ and } \mathcal{O} = [T]^{-1}(\mathcal{O}_1) \subset \mathbb{F}_q^{ln}.$$

Note that $\dim_{\mathbb{F}_q} \mathcal{O} = lo$ and for any $\mathbf{u}, \mathbf{v} \in \mathcal{O}$, $0 \leq j, k \leq l-1$, we have

$$\mathbf{u}^t \cdot \Big([\Lambda_{s^j}][P_i][\Lambda_{s^k}]\Big) \cdot \mathbf{v} = 0 \in \mathbb{F}_q \text{ for } i = 1, \cdots, m. \tag{2.1}$$

That is, each $[\Lambda_{s^j}][P_i][\Lambda_{s^k}]$ sends $\mathcal{O}$ into its own orthogonal complement $\mathcal{O}^\perp$. Since $[T]$ and $[\Lambda_s]$ are commutative and $\mathcal{O}_1$ is stable under $[\Lambda_s]$, $\mathcal{O}$ is stable under $[\Lambda_s]$. Therefore an SNOVA(v, o, q, l) scheme induces a UOV(lv, lo, q) scheme whose oil space is $\mathcal{O}$ with $l^2 o$ equations given by (2.1).

Next, we will explain how we use the oil space $\mathcal{O}$ of the UOV(lv, lo, q) scheme with $l^2 o$ equations given by (2.1) obtained from a SNOVA(v, o, q, l) to recover the oil space of SNOVA scheme. Set

$$\mathcal{O} \otimes \mathbb{F}_q^l := \{ \sum_{1 \leq i \leq lo, 1 \leq j \leq l} a_{ij} \mathbf{u}_i \otimes e_j^t \in \mathcal{R}^n : \mathbf{u}_i \in \mathcal{O}, e_j \in \mathbb{F}_q^l, a_{ij} \in \mathbb{F}_q\} \subset \mathcal{R}^n,$$

where $\{\mathbf{u}_i\}_{1 \leq i \leq lo}$(resp. $\{e_j\}_{1 \leq j \leq l}$) is a basis of $\mathcal{O}$(resp. $\mathbb{F}_q^l$) over $\mathbb{F}_q$ and $\otimes$ denotes the Kronecker product of matrices. We have $\dim_{\mathbb{F}_q} \mathcal{O} \otimes \mathbb{F}_q^l = lo^2$ and for any $\mathbf{x} \in \mathcal{O} \otimes \mathbb{F}_q^l$,

$$P(\mathbf{x}) = 0 \in \mathcal{R}^m.$$

Indeed, for any $Q_{\alpha 1}, Q_{\alpha 2} \in \mathbb{F}_q[s]$, $[\Lambda_{Q_{\alpha 1}}][P_i][\Lambda_{Q_{\alpha 2}}]$ can be written as a linear combination of $\{[\Lambda_{s^j}][P_i][\Lambda_{s^k}]\}_{0 \leq j,k \leq l-1}$, and each column of $\mathbf{x}$ in $\mathcal{O} \otimes \mathbb{F}_q^l$ belongs to $\mathcal{O}$. By (2.1), we have $\mathbf{x}^t([\Lambda_{Q_{\alpha 1}}][P_i][\Lambda_{Q_{\alpha 2}}])\mathbf{x} = 0 \in \mathcal{R}$ for each i. Hence $P(\mathbf{x}) = 0 \in \mathcal{R}^m$.

Combining with the fact that $\dim_{\mathbb{F}_q} \mathcal{O} \otimes \mathbb{F}_q^l = lo^2$, a UOV$(lv, lo, q)$ scheme with $l^2 o$ equations over $\mathbb{F}_q$ obtained from a SNOVA(v, o, q, l) can easily recover the oil space $\mathcal{O} \otimes \mathbb{F}_q^l$ of SNOVA scheme. Therefore we only need to consider the system of Eq. (2.1), which is a UOV(lv, lo, q) scheme with $l^2 o$ equations over $\mathbb{F}_q$.

Claim 2. An SNOVA(v, o, q, l) scheme can induce a standard UOV(v, o, q^l) scheme.

We know that all the eigenvalues of s lie in $\mathbb{F}_{q^l}$ due to the characteristic polynomial of s being irreducible. Let $\lambda \in \mathbb{F}_{q^l}$ be an eigenvalue of s and $\xi \in (\mathbb{F}_{q^l})^l$ an eigenvector corresponding to λ. Let τ be the Frobenius element $z \mapsto z^q$ in the Galois group Gal$(\mathbb{F}_{q^l}/\mathbb{F}_q)$. For $j = 0, \cdots, l-1$, we have

$$s\tau^j(\xi) = \tau^j(\lambda)\tau^j(\xi).$$

Thus for each j, $\tau^j(\xi)$ is an eigenvector corresponding to the eigenvalue $\tau^j(\lambda)$. In particular, $\{\xi, \tau^1(\xi), \cdots, \tau^{l-1}(\xi)\}$ are linear independent and so

$$\text{Tr}(\xi) := \sum_{j=0}^{l-1} \tau^j(\xi) \in \mathbb{F}_q^l - \{0\}.$$

Lemma 2.1. *With the notations above. Suppose that*

$$\mathcal{O}_1 = \{(0, \cdots, 0, a_{lv+1}, \cdots, a_{ln})^t \in \mathbb{F}_q^{ln} : a_i \in \mathbb{F}_q\} \text{ and } \mathcal{O} = [T]^{-1}(\mathcal{O}_1) \subset \mathbb{F}_q^{ln}.$$

There is a subspace $\mathcal{O}_2$ of $\mathbb{F}_{q^l}^{nl}$ such that

$$\mathcal{O} \otimes_{\mathbb{F}_q} \mathbb{F}_{q^l} = \mathcal{O}_2 \oplus \tau(\mathcal{O}_2) \oplus \cdots \oplus \tau^{l-1}(\mathcal{O}_2) \tag{2.2}$$

and $\dim_{\mathbb{F}_{q^l}} \mathcal{O}_2 = o$, where τ is induced from the Frobenius element. Here we use the same notation.

Proof. Take

$$\mathcal{O}_1' := \left\{(0, \cdots, 0, a_{v+1}\xi^t, \cdots, a_n\xi^t)^t \in \mathbb{F}_{q^l}^{ln} : a_i \in \mathbb{F}_{q^l}\right\} \subset \mathcal{O}_1 \otimes_{\mathbb{F}_q} \mathbb{F}_{q^l}$$

and

$$\mathcal{O}_2 := [T]^{-1}(\mathcal{O}_1') \subset \mathcal{O} \otimes_{\mathbb{F}_q} \mathbb{F}_{q^l}.$$

It is easy to know $\dim_{\mathbb{F}_{q^l}} \mathcal{O}_2 = o$. We claim that such $\mathcal{O}_2$ is what we want. Indeed, since each entry of $[T]$ belongs to $\mathbb{F}_q[s]$, we have $\mathcal{O} \otimes_{\mathbb{F}_q} \mathbb{F}_{q^l} = [T]^{-1}(\mathcal{O}_1 \otimes_{\mathbb{F}_q} \mathbb{F}_{q^l})$ and

$$[T]^{-1}(\tau^k(\mathcal{O}_1')) = \tau^k([T]^{-1}(\mathcal{O}_1')) = \tau^k(\mathcal{O}_2)$$

for $k = 1, \cdots, l-1$. Thus, it is necessary to show

$$\mathcal{O}_1 \otimes_{\mathbb{F}_q} \mathbb{F}_{q^l} = \mathcal{O}_1' \oplus \tau(\mathcal{O}_1') \oplus \cdots \oplus \tau^{l-1}(\mathcal{O}_1').$$

Since $\{\xi, \tau^1(\xi), \cdots, \tau^{l-1}(\xi)\}$ are linear independent, we have

$$\mathbb{F}_{q^l}^l = \mathbb{F}_{q^l} \cdot \xi \oplus \mathbb{F}_{q^l} \cdot \tau(\xi) \oplus \cdots \oplus \mathbb{F}_{q^l} \cdot \tau^{l-1}(\xi).$$

Thus

$$\begin{aligned}\mathcal{O}_{1i} :&= \{(0, \cdots, 0, a_{l(i-1)+1}, \cdots, a_{li}, 0, \cdots, 0)^t : a_{li+j} \in \mathbb{F}_{q^l}\} \cong \mathbb{F}_{q^l}^l \\ &= \mathcal{O}_{1i}' \oplus \tau(\mathcal{O}_{1i}') \cdots \oplus \tau^{l-1}(\mathcal{O}_{1i}'),\end{aligned}$$

where $\mathcal{O}_{1i}' := \{(0, \cdots, 0, a_i\xi^t, 0, \cdots, 0, \cdots, 0)^t : a_i \in \mathbb{F}_{q^l}\} \cong \mathbb{F}_{q^l}$. Then we have

$$\begin{aligned}\mathcal{O}_1 \otimes_{\mathbb{F}_q} \mathbb{F}_{q^l} = \bigoplus_{i=v+1}^{n} \mathcal{O}_{1i} &= \bigoplus_{i=v+1}^{n} \left(\mathcal{O}_{1i}' \oplus \tau(\mathcal{O}_{1i}') \oplus \cdots \oplus \tau^{l-1}(\mathcal{O}_{1i}')\right) \\ &= \bigoplus_{i=v+1}^{n} \mathcal{O}_{1i}' \oplus \bigoplus_{i=v+1}^{n} \tau(\mathcal{O}_{1i}') \oplus \cdots \oplus \bigoplus_{i=v+1}^{n} \tau^{l-1}(\mathcal{O}_{1i}') \\ &= \mathcal{O}_1' \oplus \tau(\mathcal{O}_1') \oplus \cdots \oplus \tau^{l-1}(\mathcal{O}_1').\end{aligned}$$

□

Note that each element of $\mathcal{O}_2$ has the form of

$$\mathbf{u} = (\lambda_1\xi^t, \cdots, \lambda_v\xi^t, a_1\xi^t, \cdots, a_o\xi^t)^t \in \mathbb{F}_{q^l}^{ln} \text{ with } \lambda_i, a_i \in \mathbb{F}_{q^l} \tag{2.3}$$

due to the fact that $[T]^{-1} \in \mathbf{M}_{n\times n}(\mathbb{F}_q[s])$ and ξ is a common eigenvector of the elements of $\mathbb{F}_q[s]$. We claim that many equations in (2.1) are redundant if $\mathbf{u}$ and $\mathbf{v}$ are elements in $\mathcal{O}_2$. Indeed, take $\mathbf{u}, \mathbf{v} \in \mathcal{O}_2$, we have

$$\mathbf{u}^t \cdot \left([\Lambda_{s^j}][P_i][\Lambda_{s^k}]\right) \cdot \mathbf{v} = \lambda^{j+k}\mathbf{u}^t \cdot [P_i] \cdot \mathbf{v},$$

where λ is the eigenvalue corresponding to ξ. Thus $\mathbf{u}^t \cdot [P_i] \cdot \mathbf{v} = 0$ will imply that $\mathbf{u}^t \cdot \left([\Lambda_{s^j}][P_i][\Lambda_{s^k}]\right) \cdot \mathbf{v} = 0$ for $0 \leq j, k \leq l-1$ and only m equations in (2.1) are effective when $\mathbf{u}, \mathbf{v} \in \mathcal{O}_2$. Therefore, after linear transformation, there is a standard UOV(v, o, q^l) scheme induced by SNOVA(v, o, q, l) scheme. In fact, take

$$\mathcal{O}_2' = \{(a_1, \cdots, a_n) : (a_1\xi^t, \cdots, a_n\xi^t)^t \in \mathcal{O}_2\} \subset \mathbb{F}_{q^l}^n.$$

It is easy to know $\dim \mathcal{O}_2' = o$. Let $[P_i] = [P_{i,jk}]$ be the public key of SNOVA scheme with $P_{i,jk} \in \mathcal{R}$. Set

$$\widetilde{P}_{i,jk} = \xi^t \cdot P_{i,jk} \cdot \xi, \quad [\widetilde{P}_i] = (\widetilde{P}_{i,jk}) \in \mathbf{M}_{n\times n}(\mathbb{F}_{q^l}). \tag{2.4}$$

We have

$$\tilde{\mathbf{u}}^t \cdot [\widetilde{P}_i] \cdot \tilde{\mathbf{v}} = (\tilde{\mathbf{u}} \otimes \xi)^t \cdot [P_i] \cdot (\tilde{\mathbf{v}} \otimes \xi) = 0 \tag{2.5}$$

for any $\tilde{\mathbf{u}}, \tilde{\mathbf{v}} \in \mathcal{O}_2'$ and $i = 1, \cdots, m$. The second equality holds because $\tilde{\mathbf{u}} \otimes \xi, \tilde{\mathbf{v}} \otimes \xi \in \mathcal{O}_2 \subset \mathcal{O} \otimes_{\mathbb{F}_q} \mathbb{F}_{q^l}$. Hence, the public keys of the induced UOV(v, o, q^l) scheme are given by $\{[\widetilde{P}_i]\}_{i=1}^m$, as defined in (2.4). The oil space of the induced UOV scheme is $\mathcal{O}_2'$, and the elements of $\mathcal{O}_2'$ satisfy equation (2.5).

Remark 2.1. If there is only one subspace of $\mathbb{F}_{q^l}^n$, whose elements satisfy equation (2.5), and the dimension of such subspace is o, it must equal to the oil space $\mathcal{O}_2'$ of the induced UOV(v, o, q^l) scheme described above. Then the oil space of SNOVA can be recovered by (2.2). Applying equivalent key attack to the induced UOV(v, o, q^l) scheme, we need solve a system of o^3 quadratic equations in vo variables over $\mathbb{F}_{q^l}$. According to the parameters given in [28], o^3 is always much larger than vo. Therefore, it may be effective for us to attack SNOVA by recovering the oil space of the induced UOV scheme. But we are not going to use the induced UOV(v, o, q^l) scheme to give specific complexity of SNOVA(v, o, q, l) scheme.

3 Security Analysis

3.1 Complexity

Given a homogeneous multivariate quadratic map $P : \mathbb{F}_q^N \to \mathbb{F}_q^M$, we use $MQ(N, M, q)$ to denote the complexity of finding a non-trivial solution $\mathbf{u}$ satisfying $P(\mathbf{u}) = 0$ if such solution exists. Several algorithms for algebraically solving the quadratic system by computing Gröbner basis [6] include F_4 [13], F_5 [14] and XL [8]. In this paper, we estimate the complexity of solving M homogeneous quadratic equations in N variables [7] as

$$3 \cdot \binom{N-1+d_{reg}}{d_{reg}}^2 \cdot \binom{N+1}{2}$$

field multiplications, where d_{reg} is equal to the degree of the first non-positive term in the series generated by

$$\frac{(1-t^2)^M}{(1-t)^N}.$$

The hybrid approach [1], which randomly guesses k ($k = 0, \cdots, N$) variables before computing a Gröbner basis. Hence the complexity are

$$\min_k q^k \cdot MQ(N-k+1, M, q)$$

field multiplications.

An underdetermined system can be reduced to an overdetermined system, then apply hybrid approach. There are many approaches listed in [28].

3.2 K-S Attack

In the UOV(v, o, q) scheme, the K-S attack [20] obtains the oil space. To obtain the oil space, the K-S attack chooses two invertible matrices W_1, W_2 from the set of linear combinations of the public keys $P_1, \cdots, P_m$ of the UOV scheme. Then, it probabilistically recovers a part of the oil space. The complexity of K-S attack is estimated by

$$\text{Comp}_{\text{K-S}}\ \text{UOV} = q^{v-o}$$

field multiplications.

In the SNOVA scheme, we have claimed that SNOVA(v, o, q, l) scheme over $\mathcal{R}$ can be regarded as a UOV(lv, lo, q) scheme in Claim 1. In such case, we have

$$\text{Comp}_{\text{K-S}}\ \text{SNOVA} = q^{lv-lo}$$

field multiplications.

3.3 Reconciliation Attack

The reconciliation attack [11] for UOV is similar to the K-S attack, trying to find an element of the oil space and hence basis of oil space can be recovered. In Sect. 2.2, we have proved that SNOVA(v, o, q, l) scheme can be regarded as a UOV(lv, lo, q) scheme with $l^2 o$ equations and the elements of oil space satisfy equation (2.1). Therefore, the reconciliation attack can be decomposed into a series of steps. Firstly, we may find an element $\mathbf{u} = (u_1, \cdots, u_{lv}, 0, \cdots, 0, 1)^t \in \mathbb{F}_q^{ln}$ such that

$$\mathbf{u}^t \cdot \Big([\Lambda_{s^j}][P_i][\Lambda_{s^k}]\Big) \cdot \mathbf{u} = 0 \in \mathbb{F}_q \tag{3.1}$$

for $i = 1, \cdots, o$ and $0 \leq j, k \leq l-1$. There are $l^2 o$ homogeneous quadratic equations in $lv+1$ variables in (3.1). Secondly, using Eq. (2.1), we get $2 \cdot o \cdot l^2$ linear equations for the other elements of $\mathcal{O}$. Hence the complexity of reconciliation attack is mainly centered on solving Eq. (3.1). Note that in the case of $vl+1 > l^2 o$, Eq. (3.1) has a lot of solutions not in the space $\mathcal{O}$. Therefore, the complexity of the reconciliation attack is evaluated by

$$\mathrm{Comp}_{\mathrm{Reconciliation}}\ \mathrm{SNOVA} = \min q^k MQ(lv+1-k, l^2 o, q), \tag{3.2}$$

where $\max\{0, lv+1-l^2 o\} \leq k \leq lv$ is the number of fixed variables in the hybrid approach.

Remark 3.1. We observe that finding solutions to Eq. (3.1) is easier in the extension field $\mathbb{F}_{q^l}$. This phenomenon does not exist in the UOV scheme. In the following, we will explain our observation. Indeed, applying the standard discussion of the reconciliation attack to the induced UOV(v, o, q^l) scheme in Claim 2, with the same notations as Sect. 2.2, Eq. (3.1) will reduce to the following equation

$$\tilde{\mathbf{u}}^t \cdot [\widetilde{P}_i] \cdot \tilde{\mathbf{u}} = 0,\ \tilde{\mathbf{u}} = (\lambda_1, \cdots, \lambda_v, 0, \cdots, 0, 1)^t \in \mathbb{F}_{q^l}^n \tag{3.3}$$

when we take

$$\mathbf{u} = \tilde{\mathbf{u}} \otimes \xi = (\lambda_1 \xi^t, \cdots, \lambda_v \xi^t, 0, \cdots, 0, \xi^t)^t \in \mathbb{F}_{q^l}^{ln}$$

in (3.1). There are only m quadratic equations and v variables over $\mathbb{F}_{q^l}$ in (3.3).

Unfortunately, we only prove the fact that Eq. (3.1) is easier to find a solution over the extension field $\mathbb{F}_{q^l}$. We don't know how to use the solution over the extension field $\mathbb{F}_{q^l}$ to get the solution over the base field $\mathbb{F}_q$. Thus, we will not use the induced UOV(v, o, q^l) scheme to give the specific complexity of SNOVA scheme. Indeed, we only have the following lemma:

Lemma 3.1. *Let* $\mathbf{u} = (\lambda_1 \xi^t, \cdots, \lambda_v \xi^t, 0, \cdots, 0, \xi^t)^t \in \mathbb{F}_{q^l}^{ln}$ *satisfying*

$$\mathbf{u}^t \cdot [P_i] \cdot \tau^j(\mathbf{u}) = 0 \in \mathbb{F}_{q^l} \tag{3.4}$$

for $i = 1, \cdots, m$ *and* $j = 0, \cdots, l-1$. *Set*

$$\mathbf{v} := \mathrm{Tr}(\mathbf{u}) = \mathbf{u} + \tau(\mathbf{u}) + \cdots + \tau^{l-1}(\mathbf{u}) \in \mathbb{F}_q^{ln}.$$

We have $\mathbf{v} \neq 0$ *and*

$$\mathbf{v}^t \cdot \Big([\Lambda_{s^j}][P_i][\Lambda_{s^k}]\Big) \cdot \mathbf{v} = 0$$

for $i = 1, \cdots, m$ *and* $0 \leq j, k \leq l-1$.

Proof. Note that $\mathbf{v} \neq 0$ due to $\mathrm{Tr}(\xi) \neq 0$. We have

$$\begin{aligned}
\mathbf{v}^t \cdot \Big([\Lambda_{s^j}][P_i][\Lambda_{s^k}]\Big) \cdot \mathbf{v} &= \sum_{0 \leq a,b \leq l-1} \tau^a(\mathbf{u}^t) \cdot \Big([\Lambda_{s^j}][P_i][\Lambda_{s^k}]\Big) \cdot \tau^b(\mathbf{u}) \\
&= \sum_{0 \leq a,b \leq l-1} \tau^a(\lambda^j)\tau^b(\lambda^k)\tau^a\Big(\mathbf{u}^t \cdot [P_i] \cdot \tau^{b-a}(\mathbf{u})\Big) \\
&= 0.
\end{aligned}$$

The last equality holds because Eq. (3.4) implies that $\mathbf{u}^t \cdot [P_i] \cdot \tau^c(\mathbf{u}) = 0$ for any $c \in \mathbb{Z}$. □

According to Lemma 3.1 above, if we want to get a solution over $\mathbb{F}_q$ from a solution $\mathbf{u}$ over $\mathbb{F}_{q^l}$ for Eq. (3.1), maybe we need to solve Eq. (3.4). But the equations in (3.4) are of degree $1 + q^j$. We could not apply the complexity formula in §3.1 directly.

3.4 Intersection Attack

Beullens proposed a new attack against UOV called the intersection attack in [2]. The intersection attack attempts to obtain an equivalent key by recovering the subspace $\mathcal{O}$ defined in Sect. 2.2. Let M_1, M_2 be two invertible matrices in the set of linear combinations of $\{[\Lambda_{s^j}][P_i][\Lambda_{s^k}]\}_{1 \leq i \leq m, 0 \leq j,k \leq l-1}$. By (2.1), we know that $M_1\mathcal{O}$ and $M_2\mathcal{O}$ are both subspaces of $\mathcal{O}^\perp$. Although $M_1\mathcal{O} \neq M_2\mathcal{O}$, we still have

$$\begin{aligned}
\dim(M_1\mathcal{O} \cap M_2\mathcal{O}) &= \dim(M_1\mathcal{O}) + \dim(M_2\mathcal{O}) - \dim(M_1\mathcal{O} + M_2\mathcal{O}) \\
&\geq 2lo - \dim(\mathcal{O}^\perp) \\
&= 2lo - lv.
\end{aligned}$$

In the Case of 2o > v. Let $\mathbf{x}$ be an element in the intersection $M_1\mathcal{O} \cap M_2\mathcal{O}$, then both $M_1^{-1}\mathbf{x}$ and $M_2^{-1}\mathbf{x}$ are in $\mathcal{O}$. Therefore, $\mathbf{x}$ is a solution to the following system of quadratic equations

$$\begin{cases}
(M_1^{-1}\mathbf{x})^t \cdot \Big([\Lambda_{s^j}][P_i][\Lambda_{s^k}]\Big) \cdot (M_1^{-1}\mathbf{x}) = 0 \\
(M_2^{-1}\mathbf{x})^t \cdot \Big([\Lambda_{s^j}][P_i][\Lambda_{s^k}]\Big) \cdot (M_2^{-1}\mathbf{x}) = 0 \\
(M_1^{-1}\mathbf{x})^t \cdot \Big([\Lambda_{s^j}][P_i][\Lambda_{s^k}]\Big) \cdot (M_2^{-1}\mathbf{x}) = 0 \\
(M_2^{-1}\mathbf{x})^t \cdot \Big([\Lambda_{s^j}][P_i][\Lambda_{s^k}]\Big) \cdot (M_1^{-1}\mathbf{x}) = 0
\end{cases} \tag{3.5}$$

Note that the third and the fourth equations in (3.5) are same when $[P_i]$ is symmetric. [19] and [28] both pointed out that there are $2l$ redundant equations in (3.5), see also [2]. Since there is a $2lo - lv$ dimensional subspace of solutions, we can impose $2lo - lv$ affine constraints on $\mathbf{x}$. Then the attack is reduced to find a solution to the above system of $4l^2o - 2l$ quadratic homogeneous equations in $ln - (2lo - lv - 1) = 2lv - lo + 1$ variables. Therefore the complexity is

$$\mathrm{Comp}_{\mathrm{Intersection}} = \min_k q^k MQ(2lv - lo + 1 - k, 4l^2o - 2l, q) \tag{3.6}$$

field multiplications, where k is the number of fixed variables in the hybrid approach.

In the Case of $2o \le v$. The intersection $M_1\mathcal{O} \cap M_2\mathcal{O}$ may have no nontrivial vector. If $M_1\mathcal{O}$ and $M_2\mathcal{O}$ are uniformly random subspaces of $\mathcal{O}^\perp$, then the probability that they have non-trivial intersection is approximately $q^{-lv+2lo-1}$. Therefore, the attack becomes a probabilistic algorithm for solving the system (3.5) with a probability of approximately $q^{-lv+2lo-1}$. Therefore the complexity is

$$\mathrm{Comp}_{\mathrm{Intersection}} = \min_k q^{lv-2lo+1} q^k MQ(ln - k + 1, 4l^2o - 2l, q) \tag{3.7}$$

field multiplications, where k is the number of fixed variables in the hybrid approach.

3.5 Security

Table 1 presents the classical complexity of respective attacks against the parameters submitted in [28], where the number of gates required for an attack is computed by

$$\#\text{gates} = \#\text{field multiplications} \cdot (2 \cdot (\log_2 q)^2 + \log_2 q).$$

In each pair of complexities, the left one denotes the complexity using the analysis results in this article, the right one denotes the complexity given by [28], where k is the number of fixed variables in the hybrid approach. Complexities that do not meet the security level of the NIST PQC project are highlighted in bold fonts. Furthermore, Table 1 also indicates that the complexity of SNOVA is generally lower than what the authors claimed in [28].

Table 1. Table of classical complexity in $\log_2(\#\text{gates})$

SL	(v, o, q, l)	K-S	Reconciliation	Intersection
I	(28, 17, 16, 2)	**93**/181	**132**/192 ($k = 2$)	**83**/275 ($k = 0$)
	(25, 8, 16, 3)	209/617	201/231 ($k = 15$)	221/819 ($k = 0$)
	(24, 5, 16, 4)	309/1221	270/286 ($k = 30$)	349/1439 ($k = 0$)
III	(43, 25, 16, 2)	**149**/293	**193**/279 ($k = 6$)	**116**/439 ($k = 0$)
	(49, 11, 16, 3)	461/1373	438/530 ($k = 66$)	529/1631 ($k = 0$)
	(37, 8, 16, 4)	469/1861	388/424 ($k = 45$)	507/2192 ($k = 0$)
V	(61, 33, 16, 2)	**229**/453	277/386 ($k = 17$)	**166**/727 ($k = 0$)
	(66, 15, 16, 3)	617/1841	575/707 ($k = 87$)	690/2178 ($k = 0$)
	(60, 10, 16, 4)	805/3205	695/812 ($k = 112$)	922/3602 ($k = 0$)

Acknowledgments. This work is supported by National Key R&D Program of China (No. 2021YFB3100100).

References

1. Bettale, L., Faugere, J.C., Perret, L.: Hybrid approach for solving multivariate systems over finite fields. J. Math. Cryptol. **3**(3), 177–197 (2009)
2. Beullens, W.: Improved cryptanalysis of UOV and rainbow. In: Canteaut, A., Standaert, F.-X. (eds.) EUROCRYPT 2021. LNCS, vol. 12696, pp. 348–373. Springer, Cham (2021). https://doi.org/10.1007/978-3-030-77870-5_13
3. Beullens, W.: MAYO: practical post-quantum signatures from oil-and-vinegar maps. In: AlTawy, R., Hülsing, A. (eds.) SAC 2021. LNCS, vol. 13203, pp. 355–376. Springer, Cham (2022). https://doi.org/10.1007/978-3-030-99277-4_17
4. Beullens, W.: Breaking rainbow takes a weekend on a laptop. In: Dodis, Y., Shrimpton, T. (eds.) CRYPTO 2022. LNCS, vol. 13508, pp. 464–479. Springer, Cham (2022). https://doi.org/10.1007/978-3-031-15979-4_16
5. Beullens, W., Preneel, B.: Field lifting for smaller UOV public keys. In: Patra, A., Smart, N.P. (eds.) INDOCRYPT 2017. LNCS, vol. 10698, pp. 227–246. Springer, Cham (2017). https://doi.org/10.1007/978-3-319-71667-1_12
6. Buchberger, B.: Ein algorithmus zum Auffinden der Basiselemente des Restklassenringes nach einem nulldimensionalen Polynomideal. Ph.D. thesis, Math. Inst., University of Innsbruck (1965)
7. Cheng, C.-M., Chou, T., Niederhagen, R., Yang, B.-Y.: Solving quadratic equations with XL on parallel architectures. In: Prouff, E., Schaumont, P. (eds.) CHES 2012. LNCS, vol. 7428, pp. 356–373. Springer, Heidelberg (2012). https://doi.org/10.1007/978-3-642-33027-8_21
8. Courtois, N., Klimov, A., Patarin, J., Shamir, A.: Efficient algorithms for solving overdefined systems of multivariate polynomial equations. In: Preneel, B. (ed.) EUROCRYPT 2000. LNCS, vol. 1807, pp. 392–407. Springer, Heidelberg (2000). https://doi.org/10.1007/3-540-45539-6_27
9. Ding, J., Gower, J.E., Schmidt, D.S.: Multivariate Public Key Cryptosystems, vol. 25. Springer, Heidelberg (2006)
10. Ding, J., Schmidt, D.: Rainbow, a new multivariable polynomial signature scheme. In: Ioannidis, J., Keromytis, A., Yung, M. (eds.) ACNS 2005. LNCS, vol. 3531, pp. 164–175. Springer, Heidelberg (2005). https://doi.org/10.1007/11496137_12
11. Ding, J., Yang, B.-Y., Chen, C.-H.O., Chen, M.-S., Cheng, C.-M.: New differential-algebraic attacks and reparametrization of rainbow. In: Bellovin, S.M., Gennaro, R., Keromytis, A., Yung, M. (eds.) ACNS 2008. LNCS, vol. 5037, pp. 242–257. Springer, Heidelberg (2008). https://doi.org/10.1007/978-3-540-68914-0_15
12. Ding, J., Zhang, Z., Deaton, J., Schmidt, K., Vishakha, F.: New attacks on lifted unbalanced oil vinegar. In: the 2nd NIST PQC Standardization Conference (2019)
13. Faugere, J.C.: A new efficient algorithm for computing Gröbner bases (F4). J. Pure Appl. Algebra **139**(1–3), 61–88 (1999)
14. Faugere, J.C.: A new efficient algorithm for computing Gröbner bases without reduction to zero (F5). In: Proceedings of the 2002 International Symposium on Symbolic and Algebraic Computation, pp. 75–83 (2002)
15. Furue, H., Ikematsu, Y., Kiyomura, Y., Takagi, T.: A new variant of unbalanced oil and vinegar using quotient ring: QR-UOV. In: Tibouchi, M., Wang, H. (eds.) ASIACRYPT 2021, Part IV. LNCS, vol. 13093, pp. 187–217. Springer, Cham (2021). https://doi.org/10.1007/978-3-030-92068-5_7

16. Furue, H., Kinjo, K., Ikematsu, Y., Wang, Y., Takagi, T.: A structural attack on block-anti-circulant UOV at SAC 2019. In: Ding, J., Tillich, J.-P. (eds.) PQCrypto 2020. LNCS, vol. 12100, pp. 323–339. Springer, Cham (2020). https://doi.org/10.1007/978-3-030-44223-1_18
17. Garey, M.R., Johnson, D.S.: Computers and Intractability, vol. 174. Freeman, San Francisco (1979)
18. Hashimoto, Y.: An elementary construction of QR-UOV. Cryptology ePrint Archive (2022). https://eprint.iacr.org/2022/145
19. Ikematsu, Y., Akiyama, R.: Revisiting the security analysis of SNOVA. Cryptology ePrint Archive (2024). https://eprint.iacr.org/2024/096
20. Kipnis, A., Shamir, A.: Cryptanalysis of the oil and vinegar signature scheme. In: Krawczyk, H. (ed.) CRYPTO 1998. LNCS, vol. 1462, pp. 257–266. Springer, Cham (1998)
21. Patarin, J.: Hidden fields equations (HFE) and isomorphisms of polynomials (IP): two new families of asymmetric algorithms. In: Maurer, U. (ed.) EUROCRYPT 1996. LNCS, vol. 1070, pp. 33–48. Springer, Heidelberg (1996). https://doi.org/10.1007/3-540-68339-9_4
22. Patarin, J.: The oil and vinegar algorithm for signatures. In: Dagstuhl Workshop on Cryptography (1997)
23. Petzoldt, A., Bulygin, S., Buchmann, J.: CyclicRainbow – a multivariate signature scheme with a partially cyclic public key. In: Gong, G., Gupta, K.C. (eds.) INDOCRYPT 2010. LNCS, vol. 6498, pp. 33–48. Springer, Heidelberg (2010). https://doi.org/10.1007/978-3-642-17401-8_4
24. Shor, P.W.: Polynomial-time algorithms for prime factorization and discrete logarithms on a quantum computer. SIAM Rev. **41**(2), 303–332 (1999)
25. Szepieniec, A., Preneel, B.: Block-anti-circulant unbalanced oil and vinegar. In: Paterson, K.G., Stebila, D. (eds.) SAC 2019. LNCS, vol. 11959, pp. 574–588. Springer, Cham (2020). https://doi.org/10.1007/978-3-030-38471-5_23
26. Tao, C., Petzoldt, A., Ding, J.: Efficient key recovery for all HFE signature variants. In: Malkin, T., Peikert, C. (eds.) CRYPTO 2021, Part I. LNCS, vol. 12825, pp. 70–93. Springer, Cham (2021). https://doi.org/10.1007/978-3-030-84242-0_4
27. Wang, L.C., Tseng, P.E., Kuan, Y.L., Chou, C.Y.: NOVA, a noncommutative-ring based unbalanced oil and vinegar signature scheme with key-randomness alignment. Cryptology ePrint Archive (2022). https://eprint.iacr.org/2022/665
28. Wang, L.C., Tseng, P.E., Kuan, Y.L., Chou, C.Y.: A simple noncommutative UOV scheme. Cryptology ePrint Archive (2022). https://eprint.iacr.org/2022/1742.pdf

One Vector to Rule Them All: Key Recovery from One Vector in UOV Schemes

Pierre Pébereau[1,2](✉)

[1] Sorbonne Université, LIP6, CNRS, Paris, France
pierre.pebereau@lip6.fr
[2] Thales SIX, Gennevilliers, France

Abstract. Unbalanced Oil and Vinegar is a multivariate signature scheme that was introduced in 1999. Most multivariate candidates for signature schemes at the NIST standardization competition are either based on UOV or closely related to it. The philosophy of the scheme is that the signer has to solve only a linear system to sign a message, while producing a forgery should be as hard as solving a random quadratic system. To achieve this, the signer uses the UOV trapdoor, which is a secret subspace, the "oil subspace".

We show how to recover an equivalent secret key from the knowledge of a single vector in the oil subspace in any characteristic. From this vector, we obtain linear equations that contain enough information to dismiss the public quadratic equations and retrieve the secret subspace with linear algebra for practical parametrizations of UOV, in at most 13 s for modern instantiations of UOV. This proves that the security of the UOV scheme lies in the complexity of finding exactly one vector in the oil space.

We show how to extend this result to schemes related to UOV, such as MAYO and VOX.

Keywords: Cryptanalysis · Unbalanced Oil and Vinegar · Multivariate Cryptography

1 Introduction

In order to replace number-theoretic problems used in cryptography that are threatened by quantum computing, such as factorization or the discrete logarithm problem, several families of problems have been extensively studied. One of them is related to multivariate polynomial system solving, and is referred to as "multivariate cryptography". The underlying problem, Polynomial System Solving "PoSSo", is NP-hard, and this gives confidence in the hardness of this problem for quantum computers. The history of this field shows that one must be very careful in order to construct secure schemes with these tools, as in the past many cryptosystems that seemed secure turned out to be broken by a wide variety of methods. Lately, the attacks on the Rainbow signature scheme have

M.-J. Saarinen and D. Smith-Tone (Eds.): PQCrypto 2024, LNCS 14772, pp. 92–108, 2024.
https://doi.org/10.1007/978-3-031-62746-0_5

motivated a return to the roots, in particular to the parent scheme "Unbalanced Oil and Vinegar" of Kipnis, Patarin and Goubin [15]. Recently, NIST has issued a call for alternate post-quantum signatures not relying on standard lattice assumptions. Among the submitted schemes, 10 out of 40 are based on multivariate polynomial systems, and 7 of them are closely related to UOV [3,5,7,8,10,14,21]. The main features of these schemes are the short signatures and quick signing time, which are competitive with classical cryptography, and suggest applications with constrained bandwidth, such as embedded systems.

1.1 Related Work in Cryptanalysis

Many contributions to the cryptanalysis of UOV stem from the study of Rainbow [11], a more structured scheme built upon the foundations of UOV. In particular, the reconciliation attack [12] targeted Rainbow but is easily applied to UOV. This attack finds vectors in the secret subspace of the UOV trapdoor by exploiting their relationship with one another. More recently, Beullens introduced the intersection attack [2] which improves the first step of the reconciliation attack (finding the first (two) vector(s)). Beullens describes this reconciliation process in more detail in [3]. In that paper, he mentions that once enough vectors of $\mathcal{O}$ are found, one can dismiss the quadratic equations and solve a linear system. Using his bound, this process requires finding α vectors in $\mathcal{O}$ before being able to conclude, where $\alpha = 2$ for modern UOV instantiations, and more generally α is the ceiling of the ratio between the number of variables and the number of equations. Another key recovery attack against UOV is the Kipnis-Shamir attack, which targets invariant subspaces of some linear functions related to the public key. This attack is the one that motivated the "unbalanced" property of UOV. The state of the art for forgery attacks against UOV (direct attacks) consists of exploiting the underdeterminedness of the system to eliminate equations with the Thomae-Wolf algorithm [20]. The attacker then has to solve a system in $m - 1$ variables and equations for modern UOV parameters.

1.2 Previous Work in Side-Channel Attacks

In the context of side-channel attacks, more precisely fault-injection attacks, Aulbach, Campos, Krámer, Samardjiska and Stöttinger recently published a paper with a similar result [1]. Their result can be stated in the same manner, namely that one vector yields a fast key recovery, which is expected to run in polynomial time but the complexity is not given. There is a fundamental difference in the reasoning and in the complexity achieved however, as they follow the intuition of Beullens' reconciliation attack as described in [3]: he observes that one needs only two vectors of the secret subspace to conclude because they induce an overdetermined linear system whose solution space is exactly $\mathcal{O}$. They use an adapted Kipnis-Shamir attack to obtain a second vector from the first one to conclude with this observation. In our case, we focus on the geometric point of view instead of the algebraic one. We show that a single vector is enough to characterize $\mathcal{O}$, without using the reconciliation modelling.

Therefore we skip directly from one vector to the full key, without using a second vector as a stepping stone. We obtain very efficient algorithms both in theory and in practice for practical parameters of UOV, while their attack suffers from the cost of the reconciliation attack. The largest instance they attack using their tools (targeting NIST security level 5) takes a total of 12 h including the Kipnis-Shamir and the reconciliation step, while our attack takes only 13 s on the same instance.

1.3 Contribution

In this paper, we prove that the difficulty of retrieving the UOV secret key is not only dominated by the complexity of finding the first vector in $\mathcal{O}$, but that, in fact, the problem becomes polynomial given a single vector in the secret subspace. Therefore, retrieving the UOV secret key is not harder than finding a single vector in the secret subspace. In addition, we show how this yields a polynomial-time answer to the question "$\boldsymbol{x} \in \mathcal{O}$?" without the secret key, which may be of independent interest, and is not possible with the tools introduced by [1] without going through the entire attack. We stated our result in a form as general as possible, enabling us to apply them to schemes based on or close to UOV. In particular, we also analyze the impact of our attack on MAYO and VOX.

We provide an implementation of our algorithms in SageMath [19] on a GitHub repository.

2 Preliminaries

2.1 Notations

Let q be a power of a prime and let $\mathbb{F}_q$ denote the finite field with q elements. If $q = p^m$ for p prime, we write p the characteristic of $\mathbb{F}_q$. Vectors are assumed to be column vectors and are denoted by bold letters: $\boldsymbol{x}, \boldsymbol{y}, \boldsymbol{o}, \ldots$. Matrices are denoted by capital letters, and transposition is written A^T. The right kernel of a matrix A is denoted by $\ker(A)$ unless mentioned otherwise: $\boldsymbol{x} \in \ker(A) \iff A\boldsymbol{x} = 0$. Given a field $\mathbb{F}$ and an integer n, we denote $\mathbb{F}[x_1, \ldots, x_n]$ or $\mathbb{F}[\boldsymbol{x}]$ the polynomial ring of $\mathbb{F}$ in the n indeterminates $x_1, \ldots, x_n$. The restriction of a function f to a set E is denoted $f_{|E}$. The cost of multiplying two square matrices of dimension n is $O(n^\omega)$, with $2 \leq \omega < 3$.

2.2 Quadratic Forms

Let f be a quadratic form over a vector space $\mathbb{F}_q^n$.

A function $\mathcal{F} : \boldsymbol{x} \mapsto (f_1(\boldsymbol{x}), \ldots, f_m(\boldsymbol{x}))$ such that each f_i is a quadratic form is called a *quadratic map*. In fields of odd characteristic, a quadratic form f is characterized by its *polar form* $f^* := (\boldsymbol{x}, \boldsymbol{y}) \mapsto f(\boldsymbol{x} + \boldsymbol{y}) - f(\boldsymbol{x}) - f(\boldsymbol{y})$ which is a symmetric bilinear form. As such, it admits a symmetric matrix representation in $\mathbb{F}_q^{n\times n}$ that we identify with it, and with the original quadratic form. In other words, given a quadratic form f, there exists $M \in \mathbb{F}_q^{n\times n}$ such that for all $\boldsymbol{x} \in \mathbb{F}_q^n, f(\boldsymbol{x}) = f^*(\boldsymbol{x}, \boldsymbol{x}) = \boldsymbol{x}^T M \boldsymbol{x}$. In fields of even characteristic, there is no longer an equivalence with symmetric bilinear forms, as symmetric forms are also antisymmetric. Instead, we can represent quadratic forms using triangular matrices. Note that this is also true in fields of odd characteristic, but the set of triangular matrices is not stable by congruence, therefore changes of variables are more delicate in this setting. If q is odd, we say that f has *rank* r if the matrix associated to f has rank r. In particular, the rank is preserved by changes of variables in odd characteristic, which is not the case in even characteristic. A subspace $V \subset \mathbb{F}^n$ is *isotropic* for f if there exists $\boldsymbol{x} \in V$ such that $f(\boldsymbol{x}) = 0$, *totally isotropic* if for all $\boldsymbol{x} \in V, f(\boldsymbol{x}) = 0$, and *anisotropic* if for all $\boldsymbol{x} \in V \setminus \{0\}, f(\boldsymbol{x}) \neq 0$. For an introduction to quadratic forms, we refer the reader to [18].

We recall here a characterisation of totally isotropic subspaces that describes the secret key of UOV:

Lemma 1. *The subspace $\mathcal{O}$ is a totally isotropic subspace of a quadratic form f if and only if for all $(\boldsymbol{x}, \boldsymbol{y}) \in \mathcal{O}^2, f^*(\boldsymbol{x}, \boldsymbol{y}) = f^*(\boldsymbol{y}, \boldsymbol{x}) = 0$.*

Proof. Assume $\mathcal{O}$ is a totally isotropic subspace of the quadratic form f. Then for all $\boldsymbol{x}$ in $\mathcal{O}$, $f(\boldsymbol{x}) = 0$ by definition. Let $\boldsymbol{y} \in \mathcal{O}$. Then $f(\boldsymbol{y}) = 0$ and since $\mathcal{O}$ is a linear subspace, $\boldsymbol{x} + \boldsymbol{y} \in \mathcal{O}$, therefore $f(\boldsymbol{x} + \boldsymbol{y}) = 0$. Therefore,

$$f^*(\boldsymbol{x}, \boldsymbol{y}) = f(\boldsymbol{x} + \boldsymbol{y}) - f(\boldsymbol{x}) - f(\boldsymbol{y}) = f(\boldsymbol{x} + \boldsymbol{y}) = 0$$

Conversely, assume for all $(\boldsymbol{x}, \boldsymbol{y}) \in \mathcal{O}^2$, $f^*(\boldsymbol{x}, \boldsymbol{y}) = 0$. Notice in particular that $(\boldsymbol{x}, \boldsymbol{x}) \in \mathcal{O}^2$ therefore for all x in $\mathcal{O}$, $f(\boldsymbol{x}) = 0$. Therefore $\mathcal{O}$ is a totally isotropic subspace of f. □

Observe that the dimension of a totally isotropic subspace of a quadratic form of a certain rank is bounded:

Lemma 2. *Let f be a quadratic form of rank n defined over a field $\mathbb{K}$. Let $\mathcal{O}$ be a totally isotropic subspace of f. Then $\mathcal{O}$ has dimension less than or equal to $\lfloor \frac{n}{2} \rfloor$.*

Proof. By contradiction, assume that $\dim(\mathcal{O}) = r > \lfloor \frac{n}{2} \rfloor$. Let B be a basis of $\mathcal{O}$, let $\hat{B}$ be a completion of B into a basis of $\mathbb{K}^n$. Then the matrix representing f^* in basis $\hat{B}$ has a block of zeros of size $r \times r$ in the top left corner. Therefore its rank is less than n, which is a contradiction. □

2.3 Cryptanalysis

Given a signature scheme instance $\Sigma = (\mathcal{S}, \mathcal{P})$ where $\mathcal{S}$ is the secret key and $\mathcal{P}$ is the public key, we define two goals of cryptanalysis:

- *Forgery*, which is achieved if an attacker can find a signature for *one* message in the message space of Σ.

- *Key recovery*, which is achieved if the attacker obtains an equivalent secret key $\mathcal{S}'$ enabling them to sign *any* message.

These notions can be refined to specify the tools and goals of the attacker, but this high-level description is enough for us.

2.4 Unbalanced Oil and Vinegar Signatures

One of the oldest multivariate signature schemes was introduced in [17], and later generalised by [15], and remains standing after more than two decades. We formulate it in a more abstract manner than in the seminal paper, following the formalism of Beullens [2].

Definition 1 (Kipnis, Patarin, Goubin [15]). *A UOV instance is parametrized by the following parameters:*

- *m, the number of equations*
- *n, the number of variables*
- *q, the size of the finite field $\mathbb{F}_q$.*

The UOV public key is a set of m quadratic forms $G = (G_1, ..., G_m)$ of rank n over $\mathbb{F}_q$. The secret key is a totally isotropic subspace $\mathcal{O}$ of dimension m of the homogeneous component of degree two of each G_i.

This property is not generic for a family of quadratic forms, and the key generation will use a trick to introduce this structure. This trick was the original formulation of UOV in [15], and corresponds to a block of zeros of size m in the top left corner of the symmetric matrices representing the key in a secret basis. In particular, the secret key is a pair (A, F) where A is a linear change of variables (that characterizes $\mathcal{O}$) and F is a quadratic map where the variables $x_i, 1 \leq i \leq m$ appear linearly. We deduce the public key as $G = F \circ A$ by composing the secret quadratic map with the secret change of variables. Write $A^{-1} = [\boldsymbol{o}_1, ..., \boldsymbol{o}_m, \boldsymbol{v}_1, ..., \boldsymbol{v}_{n-m}]$ and observe that $\mathcal{O} = \mathsf{span}(\boldsymbol{o}_1, ..., \boldsymbol{o}_m)$. For $1 \leq i \leq m$, we call x_i an "oil" variable, and the remaining ones "vinegar" variables. We write $v = n - m$, the number of vinegar variables.

To sign a message $\mu \in \{0,1\}^*$ the signer solves the system: $F(\boldsymbol{x}) = \mathcal{H}(\mu) \in \mathbb{F}_q^m$ where $\mathcal{H}$ is a *cryptographic hash function.* This is a linear system in the oil variables, with m unknowns and equations after choosing random values for the vinegar variables. The verifier, given $\boldsymbol{y} = A^{-1}\boldsymbol{x}$ and μ, checks that $G(\boldsymbol{y}) = \mathcal{H}(\mu)$.

We introduce the *forgery variety* which is the set of signatures accepted for a given vector $\boldsymbol{z} \in \mathbb{F}_q^m$. In practice, we always sign $\boldsymbol{z} = \mathcal{H}(\mu)$.

Definition 2 (Forgery variety). *Let G be a UOV public key and $\boldsymbol{z} \in \mathbb{F}_q^m$. We define the* forgery variety *associated to $\boldsymbol{z}$ as the set of signatures of the vector $\boldsymbol{z}$:*

$$\mathbb{V}(\boldsymbol{z}) = \{\boldsymbol{x} \in \overline{\mathbb{F}_q}^n, 1 \leq i \leq m, G_i(\boldsymbol{x}) = z_i\}$$

This variety has dimension $n - m$, but we only care for solutions in $\mathbb{F}_q$.

Notice that $\mathcal{O} \subset \mathbb{V}(\mathbf{0})$. It is interesting to note that the distribution of UOV signatures is not uniform in this forgery variety.

We include as a reference the parameters chosen for UOV in recent submissions to the NIST competition.

	NIST SL	n	m	$\mathbb{F}_q$	$\lvert\mathsf{pk}\rvert$ (bytes)	$\lvert\mathsf{sk}\rvert$ (bytes)	$\lvert\mathsf{cpk}\rvert$ (bytes)	$\lvert\mathsf{sig+salt}\rvert$ (bytes)
ov-Ip	1	112	44	$\mathbb{F}_{256}$	278 432	237 912	43 576	128
ov-Is	1	160	64	$\mathbb{F}_{16}$	412 160	348 720	66 576	96
ov-III	3	184	72	$\mathbb{F}_{256}$	1 225 440	1 044 336	189 232	200
ov-V	5	244	96	$\mathbb{F}_{256}$	2 869 440	2 436 720	446 992	260

Fig. 1. UOV parameters in [6]

3 Retrieving the UOV Private Key from One Secret Vector

In this section, we assume that $n \leq 3m$. This is the case for all recent instantiations of UOV, in particular the ones referred to in Fig. 1. At the end of the section, we explain how we proceed for very unbalanced cases ($n > 3m$), and give some reasons why very unbalanced instances of UOV are unlikely to be used in practice.

We assume that we have acquired a single vector $\boldsymbol{x}$ in the secret subspace $\mathcal{O}$ either via a side-channel attack or from computations, and leverage this information to complete a key recovery attack in polynomial time. To summarize, the secret subspace is included in the kernel of each dual linear form $\boldsymbol{x}^T G_i$ by definition. The intersection of the m hyperplanes defined by these kernels is of dimension $n - m$, and still contains $\mathcal{O}$. Therefore, this intersection is a smaller subspace than the ambiant space $\mathbb{F}_q^n$ that still contains the secret subspace, and even small enough to entirely retrieve the secret subspace by considering the restriction of the public key quadratic forms to this subspace.

Before we start, we recall the Kipnis-Shamir attack that justifies why the cases $n \leq 2m$ are called "easy instances of UOV".

Lemma 3 (Kipnis-Shamir cryptanalysis of Oil and Vinegar [15,16]). *Let G be a UOV public key with parameters n, m, q. Then the following holds:*

i. If $n = 2m$, there exists a probabilistic algorithm performing a key recovery attack against G in time $O(n^\omega)$.
ii. If $n > 2m$, there exists a probabilistic algorithm performing a key recovery attack against G in time $O(q^{n-2m}n^\omega)$.
iii. If $n < 2m$, there exists a deterministic algorithm performing a key recovery attack against G in time $O(n^\omega)$.

Proof. The first two cases are exactly the Kipnis-Shamir attack against OV [16] and the extension to the unbalanced case found in [15]. The last case comes from the observation that if $n < 2m$, then the existence of an m-dimensional totally isotropic subspace for a quadratic form implies by Lemma 2 that it is not full rank. Therefore we retrieve the subspace $\mathcal{O}$ by computing the kernels of the matrices representing the quadratic forms of the public key. Each kernel is a subspace included in $\mathcal{O}$ of positive dimension. Since generically a collection of m subspaces of positive dimension in $\mathcal{O}$ span a subspace of dimension at least m, we obtain a basis of $\mathcal{O}$ from the bases of these kernels. In the unlikely event where this process fails, we can repeat the procedure with the first vectors obtained. □

We note here that the Kipnis-Shamir attack described in the original paper [16] can be improved from a practical point of view. The essence of the attack resides in the fact that invariant subspaces of the public key matrices are eigenspaces of some closely related matrices in the set $\mathcal{T}$ defined as the closure of the $G_i^{-1}G_j$ under addition, mutliplication, and multiplication by an element of $\mathbb{F}_q$.

Therefore, the strategy of the attack is to find such eigenspaces by computing and factoring the characteristic polynomials of random elements of $\mathcal{T}$. The attack looks for irreducible factors of degree m which yield eigenspaces of dimension m, one of which is guaranteed to be the secret subspace $\mathcal{O}$. If the polynomial factors further than degree m, they consider that the attack has failed and move on to the next random element of $\mathcal{T}$.

This decision to dismiss such factors is coherent with the result proven in [16, Theorem 9], but experiments show that even smaller factors of the characteristic polynomial still yield part of the private key. We observe the following facts:

Fact 1. *Let $t \in \mathcal{T}$, let χ be the characteristic polynomial of t. Then χ is always a square.*

Proof. This comes from the shape of the secret key in the balanced Oil and Vinegar scheme:

$$F_1 = A^T P_1 A = \begin{pmatrix} 0 & D \\ D^T & B \end{pmatrix}$$

where D is invertible if and only if F_1 is and D, B are square blocks of size m. In this case,

$$F_1^{-1} = \begin{pmatrix} * & D^{-1} \\ (D^{-1})^T & 0 \end{pmatrix}$$

The same structure holds for all $F_i, 1 \leq i \leq m$.
Therefore, $P_1^{-1}P_2 = (AF_1^{-1}A^T)(A^{-1T}P_2A^{-1}) = AF_1^{-1}F_2A^{-1}$. From the above, $F_1^{-1}F_2$ has diagonal blocks that are transpose of each other. Therefore the characteristic polynomial of $F_1^{-1}F_2$ is square, and $P_1^{-1}P_2$ is similar to $F_1^{-1}F_2$, therefore its characteristic polynomial differs only by a constant factor. This applies immediately to linear combinations of the P_i and therefore to all $t \in \mathcal{T}$. □

Fact 2. *If $\chi = r^2$, then $\mathcal{O} = \ker(r(M))$.*

We insist on the fact that χ is always a square, because this is the main difference with the work presented in [16]: In [16, section 4.2], the authors remark that once a factorisation of $\chi(x) = P_1(x)P_2(x)$, with P_1, P_2 irreducible has been obtained, then $\mathcal{O}$ is either $\ker(P_1(M))$ or $\ker(P_2(M))$.

Since P_1 and P_2 are irreducible and χ is a square, it holds that $P_1 = P_2$. This was not exploited by [16] but it is a significant improvement from a practical point of view, as one only needs to consider one element of $\mathcal{T}$ obtained easily from the public key and never has to draw again (the original attack had a chance of failure, these observations show that the attack actually succeeds on every attempt). Technically, this observation also improves the complexity result because this turns the attack into a deterministic algorithm instead of a probabilistic one.

Lemma 4. *Let $G = (G_1, \dots, G_m)$ be a homogeneous quadratic map of rank n represented by m matrices. Let $\mathcal{O}$ be a common totally isotropic subspace of $G_1, \dots, G_m$. Let $\boldsymbol{x} \in \mathcal{O} \setminus \{\boldsymbol{0}\}$ and let $J(\boldsymbol{x}) = (\boldsymbol{x}^T G_1, \dots, \boldsymbol{x}^T G_m)$. Then $\mathcal{O} \subset \ker(J(\boldsymbol{x}))$, and $\ker(J(\boldsymbol{x}))$ is generically an $(n-m)$-dimensional linear subspace of $\mathbb{F}_q^n$.*

Remark 1. $2J(\boldsymbol{x})$ is the Jacobian of G if the characteristic is not 2, hence the notation J.

Proof. Let $\boldsymbol{x} \in \mathcal{O} \setminus \{\boldsymbol{0}\}$. By Lemma 1, for all $\boldsymbol{z} \in \mathcal{O}$ and for all $g \in G$, we have: $g(\boldsymbol{x}) = g(\boldsymbol{z}) = 0$ and $g^*(\boldsymbol{z}, \boldsymbol{x}) = 0$. In particular, this implies that the kernel of the linear form $g_{\boldsymbol{x}} = g^*(\boldsymbol{x}, .)$ contains $\mathcal{O}$. By hypothesis, all the quadratic forms are of rank n, therefore this linear form is non-zero. Since it is a non-zero linear form, its kernel is a hyperplane.

We have shown that for all $1 \le i \le m, \mathcal{O} \subset \ker(\boldsymbol{x}^T G_i)$. Therefore,

$$\mathcal{O} \subset \bigcap_{1 \le i \le m} \ker(\boldsymbol{x}^T G_i) = \ker(J(\boldsymbol{x}))$$

We assume that these hyperplanes are generic among hyperplanes that contain $\mathcal{O}$. The intersection of m hyperplanes in general position has dimension $n - m$, which yields the conclusion. The probability that these hyperplanes are not in general position can be bounded by a constant by the Schwartz-Zippel lemma. Therefore, if it is not the case, we try again with a new vector and must retry at most a constant number of times. □

This lemma is the key to our attack. We apply it to the formalism of UOV in the following theorem:

Theorem 1 (Key recovery from one vector). *Let $G = (G_1, \dots, G_m)$ be a UOV public key, let $\mathcal{O}$ be the secret subspace of G, and let $\boldsymbol{x} \in \mathcal{O} \setminus \{\boldsymbol{0}\}$.*

There exists an algorithm taking as input $(G, \boldsymbol{x})$ that outputs a basis of $\mathcal{O}$ in polynomial time. More precisely, Algorithm 2a performs this task and has complexity $O(mn^\omega)$, where $2 \le \omega \le 3$ is the exponent of matrix multiplication.

Proof. Recall that $n \leq 3m$. To keep notations simple, denote $K(\boldsymbol{x}) := \ker(J(\boldsymbol{x}))$. By Lemma 4, it holds that $\mathcal{O} \subset K(\boldsymbol{x})$. Let $B \in \mathbb{F}_q^{n\times(n-m)}$ be a basis of $K(\boldsymbol{x})$, which we can compute in time $O(n^{\omega})$. We restrict the public key to $K(\boldsymbol{x})$:

$$\forall 1 \leq i \leq m, \quad G_{i|K(\boldsymbol{x})} = B^T G_i B \tag{1}$$

Computing these restrictions requires two matrix multiplications per element of the public key, which takes time $O(mn^{\omega})$ in total.

Define $G_{|K(\boldsymbol{x})} = (G_{1|K(\boldsymbol{x})}, \ldots, G_{m|K(\boldsymbol{x})})$. By definition, $G_{|K(\boldsymbol{x})}$ is a UOV instance for parameters $(n-m, m)$. By hypothesis, $n \leq 3m$ therefore $n-m \leq 2m$. By Lemma 3, such an instance is broken in time $O(n^{\omega})$, yielding a basis of the subspace $\hat{\mathcal{O}}$, the secret subspace of $G_{|K(\boldsymbol{x})}$. More precisely, in practice $n < 3m$ therefore we use the kernel approach (Lemma 3, iii.) instead of the Kipnis-Shamir attack. Once we obtain $\hat{\mathcal{O}}$, we take it back to the initial space $\mathbb{F}_q^n$ using B:

Let $C \in \mathbb{F}_q^{(n-m)\times m}$ be a basis of $\hat{\mathcal{O}}$. Then, for all $g \in G$:

$$(B \cdot C)^T g (B \cdot C) = C^T (B^T g B) C = C^T g_{|K(\boldsymbol{x})} C = 0 \in \mathbb{F}_q^{m\times m}$$

This proves that $B \cdot C$ is a basis of $\mathcal{O}$ since it is a free family of maximal cardinality included in $\mathcal{O}$. This matrix product costs $O(n^{\omega})$, which yields a total complexity $O(mn^{\omega})$ (Fig. 2). □

```
one_vector_to_key(G, x)
m = |G|
K(x) = [x^T G_i for 1 ≤ i ≤ m]
B = ker(K(x))
Ĝ = [B^T G_i B for 1 ≤ i ≤ m]
C = []
for 1 ≤ i ≤ m :
    for z ∈ ker(Ĝ_i) :
        if z ∉ span(C) :
            C = C ∪ {z}
    if |C| = m :
        break
return BC
```

(a) Key recovery from one vector

```
in_secret_subspace(G, x)
n = |x|
m = |G|
K(x) = [x^T G_i for 1 ≤ i ≤ m]
B = ker(K(x))
Ĝ = [B^T G_i B for 1 ≤ i ≤ m]
for 1 ≤ i ≤ m :
    if rank(Ĝ_i) > 2(n − 2m) :
        return false
return true
```

(b) Fast test of $\boldsymbol{x} \in \mathcal{O}$?

Fig. 2. Algorithms

Remark 2. The previous result is true regardless of the characteristic of the field. In characteristic two, to ensure we are considering full rank matrices, we use the symmetric bilinear form defined by $G_i+G_i^T$ instead of G_i, which shares the same properties as G_i when considered as a linear map (namely a large block of zeroes in some basis). This observation is credited to Coppersmith in [16, Remark after Lemma 4.].

Remark 3. Notice that Lemma 4 relies on a genericity assumption. This assumption describes the usual case encountered in practice, but the non-generic cases are not significantly harder:

1. If $\boldsymbol{x}$ is not "generic in $\mathcal{O}$", $\boldsymbol{x}$ may be a singular point of the variety, in which case $\dim(K(\boldsymbol{x})) = n-m+1$, which does not prevent the success of Algorithm 2a unless $n \geq 3m$.
2. If the G_i are not chosen uniformly at random as required by the KeyGen algorithm, the dimension of $K(\boldsymbol{x})$ may be arbitrarily large (up to n). For example if some equation is a linear combination of the others, the variety is no longer a complete intersection and $K(\boldsymbol{x})$ has a larger dimension. But in this case, the public key system becomes easier to solve and therefore the key does not reach the claimed security level.
3. The algorithm will succeed in polynomial time as long as $\dim(K(\boldsymbol{x})) \leq 2m$ (in case of equality, we use the Kipnis-Shamir attack).

Notice that in Algorithm 2a, we include a break statement because with overwhelming probability, a subset of the kernels are enough to retrieve the secret key. We also obtain the following result as a corollary of this theorem, which was the initial motivation for this work.

Corollary 1. *Given G a UOV public key and $\boldsymbol{x} \in \mathbb{F}_q^n$, there exists a polynomial-time algorithm deciding whether $\boldsymbol{x} \in \mathcal{O}$.*

Note that this question is interesting only if $\boldsymbol{x}$ is in the forgery variety of the vector $\mathbf{0} \in \mathbb{F}_q^m$, as any vector that does not vanish the public key has no chance of being part of the secret subspace.

Intuitively, to prove the corollary, it suffices to apply the algorithm of Theorem 1 and conclude from a success or a failure. We do not need to apply all of the algorithm, as we distinguish the case $\boldsymbol{x} \in \mathcal{O}$ using the rank of the restrictions of the public key to $J(\boldsymbol{x})$. More precisely, any vector in the forgery variety induces a restriction of the public key by Lemma 4 where all the matrices have kernel of dimension at least 1. These kernels coincide on a dimension 1 subspace corresponding to the span of the original vector written in the new basis. But, if the vector belongs to a common totally isotropic subspace of dimension at least two, these kernels are larger and their intersection has a dimension that matches that of the totally isotropic subspace. This is the distinguisher we use.

We use the following lemma to specialize the algorithm of Theorem 1 for this task.

Lemma 5. *Let G be a collection of quadratic forms, $\boldsymbol{x} \in \mathbb{V}(\mathbf{0}) \setminus \{\mathbf{0}\}$ and $J(\boldsymbol{x}) = (\boldsymbol{x}^T G_1, \ldots, \boldsymbol{x}^T G_m)$. Let B be a basis of* $\ker(J(\boldsymbol{x}))$. *Then for all $g \in G$, $B^T gB$ has rank at most $n - m - 1$.*

Proof. Let $1 \leq i \leq m$. Let us show that $B^T G_i B \in \mathbb{F}_q^{n-m \times n-m}$ has rank at most $n - m - 1$. For this, we exhibit a non-zero element of the kernel of G_i. Notice that $J(\boldsymbol{x})\boldsymbol{x} = (\boldsymbol{x}^T G_1 \boldsymbol{x}, \ldots, \boldsymbol{x}^T G_m \boldsymbol{x}) = 0$ therefore $\boldsymbol{x} \in \ker(J(\boldsymbol{x}))$. Consequently there exist $(\lambda_1, ..., \lambda_{n-m}) \in \mathbb{F}_q^{n-m}$ not all zero such that $\boldsymbol{x} = \sum_{i=1}^{n-m} \lambda_i B_i$. Let $\boldsymbol{x}' = (\lambda_1, \ldots, \lambda_{n-m})^T$. Then $\boldsymbol{x}'^T B^T G_i B = \boldsymbol{x}^T (G_i B) = (\boldsymbol{x}^T G_i) B$ and by definition B is a basis of $\cap_{j \leq m} \ker(\boldsymbol{x}^T G_j)$ which implies that $\mathsf{span}(B) \subset \ker(\boldsymbol{x}^T G_i)$ and therefore $\boldsymbol{x}' \in \ker(B^T G_i B)$ (this is a left kernel!), which yields the upper bound on the rank of G_i. □

Proof (of Corollary 1).

For all i, the rank of $B^T G_i B$ is upper bounded by Lemma 5 since $\mathcal{O} \subset \mathbb{V}(\mathbf{0})$. Assume that $\cap_{i=1}^m \ker(B^T G_i B)$ has dimension at least 2. We show that this implies that $\boldsymbol{x}$ belongs to a linear subspace included in $\mathbb{V}(\mathbf{0})$ of dimension at least 2.

Let $\boldsymbol{x}', \boldsymbol{y}'$ be a basis of $\cap_{i=1}^m \ker(B^T G_i B)$. Then define $\boldsymbol{x}'' := B\boldsymbol{x}'$ and $\boldsymbol{y}'' := B\boldsymbol{y}'$. Observe that for all i, $\boldsymbol{x}''^T G_i \boldsymbol{y}'' = \boldsymbol{x}'^T B^T G_i B \boldsymbol{y}' = 0 = \boldsymbol{y}''^T G_i \boldsymbol{x}''$. $\boldsymbol{x}'', \boldsymbol{y}''$ must be linearly independent since $\boldsymbol{x}', \boldsymbol{y}'$ were and B is a free family by definition. By Lemma 1, this implies there is a dimension two totally isotropic subspace $\mathsf{span}(\boldsymbol{x}, \boldsymbol{y})$ shared by the G_i.

We obtain a more precise result if $\boldsymbol{x} \in \mathcal{O}$: the kernel of the G_i must be of a large dimension and included in $\mathcal{O}$. To prove this, assume that $B = B_1 \oplus B_2$ where B_1 is a basis of $\mathcal{O}$ which is possible since $\mathcal{O} \subset \mathsf{span}(B)$. In this case, for all i,

$$B^T G_i B = \begin{pmatrix} 0 & C_1^{(i)} \\ C_1^{(i)T} & C_2^{(i)} \end{pmatrix}$$

where $C_1^{(i)} \in \mathbb{F}_q^{m \times (n-2m)}$, $C_2^{(i)} \in \mathbb{F}_q^{(n-2m) \times (n-2m)}$ and C_2 is symmetric. Since the block of zeros have size m, such a matrix has rank at most $n - 2m + n - 2m = 2(n - 2m)$.

The variety $\mathbb{V}(0)$ generically contains no linear subspaces of dimension m by the Debarre-Manivel bounds [9, Théorème 2.1]. Therefore, we expect $\mathcal{O}$ to be the only such subspace.

By Lemma 5, we distinguish a vector of $\mathcal{O}$ from a generic vector of $\mathbb{V}(\mathbf{0})$ if $2(n-2m) < n-m-1 \iff n < 3m-1$. If the parameters are such that $n = 3m$ or $3m - 1$, we can apply the algorithm from Theorem 1 which succeeds only if $\boldsymbol{x} \in \mathcal{O}$, and is polynomial in any case. In practical instances of UOV, $n = \frac{5}{2}m$. Therefore the rank is at most $2(n - 2m) = m$, which allows us to use this more specific result.

This yields Algorithm 2b. □

3.1 Very Unbalanced Instances of UOV

The key recovery attack described in the previous section only works if $n \leq 3m$. We show here what happens in the $n > 3m$ case. The algorithm of Theorem 1 does not yield an easy UOV instance, but instead a smaller UOV instance that has a small rank deficiency.

Keeping the formalism of Theorem 1, let $\hat{G} = G_{|K(\boldsymbol{x})}$ using the basis B of $K(\boldsymbol{x})$. This restriction can be defined regardless of the ratio $\frac{n}{m}$, and always corresponds to a UOV instance in dimension $n - m$. Next, recall that $\boldsymbol{x} \in \mathsf{span}(B)$ and therefore we can define $\hat{\boldsymbol{x}} = (\lambda_1, \ldots, \lambda_{n-m})$ where $v = \sum_{i=1}^{n-m} \lambda_i B_i$. By construction, this vector $\hat{\boldsymbol{x}}$ is in the secret subspace of $\hat{G}$.

Notice that both instances are equivalent since a solution of either can be translated to the other with the restriction basis B, and the restricted one is in dimension $n - m$ instead of n.

$$(G, \boldsymbol{x}, \mathcal{O}) \overset{B}{\longleftrightarrow} (\hat{G}, \hat{\boldsymbol{x}}, \hat{\mathcal{O}})$$

Further, by Lemma 5, this new UOV instance is composed of quadratic forms that are not full rank, and in particular which share a kernel contained in $\mathcal{O}$. This information is redundant with the secret vector we had for the original instance, as this kernel corresponds to $\mathsf{span}(\hat{\boldsymbol{x}})$. We are tempted to use this new vector $\hat{\boldsymbol{x}}$ that belongs to $\hat{\mathcal{O}}$ to repeat the attack inductively, but this fails because this vector is in the kernel of each matrix of the public key, which means that the matrix $J(\boldsymbol{x})$ is the zero matrix. Therefore, we need to solve a new UOV instance (which has some more structure in the form of the kernel we observed in this paragraph) that is strictly weaker against key recovery attacks. For very unbalanced instances of UOV, we will need a constant number of vectors in the secret key to conclude, in a similar fashion as observed by Beullens in [3]. More precisely, each independent vector in $\mathcal{O}$ allows to reduce the search space by m dimensions. We can conclude with β vectors if $n - \beta m \leq 2m \iff \beta \geq \lceil \alpha - 2 \rceil$ since β is an integer. Naturally this yields $\beta = 1$ for practical instances of UOV, which is the result presented in Sect. 3.

It could thus seem to be a good idea to aim for very unbalanced parameters, but there are two reasons why these parameters are unlikely to be used in practice:

1. Random polynomial systems are easier to solve when they are heavily unbalanced. An argument that justifies this statement is the generic algorithm of Thomae and Wolf [20] (especially in characteristic two), and more generally the observation that any new variable is a degree of liberty that can be exploited for free.
2. UOV already has large keys. Linear increases in n yield quadratic increases in the key sizes.

This highlights an interesting tradeoff in the security of UOV: the larger the parameter $\alpha = \frac{n}{m}$, the stronger UOV is against key recovery attacks, and the weaker it is against forgery attacks. Reciprocally, the smaller α is, the weaker UOV is against key recovery attacks, and the stronger it is against forgery attacks.

3.2 Experimental Results

The algorithms we obtain have polynomial complexities. We show that they are also fast in practice by providing an implementation in SageMath [19], using native linear algebra functions. We test them against the parameter sets of [6]. The strategy is as follows: the oracle providing a vector in $\mathcal{O}$ is obtained by a function that chooses a random element in $\mathsf{span}(o_1, \dots, o_m)$, which are the first m columns of A^{-1}.

The code can be found at:

https://github.com/pi-r2/OneVector

We test the attack against the parameters of [6], which are representative of the state-of-the-art instantiations of UOV. We include a key size with twice as many variables as the target for NIST level 5 to demonstrate that the attack scales beyond NIST parameters. The hardware used is a laptop with an Intel CPU i7-1165G7 running at 2.80 GHz with 8 GB of RAM. All experiments were ran on a single thread (Fig. 3).

Parameters n,m,q	uov-Ip 112, 44, 256	uov-Is 160, 64, 16	uov-III 184, 72, 256	uov-V 244, 96, 256	"uov-X" (480, 192, 256)
Time	1.7s	4.4s	5.7s	13.3s	145.1s

Fig. 3. Key recovery from one vector with our attack in $\mathbb{F}_{256}$

To obtain a complete key recovery, one must first find a vector of the secret subspace $\mathcal{O}$. Then, the attacker uses the attack described in this paper to complete his basis of the secret subspace, in a matter of seconds on a laptop (Fig. 4).

Parameters n,m,q	uov-Ip 112, 44, 256	uov-Is 160, 64, 16	uov-III 184, 72, 256	uov-V 244, 96, 256	"uov-X" (480, 192, 256)
Time	0.2s	0.5s	0.7s	1.5s	9.1s

Fig. 4. "$x \in \mathcal{O}$?" with our algorithm in $\mathbb{F}_{256}$

4 Applications to UOV Variants

4.1 MAYO

The MAYO signature scheme [3] was introduced by Beullens as a generalization of UOV in which we allow the subspace $\mathcal{O}$ to have a smaller dimension than m. We switch to the notations of Beullens for clarity. The size of the secret subspace of a MAYO key is denoted o, m remains the number of quadratic forms in the public key, n remains the dimension of the vector space $\mathbb{F}_q^n$, and q is a small power of two. In the UOV formalism used so far, $m = o$. In MAYO, o is significantly smaller than m. This transformation makes the scheme much more compact, but increases signature size. Beullens introduces some additional structure in the form of a "Whipping" transformation that maps $\mathbb{F}_q^n \to \mathbb{F}_q^{ko}$, instead of UOV which maps $\mathbb{F}_q^n \to \mathbb{F}_q^m$. This is required to allow the signer to sign. We obtain the UOV scheme for $k = 1$. The following parameters of MAYO have been submitted to NIST, taken from [4].

Parameter set security level	$MAYO_1$ 1	$MAYO_2$ 1	$MAYO_3$ 3	$MAYO_5$ 5
n	66	78	99	133
m	64	64	96	128
o	8	18	10	12
k	9	4	11	12
q	16	16	16	16

If we try to attack the UOV map of MAYO, then we consider a collection of m quadratic maps P_i, the public key maps, that share an o dimensional totally isotropic subspace. The attack proceeds as follows: Given $\boldsymbol{x} \in \mathcal{O}$, we obtain m linear forms $P_i'(\boldsymbol{x}, .)$, therefore the intersection of their kernels generically defines $J(\boldsymbol{x})$ an $n-m$ dimensional subspace that still contains $\mathcal{O}$. In the context of MAYO, $n - m \leq o$. Therefore we recover $\mathcal{O}$ entirely from the kernels of the restriction of the public key to $J(\boldsymbol{x})$. Notice that this does not improve the reconciliation attack on MAYO, as this was already achieved by Beullens in [3] with an algebraic method. This shows that the work done in Sect. 3 is consistent with the state of the art when transferred to MAYO.

4.2 VOX

To have a result as general as possible, we apply our attack to $\text{UOV}^{\hat{+}}$ [13]. This corresponds to a more general formulation of VOX known as FOX, which is introduced in the same specification as VOX [8], based on [13]. Notably, it relies on less assumptions than VOX and still has competitive signature sizes with UOV, with a priori improved security. This signature scheme is a UOV-like signature scheme where t quadratic forms of the secret key are random. These random equations are called "vinegar forms" and the usual UOV quadratic forms are called 'oil forms' by analogy. This is the $\hat{+}$ perturbation. The private key is then composed with two changes of variables (S, T) where $S \in GL_o(\mathbb{F}_q), T \in GL_n(\mathbb{F}_q)$ In traditional UOV, $S = I_n$ and $T = A^{-1}$.

$$\mathcal{F} = S \circ \mathcal{P} \circ T$$

The tradeoff is that the signer now has to solve a small quadratic polynomial system with t equations to sign a message.

The transformation S adds "noise" to the equations: the oil quadratic forms are mixed with the vinegar quadratic forms. This implies that the public system does not have a high-dimensional totally isotropic subspace like the UOV one. More precisely, we have the following shape of S chosen in [8]. Here $S \circ \mathcal{P}'$ is a left product: $S \circ \mathcal{P}' = \mathcal{P}' \cdot S$.

$$S = \begin{pmatrix} I_t & S' \\ 0 & I_{o-t} \end{pmatrix}, \quad S' \in \mathbb{F}_q^{(o-t)\times t} \tag{2}$$

We have for $1 \leq i \leq o$, $f_i = \sum_{j=1}^{o} s_{i,j} p'_j$, and more precisely using (2):

$$\begin{cases} 1 \leq i \leq t : f_i = p'_i \\ t+1 \leq i \leq o : f_i = p'_i + \sum_{j=1}^{t} s'_{i,j} p'_j \end{cases} \tag{3}$$

The main takeaway is that S has $t(o-t)$ unknown coefficients. For vectors in $\mathcal{O}$, the contribution of the oil forms to these mixed equations is zero, therefore we can retrieve this linear change of variables with linear algebra from the evaluation of the public key on oil vectors. Each evaluation yields $o-t$ equations by expressing the last $o-t$ coefficients of $\mathcal{P}(\boldsymbol{x})$ as linear combinations of the first t coefficients. Therefore we need t vectors in the oil subspace to retrieve the change of variables S.

Once this is done, we can apply the tools introduced earlier to recover T from $\mathcal{P}' = S^{-1} \circ \mathcal{P}$ which is a UOV system with t random equations. If we are given $x \in \mathcal{O}$, we will observe that it only vanishes $m-t$ of the quadratic forms of $\mathcal{P}'$. Each of the remaining t vinegar forms have probability $\approx \frac{1}{q}$ to vanish coincidentally on this vector but the knowledge of S allows us to distinguish the oil forms. In any case, the algorithm $\boldsymbol{x} \in \mathcal{O}$? would enable one to distinguish oil forms from vinegar forms even if the equations were permuted.

Then, we are able to reduce the $\mathcal{P}'$ instance to a smaller subspace of dimension $n-(m-t)$, as we only consider $(m-t)$ linear forms instead of m. FOX with $S = I_n$, which is exactly what $\mathcal{P}'$ is, shares the weakness of UOV to the Kipnis-Shamir attacks (Lemma 3), therefore we complete the attack if $n-m+t \leq 2m \iff n+t \leq 3m$. The parameters of FOX from [8] are in Fig. 5.

Variant	Security Level	q	o	v	t	|sig|	|cpk|	|csk|
FOX-I	128	251	48	72	8	120 B	47,056 B	64 B
FOX-III	192	4093	68	106	8	261 B	211,156 B	64 B
FOX-V	256	65521	91	140	8	462 B	694,892 B	64 B

Fig. 5. FOX parameters in [8].

We have $n = o+v$, where $o = m$ in our formalism. In all cases $n \leq 2.55o$, and in particular we respectively have $n+t = 122, 182, 239$ versus $3o = 144, 204, 273$ for security levels 1,3,5. Therefore our attacks apply to these parameter sets of FOX, but only with knowledge of S, which we obtain from t vectors of $\mathcal{O}$.

It is interesting to note that the signer has to solve a random system involving t quadratic equations, therefore the scheme does not allow much flexibility in the choice of t, as this task can only be done quickly for small values of t.

References

1. Aulbach, T., Campos, F., Krämer, J., Samardjiska, S., Stöttinger, M.: Separating oil and vinegar with a single trace side-channel assisted Kipnis-Shamir attack on UOV. IACR Trans. Cryptogr. Hardw. Embed. Syst. **2023**(3), 221–245 (2023). https://doi.org/10.46586/tches.v2023.i3.221-245
2. Beullens, W.: Improved cryptanalysis of UOV and rainbow. In: Canteaut, A., Standaert, F.-X. (eds.) EUROCRYPT 2021. LNCS, vol. 12696, pp. 348–373. Springer, Cham (2021). https://doi.org/10.1007/978-3-030-77870-5_13
3. Beullens, W.: MAYO: practical post-quantum signatures from oil-and-vinegar maps. In: AlTawy, R., Hülsing, A. (eds.) SAC 2021. LNCS, vol. 13203, pp. 355–376. Springer, Cham (2022). https://doi.org/10.1007/978-3-030-99277-4_17
4. Beullens, W., Campos, F., Celi, S., Hess, B., Kannwischer, M.J.: Mayo (2023). https://pqmayo.org. Accessed 05 Oct 2023
5. Beullens, W., et al.: Uov (2023). https://www.uovsig.org/. Accessed 05 Oct 2023
6. Beullens, W., et al.: Oil and vinegar: modern parameters and implementations. IACR Trans. Cryptogr. Hardw. Embed. Syst. **2023**(3), 321–365 (2023). https://doi.org/10.46586/tches.v2023.i3.321-365
7. Cogliati, B., et al.: Provable unbalanced oil and vinegar (2023). http://prov-sign.github.io. Accessed 05 Oct 2023
8. Cogliati, B., et al.: Vox-sign (2023). http://vox-sign.com/files/vox_nist.pdf. Accessed 05 Oct 2023
9. Debarre, O., Manivel, L.: Sur la variété des espaces linéaires contenus dans une intersection complète. Math. Annalen **312**(1998), 549–574 (1998). https://doi.org/10.1007/s002080050235
10. Ding, J., et al.: Triangular unbalanced oil and vinegar (2023). https://www.tuovsig.org/. Accessed 05 Oct 2023
11. Ding, J., Schmidt, D.: Rainbow, a new multivariable polynomial signature scheme. In: Ioannidis, J., Keromytis, A., Yung, M. (eds.) ACNS 2005. LNCS, vol. 3531, pp. 164–175. Springer, Heidelberg (2005). https://doi.org/10.1007/11496137_12
12. Ding, J., Yang, B.-Y., Chen, C.-H.O., Chen, M.-S., Cheng, C.-M.: New differential-algebraic attacks and reparametrization of rainbow. In: Bellovin, S.M., Gennaro, R., Keromytis, A., Yung, M. (eds.) ACNS 2008. LNCS, vol. 5037, pp. 242–257. Springer, Heidelberg (2008). https://doi.org/10.1007/978-3-540-68914-0_15
13. Faugère, J.C., Macario-Rat, G., Patarin, J., Perret, L.: A new perturbation for multivariate public key schemes such as HFE and UOV. Cryptology ePrint Archive, Paper 2022/203 (2022). https://eprint.iacr.org/2022/203
14. Furue, H., Ikematsu, Y., Kiyomura, Y., Takagi, T.: A new variant of unbalanced oil and vinegar using quotient ring: QR-UOV. In: Tibouchi, M., Wang, H. (eds.) ASIACRYPT 2021. LNCS, vol. 13093, pp. 187–217. Springer, Cham (2021). https://doi.org/10.1007/978-3-030-92068-5_7
15. Kipnis, A., Patarin, J., Goubin, L.: Unbalanced oil and vinegar signature schemes. In: Stern, J. (ed.) EUROCRYPT 1999. LNCS, vol. 1592, pp. 206–222. Springer, Heidelberg (1999). https://doi.org/10.1007/3-540-48910-X_15

16. Kipnis, A., Shamir, A.: Cryptanalysis of the oil and vinegar signature scheme. In: Krawczyk, H. (ed.) CRYPTO 1998. LNCS, vol. 1462, pp. 257–266. Springer, Heidelberg (1998). https://doi.org/10.1007/BFb0055733
17. Patarin, J.: The oil and vinegar signature scheme. In: Dagstuhl Workshop on Cryptography, September 1997 (1997)
18. Serre, J.P.: A Course in Arithmetic. Springer, New York (1978)
19. The Sage Developers: SageMath, the Sage Mathematics Software System (2022). https://www.sagemath.org. https://doi.org/10.5281/zenodo.6259615
20. Thomae, E., Wolf, C.: Solving underdetermined systems of multivariate quadratic equations revisited. In: Fischlin, M., Buchmann, J., Manulis, M. (eds.) PKC 2012. LNCS, vol. 7293, pp. 156–171. Springer, Heidelberg (2012). https://doi.org/10.1007/978-3-642-30057-8_10
21. Wang, L.C., et al.: SNOVA (2023). https://csrc.nist.gov/csrc/media/Projects/pqc-dig-sig/documents/round-1/spec-files/SNOVA-spec-web.pdf. Accessed 02 Jan 2024

Polynomial XL: A Variant of the XL Algorithm Using Macaulay Matrices over Polynomial Rings

Hiroki Furue[1(✉)] and Momonari Kudo[2]

[1] NTT Social Informatics Laboratories, Tokyo, Japan
hiroki.furue@ntt.com
[2] Fukuoka Institute of Technology, Fukuoka, Japan
m-kudo@fit.ac.jp

Abstract. Solving a system of m multivariate quadratic equations in n variables over finite fields (the MQ problem) is one of the important problems in the theory of computer science. The XL algorithm (XL for short) is a major approach for solving the MQ problem with linearization over a coefficient field. Furthermore, the hybrid approach with XL (h-XL) is a variant of XL guessing some variables beforehand. In this paper, we present a variant of h-XL, which we call the *polynomial XL (PXL)*. In PXL, the whole n variables are divided into k variables to be fixed and the remaining $n-k$ variables as "main variables", and we generate a Macaulay matrix with respect to the $n-k$ main variables over a polynomial ring of the k (sub-)variables. By eliminating some columns of the Macaulay matrix over the polynomial ring before guessing k variables, the amount of operations required for each guessed value can be reduced compared with h-XL. Our complexity analysis of PXL (under some practical assumptions and heuristics) gives a new theoretical bound, and it indicates that PXL could be more efficient than other algorithms in theory on the random system with $n=m$, which is the case of general multivariate signatures. For example, on systems over the finite field with 2^8 elements with $n=m=80$, the numbers of operations deduced from the theoretical bounds of the hybrid approaches with XL and Wiedemann XL, Crossbred, and PXL with optimal k are estimated as 2^{252}, 2^{234}, 2^{237}, and 2^{220}, respectively.

Keywords: MQ problem · MPKC · XL · hybrid approach · Macaulay matrices

1 Introduction

In the field of computer science, the problem of solving a multivariate polynomial system of degree ≥ 2 over a finite field (*the MP problem*) is one of the most important problems, where "solve" means to find (at least) one root of the system. The particular case where polynomials are all quadratic is called *the MQ problem*, and both the MP and MQ problems are known to be NP-hard [30].

H. Furue—This research was conducted while at the University of Tokyo.

M.-J. Saarinen and D. Smith-Tone (Eds.): PQCrypto 2024, LNCS 14772, pp. 109–143, 2024.
https://doi.org/10.1007/978-3-031-62746-0_6

Moreover, the hardness of the MQ problem is nowadays applied to constructing various cryptosystems (e.g., multivariate public key cryptosystems (MPKCs) such as UOV [37]). Therefore, the analysis even for the quadratic case is a very important task both in theory and in practice, and thus we mainly focus on solving the MQ problem in this paper.

A precise definition of the MQ problem is the following: Let n and m be positive integers, and let q be a power of a rational prime p. Given a sequence $F = (f_1, \ldots, f_m)$ of m quadratic polynomials $f_1, \ldots, f_m$ in n variables $x_1, \ldots, x_n$ over a finite field $\mathbb{F}_q$ of q elements, the MQ problem requires to find at least one $(a_1, \ldots, a_n) \in \mathbb{F}_q^n$ such that $f_i(a_1, \ldots, a_n) = 0$ for all i with $1 \leq i \leq m$. Throughout the rest of this paper, we deal with only the case of $n \leq m$ (*overdetermined* case). This is because algorithms solving the overdetermined MQ problem can be easily applied to the case of $n > m$, since, after the values of $n - m$ variables are randomly specified, the resulting system will have a solution in most cases. Furthermore, this paper evaluates the efficiency of algorithms solving the MQ problem by substituting specific parameters into the asymptotic complexity formula following the security evaluation for various multivariate signatures [8,9,27].

In the literature, there are various methods for solving the MQ problem such as Gröbner basis method, Linearization, resultant-based method [15, Chapter 3], and Wu's method [53]. In particular, Gröbner basis method is a generic method to solve the MQ problem. The most classical method to compute Gröbner bases is Buchberger's algorithm [11], and ones of the currently most efficient algorithms are Faugère's F_4 and F_5 algorithms [23,24]. When the ideal generated by F is zero-dimensional, namely the number of (affine) roots of F over an algebraic closure of $\mathbb{F}_q$ is finite, once a Gröbner basis for the input F is computed for a given monomial order (typically a graded reverse lexicographic order is chosen for practical efficiency) with the above algorithms, the FGLM conversion [25] enables us to obtain its lexicographical Gröbner basis, from which roots of F can be easily derived [16, Chapter 3].

As a linearization-based algorithm, Courtois et al. [14] proposed the *XL algorithm* at EUROCRYPT 2000, and this algorithm is an extension of Relinearization algorithm [38]. The main idea of XL, which is already used in [41,42] by Lazard in order to analyze Buchberger's algorithm, is: Linearize the given system by regarding each monomial as one variable, and then, similarly to F_4, use linear algebra to the coefficient matrix of the linearized system. More concretely, we first construct a shift $\mathscr{S}$ of F, that is, the set of polynomials of the form $t \cdot f_i$ for all $1 \leq i \leq m$ with monomials t up to given degree. By linearizing the system defined by $\mathscr{S}$, we then generate its coefficient matrix (this matrix is nothing but a *Macaulay matrix* of $\mathscr{S}$), and compute its reduced row echelon form (RREF) by the row reduction (Gaussian elimination). If the shift $\mathscr{S}$ is sufficiently large, then the number of linearly independent polynomials in $\mathscr{S}$ becomes close to the total number of monomials of degree up to the maximal degree of polynomials in $\mathscr{S}$, and hence a univariate equation would be obtained from RREF of the Macaulay matrix. We then solve the obtained univariate equation and repeat such processes with respect to the remaining variables. Note that XL is considered to be a redundant variant of F_4 algorithm (see [1,2] for details). Furthermore, Yang et al. [56] analyzed a variant of the XL algorithm called *Wiedemann XL (WXL)*, which adopts Wiedemann's algorithm [52] instead of row reduction algorithms in the XL framework. WXL provides another complexity estimate that is used to evaluate the security of various MPKCs such as UOV [9].

One of the most effective improvements of XL is to apply the *hybrid approach* [7,55] (first proposed as FXL in [55] for XL, in which the "F" stands for "fix"), which is proposed as an approach applying an MQ solver such as F_4, F_5, or XL efficiently. This approach fixes the values of k among n variables (say $x_1, \ldots, x_k$), and then solves the remaining system in the $n-k$ variables $x_{k+1}, \ldots, x_n$ using an MQ solver. These processes are iterated until a solution is found. In the case of $n \approx m$, the hybrid approach may be effective, since the gain obtained by working on systems with less variables may overcome the loss due to the exhaustive search on the fixed variables. In this paper, we call the hybrid approach with XL (resp. WXL) *h-XL* (resp. *h-WXL*). Furthermore, Joux and Vitse proposed the Crossbred algorithm as a practical efficient algorithm for solving MQ systems over the binary field in 2017 [35]. This Crossbred is constructed based on h-XL by eliminating parts of Macaulay matrices before fixing the values of some variables. In this paper, we propose a new variant of XL following this direction to further reduce the time complexity.

Our Contributions. In this paper, we propose a new variant of the XL algorithm, which we call *polynomial XL* (PXL), as an improvement of h-XL. With notation same as in h-XL described above, the main idea of our improvement is the following: Before fixing the values of the variables $x_1, \ldots, x_k$, we partly perform Gaussian elimination on a Macaulay matrix *over the polynomial ring* $\mathbb{F}_q[x_1, \ldots, x_k]$, with keeping $x_1, \ldots, x_k$ as indeterminates. More specifically, for a given MQ system, namely a sequence $F = (f_1, \ldots, f_m) \in \mathbb{F}_q[x_1, \ldots, x_n]^m$ of m quadratic (not necessarily homogeneous) polynomials $f_1, \ldots, f_m$, we first regard each f_i as a polynomial in $(\mathbb{F}_q[x_1, \ldots, x_k])[x_{k+1}, \ldots, x_n]$, and construct a shift of F by multiplying all f_i's by monomials in $x_{k+1}, \ldots, x_n$ (up to some degree). We then generate the Macaulay matrix $\mathcal{PM}$ of the shift with respect to a *graded* monomial order in $x_{k+1}, \ldots, x_n$, where $\mathcal{PM}$ is a *polynomial* matrix with entries in the polynomial ring $\mathbb{F}_q[x_1, \ldots, x_k]$. Here, due to the gradedness of the monomial order, $\mathcal{PM}$ is *almost upper-block triangular*, and all of its (nearly-)diagonal blocks are matrices with entries in $\mathbb{F}_q$, *not* in $\mathbb{F}_q[x_1, \ldots, x_k]$. Thus we can execute row operations on these blocks efficiently, and as a result, we also obtain a partly-reduced matrix. Under some practical assumption and heuristic (Assumption 3 and Heuristic 1) such as the semi-regularity of a polynomial sequence, the size of the uneliminated part of this resulting matrix is expected to be much smaller than that of the original one (e.g., in the case where $n = m = 40$ and $k = 10$, the sizes of the original matrix and the uneliminated part are approximately 2^{30} and 2^{21}, respectively), so that the amount of manipulations for each guessed value can be reduced compared with h-XL. As we will see in Subsect. 4.3 below, this enables us to solve the system with smaller complexity for some parameters.

We also discuss the time and space complexities of our PXL, and theoretically compare them with those of h-XL, h-WXL, and Crossbred. Comparing the time complexities, we show that, under some practical assumptions and heuristic (Assumptions 2 and 3, and Heuristic 1 below) such as the affine semi-regularity of polynomial sequences, our PXL would be the most efficient in theory for the case of $n \approx m$, see Table 1 for details. For example, on the system over $\mathbb{F}_{2^8}$ with $n = m = 80$, the numbers of operations in $\mathbb{F}_q$ required for the execution of h-XL, h-WXL, Crossbred, and PXL are estimated as 2^{252}, 2^{234}, 2^{237}, and 2^{220}, respectively. On the other hand, in terms of the space complexity, PXL might be not well compared to h-WXL since the sparsity of the Macaulay matrix is not maintained through an execution of PXL. Therefore, the relationship between PXL and h-WXL can be seen as a trade-off between time and memory.

Organizations. The rest of this paper is organized as follows: Sect. 2 reviews the XL algorithm and the hybrid approach. Section 3 is devoted to describing the proposed algorithm PXL. We estimate the time complexity, and theoretically compare it with those of h-XL, h-WXL, and Crossbred in Sect. 4, and Sect. 5 introduces experimental results obtained by our (unoptimized) implementation of PXL. Finally, Sect. 6 is devoted to the conclusion, where we summarize the key points and suggest possible future works. Also in Appendix A, we recall semi-regular polynomial sequences and their properties.

2 Preliminaries

In this section, we recall the definition of the XL algorithm [14], and discuss its complexity. We also explain the hybrid approach, which combines an exhaustive search with an MQ solver such as XL.

2.1 Notation and Macaulay Matrices

We first fix the notations that are used throughout the rest of this paper. Let $X = \{x_1, \ldots, x_n\}$ be a set of n variables, and $\mathscr{T}(X)$ denote the set of monomials in $x_1, \ldots, x_n$. For each non-negative integer d, we also denote by $\mathscr{T}(X)_d$ (resp. $\mathscr{T}(X)_{\le d}$) the set of all monomials in $x_1, \ldots, x_n$ of degree d (resp. less than or equal to d). Namely, we set

$$\begin{aligned}\mathscr{T}(X) &:= \{x_1^{\alpha_1} \cdots x_n^{\alpha_n} \mid (\alpha_1, \ldots, \alpha_n) \in (\mathbb{Z}_{\ge 0})^n\},\\ \mathscr{T}(X)_d &:= \{x_1^{\alpha_1} \cdots x_n^{\alpha_n} \in \mathscr{T}(X) \mid \alpha_1 + \cdots + \alpha_n = d\},\\ \mathscr{T}(X)_{\le d} &:= \mathscr{T}(X)_0 \cup \cdots \cup \mathscr{T}(X)_d = \{x_1^{\alpha_1} \cdots x_n^{\alpha_n} \in \mathscr{T}(X) \mid \alpha_1 + \cdots + \alpha_n \le d\}.\end{aligned}$$

Once $X = \{x_1, \ldots, x_n\}$ is fixed, we may write $\mathscr{T}(X)$, $\mathscr{T}(X)_d$, and $\mathscr{T}(X)_{\le d}$ as $\mathscr{T}$, $\mathscr{T}_d$, and $\mathscr{T}_{\le d}$, respectively. For a commutative ring A of unity, we denote by $A[X] = A[x_1, \ldots, x_n]$ the polynomial ring with n variables $X = \{x_1, \ldots, x_n\}$ over A. The total degree of $f \in A[X]$ is denoted by $\deg(f)$, and for a monomial $t \in \mathscr{T}(X)$, let $\mathrm{coeff}(f, t)$ denote the coefficient of t in f. When F is a set or sequence of polynomials in $A[X]$, the ideal of $A[X]$ generated by F is denoted by $\langle F \rangle_{A[X]}$ or simply $\langle F \rangle$. In particular, when F is a finite set $\{f_1, \dots, f_m\}$, we denote it by $\langle f_1, \dots, f_m \rangle_{A[X]}$ or $\langle f_1, \dots, f_m \rangle$. For a subset or sequence F of polynomials in $A[X]$, and for a subset $T \subset \mathscr{T}(X)$, we set $T \cdot F = \{t \cdot f : t \in T,\ f \in F\}$, which is called the *shift* of F by T (we also call a union of shifts a shift). As a particular but important case, we define the following shifts:

$$\mathscr{S}_d(F) := \bigcup_{f \in F_{\leq d}} \mathscr{T}(X)_{d-\deg(f)} \cdot \{f\} = \{tf : f \in F_{\leq d},\ t \in \mathscr{T}(X)_{d-\deg(f)}\},$$

$$\mathscr{S}_{\leq d}(F) := \mathscr{S}_0(F) \cup \cdots \cup \mathscr{S}(X)_d = \{tf : f \in F_{\leq d},\ t \in \mathscr{T}(X)_{\leq d-\deg(f)}\}$$

with $F_{\leq d} := \{f \in F : \deg(f) \leq d\}$ for each non-negative integer d, where "$\mathscr{S}$" stands for "shift". In the case where $F_{\leq d}$ is empty, we set $\mathscr{S}_d(F) := \{0\}$ and $\mathscr{S}_{\leq d}(F) := \{0\}$. We may write $\mathscr{S}_d(F)$ and $\mathscr{S}_{\leq d}(F)$ simply by $\mathscr{S}_d$ and $\mathscr{S}_{\leq d}$ respectively, when F is fixed.

Here, we recall the definition of Macaulay matrices. Let $\prec$ be a monomial order on $\mathscr{T}(X)$. For a sequence $F = (f_1, \dots, f_m) \in A[X]^m$ and an ordered subset $T = \{t_1, \dots, t_\ell\} \subset \mathscr{T}(X)$ with $t_1 \succ \cdots \succ t_\ell$, we define the *Macaulay matrix* $\mathcal{M}_\prec(F, T)$ of F with respect to T as an $(m \times \ell)$-matrix over R whose (i, j)-entry is the coefficient of t_j in f_i, say

$$\mathcal{M}_\prec(F, T) := \begin{array}{c} \\ f_1 \\ \vdots \\ f_m \end{array}\!\!\begin{array}{c} \begin{array}{ccc} t_1 & \cdots & t_\ell \end{array} \\ \begin{pmatrix} \mathrm{coeff}(f_1, t_1) & \cdots & \mathrm{coeff}(f_1, t_\ell) \\ \vdots & & \vdots \\ \mathrm{coeff}(f_m, t_1) & \cdots & \mathrm{coeff}(f_m, t_\ell) \end{pmatrix} \end{array}.$$

When $\prec$ is clear from the context, we simply denote it by $\mathcal{M}(F, T)$.

Conversely, for an $(m \times \ell)$-matrix $M = (a_{i,j})$ over A and for T given as above, let $\mathcal{M}_\prec^{-1}(M, T)$ (or $\mathcal{M}^{-1}(M, T)$ simply) denote a unique list F' of polynomials in $A[X]$ such that $\mathcal{M}_\prec(F', T) = M$, namely, we set $g_i := \sum_{j=1}^{\ell} a_{i,j} t_j$ for $1 \leq i \leq m$, and $\mathcal{M}_\prec^{-1}(M, T) := (g_1, \dots, g_m)$.

Example 1. Consider the following three quadratic polynomials (over $R = \mathbb{Z}$) in two variables x_1 and x_2:

$$\begin{aligned} f_1 &= 5x_1^2 + 6x_1x_2 + 4x_1 + 5x_2 + 3, \\ f_2 &= 4x_1^2 + 5x_1x_2 + 3x_2^2 + 6x_1 + 2x_2 + 2, \\ f_3 &= 2x_1^2 + 4x_1x_2 + 2x_2^2 + 6x_1 + x_2 + 2. \end{aligned}$$

When we put $F := (f_1, f_2, f_3)$, we construct a Macaulay matrix of the shift $\mathscr{S}_3 = \mathscr{S}_3(F) = \mathscr{T}_1 \cdot F = \{x_i f_j : 1 \leq i \leq 2,\ 1 \leq j \leq 3\}$, where $\mathscr{T}_1$ is the set of monomials in x_1 and x_2 of degree one. We order elements of $\mathscr{S}_3$ as follows: $\mathscr{S}_3 = \{x_1f_1, x_1f_2, x_1f_3, x_2f_1, x_2f_2, x_2f_3\}$. Let $\prec_{\mathrm{glex}}$ be the graded lexicographic order on the monomials in x_1 and x_2 with $x_1 \succ x_2$, that is, $x_1^{\alpha_1}x_2^{\alpha_2} \prec_{\mathrm{glex}} x_1^{\beta_1}x_2^{\beta_2}$ if $\alpha_1 + \alpha_2 < \beta_1 + \beta_2$, or $\alpha_1 + \alpha_2 = \beta_1 + \beta_2$ and $x_1^{\beta_1}x_2^{\beta_2}$ is greater than $x_1^{\alpha_1}x_2^{\alpha_2}$ with respect to the lexicographical order with $x_1 \succ x_2$. When we order elements of $\mathscr{T}_{\leq 3}$ (which is the set of monomials in $X = \{x_1, x_2\}$ of degree ≤ 3) by $\prec_{\mathrm{glex}}$, the Macaulay matrix $\mathcal{M}_{\prec_{\mathrm{glex}}}(\mathscr{S}_3, \mathscr{T}_{\leq 3})$ of $\mathscr{S}_3$ with respect to $\mathscr{T}_{\leq 3}$ is given as follows:

$$\mathcal{M}_{\prec_{\mathrm{glex}}}(\mathscr{S}_3, \mathscr{T}_{\leq 3}) = \begin{array}{c} \\ x_1 f_1 \\ x_1 f_2 \\ x_1 f_3 \\ x_2 f_1 \\ x_2 f_2 \\ x_2 f_3 \end{array} \begin{array}{c} \begin{array}{cccccccccc} x_1^3 & x_1^2 x_2 & x_1 x_2^2 & x_2^3 & x_1^2 & x_1 x_2 & x_2^2 & x_1 & x_2 & 1 \end{array} \\ \begin{pmatrix} 5 & 6 & 0 & 0 & 4 & 5 & 0 & 3 & 0 & 0 \\ 4 & 5 & 3 & 0 & 6 & 2 & 0 & 2 & 0 & 0 \\ 2 & 4 & 2 & 0 & 6 & 1 & 0 & 2 & 0 & 0 \\ 0 & 5 & 6 & 0 & 0 & 4 & 5 & 0 & 3 & 0 \\ 0 & 4 & 5 & 3 & 0 & 6 & 2 & 0 & 2 & 0 \\ 0 & 2 & 4 & 2 & 0 & 6 & 1 & 0 & 2 & 0 \end{pmatrix} \end{array}.$$

In the XL algorithm in Subsect. 2.2, the reduced row echelon form of a Macaulay matrix of a shift of F is computed, with R a finite field $\mathbb{F}_q$ of order q, where q is a power of a prime. This corresponds to computing a basis G of the $\mathbb{F}_q$-vector space generated by the shift, and clearly the computed basis also generates the ideal $\langle F \rangle_{\mathbb{F}_q[X]}$, i.e., $\langle G \rangle_{\mathbb{F}_q[X]} = \langle F \rangle_{\mathbb{F}_q[X]}$. In general, G computed as above is not necessarily a Gröbner basis of $\langle F \rangle_{\mathbb{F}_q[X]}$, but we will review in Subsect. 2.3 below that for sufficiently large shifts, G becomes a Gröbner basis.

2.2 XL Algorithm

This subsection briefly reviews *the XL algorithm* (which stands for eXtended Linearizations), which is proposed in [14] by Courtois et al. to find a solution to a system of multivariate polynomials over finite fields. We write down the XL algorithm in Algorithm 1 below, where the notations are the same as in the previous subsections. We also suppose that the input system is zero-dimensional, namely, the input system has only finite (affine) roots over an algebraically closed field. Note also that the input polynomials are assumed to be all quadratic as in the original paper [14], but in fact, their idea is applicable to a general multivariate system of higher degree.

Algorithm 1 (XL, [14, Section 3, Definition 1]).

Input: A sequence $F = (f_1, \ldots, f_m) \in \mathbb{F}_q[x_1, \ldots, x_n]^m$ *of (not necessarily homogeneous) quadratic polynomials, and a natural number* D *with* $D \geq 2$.
Output: A solution over $\mathbb{F}_q$ *to* $f_i(x_1, \ldots, x_n) = 0$ *for* $1 \leq i \leq m$.

(1) ***Multiply:*** *Computing all the products* $t \cdot f_i$ *with* $t \in \mathscr{T}_{\leq D-2}$, *construct the shift* $\mathscr{S}_{\leq D} := \mathscr{S}_{\leq D}(F) = \mathscr{T}_{\leq D-2} \cdot F$, *which is the shift of* F *by* $\mathscr{T}_{\leq D-2}$.
(2) ***Linearize:*** *Make the Macaulay matrix* $M := \mathcal{M}_{\prec}(\mathscr{S}_{\leq D}, \mathscr{T}_{\leq D})$ *with respect to some elimination monomial order* $\prec$ *such that all the terms containing one variable (say* x_n*) are eliminated last. Compute the reduced row echelon form* B *of* M, *and put* $G := \mathcal{M}_{\prec}^{-1}(B, \mathscr{T}_{\leq D})$. *A univariate polynomial* $g(x_n)$ *in* x_n *of degree at most* D *is surely contained in* G *when* D *is sufficiently large.*
(3) ***Solve:*** *Compute the roots in* $\mathbb{F}_q$ *of* g *by e.g., combining square-free, distinct-degree and equal-degree factorization algorithms such as* [58], [36] *and* [31] *respectively.*

(4) ***Repeat:*** *Substitute a root into x_n, simplify the equations of G, and then find the values of the other variables.*

Note that in the generation of $\mathcal{M}_{\prec}(\mathscr{S}_{\leq D}, \mathscr{T}_{\leq D})$, one can sort elements in $\mathscr{S}_{\leq D}$ arbitrarily. We also note that, in XL, it suffices to obtain a univariate polynomial in Step (3) to continue the procedures, whence we do not need to compute a Gröbner basis. On the other hand, XL can be described as a redundant variant of F_4, supposing an assumption that the input system F has only one solution over a finite field, see [2] for details. Moreover, we remark that we can use any other monomial order (e.g., a graded monomial order), if we execute only Steps (1) and (2) to obtain a Gröbner basis of $\langle F \rangle$ (in this case, the computation can be viewed as a special case of Lazard's algorithm [41,42]). Even in this case, we can obtain a root easily from the computed Gröbner basis, under an assumption similar to [2], see Remark 1 below for details.

The condition of the natural number D for XL to continue the procedures is discussed in the next subsection.

2.3 Degree Bounds for the Success of XL

Algorithm 1 has an input parameter D called a *degree bound*, and it is known that the algorithm surely finds a zero of $\langle F \rangle$ for sufficiently large D. This subsection reviews bounds on such D both in theory and in practice. Let $R := K[x_1, \ldots, x_n]$ be the polynomial ring of n variables over a field K, and $F = (f_1, \ldots, f_m)$ be a sequence of *not necessarily homogeneous* polynomials in R of positive degrees $d_1, \ldots d_m$, respectively. We denote by f^{top} the maximal homogeneous part of $f \in R \smallsetminus \{0\}$, and put $F^{\mathrm{top}} := (f_1^{\mathrm{top}}, \ldots, f_m^{\mathrm{top}})$. Put $R' = R[y]$ for an extra variable y for homogenization. We also denote by f^h the homogenization of $f \in R \smallsetminus \{0\}$ by y, say $f^h = y^{\deg(f)} f(x_1/y, \ldots, x_n/y)$, and put $F^h := (f_1^h, \ldots, f_m^h) \in (R')^m$. For each $d \in \mathbb{Z}$, let I_d denote the degree-d homogeneous component of a homogeneous ideal I of R (resp. R'), namely $I_d = I \cap R_d$ (resp. $I_d = I \cap (R')_d$). We put $I_{\leq d} := I \cap R_{\leq d}$ with $R_{\leq d} := \bigoplus_{i=0}^{d} R_i$ for a (not necessarily homogeneous) ideal I of R, and this kind of notation is applied to R' and its arbitrary ideal.

A well-known (theoretical) upper bound is *Dubé's degree bound* [21] given by $D(n, d) := 2\left((d^2/2) + d\right)^{2^{n-1}}$ with $d := \max\{\deg(f_i) : 1 \leq i \leq m\}$. For any degree D larger than or equal to the Dubé's bound, the reduced row echelon form of $\mathcal{M}_{\prec}(\mathscr{S}_{\leq D}, \mathscr{T}_{\leq D})$ with $\mathscr{S}_{\leq D} = \mathscr{S}_{\leq D}(F)$ and $\mathscr{T}_{\leq D} = \mathscr{T}(X)_{\leq D}$ yields a Gröbner basis of $\langle F \rangle$ with respect to an elimination order $\prec$. Hence, for such a D one can obtain a root of F with Algorithm 1.

However, Dubé's degree bound would be impractical under the cryptographic setting, and we here recall quite smaller bounds under the following assumption:

Assumption 1. *The input sequence $F = (f_1, \ldots, f_m)$ is affine semi-regular, namely $F^{\mathrm{top}} = (f_1^{\mathrm{top}}, \ldots, f_m^{\mathrm{top}})$ is semi-regular.*

See Definition 4 in Appendix A below for the definition of affine semi-regular sequences. Semi-regular sequences are important in the theory of solving polynomial systems (cf. [3,5]), and often (e.g., [33, Section 4.3]) the security of multivariate cryptosystems is evaluated under Assumption 1. Under Assumption 1, a bound for the success of XL is obtained by considering the rank of the Macaulay matrix $\mathcal{M}_{\prec}(\mathscr{S}_{\le d}, \mathscr{T}_{\le d})$, denoted by $\mathrm{rank}(\mathcal{M}_{\prec}(\mathscr{S}_{\le d}, \mathscr{T}_{\le d}))$, where $\mathscr{S}_{\le d} = \mathscr{S}_{\le d}(F)$ and $\mathscr{T}_{\le d} = \mathscr{T}(X)_{\le d}$ with $X = \{x_1, \ldots, x_n\}$. This rank is clearly equal to the dimension $\dim_K(\langle \mathscr{S}_{\le d}(F)\rangle_K)$ of the K-vector space $\langle \mathscr{S}_{\le d}(F)\rangle_K$ generated by $\mathscr{S}_{\le d}(F)$, and it does not depend on the order of the monomials in $\mathscr{T}_{\le d}$. Thus, we need to investigate $\dim_K(\langle \mathscr{S}_{\le d}(F)\rangle_K)$. For this, let us first recall the following theorem, whose mathematically rigorous and correct proof is given in [40] (or [39]) by Kudo-Yokoyama:

Theorem 1 ([40, **Theorem 1 & 7, Corollary 1**], [39, **Theorem 1**]). *With notation as above, assume that the sequence $F = (f_1, \ldots, f_m)$ of not necessarily homogeneous polynomials satisfies Assumption 1. Let $d_{\mathrm{reg}}(F^{\mathrm{top}})$ denote the degree of regularity for the homogeneous ideal $\langle F^{\mathrm{top}}\rangle_R$, defined as in Definition 2. Then, for any non-negative integer d with $d < d_{\mathrm{reg}}(F^{\mathrm{top}})$, we have*

$$\dim_K(R')_d/\langle F^h\rangle_d = \sum_{i=0}^{d} \dim_K R_d/\langle F^{\mathrm{top}}\rangle_d$$

with $F^h := (f_1^h, \ldots, f_m^h)$. Hence, the Hilbert series $\mathrm{HS}_{R'/\langle F^h\rangle}(z)$ of $R'/\langle F^h\rangle$ satisfies

$$\mathrm{HS}_{R'/\langle F^h\rangle}(z) \equiv \frac{\prod_{j=1}^{m}(1 - z^{d_j})}{(1-z)^{n+1}} \pmod{z^D}$$

for $d_j := \deg(f_j)$ and $D := d_{\mathrm{reg}}(F^{\mathrm{top}})$, so that F^h is $d_{\mathrm{reg}}(F^{\mathrm{top}})$-regular. Moreover, if $d_{\mathrm{reg}}(F^{\mathrm{top}}) < \infty$ (which is equivalent to $m \ge n$ under Assumption 1), then the number of projective zeros of $\langle F^h\rangle_{R'}$ is finite at most, whence $\langle F\rangle_R$ is zero-dimensional.

Note that $d_{\mathrm{reg}}(F^{\mathrm{top}})$ in Theorem 1 is easily computed from the Hilbert series given in (A.3), and in fact it does not depend on F^{top} but is determined only by n, m, and $d_1, \ldots, d_m$. From this, for fixed m and $d_1, \ldots, d_m$, we set

$$D_{\mathrm{reg}}^{(n)} := d_{\mathrm{reg}}(F^{\mathrm{top}}) = \min\left\{ d \;\middle|\; \mathrm{coeff}\left(\frac{\prod_{j=1}^{m}(1-z^{d_j})}{(1-z)^n}, t^d\right) \le 0 \right\},$$

which we interpret as ∞ if $m < n$. In particular, if $d_1 = \cdots = d_m = 2$, we have

$$D_{\mathrm{reg}}^{(n)} = \min\left\{ d \;\middle|\; \mathrm{coeff}\left((1-z)^{m-n}(1+z)^m, t^d\right) \le 0 \right\}.$$

Here, even if we do not suppose the affine semi-regularity of F, we have

$$\langle F^h\rangle_d = \langle \mathscr{S}_d(F^h)\rangle_K \cong \langle \mathscr{S}_{\le d}(F)\rangle_K \subset \langle F\rangle_{\le d}$$

as K-vector spaces, where a K-isomorphism is given by the dehomogenization map $\langle \mathscr{S}_d(F^h)\rangle_K \ni h \longmapsto h|_{y=1} \in \langle \mathscr{S}_{\le d}(F)\rangle_K$ (see e.g., [17, Section 4] for details), and therefore

$$\dim_K\langle F^h\rangle_d = \dim_K\langle \mathscr{S}_d(F^h)\rangle_K = \dim_K\langle \mathscr{S}_{\le d}(F)\rangle_K \le \dim_K\langle F\rangle_{\le d}.$$

Moreover, it follows that $\dim_K(R')_d = |\mathcal{T}(X \cup \{y\})_d| = \dim_K R_{\leq d} = |\mathcal{T}_{\leq d}|$. Hence, as a corollary of Theorem 1, we obtain the following:

Corollary 1 (cf. [54, Proposition 1]). *Under the same setting and assumptions as in Theorem 1, for any d with $d < D_{\text{reg}}^{(n)} = d_{\text{reg}}(F^{\text{top}})$, we have*

$$|\mathcal{T}_{\leq d}| - \dim_K(\langle \mathcal{S}_{\leq d}(F) \rangle_K) = \operatorname{coeff}\left(\frac{\prod_{j=1}^{m}(1 - z^{d_j})}{(1 - z)^{n+1}}, z^d \right).$$

In particular, if the elements of F are all quadratic, then we have

$$|\mathcal{T}_{\leq d}| - \dim_K(\langle \mathcal{S}_{\leq d}(F) \rangle_K) = \operatorname{coeff}\left((1 - z)^{m-n-1} (1 + z)^m, z^d \right)$$

for any d with $d < D_{\text{reg}}^{(n)}$.

In the context of the above discussion, we here list the following two kinds of bounds on D for which Algorithm 1 finds a solution:

Heuristic but Practical Bound from Yang-Chen, Ars Et Al., and Diem's Studies. Assuming that F is an affine semi-regular sequence of quadratic polynomials, we consider a sufficient condition that a univariate polynomial in x_n is obtained in Step (2) of Algorithm 1, when we use an elimination order such that $x_n^D, x_n^{D-1}, \ldots, x_n, 1$ are listed at the end. It is straightforward that the last non-zero row vector of the reduced row echelon form of $\mathcal{M}(\mathcal{S}_{\leq D}, \mathcal{T}_{\leq D})$ yields a univariate equation of x_n if $\operatorname{rank}(\mathcal{M}(\mathcal{S}_{\leq D}, \mathcal{T}_{\leq D}))$ is larger than the number of columns minus $D + 1$, i.e.,

$$\operatorname{rank}(\mathcal{M}(\mathcal{S}_{\leq D}, \mathcal{T}_{\leq D})) \geq |\mathcal{T}_{\leq D}| - D,$$

equivalently

$$\chi(D) := |\mathcal{T}_{\leq D}| - \dim_K(\langle \mathcal{S}_{\leq D}(F) \rangle_K) \leq D, \tag{2.1}$$

which is used in [17] and [43]. Thus, it follows from Corollary 1 that the minimum D, denoted by D_{XL} here, required for the success of Step (2) of Algorithm 1 is upper-bounded by

$$D_{\text{XL}} \leq D_0 := \min\left\{ d \;\middle|\; \operatorname{coeff}\left((1 - z)^{m-n-1} (1 + z)^m, z^d \right) \leq d \right\} \tag{2.2}$$

if $D_{\text{XL}} < D_{\text{reg}}^{(n)}$. The condition $\operatorname{coeff}((1 - z)^{m-n-1}(1 + z)^m, z^d) \leq d$ is equivalent to that the z^d-coefficient of $(1 - z)^{m-n-1}(1 + z)^m - (1 - z)^{-2}$ is negative (cf. [2, Section 5.1]). Note that, even when $D_{\text{XL}} \geq D_{\text{reg}}^{(n)}$, it would be possible that Step (2) of Algorithm 1 produces a univariate polynomial at the degree equal to this upper-bound: See [54, Section 4], where the authors of [54] say "the minimum D required for the reliable termination of XL is given by D_0". From this, we may estimate $D_{\text{XL}} \approx D_0$. Assuming the *Maximum Rank Conjecture* (which is equivalent over an infinite field to Fröberg conjecture [26], see [47] for a proof of the equivalency), Diem also proved in [17, Theorem 1] that D_0 is a lower bound for (2.1) to be satisfied. One can easily confirm that D_0 tends to be much smaller than Dubé's degree bound (e.g., the value of D_0 on systems with $n = 10$ and $m = 11$ is 11, whereas Dubé's degree bound on the same system is approximately 10^{309}).

Remark 1. In the case where we use a graded monomial order as noted in Subsect. 2.2, we consider the inequality $\chi(D) \leq 1$ instead of (2.1) as a sufficient condition for XL to compute a solution, supposing the following (i) and (ii):

(i) F has at most one root (counted with multiplicity) over an algebraic closure $\overline{K}$ of K (cf. [2, Condition 1] for a similar condition).
(ii) F^{top} has no root other than $(0, \ldots, 0)$.

Under these assumptions, there exists a sufficiently large integer d such that the above inequality definitely holds for any D with $D \geq d$. Indeed, it follows from (i) and (ii) that the number of projective zeros over $\overline{K}$ of F^h is also finite (in fact one at most), whence there exists $d > 0$ such that for any D with $D \geq d$, the value of the Hilbert function $\mathrm{HF}_{R'/\langle F^h \rangle}(D) = \dim_K(R'/\langle F^h \rangle)_D = \chi(D)$ is equal to the number of roots (counted with multiplicity) over $\overline{K}$ of F, see e.g., [13, Proposition 3.3.6] or [54, Corollary 10] for a proof (see also [39, Lemma 2.2.2]). In this case, we remark that the reduced Gröbner basis of $\langle F \rangle$ is $\{x_1 - a_1, \ldots, x_n - a_n\}$, where $(a_1, \ldots, a_n)$ is the unique root of F. For $m > n$, we estimate

$$D_{\mathrm{XL}} \approx D_1 := \min \left\{ d \geq 2 \,\middle|\, \operatorname{coeff}\left((1-z)^{m-n-1} (1+z)^m, t^d \right) \leq 1 \right\}, \tag{2.3}$$

by a discussion following [54, Section 4], similarly to the case of elimination order. Note that the cases $d = 0$ and $d = 1$ are removed in (2.3), since $\chi(0) = 1$ and $\chi(1) = n + 1$. We also note that $D_1 \geq D_0$. We experimentally confirmed that, in most cases, XL for $D = D_1$ computes a Gröbner basis of the input system: In our experiments, we randomly generated sequences $H = (h_1, \ldots, h_m)$ of quadratic non-homogeneous polynomials over $\mathbb{F}_{31}$ with no constant term for several small n and for all m with $n < m \leq 2n$. For each generated sequence H, we choose $(a_1, \ldots, a_n) \in \mathbb{F}_{31}^n$ at random, and then put $f_i := h_i(x_1, \ldots, x_n) - h_i(a_1, \ldots, a_n)$ for $1 \leq i \leq m$ and $F := (f_1, \ldots, f_m)$. Then each sequence F constructed as above would satisfy the above assumptions (i) and (ii) (in fact, F^{top} would be semi-regular) with its unique root $(a_1, \ldots, a_n)$, in most cases. This construction of H and F may correspond to the general construction of multivariate public key encryption (see e.g., [19, Section 2.2], [33, Section 4.3]). Therefore, our experiments would be meaningful.

Expected Theoretical Bound from Semaev-Tenti and Kudo-Yokoyama's Results. We also note that, as a theoretical upper-bound on D_{XL}, we may apply the following upper-bound on the *solving degree* of Gröbner basis computation:

Theorem 2 ([40, Lemma 4], [39, Theorem 3]). *Let $F = (f_1, \ldots, f_m)$ be a (not necessarily semi-regular) sequence of polynomials in $K[x_1, \ldots, x_n]$, and $\prec$ be a graded reverse lexicographic order on the monomials in $x_1, \ldots, x_n$. If*

$d_{\mathrm{reg}}(F^{\mathrm{top}}) < \infty$, then there constructively exists a Buchberger-like algorithm $\mathcal{A}$ for computing a Gröbner basis for F with respect to $\prec$ such that the degree of critical S-pairs (resp. S-polynomials) appearing in the execution of $\mathcal{A}$ is upper-bounded by $2d_{\mathrm{reg}}(F^{\mathrm{top}}) - 1$ (resp. $2d_{\mathrm{reg}}(F^{\mathrm{top}}) - 2$).

These upper-bounds had been proved by Tenti in his PhD thesis [51, Theorem 3.65] (see also [49, Theorem 2.1] by Semaev-Tenti) under some constraints (e.g., F contains field equations $x_i^q - x_i$ for $1 \le i \le n$), and Kudo-Yokoyama extended his result to a general case in [40, Section 5] (see also [39, Section 4] for algorithmic details). Since we can interpret the Gröbner basis computation as repeating to execute row reductions on Macaulay matrices as in F_4 [23] and (matrix-)F_5 [24], we *expect* that $D_{\mathrm{XL}} \le 2d_{\mathrm{reg}}(F^{\mathrm{top}}) - 1$. As for the magnitude relation between D_1 and $2d_{\mathrm{reg}}(F^{\mathrm{top}})-1$, they are not equal to each other in general, and both $D_1 < 2d_{\mathrm{reg}}(F^{\mathrm{top}}) - 1$ and $D_1 > 2d_{\mathrm{reg}}(F^{\mathrm{top}}) - 1$ occur depending on parameters; the former case tend to hold as m is larger than n.

Salizzoni also proved in [48] that the solving degree of *mutant algorithms* (tamed in [28]) such as MutantXL [12] and MXL2 [44] is upper-bounded by $d_{\mathrm{reg}}(F^{\mathrm{top}}) + 1$, but this is not the case that we consider in this paper, since we will construct our algorithm based on the original XL [14], not on mutant algorithms.

2.4 Complexity

In this subsection, we estimate the time complexity of (plain) XL together with that of its variant Wiedemann XL (WXL). Here WXL uses Wiedemann's algorithm [52] instead of Gaussian elimination in the XL framework, which was first analyzed in [56]. Wiedemann's algorithm generally solves sparse linear systems more efficiently than Gaussian elimination.

Complexity of XL. We first consider plain XL (Algorithm 1), where the **Linearize** step is clearly dominant in terms of the time complexity. Recall from Subsect. 2.3 that XL could output a solution of the input system for D equal to or larger than D_0 given in (2.2), and here we assume to take D to be this bound D_0. In the **Linearize** step, one uses linear algebra to obtain the reduced row echelon form of a Macaulay matrix with $m \cdot \binom{n+D-2}{D-2}$ rows and $\binom{n+D}{D}$ columns. However, in fact, the cost of this step can be estimated as that of Gaussian elimination on a matrix with $\binom{n+D}{D}$ rows and columns, assuming the following practical heuristic as in [45]:

Heuristic 1. *In XL, if we pick rows in $\mathcal{M}(\mathscr{S}_{\le D}, \mathscr{T}_{\le D})$ at random under the constraint that we have enough equations at each degree $d \le D$, then usually we have a linearly independent set.*

From this heuristic, the complexity of XL is roughly estimated as

$$O\left(\binom{n+D}{D}^{\omega}\right), \tag{2.4}$$

where $2 \le \omega < 3$ is the exponent of matrix multiplication.

Complexity of WXL. According to [9], the complexity of WXL is estimated as

$$O\left(\binom{n}{2} \cdot \binom{n+D}{D}^2\right), \tag{2.5}$$

where D can be taken to be D_0 given in (2.2). (We remove the constant part from the complexity in [9], since we focus on asymptotic complexity.) WXL consumes less memory than the plain XL, since it can deal with the Macaulay matrix as a sparse matrix, and its memory consumption is estimated as $O\left(\binom{n}{2} \cdot \binom{n+D}{D}\right)$, see [52] for details.

2.5 Improving XL via Hybrid Approach

One of the most effective improvements of XL (Algorithm 1) is to apply the *hybrid approach* [7,55], which is the best known technique for solving the MQ problem. The hybrid approach combines an exhaustive search with an MQ solver, and it was proposed in [7] (resp. [55]) for Gröbner basis algorithms such as F_4 and F_5 (resp. XL). Specifically, given an MQ system of m equations in n variables, the values for k ($0 \leq k \leq n$) variables are randomly guessed and fixed before an MQ solver is applied to the system in the remaining $n-k$ variables; this is repeated until a solution is obtained. The hybrid approach for XL presented in [55] is called FXL, where "F" stands for "fix", and it is constructed by adding the first and last steps below into Algorithm 1:

Algorithm 2 (Hybrid approach with XL (h-XL)).

Input: A sequence $F = (f_1, \dots, f_m) \in \mathbb{F}_q[x_1, \dots, x_n]^m$ of (not necessarily homogeneous) quadratic polynomials, the number k of guessed variables, and a degree bound D.
Output: A solution over $\mathbb{F}_q$ to $f_i(x_1, \dots, x_n) = 0$ for $1 \leq i \leq m$.

(1) ***Fix:*** *Fix the values $a_1, \dots, a_k \in \mathbb{F}_q$ for the k variables $x_1, \dots, x_k$ randomly. In the following two steps, we set $f_i^{(\mathbf{a})} := f_i(a_1, \dots, a_k, x_{k+1}, \dots, x_n)$ and $F^{(\mathbf{a})} := (f_1^{(\mathbf{a})}, \dots, f_m^{(\mathbf{a})})$ with $\mathbf{a} = (a_1, \dots, a_k)$.*
(2) ***Multiply:*** *Construct the shift $\mathscr{S}_{\leq D}^{(k)}(F^{(\mathbf{a})}) := \mathscr{T}_{\leq D-2}^{(k)} \cdot F^{(\mathbf{a})}$, where we set $\mathscr{T}_{\leq D-2}^{(k)} := \mathscr{T}(X^{(k)})_{\leq D-2}$ with $X^{(k)} = \{x_{k+1}, \dots, x_n\}$.*
(3) ***Linearize:*** *Compute the reduced row echelon form of $\mathcal{M}(\mathscr{S}_{\leq D}^{(k)}(F^{(\mathbf{a})}), \mathscr{T}_{\leq D}^{(k)})$, where we set $\mathscr{T}_{\leq D}^{(k)} := \mathscr{T}(X^{(k)})_{\leq D}$.*
(4) ***Solve:*** *Compute the root of a univariate polynomial obtained in* ***Linearize****.*
(5) ***Repeat:*** *Find the values of the other variables.*
(6) If there exists no solution, return to (1) ***Fix****.*

The complexities of the hybrid approaches using the plain XL and WXL as MQ solvers are estimated as

$$O\left(q^k \cdot \binom{n-k+D}{D}^\omega\right), \tag{2.6}$$

$$O\left(q^k \cdot \binom{n-k}{2} \cdot \binom{n-k+D}{D}^2\right), \tag{2.7}$$

respectively, by using the estimations (2.4) and (2.5). Here D can be taken as

$$D_0^{(n-k)} := \min \left\{ d \;\middle|\; \mathrm{coeff} \left((1-t)^{m-(n-k)-1} (1+t)^m , t^d \right) \leq d \right\} \tag{2.8}$$

from (2.2). In the use of the hybrid approach, the number k of guessed variables is chosen such that the function inside brackets in (2.6) or (2.7) takes the minimum value.

2.6 Crossbred Algorithm

This subsection recalls the Crossbred algorithm proposed by Joux and Vitse, which is a practical efficient algorithm for solving MQ systems over the binary field [35]. Our proposed algorithm described in Sect. 3 follows a framework similar to the Crossbred algorithm. Note that we here change the notation of Crossbred such that it fixes the values of k variables randomly for consistency with the description of our proposed algorithm.

We here roughly describe the Crossbred algorithm. The Crossbred algorithm takes the number k of guessed variables and the degrees d and D with $d \leq D$ as parameters. In this Crossbred algorithm, we perform some linear algebra operations on Macaulay matrices before fixing the values of the k variables as in h-XL. More specifically, for a given MQ system $F \in \mathbb{F}_{2^r}[x_1, \ldots, x_n]^m$, the Crossbred algorithm can be described by the following two steps: The first step generates the Macaulay matrix of the shift of F with degree $\leq D$, and then by linear algebra on the Macaulay matrix obtains a sequence $P = (p_1, \ldots, p_r)$ of some polynomials whose degrees in the remaining $n-k$ variables are lower than or equal to d. The second step then performs linear algebra on the Macaulay matrix of the shift of the polynomials obtained by fixing the value of k variables in F and P with degree $\leq d$. If the second step obtains a univariate polynomial, then one can find a solution as in the plain XL algorithm. This second step is iterated $O(q^k)$ times until one solution is found.

In Subsect. 4.3 below, we estimate the complexity of the Crossbred algorithm by Multivariate Quadratic Estimator by the Technology Innovation Institute [22,34]. We refer to [6,20,46] for details on the complexity of the Crossbred algorithm.

3 Main Algorithm

In this section, we propose a new variant of the XL algorithm for solving the MQ problem of m equations in n variables over $\mathbb{F}_q$, in the case where $n \leq m$. We first discuss Macaulay matrices over polynomial rings, and second describe the outline of our proposed algorithm "polynomial XL (PXL)". After that, details of the most technical step will be described in Subsect. 3.3, and degree bounds for the success of PXL will be discussed in Subsect. 3.4. Furthermore, Subsect. 3.5 explains the relationship of PXL with FXL and Crossbred, and Subsect. 3.6 gives a toy example. Throughout this section, let $F = (f_1, \ldots, f_m) \in \mathbb{F}_q[x_1, \ldots, x_n]^m$ be a sequence of m quadratic (and not necessarily homogeneous) polynomials in n variables $x_1, \ldots, x_n$ over $\mathbb{F}_q$, where q is a power of a prime.

3.1 Macaulay Matrices over Polynomial Rings

In this subsection, we fix the notations that are used in the rest of this section. In particular, we construct a Macaulay matrix *over the polynomial ring* $\mathbb{F}_q[x_1,\ldots,x_k]$ with respect to $x_{k+1},\ldots,x_n$ for $1 \le k \le n$, where each entry belongs to $\mathbb{F}_q[x_1,\ldots,x_k]$. Namely, a Macaulay matrix whose coefficient ring is $\mathbb{F}_q[x_1,\ldots,x_k]$ will be constructed. Such a Macaulay matrix, together with our construction, plays a key role in the main algorithm in Subsect. 3.2 below. Note that most of the notations given below are similar to those defined in Subsect. 2.1 for the case where the coefficient ring is a general ring.

In the following, an integer k is fixed, unless otherwise noted. Similarly to the hybrid approach reviewed in Subsect. 2.5, the main algorithm divides $x_1,\ldots,x_n$ into k variables $x_1,\ldots,x_k$ and the remaining $n-k$ variables $x_{k+1},\ldots,x_n$, and then regards $f_1,\ldots,f_m$ as elements of the polynomial ring $(\mathbb{F}_q[x_1,\ldots,x_k])[x_{k+1},\ldots,x_n]$. As in Subsect. 2.1, we define subsets $\mathscr{T}_d^{(k)}$, $\mathscr{T}_{d';d}^{(k)}$, $\mathscr{T}_{\le d}^{(k)}$, $\mathscr{S}_d^{(k)}$, $\mathscr{S}_{d';d}^{(k)}$, and $\mathscr{S}_{\le d}^{(k)}$ of $(\mathbb{F}_q[x_1,\ldots,x_k])\,[x_{k+1},\ldots,x_n]$ as follows: Putting $X^{(k)} = \{x_{k+1},\ldots,x_n\}$, we set

$$\mathscr{T}_d^{(k)} := \mathscr{T}(X^{(k)})_d = \left\{ x_{k+1}^{\alpha_{k+1}} \cdots x_n^{\alpha_n} \in \mathscr{T}(X^{(k)}) : \sum_{i=k+1}^{n} \alpha_i = d \right\},$$

$$\mathscr{T}_{d';d}^{(k)} := \mathscr{T}_{d'}^{(k)} \cup \mathscr{T}_{d'+1}^{(k)} \cup \cdots \cup \mathscr{T}_d^{(k)}, \qquad \mathscr{T}_{\le d}^{(k)} := \mathscr{T}_{0;d}^{(k)} = \mathscr{T}(X^{(k)})_{\le d}$$

for $0 \le d' \le d$, and

$$\mathscr{S}_d^{(k)} := \bigcup_{1 \le i \le d} \mathscr{T}(X^{(k)})_{d-2} \cdot \{f_i\} = \{tf_i : 1 \le i \le m,\ t \in \mathscr{T}(X^{(k)})_{d-2}\}$$

for $2 \le d$. We also set $\mathscr{S}_0^{(k)} := \{0\}$, $\mathscr{S}_1^{(k)} := \{0\}$, and

$$\mathscr{S}_{d';d}^{(k)} := \mathscr{S}_{d'}^{(k)} \cup \mathscr{S}_{d'+1}^{(k)} \cup \cdots \cup \mathscr{S}_d^{(k)}, \qquad \mathscr{S}_{\le d}^{(k)} := \mathscr{S}_{0;d}$$

for $0 \le d' \le d$. In particular, $\mathscr{S}_{\le d}^{(k)}$ is the shift of F by the set $\mathscr{T}_{\le d-2}^{(k)}$ of monomials in $x_{k+1},\ldots,x_n$ of degree $\le d-2$.

Here, we construct a Macaulay matrix of the shift $\mathscr{S}_{\le D}^{(k)}$ with respect to $\mathscr{T}_{\le D}^{(k)}$ for $D \ge 2$, as in the plain XL. For this, unlike the plain XL (mainly adopting an elimination order described in Sect. 2), we use a *graded* monomial order (e.g., graded lexicographic order), which is a monomial order first comparing the total degree of two monomials. Furthermore, as for the order of elements in $\mathscr{S}_{\le D}^{(k)}$, we also use an order that first compares the degree of two polynomials.

To simplify the notation, once F, k, and D are fixed, we denote the Macaulay matrix $\mathcal{M}(\mathscr{S}_{\le D}^{(k)}, \mathscr{T}_{\le D}^{(k)})$ constructed as above by $\mathcal{PM}$ to emphasize that it is a *polynomial matrix*, and call it a *Macaulay matrix of F at degree D over* $\mathbb{F}_q[x_1,\ldots,x_k]$. For two integers d_1 and d_2 with $2 \le d_1 \le D$ and $0 \le d_2 \le D$, we also denote by $\mathcal{PM}[\mathscr{S}_{d_1}^{(k)}, \mathscr{T}_{d_2}^{(k)}]$ the submatrix of $\mathcal{PM}$ whose rows (resp.

columns) correspond to polynomials of $\mathscr{S}_{d_1}^{(k)}$ (resp. monomials of $\mathscr{T}_{d_2}^{(k)}$). Then, $\mathcal{PM}$ is divided by submatrices $\mathcal{PM}[\mathscr{S}_{d_1}^{(k)}, \mathscr{T}_{d_2}^{(k)}]$ for $2 \le d_1 \le D$ and $0 \le d_2 \le D$.

Thanks to our choice of a graded monomial order together with the quadraticity of F, the following lemma holds:

Lemma 1. *For a sequence $F = (f_1, \ldots, f_m)$ of quadratic and not necessarily homogeneous polynomials in $\mathbb{F}_q[x_1, \ldots, x_n]$ and for positive integers k and D with $1 \le k \le n$ and $D \ge 2$, let $\mathcal{PM}$ be a Macaulay matrix of F at degree D over $\mathbb{F}_q[x_1, \ldots, x_k]$. Then, for each integer d with $2 \le d \le D$, the submatrix $\mathcal{PM}[\mathscr{S}_d^{(k)}, \mathscr{T}_{d'}^{(k)}]$ with $d' \notin \{d, d-1, d-2\}$ is a zero matrix, and all elements of $\mathcal{PM}[\mathscr{S}_d^{(k)}, \mathscr{T}_d^{(k)}]$ belong to $\mathbb{F}_q$.*

Proof. Each f_i is written as

$$f_i = q_i(x_{k+1}, \ldots, x_n) + \sum_{j=k+1}^{n} \ell_{i,j}(x_1, \ldots, x_k)x_j + c_i(x_1, \ldots, x_k) \tag{3.1}$$

for a quadratic form $q_i(x_{k+1}, \ldots, x_n)$ in $\mathbb{F}_q[x_{k+1}, \ldots, x_n]$, linear polynomials $\ell_{i,j}(x_1, \ldots, x_k)$'s in $\mathbb{F}_q[x_1, \ldots, x_k]$, and a quadratic polynomial $c_i(x_1, \ldots, x_k)$ in $\mathbb{F}_q[x_1, \ldots, x_k]$. Therefore, multiplying it by a monomial $t \in \mathscr{T}_{d-2}^{(k)}$ in $x_{k+1}, \ldots, x_n$ of degree $d-2$, we have

$$tf_i = tq_i(x_{k+1}, \ldots, x_n) + \sum_{j=k+1}^{n} \ell_{i,j}(x_1, \ldots, x_k)tx_j + c_i(x_1, \ldots, x_k)t,$$

where tq_i is a form in $\mathbb{F}_q[x_{k+1}, \ldots, x_n]$ of degree d and where each tx_j is a monomial in $\mathbb{F}_q[x_{k+1}, \ldots, x_n]$ of degree $d-1$. This expression of the shift tf_i, which corresponds to a row of $\mathcal{PM}[\mathscr{S}_d^{(k)}, \mathscr{T}_{\le d}^{(k)}]$ and vice versa, implies the assertions of the lemma. □

Due to this lemma, we can partly perform row reduction on $\mathcal{PM}$, which is a key operation of the proposed algorithm in the next subsection.

3.2 Outline of Our Algorithm PXL

This subsection describes the proposed algorithm polynomial XL (PXL). As in the h-XL described in Subsect. 2.5, PXL first sets the first k variables $x_1, \ldots, x_k$ as guessed variables, whereas the main difference between our PXL and h-XL is the following: While h-XL performs row reduction after substituting actual k values to $x_1, \ldots, x_k$, PXL *partly* performs Gaussian elimination *before* fixing k variables. These manipulations are possible due to our construction of Macaulay matrices over $\mathbb{F}_q[x_1, \ldots, x_k]$ described in Lemma 1.

Here, we give the outline of PXL. The notations are same as those in Subsect. 3.1.

Algorithm 3 (Polynomial XL).

Input: A sequence $F = (f_1, \ldots, f_m) \in \mathbb{F}_q[x_1, \ldots, x_n]^m$ *of not necessarily homogeneous polynomials of degree 2, the number k of guessed variables, and a degree bound D.*
Output: A solution over $\mathbb{F}_q$ *to* $f_i(x_1, \ldots, x_n) = 0$ *for* $1 \leq i \leq m$.

(1) ***Multiply****: Compute the set* $\mathscr{S}^{(k)}_{\leq D}$ *of all the products* $t \cdot f_i$ *with* $t \in \mathscr{T}^{(k)}_{\leq D-2}$.
(2) ***Linearize(1)****: Generate* $\mathcal{PM} := \mathcal{M}(\mathscr{S}^{(k)}_{\leq D}, \mathscr{T}^{(k)}_{\leq D})$*, which is the Macaulay matrix of F at degree D over* $\mathbb{F}_q[x_1, \ldots, x_k]$*, and partly perform Gaussian elimination on it. (The details will be described in Subsect. 3.3 below.)*
(3) ***Fix****: Fix randomly the values for the k variables* $x_1, \ldots, x_k$ *in the resulting matrix of* **Linearize(1)**.
(4) ***Linearize(2)****: Compute the reduced row echelon form of the resulting matrix of step 3.*
(5) ***Solve****: If step 4 yields a univariate polynomial, compute its root.*
(6) ***Repeat****: Substitute the root, simplify the equations, and then repeat the process to find the values of the other variables.*
(7) If there exists no solution, return to (3) ***Fix****.*

Note that the definition of 'the resulting matrix of **Linearize(1)**' is given in the next paragraph.

Let us here describe only the first two steps, since the last four steps are executed similarly to h-XL. The **Multiply** step generates the shift $\mathscr{S}^{(k)}_{\leq D}$ of F by $\mathscr{T}^{(k)}_{\leq D-2}$, defined in Subsect. 3.1, by regarding each polynomial as one in $(\mathbb{F}_q[x_1, \ldots, x_k])[x_{k+1}, \ldots, x_n]$. At the beginning of the **Linearize(1)** step, $\mathcal{PM}$ is a polynomial matrix with entries in the polynomial ring $\mathbb{F}_q[x_1, \ldots, x_k]$, but by Lemma 1 it is almost upper-block triangular, and all of its (nearly-)diagonal blocks are matrices with entries in $\mathbb{F}_q$. By utilizing this property, the **Linearize(1)** step repeats to transform such a block into the row echelon form and to eliminate entries of its upper blocks. After the **Linearize(1)** step, the resulting Macaulay matrix is supposed to be of the form $\begin{pmatrix} I & * \\ 0 & A \end{pmatrix}$, by interchanging rows (and columns). Here I is an identity matrix, and A is a matrix over $\mathbb{F}_q[x_1, \ldots, x_k]$. Then, the last four steps deal with only the submatrix composed of rows and columns including no leading coefficient of the reduced part, which corresponds to A. We call this submatrix A the *resulting matrix of* **Linearize(1)**.

3.3 Details of Linearize(1) Step

In this subsection, we describe the details of the **Linearize(1)** step in the proposed algorithm, and show that it works well as row operations on $\mathcal{PM}$. We use the same notations as in Subsect. 3.1. In the following, we also denote by $\mathcal{PM}[\mathscr{S}^{(k)}_d, \mathscr{T}^{(k)}_{d'}]$ the same part even after $\mathcal{PM}$ is transformed.

The **Linearize(1)** step is mainly performed on each $\mathcal{PM}[\mathscr{S}^{(k)}_d, \mathscr{T}^{(k)}_{(d-2);d}]$, starting from $d = D$ down to 2. Each iteration d consists of the following three substeps:

(d)-1. Perform Gaussian elimination on $\mathcal{PM}[\mathscr{S}_d^{(k)}, \mathscr{T}_d^{(k)}]$.
(d)-2. Perform the same row operations as those of (d)-1 on the submatrix $\mathcal{PM}[\mathscr{S}_d^{(k)}, \mathscr{T}_{(d-2);(d-1)}^{(k)}]$.
(d)-3. Using the *leading coefficients* of the resulting $\mathcal{PM}[\mathscr{S}_d^{(k)}, \mathscr{T}_d^{(k)}]$ (namely the reduced row echelon form of the initial $\mathcal{PM}[\mathscr{S}_d^{(k)}, \mathscr{T}_d^{(k)}]$), eliminate the corresponding columns of $\mathcal{PM}$. Here, a leading coefficient is the leftmost nonzero entry in each row of a row echelon form of a matrix.

Here, we show that the **Linearize(1)** step described above works well as row operations on $\mathcal{PM}$. Note that for any $3 \le d \le D$, the (d)-3 step does not affect the submatrix $\mathcal{PM}[\mathscr{S}_{\le(d-1)}^{(k)}, \mathscr{T}_d^{(k)}]$, since $\mathcal{PM}[\mathscr{S}_{\le(d-1)}^{(k)}, \mathscr{T}_d^{(k)}]$ is always a zero matrix by Lemma 1. This indicates that $\mathcal{PM}[\mathscr{S}_d^{(k)}, \mathscr{T}_{\le D}^{(k)}]$ does not change from the original structure at the beginning of the (d)-1 step. Therefore, from Lemma 1, the manipulations in the (d)-1 and (d)-2 steps can be performed correctly and seen as row operations on $\mathcal{PM}$. Furthermore, the (d)-3 step can be also performed correctly, since the leading coefficients of the resulting $\mathcal{PM}[\mathscr{S}_d^{(k)}, \mathscr{T}_d^{(k)}]$ belong to $\mathbb{F}_q$. As a result, we have that all the manipulations are practicable and regarded as row operations on the whole $\mathcal{PM}$.

After the **Linearize(1)** step, all manipulations are performed on the resulting matrix of **Linearize(1)** obtained by concatenating rows and columns including no leading coefficient of the row echelon form $\mathcal{PM}[\mathscr{S}_d^{(k)}, \mathscr{T}_d^{(k)}]$ with $2 \le d \le D$.

Remark 2. As in the XL algorithm, in practice, PXL randomly chooses approximately $|\mathscr{T}_{\le D}^{(k)}|$ independent rows from the Macaulay matrix with $|\mathscr{S}_{\le D}^{(k)}|$ rows (namely we suppose a heuristic similar to Heuristic 1), and executes the **Linearize(1)** step on the submatrix composed of chosen row vectors. We then assume that the rank of the resulting matrix of **Linearize(1)** is large enough to yield a univariate equation, and we experimentally confirmed that this assumption is correct in most cases.

3.4 Degree Bounds for the Success of PXL

This subsection estimates the minimum value D_{PXL} where PXL with input $D = D_{\mathrm{PXL}}$ succeeds in finding a solution, under a practical assumption (Assumption 2 below), which requires conditions similar to (i) and (ii) in Remark 1. Note that the success of PXL means the following: For some evaluation of $\mathbf{a} = (a_1, \dots, a_k) \in \mathbb{F}_q^k$ to $(x_1, \dots, x_k)$ in the **Fix** step, the remaining steps finds a solution $(a_{k+1}, \dots, a_n) \in \mathbb{F}_q^{n-k}$ to the multivariate system in $x_{k+1}, \dots, x_n$ corresponding to the resulting matrix of the **Linearize(1)** step, and then $(a_1, \dots, a_n)$ is exactly a solution to the original system.

To estimate the value of D_{PXL}, we discuss the rank of the resulting matrix of **Linearize(1)**. Recall from Subsect. 3.2 that the **Linearize(1)** step transforms the Macaulay matrix into a matrix of the form $\begin{pmatrix} I & * \\ 0 & A \end{pmatrix}$, by interchanging rows (and columns). Here I is an identity matrix, and A is a matrix over

$\mathbb{F}_q[x_1,\ldots,x_k]$. The resulting matrix of the **Linearize(1)** step is A, and let α be the number of columns of A. For $\mathbf{a} = (a_1,\ldots,a_k) \in \mathbb{F}_q^k$, we denote by $A^{(\mathbf{a})}$ (resp. $\mathcal{M}(\mathscr{S}^{(k)}_{\leq D}, \mathscr{T}^{(k)}_{\leq D})^{(\mathbf{a})}$) the matrix obtained by substituting $(a_1,\ldots,a_k)$ to $(x_1,\ldots,x_k)$ in A (resp. $\mathcal{M}(\mathscr{S}^{(k)}_{\leq D}, \mathscr{T}^{(k)}_{\leq D})$). Since an evaluation of $x_1,\ldots,x_k$ and elementary row operations over $\mathbb{F}_q[x_1,\ldots,x_k]$ (without multiplying rows by elements in $\mathbb{F}_q[x_1,\ldots,x_k]$ of degree ≥ 1) are commutative, we have the following:

Lemma 2. *With notation as above, we have*

$$\alpha - \mathrm{rank}(A^{(\mathbf{a})}) = |\mathscr{T}^{(k)}_{\leq D}| - \mathrm{rank}(\mathcal{M}(\mathscr{S}^{(k)}_{\leq D}, \mathscr{T}^{(k)}_{\leq D})^{(\mathbf{a})}).$$

Furthermore, we also suppose the following assumption, in order to estimate the value of D_{PXL}:

Assumption 2.. *For any* $\mathbf{a} = (a_1,\ldots,a_k) \in \mathbb{F}_q^k$, *we have that the sequence* $F^{(\mathbf{a})} := (f_1^{(\mathbf{a})},\ldots,f_m^{(\mathbf{a})})$ *with* $f_i^{(\mathbf{a})} := f_i(a_1,\ldots,a_k,x_{k+1},\ldots,x_n)$ *satisfies the following conditions.*

(i) $F^{(\mathbf{a})}$ *has at most one root (counted with multiplicity) over an algebraic closure* $\overline{\mathbb{F}}_q$ *of* $\mathbb{F}_q$.
(ii) $(F^{(\mathbf{a})})^{\mathrm{top}}$ *is semi-regular (hence it has no root other than* $(0,\ldots,0) \in \mathbb{F}_q^{n-k}$*).*

This assumption is expected to hold since $F^{(\mathbf{a})}$ is highly overdetermined (see [33, Section 4.4] for arguments on (ii)). From the above lemma and assumption, we then obtain

$$\alpha - \mathrm{rank}(A^{(\mathbf{a})}) = \mathrm{coeff}\left((1-z)^{m-(n-k)-1}(1+z)^m, z^D\right),$$

if D is lower than $D^{(n-k)}_{\mathrm{reg}}$ as in Corollary 1, where

$$D^{(n-k)}_{\mathrm{reg}} = \min\left\{ d \;\middle|\; \mathrm{coeff}\left((1-z)^{m-(n-k)}(1+z)^m, z^d\right) \leq 0 \right\}. \tag{3.2}$$

Similarly to Remark 1, from Assumption 2, we obtain a *practical* estimation

$$D_{\mathrm{PXL}} \approx D_1^{(n-k)} := \min\left\{ d \geq 2 \;\middle|\; \mathrm{coeff}\left((1-z)^{m-(n-k)-1}(1+z)^m, z^d\right) \leq 1 \right\}. \tag{3.3}$$

Indeed, we experimentally confirmed that PXL finds a solution at $D = D_1^{(n-k)}$. Note that $D_1^{(n-k)} \geq D_0^{(n-k)}$ for the bound $D_0^{(n-k)}$ given in (2.8) for h-XL, but the equality holds in most cases. We also note that, as a *theoretical* upper-bound on D_{PXL} in the *worst* case, we expect from Theorem 2 that $D_{\mathrm{PXL}} \leq 2D^{(n-k)}_{\mathrm{reg}} - 1$.

3.5 Relationships with XFL and Crossbred

Remark 3 (Relationships with XFL [14,54]*).* We here briefly discuss the relationship between our algorithm PXL and XFL [14,54] proposed as a variant of h-XL.

XFL is roughly described as follows: First, the k variables to be fixed are chosen and generate a shift of the given system by all monomials in the remaining $n-k$ variables up to some degree $D-2$. Second, construct a Macaulay matrix (over $\mathbb{F}_q$, but not over $\mathbb{F}_q[x_1,\ldots,x_k]$) of the shift with respect to all monomials in the whole n variables up to the degree D, and then eliminate only monomials of degree D including only the $n-k$ variables. Third, substitute actual values for the k variables, and execute XL for a system in $n-k$ variables obtained by the substitution.

The first step of XFL clearly coincides with the **Multiply** step of our PXL. The main difference of XFL from PXL is the second step: The second step of XFL eliminates monomials in the $n-k$ variables of degree D, and it corresponds to eliminating only $\mathcal{PM}[\mathscr{S}_D^{(k)}, \mathscr{T}_D^{(k)}]$ in the second step of our PXL (in fact, PXL eliminates every block $\mathcal{PM}[\mathscr{S}_d^{(k)}, \mathscr{T}_d^{(k)}]$ with $2 \le d \le D$). Therefore, PXL can be regarded as an extension of XFL, and the size of the uneliminated part of the second step of XFL is larger than that of PXL.

Remark 4 (Relationships with Crossbred [35]*).* This remark explains the difference between our PXL and the Crossbred algorithm proposed by Joux and Vitse [35], from the following two points: (i) The parts of Macaulay matrices echelonized before the fixing step, and (ii) Our original structure of Macaulay matrices over the polynomial ring $\mathbb{F}_q[x_1,\ldots,x_k]$, where $x_1,\ldots,x_k$ are variables to be fixed.

First, the parts of Macaulay matrices echelonized before the fixing step for PXL are definitely different from those for Crossbred by the following reason: Crossbred eliminates monomials in which the degree of the remaining $n-k$ variables is larger than a given degree, whereas our algorithm PXL eliminates $\mathrm{rank}\left(\mathcal{PM}[\mathscr{S}_d^{(k)}, \mathscr{T}_d^{(k)}]\right)$ monomials among degree d monomials in the $n-k$ variables for each $2 \le d \le D$. This could cause a difference in the estimations of the degrees D (for which a root is found) and the complexities.

Second, our Macaulay matrix is constructed over $\mathbb{F}_q[x_1,\ldots,x_k]$ by regarding each polynomial in $\mathbb{F}_q[x_1,\ldots,x_n]$ as an element of the polynomial ring in the $n-k$ variables over $\mathbb{F}_q[x_1,\ldots,x_k]$, unlike Crossbred, which uses a Macaulay matrix over the base field $\mathbb{F}_q$. In our Macaulay matrix over $\mathbb{F}_q[x_1,\ldots,x_k]$, row operations adding a multiple of one row with one variable x_i with $1 \le i \le k$ into another row can be realized. By contrast, such a row operation cannot be performed in the standard Macaulay matrix over $\mathbb{F}_q$ clearly. Therefore, row reductions performed in our PXL cannot be duplicated in the standard Macaulay matrix over $\mathbb{F}_q$, and thus row reductions of our PXL performed before fixing the values of k variables are different from those of Crossbred.

3.6 Toy Example

We here solve an MQ system $F = (f_1, f_2, f_3)$ in $n = 3$ variables (x_1, x_2, x_3) over $\mathbb{F}_7$ of $m = 3$ polynomials

$$\begin{aligned} f_1 &= 5x_1^2 + 6x_1x_2 + 4x_1x_3 + x_2x_3 + 5x_3^2 + 4x_1 + 5x_2 + 3, \\ f_2 &= 4x_1^2 + 5x_1x_2 + 4x_1x_3 + 3x_2^2 + 5x_2x_3 + x_3^2 + 6x_1 + 2x_2 + 3x_3 + 2, \\ f_3 &= 2x_1^2 + 4x_1x_2 + 2x_2^2 + 6x_3^2 + 6x_1 + x_2 + 3x_3 + 2, \end{aligned}$$

by our PXL with $k = 1$ and $D = 4$; in fact, we can take $D = 3$ by $D_1^{(n-k)} = 3$ from (3.3) (or $2d_{\mathrm{reg}}(F^{\mathrm{top}}) - 1 = 3$ in Theorem 2), but we take $D = 4$ for a demonstration.

Then the Macaulay matrix $\mathcal{PM}$ of F at degree D over $\mathbb{F}_7[x_1]$ is given as

$$\begin{array}{c|ccccc|cccc|ccc|cc|c}
 & x_2^4 & x_2^3x_3 & x_2^2x_3^2 & x_2x_3^3 & x_3^4 & x_2^3 & x_2^2x_3 & x_2x_3^2 & x_3^3 & x_2^2 & x_2x_3 & x_3^2 & x_2 & x_3 & 1 \\
x_2^2f_1 & & 1 & 5 & & & 6x_1+5 & 4x_1 & & & 5x_1^2+4x_1+3 & & & & & \\
x_2^2f_2 & 3 & 5 & 1 & & & 5x_1+2 & 4x_1+3 & & & 4x_1^2+6x_1+2 & & & & & \\
x_2^2f_3 & 2 & & 6 & & & 4x_1+1 & 3 & & & 2x_1^2+6x_1+2 & & & & & \\
x_2x_3f_1 & & & 1 & 5 & & & 6x_1+5 & 4x_1 & & & 5x_1^2+4x_1+3 & & & & \\
x_2x_3f_2 & & 3 & 5 & 1 & & & 5x_1+2 & 4x_1+3 & & & 4x_1^2+6x_1+2 & & & & \\
x_2x_3f_3 & & 2 & & 6 & & & 4x_1+1 & 3 & & & 2x_1^2+6x_1+2 & & & & \\
x_3^2f_1 & & & & 1 & 5 & & & 6x_1+5 & 4x_1 & & & 5x_1^2+4x_1+3 & & & \\
x_3^2f_2 & & & 3 & 5 & 1 & & & 5x_1+2 & 4x_1+3 & & & 4x_1^2+6x_1+2 & & & \\
x_3^2f_3 & & & 2 & & 6 & & & 4x_1+1 & 3 & & & 2x_1^2+6x_1+2 & & & \\
\hline
x_2f_1 & & & & & & & 1 & 5 & & 6x_1+5 & 4x_1 & & 5x_1^2+4x_1+3 & & \\
x_2f_2 & & & & & & 3 & 5 & 1 & & 5x_1+2 & 4x_1+3 & & 4x_1^2+6x_1+2 & & \\
x_2f_3 & & & & & & 2 & & 6 & & 4x_1+1 & 3 & & 2x_1^2+6x_1+2 & & \\
x_3f_1 & & & & & & & & 1 & 5 & & 6x_1+5 & 4x_1 & & 5x_1^2+4x_1+3 & \\
x_3f_2 & & & & & & & 3 & 5 & 1 & & 5x_1+2 & 4x_1+3 & & 4x_1^2+6x_1+2 & \\
x_3f_3 & & & & & & & 2 & & 6 & & 4x_1+1 & 3 & & 2x_1^2+6x_1+2 & \\
\hline
f_1 & & & & & & & & & & & 1 & 5 & 6x_1+5 & 4x_1 & 5x_1^2+4x_1+3 \\
f_2 & & & & & & & & & & 3 & 5 & 1 & 5x_1+2 & 4x_1+3 & 4x_1^2+6x_1+2 \\
f_3 & & & & & & & & & & 2 & & 6 & 4x_1+1 & 3 & 2x_1^2+6x_1+2
\end{array},$$

and this can be regarded as a block matrix with the following form:

$$\begin{pmatrix}
\mathcal{PM}[\mathscr{S}_4^{(1)}, \mathscr{T}_4^{(1)}] & \mathcal{PM}[\mathscr{S}_4^{(1)}, \mathscr{T}_3^{(1)}] & \mathcal{PM}[\mathscr{S}_4^{(1)}, \mathscr{T}_2^{(1)}] & \mathcal{PM}[\mathscr{S}_4^{(1)}, \mathscr{T}_1^{(1)}] & \mathcal{PM}[\mathscr{S}_4^{(1)}, \mathscr{T}_0^{(1)}] \\
\mathcal{PM}[\mathscr{S}_3^{(1)}, \mathscr{T}_4^{(1)}] & \mathcal{PM}[\mathscr{S}_3^{(1)}, \mathscr{T}_3^{(1)}] & \mathcal{PM}[\mathscr{S}_3^{(1)}, \mathscr{T}_2^{(1)}] & \mathcal{PM}[\mathscr{S}_3^{(1)}, \mathscr{T}_1^{(1)}] & \mathcal{PM}[\mathscr{S}_3^{(1)}, \mathscr{T}_0^{(1)}] \\
\mathcal{PM}[\mathscr{S}_2^{(1)}, \mathscr{T}_4^{(1)}] & \mathcal{PM}[\mathscr{S}_2^{(1)}, \mathscr{T}_3^{(1)}] & \mathcal{PM}[\mathscr{S}_2^{(1)}, \mathscr{T}_2^{(1)}] & \mathcal{PM}[\mathscr{S}_2^{(1)}, \mathscr{T}_1^{(1)}] & \mathcal{PM}[\mathscr{S}_2^{(1)}, \mathscr{T}_0^{(1)}]
\end{pmatrix}.$$

In the **Linearize(1)** step, we first perform the Gaussian elimination on $\mathcal{PM}[\mathscr{S}_4^{(1)}, \mathscr{T}_4^{(1)}]$, and then $\mathcal{PM}[\mathscr{S}_4^{(1)}, \mathscr{T}_{2;4}^{(1)}]$ is changed into

$$
\begin{array}{ccccc|cccc|ccc}
x_2^4 & x_2^3x_3 & x_2^2x_3^2 & x_2x_3^3 & x_3^4 & x_2^3 & x_2^2x_3 & x_2x_3^2 & x_3^3 & x_2^2 & x_2x_3 & x_3^2 \\
\hline
1 & & & & & 4x_1+3 & 2 & 6x_1+3 & & 6x_1^2+2x_1+3 & 3x_1^2+x_1 & \\
 & 1 & & & & 5x_1+3 & 3x_1+2 & 5x_1+6 & & 3x_1^2+x_1+6 & 6x_1^2+2x_1 & \\
 & & 1 & & & 3x_1+6 & 3x_1+1 & 6x_1+3 & & 6x_1^2+2x_1+5 & 3x_1^2+x_1 & \\
 & & & 1 & & 5x_1+3 & 2x_1+5 & x_1+5 & & 3x_1^2+x_1+6 & 6x_1^2+2x_1+2 & \\
 & & & & 1 & 6x_1+5 & x_1+6 & x_1 & 5x_1 & 5x_1^2+4x_1+3 & 3x_1^2+x_1+1 & x_1^2+5x_1+2 \\
 & & & & & 2x_1+5 & x_1 & 5x_1+6 & & x_1^2+6x_1+5 & 6x_1^2+2x_1 & \\
 & & & & & 3x_1+6 & 3 & 4x_1+1 & & 6x_1^2+2x_1+5 & x_1^2+6x_1+6 & \\
 & & & & & & 3x_1+6 & 3 & 4x_1+1 & & 6x_1^2+2x_1+5 & x_1^2+6x_1+6 \\
 & & & & & 6x_1+5 & 3x_1+3 & 6x_1+2 & 4x_1+2 & 5x_1^2+4x_1+3 & 2 & 2x_1^2+3x_1
\end{array}.
$$

Note that the first five rows of the above matrix can be ignored after this elimination. We then eliminate elements of $\mathcal{PM}[\mathscr{S}_3^{(1)}, \mathscr{T}_3^{(1)}]$, and then $\mathcal{PM}[\mathscr{S}_3^{(1)}, \mathscr{T}_{1;3}^{(1)}]$ is changed into

$$
\begin{array}{cccc|ccc|cc}
x_2^3 & x_2^2x_3 & x_2x_3^2 & x_3^3 & x_2^2 & x_2x_3 & x_3^2 & x_2 & x_3 \\
\hline
1 & & & & 4x_1+3 & 2 & 6x_1+3 & 6x_1^2+2x_1+3 & 3x_1^2+x_1 \\
 & 1 & & & 5x_1+3 & 3x_1+2 & 5x_1+6 & 3x_1^2+x_1+6 & 6x_1^2+2x_1 \\
 & & 1 & & 3x_1+6 & 3x_1+1 & 6x_1+3 & 6x_1^2+2x_1+5 & 3x_1^2+x_1 \\
 & & & 1 & 5x_1+3 & 2x_1+5 & x_1+5 & 3x_1^2+x_1+6 & 6x_1^2+2x_1+2 \\
 & & & & 3x_1+6 & 3 & 4x_1+1 & 6x_1^2+2x_1+5 & x_1^2+6x_1+6 \\
 & & & & 4x_1+3 & 2x_1 & 3x_1+5 & 2x_1^2+5x_1+3 & 5x_1^2+4x_1
\end{array}.
$$

Then using the leading coefficient of this partly reduced $\mathcal{PM}[\mathscr{S}_3^{(1)}, \mathscr{T}_3^{(1)}]$, we eliminate nonzero elements of the last four rows of $\mathcal{PM}[\mathscr{S}_4^{(1)}, \mathscr{T}_3^{(1)}]$, and then the last four rows of $\mathcal{PM}[\mathscr{S}_4^{(1)}, \mathscr{T}_{1;2}^{(1)}]$ becomes the following form

$$
\begin{array}{ccc|cc}
x_2^2 & x_2x_3 & x_3^2 & x_2 & x_3 \\
\hline
x_1^2+6x_1+3 & 2x_1^2+x_1+5 & 2x_1^2+5x_1+2 & 4x_1^3+3x_1^2+4x_1+4 & x_1^3+3x_1 \\
3x_1^2+4x_1 & 3x_1^2+5x_1+1 & 6x_1+3 & 5x_1^2+3x_1+1 & 3x_1^2+x_1 \\
5x_1+3 & 3x_1^2+3x_1+6 & 3x_1^2+3x_1+5 & 3x_1^2+x_1+6 & 5x_1^2+3x_1+5 \\
5x_1^2+4x_1+3 & 2 & 2x_1^2+3x_1 & 5x_1^3+3x_1^2+3x_1+1 & 6x_1^3+3x_1+3
\end{array}.
$$

Similarly, we perform the (d)-1, (d)-2, and (d)-3 steps with $d = 2$, and then the resulting matrix of the **Linearize(1)** step is given as

$$
\begin{array}{ccc}
x_2 & x_3 & 1 \\
5x_1^3+3x_1+2 & 3x_1^3+5x_1^2+2x_1+3 & 4x_1^4+3x_1^3+6x_1^2+3x_1+6 \\
3x_1^3+2x_1^2+2x_1+3 & 6x_1^3+3x_1^2+6x_1+2 & 2x_1^4+2x_1^3+5x_1^2+2 \\
6x_1^3+6x_1+6 & 4x_1^3+6x_1^2+3x_1+3 & 2x_1^4+3x_1^3+2x_1^2+4x_1+1 \\
3x_1^2+3x_1+1 & 3x_1^2+x_1+1 & x_1^2+2 \\
6x_1^2+2x_1+5 & 6x_1^2+6x_1+3 & 3x_1^3+x_1^2
\end{array}.
$$

In the **Fix** step, we here substitute $x_1 = 3$ and obtain the following matrix by the Gaussian elimination

$$\begin{array}{c} \quad x_2\ x_3\ 1 \\ \begin{pmatrix} 1 & & 4 \\ & 1 & 1 \end{pmatrix}. \end{array}$$

Then, we can obtain two univariate equations $x_2 + 4 = 0$ and $x_3 + 1 = 0$, and thus a solution is $(x_1, x_2, x_3) = (3, 3, 6)$.

4 Complexity

In this section, we first estimate the size of the resulting matrix of **Linearize(1)**. After that, we estimate the time complexity of PXL and compare it with those of h-XL, h-WXL, and Crossbred. We take D to be $D_1^{(n-k)}$ so that PXL can find a solution (as described in Subsect. 3.4).

4.1 Size of Resulting Matrix of Linearize(1)

Let α be the number of columns of the resulting matrix of **Linearize(1)**. In the following, we estimate the value of this α, and show that it can be quite smaller than the number of the columns of the original Macaulay matrix $\mathcal{PM}$. We also describe that the resulting matrix of **Linearize(1)** can be assumed to be an $\alpha \times \alpha$ matrix.

As in the proof of Lemma 1, we denote by q_i the sum of degree-2 terms with respect to $x_{k+1}, \ldots, x_n$ in f_i. Note that $q_i = f_i^{\mathrm{top}}(0, \ldots, 0, x_{k+1}, \ldots, x_n)$ for each i with $1 \leq i \leq m$. Then, by putting $F^{(\mathrm{top},k)} := (q_1, \ldots, q_m)$, it is straightforward that the elements in the shift $\mathscr{S}_d^{(k)}(F^{(\mathrm{top},k)})$, which is equal to $((\mathscr{S}_d^{(k)})^{\mathrm{top}})|_{(x_1,\ldots,x_k)=(0,\ldots,0)}$, correspond to the rows of $\mathcal{PM}[\mathscr{S}_d^{(k)}, \mathscr{T}_d^{(k)}]$, for each non-negative integer d. We have that the number of columns eliminated in the step (d)-1 of **Linearize(1)** on $\mathcal{PM}[\mathscr{S}_d^{(k)}, \mathscr{T}_d^{(k)}]$ is equal to the rank of $\mathcal{PM}[\mathscr{S}_d^{(k)}, \mathscr{T}_d^{(k)}]$, that is $\dim_{\mathbb{F}_q} \langle \mathscr{S}_d^{(k)}(F^{(\mathrm{top},k)}) \rangle_{\mathbb{F}_q}$. Therefore, we have

$$\begin{aligned} \alpha &= |\mathscr{T}_{\leq D}^{(k)}| - \sum_{d=0}^{D} \dim_{\mathbb{F}_q} \langle \mathscr{S}_d^{(k)}(F^{(\mathrm{top},k)}) \rangle_{\mathbb{F}_q} \\ &= \sum_{d=0}^{D} \left(|\mathscr{T}_d^{(k)}| - \dim_{\mathbb{F}_q} \langle \mathscr{S}_d^{(k)}(F^{(\mathrm{top},k)}) \rangle_{\mathbb{F}_q} \right) \\ &= \sum_{d=0}^{D} \left(\dim_{\mathbb{F}_q} \mathbb{F}_q[x_{k+1}, \ldots, x_n]_d - \dim_{\mathbb{F}_q} \langle F^{(\mathrm{top},k)} \rangle_d \right) \\ &= \sum_{d=0}^{D} \dim_{\mathbb{F}_q} \mathbb{F}_q[x_{k+1}, \ldots, x_n]_d / \langle F^{(\mathrm{top},k)} \rangle_d, \end{aligned} \tag{4.1}$$

where we used $\langle \mathscr{S}_d^{(k)}(F^{(\mathrm{top},k)})\rangle_{\mathbb{F}_q} = \langle F^{(\mathrm{top},k)}\rangle_d$ since all the elements in the sequence $F^{(\mathrm{top},k)} = (q_1,\ldots,q_m)$ are homogeneous. Here, we suppose the following:

Assumption 3. *The sequence $F^{(\mathrm{top},k)} = (q_1,\ldots,q_m)$ of homogeneous polynomials in $\mathbb{F}_q[x_{k+1},\ldots,x_n]$ is semi-regular, where q_i is given in* (3.1) *of the proof of Lemma 1.*

Under this assumption, the value of (4.1) can be estimated as

$$\alpha = \sum_{d=0}^{D} \max\left\{\mathrm{coeff}\left((1-t)^{m-(n-k)}(1+t)^m, t^d\right), 0\right\} \tag{4.2}$$

by Proposition 1. Note that this can be quite smaller than $\binom{n-k+D}{D}$, which is the number of the columns of the whole Macaulay matrix $\mathcal{PM}$. For example, when $n = m = 40$ and $k = 10$, the degree D for which PXL could succeed is estimated as 10 by (3.3), and then α and $\binom{n-k+D}{D}$ are approximately 2^{21} and 2^{30}, respectively.

Recall from Remark 2 that PXL randomly chooses approximately $|\mathscr{T}_{\le D}^{(k)}|$ independent rows from the whole Macaulay matrix $\mathcal{PM}$. When $\tilde{\mathscr{S}}_d^{(k)}$ denotes the subset of $\mathscr{S}_d^{(k)}$ including polynomials corresponding to randomly chosen rows and $r_d^{(k)}$ denotes the rank of $\mathcal{PM}[\tilde{\mathscr{S}}_d^{(k)}, \mathscr{T}_d^{(k)}]$, the number of rows of the resulting matrix of **Linearize(1)** is equal to $\sum_{d=2}^{D}\left(|\tilde{\mathscr{S}}_d^{(k)}| - r_d^{(k)}\right)$, and we *suppose* the following approximation:

$$\sum_{d=2}^{D}\left(|\tilde{\mathscr{S}}_d^{(k)}| - r_d^{(k)}\right) \approx \alpha. \tag{4.3}$$

This can be realized by avoiding choosing too many rows from $\mathscr{S}_D^{(k)}$, and, by doing so, the size of the resulting matrix of **Linearize(1)** is approximately $\alpha\times\alpha$.

4.2 Time Complexity

In this subsection, we estimate the time complexity of PXL. Here, $C_{(d)1}$ (resp. $C_{(d)2}$, $C_{(d)3}$) denotes the estimation of the sum of the number of operations in $\mathbb{F}_q$ required for $(d)-1$ (resp. $(d)-2$, $(d)-3$) in the **Linearize(1)** step for all d with $2 \le d \le D$. Furthermore, C_{fix} (resp. C_{li2}) denote the estimation of the number of operations in $\mathbb{F}_q$ required for the **fix** (resp. **Linearize(2)**) step. These estimations are determined from the number n of all variables, the number k of guessed variables, the degree bound D (which can be taken to be $D_1^{(n-k)}$ given in (3.3)), and the size α of the resulting matrix of **Linearize(1)**. After obtaining each of these five estimations, we give a practical estimation of total time complexity by (4.8) below.

Time Complexity of (d)-1. Recall that the (d)-1 step performs Gaussian elimination on $\mathcal{PM}[\tilde{\mathscr{S}}_d^{(k)}, \mathscr{T}_d^{(k)}]$, and its complexity is given as $\max\{|\tilde{\mathscr{S}}_d^{(k)}|, |\mathscr{T}_d^{(k)}|\}^{\omega}$

for each d with $2 \le d \le D$. Since we have $\sum_{d=2}^{D} \max\{|\tilde{\mathscr{S}}_d^{(k)}| - |\mathscr{T}_d^{(k)}|, 0\} \le \alpha$ from (4.3), an upper bound on the sum of the complexity estimation of the (d)-1 step for all $2 \le d \le D$ is given by

$$\sum_{d=2}^{D} \max\{|\tilde{\mathscr{S}}_d^{(k)}|, |\mathscr{T}_d^{(k)}|\}^{\omega} \le \left(\sum_{d=2}^{D} \max\{|\tilde{\mathscr{S}}_d^{(k)}|, |\mathscr{T}_d^{(k)}|\}\right)^{\omega} \le \left(|\mathscr{T}_{\le D}^{(k)}| + \alpha\right)^{\omega}$$
$$\le (2 \cdot |\mathscr{T}_{\le D}^{(k)}|)^{\omega} = O\left(\binom{n-k+D}{D}^{\omega}\right),$$

where we used the equality

$$\sum_{d=2}^{D} \max\{|\tilde{\mathscr{S}}_d^{(k)}|, |\mathscr{T}_d^{(k)}|\} = \sum_{d=2}^{D} \max\{|\tilde{\mathscr{S}}_d^{(k)}| - |\mathscr{T}_d^{(k)}|, 0\} + |\mathscr{T}_{\le D}^{(k)}|.$$

Therefore, we set $C_{(d)1}$ to be $\binom{n-k+D}{D}^{\omega}$.

Time Complexity of (d)-2. In each (d)-2 step, the complexity of executing the same row operations as those in (d)-1 step is estimated as that of multiplying a square matrix over $\mathbb{F}_q$ of size $|\tilde{\mathscr{S}}_d^{(k)}| \times |\tilde{\mathscr{S}}_d^{(k)}|$ to the polynomial matrix $\mathcal{PM}[\tilde{\mathscr{S}}_d^{(k)}, \mathscr{T}_{(d-2);(d-1)}^{(k)}]$ from the left. Note that $\mathcal{PM}[\tilde{\mathscr{S}}_d^{(k)}, \mathscr{T}_{(d-2);(d-1)}^{(k)}]$ is a sparse matrix, since $\mathcal{PM}[\mathscr{S}_d^{(k)}, \mathscr{T}_{\le(d-1)}^{(k)}]$ does not change from the original structure at the beginning of the (d)-2 step by the same discussion as in Subsect. 3.3, where each row of it has at most $n-k+1$ non-zero entries. Thus, multiplying the two matrices are done in $O((n-k) \cdot |\tilde{\mathscr{S}}_d^{(k)}|^2)$ additions and scalar multiplications in $\mathbb{F}_q[x_1, \dots, x_k]$. Since polynomials appearing in each addition or scalar multiplication have degree ≤ 2, its cost is bounded by $O\left(\binom{k+2}{2}\right)$ with naive approach. Considering above together, each (d)-2 step has complexity $O\left(\binom{k+2}{2} \cdot (n-k) \cdot |\tilde{\mathscr{S}}_d^{(k)}|^2\right)$, and hence the total complexity of (d)-2 for all $2 \le d \le D$ is given by

$$\sum_{d=2}^{D} \left(\binom{k+2}{2} \cdot (n-k) \cdot |\tilde{\mathscr{S}}_d^{(k)}|^2\right) \le \binom{k+2}{2} \cdot (n-k) \cdot \left(\sum_{d=2}^{D} |\tilde{\mathscr{S}}_d^{(k)}|\right)^2$$
$$= \binom{k+2}{2} \cdot (n-k) \cdot |\mathscr{T}_{\le D}^{(k)}|^2$$
$$= O\left(k^2 \cdot (n-k) \cdot \binom{n-k+D}{D}^2\right),$$

and thus $C_{(d)2}$ is set to be $k^2 \cdot (n-k) \cdot \binom{n-k+D}{D}^2$.

Time Complexity of (d)-3. To estimate the time complexity of (d)-3 for all d with $2 \le d \le D$, we use the following lemma:

Lemma 3. *At the time of executing the (d)-3 step with $2 \le d \le D-1$, the degree of every element of $\mathcal{PM}[\tilde{\mathscr{S}}_{(d+1);D}^{(k)}, \mathscr{T}_d^{(k)}]$ is lower than or equal to $D-d$.*

Proof. By the induction, we prove that, at the time of starting the (d)-3 step, the degree of every element of $\mathcal{PM}[\tilde{\mathscr{S}}^{(k)}_{(d+1);D}, \mathscr{T}^{(k)}_{d}]$ and $\mathcal{PM}[\tilde{\mathscr{S}}^{(k)}_{(d+1);D}, \mathscr{T}^{(k)}_{d-1}]$ is lower than or equal to $D-d$ and $D-d+1$, respectively. In the case of $d = D-1$, the above statement clearly holds. In the following, we show that, if the statement holds when $d = d'$ with $3 \leq d' \leq D-1$, then it also holds when $d = d'-1$. Before executing the step (d')-3, it is clear that $\mathcal{PM}[\tilde{\mathscr{S}}^{(k)}_{(d'+1);D}, \mathscr{T}^{(k)}_{d'-2}]$ is a zero matrix. Then, the (d')-3 step adds row vectors, which are obtained by multiplying rows corresponding to $\tilde{\mathscr{S}}^{(k)}_{d'}$ by a polynomial with the degree $D-d'$, to rows corresponding to $\tilde{\mathscr{S}}^{(k)}_{(d'+1);D}$. Here, the degree of each entry of $\mathcal{PM}[\tilde{\mathscr{S}}^{(k)}_{d'}, \mathscr{T}^{(k)}_{d'-1}]$ and $\mathcal{PM}[\tilde{\mathscr{S}}^{(k)}_{d'}, \mathscr{T}^{(k)}_{d'-2}]$ are at most 1 and 2, respectively. Hence, through (d')-3, the degree of each entry of $\mathcal{PM}[\tilde{\mathscr{S}}^{(k)}_{(d'+1);D}, \mathscr{T}^{(k)}_{d'-2}]$ becomes at most $D-d'+2$ and that of $\mathcal{PM}[\tilde{\mathscr{S}}^{(k)}_{(d'+1);D}, \mathscr{T}^{(k)}_{d'-1}]$ remains at most $D-d'+1$, Therefore, the statement holds in the case where $d = d'-1$, as desired. □

Each (d)-3 step eliminates the corresponding columns using the leading coefficients of $\mathcal{PM}[\tilde{\mathscr{S}}^{(k)}_{d}, \mathscr{T}^{(k)}_{d}]$. More concretely, for each i with $1 \leq i \leq r_d$, we conduct row operations to eliminate the non-zero entries in the column to which the leading coefficient of the i-th row of $\mathcal{PM}[\tilde{\mathscr{S}}^{(k)}_{d}, \mathscr{T}^{(k)}_{d}]$ (in reduced row echelon form) belong, where r_d is the rank of $\mathcal{PM}[\tilde{\mathscr{S}}^{(k)}_{d}, \mathscr{T}^{(k)}_{d}]$. Such the non-zero entries to be eliminated are ones of $\mathcal{PM}[\tilde{\mathscr{S}}^{(k)}_{(d+1);D}, \mathscr{T}^{(k)}_{d}]$, and we suppose from (4.3) that the number of them is at most α for each i. In each elimination process, we multiply the i-th row of $\mathcal{PM}[\tilde{\mathscr{S}}^{(k)}_{d}, \mathscr{T}^{(k)}_{(d-2);d}]$ by a non-zero polynomial in $\mathbb{F}_q[x_1, \ldots, x_k]$ of degree at most $D-d$ (this degree bound comes from Lemma 3), and then add the multiple to a row of $\mathcal{PM}[\tilde{\mathscr{S}}^{(k)}_{(d+1);D}, \mathscr{T}^{(k)}_{(d-2);d}]$. Since each entry of $\mathcal{PM}[\tilde{\mathscr{S}}^{(k)}_{d}, \mathscr{T}^{(k)}_{(d-2);d}]$ is a polynomial in $\mathbb{F}_q[x_1, \ldots, x_k]$ of degree ≤ 2 at this point, and since $\mathcal{PM}[\tilde{\mathscr{S}}^{(k)}_{d}, \mathscr{T}^{(k)}_{(d-2);d}]$ has $|\mathscr{T}^{(k)}_{(d-2);d}| = O(|\mathscr{T}^{(k)}_{d}|)$ columns, each elimination process is done in $O\left(\binom{k+2}{2} \cdot \binom{k+D-d}{D-d} \cdot |\mathscr{T}^{(k)}_{d}|\right)$ with a naive approach. The total number of these elimination processes is upper-bounded by $r_d \cdot \alpha$, we estimate the complexity of the (d)-3 step as

$$O\left(\binom{k+D-d}{D-d} \cdot \binom{k+2}{2} \cdot \alpha \cdot r_d \cdot |\mathscr{T}^{(k)}_{d}|\right) \leq O\left(\binom{k+D-d}{D-d} \cdot \binom{k+2}{2} \cdot \alpha \cdot \binom{n-k+d-1}{d}^2\right).$$

Note that the (D)-3 step can be omitted since $\mathcal{PM}[\tilde{\mathscr{S}}^{(k)}_{\leq(D-1)}, \mathscr{T}^{(k)}_{D}]$ is a zero matrix. Consequently, the sum of the complexities of the (d)-3 step for all d with $2 \leq d \leq D-1$ is estimated by

$$\sum_{d=2}^{D-1} \left(\binom{k+D-d}{D-d} \cdot \binom{k+2}{2} \cdot \alpha \cdot \binom{n-k+d-1}{d}^2\right)$$
$$\leq \binom{k+2}{2} \cdot \alpha \cdot \left(\sum_{d=2}^{D-1} \binom{n-k+d-1}{d}\right) \cdot \left(\sum_{d=2}^{D-1} \binom{k+D-d}{k} \cdot \binom{n-k+d-1}{n-k-1}\right). \quad (4.4)$$

Putting $d' = k + D - d$, one has

$$\sum_{d=2}^{D-1} \binom{k+D-d}{k} \cdot \binom{n-k+d-1}{n-k-1} = \sum_{d'=k+1}^{k+D-2} \binom{d'}{k}\binom{(n+D-1)-d'}{(n-1)-k}$$
$$\leq \sum_{d'=0}^{n+D-1} \binom{d'}{k}\binom{(n+D-1)-d'}{(n-1)-k} = \binom{(n+D-1)+1}{(n-1)+1} = \binom{n+D}{D}$$

from a formula similar to Vandermonde's identity. Therefore, the right hand side of (4.4) is upper-bounded by

$$O\left(k^2 \cdot \alpha \cdot \binom{n-k+D}{D} \cdot \binom{n+D}{D}\right),$$

and thus we set $C_{(d)3}$ to be $k^2 \cdot \alpha \cdot \binom{n-k+D}{D} \cdot \binom{n+D}{D}$.

Time Complexity of Fix. The size of the resulting matrix of **Linearize(1)** is approximately $\alpha \times \alpha$ due to the discussion in Subsect. 4.1, and the degree of every element in the matrix is lower than or equal to D from Lemma 3. Therefore, the time complexity of **Fix** is estimated as that of substituting k values to $x_1, \dots, x_k$ in α^2 polynomials with degree D in $\mathbb{F}_q[x_1, \dots, x_k]$. When we use a naive approach, the complexity of evaluation of a polynomial with degree d in k variables is estimated by $\binom{k+d}{d}$. Therefore, C_{fix} is given by

$$C_{\mathsf{fix}} = q^k \cdot \alpha^2 \cdot \binom{k+D}{D}, \tag{4.5}$$

since the **Fix** step is iterated for any values of $x_1, \dots, x_k$.

Time Complexity of Linearize(2). The **Linearize(2)** step performs Gaussian elimination on an $\alpha \times \alpha$ matrix over $\mathbb{F}_q$, and thus we estimate C_{li2} by

$$C_{\mathsf{li2}} = q^k \cdot \alpha^\omega, \tag{4.6}$$

considering q^k times iterations.

Rough Estimations of Time Complexity. Here, we present a more compact formula for the time complexity of PXL. Comparing the estimations $C_{(d)2}$ and $C_{(d)3}$, we can easily confirm that the value of $C_{(d)3}$ is larger than that of $C_{(d)2}$. Furthermore, comparing the estimations $C_{(d)1}$ and $C_{(d)3}$, we experimentally confirmed that, for the case where $10 \leq n \leq 100$, $m = n, 1.5n, 2n$, and k is the value minimizing the sum of the above five estimations, the value of $C_{(d)3}$ is always much larger than that of $C_{(d)1}$ (e.g., $C_{(d)1}$ and $C_{(d)3}$ in the case where $n = m = 100$ with $q = 2^8$ is approximately 2^{210} and 2^{259}, respectively). These facts indicate that the complexity of the **Linearize(1)** step is dominated by $C_{(d)3}$ for practical cases, and it is estimated as follows:

$$O\left(k^2 \cdot \alpha \cdot \binom{n-k+D}{D} \cdot \binom{n+D}{D}\right). \tag{4.7}$$

Table 1. The number of field operations approximated by power of 2 between PXL (4.8), h-XL (2.6), h-WXL (2.7), and Crossbred [22], the optimal number k of guessed variables of PXL, the value of $D = D_1^{(n-k)}$ estimated in (3.3), and the estimated size α of the resulting matrix of **Linearize(1)** on the MQ system with $n = m = 20$, 40, 60, and 80 over $\mathbb{F}_{2^8}$ (above) and over $\mathbb{F}_{31}$ (below).

	$n = m$	20		40		60		80	
	ω	2.37	2.81	2.37	2.81	2.37	2.81	2.37	2.81
$\mathbb{F}_{2^8}$	h-XL	2^{75}	2^{85}	2^{134}	2^{153}	2^{194}	2^{221}	2^{252}	2^{287}
	h-WXL	2^{75}	2^{75}	2^{129}	2^{129}	2^{182}	2^{182}	2^{234}	2^{234}
	Crossbred	2^{65}	2^{74}	2^{123}	2^{137}	2^{180}	2^{201}	2^{237}	2^{265}
	PXL	$\mathbf{2^{62}}$	$\mathbf{2^{64}}$	$\mathbf{2^{117}}$	$\mathbf{2^{121}}$	$\mathbf{2^{169}}$	$\mathbf{2^{178}}$	$\mathbf{2^{220}}$	$\mathbf{2^{233}}$
	k	3	3	6	5	8	7	10	8
	D	9	9	14	15	19	20	24	27
	α	2^{14}	2^{14}	2^{27}	2^{29}	2^{42}	2^{44}	2^{56}	2^{60}

	$n = m$	20		40		60		80	
	ω	2.37	2.81	2.37	2.81	2.37	2.81	2.37	2.81
$\mathbb{F}_{31}$	h-XL	2^{66}	2^{73}	2^{119}	2^{131}	2^{170}	2^{191}	2^{221}	2^{246}
	h-WXL	2^{65}	2^{65}	2^{116}	2^{116}	2^{162}	2^{162}	2^{208}	2^{208}
	Crossbred	2^{57}	2^{62}	2^{109}	2^{117}	2^{158}	2^{170}	2^{208}	2^{224}
	PXL	$\mathbf{2^{57}}$	$\mathbf{2^{57}}$	$\mathbf{2^{105}}$	$\mathbf{2^{107}}$	$\mathbf{2^{152}}$	$\mathbf{2^{158}}$	$\mathbf{2^{197}}$	$\mathbf{2^{208}}$
	k	5	5	8	8	11	10	13	12
	D	7	7	12	12	16	17	21	22
	α	2^{11}	2^{11}	2^{24}	2^{24}	2^{37}	2^{38}	2^{51}	2^{53}

By using this estimation on $C_{(d)3}$, the time complexity of PXL is roughly estimated by $C_{(d)3} + C_{\mathsf{fix}} + C_{\mathsf{li2}}$, say

$$O\left(k^2 \cdot \alpha \cdot \binom{n-k+D}{D} \cdot \binom{n+D}{D} + q^k \cdot \left(\alpha^2 \cdot \binom{k+D}{D} + \alpha^\omega\right)\right). \tag{4.8}$$

4.3 Comparison

We compare the complexity of our PXL with those of h-XL, h-WXL, and Crossbred with our motivation towards contribution of PXL to evaluating the security of MPKCs. Following the security estimation of [9], we choose h-WXL among the XL family as a target for comparison. We also adopt the complexity of h-XL on which h-WXL is originally based (in fact, h-XL is the most basic method in the framework of the hybrid approaches with XL) and that of Crossbred recognized as the theoretical most efficient algorithm for some parameter sets in [6]. Recall that the complexities of h-XL, h-WXL, Crossbred, and PXL are estimated by

(2.6), (2.7), [22] and (4.8), respectively, where the estimation (4.8) for our PXL is obtained by supposing practical Assumptions 2 and 3, and Heuristic 1. Note that, for fixed n, m, and q, each of the four approaches chooses the number k of guessed variables (and D and d for Crossbred) so that its complexity estimation becomes the smallest value, and thus the value of k depends on each approach. Furthermore, we here take the exponent of matrix multiplication ω as 2.37 [29] and 2.81 [50]. As we will see below, PXL is theoretically more efficient than other algorithms in the case of $n = m$ (this is the case where hybrid approaches for the MQ problem work most efficiently).

Table 1 compares the bit complexities of PXL, h-XL, h-WXL, and Crossbred on the MQ system of m equations in n variable with $n = m$ over $\mathbb{F}_{2^8}$ and $\mathbb{F}_{31}$. These orders of the finite fields are chosen following the MQ challenge [57], and in particular, $q = 2^8 = 256$ is also suggested as a parameter of [9]. Note also that we do not choose $q = 2$ since exhaustive searches are known to be effective in this case. Specifically, Table 1 shows the bit complexities of the four approaches, the optimal k of PXL minimizing the value of (4.8), the value of $D = D_1^{(n-k)}$ estimated in (3.3), and the estimated size α of the resulting matrix of **Linearize(1)** obtained from (4.2) for the case where $n = m$ with $n \in \{20, 40, 60, 80\}$. For example, when $q = 2^8$, $n = m = 80$, and $\omega = 2.37$, the complexities of h-XL, h-WXL, Crossbred, and PXL are approximately estimated as 2^{252}, 2^{234}, 2^{237}, and 2^{220}, respectively. As a result, we expect that PXL has the less complexity than those of other algorithms especially in the case of $\omega = 2.37$; we also expect that similar results will be obtained in other finite fields from the form of the complexity estimation (4.8).

On the other hand, we confirmed that PXL is not efficient in highly overdetermined cases. This is because, in such overdetermined cases, k is set to be a very small value for efficiency.

Remark 5 (Space Complexity). The memory space consumed by PXL is upper-bounded by $O\left(\binom{k+D}{D} \cdot \binom{n-k+D}{D}^2\right)$, since the degree of every element of the Macaulay matrix and its transformed matrices in **Linearize(1)** is at most D through an execution of PXL from Lemma 3. This estimation cannot be directly compared with other algorithms, since the values of the following two parameters depend on one's choice of an algorithm: The degree bound D (for the success of the algorithm) and the number k of fixed values.

On the other hand, focusing on the sparsity/density of matrices, we predict that PXL is not efficient compared with h-WXL in terms of the space complexity for the following reason: Through the elimination process of Macaulay matrices, WXL can deal with a Macaulay matrix as a sparse matrix due to Wiedemann's algorithm, whereas PXL maintains some dense submatrices. Considering this together with the time complexities for practical parameters, we conclude that the relationship between PXL and h-WXL would be a trade-off between time and memory.

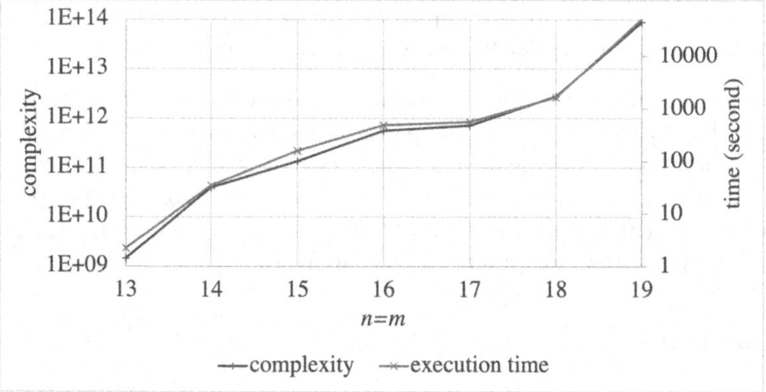

Fig. 1. Comparison between the estimation of complexity by (4.7) and the execution time of the **Linearize(1)** step on an MQ system with $n = m$ over $\mathbb{F}_{2^4}$.

5 Experimental Results

We implemented the proposed algorithm PXL in the Magma computer algebra system (V2.26-10) [10], in order to examine that it behaves as our complexity estimation provided in Sect. 4. (As it will be described below, note that our current implementation is not optimized one, see also Remark 6.) We also confirmed in our experiments that PXL outputs a solution correctly at $D = D_1^{(n-k)}$ as estimated in (3.3).

First, we confirmed that the **Linearize(1)** step behaves as in (4.7). The reason why we focus on the behavior of the **Linearize(1)** step is the following: In the estimation (4.8) of the total time complexity, only $C_{(d)3}$ is specific to our estimation in theory, while the later parts C_{fix} and C_{li2} for the **Fix** and **Linearize(2)** steps just come from known complexity estimations. Figure 1 compares the execution time of the **Linearize(1)** step and the bit complexity (4.7) on the system with $n = m$ from $n = 13$ to $n = 19$ over $\mathbb{F}_{2^4}$, and the number k of fixed variables is chosen so as to minimize the value of (4.8). As a result, Fig. 1 shows that the execution time and our estimation (4.7) have almost the same behavior, which indicates that the estimation (4.7) would be reliable.

On the other hand, our current Magma implementation of the **Fix** and **Linearize(2)** steps does not show the similar behavior as our complexity estimation, due to the use of unoptimized implementation. For example, in the case of $n = m = 16$ with $k = 5$, **Linearize(1)**, **Fix**, and **Linearize(2)** took 10 min., 40 hr., and 30 min., respectively, whereas the estimated numbers of field operations of these three steps from (4.7), (4.5), and (4.6) are 2^{39}, 2^{44}, and 2^{39}, respectively. We observe that this inefficiency of the latter two steps (in particular **Fix** with a lot of for-loops) is due to the use of Magma's interpreter language. Using compiler languages such as C instead could be a solution to resolve this problem, but we must newly implement the arithmetic of matrices and polynomials efficiently, which is not the topic of this paper. We leave such an efficient implementation with compiler languages to future work.

Remark 6. We remark that here we do not compare the execution time of our PXL with that of any other variant of XL, since the practical behavior deeply depends on how one implements the arithmetic of matrices (and polynomials) efficiently, which is not the topic of this paper. For a fair comparison, providing optimized implementations of several variants including PXL is required, and it is a very important task for practical cryptanalysis.

6 Conclusion

We presented a new variant of XL, which is a major approach for solving the MQ problem. Our proposed polynomial XL (PXL) eliminates the linearized monomials in polynomial rings to solve the system efficiently, and we estimated its complexities. Given an MQ system of m equations in n variables, the proposed algorithm first regards each polynomial in n variable as one in $n-k$ variables $x_{k+1}, \ldots, x_n$, whose coefficients belong to the polynomial ring $\mathbb{F}_q[x_1, \ldots, x_k]$. We then generate a Macaulay matrix over $\mathbb{F}_q[x_1, \ldots, x_k]$, and partly perform the row reduction (Gaussian elimination). Finally, random values are substituted for the k variables, and the remaining part of the (partly-reduced) Macaulay matrix is transformed into the reduced row echelon form. Partly reducing the (polynomial) Macaulay matrix is done mainly on submatrices over $\mathbb{F}_q$ (not over $\mathbb{F}_q[x_1, \ldots, x_k]$) with arithmetic of polynomials in $\mathbb{F}_q[x_1, \ldots, x_k]$ of bounded degree, and under some practical assumption and heuristic (Assumption 3 and Heuristic 1), the remaining part is expected to have size much smaller than the original one. This construction can reduce the amount of field operations for each guessed value, compared to h-XL. Supposing the above assumption and heuristic and additional but still practical one (Assumption 2), which assumes the affine semi-regularity of polynomial sequences, we gave an asymptotic estimation of the time complexity of PXL, which implies that PXL could solve the system faster in theory for the case of $n \approx m$ than h-XL, h-WXL, and Crossbred. On the other hand, PXL might be less efficient than h-WXL with respect to the space complexity.

This paper discusses only the quadratic case, but, as in the plain XL, the proposed algorithm can be also generalized to higher degree cases. Therefore, one considerable future work is to analyze the complexity of PXL on such higher degree systems. Furthermore, for a comparison of the practical time-efficiencies of our PXL and other XL variants, it is important to implement PXL (and the other variants) efficiently. In our experiments, we implemented PXL over Magma, but this can be more optimized by using an alternative (compiler) programming language, e.g., C. Note that there will be a drawback that the construction of our PXL over the polynomial ring prohibits the use of existing linear algebra libraries, which are often heavily optimized. Therefore, to provide such an optimized code for PXL will be a challenging task. Finally, we leave the analysis of the effect of PXL on the security of various multivariate signature schemes to a future work.

Acknowledgements. The authors thank the anonymous referees for helpful comments and suggestions. The authors also thank Tsuyoshi Takagi and Kazuhiro Yokoyama for helpful comments and suggestions. The authors are grateful to Kosuke Sakata for his advice on the implementation of our proposed algorithm.

This work was supported by JST CREST Grant Number JPMJCR2113, Japan, JSPS KAKENHI Grant Number JP22KJ0554, Japan, and JSPS Grant-in-Aid for Young Scientists 20K14301 and 23K12949, Japan.

A Semi-regular Sequences

We here review the notion of *semi-regular* sequence, which is introduced first by Bardet et al. (e.g., [3–5]). Semi-regular sequences are formulated also by Diem [18] in terms of commutative and homological algebra. See also [40, Section 2] for a survey.

We use the following notation: Let $R = K[x_1, \ldots, x_n]$ be the polynomial ring of n variables $x_1, \ldots, x_n$ over a field K. For a finitely generated graded R-module $M = \bigoplus_{d\in\mathbb{Z}} M_d$ (namely M_d is the degree-d homogeneous component), we denote by HF_M its Hilbert function, namely $\mathrm{HF}_M(d) = \dim_K M_d$ for each integer d, and denote by HS_M the Hilbert series of M, say $\mathrm{HS}_M(z) = \sum_{d=0}^{\infty} \mathrm{HF}_M(d)z^d \in \mathbb{Z}[\![z]\!]$. For a sequence $(f_1, \ldots, f_m)$ of *homogeneous* polynomials in R of positive degrees, let $K_\bullet(f_1, \ldots, f_m)$ denote the Koszul complex on the sequence (see e.g., [32, Section 7.6] for its definition), and let $H_i(K_\bullet(f_1, \ldots, f_m))$ be its i-th homology group. In particular, the first homology group is a finitely generated graded R-module given by

$$H_1(K_\bullet(f_1, \ldots, f_m)) = \mathrm{syz}(f_1, \ldots, f_m)/\mathrm{tsyz}(f_1, \ldots, f_m), \tag{A.1}$$

the sum of whose homogeneous components of degree less than or equal to d is denoted by $H_1(K_\bullet(f_1, \ldots, f_m))_{\leq d}$ for each $d \in \mathbb{Z}$. Here, $\mathrm{syz}(f_1, \ldots, f_m)$ denotes the module of syzigies on $(f_1, \ldots, f_m)$, say

$$\mathrm{syz}(f_1, \ldots, f_m) = \left\{ (h_1, \ldots, h_m) \in \bigoplus_{j=1}^{m} R(-d_j)\mathbf{e}_j \right\},$$

where each $R(-d_j)$ is the shifted graded ring given by $R(-d_j)_d = R_{d-d_j}$ for $d \in \mathbb{Z}$, and where each $\mathbf{e}_j$ denotes a standard basis element. On the other hand, $\mathrm{tsyz}(f_1, \ldots, f_m)$ is defined as an R-submodule of $\mathrm{syz}(f_1, \ldots, f_m)$ given by

$$\mathrm{tsyz}(f_1, \ldots, f_m) := \langle \mathbf{t}_{i,j} := f_i\mathbf{e}_j - f_j\mathbf{e}_i : 1 \leq i < j \leq m \rangle_R,$$

which is called the module of trivial syzigies on $(f_1, \ldots, f_m)$.

We first recall the definiton of d-regular sequences:

Definition 1 ([4, Definition 3], [18, Definition 1]). *Let $f_1, \ldots, f_m \in R$ be homogeneous polynomials of positive degrees $d_1, \ldots, d_m$ respectively, and put $I = \langle f_1, \ldots, f_m \rangle_R$. For each integer d with $d \geq \max\{d_i : 1 \leq i \leq m\}$, we say that a sequence $(f_1, \ldots, f_m)$ is d-regular if it satisfies the following condition:*

- *For each i with $1 \leq i \leq m$, if a homogeneous polynomial $g \in R$ satisfies $gf_i \in \langle f_1, \dots, f_{i-1} \rangle_R$ and $\deg(gf_i) < d$, then we have $g \in \langle f_1, \dots, f_{i-1} \rangle_R$.*

The (truncated) Hilbert series of d-regular sequences was determined by Diem [18], as in the following proposition:

Theorem 3 (cf. [18, Theorem 1]). *We use the same notation as in Definition 1. Then, the following are equivalent for each d with $d \geq \max\{d_i : 1 \leq i \leq m\}$:*

(1) The sequence $(f_1, \dots, f_m)$ of homogeneous polynomials is d-regular.
(2) We have

$$\mathrm{HS}_{R/\langle f_1, \dots, f_m \rangle}(z) \equiv \frac{\prod_{j=1}^{m}(1 - z^{d_j})}{(1 - z)^n} \pmod{z^d}. \tag{A.2}$$

(3) $H_1(K_\bullet(f_1, \dots, f_m))_{\leq d-1} = 0$.

Recall that a finitely generated graded R-module M is said to be *Artinian* if there exists a sufficiently large $D \in \mathbb{Z}$ such that $M_d = 0$ for all $d \geq D$.

Definition 2 ([4, Definition 4], [5, Definition 4]). *For a homogeneous ideal I of R, we define its degree of regularity $d_{\mathrm{reg}}(I)$ as follows: If the finitely generated graded R-module R/I is Artinian, we set $d_{\mathrm{reg}}(I) := \min\{d : R_d = I_d\}$ with $I_d = I \cap R_d$, and otherwise we set $d_{\mathrm{reg}}(I) := \infty$. We also denote $d_{\mathrm{reg}}(I)$ by $d_{\mathrm{reg}}(F)$ for a subset or a sequence F of homogeneous elements in R generating the homogeneous ideal I.*

Definition 3 ([4, Definition 5], [5, Definition 5]; *see also* [18, §2]). *A sequence $(f_1, \dots, f_m) \in R^m$ of homogeneous polynomials of positive degrees is said to be semi-regular if it is $d_{\mathrm{reg}}(I)$-regular, where we set $I = \langle f_1, \dots, f_m \rangle_R$.*

The semi-regularity is characterized by equivalent conditions in the following proposition:

Proposition 1 ([18, Proposition 1 (d)]; *see also* [5, Proposition 6]). *With the same notation as in Definition 1, we put $D = d_{\mathrm{reg}}(I)$. Then, the following are equivalent:*

(1) The sequence $(f_1, \dots, f_m)$ of homogeneous polynomials is semi-regular.
(2) We have

$$\mathrm{HS}_{R/I}(z) = \left[\frac{\prod_{j=1}^{m}(1 - z^{d_j})}{(1 - z)^n} \right], \tag{A.3}$$

where $[\cdot]$ means truncating a formal power series over $\mathbb{Z}$ after the last consecutive positive coefficient.
(3) $H_1(K_\bullet(f_1, \dots, f_m))_{\leq D-1} = 0$.

Note that, by Definition 3, if $(f_1, \dots, f_m)$ is semi-regular, then the degree of regularity $d_{\mathrm{reg}}(I)$ coincides with $\deg(\mathrm{HS}_{R/I})+1$, where we set $I = \langle f_1, \dots, f_m \rangle_R$.

Finally, we recall the definition of an affine semi-regular sequence:

Definition 4 ([5, Definition 5]). *A sequence $F = (f_1, \dots, f_m) \in R^m$ of not necessarily homogeneous polynomials of positive degrees is said to be semi-regular if the sequence $F^{\mathrm{top}} = (f_1^{\mathrm{top}}, \dots, f_m^{\mathrm{top}})$ is semi-regular . In this case, the sequence F is said to be affine semi-regular.*

References

1. Albrecht, M.-R., Cid, C., Faugère, J.-C., Perret, L.: On the relation between the MXL family of algorithms and Gröbner basis algorithms. J. Symb. Comput. **47**(8), 926–941 (2012)
2. Ars, G., Faugère, J.-C., Imai, H., Kawazoe, M., Sugita, M.: Comparison between XL and Gröbner basis algorithms. In: Lee, P.J. (ed.) ASIACRYPT 2004. LNCS, vol. 3329, pp. 338–353. Springer, Heidelberg (2004). https://doi.org/10.1007/978-3-540-30539-2_24
3. Bardet, M.: *Étude des systèms algébriques surdéterminés. Applications aux codes correcteurs et à la cryptographie*. PhD thesis, Université Pierre et Marie Curie-Paris VI, 2004
4. Bardet, M., Faugére, J.-C., Salvy, B.: On the complexity of Gröbner basis computation of semi-regular overdetermined algebraic equations (extended abstract). In: ICPSS 2004, pp. 71–74 (2004)
5. Bardet, M., Faugére, J.-C., Salvy, B., Yang, B.-Y.: Asymptotic behaviour of the degree of regularity of semi-regular polynomial systems. In: MEGA 2005 (2005)
6. Bellini, E., Makarim, R.H., Sanna, C., Verbel, J.: An estimator for the hardness of the MQ problem. In: Batina, L., Daemen, J. (eds.) Progress in Cryptology - AFRICACRYPT 2022. AFRICACRYPT 2022. LNCS, vol. 13503, pp. 323–347. Springer, Cham (2022). https://doi.org/10.1007/978-3-031-17433-9_14
7. Bettale, L., Faugère, J.-C., Perret, L.: Hybrid approach for solving multivariate systems over finite fields. J. Math. Cryptol. **3**, 177–197 (2009)
8. Beullens, W., Campos, F., Celi, S., Hess, B., Kannwischer, M.J.: MAYO specification, 2023. https://csrc.nist.gov/csrc/media/Projects/pqc-dig-sig/documents/round-1/spec-files/mayo-spec-web.pdf
9. Beullens, W., et al.: UOV: unbalanced oil and vinegar algorithm specifications and supporting documentation version 1.0. https://csrc.nist.gov/csrc/media/Projects/pqc-dig-sig/documents/round-1/spec-files/UOV-spec-web.pdf
10. Bosma, W., Cannon, J., Playoust, C.: The Magma algebra system. I. The user language. J. Symb. Comput. **24**(3-4), 235–265 (1997)
11. Buchberger, B.: Ein algorithmus zum auffinden der basiselemente des restklassenringes nach einem nulldimensionalen polynomideal. PhD thesis, Universität Innsbruck, 1965
12. Buchmann, J.A., Ding, J., Mohamed, M.S.E., Mohamed, W.S.A.E.: MutantXL: solving multivariate polynomial equations for cryptanalysis. In: Dagstuhl seminar proceedings. Schloss Dagstuhl-Leibniz-Zentrum für Informatik (2009)
13. Capaverde, J.G.: Gröbner Bases: Degree Bounds and Generic Ideals. PhD thesis, Clemson University, 2014
14. Courtois, N., Klimov, A., Patarin, J., Shamir, A.: Efficient algorithms for solving overdefined systems of multivariate polynomial equations. In: Preneel, B. (ed.) EUROCRYPT 2000. LNCS, vol. 1807, pp. 392–407. Springer, Heidelberg (2000). https://doi.org/10.1007/3-540-45539-6_27
15. Cox, D.-A., Little, J., O'Shea, D.: Using Algebraic Geometry, second edn. Springer, New York (2005). https://doi.org/10.1007/b138611
16. Cox, D.-A. , Little, J., O'Shea, D.: Ideals, Varieties, and Algorithms, fourth edn. Springer, Cham (2015). https://doi.org/10.1007/978-3-319-16721-3
17. Diem, C.: The XL-algorithm and a conjecture from commutative algebra. In: Lee, P.J. (ed.) ASIACRYPT 2004. LNCS, vol. 3329, pp. 323–337. Springer, Heidelberg (2004). https://doi.org/10.1007/978-3-540-30539-2_23

18. Diem, C.: Bounded regularity. J. Algebra **423**, 1143–1160 (2015)
19. Ding, J., Petzoldt, A., Schmidt, D.S.: Multivariate Public Key Cryptosystems. AIS, vol. 80. Springer, New York (2020). https://doi.org/10.1007/978-1-0716-0987-3
20. Duarte, J.D.: On the complexity and admissible parameters of the Crossbred algorithm in $\mathbb{F}_{q\geq 2}$. Cryptology ePrint Archive, Paper 2023/1664, 2023
21. Dubé, T.-W.: The structure of polynomial ideals and Gröbner bases. SIAM J. Comput. **19**(4), 750–773 (1990)
22. Esser, A., Verbel, J., Zweydinger, F., Bellini, E.: NonProportional CryptographicEstimators software library for cryptographic hardness estimation. Cryptology ePrint Archive, Paper 2023/589, 2023. Paper 2023/589, 2023
23. Faugère, J.-C.: A new efficient algorithm for computing Gröbner bases (F4). J. Pure Appl. Algebra **139**(1–3), 61–88 (1999)
24. Faugère, J.-C.: A new efficient algorithm for computing Gröbner bases without reduction to zero (F5). In: ISSAC 2002, pp. 75–83. ACM (2002)
25. Faugère, J.-C., Gianni, P., Lazard, D., Mora, T.: Efficient computation of zero-dimensional Gröbner bases by change of ordering. J. Symb. Comput. **16**(4), 329–344 (1993)
26. Fröberg, R.: An inequality for Hilbert series of graded algebras. Math. Scand. **56**, 117–144 (1985)
27. Furue, H., et al.: QR-UOV specification document, 2023. https://csrc.nist.gov/csrc/media/Projects/pqc-dig-sig/documents/round-1/spec-files/qruov-spec-web.pdf
28. Gaggero, G., Gorla, E.: The complexity of solving a random polynomial system, 2023. arxiv:2309.03855
29. Gall, F.L.: Powers of tensors and fast matrix multiplication. In: ISSAC 2014, pp. 296–303. ACM (2014)
30. Garey, M.-R., Johnson, D.-S.: Computers and Intractability: A Guide to the Theory of NP-Completeness. W. H. Freeman, New York (1979)
31. Gathen, J.V.Z., Shoup, V.: Computing Frobenius maps and factoring polynomials. Comput. Complex. **2**(3), 87–224 (1992)
32. Greuerl, G.-M., Pfister, G.: A Singular Introduction to Commutative Algebra (2nd Edition). Springer, Berlin, Heidelberg (2007). https://doi.org/10.1007/978-3-662-04963-1
33. Ikematsu, Y., Nakamura, S., Takagi, T.: Recent progress in the security evaluation of multivariate public-key cryptography. IET Inf. Secur. **17**(2), 210–226 (2023)
34. Technology Innovation Institute. Multivariate quadratic estimator. https://estimators.crypto.tii.ae/configuration?id=MQEstimator
35. Joux, A., Vitse, V.: A crossbred algorithm for solving Boolean polynomial systems. In: Kaczorowski, J., Pieprzyk, J., Pomykała, J. (eds.) NuTMiC 2017. LNCS, vol. 10737, pp. 3–21. Springer, Cham (2018). https://doi.org/10.1007/978-3-319-76620-1_1
36. Kaltofen, E., Shoup, V.: Subquadratic-time factoring of polynomials over finite fields. Math. Comp. **67**(223), 1179–1197 (1998)
37. Kipnis, A., Patarin, J., Goubin, L.: Unbalanced oil and vinegar signature schemes. In: Stern, J. (ed.) EUROCRYPT 1999. LNCS, vol. 1592, pp. 206–222. Springer, Heidelberg (1999). https://doi.org/10.1007/3-540-48910-X_15
38. Kipnis, A., Shamir, A.: Cryptanalysis of the HFE public key cryptosystem by relinearization. In: Wiener, M. (ed.) CRYPTO 1999. LNCS, vol. 1666, pp. 19–30. Springer, Heidelberg (1999). https://doi.org/10.1007/3-540-48405-1_2
39. Kudo, M., Yokoyama, K.: The solving degrees for computing Gröbner bases of affine semi-regular polynomial sequences, 2024. arXiv:2404.03530

40. Kudo, M., Yokoyama, K.: On Hilbert-Poincaré series of affine semi-regular polynomial sequences and related Gröbner bases. In *Mathematical Foundations for Post-Quantum Cryptography*, page 26 pages. Springer, 2024, to appear arXiv:2401.07768
41. Lazard, D.: Systems of algebraic equations. In: Ng, E.W. (ed.) Symbolic and Algebraic Computation. LNCS, vol. 72, pp. 88–94. Springer, Heidelberg (1979). https://doi.org/10.1007/3-540-09519-5_62
42. Lazard, D.: Gröbner bases, Gaussian elimination and resolution of systems of algebraic equations. In: van Hulzen, J.A. (ed.) EUROCAL 1983. LNCS, vol. 162, pp. 146–156. Springer, Heidelberg (1983). https://doi.org/10.1007/3-540-12868-9_99
43. McGuire, G., O'Hara, D.: On the termination of the general XL algorithm and ordinary multinomials. J. Symb. Comput. **104**, 90–104 (2021)
44. Mohamed, M.S.E., Mohamed, W.S.A.E., Ding, J., Buchmann, J.: MXL2: solving polynomial equations over GF(2) using an improved mutant strategy. In: Buchmann, J., Ding, J. (eds.) PQCrypto 2008. LNCS, vol. 5299, pp. 203–215. Springer, Heidelberg (2008). https://doi.org/10.1007/978-3-540-88403-3_14
45. Mohamed, W.S.A.: Improvements for the XL algorithm with applications to algebraic cryptanalysis. PhD thesis, TU Darmstadt (2011)
46. Nakamura, S.: Admissible parameter sets and complexity estimation of Crossbred algorithm. Cryptology ePrint Archive, Paper 2023/1687 (2023)
47. Pardue, K.: Generic sequences of polynomials. J. Algebra **324**(4), 579–590 (2010)
48. Salizzoni, F.: An upper bound for the solving degree in terms of the degree of regularity, 2023. arXiv:2304.13485
49. Semaev, I., Tenti, A.: Probabilistic analysis on Macaulay matrices over finite fields and complexity constructing Gröbner bases. J. Algebra **565**, 651–674 (2021)
50. Strassen, V.: Gaussian elimination is not optimal. Numer. Math. **13**(4), 354–356 (1969)
51. Tenti, A.: Sufficiently overdetermined random polynomial systems behave like semiregular ones. PhD thesis, University of Bergen (2019)
52. Wiedemann, D.H.: Solving sparse linear equations over finite fields. IEEE Trans. Inf. Theor. **32**(1), 54–62 (1986)
53. Wu, W.-T.: Basic principles of mechanical theorem proving in elementary geometries. J. Autom. Reason. **2**(3), 221–252 (1986)
54. Yang, B.-Y., Chen, J.-M.: All in the XL family: theory and practice. In: Park, C., Chee, S. (eds.) ICISC 2004. LNCS, vol. 3506, pp. 67–86. Springer, Heidelberg (2005). https://doi.org/10.1007/11496618_7
55. Yang, B.-Y., Chen, J.-M., Courtois, N.T.: On asymptotic security estimates in XL and Gröbner bases-related algebraic cryptanalysis. In: Lopez, J., Qing, S., Okamoto, E. (eds.) ICICS 2004. LNCS, vol. 3269, pp. 401–413. Springer, Heidelberg (2004). https://doi.org/10.1007/978-3-540-30191-2_31
56. Yang, B.-Y., Chen, O.C.-H., Bernstein, D.J., Chen, J.-M.: Analysis of QUAD. In: Biryukov, A. (ed.) FSE 2007. LNCS, vol. 4593, pp. 290–308. Springer, Heidelberg (2007). https://doi.org/10.1007/978-3-540-74619-5_19
57. Yasuda, T., Dahan, X., Huang, Y.-J., Takagi, T., Sakurai, K.: MQ challenge: hardness evaluation of solving multivariate quadratic problems, 2015. NIST Workshop on Cybersecurity in a Post-Quantum World
58. Yun, D.Y.Y.: On square-free decomposition algorithm. In: ISSAC 1976, pp. 26–35. ACM (1976)

State of the Art of HFE Variants

Is It Possible to Repair HFE with Appropriate Modifiers?

Benoît Cogliati[1], Gilles Macariot-Rat[2], Jacques Patarin[1], and Pierre Varjabedian[1](✉)

[1] THALES, Meudon, France
{benoit-michel.cogliati,jacques.patarin, pierre.varjabedian}@thalesgroup.com
[2] Orange, Chatillon, France
gilles.macariorat@orange.com

Abstract. HFE (that stands for Hidden Field Equations) belongs to multivariate cryptography and was designed by Jacques Patarin in 1996 as a public key trapdoor suitable for encryption or signature. This original basic version is unfortunately known to have a super-polynomial attack, but as imagined since the beginning, it comes with various variants, one can describe as combinations of "modifiers".

In this work, we first present the state of the art of these HFE modifiers, along with their effect on the complexity of the main cryptanalysis techniques against HFE-based schemes. This allows us, in a second time, to identify a combination of two modifiers that has not yet been explored and may still be secure with efficient parameters. Based on our analysis, we propose a new signature scheme that offers extremely short signature sizes, with reasonable public key sizes and performance. In particular, we rely on the classical Feistel-Patarin technique to reduce signature sizes below two times the security parameter.

Keywords: Multivariate Cryptography · Short Signature · HFE · HFE variants · MinRank attacks

1 Introduction

The cryptosystem and signature scheme HFE was created in 1996 by Jacques Patarin [Pat96b] in order to repair the Matsumoto-Imai cypher [MI88]. In this initial paper, it was already mentioned that many variants of HFE exist since many "modifiers" can be added to the scheme. We will call "unmodified" HFE the simplest variant, i.e. HFE with no additional modifiers. In [Pat96b] it was mentioned that when the degree d of the hidden polynomial is fixed, some polynomial attacks are possible, but at that time the scheme was nevertheless efficient even with small parameters. Since 1996 many other papers have been published, with the discovery of many more variants, along with many more possible attacks. On "unmodified" HFE for example, super-polynomial attacks were published in [FJ03] even when the degree d increases. Therefore "unmodified" HFE

M.-J. Saarinen and D. Smith-Tone (Eds.): PQCrypto 2024, LNCS 14772, pp. 144–167, 2024.
https://doi.org/10.1007/978-3-031-62746-0_7

is at present only interesting for very specific needs: very short public signatures and a security level of only about 80 bits (see [PMBK20]), since for larger security the size of the public key becomes too large.

The two main families of attacks on HFE and HFE variants are direct attacks using Gröbner bases [FJ03], and full key recovery attacks using MinRank problem. The first MinRank attack was published in [KS99]. Recently great improvements have been done on these MinRank attacks. In fact many different MinRank attacks exist: some that first target the secret matrix $\mathbf{T}$ of HFE [BFP11] and some that will first attack the secret matrix $\mathbf{S}$ of HFE. Improvements have also been made in the resolution of the MinRank problem. The first methods were the use of the so called minor modelling, while today we are using an improved version called the Support minor modelling [BBB+22].

It is relatively easy to add a simple modifier to resist one of these attacks, but, as we will see in this paper, it is difficult to resist all of them. In fact, the most impressive recent cryptanalysis result on HFE variants was the cryptanalysis of GeMSS done in [TPD21,BBC+22] by a MinRank attack (following the idea of Beullens [Beu21] on the rainbow scheme). GeMSS is a HFE$v-$ signature scheme i.e. HFE with modifier v and - (these modifiers will be defined later) submitted to the NIST-PQ competition. The scheme was broken due to these attacks. The aim of this paper will be to see if some combination of two HFE variants can resist all known attacks (Gröbner basis attack, all the MinRank attack variants, differential attacks etc...). We think that it is also interesting to have a general view of the state of the art on this subject because there are so many papers on HFE that the situation may look confusing. As we will see, in encryption we did not find any solution from the known modifiers. However in signature, one of the variants, called HFE$IP-$ (for HFE with the Internal Perturbation and the minus modifier) may still be secure with efficient parameters. Of course, since the analysis of this design is recent, and since many HFE variants have been broken, we do not recommend to use it yet for critical application, but rather to continue the theoretical analysis to see if this variant can really be secure and resist the test of time.

In this paper we provide a summary of the situation of the research on HFE variants. We are making in the first part a cryptanalysis on every variant found on HFE with the most modern attacks available. Hence, we provide cryptanalysis that were not made on certain variants such a "plus" or "internal perturbation". In this section we focus on MinRank attacks and give a slight insight on Gröbner bases attacks or attacks specific to a said variant. In the second part we propose a new scheme based on HFE, we also give a set of parameters for this scheme.

2 Preliminary

2.1 Notations

For our notations, the set of all integers between integers a, b (a and b included) is $\{a \dots b\}$. Row vectors and matrices will be written in **bold**. On this paper we will sometimes switch to a polynomial notation or a function notation so the function represented by the matrix will sometimes be implicitly called by the same letter that was used for the matrix. For example the function H will be associated with the matrix $\mathbf{H}$. We denote by v_i the i-th component of a vector $\mathbf{v}$, and the entries of a matrix $\mathbf{M}$ of size $n_r \times n_c$ will be denoted by $\mathbf{M}_{i,j}$, where i (resp. j) is an integer in $\{1..n_r\}$ (resp. $\{1..n_c\}$). If one consider the subsets $I \subset \{1..n_r\}$ and $J \subset \{1..n_c\}$, we use the notation $\mathbf{M}_{I,J}$ for the submatrix of $\mathbf{M}$ formed by its rows (resp. columns) with indexes in I (resp. J), and we adopt the shorthand notation $\mathbf{M}_{*,J} = \mathbf{M}_{\{1..n_r\},J}$ and $\mathbf{M}_{I,*} = \mathbf{M}_{I,\{1..n_c\}}$. We also denote by $|\mathbf{M}|$ the determinant of $\mathbf{M}$. Finally, we use $\#I$ to denote the number of elements of a set I.

A field with q elements is denoted $\mathbb{F}_q$.

For $X \in \mathbb{F}_{q^n}$, we define $X^{\square} := (X^{q^0}, \ldots, X^{q^{n-1}})$, that is the vector of the conjugates of X.

We note $\mathbf{I}_n$ the identity matrix of size n.

Finally we note Tr_n the well known linear mapping trace defined by $\mathrm{Tr}_n : \mathbb{F}_{q^n} \to \mathbb{F}_q, x \mapsto \sum_{i=0}^{n-1} x^{q^i}$.

2.2 Univariate and Multivariate Representations

An extension $\mathbb{F}_{q^n}$ of $\mathbb{F}_q$ can be classically defined as $\mathbb{F}_q[\alpha]$ where α is a primitive element of degree n. $\mathbb{F}_{q^n}$ can be then considered as a vector space over $\mathbb{F}_q$ with basis $(1, \alpha, \ldots, \alpha^{n-1})$. So let X be an element of $\mathbb{F}_{q^n}$ and $(x_1, \ldots, x_n)$ its coordinates over this basis, such that $X = \sum_{i=1}^n x_i \alpha^{i-1}$. Let $\mathbf{M}_n$ be the matrix of $\mathcal{M}_{n\times n}(\mathbb{F}_{q^n})$ whose (i,j)-coefficient is $\alpha^{(i-1)q^{j-1}}$. One can see that the ith row of $\mathbf{M}_n$ is $(\alpha^{i-1})^{\square}$. By construction of $\mathbf{M}_n$, we have $(x_1, \ldots, x_n)\mathbf{M}_n = X^{\square}$ and therefore also $(x_1, \ldots, x_n) = X^{\square}\mathbf{M}_n^{-1}$. So if we define $\phi : \mathbb{F}_{q^n} \to \mathbb{F}_q^n$, $X \mapsto X^{\square}\mathbf{M}_n^{-1}$, then ϕ converts X to its coordinates, and vice-versa for ϕ^{-1}. Additionally, $\phi^{-1}(x_1, \ldots, x_n) = \sum_{i=1}^n x_i \alpha^{i-1}$ can also be seen as the first component of $(x_1, \ldots, x_n)\mathbf{M}_n$.

Linear Mappings and Matrices: The $\mathbb{F}_q$-linear polynomial $\mathbf{T}(X) = \sum_{i=0}^{n-1} t_i X^{q^i}$ over $\mathbb{F}_{q^n}$, can be represented by the matrix T given by:

$$T = (t_{i,j})_{i,j} = \mathbf{M}_n \begin{pmatrix} t_0^{\square} \\ \vdots \\ t_{n-1}^{\square} \end{pmatrix} \mathbf{M}_n^{-1}.$$

Proof. Let's write $\mathbf{T}(X) = \sum_{j=1}^n (\sum_{i=1}^n x_i t_{i,j})\alpha^{j-1}$ using the coordinates over $\mathbb{F}_q$ of $T(X)$. In one hand we have:

$$\mathbf{T}(X)^{\square} = X^{\square} \begin{pmatrix} t_0^{\square} \\ \vdots \\ t_{n-1}^{\square} \end{pmatrix}.$$

On the other hand, $\mathbf{T}(X)^{\square}\mathbf{M}_n^{-1} = (x_1, \ldots, x_n)(t_{i,j})$. Replacing $(x_1, \ldots, x_n)$ by $X^{\square}\mathbf{M}_n^{-1}$ gives

$$X^{\square}\mathbf{M}_n^{-1}(t_{i,j}) = X^{\square} \begin{pmatrix} t_0^{\square} \\ \vdots \\ t_{n-1}^{\square} \end{pmatrix} \mathbf{M}_n^{-1}.$$

Identifying and multiplying by $\mathbf{M}_n$ on the left gives the result. □

2.3 The HFE Cryptosystem

We describe here the HFE cryptosystem mostly as in [Pat96a]: the secret trapdoor is a univariate polynomial over a finite field $\mathbb{F}_{q^n}$:

$$H(X) = \sum_{0 \leq i,j \leq d} \alpha_{i,j} X^{q^i + q^j}. \quad (1)$$

There are two reasons for this special form. First d and mostly $D = q^d$ are chosen not too big so that any equation $H(X) = h$ can be solved efficiently[1], and second the polynomial H has only monomials of degrees that are sum of two powers of q, so that it has a multivariate representation over $\mathbb{F}_q$ that is quadratic.

There are two more elements in the secret key, they are bijective linear mappings, that can be represented as univariate polynomials over $\mathbb{F}_{q^n}$: $S(X) = \sum_{0 \leq i < n} s_i X^{q^i}$ and $T(X) = \sum_{0 \leq i < n} t_i X^{q^i}$. Finally, the public key is the composition

$$P = T \circ H \circ S, \quad (2)$$

where the structure of H is supposed to be hidden by S and T, and therefore P is deemed to be hard to invert without the knowledge of S and T. Equivalently, $\phi \circ P \circ \phi^{-1}$ can be used to describe the public key as a multivariate quadratic system of n equations in n variables.

The HFE polynomial can be used as a trapdoor function both for encryption and signature. The reason is that it is an almost bijective function: for a random h, the equation $H(X) = h$ has only one[2] solution with probability around e^{-1}.

Encryption: HFE can be used in encryption in the following way. Let a be the sender and b the receiver. a only has the public key P in its possession and wants to send the message $\mathbf{x} = \{x_1, \ldots, x_n\}$. b has the secret key. To encrypt a computes the vector $P(\mathbf{x}) = \{P_1(x_1, \ldots, x_n), \ldots, P_n(x_1, \ldots, x_n)\}$ and sends it to b. To decrypt

1. b inverts the linear map and T and uses the natural morphism to obtain $H(\phi(S(\mathbf{x})))$

[1] We assume simply here that the effective degree of H is between $q^d + 1$ and $2q^d$.

[2] When q is odd, an homogeneous equation has a even number of non zero solutions since $H(-X) = H(X)$.

2. b then uses an algorithm like Berlekamp to find $\phi(S(\mathbf{x}))$ (there may be an ambiguity in the value of $\phi(\mathbf{x})$ as H got several roots but a sends a small vector as well to help b decide which root is the right one).
3. Finally b invert S and ϕ to obtain the value of $\mathbf{x}$.

Signature: HFE can be used in signature in the following way. Let a be the signing party and b be the verifier. b only have the public key P in its possession a has the secret key and wants to sign a message $\mathbf{y}$.

At first a wants to sign the message $\mathbf{y} = \{y_1, \ldots, y_n\}$ to b

1. a must send a vector $\mathbf{x} = \{x_1, \ldots, x_n\}$ that verifies the property

$$\{P_1(x_1, \ldots x_n) = y_1, \ldots, P_n(x_1, \ldots, x_n) = y_n\}$$

2. a uses the private key obtain the problem $H(\phi(S(\mathbf{x}))) = \phi^{-1}(T^{-1}(\mathbf{y}))$, and then uses a root finding algorithm (such as Berlekamp algorithm) to find a solution $\mathbf{x}$.
3. a inverts S and ϕ to obtain a message $\mathbf{x}$ that verifies the property.
4. a send $\mathbf{x}$ to b and b uses the public key to check if

$$\{P_1(x_1, \ldots x_n) = y_1, \ldots, P_n(x_1, \ldots, x_n) = y_n\}.$$

3 Full Key Recovery Attack on HFE

The attacks described in this section aim to find an equivalent secret key for HFE. The goal is to exploit a rank defect in the HFE structure. Usually, the tool used is the resolution of a MinRank problem. Hence, we will make a full introduction of this problem and a way to solve it. In the rest of the paper, we will call this attack MinRank attack instead of Full key recovery attack by abuse of language.

3.1 Introduction to the MinRank Problem

Being one of the main tool used to attack HFE it is important to make a quick introduction to the MinRank problem. This problem was first introduced in [BFS99], the authors proved in this paper the NP-completeness of the problem. Then it was used by Kipnis and Shamir in [KS99] in order to attack "unmodified HFE". Since then, it remained a keystone in the Multivariate Quadratic (MQ) cryptography. It is a linear algebra problem that involves minimizing the rank of a linear combination of matrices.

The MinRank problem can be expressed this way:

Definition 1. *Let n, m, r, $k \in \mathbb{N}$ and let $\mathbf{M}_1, \mathbf{M}_2, \ldots \mathbf{M}_k$ $n \times m$ matrices over the field $\mathbb{F}$. The MinRank problem consists to find $u_1, u_2, \ldots u_k$ over $\mathbb{F}$ such that* $\mathrm{rank}(\sum_{i=1}^{k} u_i \mathbf{M}_i) \leq r$.

3.2 Resolution of the MinRank Problem

We will present here a quick explanation on the method used to solve the MinRank problem. We will only introduce the support-minors method as it is the one used nowadays. This technique was first introduced by Bardet *et al.* [BBB+22].

Let n, m, r, $k \in \mathbb{N}$ and let $\mathbf{M}_1, \mathbf{M}_2, \ldots \mathbf{M}_k$ be $n \times m$ matrices over the field $\mathbb{F}$. Let $\mathbf{M} = \sum_{i=1}^{k} u_i \mathbf{M}_i$ such that $\text{rank}(\mathbf{M}) \leq r$ then there exist $\mathbf{S}$ and $\mathbf{C}$ respectively of size $n \times r$ and $r \times m$ such that $\mathbf{M} = \mathbf{SC}$. If one considers $\mathbf{r}_j$ the j-th row of the matrix $\mathbf{M}$, then the rank of the matrix $\mathbf{R}_j = \binom{\mathbf{r}_j}{\mathbf{C}}$ is at most r. Therefore, all maximum minors of $\mathbf{R}_j$ all null, hence we have a new system where the unknown values are the u_i and the maximal minors of $\mathbf{C}$. The system is nonlinear but can be solved through linearization.

3.3 Application to HFE

First of all we will write the polynomial central map h in a matrix form, using the Macaulay writing meaning that we write $h(X) = \underline{X}\mathbf{H}\underline{X}^t$ where $\underline{X} = (X, X^q, \ldots, X^{q^{n-1}})$.

Lemma 1. *Let* $\mathbf{S}, \mathbf{T} \in M_{n \times n}(\mathbb{F}_q)$ *then the public key* P *can be written*

$$P = (\mathbf{P}_1, \ldots \mathbf{P}_n) = (\mathbf{SM}_n\mathbf{H}^{*0}\mathbf{M}_n^t\mathbf{S}^t, \ldots, \mathbf{SM}_n\mathbf{H}^{*n}\mathbf{M}_n^t\mathbf{S}^t)\mathbf{M}_n^{-1}\mathbf{T}$$

where $\mathbf{H}^{*i}$ *is the matrix representation of the* q^i*th power of the secret polynomial* h.

A detailed proof of this lemma can be found in [BFP11], it is essentially based on the formula of ϕ and ϕ^{-1}. The main problem in order to recover the secret key is to find either $\mathbf{T}$ or $\mathbf{S}$, once it is done it is relatively easy to find an equivalent key [BFP11,TPD21]. We can then extract two different MinRank problems on HFE, one attacking $\mathbf{S}$ the other attacking $\mathbf{T}$.

1. Attack on T. We will first show how to attack $\mathbf{T}$ [BFP11].

Let q, n, D be standard HFE parameters, $(\mathbf{P}_1, \ldots \mathbf{P}_n)$ the public key and $\mathbf{T}, \mathbf{S}, \mathbf{H}$ the secret key as defined earlier. Then we have

$$(\mathbf{P}_1, \ldots, \mathbf{P}_n) = (\mathbf{SM}_n\mathbf{H}^{*0}\mathbf{M}_n^t\mathbf{S}^t, \ldots, \mathbf{SM}_n\mathbf{H}^{*n}\mathbf{M}_n^t\mathbf{S}^t)\mathbf{M}_n^{-1}\mathbf{T}.$$

So we can write

$$(\mathbf{P}_1, \ldots \mathbf{P}_n)\mathbf{T}^{-1}\mathbf{M}_n = (\mathbf{SM}_n\mathbf{H}^{*0}\mathbf{M}_n^t\mathbf{S}^t, \ldots, \mathbf{SM}_n\mathbf{H}^{*n-1}\mathbf{M}_n^t\mathbf{S}^t).$$

We will write $\mathbf{U} = \mathbf{T}^{-1}\mathbf{M}_n$ and $\mathbf{W} = \mathbf{SM}_n$. Then we have

$$(\mathbf{P}_1, \ldots, \mathbf{P}_n)\mathbf{U} = (\mathbf{WH}^{*0}\mathbf{W}^t, \ldots, \mathbf{WH}^{*n}\mathbf{W}^t).$$

Let $(u_{0,0}, u_{1,0}, \ldots, u_{n-1,0})$ be the first column of $\mathbf{U}$ then we have

$$\sum_{i=0}^{n-1} u_{0,i}\mathbf{P}_i = \mathbf{WHW}^t.$$

Recall that

$$\mathbf{H} = \begin{pmatrix} \mathbf{A} & 0 \\ 0 & 0 \end{pmatrix}$$

where $\mathbf{A}$ is a matrix of size $d = \log_q(D)$. Hence

$$\mathrm{rank}(\sum_{i=0}^{n-1} u_{0,i}\mathbf{P}_i) = \log_q(D)$$

which is small so finding the first column of $\mathbf{U}$ reduces to solve a MinRank instance with $k = n$ and $r = \log_q(D)$ on the matrices $\mathbf{P}_1, \ldots, \mathbf{P}_n$.

Remark that the matrix product $\mathbf{T}^{-1}\mathbf{M}_n$ is special as finding the first column means finding the whole matrix because one has

$$\forall (i,j) \in \{0 \ldots n-1\} \times \{1 \ldots n-1\}\, u_{i,j} = u_{i,j-1}^q.$$

Hence, we are able to find $\mathbf{T}$ by solving the previous MinRank instance.

2. Attack on S. Now we can do a similar thing in order to attack $\mathbf{S}$. It was first proposed by Ward Beullens and by Tao *et al.* [TPD21].

Proposition 1. *Retaining the notations* $\mathbf{U}$ *and* $\mathbf{W}$ *from the previous attack, we have* $(\mathbf{P}_1, \ldots \mathbf{P}_{n-1}) = (\mathbf{W}\mathbf{H}^{*0}\mathbf{W}^t, \ldots, \mathbf{W}\mathbf{H}^{*n-1}\mathbf{W}^t)\mathbf{U}^{-1}$. *Then we obtain*

$$(\mathbf{W}^{-1}\mathbf{P}_1\mathbf{W}^{-1,t}, \ldots, \mathbf{W}^{-1}\mathbf{P}_{n-1}\mathbf{W}^{-1,t}) = (\mathbf{H}^{*0}, \ldots, \mathbf{H}^{*n-1})\mathbf{U}^{-1}.$$

If one notes $\mathbf{Q} = (\mathbf{U}^{-1})^t \begin{pmatrix} a_0 \\ \vdots \\ a_n \end{pmatrix}$ *where* a_i *is the first row of the matrix* $\mathbf{H}^{*i}$ *then* $\mathbf{Q} = (\mathbf{U}^{-1})^t \begin{pmatrix} \mathbf{A}_1 \\ 0 \\ \mathbf{A}_2 \end{pmatrix}$ *where* $\mathbf{A}_1$ *is an* $1 \times n$ *matrix, and* $\mathbf{A}_2$ *is a* $(d-1) \times n$ *matrix and* $\mathrm{rank}(\mathbf{Q}) \leq d$ *where* $d = \log_q(D)$.

Furthermore, using the proposition above and the matrix equation of HFE:

Theorem 1. *Let* $\mathbf{P}_1, \ldots, \mathbf{P}_n$ *matrices of the public key and* $\mathbf{W}$ *the matrix previously defined. If one notes* $(w_0^{-1}, w_1^{-1}, \ldots w_{n-1}^{-1})$ *the first row of the matrix* $\mathbf{W}^{-1}$, *and* $b_i = (w_0^{-1}, w_1^{-1}, \ldots w_{n-1}^{-1})\mathbf{P}_i$, *then the matrix* $\mathbf{Z}$ *whose rows are the* b_i *has a rank at most* d.

Proof. From the previous proposition we know that the rank of $\mathbf{Z}\mathbf{W}^{-1^t}$ is bounded by d, hence the rank of $\mathbf{Z}$ is bounded by d

We then have a MinRank attack on $\mathbf{S}$ with $\mathbf{P}_i$ as the matrices, d as the rank and w_i^{-1} as the target vector. Just like for $\mathbf{T}$, once we have the first row of $\mathbf{W}^{-1}$ we have the whole matrix. Hence, we can recover $\mathbf{S}$.

We will not describe how we recover the whole key once $\mathbf{T}$ or $\mathbf{S}$ is discovered as the complexity of the attack is mainly the complexity of solving the MinRank problem. For more details for the recovery of the totality of the key please refer to [BFP11,TPD21].

3. Complexity of the Attacks. The complexity of these attacks is the same, as they both only involve solving a MinRank problem. We have a complexity of $\mathcal{O}\left(d(n-1)^4\binom{2d+1}{d}^2\right)$ [BBC+22]. One may note that at first glance the two attacks are extremely similar, and it seems that there is no point having two of them. In fact, this is true for plain HFE, however when we consider variants of HFE we will see that there is often an attack that is more efficient than the other. It is also important to note that it is possible to use two or more variants at the same time, indeed published scheme like GeMSS were using two variants (vinegar and minus). Nevertheless in Sect. 5 we will only consider variants used alone.

3.4 About Characteristic 2

The MinRank attack requires a discussion on the characteristic on the field and on the parity of the rank of the HFE central map. Indeed, when used on characteristic 2, the resolution of the MinRank instance may yield too many solutions if the targeted rank is even. Then some of the solutions must be discarded as they do not yield an equivalent key. However, previous work on HFE like the paper [BFP11] found a variant of the attack that has the same complexity that we mentioned. So in the rest of the paper, we will not mention the special case of characteristic 2 as it will not change the complexity of the cryptanalysis.

4 Direct Attacks on HFE

In this section we will discuss direct attacks on HFE. The aim is not to find an equivalent key but rather to invert the system in order to find the original message or forge a signature. Many tools can be used like XL or Gröbner basis, but we will focus on the Gröbner basis approach. Usually instead of direct attack we call this attack Gröbner basis attack by abuse of language. We will not describe the main algorithms used nowadays (F4, F5 [Fau99] [Fau02]) rather present the general ideas on Gröbner basis. Let I be an ideal of $\mathbb{F}[X_1, X_2, \dots X_n]$ where $\mathbb{F}$ is a field. Basically a Gröbner basis is a set of polynomials G that are generator of I. We add a few properties to make this set G unique for each ideal I. The set G depends on the order you take on the monomials. For our purpose the important order will be the lexicographic order. Indeed this order gives the property that the set G forms a triangular system, in other words if one considers a set of polynomials $\{P_1(x_1, \dots, x_n), \dots, P_k(x_1, \dots, x_n)\}$ then the lexicographic Gröbner basis of the ideal generated by the P_i will be of the form: $G = \{G_1(x_1), G_2(x_1, x_2), \dots G_m(x_1, \dots x_n)\}$. Hence it can be used to find a solution $(x_1, \dots, x_n)$ of a system

$$\begin{aligned} P_1(x_1, \dots, x_n) &= y_1 \\ P_2(x_1, \dots, x_n) &= y_2 \\ &\vdots \\ P_k(x_1, \dots, x_n) &= y_k. \end{aligned}$$

Indeed let $G = \{G_1(X_1), G_2(X_1, X_2), \dots G_m(X_1, \dots X_n)\}$ be the Gröbner basis of the ideal generated by $P_1(X_1, \dots, X_n) - y_1, \dots, P_k(X_1, \dots, X_n) - y_k$. We then have an equivalent system of equation:

$$\begin{aligned} G_1(x_1) &= 0 \\ G_2(x_1, x_2) &= 0 \\ &\vdots \\ G_m(x_1, \dots, x_n) &= 0. \end{aligned}$$

So the resolution is simply to find first x_1 as root of $G_1(X)$ (with an algorithm like Cantor-Zassenhauss for finite fields [CZ81]), then the roots of the polynomial $G_2(x_1, X)$ and so on. In other words, Gröbner bases can be used to solve multivariate systems of polynomials. We can then use Gröbner bases to attack HFE and its variants. It will not be a full key recovery like MinRank attacks but rather a forgery tool in the case of signature or a plain text recovery in the case of encryption.

The complexity of the computation of a Gröbner basis is hard to determine. Indeed we can write the complexity as $\mathcal{O}\binom{n+d_{reg}}{n}^{\omega}$, ($\omega$ is the linear algebra constant, usually we consider $\omega \approx 2.81$). The problem is to determine the value of d_{reg} or "degree of regularity".

Definition 2 [DS13]. *We define $B = \mathbb{F}[X_1, \dots, X_n]/\langle X_1{}^q, \dots, X_n{}^q \rangle$ and B_d it's degree d subspace. Let P be a set of homogeneous polynomial $P = \{P_1, \dots, P_m\} \subset B_2^m$.*

Let ψ_d be the map $\psi_d : B_d^m \to B_{d+2}$ defined as

$$\psi(b_1, \dots, b_m) = \sum_{i=1}^{m} b_i P_i$$

Then

$$R_d(P_1, \dots, P_m) := \ker(\psi_d).$$

Further let $T_d(P_1, \dots, P_m)$ be the subspace of trivial relations generated by the elements

$$\{b(P_i e_j - P_j e_i) | 1 \le i < j \le m, b \in B_{d-2}\},$$

and

$$\{b(P_i^{q-1})e_i | 1 \le i \le m, b \in B_{d-2(q-1)}\}.$$

Here e_i means the i-th unit vector consisting of all zeros except 1 at the i-th position $e_i = (0,\ldots,0,1,0,\ldots,0)$. The degree of regularity of a homogeneous quadratic set is then

$$Dreg(P_1,\ldots,P_m) := min\{d|R_{d-2}(P_1,\ldots,P_m)/T_{d-2}(P_1,\ldots,P_m) \neq \{0\}\}.$$

For a general system of polynomial, it is not possible to compute the degree of regularity without computing the Gröbner basis. However in the case of HFE, it is possible to find an upper bound for the degree of regularity [DY13]. The upper bound Ding and Yang have found is: $\frac{(q-1)(d-1)}{2} + 2$ if q is even and d is odd, $\frac{(q-1)d}{2} + 2$ otherwise ($d = \log_q(D)$). This upper bound is close to real values of degree of regularity. Although this upper bound is as tight as possible, Petzoldt [Pet17] has found a lower bound allowing us to have a more precise idea on the value of the degree of regularity. Indeed for $q = 2$ we have $d_{reg} \geq \lfloor \frac{d}{3} \rfloor + 2$. We will keep this value for the rest of the paper.

5 Variants of HFE

5.1 Vinegar (v) Variant

The first modifier that we will consider is v. It adds variables y_i into the system. The v stands for vinegar, in an analogue to the scheme UOV (Unbalanced Oil and Vinegar). To decipher one will fix the vinegar variables and solve the system. We can define this modifier that way:

Definition 3. *Let $v \in \mathbb{N}$ and $y = (y_1,\ldots,y_v)$, then the new secret polynomial $f : \mathbb{F}_{q^n} \times \mathbb{F}_q^v \to \mathbb{F}_{q^n}$ is of the form:*

$$\sum_{i,j \in \mathbb{N}, q^i+q^j \leq D} \alpha_i X^{q^i+q^j} + \sum_{i, q^i \leq D} \beta_i(y) X^{q^i} + \gamma(y)$$

where $\beta_i : \mathbb{F}_q^v \to \mathbb{F}_{q^n}$ are linear maps and $\gamma : \mathbb{F}_q^v \to \mathbb{F}_{q^n}$ is a quadratic map. So the central map becomes $\tilde{\mathbf{H}} = \begin{pmatrix} \mathbf{H} & A \\ B & C \end{pmatrix}$. where $\mathbf{A}$, $\mathbf{B}$, $\mathbf{C}$ are random matrices. remark however that $\mathbf{A} = \begin{pmatrix} 0 & 0 \\ \mathbf{A}' & 0 \end{pmatrix}$ where $\mathbf{A}$' is a block of size $d \times v$,

$\mathbf{B} = \begin{pmatrix} 0 & \mathbf{B}' \\ 0 & 0 \end{pmatrix}$ where $\mathbf{B}$' is a block of size $v \times d$ and $\mathbf{C}$ a matrix of size $v \times v$ hence the rank of the matrix $\tilde{\mathbf{H}}$ is $d + v$.

Furthermore, the linear transformations must also change accordingly. Indeed $\mathbf{S}$ is now a full rank linear map $\mathbb{F}_q^{n+v} \to \mathbb{F}_q^{n+v}$. $\mathbf{T}$ remains unchanged. If we use the previous notation $\mathbf{U}$ and $\mathbf{W}$ recall that $\mathbf{W} = \mathbf{S}\mathbf{M}_n$ and $\mathbf{U} = \mathbf{T}^{-1}\mathbf{M}_n$. Obviously as $\mathbf{S}$ is no more of size n, $\mathbf{M}_n$ in $\mathbf{W}$ must change. So $\mathbf{W}$ becomes $\mathbf{W} = \mathbf{S}\tilde{\mathbf{M}}_n$ where $\tilde{\mathbf{M}}_n = \begin{pmatrix} \mathbf{M_n} & 0 \\ 0 & \mathbf{I}_v \end{pmatrix}$.

We can note that $\mathbf{U}$ remains unchanged.

This variant has negligible cost when used in signature as the signer only needs to solve a system $z = H_v(x)$ where H_v is the central map of a HFEv. In order to do so he simply fixes randomly the variable v until he is able to find a solution to the rest of the system.

However, this variant is costly in encryption. In order to decrypt the system, one must find the exact x that works hence he needs to do a exhaustive search on the y_i which means a cost of q^v times the complexity of HFE it means that it is extremely costly in encryption.

To make a cryptanalysis of this variant we can do an attack on $\mathbf{S}$. We use the equation we wrote in the previous Sect. 3 but with the new $\mathbf{W} = \mathbf{S}\tilde{\mathbf{M}}_n$:

$$(\mathbf{W}^{-1}\mathbf{P}_1\mathbf{W}^{-1,t}, \ldots, \mathbf{W}^{-1}\mathbf{P}_{n-1}\mathbf{W}^{-1,t}) = (\mathbf{H}^{*0}, \ldots, \mathbf{H}^{*n-1})\mathbf{U}^{-1}.$$

However the matrix $\mathbf{Q}$ previously defined is still of the form: $\mathbf{Q} = (\mathbf{U}^{-1})^t \begin{pmatrix} \mathbf{A}_1 \\ 0 \\ \mathbf{A}_2 \end{pmatrix}$, thus the rank has not changed ($r = d$). The only difference is the number of equations we get, indeed we now have $(n+v)\binom{2d+1}{d}$ equations. It leads to a slight increase in complexity, which is now $\mathcal{O}\left(dn(n+v-1)^3\binom{2d+1}{d}^2\right)$.

If we had done the attack on the other way meaning that we try to break $\mathbf{T}$ we would have had: $(\mathbf{P}_0, \ldots, \mathbf{P}_{n-1})\mathbf{U} = (\mathbf{W}\tilde{\mathbf{H}}^{*0}\mathbf{W}^t, \ldots, \mathbf{W}\tilde{\mathbf{H}}^{*n}\mathbf{W}^t)$. As stated earlier the rank of the matrix $\tilde{\mathbf{H}}^{*0}$ is now $r = d + v$. Which means we now have a complexity of $\mathcal{O}\left((d+v)(n-1)^4\binom{2(d+v)+1}{d+v}^2\right)$.

If we look at the direct attack (Gröbner basis), it seems that the result resembles what was found for the MinRank attack on $\mathbf{T}$. Indeed one should replace d by $d+v$ in the formula we introduced in Sect. 4 $\frac{(q-1)(d+v-1)}{2} + 2$ if q is even and d is odd, $\frac{(q-1)(d+v)}{2} + 2$ otherwise. The lower bound becomes for $q = 2$, $d_{reg} \geq \lfloor \frac{d+v}{3} \rfloor + 2$.

5.2 Minus

The variant $-$ is simply a suppression of some polynomials of the public key of a unmodified HFE. For example if the public key of a HFE is $P = (\mathbf{P}_0, \ldots, \mathbf{P}_{n-1})$ then the public key a HFE$-$ will be $P_- = (\mathbf{P}_0, \mathbf{P}_1, \ldots, \mathbf{P}_{n-1-a})$ where a is the number of equations that were suppressed. If we rewrite it in a matrix form it simply means that T is a full rank linear map ${\mathbb{F}_q}^n \to {\mathbb{F}_q}^{n-a}$. $\mathbf{S}$ and $\mathbf{M}_n$ remains unchanged.

This variant cost is almost negligible when using HFE in signature as the signer can randomly complete the matrix $\mathbf{T}$ to make it invertible and solve it like a unmodified HFE. Indeed, this variant does not change the central map.

However, this variant is costly in encryption. In order to decrypt the system, one must find the exact x that works hence he needs to do a exhaustive search on the missing polynomials it means a cost of q^a times the complexity of HFE it means that it is extremely costly in encryption.

We can try an attack on $\mathbf{T}$: we however cannot write

$$(\mathbf{P}_0, \ldots, \mathbf{P}_{n-1})\mathbf{U} = (\mathbf{W}\mathbf{H}^{*0}\mathbf{W}^t, \ldots, \mathbf{W}\mathbf{H}^{*n}\mathbf{W}^t)$$

as $\mathbf{U}$ is not invertible any more we can however rewrite $T = T^+ \circ L_a$ where $T^+ : \mathbb{F}_q{}^n \to \mathbb{F}_q{}^n$ is a bijective extension of T and L_a is a linear polynomial of degree q^a. It means that our central map is equivalent to a standard HFE with $D' = q^a D$ [VS17]. We note $\tilde{H} = L_a \circ H$. So we now have

$$(\mathbf{P}_0, \ldots, \mathbf{P}_{n-1})\mathbf{T}^{+^{-1}}\mathbf{M}_n = (\mathbf{W}\tilde{\mathbf{H}}^{*0}\mathbf{W}^t, \ldots, \mathbf{W}\tilde{\mathbf{H}}^{*n}\mathbf{W}^t).$$

We have now the same equation as in Proposition 2 but with a target rank of $r = d + a$. So the complexity is now: $\mathcal{O}\left((d+a)(n-1)^4\binom{2(d+a)+1}{d+a}^2\right)$.

We can also try an attack on $\mathbf{S}$: as in [BBC+22] we can write

$$(\mathbf{W}^{-1}\mathbf{P}_1\mathbf{W}^{-1,t}, \ldots, \mathbf{W}^{-1}\mathbf{P}_{n-1}\mathbf{W}^{-1,t}) = (\mathbf{H}^{*0}, \ldots, \mathbf{H}^{*n-1})\mathbf{U}^{-1}.$$

However this time the rank on the right has not changed ($r = d$) so we have the exact same attack so the complexity is still

$$\mathcal{O}\left(d(n-1)^4\binom{2d+1}{d}^2\right).$$

If we look at the direct attack (Gröbner), it seems that the result resembles what was found for the MinRank attack on $\mathbf{T}$. Indeed one should replace d by $d + a$ in the upper bound we introduced in Sect. 4 $\frac{(q-1)(d+a-1)}{2} + 2$ if q is even and $d + a$ is odd, $\frac{(q+a)(d)}{2} + 2$ otherwise. The lower bound becomes for $q = 2$, $d_{reg} \geq \lfloor \frac{d+a}{3} \rfloor + 2$.

5.3 Plus

The variant + adds random equations on the public key. This means that if $P = (\mathbf{P}_0, \ldots, \mathbf{P}_{n-1})$ is the public key then the public key of HFE+ is $P_+ = (\mathbf{P}_0, \ldots, \mathbf{P}_{n-1}, \mathbf{P}_n, \ldots, \mathbf{P}_{n-1+k})$ where $P_i, n < i : \mathbb{F}_q \to \mathbb{F}_q$ and k the number of added equations. Note that the equations of the public key are then linearly mixed.

This variant has a negligible cost in encryption, as to decipher one can ignore the added equations. So, it can be inverted. However, it costs q^k in signature because one must first solve the system ignoring the added polynomials and then check if it is compatible with the added polynomials. Obviously as the n first polynomials remain untouched by the modifiers we can still find a linear combination of the n first polynomials of small rank. Hence, we can find a combination of all the polynomials of small rank.

5.4 Projection

The variant p or projection [CS17] consists in replacing the map $S : \mathbb{F}_q{}^n \to \mathbb{F}_q{}^n$ by $S = L \circ S' : \mathbb{F}_q{}^{n-p} \to \mathbb{F}_q{}^n$ where $S' : \mathbb{F}_q{}^{n-p} \to \mathbb{F}_q{}^{n-p}$ is full rank and $L : \mathbb{F}_q{}^{n-p} \to \mathbb{F}_q{}^n$ is a linear polynomial of degree p that is also full rank. This time $\mathbf{W} = \mathbf{S}'\mathbf{M}_n$.

The complexity of this variant in encryption, is almost the same as a plain HFE as to decipher one can ignore the modifier because it is an injective linear map. So it can be inverted. However it costs a factor q^p in signature because one must first solve the system ignoring the projection and then check if it is compatible with the projection.

We can try an attack on $\mathbf{S}$: we can write

$$(\mathbf{W}^{-1}\mathbf{P}_1\mathbf{W}^{-1,t}, \dots, \mathbf{W}^{-1}\mathbf{P}_{n-1}\mathbf{W}^{-1,t}) = (\mathbf{L}\mathbf{H}^{*0}\mathbf{L}^t, \dots, \mathbf{L}\mathbf{H}^{*n-1}\mathbf{L}^t)\mathbf{U}^{-1}.$$

Indeed, taking the first row of each matrix on the right, we have now the same equation as in Proposition 3 but with a target rank of $r = d + p$. So the complexity is now: $\mathcal{O}\left((d+p)(n-1)^4\binom{2(d+p)+1}{d+p}^2\right)$ [BBC+22]. However, if we do an attack on $\mathbf{T}$, the equation becomes $(\mathbf{P}_0, \dots, \mathbf{P}_{n-1})\mathbf{U} = (\mathbf{W}\mathbf{L}\mathbf{H}^{*0}\mathbf{L}^t\mathbf{W}^t, \dots, \mathbf{W}\mathbf{L}\mathbf{H}^{*n}\mathbf{L}^t\mathbf{W}^t)$ and the targeted rank is the rank of the matrix $\mathbf{W}\mathbf{L}\mathbf{H}^{*0}\mathbf{L}^t\mathbf{W}^t$. However, the p modifier does not change the rank of the central map. Indeed the rank of $\mathbf{H}$ is at most d so the rank of $\mathbf{W}\mathbf{L}\mathbf{H}^{*0}\mathbf{L}^t\mathbf{W}^t$ is at most $r = d$ because it is a matrix product. So the complexity is $\mathcal{O}\left(d(n-1)^4\binom{2d+1}{d}^2\right)$.

5.5 Internal Plus ($\hat{+}$)

In this section we are going to describe the internal plus ($\hat{+}$) variant as introduced in the paper [FmRPP22]. It adds new equations internally in order to increase the rank of the central map. Formally, let t be the parameter of the modifier, let $\beta_i \in \mathbb{F}_{q^n}$ for $i \in \{1 \dots t\}$ be random elements, and $\hat{p}_i(x) = \mathrm{Tr}_n\left(\sum_{j,k} \alpha_{i,j,k} x^{q^j+q^k}\right)$ where $\alpha_{i,j,k}$ are random element of $\mathbb{F}_{q^n}$ and let $Q(x) = \sum_i \beta_i \hat{p}_i(x)$. The central map of the modifier is $F(x) = H(x) + Q(x)$ where $H(x)$ is the central map of a "unmodified HFE" and $Q(x)$ the polynomial previously defined.

The degree of $F(x)$ is much greater than the degree of $H(x)$. Due to the presence of $Q(x)$ it will be q^{n-1}. It means that direct methods of resolution such as Berlekamp algorithm are no longer possible. We can however use the fact that $\hat{p}_i(x)$ is a polynomial in $\mathbb{F}_q$ so we can make an exhaustive search of the value of each $\hat{p}_i(x)$ which means that $Q(x)$ can take at most q^t possibilities. Thus we end up with a variant q^t times slower in decryption or signature than a "unmodified" HFE.

It is important to note that the rank of the central map is very likely to be maximal even with a small t since β_i are chosen randomly hence the polynomial $F(x)$ can have a very high degree. However, it does not mean that MinRank attacks will not work. We have:

$$(\mathbf{P}_1, \dots \mathbf{P}_n) = (\mathbf{W}\mathbf{F}^{*0}\mathbf{W}^t, \dots, \mathbf{W}\mathbf{F}^{*n-1}\mathbf{W}^t)\mathbf{U}^{-1},$$

which gives

$$(\mathbf{W}^{-1}\mathbf{P}_1\mathbf{W}^{-1,t},\ldots,\mathbf{W}^{-1}\mathbf{P}_n\mathbf{W}^{-1,t}) = (\mathbf{F}^{*0},\ldots,\mathbf{F}^{*n-1})\mathbf{U}^{-1}.$$

Let us note $\mathbf{Z} = (\mathbf{U}^{-1})^t \begin{pmatrix} \mathbf{a}_0 \\ \vdots \\ \mathbf{a}_n \end{pmatrix}$ where $\mathbf{a}_i$ is the first row of the matrix $\mathbf{F}^{*i}$. Recall that for previous attacks on $\mathbf{S}$ we had:

$\mathbf{Z} = (\mathbf{U}^{-1})^t \begin{pmatrix} \mathbf{A}_1 \\ 0 \\ \mathbf{A}_2 \end{pmatrix}$. Unfortunately, it is no longer the case. Indeed, the matrix that represents $\mathbf{F}$ is now full. However, we can decompose $\mathbf{F} = \mathbf{H} + \mathbf{Q}$. Then $\mathbf{Z} = (\mathbf{U}^{-1})^t \times \left(\begin{pmatrix} \mathbf{A}_1 \\ 0 \\ \mathbf{A}_2 \end{pmatrix} + \begin{pmatrix} \mathbf{q}_0 \\ \vdots \\ \mathbf{q}_n \end{pmatrix} \right)$.

The Froebenius operation being linear we will study the matrix $\begin{pmatrix} \mathbf{q}_0 \\ \vdots \\ \mathbf{q}_n \end{pmatrix}$ separately.

We can write that $\mathbf{q}_i$ is the first row of the matrix $\sum_{i=0}^{t} \beta_i^{q^i} \mathbf{Q}_i$. Indeed $\mathbf{Q}_i$ is the representative matrix of the polynomial $\hat{p}_i(x)$ whose image is in $\mathbb{F}_q$. Hence the polynomial is unchanged by the Froebenius.

It means that the rank of the matrix $\mathbf{Q}$ is at most t and thus the rank of the matrix $\begin{pmatrix} \mathbf{A}_1 \\ 0 \\ \mathbf{A}_2 \end{pmatrix} + \begin{pmatrix} \mathbf{q}_0 \\ \vdots \\ \mathbf{q}_n \end{pmatrix}$ is at most $r = d + t$.

So the complexity of the attack is the complexity of a MinRank whose target rank is $r = d + t$: $\mathcal{O}\left((d+t)(n-1)^4 \binom{2(d+t)+1}{d+t}^2\right)$.

The attack on $\mathbf{T}$ remains quite unchanged as all the previous equations applies however the rank of the central map $\mathbf{H}$ is now $r = d + t$ so we obtain the same complexity as the attack on $\mathbf{T}$: $\mathcal{O}\left((d+t)(n-1)^4 \binom{2(d+t)+1}{d+t}^2\right)$.

5.6 Internal Perturbation

The idea of this modifier is similar to the vinegar modifier, it was first introduced in [DS05]. We add a variable Y that is linear combination of X variable, that combination should be of small rank to be able to invert the system. So we have a linear map $Z : \mathbb{F}_{q^n} \to \mathbb{F}_{q^n}$ of low rank π. Then the central map $f : \mathbb{F}_{q^n} \to \mathbb{F}_{q^n}$ is of the form: $\sum_{i,j\in\mathbb{N}, q^i+q^j \leq D} \alpha_i X^{q^i+q^j} + \sum_{i,q^i\leq D} \beta_i(Y) X^{q^i} + \bar{P}(Y)$ where $\beta_i : \mathbb{F}_{q^n} \to \mathbb{F}_{q^n}$ are linear maps and $\bar{P} : \mathbb{F}_{q^n} \to \mathbb{F}_{q^n}$ is a quadratic map and $Y = Z(X)$. A description of this modifier can be found in [DS05].

To decrypt one must try to solve the system without the modifier and hope it will nullify the modifier as well, meaning an increase of a factor q^π times the complexity to decrypt or to sign compared to "unmodified HFE".

In terms of rank, it means that the rank of the central map has increased by π. It means that when attacking $\mathbf{T}$ the target rank will be the one of the central maps. It means that the attack the complexity will be:

$$\mathcal{O}\left((d+\pi)(n-1)^4\binom{2(d+\pi)+1}{d+\pi}^2\right).$$

However, the effect is drastically different when attacking via $\mathbf{S}$. Indeed, recall that when attacking S one consider the rank of the matrix $\mathbf{Q} = (\mathbf{U}^{-1})^t \begin{pmatrix} \mathbf{a}_0 \\ \vdots \\ \mathbf{a}_n \end{pmatrix}$ where $\mathbf{a}_i$ is the first row of the matrix F^{*i}. Although the rank of the F^{*i} is $d+\pi$ the matrix F^{*i} is full. Indeed, the polynomial $F(X)$ have a degree $q^n - 1$. Thus, one cannot write $\mathbf{Q} = (\mathbf{U}^{-1})^t \begin{pmatrix} \mathbf{A}_1 \\ 0 \\ \mathbf{A}_2 \end{pmatrix}$.

We cannot evaluate easily the rank of $\mathbf{Q}$, but we have observed that for small values of $\pi = (1, 2, 3, 4, 5)$ the rank of $\mathbf{Q}$ is far greater than $d + \pi$. For example, for $n = 20, q = 2, D = 9, \pi = 1$ we observe that the rank of $\mathbf{Q}$ is between 11 and 15 far greater than $d + \pi = 5$. Overall, we have observed that for $1 < \pi$ the rank of the matrix $\mathbf{Q}$ is above $n/2$. It is the rank we will retain for our complexity evaluation (when π grows the rank quickly becomes far above $n/2$).

It is important to note that there is another type of attack specific to this variant. Dubois *et al.* [DGS07] have found a differential attack on this variant. They can make a recovery of the kernel of the linear map Z. Once the linear map is discovered, the internal perturbation can be negated. In the following section we will note $DP_{\mathbf{y}}(x) = P(a+x) - P(x) - P(a) + P(0)$ as the discrete differential of P in the vector $\mathbf{y}$ The key to this attack is the following observation:

- If $\mathbf{a}$ is a vector that is not in the kernel of Z then the differential of the public key in $\mathbf{a}$ will be written with the form: $D\tilde{P_{\mathbf{a}}}(x) = DP_{\mathbf{a}}(x) + M(x, Z(\mathbf{a})) + M(\mathbf{a}, Z(x)) + D\bar{P}_{Z(\mathbf{a})}(Z(x))$, where $\tilde{P}$ is the public key, P is the public key without the internal perturbation, M the mixing part and $\bar{P}$ the polynomial in y.
- However when $\mathbf{a}$ is in $\ker(Z)$ then $D\tilde{P_{\mathbf{a}}}(x) = DP_{\mathbf{a}}(x) + M(\mathbf{a}, Z(x))$.

Clearly the two forms are quite different. Hence the authors are using these differences to create a non-deterministic distinguisher that can detect whether or not an element $\mathbf{a}$ is in $\ker(Z)$. In order to make a recovery of the kernel to obtain n distinct element of $\ker(Z)$, and the number of element that are in $\ker(Z)$ is $q^{n-\pi}$ so the number of utilisation of the distinguisher is about $n \times q^{\pi+1}$. The complexity of the attack is then $n \times q^{\pi+1}N$. where N is the complexity of the distinguisher.

The complexity of the distinguisher is difficult to describe briefly. Indeed its calculation is not given by a simple direct formula but requires to solve linear systems. Nonetheless our tests showed that on modern parameters the complexity is high. More details on this matter can be found on the paper [DGS07]. We have computed the complexity of the attack and found that for parameters of HFE with $q = 2$, $n = 177$, $D = 17$ (one can note we used red-GeMSS-128 parameters where we got rid of the modifiers used in GeMSS) with a rank of the internal perturbation of (1, 2, 3, 4, 5). Our results are recapped in Table 1

Table 1. Complexity of the attack from [DGS07] on HFEIP with $q = 2$, $n = 177$, $D = 17$, the complexity are given in $\log_2$.

IP	complexity
1	106.26
2	130.92
3	150.20
4	173.58
5	196.70

It means that with few of these modifiers we have attacks less effective than MinRank attacks.

We can also look at a Gröbner basis perspective. This variant is very similar to the v variant so the degree of regularity is the same. Indeed one should replace $d + v$ by $d + \pi$ in the formula we introduced in Sect. 4: $\frac{(q-1)(d+\pi-1)}{2} + 2$ if q is even and d is odd, $\frac{(q-1)(d+\pi)}{2} + 2$ otherwise [DY13]. Although the lower bound was not computed in [Pet17] we can easily conjecture that it will be for $q = 2$, $d_{reg} \geq \lfloor \frac{r+\pi}{3} \rfloor + 2$ due to the similarities with v variant.

In Table 2 we have recapped all complexity results. On the rows we have each variant, and the type of attack by column table of all results:

Table 2. Table of the complexity of each attack on each variant, for the Gröbner Basis column we have not written the complexity but the upper bound of the degree of regularity so the real complexity is $\mathcal{O}(\binom{n+d_{reg}}{n}^{\omega})$. Empty cells correspond to unknown complexity. Here $n_p = n - 1$, $d_a = d + a$, $d_p = d + p$, $d_t = d + t$, $d_\pi = d + \pi$.

	MinRank T	MinRank S	Gröbner basis
v	$\mathcal{O}\left(d_v(n_p)^4\binom{2(d_v)+1}{d}^2\right)$	$\mathcal{O}\left(d(n_p+v)^4\binom{2d+1}{d}^2\right)$	$\frac{(q-1)(d+v)}{2}+2$
+	$\mathcal{O}\left(d(n_p)^4\binom{2d+1}{d}^2\right)$	$\mathcal{O}\left(d(n_p)^4\binom{2d+1}{d}^2\right)$	
−	$\mathcal{O}\left((d_a)(n_p)^4\binom{2(d_a)+1}{d_a}^2\right)$	$\mathcal{O}\left(d(n_p)^4\binom{2d+1}{d}^2\right)$	$\frac{(q-1)(d+a)}{2}+2$
p	$\mathcal{O}\left(d(n_p)^4\binom{2d+1}{d}^2\right)$	$\mathcal{O}\left((d_t)(n_p)^4\binom{2(d_t)+1}{d+t}^2\right)$	
$\hat{+}$	$\mathcal{O}\left((d_t)(n_p)^4\binom{2(d_t)+1}{d+t}^2\right)$	$\mathcal{O}\left((d_p)(n_p)^4\binom{2(d_p)+1}{d_p}^2\right)$	
IP	$\mathcal{O}\left((d_\pi)(n_p)^4\binom{2(d_\pi)+1}{d_\pi}^2\right)$	$\mathcal{O}\left((n/2)(n_p)^4\binom{2(n/2)+1}{n/2}^2\right)$	$\frac{(q-1)(d+\pi)}{2}+2$

Table 3 shows the cost to sign/encrypt of every variant. These costs do limit the combinations we are able to use without making the scheme too slow.

6 On the Security of *p*HFE*v*−

The HFE*v*− combination has already been explored for signature schemes, for example in the GeMSS NIST-PQ submission [CFMR+20]. This scheme has later

Table 3. Table of the cost of each variant in order to sign or encrypt a message depending of the parameter of the said variant

	Signature	Decryption
v	$\mathcal{O}(1)$	$\mathcal{O}(q^v)$
+	$\mathcal{O}(q^t)$	$\mathcal{O}(1)$
−	$\mathcal{O}(1)$	$\mathcal{O}(q^a)$
p	$\mathcal{O}(q^p)$	$\mathcal{O}(1)$
$\hat{+}$	$\mathcal{O}(q^t)$	$\mathcal{O}(q^t)$
IP	$\mathcal{O}(q^\pi)$	$\mathcal{O}(q^\pi)$

been broken in [BBC+22]. The projection variant that we introduced earlier was quite recently used to try to repair HFE*v*− and GeMSS [CFMR+20]. This reparation was first mentioned in [ØSV21]. The new scheme would have been called *p*HFE*v*−. The reason for this scheme was to counter attacks on **S** because both variant v and minus don't have any effect on this attack. However, with the projection modifier the rank of the matrix we were attacking is increased by p (projection parameter). Nonetheless as GeMSS is a signature scheme, the use of the projection variant induces an increase of the complexity of the signature by a factor q^p. Hence in order to have an efficient scheme, p must remain small. But improvement of **S** attacks discovered by [BBC+22] made *p*HFE*v*− again vulnerable. For example, for GeMSS-128 parameters we would require $p = 15$ to be again above 128 bits of security. It means a signature 2^{15} slower than GeMSS. With GeMSS specification we can make the estimation that it would require $24576000M$ of cycles to sign ($M = 10^6$). Obviously, these times are completely unrealistic. Hence *p*HFE*v*− was discarded.

7 New Scheme

7.1 Design Rationale

The problem we had with all previous schemes was that either a MinRank attack on **S** or **T** was threatening for their security. Technically for all attacks there exist a countermeasure, but the problem was the cost in complexity of the countermeasure. To be more specific when we use HFE in signature then we can use variants like – (minus) that will easily counter attacks through **T** because – is not costly in signature. However, it is hard to defend from attacks on **S** as we can totally negate – and variants that counter attacks on **S** are very costly in signature. On the other hand, in encryption, we can easily counter attacks on **S** with variants like p however all variants that protect **T** are very costly.

Nevertheless, the internal perturbation variant may lead to a new signature scheme. Indeed, as we have found it is highly effective against attacks on **S** with little modifier required. It means that we can have a small rank π for **Z** between 3 and 5 and avoid all attacks through **S** which means a reasonable increase of the complexity of the signature by a factor q^{π}.

On the other hand, we can avoid attacks on **T** by adding a lot of – modifier. Indeed, as we mentioned earlier the – modifier is not costly at all in signature and it is effective against attacks on **T**.

So our idea is to uses both of these modifiers in order to make a new signature scheme based of HFE.

In order to further reduce the signature size without being vulnerable to a meet in the middle attack, we are using the Feistel-Patarin Technique like, for example, GeMSS. This technique was introduced in [Cou03] as a solution to obtain short signatures. Its principle is, as the name suggests, inspired from a Feistel Scheme.

Naively the signature of a HFE scheme is built in the following way: given a message $\mathbf{y}$, one needs to find a vector $\mathbf{x}$ such that $P(\mathbf{x}) = B(\mathbf{y})$, where B is a hash function. In order to avoid generic attacks such as meet-in-the-middle attacks or collision attacks on B, we need to choose n to be at least two times the security parameter. Let us now describe how the 2-round Feistel-Patarin technique can improve signature sizes.

For now, we will consider that $m = n$. By abuse of language we note $P^{-1}(\mathbf{y})$ a solution $\mathbf{x}$ of the problem $P(\mathbf{x}) = \mathbf{y}$. Dividing the hash of $\mathbf{y}$ in two pieces $B(\mathbf{y}) = (B_1(\mathbf{y}), B_2(\mathbf{y}))$, the signature of $\mathbf{y}$ would be $\mathbf{x} = B_1(\mathbf{y}) \oplus P^{-1}(B_2(\mathbf{y}) \oplus P^{-1}(B_1(\mathbf{y})))$. We can easily see the similarity with a Feistel scheme with two rounds. Hence, this definition can easily be extended to a higher number of rounds.

However in the case of our scheme we have $m < n$, which creates an issue of dimension in the definition we gave. Indeed, $P^{-1}(B_1(\mathbf{y}))$ has a size of n but $B_2(\mathbf{y})$ is of size $m < n$ due to the use of the minus modifier. It means that it misses some bits, and that we will need to give for each round k the missing bits a_k as part of the signature. We will then obtain $\mathbf{x} = (B_1(\mathbf{y})||a_2) \oplus P^{-1}((B_2(\mathbf{y})||a_1) \oplus P^{-1}(B_1(\mathbf{y})))$. Overall, the signature will be $\mathbf{x}||a_1||a_2||\ldots||a_r$ each a_i has a length of a the number of missing equations. We can then compute the length of the signature in bits by $(n-a) + Nb_{ite} \times a$ where N_{ite} is the number of rounds used in the Feistel-Patarin.

7.2 Parameters

One of the advantages of the scheme HFE is the fact that we can get short signatures. Already in 2020 Bros *et al.* [PMBK20] tried to optimize HFE and variants parameters in order to get the shortest possible signatures.

We propose 8 sets of parameters that we can regroup in two groups of four. The first group is a set of parameters for each expected security 80, 128, 192, 256 bits that tries to optimize the size of the signature but with no regard to the time to sign. The nomenclature of the scheme will be "HFE$^s IP-$ *" where s stands for Short Signature and * the expected security. The second group of four set of parameters for each expected security 80, 128, 192, 256 that tries to optimize the size of the signature but with reasonable time to sign. The nomenclature of the scheme will be "HFE$^f IP-$ *" where f stands for Fast Signature and * the expected security.

Table 4. Parameter and performance of a HFE$^s IP-$ schemes

Name	param. (q, n, D, π, a)	Cycles to sign	$\|pk\|$ (KB)	$\|sign\|$ (b)	N_{ite}
HFE$^s IP-$ 80	(2, 102, 513, 2, 2)	3735M	66	113	4
HFE$^s IP-$ 128	(2, 182, 513, 4, 11)	42296M	356	204	3
HFE$^s IP-$ 192	(2, 283, 513, 4, 27)	133564M	1286	337	3
HFE$^s IP-$ 256	(2, 385, 513, 3, 43)	213304M	3177	468	3

Here on Table 4 is the scheme built to optimize the size of signature but too slow to be used.

Table 5. Parameter and performance of a HFE$^f IP-$ schemes

Name	Param. (q, n, D, π, a)	Cycles to sign	$\|pk\|$ (KB)	$\|sign\|$ (b)	N_{ite}
HFE$^f IP-$ 80	(2, 107, 17, 2, 7)	35M	73	128	4
HFE$^f IP-$ 128	(2, 189, 17, 3, 17)	56M	387	223	3
HFE$^f IP-$ 192	(2, 289, 17, 3, 33)	120M	1341	355	3
HFE$^f IP-$ 256	(2, 390, 17, 4, 48)	160M	3260	486	3

The second set of parameters (Table 5) or HFE$^f IP-$ is the set we consider the most efficient as it is reasonably fast and still have very good signature size. On the other hand, the first set of parameters should be more considered as a demonstrators as the slow signature limits its uses. Note that we did not mention the verification time because it is extremely faster than the time to sign.

Performance Results. Our results are estimates of the real number of cycles required to sign, as we made our tests using the reference implementation of GeMSS (HFE$v-$) and estimated the impact of the IP modifier. We could not use the optimized version as it did not allow for re-parametrization. The code was made in C++ and used the library NTL for the operations on $\mathbb{F}_2$. Benchmarking was done on an Intel Core i7-10850H CPU with 32GB of RAM.

7.3 Cryptanalysis

In this section we will give security complexity for HFE$^f IP-$, we have similar results for HFE$^s IP-$. The complexity of the direct attack depends on the degree of regularity d_{reg} of the public key which satisfies $d_{reg} \geq \lfloor \frac{r+\pi+a}{3} \rfloor + 2$. We have then the following lower bound for the complexity in the following Table 6.

As this variant uses internal perturbation we have to take into account the differential attack of Dubois *et al.* [DGS07]. With the parameters of HFE$^f IP-$ 128 we have found a complexity of 2^{150} far above the level of security of 128 bits. For HFE$^f IP-$ 80 we have found a complexity of 2^{130}. For all other parameters the attack fails as the advantage of the opponent is far too small (almost 0) (Table 7).

Table 6. Complexity of direct attacks based on Gröbner basis over HFE$^f IP-$ with their respective parameters.

Name	Security
HFE$^f IP-$ 80	99 bits
HFE$^f IP-$ 128	164 bits
HFE$^f IP-$ 192	245 bits
HFE$^f IP-$ 256	326 bits

Table 7. Complexity of direct attacks based on Gröbner basis over HFE$^s IP-$ with their respective parameters.

Name	Security
HFE$^s IP-$ 80	98 bits
HFE$^s IP-$ 128	163 bits
HFE$^s IP-$ 192	244 bits
HFE$^s IP-$ 256	326 bits

We can also try MinRank attacks. Because of the presence of minus and IP modifiers the target rank via $\mathbf{T}$ will be $d+a+\pi$. For MinRank attacks that target $\mathbf{S}$ we require an evaluation of the rank of the target matrix. Indeed, we know that minus modifier have no effect on this attack however we have no proper formula for the effect of IP. The tests we have performed however showed that we can expect a very high rank, namely at least $n/2$ for a parameter of $IP = 1$. In reality for the parameters we used, our tests showed that we ought to obtain almost a full rank matrix. But in the following Table 8 we will keep a pessimistic lower bound for the rank of $n/2$.

Table 8. Complexity of the best MinRank attacks (in bold) over HFE$^f IP-$ with their respective parameters.

Name	**Attack on T**	Attack on **S**
HFE$^f IP-$ 80	**81 bits**	240 bits
HFE$^f IP-$ 128	**128 bits**	406 bits
HFE$^f IP-$ 192	**195 bits**	609 bits
HFE$^f IP-$ 256	**257 bits**	812 bits

Obviously, the results show that any attack on **S** with the current form of MinRank is impossible. The attack on **T** remains our best attack, and any moderate improvement in the complexity of the attack could be countered by increasing a. Note that this would not dramatically worsen our performance, the size of the signature or the public key. On the other hand, it seems unlikely that an attack on **S** in its current form could threaten our scheme without a way to somehow eliminate the effect of the IP variant (Table 9).

Table 9. Complexity of the best MinRank attacks (in bold) over HFE$^s IP-$ with their respective parameters.

Name	**Attack on T**	Attack on **S**
HFE$^s IP-$ 80	**81 bits**	228 bits
HFE$^s IP-$ 128	**128 bits**	392 bits
HFE$^s IP-$ 192	**195 bits**	597 bits
HFE$^s IP-$ 256	**257 bits**	803 bits

8 Conclusion

Consequently to the new MinRank attacks that broke the NIST submission GeMSS, it is generally considered that HFE and all its variants do not allow interesting signatures with a security of at least 128 bits. This is because the size of the public key would then be unrealistic (although for 80 bits of security unmodified HFE is still competitive but for most usage 80 bits remains insufficient). In this article however, we showed that a small range of parameters still offers a good security against all known attacks (with 128 or even 256 bits of security) and a reasonable time to sign. Furthermore, with these parameters we obtain very short signatures (less than 2λ bits where λ is the required security). This is the variant HFE$IP-$. It uses two modifiers, namely IP and minus. Both are required to counter all attack types, especially MinRank attacks. Naturally only the future will tell if this range of parameters remains unbroken or if new attacks will make this scheme vulnerable again. Hence, we do not recommend using this scheme for sensitive applications. The most important aspect of this scheme is that it currently offers the shortest public key signatures (quantum resistant or not). For example, ECDSA (Elliptic Curve Digital Signature Algorithm) is only able to have signatures at least three time the length of the security parameter or up to 2.5 in some variants (and is not post quantum), while we can get with HFE IP - a signature length less than twice the size of the security parameter and still expect it to be post quantum.

References

[BBB+22] Bardet, M., Briaud, P., Bros, M., Gaborit, P., Tillich, J.-P.: Revisiting algebraic attacks on MinRank and on the rank decoding problem. Cryptology ePrint Archive, Report 2022/1031 (2022). https://eprint.iacr.org/2022/1031

[BBC+22] Baena, J., Briaud, P., Cabarcas, D., Perlner, R.A., Smith-Tone, D., Verbel, J.A.: Improving support-minors rank attacks: applications to GeMSS and rainbow. In: Dodis, Y., Shrimpton, T. (eds.) CRYPTO 2022, Part III. LNCS, vol. 13509, pp. 376–405. Springer, Heidelberg (2022). https://doi.org/10.1007/978-3-031-15982-4_13

[Beu21] Beullens, W.: Improved cryptanalysis of UOV and rainbow. In: Canteaut, A., Standaert, F.-X. (eds.) EUROCRYPT 2021, Part I. LNCS, vol. 12696, pp. 348–373. Springer, Cham (2021). https://doi.org/10.1007/978-3-030-77870-5_13

[BFP11] Bettale, L., Faugère, J.-C., Perret, L.: Cryptanalysis of multivariate and odd-characteristic HFE variants. In: Catalano, D., Fazio, N., Gennaro, R., Nicolosi, A. (eds.) PKC 2011. LNCS, vol. 6571, pp. 441–458. Springer, Heidelberg (2011). https://doi.org/10.1007/978-3-642-19379-8_27

[BFS99] Buss, J.F., Frandsen, G.S., Shallit, J.O.: The computational complexity of some problems of linear algebra. J. Comput. Syst. Sci. **58**(3), 572–596 (1999)

[CFMR+20] Casanova, A., Faugère, J.C., Macario-Rat, G., Patarin, J., Perret, L., Ryckeghem, J.: GeMSS: a great multivariate short signature. In: NIST CSRC (2020)

[Cou03] Courtois, N.T.: Generic attacks and the security of Quartz. In: Desmedt, Y.G. (ed.) PKC 2003. LNCS, vol. 2567, pp. 351–364. Springer, Heidelberg (2003). https://doi.org/10.1007/3-540-36288-6_26

[CS17] Cartor, R., Smith-Tone, D.: An updated security analysis of PFLASH. In: Lange, T., Takagi, T. (eds.) PQCrypto 2017. LNCS, vol. 10346, pp. 241–254. Springer, Cham (2017). https://doi.org/10.1007/978-3-319-59879-6_14

[CZ81] Cantor, D.G., Zassenhaus, H.: A new algorithm for factoring polynomials over finite fields. Math. Comput. **36**(154), 587–592 (1981)

[DGS07] Dubois, V., Granboulan, L., Stern, J.: Cryptanalysis of HFE with internal perturbation. In: Okamoto, T., Wang, X. (eds.) PKC 2007. LNCS, vol. 4450, pp. 249–265. Springer, Heidelberg (2007). https://doi.org/10.1007/978-3-540-71677-8_17

[DS05] Ding, J., Schmidt, D.: Cryptanalysis of HFEv and internal perturbation of HFE. In: Vaudenay, S. (ed.) PKC 2005. LNCS, vol. 3386, pp. 288–301. Springer, Heidelberg (2005). https://doi.org/10.1007/978-3-540-30580-4_20

[DS13] Ding, J., Schmidt, D.: Solving degree and degree of regularity for polynomial systems over a finite fields. In: Fischlin, M., Katzenbeisser, S. (eds.) Number Theory and Cryptography. LNCS, vol. 8260, pp. 34–49. Springer, Heidelberg (2013). https://doi.org/10.1007/978-3-642-42001-6_4

[DY13] Ding, J., Yang, B.-Y.: Degree of regularity for HFEv and HFEv-. In: Gaborit, P. (ed.) PQCrypto 2013. LNCS, vol. 7932, pp. 52–66. Springer, Heidelberg (2013). https://doi.org/10.1007/978-3-642-38616-9_4

[Fau99] Faugère, J.-C.: A new efficient algorithm for computing Gröbner bases (F_4). J. Pure Appl. Algebra **139**(1), 61–88 (1999)

[Fau02] Faugère, J.C.: A new efficient algorithm for computing Gröbner bases without reduction to zero (F_5). In: Proceedings of the 2002 International Symposium on Symbolic and Algebraic Computation, ISSAC 2002, pp. 75–83. Association for Computing Machinery, New York (2002)

[FJ03] Faugère, J.-C., Joux, A.: Algebraic cryptanalysis of hidden field equation (HFE) cryptosystems using Gröbner bases. In: Boneh, D. (ed.) CRYPTO 2003. LNCS, vol. 2729, pp. 44–60. Springer, Heidelberg (2003). https://doi.org/10.1007/978-3-540-45146-4_3

[FmRPP22] Faugère, J.-C., Macario Rat, G., Patarin, J., Perret, L.: A new perturbation for multivariate public key schemes such as HFE and UOV. Cryptology ePrint Archive, Report 2022/203 (2022). https://eprint.iacr.org/2022/203

[KS99] Kipnis, A., Shamir, A.: Cryptanalysis of the HFE public key cryptosystem by relinearization. In: Wiener, M. (ed.) CRYPTO 1999. LNCS, vol. 1666, pp. 19–30. Springer, Heidelberg (1999). https://doi.org/10.1007/3-540-48405-1_2

[LT17] Lange, T., Takagi, T. (eds.): Post-Quantum Cryptography - 8th International Workshop, PQCrypto 2017. Springer, Heidelberg (2017). https://doi.org/10.1007/978-3-319-59879-6

[MI88] Matsumoto, T., Imai, H.: Public quadratic polynomial-tuples for efficient signature-verification and message-encryption. In: Barstow, D., et al. (eds.) EUROCRYPT 1988. LNCS, vol. 330, pp. 419–453. Springer, Heidelberg (1988). https://doi.org/10.1007/3-540-45961-8_39

[ØSV21] Øygarden, M., Smith-Tone, D., Verbel, J.: On the effect of projection on rank attacks in multivariate cryptography. In: Cheon, J.H., Tillich, J.-P. (eds.) PQCrypto 2021 2021. LNCS, vol. 12841, pp. 98–113. Springer, Cham (2021). https://doi.org/10.1007/978-3-030-81293-5_6

[Pat96a] Patarin, J.: Asymmetric cryptography with a hidden monomial. In: Koblitz, N. (ed.) CRYPTO 1996. LNCS, vol. 1109, pp. 45–60. Springer, Heidelberg (1996). https://doi.org/10.1007/3-540-68697-5_4

[Pat96b] Patarin, J.: Hidden fields equations (HFE) and isomorphisms of polynomials (IP): two new families of asymmetric algorithms. In: Maurer, U. (ed.) EUROCRYPT 1996. LNCS, vol. 1070, pp. 33–48. Springer, Heidelberg (1996). https://doi.org/10.1007/3-540-68339-9_4

[Pet17] Petzoldt, A.: On the complexity of the hybrid approach on HFEv-. Cryptology ePrint Archive, Report 2017/1135 (2017). https://eprint.iacr.org/2017/1135

[PMBK20] Patarin, J., Macario-Rat, G., Bros, M., Koussa, E.: Ultra-short multivariate public key signatures. Cryptology ePrint Archive, Report 2020/914 (2020). https://eprint.iacr.org/2020/914

[TPD21] Tao, C., Petzoldt, A., Ding, J.: Efficient key recovery for all HFE signature variants. In: Malkin, T., Peikert, C. (eds.) CRYPTO 2021. LNCS, vol. 12825, pp. 70–93. Springer, Cham (2021). https://doi.org/10.1007/978-3-030-84242-0_4

[VS17] Vates, J., Smith-Tone, D.: Key recovery attack for all parameters of HFE-. In: Lange, T., Takagi, T. (eds.) PQCrypto 2017. LNCS, vol. 10346, pp. 272–288. Springer, Cham (2017). https://doi.org/10.1007/978-3-319-59879-6_16

Practical Key-Recovery Attack on MQ-Sign and More

Thomas Aulbach[1](✉), Simona Samardjiska[2], and Monika Trimoska[3]

[1] University of Regensburg, Regensburg, Germany
thomas.aulbach@ur.de
[2] Radboud Universiteit, Nijmegen, The Netherlands
simonas@cs.ru.nl
[3] Eindhoven University of Technology, Eindhoven, The Netherlands
m.trimoska@tue.nl

Abstract. In this paper we describe attacks on the UOV-based signature scheme called MQ-Sign. MQ-Sign was submitted by Shim, Kim, and An as a first-round candidate for standardization in the (South) Korean post-quantum cryptography competition (KpqC). The scheme makes use of sparseness of the secret central polynomials and equivalent key construction to reduce the size of the private key. The authors propose four variants exploiting different levels of sparsity, MQ-Sign-SS, MQ-Sign-RS, MQ-Sign-SR, and MQ-Sign-RR with the last one being the standard UOV signature scheme.

We show that apart from the MQ-Sign-RR variant, all the others are insecure. Namely, we present a polynomial-time key-recovery attack on the variants MQ-Sign-SS and MQ-Sign-RS and a forgery attack on the variant MQ-Sign-SR below the claimed security level. Our attack exploits exactly the techniques used for reduction of keys - the sparsity of the central polynomials in combination with the specific structure of the secret linear map **S**.

We provide a verification script for the polynomial-time key-recovery attack, that recovers the secret key in less than seven seconds for security level V. Furthermore, we provide an implementation of the non-guessing part of the forgery attack, confirming our complexity estimates.

1 Introduction

In recent years we have witnessed a substantial effort from standardization bodies and the cryptographic community to design, develop and scrutinize candidates for post-quantum secure key-encapsulation mechanisms and digital signatures [7,12,14,20,26]. This effort is racing an equally fuelled one for developing a large scale error-tolerant universal quantum computer which, although still very much elusive, will likely be reality in a decade or so [19]. When this happens, all the classical cryptography we are happily using today will be immediately rendered insecure. Therefore, as the community widely agrees upon, we need to move as fast as possible with the standardization of post-quantum cryptosystems that we believe are secure even against quantum adversaries.

M.-J. Saarinen and D. Smith-Tone (Eds.): PQCrypto 2024, LNCS 14772, pp. 168–185, 2024.
https://doi.org/10.1007/978-3-031-62746-0_8

On the other hand, we need to be extremely careful in the assessment of the level of scrutiny put into these standardization processes. For example, a major disruption in NIST's standardization process, and certainly a shock for the crypto community, was the cryptanalysis [3, 28] of the two multivariate quadratic ($\mathcal{MQ}$) signature schemes - GeMSS [6] and Rainbow [8] after they were chosen as finalists [20]. Both of these schemes were thought to be well understood, with solid security analysis, albeit both with ad-hoc designs and no security proof.

These developments resulted in NIST choosing two lattice-based signature schemes in the new standard [18,25] in addition to the heavy SPHINCS+ [13], and no adequate solution for use-cases in need of very small signatures. NIST reopened the call for post-quantum digital signature proposals, specifying the need for shorter signatures with fast verification. This spurred a huge number of new multivariate signatures, many of which are variants of UOV (Unbalanced Oil and Vinegar) [16]. UOV is one of the oldest, simplest and most studied ad-hoc multivariate signature schemes. It has very short signatures, but the public key is huge. Therefore, it was not particularly interesting for a very long time, especially since the alternative Rainbow seemed to be more efficient for the same security level (after the attack by Beullens [3] this advantage disappeared). After Rainbow was out of the game, the community returned to UOV in a new round of attempts to reduce the size of the public key while not compromising the security.

One of those efforts is the MQ-Sign [27] signature scheme submitted to the Korean Post-Quantum Cryptography Competition [26], and since recently selected to advance to the 2nd round. The MQ-Sign submission combines two known techniques from multivariate cryptography - equivalent keys [24] and sparse central polynomials [30]. The central map is a standard UOV map that can additionally exhibit sparseness in either the vinegar-vinegar part or the vinegar-oil part. The authors propose four different variants. Both the vinegar-vinegar and vinegar-oil parts being sparse corresponds to the MQ-Sign-SS variant, which yields the smallest private keys. In the variant MQ-Sign-RS, the vinegar-vinegar part is random and the vinegar-oil part is sparse. The two parts switch their structure in the MQ-Sign-SR variant. Finally, the variant MQ-Sign-RR, where both parts are random, corresponds to the standard UOV signature scheme.

1.1 Our Contribution

In this work, we study the security of the MQ-Sign signature scheme. We propose two attacks that cover all variants using sparseness, i.e. every except the last, MQ-Sign-RR variant.

First, we show how the property of using sparse polynomials can be exploited to develop a polynomial time key-recovery attack on the variants MQ-Sign-SS and MQ-Sign-RS. Our attack relies on two key properties – the sparseness property of the vinegar-oil quadratic part and the specific structure of the linear transformation $\mathbf{S}$, as per the *equivalent keys* key generation technique. We first recover the linear transformation $\mathcal{S}$, which allows to subsequently compute the central map $\mathcal{F}$. Our attack is very efficient, and recovers the key in just seconds regardless of the security level.

Second, we introduce a forgery attack on the variant MQ-Sign-SR which is actually a direct attack using only the public key. Our attack exploits a bilinear substructure emerging as a result of the sparse secret polynomials. The attack is not practical, but still shows that MQ-Sign-SR falls short of the claimed security levels by about 30 bits.

We perform a complexity analysis of both attacks, showing that these three variants do not reach the originally estimated security levels. The claims in our complexity analysis are additionally backed up with experimental results. Most notably, we provide an implementation of the practical key-recovery attack that is executed in less than seven seconds for all security levels. We also provide an implementation of the non-guessing part of the forgery attack, confirming our complexity estimates. Both the implementation of attacks and the code used for confirming the complexity estimates are open source.

1.2 Timeline

Our key recovery attack on MQ-Sign-RS and MQ-Sign-SS with $\mathcal{S}$ in block matrix structure (using the equivalent keys optimization) was announced in March 2023. Shortly afterwards, Ikematsu, Jo, and Yasuda [15] generalized our approach and gave an efficient attack that also works with general $\mathcal{S}$. As a result of the two attacks, the authors of MQ-Sign removed the two variants MQ-Sign-RS and MQ-Sign-SS from their specifications in the ongoing KpqC competition. Note that in the current version of the specifications, both remaining variants still use the equivalent key optimization, and do not use a random linear transformation $\mathcal{S}$.

1.3 Organization of the Paper

In Sect. 2 we provide the necessary background on multivariate cryptography, in particular the UOV signature scheme and the optimization choices used in MQ-Sign. We introduce the announced attacks in Sect. 3 and 4. In more detail, we first show in Sect. 3 that the sparse vinegar-oil polynomials in MQ-Sign-RS and MQ-Sign-SS let us derive enough linear equations to compute the secret linear transformation $\mathcal{S}$ in a matter of seconds. Section 4 demonstrates a strategy to attack MQ-Sign-SR by first guessing a selection of variables and subsequently solving a part of the equations for the remaining ones. Even though the cost of the guessing part remains quite high, this shows that the remaining sparse variant slightly fails to provide the required security levels. We provide verification scripts of the stated attacks in Sect. 5 and discuss the impact on the MQ-Sign variants in Sect. 6. Finally, we debate about the still appealing question of using sparse polynomials in UOV and shift attention to the public equations instead.

2 Preliminaries

Throughout the text, $\mathbb{F}_q$ will denote the finite field of q elements, and $\mathrm{GL}_n(\mathbb{F}_q)$ and $\mathrm{AGL}_n(\mathbb{F}_q)$ will denote respectively the general linear group and the general affine group of degree n over $\mathbb{F}_q$. We will also use the notation $\mathbf{x} = (x_1, \ldots, x_n)^\intercal$ for the vector $(x_1, \ldots, x_n) \in \mathbb{F}_q^n$.

2.1 Multivariate Signatures

First, we recall the general principle of $\mathcal{MQ}$ public key cryptosystems. A typical $\mathcal{MQ}$ public key cryptosystem relies on the knowledge of a trapdoor for a particular system of polynomials over the field $\mathbb{F}_q$. The public key of the cryptosystem is usually given by a multivariate quadratic map $\mathcal{P} = (\mathcal{P}^{(1)}, \ldots, \mathcal{P}^{(m)}) : \mathbb{F}_q^n \to \mathbb{F}_q^m$, where

$$\mathcal{P}^{(k)}(x_1, \ldots, x_n) = \sum_{1 \le i \le j \le n} \gamma_{ij}^{(k)} x_i x_j + \sum_{i=1}^{n} \beta_i^{(k)} x_i + \alpha^{(k)}$$

for some coefficients $\gamma_{ij}^{(k)}, \beta_i^{(k)}, \alpha^{(k)} \in \mathbb{F}_q$. It is obtained by obfuscating a structured central map

$$\mathcal{F} : (x_1, \ldots, x_n) \in \mathbb{F}_q^n \to \left(\mathcal{F}^{(1)}(x_1, \ldots, x_n), \ldots, \mathcal{F}^{(m)}(x_1, \ldots, x_n)\right) \in \mathbb{F}_q^m,$$

using two bijective affine mappings $\mathcal{S}, \mathcal{T} \in \mathrm{AGL}_n(\mathbb{F}_q)$ that serve as a sort of mask to hide the structure of $\mathcal{F}$. The public key is defined as

$$\mathcal{P} = \mathcal{T} \circ \mathcal{F} \circ \mathcal{S}.$$

The mappings $\mathcal{S}$ and $\mathcal{T}$ are part of the private key s. Besides them, the private key may also contain other secret parameters that allow creation, but also easy inversion of the transformation $\mathcal{F}$. Without loss of generality, we can assume that the private key is $s = (\mathcal{F}, \mathcal{S}, \mathcal{T})$.

Signature Generation. To generate a signature for a message d, the signer uses a hash function $\mathcal{H} : \{0,1\}^\star \to \mathbb{F}_q^m$ to compute the hash value $\mathbf{w} = \mathcal{H}(d) \in \mathbb{F}_q^m$ and computes recursively $\mathbf{x} = \mathcal{T}^{-1}(\mathbf{w}) \in \mathbb{F}_q^m$, $\mathbf{y} = \mathcal{F}^{-1}(\mathbf{x}) \in \mathbb{F}_q^n$, and $\mathbf{z} = \mathcal{S}^{-1}(\mathbf{y})$. The signature of the message d is $\mathbf{z} \in \mathbb{F}_q^n$. Here, $\mathcal{F}^{-1}(\mathbf{x})$ means finding one (of possibly many) preimages of $\mathbf{x}$ under the central map $\mathcal{F}$.

Verification. To check if $\mathbf{z} \in \mathbb{F}_q^n$ is indeed a valid signature for a message d, one computes $\mathbf{w} = \mathcal{H}(d)$ and $\mathbf{w}' = \mathcal{P}(\mathbf{z}) \in \mathbb{F}_q^m$. If $\mathbf{w}' = \mathbf{w}$ holds, the signature is accepted, otherwise it is rejected.

The standard signature generation and verification process of a multivariate signature scheme works as shown in Fig. 1.

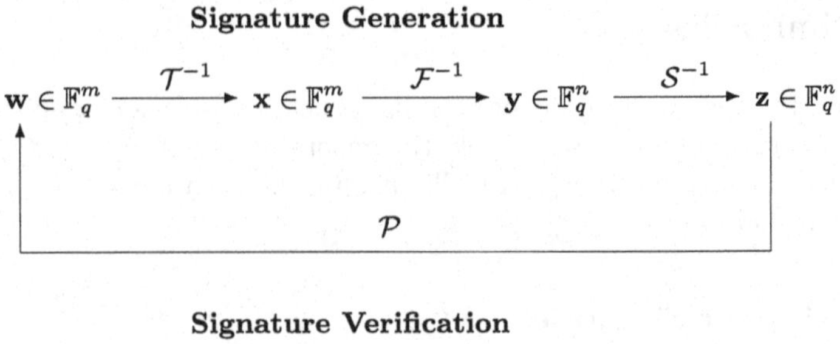

Fig. 1. General workflow of multivariate signature schemes.

2.2 Unbalanced Oil and Vinegar

The Unbalanced Oil and Vinegar signature scheme is one of the oldest multivariate signature schemes. It was proposed by Kipnis, Patarin, and Goubin at EUROCRYPT'99 [16] as a modification of the oil and vinegar scheme of Patarin [22] that was broken by Kipnis and Shamir in 1998 [17].

The characteristic of the oil and vinegar construction is in the special structure of the central map in which the variables are divided in two distinct sets, vinegar variables and oil variables. The vinegar variables are combined quadratically with all of the variables, while the oil variables are only combined quadratically with vinegar variables and not with other oil variables. Formally, the central map is defined as $\mathcal{F} : \mathbb{F}_q^n \to \mathbb{F}_q^m$, with central polynomials

$$\mathcal{F}^{(k)}(x_1, \dots, x_n) = \sum_{i \in V, j \in V} \gamma_{ij}^{(k)} x_i x_j + \sum_{i \in V, j \in O} \gamma_{ij}^{(k)} x_i x_j + \sum_{i=1}^{n} \beta_i^{(k)} x_i + \alpha^{(k)} \quad (1)$$

where $n = v + m$, and $V = \{1, \dots, v\}$ and $O = \{v + 1, \dots, n\}$ denote the index sets of the vinegar and oil variables, respectively.

It can be shown that if an oil and vinegar central map is used in the standard $\mathcal{MQ}$ construction the affine mapping $\mathcal{T}$ does not add to the security of the scheme and is therefore not necessary. Hence the secret key consists of a linear transformation $\mathcal{S}$ and central map $\mathcal{F}$, while the public key is defined as $\mathcal{P} = \mathcal{F} \circ \mathcal{S}$. In order to sign a message, we need to find a preimage of $\mathcal{F}$. This can be done by simply fixing the vinegar variables to some random values. In this way, we obtain a system of m linear equations in m variables, which has a solution with probability around $1 - 1/q$. If the obtained system does not have a solution, we repeat the procedure with different values for the vinegar variables.

Key Generation. It was shown in [23] that for any instance of a UOV secret key $(\mathcal{F}, \mathcal{S})$, there exists an equivalent secret key $(\mathcal{F}, \mathbf{S})$ with

$$\mathbf{S} = \begin{pmatrix} \mathbf{I}_{v \times v} & \mathbf{S}_1 \\ \mathbf{0}_{m \times v} & \mathbf{I}_{m \times m} \end{pmatrix}. \quad (2)$$

Furthermore, the quadratic polynomials of the central map $\mathcal{F} : \mathbb{F}_q^n \to \mathbb{F}_q^m$ can be represented using upper triangular matrices $\mathbf{F}^{(1)}, \ldots, \mathbf{F}^{(m)} \in \mathbb{F}_q^{n\times n}$ where each nonzero coefficient (i,j) in $\mathbf{F}^{(k)}$ corresponds to the nonzero coefficient of $x_i x_j$ in $\mathcal{F}^{(k)}$. Note that the $m \times m$ block on the bottom right of these matrices is empty, since the polynomials of the central map have no quadratic oil terms. Thus, these matrices contain an upper triangular block $\mathbf{F}_1^{(k)} \in \mathbb{F}_q^{v\times v}$ and a block $\mathbf{F}_2^{(k)} \in \mathbb{F}_q^{v\times m}$ on the top right. In other words, the matrices are of the form:

$$\mathbf{F}^{(k)} = \begin{pmatrix} \mathbf{F}_1^{(k)} & \mathbf{F}_2^{(k)} \\ \mathbf{0} & \mathbf{0} \end{pmatrix}.$$

Thus, in order to obtain a key pair, it suffices to first randomly generate $(\mathbf{S}_1, \mathbf{F}^{(1)}, \ldots, \mathbf{F}^{(m)})$ and then compute $(\mathbf{P}^{(1)}, \ldots, \mathbf{P}^{(m)})$ by evaluating $\mathbf{P}^{(k)} = \mathbf{S}^\top \mathbf{F}^{(k)} \mathbf{S}$ and bringing the resulting matrices to upper triangular form.

2.3 MQ-Sign

MQ-Sign is a signature scheme based on UOV. The scheme uses inhomogenous polynomials and each polynomial of the central map can be written as

$$\mathcal{F}^{(k)} = \mathcal{F}_V^{(k)} + \mathcal{F}_{OV}^{(k)} + \mathcal{F}_{L,C}^{(k)}$$

where

$$\mathcal{F}_V^{(k)}(x_1, \ldots, x_n) = \sum_{i\in V, j\in V} \gamma_{ij}^{(k)} x_i x_j, \text{ and } \mathcal{F}_{OV}^{(k)}(x_1, \ldots, x_n) = \sum_{i\in V, j\in O} \gamma_{ij}^{(k)} x_i x_j.$$

These can alternatively be referred to as the vinegar-vinegar quadratic part and the vinegar-oil quadratic part. Finally, $\mathcal{F}_{L,C}^{(k)}$ refers to the linear and constant part of the polynomials. In the following, we ignore the linear and constant parts, since our attack does not use them.

The main design goal of MQ-Sign is to reduce the size of the secret key compared to traditional UOV. This is achieved using sparse polynomials for the quadratic part of the central map. If sparseness is introduced in the $\mathcal{F}_V^{(k)}$ part, then it is defined as

$$\mathcal{F}_{V,S}^{(k)}(x_1, \ldots, x_n) = \sum_{i=1}^{v} \alpha_i^k x_i x_{(i+k-1(\bmod v))+1} \tag{3}$$

If, on the other hand, sparseness is introduced in the $\mathcal{F}_{OV}^{(k)}$ part, then it is defined as

$$\mathcal{F}_{OV,S}^{(k)}(x_1, \ldots, x_n) = \sum_{i=1}^{v} \beta_i^k x_i x_{(i+k-2(\bmod m))+v+1}. \tag{4}$$

The MQ-Sign proposal provides a parameter selection for four variants of the scheme: MQ-Sign-SS, MQ-Sign-RS, MQ-Sign-SR and MQ-Sign-RR. The first

S/R in the suffix specifies whether $\mathcal{F}_V$ is defined with sparse ($\mathcal{F}_{V,S}$) or random polynomials ($\mathcal{F}_{V,R}$). The second S/R refers to the same property, but for $\mathcal{F}_{OV}$. Note that the variant MQ-Sign-RR corresponds to the standard UOV scheme defined with inhomogenous polynomials.

If both $\mathcal{F}_{V,S}$ and $\mathcal{F}_{OV,S}$ are used, the size of the secret key is reduced to $2vm$ field elements.

The authors provide an elaborate security analysis including all known relevant attacks on UOV. However, they do not consider the sparseness of (parts of) the secret polynomials in any of the attacks. Their assumption is that it is not exploitable within the known cryptanalytic techniques. Table 1 summarizes the parameters chosen by the authors for security levels I, III, and V.

Note that when $\mathcal{F}_{V,S}$ is used, the size of the public key can also be reduced, as, due to the equivalent keys structure of $\mathbf{S}$ as in (2), a part of the public key is equivalent to a part of the secret key and thus sparse. This is however not taken into consideration in the implementation of MQ-Sign or in the public key sizes reported in Table 1.

Table 1. The parameter selection for security category I, III and V for the variants SS, RS, SR and RR of MQ-Sign with key sizes in bytes.

Sec. level	Parameters (q, v, m)	sig	PK	SK (SS)	SK (RS)	SK (SR)	SK (RR)
I	$(2^8, 72, 46)$	134	328 441	15 561	133 137	164 601	282 177
III	$(2^8, 112, 72)$	200	1 238 761	37 729	485 281	610 273	1 057 825
V	$(2^8, 148, 96)$	260	2 892 961	66 421	1 110 709	1 416 181	2 460 469

3 An Efficient Key-Recovery Attack on Variants Using Sparse $\mathcal{F}_{OV}$

In the following, we consider $\mathcal{C}$ to be the class of polynomials defined by $\mathcal{F}_{V,R} + \mathcal{F}_{OV,S}$, denoting that only $\mathcal{F}_{OV}$ needs to be defined as in (4), i.e. with sparse polynomials. This corresponds to the MQ-Sign-SS and MQ-Sign-RS variants.

In this section we show that the usage of $\mathcal{F}_{OV,S}$ introduces weaknesses that enable a practical key-recovery attack that takes merely seconds to mount. In the attack, we essentially solve the Extended Isomorphism of Polynomials (EIP) problem as defined in [9] (see also [27]). We recall here its definition.

$\mathsf{EIP}(n, m, \mathcal{P}, \mathcal{C})$:
Input: An m-tuple of multivariate polynomials $\mathcal{P} = (\mathcal{P}^{(1)}, \mathcal{P}^{(2)}, \ldots, \mathcal{P}^{(m)}) \in \mathbb{F}_q[x_1, \ldots, x_n]^m$ and a special class of m-tuples of multivariate polynomials $\mathcal{C} \subseteq \mathbb{F}_q[x_1, \ldots, x_n]^m$.
Question: Find – if any – $\mathbf{S} \in \mathrm{GL}_n(q)$ and $\mathcal{F} = (\mathcal{F}^{(1)}, \mathcal{F}^{(2)}, \ldots, \mathcal{F}^{(m)}) \in \mathcal{C}$ such that $\mathcal{P} = \mathcal{F} \circ \mathbf{S}$.

Solving this problem is in general not easy. In fact, the security of ad-hoc multivariate schemes is based on the hardness on this problem. However, if $\mathcal{F}$ exhibits enough structure, then the problem can become easy to solve.

We next show that the sparse structure present in MQ-Sign-SS and MQ-Sign-RS is enough to solve the corresponding EIP problem very efficiently. In order to see this, note that the computation of the public key for UOV-like signature schemes can be written in matrix form as:

$$\begin{pmatrix} \mathbf{P}_1^{(k)} & \mathbf{P}_2^{(k)} \\ \mathbf{0} & \mathbf{P}_4^{(k)} \end{pmatrix} = \begin{pmatrix} \mathbf{I} & \mathbf{0} \\ \mathbf{S}_1^\top & \mathbf{I} \end{pmatrix} \begin{pmatrix} \mathbf{F}_1^{(k)} & \mathbf{F}_2^{(k)} \\ \mathbf{0} & \mathbf{0} \end{pmatrix} \begin{pmatrix} \mathbf{I} & \mathbf{S}_1 \\ \mathbf{0} & \mathbf{I} \end{pmatrix},$$

for all $k \in \{1, \ldots, m\}$. From this we deduce

$$\begin{pmatrix} \mathbf{P}_1^{(k)} & \mathbf{P}_2^{(k)} \\ \mathbf{0} & \mathbf{P}_4^{(k)} \end{pmatrix} = \begin{pmatrix} \mathbf{F}_1^{(k)} & (\mathbf{F}_1^{(k)} + \mathbf{F}_1^{(k)\top})\mathbf{S}_1 + \mathbf{F}_2^{(k)} \\ \mathbf{0} & \mathsf{Upper}(\mathbf{S}_1^\top \mathbf{F}_1^{(k)} \mathbf{S}_1 + \mathbf{S}_1^\top \mathbf{F}_2^{(k)}) \end{pmatrix}, \tag{5}$$

where $\mathsf{Upper}(\mathbf{M})$ denotes the unique upper triangular matrix $\tilde{\mathbf{M}}$ such that the difference $\tilde{\mathbf{M}} - \mathbf{M}$ is skew-symmetric. Equation (5) shows how different blocks of the public key are obtained from the blocks of the secret key, and having these relations allows us to mount an algebraic attack that will recover all of the entries of the secret key. We first model this correspondence between the public and the secret key as a system of equations where the variables are the entries of $\mathbf{S}_1$ and $\mathbf{F}_1^{(k)}$. From the two upper blocks we obtain the following two equations

$$\begin{aligned} \mathbf{P}_1^{(k)} &= \mathbf{F}_1^{(k)} \\ \mathbf{P}_2^{(k)} &= (\mathbf{F}_1^{(k)} + \mathbf{F}_1^{(k)\top})\mathbf{S}_1 + \mathbf{F}_2^{(k)}. \end{aligned}$$

From these, we infer that

$$\mathbf{P}_2^{(k)} = (\mathbf{P}_1^{(k)} + \mathbf{P}_1^{(k)\top})\mathbf{S}_1 + \mathbf{F}_2^{(k)}. \tag{6}$$

Ignoring the sparseness at first, from (6) we can derive a linear system of vm^2 equations in $v(m^2 + m)$ variables (vm that correspond to the entries of the unknown block of the linear transformation $\mathbf{S}$, and vm^2 from the entries of $\mathbf{F}_2^{(k)}$). Even though the system is linear, a solution cannot be extracted easily as it is highly underdetermined. But considering the sparseness in the MQ-Sign-SS and MQ-Sign-RS instances, the following key observation allows us to solve the system easily in practice.

The matrices $\mathbf{F}_2^{(k)}$ are part of the secret key, but we know that they are sparse. From the description of $\mathcal{F}_{OV}$ in (4) we can see that the value of $\mathbf{F}_2^{(k)}$ is known on $(vm - v)$ entries. Since $\mathbf{F}_2^{(k)}$ appears linearly in (6), we can extract constraints from the entries where the value of $\mathbf{F}_2^{(k)}$ is zero and obtain a system that is only in the $\mathbf{S}_1$ variables. Let $\widetilde{\mathbf{P}}_1^{(k)} = \mathbf{P}_1^{(k)} + \mathbf{P}_1^{(k)\top}$. We obtain the following system of equations, where we denote by $\tilde{p}_{i,j}^{(k)}$ the entries of $\widetilde{\mathbf{P}}_1^{(k)}$, by $s_{i,j}$ the entries of $\mathbf{S}_1$, by $p_{i,j}^{(k)}$ the entries of $\mathbf{P}_2^{(k)}$, and by $f_{i,j}^{(k)}$ the entries of $\mathbf{F}_2^{(k)}$.[1]

$$\sum_{1 \leqslant p \leqslant v} \tilde{p}_{i,p}^{(k)} s_{p,j} - p_{i,j}^{(k)} = 0, \quad \forall (i,j,k) \text{ s.t. } f_{i,j}^{(k)} = 0. \tag{7}$$

This is a linear system in vm variables. The number of equations that we can obtain if we use all of the m quadratic maps from the public key is $mv(m-1)$. Hence, the system has vm linearly independent equations with overwhelming probability. As such, it can be solved efficiently through Gaussian Elimination. This is under the assumption that the system behaves as a random system and has no specific structure that results in non-trivial dependencies between the equations, which will be argued below as part of the complexity analysis. We conclude that, ignoring some of the equations from (6), specifically those where $f_{i,j}^{(k)}$ is not zero, allowed us to derive a linear system that is only in variables from $\mathbf{S}_1$. Once we recover the secret map $\mathbf{S}$, computing $\mathcal{F}$ is easy, as we just need to apply the inverse linear transformation on $\mathcal{P}$.

We further refine our modeling to obtain a more efficient attack, using the following strategy. Note from (7) that each equation in the system contains variables from only one column of $\mathbf{S}_1$. This observation allows us to optimize the attack by solving for one column at a time. This is more evident when we look at the matrix representation of our linear system. Let us define a matrix $\mathbf{A}'$ as

$$\begin{pmatrix} \widetilde{\mathbf{P}}_1^{(1)} \\ \widetilde{\mathbf{P}}_1^{(2)} \\ \vdots \\ \widetilde{\mathbf{P}}_1^{(m)} \end{pmatrix},$$

i.e. a block matrix obtained by concatenating vertically the quadratic maps $\widetilde{\mathbf{P}}_1^{(k)}$. Then, let $\mathbf{A}$ be a block matrix that has copies of $\mathbf{A}'$ on the main diagonal and zeros everywhere else

$$\mathbf{A} = \begin{pmatrix} \mathbf{A}' & \mathbf{0} & \cdots & \mathbf{0} \\ \mathbf{0} & \mathbf{A}' & \cdots & \mathbf{0} \\ \vdots & & \ddots & \\ \mathbf{0} & \mathbf{0} & \cdots & \mathbf{A}' \end{pmatrix}.$$

Now, let $\mathbf{x}^\top = (\mathbf{x}_1, \mathbf{x}_2, \ldots, \mathbf{x}_m)$ be a vector obtained by concatenating the columns of $\mathbf{S}_1$. Finally, let $\mathbf{b}^\top = \mathbf{b}_1, \mathbf{b}_2, \ldots, \mathbf{b}_m$, be a vector that is obtained by concatenating the first column of each quadratic map $\mathbf{P}_2^{(k)}$, followed by the second column of each map, etc.

[1] Here, and in the following, the submatrix indices are ommited where there is no ambiguity.

We can then rewrite $\widetilde{\mathbf{P}}_1^{(k)}\mathbf{S}_1 = \mathbf{P}_2^{(k)}$, for all $k \in \{1,\ldots,m\}$, as $\mathbf{Ax} = \mathbf{b}$. Indeed, we have

$$\begin{pmatrix} \mathbf{A}' & \mathbf{0} & \cdots & \mathbf{0} \\ \mathbf{0} & \mathbf{A}' & \cdots & \mathbf{0} \\ \vdots & & \ddots & \\ \mathbf{0} & \mathbf{0} & \cdots & \mathbf{A}' \end{pmatrix} \cdot \begin{pmatrix} \mathbf{x}_1 \\ \mathbf{x}_2 \\ \vdots \\ \mathbf{x}_m \end{pmatrix} = \begin{pmatrix} \mathbf{b}_1 \\ \mathbf{b}_2 \\ \vdots \\ \mathbf{b}_m \end{pmatrix},$$

where

$$\mathbf{A}' = \begin{pmatrix} \tilde{p}_{1,1}^{(1)} \cdots \tilde{p}_{1,v}^{(1)} \\ \tilde{p}_{2,1}^{(1)} \cdots \tilde{p}_{2,v}^{(1)} \\ \vdots \\ \tilde{p}_{v,1}^{(1)} \cdots \tilde{p}_{v,v}^{(1)} \\ \vdots \\ \tilde{p}_{1,1}^{(m)} \cdots \tilde{p}_{1,v}^{(m)} \\ \tilde{p}_{2,1}^{(m)} \cdots \tilde{p}_{2,v}^{(m)} \\ \vdots \\ \tilde{p}_{v,1}^{(m)} \cdots \tilde{p}_{v,v}^{(m)} \end{pmatrix}, \quad \mathbf{x}_i = \begin{pmatrix} s_{1,i} \\ s_{2,i} \\ \vdots \\ s_{v,i} \end{pmatrix}, \quad \text{and } \mathbf{b}_i = \begin{pmatrix} p_{1,i}^{(1)} \\ p_{2,i}^{(1)} \\ \vdots \\ p_{v,i}^{(1)} \\ \vdots \\ p_{1,i}^{(m)} \\ p_{2,i}^{(m)} \\ \vdots \\ p_{v,i}^{(m)} \end{pmatrix}.$$

Looking at where the zero entries lie in $\mathbf{A}$, we can now split the problem. We solve $\mathbf{A}'\mathbf{x}_i = \mathbf{b}_i$ for all $i \in \{1,\ldots,m\}$, and for every system that we solve, we reveal one column of $\mathbf{S}_1$.

3.1 Complexity Analysis

Using this strategy, instead of solving one linear system in vm variables, we solve m linear systems in v variables. Thus, our attack has only $\mathcal{O}(mv^\omega)$ time complexity, where ω is the linear algebra constant. A strong requirement for the success of the attack is that all of the linear subsystems that we need to solve are determined. Since we are combining solutions of subsystems to recover the entire solution, having even a small nonzero number of solutions to the subsystems would rapidly increase the complexity of the attack. However, in the following, we argue that we can rely on the assumption that all subsystems have exactly one solution.

Table 2. Theoretical complexity of our attack against the MQ-Sign-SS and MQ-Sign-RS variants.

Security level	Parameters (q, v, m)	Attack complexity
I	$(2^8, 72, 46)$	2^{24}
III	$(2^8, 112, 72)$	2^{27}
V	$(2^8, 148, 96)$	2^{29}

As per the analysis in the previous section, the ith subset of equations is obtained from

$$\begin{pmatrix} \tilde{p}^{(1)}_{1,1} & \cdots & \tilde{p}^{(1)}_{1,v} \\ \tilde{p}^{(1)}_{2,1} & \cdots & \tilde{p}^{(1)}_{2,v} \\ & \vdots & \\ \tilde{p}^{(1)}_{v,1} & \cdots & \tilde{p}^{(1)}_{v,v} \\ & \vdots & \\ \tilde{p}^{(m)}_{1,1} & \cdots & \tilde{p}^{(m)}_{1,v} \\ \tilde{p}^{(m)}_{2,1} & \cdots & \tilde{p}^{(m)}_{2,v} \\ & \vdots & \\ \tilde{p}^{(m)}_{v,1} & \cdots & \tilde{p}^{(m)}_{v,v} \end{pmatrix} \cdot \begin{pmatrix} s_{1,i} \\ s_{2,i} \\ \vdots \\ s_{v,i} \end{pmatrix} = \begin{pmatrix} p^{(1)}_{1,1} \\ p^{(1)}_{2,1} \\ \vdots \\ p^{(1)}_{v,1} \\ \vdots \\ p^{(m)}_{1,1} \\ p^{(m)}_{2,1} \\ \vdots \\ p^{(m)}_{v,1} \end{pmatrix}. \tag{8}$$

From this equality, we extract $v(m-1)$ equations. That is, one equation for each entry from $\mathbf{b}_i$, ignoring entries (i, j) where $f^{(k)}_{i,j}$ is not zero. We are interested in how many of these equations are linearly independent. From (8) we can see that each equation can be viewed as a linear combination of the $s_{\_,i}$ variables where the coefficients come from a row of $\widetilde{\mathbf{P}}^{(k)}_1$, plus a constant that corresponds to an entry of $\mathbf{P}^{(k)}_2$. Hence, the number of linearly independent equations is exactly determined by the rank of $\mathbf{A}'$. It is actually the rank of $(\mathbf{A}'\ \mathbf{b}_i)$, but we can ignore the constant in our case. Indeed, if the rank of $\mathbf{A}'$ is smaller than the rank of $(\mathbf{A}'\ \mathbf{b}_i)$, this would result in the system derived from (8) being inconsistent. This case cannot happen when we model a coherent instance of UOV key generation. Now, recall that public key in UOV-based schemes is generated randomly (or derived from a randomly generated central map) and thus it is comprised of matrices of full rank with high probability. Hence, a concatenation of several such matrices is also full rank, which is v in this case (the dimension of the column space being v) – equal to the number of variables. We have also performed experiments to verify this claim, and out of 500 runs of the attack on MQ-Sign-SS with level I parameters, not once did the attack fail for not having enough independent equations in any of the subsystems. Table 2 summarizes the effect of the attack on the different MQ-Sign parameters.

4 A Forgery Attack on Variants Using Sparse $\mathcal{F}_V$

In this section we show a forgery attack on the MQ-Sign-SR variant, where the polynomials of $\mathcal{F}_V$ are defined as in Eq. (3). A forgery attack on a multivariate signature scheme aims at finding a signature $\mathbf{z} \in \mathbb{F}_q^n$ for a given target value $\mathbf{t} \in \mathbb{F}_q^m$, such that $\mathcal{P}(\mathbf{z}) = \mathbf{t}$ is fulfilled. We show that in the case of MQ-Sign-SR, a forgery is directly possible using only the public key.

Recall from Sect. 3, that, when the linear transformation $\mathcal{S}$ is given as in Eq. (2), it holds that $\mathbf{P}_1^{(k)} = \mathbf{F}_1^{(k)}$. This means that the sparsity of the secret coefficient matrices gets transferred to the public system. In more detail, an attacker faces the task of finding $(\mathbf{z}_v, \mathbf{z}_o) \in \mathbb{F}_q^n$ such that

$$(\mathbf{z}_v, \mathbf{z}_o) \begin{pmatrix} \mathbf{P}_1^{(k)} & \mathbf{P}_2^{(k)} \\ \mathbf{0} & \mathbf{P}_4^{(k)} \end{pmatrix} \begin{pmatrix} \mathbf{z}_v \\ \mathbf{z}_o \end{pmatrix} = \mathbf{z}_v \mathbf{P}_1^{(k)} \mathbf{z}_v + \mathbf{z}_v \mathbf{P}_2^{(k)} \mathbf{z}_o + \mathbf{z}_o \mathbf{P}_4^{(k)} \mathbf{z}_o = t_k \tag{9}$$

holds for all $k \in \{1, \ldots, m\}$, where $\mathbf{P}_1^{(k)}$ are sparse as in Eq. (3). The parameters $n \approx 2.5m$ allow us to fix the m entries of $\mathbf{z}_o \in \mathbb{F}_q^m$ and thereby remove the non-sparse submatrices $\mathbf{P}_2^{(k)}$ and $\mathbf{P}_4^{(k)}$ from the quadratic part of this system of equations. This leads us to equations of the form

$$\mathbf{z}_v \mathbf{P}_1^{(k)} \mathbf{z}_v + \text{lin}(\mathbf{z}_v) = \sum_{i=1}^{v} \alpha_i^k z_i z_{(i+k-1(\bmod v))+1} + \text{lin}(\mathbf{z}_v) = t_k. \tag{10}$$

The term $\text{lin}(\mathbf{z}_v)$ summarizes the linear and constant terms emerging from Eq. (9) after fixing the entries of $\mathbf{z}_o$. Note that the resulting system is a system of m equations in v variables, and since v is greater than m, we can fix another $(v - m)$ variables and still expect to have a solution.

At the core of this attack is the observation that, due to the sparsity in $\mathbf{P}_1^{(k)}$, the resulting system has subsets of equations that are bilinear in some subsets of variables. Specifically, upon closer examination of the indices in Eq. (10), one notices that for odd k, the quadratic monomials appearing in the polynomial equation each consist of a variable with an odd and an even index. This implies that these $\frac{m}{2}$ equations are bilinear in the sets of variables $\{z_1, z_3, \ldots, z_{m-1}\}$ and $\{z_2, z_4, \ldots, z_m\}$, where we denote by z_i the variables in vector $\mathbf{z}_v$. Hence, randomly guessing e.g., the $\frac{v}{2}$ odd-indexed variables gives us a $\frac{v-m}{2}$-dimensional linear solution space for the even-indexed variables in the $\frac{m}{2}$ bilinear equations. Let us denote by $\tilde{\mathbf{z}}_v$ the vector comprised of the vinegar variables that have not yet been assigned, i.e. the even-indexed vinegar variables. At this point, the overall system is of the following form

$$\sum_{i=0}^{\frac{v}{2}-1} \alpha_{2i+1}^k z_{((2i+1)+k-1(\bmod v))+1} + \alpha_{2i+2}^k z_{2i+2} + \text{lin}(\tilde{\mathbf{z}}_v) = t_k, \qquad \text{if } k \text{ odd}$$

$$\sum_{i=1}^{\frac{v}{2}} \alpha_{2i}^k z_{2i} z_{(2i+k-1(\bmod v))+1} + \text{lin}(\tilde{\mathbf{z}}_v) = t_k, \qquad \text{if } k \text{ even.}$$

The probability that there exists a solution to the complete system - including the remaining $\frac{m}{2}$ quadratic (non-bilinear) equations - with the previously guessed odd variables is around $q^{-(\frac{v}{2}-(v-m))}$, since we can only fix $v-m$ variables in a quadratic system with v variables in m equations and still expect to find a solution. An alternative view is that, to obtain the $\frac{v-m}{2}$-dimensional linear solution space, we can fix $(v-m)$ variables and enumerate the rest with the usual cost of enumeration. This is the first step of our attack and its cost will be denoted by $C_{\text{ENUM}(q,\frac{v}{2}-(v-m))}$.

In the second step, we need to find an assignment to the even-indexed variables that also validate the remaining $\frac{m}{2}$ equations. Using the description of the linear solution space obtained from the bilinear equations, this step boils down to solving a quadratic system of $\frac{m}{2}$ equations in $\frac{v-m}{2}$ variables. We denote the complexity of this step by $C_{\text{MQ}(q,\frac{v-m}{2},\frac{m}{2})}$.

4.1 Complexity Analysis

The cost of the first step of the algorithm corresponds to the usual cost of enumeration over $\mathbb{F}_q$. In the second step, the complexity is dominated by the algorithm for solving the quadratic systems of equations. For the choice of $q = 2^8$, as per the MQ-Sign parameters, the best strategy would be to solve the system with a Gröbner-based algorithm (such as F4 or F5 [10,11]), without the use of hybridization. Assuming that the quadratic systems we obtain behave as semi-regular non-boolean systems of s equations in n variables, the complexity [2] of the solving algorithm is approximated by

$$\mathcal{O}\left(sD\binom{n+D-1}{D}^{\omega}\right),$$

where D denotes the *degree of regularity* and is computed as the power of the first non-positive coefficient in the expansion of

$$\frac{(1-t^2)^s}{(1-t)^n}.$$

Then, the complexity of the whole attack is given by

$$C_{\text{ENUM}(q,\frac{v}{2}-(v-m))} \cdot C_{\text{MQ}(q,\frac{v-m}{2},\frac{m}{2})},$$

since the second step has to be repeated until the odd variables are guessed correctly in the first step. In Table 3 we present an overview of the approximate costs for the parameter sets of MQ-Sign. We conclude that because of this attack, the proposed parameters of the MQ-Sign-SR variant slightly fail to provide the required security levels. Note that the algorithm described here uses the most straighforward approach to exploit the bilinearity of the subsystems, but more advanced techniques can potentially result in attacks with lower complexity.

Table 3. Theoretical complexity of our direct attack using the bilinear structure of the odd equations.

Security level	Parameters (q, v, m)	$C_{\mathrm{ENUM}(q, \frac{v}{2}-(v-m))}$	$C_{\mathrm{MQ}(q, \frac{v-m}{2}, \frac{m}{2})}$	Complexity
I	$(2^8, 72, 46)$	2^{80}	2^{31}	2^{111}
III	$(2^8, 112, 72)$	2^{128}	2^{42}	2^{170}
V	$(2^8, 148, 96)$	2^{176}	2^{52}	2^{228}

Our attack again relies on the sparseness property of the vinegar-vinegar quadratic part and the specific structure of the linear transformation $\mathbf{S}$, as per the *equivalent keys* key generation technique.

5 Implementation

5.1 Sparse $\mathcal{F}_{OV}$

To confirm the practicality of our attack in Sect. 3, we provide a verification script in MAGMA [5] where we implement the key generation of MQ-Sign-{S/R}S and then run the main algorithm for recovering the secret key from the public key as input. The running time of the attack on a laptop is 0.6 s for the proposed parameters for security level I, 2.3 s for security level III and 6.9 s for security level V. We also provide an equivalent SageMath [29] script that is slower.

5.2 Sparse $\mathcal{F}_V$

Complexity estimates in Sect. 4 show that MQ-Sign-SR falls below the required security level, but the attack is not practical for the chosen parameter sizes. We nevertheless implemented the attack as a proof-of-concept and to confirm practically our complexity estimations. The cost of enumeration is straightforward, but the second part of the attack involves Gröbner-based algorithms, whose complexity rely on heuristic assumptions of semi-regularity. Hence, our primary goal in this experimental work was to verify that the degree of regularity reached by the F4/F5 algorithm is estimated correctly. The verification script for this attack consists of generating the polynomial system in (9), fixing all variables in $\mathbf{z}_o$ and in the odd-indexed subset, and finally, solving the resulting system using the F4 algorithm implemented in MAGMA. When fixing the variables, we experimented both with a correct assignment that subsequently leads to a solution, and a random assignment that leads to an inconsistent system. As expected, there is no difference in the solving running times between the two cases.

Table 4. Experimental results of the direct attack.

Security level	Parameters (q, v, m)	D estimated	D reached	Runtime (s)	Memory (MB)
I	$(2^8, 72, 46)$	4	4	0.6	32
III	$(2^8, 112, 72)$	5	5	90.2	534
V	$(2^8, 148, 96)$	6			>32000

The results of our experiments are in Table 4. Most notably, we confirm that the degree of regularity reached during the execution of the algorithm matches the theoretical estimation. This holds for both security level I and III. For security level V, the degree of regularity is expected to be six, hence we could not perform the verification due to the high memory requirements. For further assurance, we verified our complexity estimation on other parameter sets that are not part of the MQ-Sign specification, but follow the usual UOV ratios. We conclude that the MQ instances that need to be solved in the second part of the algorithm behave as semi-regular instances and the complexity of finding a solution can reliably be estimated using the analysis in [2].

Verification scripts for both attacks outlined in this paper can be found at

https://github.com/mtrimoska/MQ-Sign-attack.

6 Impact on the MQ-Sign Variants

Both attacks presented in this paper rely on the specific structure of the linear transformation **S**, as per the *equivalent keys* key generation technique. This technique is used in most modern UOV-based signature schemes, including MQ-Sign. If the equivalent keys structure is removed and **S** is a random affine map[2], this change of representation comes with additional memory cost. Specifically, Table 5 shows the impact of this modification on the secret key sizes, compared to the sizes reported in the MQ-Sign specification. The comparison is shown for the three MQ-Sign variants that are concerned by the two attacks proposed in this paper. The fourth variant, MQ-Sign-RR, is equivalent to the traditional UOV scheme and is not affected by our attacks. For this variant, the use of the equivalent keys structure of **S** is still a concern for side-channel attacks [1,21].

[2] This was suggested by the authors of MQ-Sign as a countermeasure when the attack in Sect. 3 was first announced.

Table 5. Size (in Bytes) of the secret key of MQ-Sign with and without the equivalent keys structure of **S**.

Variant	Security Level					
	I		III		V	
	equivalent keys **S**	random **S**	equivalent keys **S**	random **S**	equivalent keys **S**	random **S**
MQ-Sign-SS	15 561	26 173	37 729	63 521	66 421	111 749
MQ-Sign-RS	133 137	143 749	485 281	511 073	1 110 709	1 156 037
MQ-Sign-SR	164 601	175 213	610 273	636 065	1 416 181	1 461 509

Furthermore, this countermeasure was shown to be insufficient for the variants where the vinegar-oil space is sparse. In subsequent work, Ikematsu, Jo, and Yasuda [15] propose an attack that does not rely on the equivalent structure of **S** and remains practical: it runs in no more than 30 min for all security levels.

For the MQ-Sign-SR variant, further research is needed to determine whether the sparseness of $\mathcal{F}_V$ can still be exploited in a similar manner when **S** is random.

7 Discussion on Using Sparse Matrices

MQ-Sign follows the UOV construction that is widely believed to be solid. Yet, as we have demonstrated, bad choices for optimization have significantly damaged its security. The aforementioned attacks were possible due to mainly two reasons. First, the *secret* polynomials were chosen sparse. Thus, we could derive more equations from the public key entries and their computation in Eq. (6) than there are secret key entries to obscure them. Second, the secret key polynomials were chosen so sparse, that half of the public key equations turned bilinear after fixing certain variables. The question that remains is whether we can still make use of sparseness to reduce the size of the (expanded) keys.

As an alternative, we could, instead of choosing sparse secret submatrices $\mathbf{F}_1^{(k)}$ and $\mathbf{F}_2^{(k)}$, choose the public $\mathbf{P}_1^{(k)}$ and $\mathbf{P}_2^{(k)}$ sparse. Our key-recovery attack does not work anymore, but, we would need to add more coefficients to the matrices, so that the strategy in Sect. 4 does not apply anymore.

The approach complements current UOV instantiations [4] which use key compression techniques. The authors of [4] expand the matrices $\mathbf{P}_1^{(k)}$ and $\mathbf{P}_2^{(k)}$ from a seed $\texttt{seed}_{pk}$ and only store $cpk = (\texttt{seed}_{pk}, \mathbf{P}_3^{(k)})$. Therefore, making these two matrices sparse will not result in a smaller compressed public key, but the size of the expanded secret key and the expanded public key would be reduced, which implies a lower overall storage requirement.

However, caution should be put into the choice of the sparse public matrices. The strategy of using "rotating diagonals" seems to work well with regards to the standard attacks against UOV analyzed in the specs. However, the sparse equations introduce enough structure to make a direct attack cheaper than in the no-sparse case. An option could be to slightly increase the number of non-zero coefficients in $\mathbf{P}_1^{(k)}$ and $\mathbf{P}_2^{(k)}$, enough to increase the cost of our attack or a similar direct attack. This is of course an ad-hoc solution, and more scrutiny is required in order to determine whether a secure balance can be found that is a better solution than simply increasing the parameters. We leave this question as future work.

References

1. Aulbach, T., Campos, F., Krämer, J., Samardjiska, S., Stöttinger, M.: Separating oil and vinegar with a single trace side-channel assisted Kipnis-Shamir attack on UOV. IACR Trans. Cryptogr. Hardw. Embed. Syst. **2023**(3), 221–245 (2023)
2. Bardet, M.: Étude des systèmes algébriques surdéterminés. Applications aux codes correcteurs et à la cryptographie. Ph.D. thesis, Université de Paris VI (2004)
3. Beullens, W.: Breaking rainbow takes a weekend on a laptop. In: Dodis, Y., Shrimpton, T. (eds.) CRYPTO 2022. LNCS, vol. 13508, pp. 464–479. Springer, Cham (2022). https://doi.org/10.1007/978-3-031-15979-4_16
4. Beullens, W., et al.: Oil and vinegar: modern parameters and implementations. IACR Trans. Cryptogr. Hardw. Embed. Syst. **321–365**, 2023 (2023)
5. Bosma, W., Cannon, J., Playoust, C.: The magma algebra system. I. The user language. J. Symbolic Comput. **24**(3–4), 235–265 (1997). Computational algebra and number theory (London, 1993)
6. Casanova, A., Faugère, J.-C., Macario-Rat, G., Patarin, J., Perret, L., Ryckeghem, J.: GeMSS. Technical report, National Institute of Standards and Technology (2020)
7. Chinese Association for Cryptologic Research (CACR). CACR post-quantum competition (2018)
8. Ding, J., et al.: Rainbow. Technical report, National Institute of Standards and Technology (2020)
9. Ding, J., Hu, L., Yang, B.-Y., Chen, J.-M.: Note on design criteria for rainbow-type multivariates. Cryptology ePrint Archive, Report 2006/307 (2006)
10. Faugère, J.-C.: A new efficient algorithm for computing Gröbner bases (F_4). J. Pure Appl. Algebra **139**, 61–88 (1999)
11. Faugère, J.-C.: A new efficient algorithm for computing Gröbner bases without reduction to zero (F_5). In: Proceedings of the 2002 International Symposium on Symbolic and Algebraic Computation, ISSAC, pp. 75–83. ACM Press (2002)
12. I. O. for Standardization ISO/IEC JTC 1/SC 27 (WG2). Information security, cybersecurity and privacy protection: ISO/IEC WD 14888-4 Information technology - Security techniques - Digital signatures with appendix - Part 4: Stateful hash-based mechanisms. https://www.iso.org/standard/80492.html
13. Hulsing, A., et al.: SPHINCS+. NIST PQC Submission (2020)
14. Hülsing, A., Butin, D., Gazdag, S.-L., Rijneveld, J., Mohaisen, A.: XMSS: extended hash-based signatures. RFC 8391 (2018)
15. Ikematsu, Y., Jo, H., Yasuda, T.: A security analysis on MQ-Sign. In: Kim, H., Youn, J. (eds.) WISA 2023. LNCS, vol. 14402, pp. 40–51. Springer, Singapore (2024). https://doi.org/10.1007/978-981-99-8024-6_4
16. Kipnis, A., Patarin, J., Goubin, L.: Unbalanced oil and vinegar signature schemes. In: Stern, J. (ed.) EUROCRYPT 1999. LNCS, vol. 1592, pp. 206–222. Springer, Heidelberg (1999). https://doi.org/10.1007/3-540-48910-X_15
17. Kipnis, A., Shamir, A.: Cryptanalysis of the oil and vinegar signature scheme. In: Krawczyk, H. (ed.) CRYPTO 1998. LNCS, vol. 1462, pp. 257–266. Springer, Heidelberg (1998). https://doi.org/10.1007/BFb0055733

18. Lyubashevsky, V., et al.: Crystals-dilithium. NIST PQC Submission (2020)
19. Mosca, M., Piani, M.: 2021 quantum threat timeline report (2022)
20. National Institute for Standards and Technology. Post-Quantum Cryptography Standardization (2017)
21. Park, A., Shim, K.-A., Koo, N., Han, D.-G.: Side-channel attacks on post-quantum signature schemes based on multivariate quadratic equations **2018**(3), 500–523 (2018). https://tches.iacr.org/index.php/TCHES/article/view/7284
22. Patarin, J.: The oil and vinegar signature scheme (1997)
23. Petzoldt, A.: Selecting and reducing key sizes for multivariate cryptography. Ph.D. thesis, Darmstadt University of Technology, Germany (2013)
24. Petzoldt, A., Bulygin, S., Buchmann, J.: CyclicRainbow - a multivariate signature scheme with a partially cyclic public key based on rainbow. Cryptology ePrint Archive, Report 2010/424 (2010)
25. Prest, T., et al.: FALCON. NIST PQC Submission (2020)
26. Quantum Resistant Cryptography Research Center. Korean post-quantum cryptographic competition (2022)
27. Shim, K.-A., Kim, J., An, Y.: MQ-Sign: a new post-quantum signature scheme based on multivariate quadratic equations: shorter and faster (2022). https://www.kpqc.or.kr/images/pdf/MQ-Sign.pdf
28. Tao, C., Petzoldt, A., Ding, J.: Efficient key recovery for all HFE signature variants. In: Malkin, T., Peikert, C. (eds.) CRYPTO 2021. LNCS, vol. 12825, pp. 70–93. Springer, Cham (2021). https://doi.org/10.1007/978-3-030-84242-0_4
29. The Sage Developers. SageMath, the Sage Mathematics Software System (Version 9.5) (2022). https://www.sagemath.org
30. Yang, B.-Y., Chen, J.-M., Chen, Y.-H.: TTS: high-speed signatures on a low-cost smart card. In: Joye, M., Quisquater, J.-J. (eds.) CHES 2004. LNCS, vol. 3156, pp. 371–385. Springer, Heidelberg (2004). https://doi.org/10.1007/978-3-540-28632-5_27

Practical and Theoretical Cryptanalysis of VOX

Hao Guo[1,2], Yi Jin[3], Yuansheng Pan[3], Xiaoou He[3], Boru Gong[3], and Jintai Ding[1,2](✉)

[1] Beijing Institute of Mathematical Sciences and Applications, Beijing, China
jintai.ding@gmail.com
[2] Yau Mathematical Sciences Center, Tsinghua University, Beijing, China
guoh22@mails.tsinghua.edu.cn
[3] CCBFT, Shanghai, China

Abstract. VOX is a UOV-like hash-and-sign signature scheme from the Multivariate Quadratic (MQ) family, which has been submitted to NIST Post-Quantum Cryptography Project, in response to NIST's Call for Additional Digital Signature Schemes for the PQC Standardization Process. In 2023, the submitters of VOX updated the sets of recommended parameters of VOX, due to the rectangular MinRank attack proposed by Furue and Ikematsu.

In this work we demonstrate the insecurity of the updated VOX from both the practical and the theoretical aspects.

First, we conduct a practical MinRank attack against VOX, which uses multiple matrices from matrix deformation of public key to form a large rectangular matrix and evaluate the rank of this new matrix. By using Kipnis–Shamir method and Gröbner basis calculation only instead of support-minors method, our experiment shows it could recover, *within two seconds*, the secret key of almost every updated recommended instance of VOX.

Moreover, we propose a theoretical analysis on VOX by expressing public/secret key as matrices over a smaller field to find a low-rank matrix, resulting in a more precise estimation on the concrete hardness of VOX; for instance, the newly recommended VOX instance claimed to achieve NIST security level 3 turns out to be 69-bit-hard, as our analysis shows.

Keywords: PQC · MPKC · VOX

1 Introduction

The UOV signature scheme has been introduced for more than 20 years, and remains competitive in its short signature and fast verification. However, UOV and its variants suffer from long public key length. Therefore the researchers have been devoted to compressing the public key size of UOV as well as its variants. Recently NIST announced an additional round for post-quantum signatures and

M.-J. Saarinen and D. Smith-Tone (Eds.): PQCrypto 2024, LNCS 14772, pp. 186–208, 2024.
https://doi.org/10.1007/978-3-031-62746-0_9

received about 40 submissions. Among the submissions seven of them are UOV-like schemes: MAYO [5], PROV [19], QR-UOV [17], SNOVA [29], TUOV [9], UOV [6] and VOX [26].

In this work we concentrate on the VOX scheme [26], which was proposed by Patarin et al., and it combines the idea of QR-UOV [18] and plus modification [15]. After the publication of VOX, Furue and Ikematsu [16] proposed an equivalent key recovery attack using rectangular MinRank attack. Rectangular MinRank attack was proposed by Beullens in [3], and the idea has also been found in [27]. In [16] the authors showed that MAYO and QR-UOV remains secure under the rectangular MinRank attack. However VOX turned out to be vulnerable under their traditional rectangular MinRank attack, due to the fact that $O > t$ in its previously recommended parameters, where O and t denote the number of oil variables and that of random polynomials, respectively. Consequently, the submitters of VOX updated their recommended parameters by requiring that $O \leq t$ and claimed that the new design will withstand the rectangular MinRank attack [24].

In this work we demonstrate that VOX equipped with its newly updated recommended parameters [24] is still *insecure* from both the practical and theoretical aspects, and more work should be done in respect of security analysis of VOX.

Practical attack against VOX. First, the main contribution of this work is a MinRank attack against VOX even if $t \geq O$. Its general idea is to concatenate l matrices from matrix deformation [22] of public key matrices vertically and evaluate the rank of this new matrix. By observing that columns of central map shuffle consistently thanks to matrix deformation formula, we find that such vertical concatenationof multiple matrices can not only be done on rectangular central map to form a matrix of rank at most $lV + t$, but also be done on rectangular public key matrices and also form a matrix of the same rank.

Compared with the attack in [16] which only uses one matrix from matrix deformation, our attack uses multiple matrices to form the target matrix, making our attack work as long as $O \leq t < O(O+1)/2$. Moreover, when solving this MinRank instance, we use Kipnis–Shamir method instead of support-minors method, and we solve the equations generated by Kipnis–Shamir method using only Gröbner basis calculation, which is in sharp contrast with other algorithms for the MinRank problem. The power of our attack can be fully demonstrated by the following experiment: when running on a server with a 2.40GHz CPU and 32GB memory, the first attack can quickly recover, within 1 min, the secret key of almost every VOX recommended instance; in particular, it takes less than 2 s for six out of nine recommended instances of VOX. However, we do not know why our first attack can break VOX in such an efficient manner, and more work need to be done in terms of its theoretical analysis (Table 1).

Theoretical analysis against VOX. Furthermore, we propose a theoretical analysis against VOX, which could be traced back to the QR-structure in VOX. As shown in Sect. 4, when the dimension c has a proper factor, say c_1, the field

Table 1. Experiment result of our practical attack.

λ	q	O	V	c	t	Running time (second)	Total Memory Usage (MB)
128	251	4	5	13	6	0.170	32.09
		5	6	11	6	0.510	32.09
		6	7	9	6	27357.799	6147.06
192	1021	5	6	15	7	0.440	32.09
		6	7	13	7	0.790	32.09
		7	8	11	7	26.170	157.69
256	4093	6	7	17	8	1.240	64.12
		7	8	14	8	1.870	64.12
		8	9	13	8	51.530	256.00

extension $\mathbb{F}_q \subset \mathbb{F}_{q^c}$ in the VOX has a nontrivial intermediate field $\mathbb{F}_{q^{c_1}}$, and the public/secret keys could be seen as matrices over this intermediate field obviously; moreover, direct verification shows that when the degree of extension $[\mathbb{F}_{q^c} : \mathbb{F}_{q^{c_1}}]$ is larger than t/O, we can always construct from the secret key a matrix that is not full-rank, and then use Kipnis-Shamir method to solve this MinRank problem over this intermediate extension field. Compared with previous MinRank attacks, our theoretical analysis aims to find low-rank matrices in an intermediate field by fully utilizing properties of the QR-structure, provided that c is composite. The strength of our second attack can be gleaned from the fact that for the the newly updated recommended parameter sets of VOX claimed to achieve NIST security 1, 3, and 5, their concrete hardness are actually 112-, 69-, and 48-bits-hard, respectively (Table 2).

Table 2. Estimated complexity of our theoretical attack.

λ	q	$O = m/c$	$V = v/c$	c	c_1	t	d	D_{mgd}	$\log_2 C$
128	251	6	7	9	3	6	2	12	112.46
	251	5	6	10	5	6	1	6	49.64
192	1021	5	6	15	5	7	1	8	69.48
256	4093	7	8	14	7	8	1	5	48.04

Organization. Our paper is organized as follows. Section 2 contains some preliminaries including the VOX scheme, MinRank problem and rectangular MinRank attack. In Sect. 3, we first introduce our padded MinRank attack, then show its practical performance against VOX parameters, and finally give our explanation of why it works. In Sect. 4, we first show the idea of intermediate field attack, explaining its construction, then give our hypothetical complexity analysis for the parameters that this attack can be used on. We conclude this work in Sect. 5.

2 Preliminaries

2.1 About the VOX Scheme

Generally speaking, a UOV-like digital signature follows the bipolar form [10]. The private key is $(\mathcal{S}, \mathcal{F}, \mathcal{T})$, where $\mathcal{S} : \mathbb{F}_q^n \to \mathbb{F}_q^n$ and $\mathcal{T} : \mathbb{F}_q^m \to \mathbb{F}_q^m$ are both invertible linear transformations, and $\mathcal{F} : \mathbb{F}_q^n \to \mathbb{F}_q^m$ consists of m homogeneous quadratic polynomials f_1, \ldots, f_m that can be somehow efficiently invertible. The public key \mathcal{P} satisfies $\mathcal{P} = \mathcal{T} \circ \mathcal{F} \circ \mathcal{S}$. For simplicity, we would identify maps $\mathcal{S}, \mathcal{T}, \mathcal{F}, \mathcal{P}$ with square matrices $\mathbf{S} \in \mathrm{GL}_n(\mathbb{F}_q), \mathbf{T} \in \mathrm{GL}_m(\mathbb{F}_q)$ and symmetric matrices $\mathbf{F} \in \mathrm{Mat}_n(\mathbb{F}_q), \mathbf{P} \in \mathrm{Mat}_m(\mathbb{F}_q)$ respectively.

$$\begin{array}{ccc} \mathbb{F}_q^n & \xrightarrow{\;\mathcal{F}\;} & \mathbb{F}_q^m \\ {\scriptstyle \mathcal{S}} \big\uparrow & & \big\downarrow {\scriptstyle \mathcal{T}} \\ \mathbb{F}_q^n & \xrightarrow{\;\mathcal{P}\;} & \mathbb{F}_q^m \end{array}$$

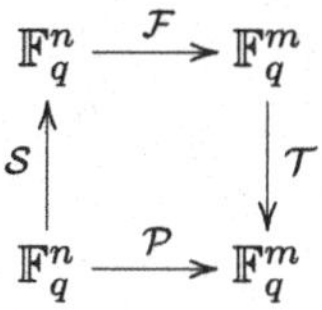

To invert \mathcal{F} efficiently, OV polynomial comes to attention. An $(n, n-m)$-OV polynomial f_k can be defined as

$$f_k(x_1, \ldots, x_n) = \sum_{i=1}^{n-m} \sum_{j=i}^{n} a_{ij}^{(k)} x_i x_j$$

with $a_{ij}^{(k)} \in \mathbb{F}_q$. Notice that f_k is linear in x_{n-m+1}, \ldots, x_n when x_1, \ldots, x_{n-m} are fixed. Then we say there are $v = n - m$ vinegar-variables x_1, \ldots, x_v and $o = m$ oil-variables x_{v+1}, \ldots, x_{v+o}.

VOX is a UOV-like scheme that constructs the secret key \mathcal{F} by mixing t totally random quadratic polynomials and $o - t$ OV polynomials with quotient ring structure. Let c be a common divisor of o and v, we denote $O = o/c$, $V = v/c$ and $N = n/c$. Then there are V vinegar-variables, O oil-variables and o equations over \mathbb{F}_{q^c} utilizing the QR-structure. Specifically, we have private key $(\mathcal{S}, \mathcal{F}, \mathcal{T})$ where $\mathcal{S} : \mathbb{F}_{q^c}^N \to \mathbb{F}_{q^c}^N$ and $\mathcal{T} : \mathbb{F}_q^o \to \mathbb{F}_q^o$ are both invertible linear transformations, and $\mathcal{F} : \mathbb{F}_{q^c}^N \to \mathbb{F}_{q^c}^o$ consists of t totally random quadratic polynomials and $o - t$ (N, V)-OV polynomials. Notice that \mathcal{T} has matrix representation $\mathbf{T} \in \mathrm{GL}_o(\mathbb{F}_q) \subseteq \mathrm{GL}_o(\mathbb{F}_{q^c})$, thus it can be directly induced as transformation over $\mathbb{F}_{q^c}^o$ that is also denoted by \mathcal{T}. And we can obtain the following commutative diagram where $\mathrm{Tr} : \mathbb{F}_{q^c} \to \mathbb{F}_q$ is the trace function. Basically, VOX's signing process is to find pre-image of $\mathrm{Tr}^{\oplus o} \circ \mathcal{F}$ and its verification should operate computation of $\mathrm{Tr}^{\oplus o} \circ \mathcal{P}$. However, for simplicity, we denote the public key as $\mathcal{P} = \mathcal{T} \circ \mathcal{F} \circ \mathcal{S} : \mathbb{F}_{q^c}^N \to \mathbb{F}_{q^c}^o$.

$$\begin{array}{ccccc} \mathbb{F}_{q^c}^N & \xrightarrow{\;\mathcal{F}\;} & \mathbb{F}_{q^c}^o & \xrightarrow{\;\mathrm{Tr}^{\oplus o}\;} & \mathbb{F}_q^o \\ {\scriptstyle \mathcal{S}} \big\uparrow & & \big\downarrow {\scriptstyle \mathcal{T}} & & \big\downarrow {\scriptstyle \mathcal{T}} \\ \mathbb{F}_{q^c}^N & \xrightarrow{\;\mathcal{P}\;} & \mathbb{F}_{q^c}^o & \xrightarrow{\;\mathrm{Tr}^{\oplus o}\;} & \mathbb{F}_q^o \end{array}$$

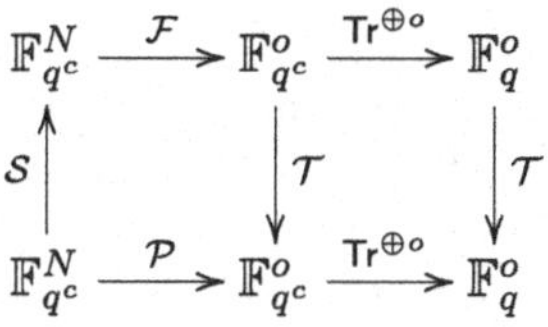

Here we list the current parameters given in [24] in Table 3.

Table 3. Current parameters of VOX.

λ	q	$O = m/c$	$V = v/c$	c	t
128	251	4	5	13	6
		5	6	11	6
		6	7	9	6
192	1021	5	6	15	7
		6	7	13	7
		7	8	11	7
256	4093	6	7	17	8
		7	8	14	8
		8	9	13	8

2.2 The MinRank Problem

Put it simply, the MinRank problem asks for a linear (or affine) combination of given matrices that has a small rank. This problem is first abstracted by Courtois [8], where he generalized the problem of Syndrome Decoding from coding theory. The problem we are interested in is the search version of the MinRank problem:

Definition 1 (Homogeneous MinRank problem). *Let* $\mathbf{M}_1, \ldots, \mathbf{M}_K$ *be some* m*-by-*n *matrices over a* finite *field* $\mathbb{F}_q$, *and let* $r < \min(m, n)$. *The problem asks for* $x_1, \ldots, x_K \in \mathbb{F}_q$ *which are not all zero, such that*

$$\mathbf{M} := \sum_{k=1}^{K} x_k \mathbf{M}_k$$

has rank no more than r.

We denote the set of instances with parameter (m, n, K, r, q) as $\mathrm{MR}(m, n, K, r, q)$. When the field is clear from context we also omit q. There is also the inhomogeneous version:

Definition 2 (Inhomogeneous MinRank problem). *Let* $\mathbf{M}_0; \mathbf{M}_1, \ldots, \mathbf{M}_K$ *be some* m*-by-*n *matrices over a* finite *field* $\mathbb{F}_q$, *and let* $r < \min(m, n)$. *The problem asks for* $x_1, \ldots, x_K \in \mathbb{F}_q$, *such that*

$$\mathbf{M} := \mathbf{M}_0 + \sum_{k=1}^{K} x_k \mathbf{M}_k$$

has rank no more than r.

We denote the set of problems with parameter (m, n, K, r, q) as $\overline{\mathrm{MR}}(m, n, K, r, q)$. When the field is clear from context we also omit q.

In homogeneous case, we require that all the $\mathbf{M}_k$'s are of rank at least $r + 1$; In inhomogeneous case, we require that $\mathbf{M}_0$ is of rank at least $r + 1$. This is to avoid trivial solutions.

2.3 Combinatorial and Algebraic Methods for Solving the MinRank problem

Courtois mentioned in [8] that the MinRank problem is NP-hard via reduction from syndrome decoding problem of a linear error correcting code which is NP-complete. Faugère [14] on another hand gives a reduction from rank decoding problem, also showing its hardness. Nonetheless, there have been many methods to solve the MinRank problem. These methods fall into two categories: combinatorial method, and algebraic method.

Kernel attack [20] is the first method proposed to solve the MinRank problem. It is proposed by Goubin and Courtois. The idea is to choose vectors $\mathbf{y}_k \in \mathbb{F}_q^n$ randomly, hoping they could fall into the kernel of $\mathbf{M}$, the linear (affine) combination of given matrices, then solve for the coefficient x_k's using the linear equations $\mathbf{M}\mathbf{y}_k = \mathbf{0}$. This is a combinatorial method, and the complexity of kernel attack is $O(q^{\lceil K/m \rceil r} K^3)$.

Minors attack [12] is the simple algebraic method, which takes out all $(r+1)$-minors of $\mathbf{M}$, and solving the system equations where all these minors are equal to zero. While it only involves the x_k variables, the degree of each equation is $r+1$. This causes complexity of the method to rely heavily on the general method of solving system of multivariate equations using Gröbner basis, which has complexity $O(\binom{K+d}{d}^{\omega})$ where d is the degree of regularity for the determinant ideal, and ω is the constant for matrix multiplication.

Kipnis–Shamir attack [23] tries to solve for the right kernel of $\mathbf{M}$. Since $\mathbf{M}$ is of size m-by-n and has rank at most r, its right kernel has at least $n-r$ dimensions, which means $n-r$ linear independent vectors $\mathbf{y}_k$ can be chosen such that $\mathbf{M}\mathbf{y}_k = \mathbf{0}$. Different with kernel attack, Kipnis–Shamir attack sets new variables as coordinates of $\mathbf{y}_k$'s, and gets bilinear quadratic equations. Kipnis–Shamir attack is analyzed [14] to contain equations in Minors attack. For more information about the complexity of Kipnis–Shamir attack we refer the readers to [12–14,25,28,30].

Support-Minors attack is the state-of-the-art method of solving homogeneous MinRank problems. It decomposes the matrix $\mathbf{M}$ as product of two rank r matrices $\mathbf{M} = \mathbf{S}\mathbf{C}$ where $\mathbf{C}$ is a r-by-n matrix, and sets the maximal minors of $\mathbf{C}$ as new variables. Equations are obtained by augmenting $\mathbf{C}$ with each row of $\mathbf{M}$, and letting the new maximal minors (the size increased by one) be zero. This new attack has been analyzed [1,21] to contain the equations in Kipnis–Shamir attack. For complexity of Support-Minors attack we refer the readers to [2].

2.4 Previous MinRank Attacks on UOV-Like Schemes

Among UOV-like schemes, MinRank attack was first applied to Rainbow [11], where a linear combination of public key matrices has exceptionally small rank. In this attack the matrices are chosen as the public key itself. In [3] the author introduced a new type of MinRank attack on Rainbow, called *rectangular* MinRank attack. The idea can be abstracted using Ikematsu's matrix deformation [22]: Let $(\mathbf{Q}_1, \ldots, \mathbf{Q}_m)$ be a set of n-by-n matrices over $\mathbb{F}_q$, and let $\mathbf{q}_k^{(j)}$

denote the j-th column vector of $\mathbf{Q}_k$. Then we define the new set $(\tilde{\mathbf{Q}}_1, \ldots, \tilde{\mathbf{Q}}_n)$ of n-by-m matrices as

$$\begin{aligned} \tilde{\mathbf{Q}}_1 &= \left[\mathbf{q}_1^{(1)}\ \mathbf{q}_2^{(1)} \cdots \mathbf{q}_m^{(1)}\right] \\ \tilde{\mathbf{Q}}_2 &= \left[\mathbf{q}_1^{(2)}\ \mathbf{q}_2^{(2)} \cdots \mathbf{q}_m^{(2)}\right] \\ &\vdots \\ \tilde{\mathbf{Q}}_n &= \left[\mathbf{q}_1^{(n)}\ \mathbf{q}_2^{(n)} \cdots \mathbf{q}_m^{(n)}\right] \end{aligned} \tag{1}$$

It is stated in [22] that if $\mathbf{S}$ is an n-by-n matrix and $\mathbf{T}$ is an m-by-m matrix, and $(\mathbf{F}_1, \ldots, \mathbf{F}_m)$ is a set of n-by-n matrices, then the matrix deformation of $(\mathbf{P}_1, \ldots, \mathbf{P}_m) = (\mathbf{S}\mathbf{F}_1\mathbf{S}^\top, \ldots, \mathbf{S}\mathbf{F}_m\mathbf{S}^\top)\mathbf{T}$ is

$$(\tilde{\mathbf{P}}_1, \ldots, \tilde{\mathbf{P}}_n) = (\mathbf{S}\tilde{\mathbf{F}}_1\mathbf{T}, \ldots, \mathbf{S}\tilde{\mathbf{F}}_n\mathbf{T})\mathbf{S}^\top \tag{2}$$

Therefore if some of the $\tilde{\mathbf{F}}_i$'s have some low rank property, then a linear combination of $\tilde{\mathbf{P}}_i$ should also be low rank.

[16] also applied rectangular MinRank attack on MAYO [4] and QR-UOV [18], and confirmed that MAYO and QR-UOV are secure under rectangular MinRank attack. VOX, however, is shown to be weak under this attack. In [24], the authors summarized the attack given by [16]. The idea is to notice that if we view the UOV map as on extension field $\mathbb{F}_{q^c}$ and generate the $\mathbf{F}_i$'s and $\mathbf{P}_i$'s correspondingly, the matrix deformation $\tilde{\mathbf{F}}_N$ have rank at most $V + t$, due to its special shape: the last $m - t$ columns of $\tilde{\mathbf{F}}_N$ have the last O rows as zero rows, so the rank they can contribute is at most V; the first t columns of $\tilde{\mathbf{F}}_N$ are random, however since $O > t$, the rank they can contribute additionally is at most t (Fig. 1).

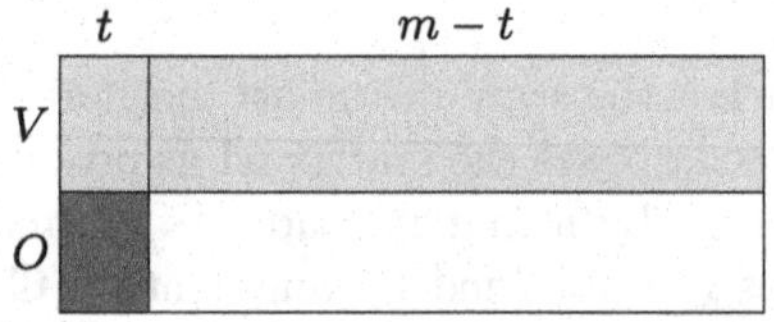

Fig. 1. Shape of $\tilde{\mathbf{F}}_N$. The rank does not exceed $V + t$.

Since $\mathbf{S}\tilde{\mathbf{F}}_N\mathbf{T}$ is a linear combination of $\tilde{\mathbf{P}}_1, \ldots, \tilde{\mathbf{P}}_N$, this creates a MinRank instance. The authors used the support minors method to estimate the complexity of the attack, and the results are listed in Table 4.

3 A Practical Attack Against VOX

Our first idea comes from the disadvantage that rectangular MinRank attack cannot be applied to VOX, due to the fact that $\tilde{\mathbf{F}}_i$'s are all full row rank now.

Table 4. Complexity of the Rectangular MinRank attack on VOX parameters

λ	q	$O = m/c$	$V = v/c$	c	t	$\log_2 C$
128	251	8	9	6	6	50.8
192	1021	10	11	7	7	54.8
256	4093	12	13	8	8	55.3

However, if we concatenate $\tilde{\mathbf{F}}_{N-1}$ and $\tilde{\mathbf{F}}_N$ vertically, the concatenated matrix will have rank at most $2V + t$, due to the fact that $2O > t$ and $m - t > 2V$ for the parameters in Table 3 (Fig. 2).

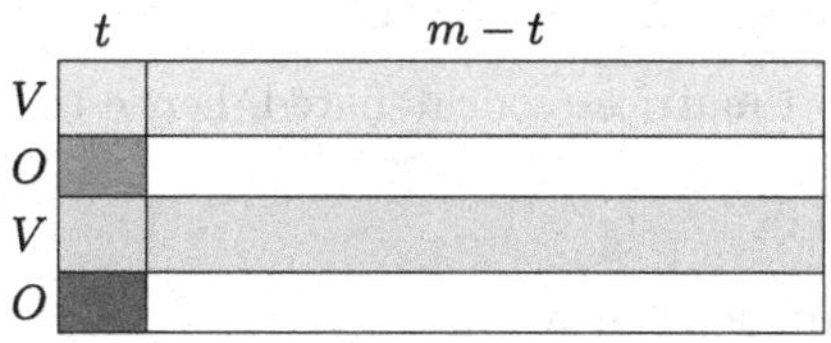

Fig. 2. The shape of $\begin{bmatrix}\tilde{\mathbf{F}}_{N-1}\\ \tilde{\mathbf{F}}_N\end{bmatrix}$. The rank does not exceed $2V + t$.

Generally, for $l \leq O$, if $m - t > lV$ and $lO > t$, then the following matrix

$$\mathbf{M}'_{\mathbf{s}} = \begin{bmatrix}\mathbf{S}\tilde{\mathbf{F}}_{N-l+1}\mathbf{T}\\ \vdots \\ \mathbf{S}\tilde{\mathbf{F}}_N\mathbf{T}\end{bmatrix} = \begin{bmatrix}\mathbf{S}\tilde{\mathbf{F}}_{N-l+1}\\ \vdots \\ \mathbf{S}\tilde{\mathbf{F}}_N\end{bmatrix}\mathbf{T} = (\mathbf{I}_l \otimes \mathbf{S})\begin{bmatrix}\tilde{\mathbf{F}}_{N-l+1}\\ \vdots \\ \tilde{\mathbf{F}}_N\end{bmatrix}\mathbf{T}$$

has rank at most $lV + t$. Using the formula (2), since $\mathbf{S}\tilde{\mathbf{F}}_{N-l+1}\mathbf{T}, \ldots, \mathbf{S}\tilde{\mathbf{F}}_N\mathbf{T}$ are all linear combinations of $\tilde{\mathbf{P}}_1, \ldots, \tilde{\mathbf{P}}_N$, it seems that we need to find choices of $x_{1,i}, \ldots, x_{l,i}$ such that

$$\mathbf{M}'_{\mathbf{s}} = \begin{bmatrix}\sum_{i=1}^N x_{1,i}\tilde{\mathbf{P}}_i\\ \vdots \\ \sum_{i=1}^N x_{l,i}\tilde{\mathbf{P}}_i\end{bmatrix}$$

has rank at most $lV + t$. However, if we naively solve this, we will get many spurious solutions which we do not really want. For example, if we choose $x_{1,i} = \cdots = x_{l,i}$ for all i, then $\mathbf{M}'_{\mathbf{s}}$ will have rank at most N, which is not what we want. However, from (2) notice that $\mathbf{x}_j = (x_{j,1}, \ldots, x_{j,N})$ should be the $N - l + j$ column of $(\mathbf{S}^\top)^{-1}$, which is a block upper triangular matrix, therefore we have for $i > V$ that

$$x_{j,i} = \begin{cases}1, & i = N - l + j\\ 0, & \text{otherwise}\end{cases}$$

As such we have

$$\mathbf{M_s} = \begin{bmatrix} \sum_{i=1}^{V} x_{1,i}\tilde{\mathbf{P}}_i + \tilde{\mathbf{P}}_{N-l+1} \\ \vdots \\ \sum_{i=1}^{V} x_{l,i}\tilde{\mathbf{P}}_i + \tilde{\mathbf{P}}_N \end{bmatrix} \tag{3}$$

which is an inhomogeneous MinRank instance. If we write out each component of linear combination, we notice that each component has the form of

$$\tilde{\mathbf{F}}_i^{(j,l)} = \begin{bmatrix} \mathbf{0} \\ \vdots \\ \tilde{\mathbf{F}}_i \\ \vdots \\ \mathbf{0} \end{bmatrix} \tag{4}$$

where l is the number of matrices concatenated, hence the name "padded" rectangular MinRank.

3.1 Nontrivial Rank Fall of $\mathbf{M_s}$

In this subsection we show that, due to the symmetry property of public key and central map, the rows of $\mathbf{M_s}$ have a structured linear combination which amounts to zero. Recall that if the central map $\mathbf{F}_i$'s are symmetric, so are the public keys $\mathbf{P}_i$. Now we have $\mathbf{x}_j = (x_{j,1}, \ldots, x_{j,N})$, so

$$\sum_{i=1}^{V} x_{1,i}\tilde{\mathbf{P}}_i + \tilde{\mathbf{P}}_{N-l+1} = \left[\mathbf{P}_1\mathbf{x}_1{}^\top\ \mathbf{P}_2\mathbf{x}_1{}^\top \cdots \mathbf{P}_o\mathbf{x}_1{}^\top\right]$$

Similarly we have

$$\sum_{i=1}^{V} x_{2,i}\tilde{\mathbf{P}}_i + \tilde{\mathbf{P}}_{N-l+2} = \left[\mathbf{P}_1\mathbf{x}_2{}^\top\ \mathbf{P}_2\mathbf{x}_2{}^\top \cdots \mathbf{P}_o\mathbf{x}_2{}^\top\right]$$

Therefore

$$\begin{aligned} \mathbf{x}_2\left(\sum_{i=1}^{V} x_{1,i}\tilde{\mathbf{P}}_i + \tilde{\mathbf{P}}_{N-l+1}\right) &= \left[\mathbf{x}_2\mathbf{P}_1\mathbf{x}_1{}^\top\ \mathbf{x}_2\mathbf{P}_2\mathbf{x}_1{}^\top \cdots \mathbf{x}_2\mathbf{P}_o\mathbf{x}_1{}^\top\right] \\ &= \left[\mathbf{x}_1\mathbf{P}_1\mathbf{x}_2{}^\top\ \mathbf{x}_1\mathbf{P}_2\mathbf{x}_2{}^\top \cdots \mathbf{x}_1\mathbf{P}_o\mathbf{x}_2{}^\top\right] \\ &= \mathbf{x}_1\left(\sum_{i=1}^{V} x_{2,i}\tilde{\mathbf{P}}_i + \tilde{\mathbf{P}}_{N-l+2}\right) \end{aligned}$$

which shows that a nonzero linear combination of the first $2N$ rows is zero. For every pair of blocks such syzygy exists, so we expect $\mathbf{M_s}$ to have rank at most $lN - \binom{l}{2}$. This means that for our attack to really works, the parameters should satisfy $lV + t < lN - \binom{l}{2}$, or equivalently $t < lO - \binom{l}{2}$. Since l can be $1, 2, \ldots, O$, we expect that such attack works when $t < O(O+1)/2$.

3.2 Experimental Results

Since we are dealing with an inhomogeneous MinRank instance, we adapt the Kipnis–Shamir attack and solve for the left kernel of $\mathbf{M_s}$. The equations come from the following matrix equation:

$$\left[\mathbf{K}\;\mathbf{I}_{2N-r}\right]\mathbf{M_s} = \mathbf{0} \tag{5}$$

where $\mathbf{K}$ is an $(2N-r)$-by-r matrix whose entries form the kernel variables.

To solve for the Gröbner basis of the ideal generated by the Kipnis–Shamir attack, we used the Gröbner basis algorithm F4 with respect to the graded reverse lexicographic monomial order in Magma V2.28-2 [7] on CPU a 2.40GHz Intel Xeon Silver 4214R CPU. The Magma code we use can be viewed in Appendix A and on Github[1]. The detailed running time of the Gröbner basis solving is listed in Table 5.

Table 5. Experiment result of our attack.

λ	q	O	V	c	t	Running time (second)	Total Memory Usage (MB)
128	251	4	5	13	6	0.170	32.09
		5	6	11	6	0.510	32.09
		6	7	9	6	27357.799	6147.06
192	1021	5	6	15	7	0.440	32.09
		6	7	13	7	0.790	32.09
		7	8	11	7	26.170	157.69
256	4093	6	7	17	8	1.240	64.12
		7	8	14	8	1.870	64.12
		8	9	13	8	51.530	256.00

The attack costs less than one second for the first two parameters of level 1 and level 3, less than two seconds for the first two parameters of level 5, and less than one minute for the other parameters except the slowest one. In the experiment, we saw that all the nine systems have first degree fall at degree 3, which matches the analysis above.

3.3 Our Hypothetical Analysis for the Result

To give a theoretical upper bound for the complexity of our attack, here we adopt the analysis of [25], and introduce the monomial graded degree D_{mgd} which is the smallest total degree of monomials in

$$\frac{\prod_{i=1}^{d}(1-t_0t_i)^m}{(1-t_0)^{lV}(1-t_1)^r\dots(1-t_d)^r}$$

[1] https://github.com/tuovsig/analysis.

whose coefficient is negative. The monomial D_{mgd} is believed to bound from above the solving degree, hence it gives an upper bound for the complexity estimation. d is the number of kernel vectors we choose, and should range between 1 and $lN - r$. Using the formula $\binom{lV+dr+D_{mgd}}{D_{mgd}}^{\omega}$ to estimate the complexity C, we list the complexity estimation in Table 6.

Table 6. Estimated complexity of our practical attack.

λ	q	$O = m/c$	$V = v/c$	c	t	d	D_{mgd}	$\log_2 C$
128	251	4	5	13	6	1	5	41.28
		5	6	11	6	1	6	49.64
		6	7	9	6	1	7	58.02
192	1021	5	6	15	7	2	4	43.41
		6	7	13	7	1	5	45.92
		7	8	11	7	1	6	54.54
256	4093	6	7	17	8	1	4	45.35
		7	8	14	8	1	5	48.04
		8	9	13	8	2	6	56.83

Using this estimation, we try to fix the parameters for VOX. It is hard to tweak t respect to O, because small t will not exceed $lO - \binom{l}{2}$, while large t will make signature harder due to Gröbner basis calculation. While making c smaller can reduce the equations occurred in Kipnis–Shamir method, it will decrease the number of variables when viewed over $\mathbb{F}_q$, resulting in a decrease of security. Therefore we decided to only tweak V. We found that the complexity grows as V increases, and we checked the parameters for $V < 2O$. We found that all of the parameters still fail the estimation, with complexity less than 140 bits.

Table 7. Estimated complexity of our attack on possible VOX parameters.

λ	q	$O = m/c$	$V = v/c$	c	t	d	D_{mgd}	$\log_2 C$
128	251	4	7	13	6	1	8	78.10
		5	9	11	6	1	11	99.80
		6	11	9	6	2	13	133.96
192	1021	5	9	15	7	1	8	84.95
		6	11	13	7	1	10	101.51
		7	13	11	7	1	14	129.55
256	4093	6	11	17	8	1	8	90.60
		7	13	14	8	1	11	113.72
		8	15	13	8	1	13	130.61

4 Another Attack Against VOX

Our second idea comes from QR-structure of VOX, specifically when parameter c is a composite number, which results in the presence of an intermediate field within the field extension $\mathbb{F}_q \subset \mathbb{F}_{q^c}$ used in the VOX. Consequently, we can consider the public key as a polynomial over this intermediate field, and subsequently construct a matrix that is not full rank.

Recall that in the QR-structure, every $a \in \mathbb{F}_{q^c}$ can be expressed as a $c \times c$ matrix over $\mathbb{F}_q$ [18,26]. Specifically, let $g \in \mathbb{F}_{q^c}$ be a root of an irreducible polynomial of degree c over $\mathbb{F}_q$. The matrix expression $\Phi(a)$ is given by the following ring homomorphism:

$$\begin{aligned} \Phi :& \mathbb{F}_{q^c} \hookrightarrow \mathsf{Mat}_c(\mathbb{F}_q) \\ & a \mapsto \Phi(a), \qquad\qquad \text{where } (1, g, \dots, g^{c-1})\Phi(a) = (a, ag, \dots, ag^{c-1}). \end{aligned}$$

In order to realize this attack, we focus on the case where c is a composite number and can be factored as $c = c_1 c_2$, allowing us to express $a \in \mathbb{F}_{q^c}$ as a matrix over an intermediate field. In this case, the matrix expression is given by a ring homomorphism $\Psi : \mathbb{F}_{q^c} \hookrightarrow \mathsf{Mat}_{c_2}(\mathbb{F}_{q^{c_1}})$. The design of Ψ will be detailed in the following section.

Moreover, we can induce a map on matrix ring from Ψ

$$\begin{aligned} \mathsf{Mat}_N(\Psi) :& \mathsf{Mat}_N(\mathbb{F}_{q^c}) \rightarrow \mathsf{Mat}_N(\mathsf{Mat}_{c_2}(\mathbb{F}_{q^{c_1}})) = \mathsf{Mat}_{c_2 N}(\mathbb{F}_{q^{c_1}}) \\ & (a_{ij})_{N\times N} \mapsto (\Psi(a_{ij}))_{N\times N} \end{aligned}$$

It is straightforward to observe that this is also a ring homomorphism owing to the homomorphic property of Ψ. For matrix $\mathbf{P} \in \mathsf{Mat}_N(\mathbb{F}_{q^c})$, we denote $\mathbf{P}^{\Psi} \in \mathsf{Mat}_{c_2 N}(\mathbb{F}_{q^{c_1}})$ as the image $\mathbf{P}$ under map $\mathsf{Mat}_N(\Psi)$ in the following.

Applying the ring homomorphism $\mathsf{Mat}_N(\Psi)$ to VOX public keys, we have

$$(\mathbf{P}_1^{\Psi}, \dots, \mathbf{P}_m^{\Psi}) = (\mathbf{S}^{\Psi}\mathbf{F}_1^{\Psi}\mathbf{S}^{t\Psi}, \dots, \mathbf{S}^{\Psi}\mathbf{F}_m^{\Psi}\mathbf{S}^{t\Psi})\mathbf{T}$$

The matrix deformation of $(\mathbf{P}_1^{\Psi}, \dots, \mathbf{P}_m^{\Psi})$ (*resp.* $(\mathbf{F}_1^{\Psi}, \dots, \mathbf{F}_m^{\Psi})$) is denoted as $(\widetilde{\mathbf{P}_1^{\Psi}}, \dots, \widetilde{\mathbf{P}_{c_2 N}^{\Psi}})$ (*resp.* $(\widetilde{\mathbf{F}_1^{\Psi}}, \dots, \widetilde{\mathbf{F}_{c_2 N}^{\Psi}})$). As (2), we have

$$(\widetilde{\mathbf{P}_1^{\Psi}}, \dots, \widetilde{\mathbf{P}_{c_2 N}^{\Psi}}) = (\mathbf{S}^{\Psi}\widetilde{\mathbf{F}_1^{\Psi}}\mathbf{T}, \dots, \mathbf{S}^{\Psi}\widetilde{\mathbf{F}_{c_2 N}^{\Psi}}\mathbf{T})\mathbf{S}^{t\Psi} \tag{6}$$

We can choose a factor c_2 of c such that $c_2 V + t < c_2 N$, then the matrices $\widetilde{\mathbf{F}_i^{\Psi}}$, $i = c_2 V + 1, \dots, c_2 N$ have low rank (Fig. 3).

Generally, for a factor c_2 of c, if $m - t > c_2 V$ and $c_2 O > t$, then the matrix $\mathbf{M_s} = \mathbf{S}^{\Psi}\widetilde{\mathbf{F}_{c_2 N}^{\Psi}}\mathbf{T}$ has rank at most $c_2 V + t$. Using the formula (6), since $\mathbf{M_s}$ is linear combinations of $\widetilde{\mathbf{P}_1^{\Psi}}, \dots, \widetilde{\mathbf{P}_{c_2 N}^{\Psi}}$, it seems that we need to find choices of $x_1, \dots, x_{c_2 N}$ such that $\mathbf{M_s} = \sum_{i=1}^{c_2 N} x_i \tilde{\mathbf{P}}_i$ has rank at most $c_2 V + t$. From (6) notice that $\mathbf{x} = (x_1, \dots, x_{c_2 N})$ should be the last column of $(\mathbf{S}^{t\Psi})^{-1}$, which is a block upper triangular matrix, therefore we have $x_i = \delta_{i, c_2 N}$ for $i > V$.

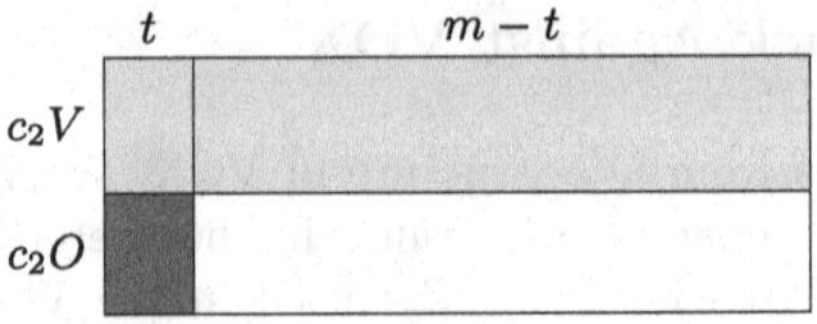

Fig. 3. Shape of $\widetilde{\mathbf{F}^{\Psi}_{c_2N}}$. The rank does not exceed $c_2V + t$.

4.1 Matrix Expression over Intermediate Field

In this section, we show the design of ring homomorphism $\Psi : \mathbb{F}_{q^c} \hookrightarrow \mathsf{Mat}_{c_2}(\mathbb{F}_{q^{c_1}})$ which brings the matrix expression over intermediate field $\mathbb{F}_{q^{c_1}}$ of element in $\mathbb{F}_{q^c}$.

In general, $\mathbb{F}_{q^c}$ is a linear space over intermediate field $\mathbb{F}_{q^{c_1}}$ of dimension c_2. Fix a basis of $\mathbb{F}_{q^c}$, denoted as $(\alpha_0, \alpha_1, \ldots, \alpha_{c_2-1})$, then we have a nature ring homomorphism

$$\begin{aligned}\Psi' :&\mathbb{F}_{q^c} \hookrightarrow \mathsf{Mat}_{c_2}(\mathbb{F}_{q^{c_1}})\\ &a \mapsto \Psi(a), \qquad\qquad \text{where } (\alpha_0, \alpha_1, \ldots, \alpha_{c_2-1})\Psi(a) = (a\alpha_0, a\alpha_1, \ldots, a\alpha_{c_2-1})\end{aligned}$$

Specifically, let $g \in \mathbb{F}_{q^c}$ be a root of an irreducible polynomial of degree c over $\mathbb{F}_q$ and $h \in \mathbb{F}_{q^c}$ be a root of an irreducible polynomial of degree c_1 over $\mathbb{F}_q$, then we get the intermediate field $\mathbb{F}_q[h]$ and field extension $\mathbb{F}_q[h][g] = \mathbb{F}_{q^{c_1}}[g] = \mathbb{F}_{q^c}$. Note that $\mathbb{F}_q[g]$ is a linear space over $\mathbb{F}_q[h]$ with basis $(1, g, \ldots, g^{c_2-1})$, then we can construct the ring homomorphism

$$\begin{aligned}\Psi :&\mathbb{F}_{q^c} \hookrightarrow \mathsf{Mat}_{c_2}(\mathbb{F}_q[h])\\ &a \mapsto \Psi(a), \qquad\qquad \text{where } (1, g, \ldots, g^{c_2-1})\Psi(a) = (a, ag, \ldots, ag^{c_2-1})\end{aligned}$$

Every column of matrix $\Psi(a)$ is the coordinates of ag^i under the basis $(1, g, \cdots, g^{c_2-1})$. For every $a = \sum_{i=0}^{c-1} x_i g^i \in \mathbb{F}_q[g]$, we can compute the coordinates easily. Since $(1, g, \ldots, g^{c-1})$ and

$$(1, h, \ldots, h^{c_1-1}, g, gh, \ldots, gh^{c_1-1}, \ldots, g^{c_2-1}, g^{c_2-1}h, \ldots, g^{c_2-1}h^{c_1-1})$$

form two $\mathbb{F}_q$-bases of $\mathbb{F}_{q^c}$. We set $\mathbf{G}$ as the transition matrix between the two bases. We can also written a as $\sum_{i,j} y_{c_1 i+j} g^i h^j$, where $y_k \in \mathbb{F}_q$, and if we set $\mathbf{x} = (x_0, x_1, \ldots, x_{c-1})^t$, $\mathbf{y} = (y_0, y_1, \ldots, y_{c-1})^t$, we have $\mathbf{y} = \mathbf{G}\mathbf{x}$. Then we get the coordinate of a under $(1, g, \ldots, g^{c-1})$.

$$\begin{aligned}a &= \left(1, g, \cdots, g^{c-1}\right)\mathbf{x}\\ &= \left(1, h, \ldots, h^{c_1-1}, g, gh, \ldots, gh^{c_1-1}, \ldots, g^{c_2-1}, g^{c_2-1}h, \ldots, g^{c_2-1}h^{c_1-1}\right)\mathbf{G}\mathbf{x}\\ &= \left(1, g, \cdots, g^{c_2-1}\right)\begin{pmatrix}\sum_{i=0}^{c_1-1} y_i h^i\\ \sum_{i=0}^{c_1-1} y_{i+c_1} h^i\\ \vdots\\ \sum_{i=0}^{c_1-1} y_{i+c_1(c_2-1)} h^i\end{pmatrix}\end{aligned}$$

4.2 Our Hypothetical Analysis for the Result

We adapt the Kipnis-Shamir method for solving MinRank problem. We can estimate the complexity of our attack following the complexity analysis detailed in Sect. 3.3. The estimated complexity is listed in Table 8.

Table 8. Estimated complexity of MinRank attack over the intermediate field $\mathbb{F}_{q^{c_1}}$ on VOX parameters.

λ	q	$O = m/c$	$V = v/c$	c	c_1	t	d	D_{mgd}	$\log_2 C$
128	251	6	7	9	3	6	2	12	112.46
	251	5	6	10	5	6	1	6	49.64
192	1021	5	6	15	5	7	1	8	69.48
256	4093	7	8	14	7	8	1	5	48.04

To investigate whether the estimated complexity accurately reflects the actual complexity, we experimented for VOX with such a smaller parameter. We used the Gröbner basis algorithm F4 with respect to the graded reverse lexicographic monomial order in Magma V2.28-2 [7] on CPU a 2.40GHz Intel Xeon Silver 4214R CPU. The Magma code we use can be viewed in Appendix B and on Github[2]. The detailed running time of the Gröbner basis solving is listed in Table 9.

Table 9. Experiment results of MinRank attack over the intermediate field $\mathbb{F}_{q^{c_1}}$ on smaller VOX parameters.

q	$O = m/c$	$V = v/c$	c	c_1	t	d	D_{mgd}	$\log_2 C$	Running time(s)	Memory Usage(MB)
251	4	5	14	7	5	1	4	34.54	6.219	32.09
251	4	5	16	8	5	1	4	34.54	5.750	32.09
251	4	5	14	7	6	1	4	41.14	120.969	86.56
251	5	6	14	7	6	1	5	43.5	769.649	310.62
251	5	6	14	7	6	2	4	42.88	942.580	448.16
251	5	6	16	8	6	1	4	36.83	11.980	32.09
1021	5	6	16	8	7	1	4	37.25	49.789	64.12
1021	5	6	16	8	7	2	4	43.41	1374.059	499.12

From the experimental results, we observe that there is a nearly direct proportional relationship between the logarithm base 2 of running time and the logarithm base 2 of the estimated complexity, which we denote as $\log_2 C$. By applying linear regression, the fitting equation is $y = 1.15x + 31.86$ which has a slope near 1. This suggests that the estimated complexity provides a good prediction of the actual complexity. The fitted line is depicted in Fig. 4.

[2] https://github.com/tuovsig/analysis.

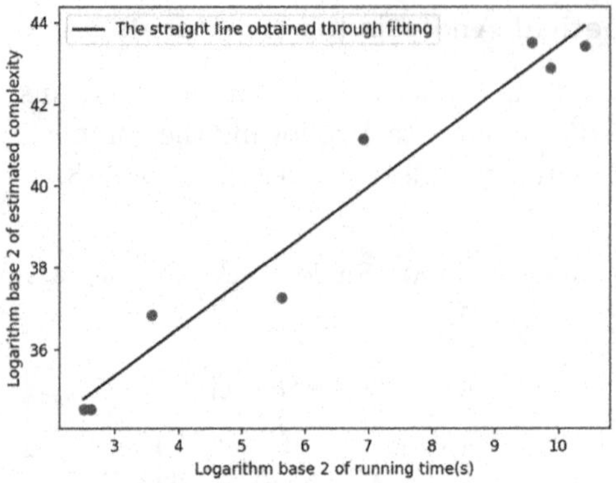

Fig. 4. Experiment running time and estimated complexity as well as the related fitted line of MinRank attack over the intermediate field $\mathbb{F}_{q^{c_1}}$ on smaller VOX parameters.

5 Conclusion

This paper presents two MinRank-based attacks against new parameters of VOX scheme, which has been submitted to NIST Post-Quantum Cryptography Project. The first attack pads public matrices vertically, and it can recover most of VOX oil spaces in seconds. While practically powerful, the padding attack lacks theoretic analysis. Hence we introduce another attack that can drastically decrease VOX security level in theory. It constructs intermediate field when"c" is co-prime and experiments on small parameters substantiate the hypothetical analysis.

With these two attacks breaking VOX in different approaches, we suspect that there might be some unspecified vulnerabilities in the scheme construction that could induce more fundamental security problems. Moreover, we presume that, in the practical attack, the gap between the passable hypothetical analysis and marvelous experiment results comes from the sparseness in matrices. It would be interesting to reason the discrepancy. Last but not the least, we expect that our attacks could be further applied to other UOV-like schemes.

Acknowledgments. This work is supported by National Key R&D Program of China (No. 2021YFB3100100) and Beijing Natural Science Foundation (No. M22001).

Disclosure of Interests. The authors have no competing interests to declare that are relevant to the content of this article.

A Magma code for our practical attack

Here we list the Magma code we used in Sect. 3.

```
// parameters for VOX
q := 251;
O := 6;
V := 7;
c := 9;
t := 6;
o := O*c;
v := V*c;
N := O+V;
n := N*c;
m := o;
l := 2;
r := l*V+t;
field<z> := GF(q^c);

// Generation of central map
F0 := [RandomMatrix(field, N, N): i in [1..t]];
F1 := [RandomMatrix(field, V, V): i in [1..m-t]];
F2 := [RandomMatrix(field, V, O): i in [1..m-t]];
F3 := [RandomMatrix(field, O, V): i in [1..m-t]];
FF := F0 cat [VerticalJoin(
    HorizontalJoin(F1[i], F2[i]),
    HorizontalJoin(F3[i], ZeroMatrix(field, O, O))
): i in [1..m-t]];

// Generation of linear map
S2 := RandomMatrix(field, V, O);
S := VerticalJoin(
    HorizontalJoin(
        ScalarMatrix(V, One(field)), S2
    ),
    HorizontalJoin(
        ZeroMatrix(field, O, V), ScalarMatrix(O, One(field))
    )
);
T2 := RandomMatrix(BaseField(field), t, m-t);
T := VerticalJoin(
    HorizontalJoin(
        ScalarMatrix(t, One(BaseField(field))), T2
    ),
    HorizontalJoin(
        ZeroMatrix(BaseField(field), m-t, t),
        ScalarMatrix(m-t, One(BaseField(field)))
    )
);
```

```
// Generation of public key
P := [Transpose(S)*FF[i]*S: i in [1..m]];
PP := [
    &+[T[i][j]*P[j]: j in [1..m]]
    : i in [1..m]
];
PTP := [(Transpose(PP[i]) + PP[i]): i in [1..m]];
PMD := [(Matrix(
    [PTP[j][i]: j in [1..m]]
)): i in [1..N]];

Z := ZeroMatrix(field, m, N*l);
RM := [
    [InsertBlock(Z, PMD[i], 1, N*j+1): i in [1..N]]: j in [0..l-1]
];

// The answer matrix for check
Ans := &+[
    &+[
        -S2[j][O-l+i] * RM[i][j]: j in [1..V]
    ]: i in [1..l]
]
+
&+[
    RM[i][i+N-l]: i in [1..l]
];

// Polynomial Ring, linear variables and kernel variables
PP<[w]> := PolynomialRing(field, l*V+r*(l*N-r), "glex");
X := [Eltseq(w)[(i-1)*V+1..i*V]: i in [1..l]];
Y := [Eltseq(w)[l*V+(i-1)*r+1..l*V+i*r]: i in [1..l*N-r]];

// Matrix M_s and Kernel matrix
MatX := &+[
    &+[
        X[i][j] * RMatrixSpace(PP, m, N*l)!RM[i][j]: j in [1..V]
    ]: i in [1..l]
]
+
&+[
    RMatrixSpace(PP, m, N*l)!RM[i][i+N-l]: i in [1..l]
];
MatY := Matrix([
    Y[i][1..r] cat [0: j in [r+1..l*N]]: i in [1..l*N-r]
```

```
]);
for i in [1..l*N-r] do
    MatY[i][r+i] := 1;
end for;
MatY := Transpose(MatY);

// Generation of equations
KS := MatX * MatY;
Poly := &cat[&cat[[KS[i][j]: j in [1..l*N-r]]: i in [1..m]]];
I := ideal<PP | Poly>;

// Calculate Groebner basis
SetVerbose("Groebner", 1);
time Groebner(I);
print("");
I;
```

B Magma code for our theoretical attack

Here we list the Magma code we used in Sect. 4.

```
q := 251;
O := 4;
V := 5;
c := 14;
t := 5;
// set d for ks model
d := 1;

o := O*c;
v := V*c;
N := O+V;
n := N*c;
m := o;

c1 := 1;
c2 := c;

for i in [2 .. c] do
    if c mod i eq 0 then
c1 := Round(c/i);
c2 := i;
        break;
    end if;
end for;
```

```
r := c2*V+t;
colstokeep := Minimum(d, c2*N-r);

Fq := GF(q);
R<x> := PolynomialRing(Fq);
f := IrreduciblePolynomial(Fq, c);
fi := IrreduciblePolynomial(Fq, c1);
field<g> := ext< Fq | f >;
interfield<h> := ext< Fq | fi>;
roots := Roots(fi, field);
mu := roots[1][1];
//print(mu);

function EletoMat(a)
    return Transpose(
        Matrix([ElementToSequence(a*g^i): i in [0..c-1]])
    );
end function;

function MattoEle(A)
    return &+ [A[i][1]*h^(i-1) : i in [1..Nrows(A)]];
end function;

function EletoIntermat(a)
    PHIa := EletoMat(a);
    M := Transpose(Matrix(
        &cat [
            [
                ElementToSequence(g^i*mu^j): j in [0..c1-1]
            ]: i in [0..c2-1]
        ]
    ));
    PSIa := M^-1*PHIa*M;
    return Matrix(
        [[MattoEle(
            Submatrix(PSIa,[c1*(i-1)+1..c1*i],[c1*(j-1)+1..c1*j])
        ) : j in [1..c2]] : i in [1..c2]]
    );
end function;

function MatInter(A)
    return VerticalJoin(
        [HorizontalJoin(
            [ EletoIntermat(A[i][j]) : j in [1..Ncols(A)] ]
        ) : i in [1..Nrows(A)]]
    );
end function;

F0 := [RandomMatrix(field, N, N): i in [1..t]];
```

```
F1 := [RandomMatrix(field, V, V): i in [1..m-t]];
F2 := [RandomMatrix(field, V, O): i in [1..m-t]];
F3 := [RandomMatrix(field, O, V): i in [1..m-t]];

FF := F0 cat [VerticalJoin(
    HorizontalJoin(F1[i], F2[i]),
    HorizontalJoin(F3[i], ZeroMatrix(field, O, O))
): i in [1..m-t]];

S2 := RandomMatrix(field, V, O);
S := VerticalJoin(
    HorizontalJoin(
        ScalarMatrix(V, One(field)), S2
    ),
    HorizontalJoin(
        ZeroMatrix(field, O, V), ScalarMatrix(O, One(field))
    )
);

T2 := RandomMatrix(BaseField(field), t, m-t);
T := VerticalJoin(
    HorizontalJoin(
        ScalarMatrix(t, One(BaseField(field))), T2
    ),
    HorizontalJoin(
        ZeroMatrix(
            BaseField(field), m-t, t),
            ScalarMatrix(m-t, One(BaseField(field))
        )
    )
);

P := [Transpose(S)*FF[i]*S: i in [1..m]];
PP := [
    &+[T[i][j]*P[j]: j in [1..m]]
    : i in [1..m]
];

PTP := [(Transpose(PP[i]) + PP[i]): i in [1..m]];

PTPInter := [MatInter(PTP[i]): i in [1..m]];

PMD := [(Matrix(
    [PTPInter[j][i]: j in [1..m]]
)): i in [1..c2*N]];

result := MatInter(Transpose(S^-1))[c2*V+1];

PR<[w]> := PolynomialRing(interfield, c2*V+r*colstokeep, "glex");
X := Eltseq(w)[1..c2*V];
```

```
Y := [Eltseq(w)[c2*V+(i-1)*r+1..c2*V+i*r]: i in [1..colstokeep]];
//print(Y);

MatX := &+[X[i]*ChangeRing(PMD[i], PR): i in [1..c2*V]] + PMD[c2*V+1];

MatY := Matrix([
    Y[i][1..r] cat [0: j in [r+1..c2*N]]: i in [1..colstokeep]
]);
for i in [1..colstokeep] do
    MatY[i][r+i] := 1;
end for;
MatY := Transpose(MatY);

KS := MatX * MatY;
//print(KS);

Poly := &cat[&cat[[KS[i][j]: j in [1..colstokeep]]: i in [1..m]]];
//print(Poly);


I := ideal<PR | Poly>;
//print(result);
SetVerbose("Groebner", 1);
time Groebner(I);
print("");
I;
```

References

1. Bardet, M., Bertin, M.: Improvement of algebraic attacks for solving super determined min rank instances. In: Cheon, J.H., Johansson, T. (eds.) PQCrypto 2022. LNCS, vol. 13512, pp. 107–123. Springer, Cham (2022). https://doi.org/10.1007/978-3-031-17234-2_6
2. Bardet, M., et al.: Improvements of algebraic attacks for solving the rank decoding and MinRank problems. In: Moriai, S., Wang, H. (eds.) ASIACRYPT 2020. LNCS, vol. 12491, pp. 507–536. Springer, Cham (2020). https://doi.org/10.1007/978-3-030-64837-4_17
3. Beullens, W.: Improved cryptanalysis of UOV and rainbow. In: Canteaut, A., Standaert, F.-X. (eds.) EUROCRYPT 2021. LNCS, vol. 12696, pp. 348–373. Springer, Cham (2021). https://doi.org/10.1007/978-3-030-77870-5_13
4. Beullens, W.: MAYO: practical post-quantum signatures from oil-and-vinegar maps. In: AlTawy, R., Hülsing, A. (eds.) SAC 2021. LNCS, vol. 13203, pp. 355–376. Springer, Cham (2022). https://doi.org/10.1007/978-3-030-99277-4_17
5. Beullens, W., Campos, F., Celi, S., Hess, B., Kannwischer, M.J.: MAYO. Round 1 Additional Signatures, Post-Quantum Cryptography: Digital Signature Schemes (2023). https://csrc.nist.gov/csrc/media/Projects/pqc-dig-sig/documents/round-1/spec-files/mayo-spec-web.pdf
6. Beullens, W., et al.: UOV: Unbalanced Oil and Vinegar - Algorithm Specifications and Supporting Documentation Version 1.0. Round 1 Additional Signatures, Post-Quantum Cryptography: Digital Signature Schemes

(2023). https://csrc.nist.gov/csrc/media/Projects/pqc-dig-sig/documents/round-1/spec-files/UOV-spec-web.pdf
7. Bosma, W., Cannon, J., Playoust, C.: The Magma algebra system. I. The user language. J. Symbolic Comput. **24**(3-4), 235–265 (1997). https://doi.org/10.1006/jsco.1996.0125, computational algebra and number theory, London (1993)
8. Courtois, N.T.: Efficient zero-knowledge authentication based on a linear algebra problem MinRank. In: Boyd, C. (ed.) ASIACRYPT 2001. LNCS, vol. 2248, pp. 402–421. Springer, Heidelberg (2001). https://doi.org/10.1007/3-540-45682-1_24
9. Ding, J., et al.: TUOV: Triangular Unbalanced Oil and Vinegar - Algorithm Specifications and Supporting Documentation Version 1.0. Round 1 Additional Signatures, Post-Quantum Cryptography: Digital Signature Schemes (2023). https://csrc.nist.gov/csrc/media/Projects/pqc-dig-sig/documents/round-1/spec-files/TUOV-spec-web.pdf
10. Ding, J., Petzoldt, A., Schmidt, D.S.: Multivariate Public Key Cryptosystems. AIS, vol. 80. Springer, New York (2020). https://doi.org/10.1007/978-1-0716-0987-3
11. Ding, J., Schmidt, D.: Rainbow, a new multivariable polynomial signature scheme. In: Ioannidis, J., Keromytis, A., Yung, M. (eds.) ACNS 2005. LNCS, vol. 3531, pp. 164–175. Springer, Heidelberg (2005). https://doi.org/10.1007/11496137_12
12. Faugère, J., Din, M.S.E., Spaenlehauer, P.: Computing loci of rank defects of linear matrices using gröbner bases and applications to cryptology. In: Koepf, W. (ed.) Symbolic and Algebraic Computation, International Symposium, ISSAC 2010, Munich, Germany, 25–28 July 2010, Proceedings, pp. 257–264. ACM (2010). https://doi.org/10.1145/1837934.1837984
13. Faugère, J., Din, M.S.E., Spaenlehauer, P.: On the complexity of the generalized MinRank problem. J. Symb. Comput. **55**, 30–58 (2013). https://doi.org/10.1016/J.JSC.2013.03.004
14. Faugère, J.-C., Levy-dit-Vehel, F., Perret, L.: Cryptanalysis of MinRank. In: Wagner, D. (ed.) CRYPTO 2008. LNCS, vol. 5157, pp. 280–296. Springer, Heidelberg (2008). https://doi.org/10.1007/978-3-540-85174-5_16
15. Faugère, J.C., Macario-Rat, G., Patarin, J., Perret, L.: A New Perturbation for Multivariate Public Key Schemes such as HFE and UOV. Cryptology ePrint Archive, Paper 2022/203 (2022). https://eprint.iacr.org/2022/203
16. Furue, H., Ikematsu, Y.: A new security analysis against MAYO and QR-UOV using rectangular MinRank attack. In: Shikata, J., Kuzuno, H. (eds.) IWSEC 2023. LNCS, vol. 14128, pp. 101–116. Springer, Cham (2023). https://doi.org/10.1007/978-3-031-41326-1_6
17. Furue, H., et al.: QR-UOV. Round 1 Additional Signatures, Post-Quantum Cryptography: Digital Signature Schemes (2023). https://csrc.nist.gov/csrc/media/Projects/pqc-dig-sig/documents/round-1/spec-files/qruov-spec-web.pdf
18. Furue, H., Ikematsu, Y., Kiyomura, Y., Takagi, T.: A new variant of unbalanced oil and vinegar using quotient ring: QR-UOV. In: Tibouchi, M., Wang, H. (eds.) ASIACRYPT 2021. LNCS, vol. 13093, pp. 187–217. Springer, Cham (2021). https://doi.org/10.1007/978-3-030-92068-5_7
19. Goubin, L., et al.: PROV: PRovable unbalanced Oil and Vinegar Specification v1.0 - 06/01/2023. Round 1 Additional Signatures, Post-Quantum Cryptography: Digital Signature Schemes (2023). https://csrc.nist.gov/csrc/media/Projects/pqc-dig-sig/documents/round-1/spec-files/prov-spec-web.pdf
20. Goubin, L., Courtois, N.T.: Cryptanalysis of the TTM cryptosystem. In: Okamoto, T. (ed.) ASIACRYPT 2000. LNCS, vol. 1976, pp. 44–57. Springer, Heidelberg (2000). https://doi.org/10.1007/3-540-44448-3_4

21. Guo, H., Ding, J.: Algebraic relation of three MinRank algebraic modelings. In: Mesnager, S., Zhou, Z. (eds.) WAIFI 2022. LNCS, vol. 13638, pp. 239–249. Springer, Cham (2022). https://doi.org/10.1007/978-3-031-22944-2_15
22. Ikematsu, Y., Nakamura, S., Takagi, T.: Recent progress in the security evaluation of multivariate public-key cryptography. IET Inf. Secur. **17**(2), 210–226 (2023). https://doi.org/10.1049/ISE2.12092
23. Kipnis, A., Shamir, A.: Cryptanalysis of the HFE public key cryptosystem by relinearization. In: Wiener, M. (ed.) CRYPTO 1999. LNCS, vol. 1666, pp. 19–30. Springer, Heidelberg (1999). https://doi.org/10.1007/3-540-48405-1_2
24. Macario-Rat, G., et al.: Rectangular attack on VOX. IACR Cryptology ePrint Archive, p. 1822 (2023). https://eprint.iacr.org/2023/1822
25. Nakamura, S., Wang, Y., Ikematsu, Y.: A new analysis of the kipnis-shamir method solving the MinRank problem. IEICE Trans. Fundam. Electron. Commun. Comput. Sci. **106**(3), 203–211 (2023). https://doi.org/10.1587/TRANSFUN.2022CIP0014
26. Patarin, J., et al.: Vox specification v1.0 - 06/01/2023. Round 1 Additional Signatures, Post-Quantum Cryptography: Digital Signature Schemes (2023). https://csrc.nist.gov/csrc/media/Projects/pqc-dig-sig/documents/round-1/spec-files/vox-spec-web.pdf
27. Tao, C., Petzoldt, A., Ding, J.: Efficient key recovery for All HFE signature variants. In: Malkin, T., Peikert, C. (eds.) CRYPTO 2021. LNCS, vol. 12825, pp. 70–93. Springer, Cham (2021). https://doi.org/10.1007/978-3-030-84242-0_4
28. Verbel, J., Baena, J., Cabarcas, D., Perlner, R., Smith-Tone, D.: On the complexity of "Superdetermined" Minrank instances. In: Ding, J., Steinwandt, R. (eds.) PQCrypto 2019. LNCS, vol. 11505, pp. 167–186. Springer, Cham (2019). https://doi.org/10.1007/978-3-030-25510-7_10
29. Wang, L.C., et al.: SNOVA - Proposal for NISTPQC: Digital Signature Schemes project. Round 1 Additional Signatures, Post-Quantum Cryptography: Digital Signature Schemes (2023). https://csrc.nist.gov/csrc/media/Projects/pqc-dig-sig/documents/round-1/spec-files/SNOVA-spec-web.pdf
30. Wang, Y., Ikematsu, Y., Nakamura, S., Takagi, T.: Revisiting the minrank problem on multivariate cryptography. In: You, I. (ed.) WISA 2020. LNCS, vol. 12583, pp. 291–307. Springer, Cham (2020). https://doi.org/10.1007/978-3-030-65299-9_22

Quantum Algorithms

Extending Regev's Factoring Algorithm to Compute Discrete Logarithms

Martin Ekerå[1,2](✉) and Joel Gärtner[1,2]

[1] KTH Royal Institute of Technology, Stockholm, Sweden
{ekera,jgartner}@kth.se
[2] Swedish NCSA, Swedish Armed Forces, Stockholm, Sweden

Abstract. Regev recently introduced a quantum factoring algorithm that may be perceived as a d-dimensional variation of Shor's factoring algorithm. In this work, we extend Regev's factoring algorithm to an algorithm for computing discrete logarithms in a natural way. Furthermore, we discuss natural extensions of Regev's factoring algorithm to order finding, and to factoring completely via order finding. For all of these algorithms, we discuss various practical implementation considerations, including in particular the robustness of the post-processing.

Keywords: Quantum cryptanalysis · Discrete logarithms · Factoring

1 Introduction

Regev [20] recently introduced a d-dimensional variation of Shor's algorithm [23, 24] for factoring integers. The quantum circuit for Regev's algorithm is asymptotically smaller than the circuit for Shor's algorithm, but the reduction in circuit size comes at the expense of using more space, and of many runs of the circuit being required to achieve a successful factorization.

In this work, we show how Regev's algorithm can be extended to compute discrete logarithms in finite cyclic groups. In particular, we focus on computing discrete logarithms in $\mathbb{Z}_p^*$ for p a large prime, although the algorithm we present may be generalized to other cyclic groups—and by extension to Abelian groups. By comparison, since Regev factors composite N, he implicitly works in $\mathbb{Z}_N^*$.

For Regev's algorithm and our extension thereof to reach an advantage over Shor's original algorithms [23, 24], and the variations thereof [2–8, 12, 21] already in the literature, there must exist a notion of *small* elements in the group.

More specifically, there must exist a set of small group elements such that any composition of a subset of these elements under the group operation is also a comparatively small element, and such that small elements are much more efficient to compose than arbitrary elements.

A natural notion of small group elements exists for $\mathbb{Z}_p^*$ and $\mathbb{Z}_N^*$, for p a large prime and N a large composite, respectively. As such, our extension of Regev's algorithm can compute discrete logarithms in $\mathbb{Z}_p^*$ with an asymptotically smaller

M.-J. Saarinen and D. Smith-Tone (Eds.): PQCrypto 2024, LNCS 14772, pp. 211–242, 2024.
https://doi.org/10.1007/978-3-031-62746-0_10

quantum circuit than the circuits for existing variations of Shor's algorithm. To the best of our current knowledge, it is however not straightforward to extend the notion of small group elements to elliptic curve groups.

Besides our extension to computing discrete logarithms, we furthermore discuss natural extensions of Regev's algorithm to order finding, and to factoring completely via order finding, in Appendix A. We note that our extension to factoring completely via order finding is in fact somewhat more efficient than Regev's original factoring algorithm. For further details, see Appendix A.3–A.4.

For Regev's original algorithm, the asymptotic reduction in the circuit size comes at the expense of using asymptotically more space, and of having to perform many runs of the circuit, as stated above. Ragavan and Vaikuntanathan [18] have however developed space-saving optimizations for Regev's algorithm, that decrease the space usage to be within a constant factor of Shor's algorithm. We apply these optimizations to our extensions of Regev's algorithm.

The quantum circuit for our extensions of Regev's algorithm, with the optimizations of Ragavan and Vaikuntanathan, is therefore asymptotically smaller compared to Shor's original algorithms [23, 24], and the variations thereof [2–8, 12, 21], while asymptotically using the same space up to a constant factor. There is, however, a lot of existing work on optimizing the performance of Shor's original algorithms, and the variations thereof, for cryptographically relevant problem instances, and constants matter in practice. As such, without further optimizations, it is not clear that our extensions of Regev's algorithm have a smaller circuit for cryptographically relevant problem instances of limited size.

The many outputs from the runs of the quantum algorithm are jointly post-processed classically. A practical problem that arises in this context is that the quantum error correction may fail to correct all errors that arise during the course of a run, resulting in an erroneous output being passed to the post-processing.

For this reason, we analyze the robustness of the classical post-processing to errors. In particular, based on a heuristic assumption, we show that it can handle an arbitrarily large fraction of erroneous outputs, as long as the algorithm parameters are increased to compensate for the failure rate.

Recent Independent Work. Shortly after our robustness result had appeared as a pre-print, Ragavan and Vaikuntanathan independently established a similar result in a revised version [19] of their pre-print [18].

Whereas we show that, under an additional assumption, Regev's original post-processing is robust to erroneous outputs being passed to it, Ragavan and Vaikuntanathan show that, under certain conditions, it is possible to detect and filter out the erroneous outputs. In particular, Ragavan and Vaikuntanathan prove, without relying on any additional assumptions, that their filtered post-processing succeeds if the erroneous outputs follow a uniform distribution.

In their revised pre-print [19], Ragavan and Vaikuntanathan also make some further improvements to the space efficiency of their optimizations. We note that it should be straightforward to transfer these improvements to our work.

2 Preliminaries

Throughout this work, we write generic Abelian groups multiplicatively, and denote by 1 the identity in such groups. Furthermore, we let ρ_s be a Gaussian function, defined for $s > 0$ as

$$\rho_s(\boldsymbol{z}) = \exp\left(-\pi \frac{\|\boldsymbol{z}\|^2}{s^2}\right)$$

where $\boldsymbol{z}$ is some vector.

2.1 Recalling Regev's Factoring Algorithm

To factor an n-bit composite N, Regev [20] defines the lattice

$$\mathcal{L} = \left\{ (z_1, \ldots, z_d) \in \mathbb{Z}^d \;\middle|\; \prod_{i=1}^{d} a_i^{z_i} = 1 \pmod N \right\}$$

where $a_i = b_i^2$ for $i \in [1, d] \cap \mathbb{Z}$, and where $b_1, \ldots, b_d$ are some small $O(\log n)$-bit integers. In what follows, we assume $b_1, \ldots, b_d$ to be the first $d = \lceil \sqrt{n} \rceil$ primes for simplicity, although other choices are possible, see Sect. 2.2.

The quantum part of Regev's algorithm is run $m \geq d + 4$ times to sample a set of m vectors that can be proved to be close to cosets of $\mathcal{L}^* / \mathbb{Z}^d$. A classical post-processing algorithm then recovers vectors in $\mathcal{L}$ from this set of vectors.

If one of the vectors thus recovered is in fact in $\mathcal{L} \backslash \mathcal{L}^0$, where

$$\mathcal{L}^0 = \left\{ (z_1, \ldots, z_d) \in \mathbb{Z}^d \;\middle|\; \prod_{i=1}^{d} b_i^{z_i} \in \{-1, 1\} \pmod N \right\},$$

the vector gives rise to a non-trivial split of N. In practice, our simulations [9] show that the recovered vectors often give rise to a sufficient number of distinct non-trivial splits so as to yield the complete factorization of N.

In this work, we extend Regev's factoring algorithm to computing discrete logarithms, to order finding, and to factoring completely via order-finding.

Recalling and Adapting Regev's Classical Post-processing. To start off, let us recall a claim and a lemma from [20] as they form the basis for the classical post-processing in both Regev's algorithm and in the extended algorithms that we introduce in this work:

Claim 1 (Claim 5.1 from [20]). *There is an efficient classical algorithm that given a basis of a lattice $\mathcal{L} \subset \mathbb{R}^k$, and some norm bound $T > 0$, outputs a list of $\ell \leq k$ vectors $\boldsymbol{z}_1, \ldots, \boldsymbol{z}_\ell \in \mathcal{L}$ of norm at most $2^{k/2}\sqrt{k}\,T$ with the property that any vector in $\mathcal{L}$ of norm at most T must be an integer combination of them. In other words, the sublattice they generate contains all the vectors in $\mathcal{L}$ of norm at most T.*

The factor $2^{k/2}$ in the above claim comes from the use of LLL [14]. It can be improved by the use of more powerful lattice reduction algorithms, such as BKZ [22], but for simplicity we follow Regev and use the above version of the claim based on LLL throughout this work.

Lemma 1 (Lemma 4.4 from [20]). *Let $\mathcal{L} \subset \mathbb{Z}^d$ and $m \geq d+4$. Let $\boldsymbol{v}_1, \ldots, \boldsymbol{v}_m$ be uniformly chosen cosets from $\mathcal{L}^*/\mathbb{Z}^d$. For some $\delta > 0$, let $\boldsymbol{w}_1, \ldots, \boldsymbol{w}_m \in [0,1)^d$ be such that $\mathrm{dist}_{\mathbb{R}^d/\mathbb{Z}^d}(\boldsymbol{w}_i, \boldsymbol{v}_i) < \delta$ for all $i \in [1,d] \cap \mathbb{Z}$. For some scaling factor $S > 0$, define the $d+m$-dimensional lattice $\mathcal{L}'$ generated by the rows of $\boldsymbol{B}$ where*

$$\boldsymbol{B} = \left(\begin{array}{c|ccc} \boldsymbol{I}_{d \times d} & S \cdot \boldsymbol{w}_1^T & \cdots & S \cdot \boldsymbol{w}_m^T \\ \hline \boldsymbol{0}_{m \times d} & & S \cdot \boldsymbol{I}_{m \times m} & \end{array} \right).$$

Then, for any $\boldsymbol{u} \in \mathcal{L}$, there exists a vector $\boldsymbol{u}' \in \mathcal{L}'$ whose first d coordinates are equal to $\boldsymbol{u}$, and whose norm is at most $\|\boldsymbol{u}\| \cdot (1 + m \cdot S^2 \cdot \delta^2)^{1/2}$. Moreover, with probability at least $1/4$ (over the choice of the $\boldsymbol{v}_i$), any non-zero $\boldsymbol{u}' \in \mathcal{L}'$ of norm $\|\boldsymbol{u}'\| < \min(S, \delta^{-1}) \cdot \varepsilon/2$ satisfies that its first d coordinates are a non-zero vector in $\mathcal{L}$, where $\varepsilon = (4 \det \mathcal{L})^{-1/m}/3$.

Regev's classical post-processing in [20] essentially follows by combining Lemma 1 and Claim 1 above, as does our classical post-processing. However, in [20], Regev only describes the classical post-processing as a part of the main theorem, and not as a separate lemma. Since we only need the post-processing part of the theorem, we extract this part and give the below lemma that is strongly influenced by Regev's main theorem:

Lemma 2 (Lemma derived from Theorem 1.1 in [20]). *Let $m = O(d)$ be an integer not smaller than $d + 4$ and let $T = \exp(O(d))$. Furthermore, let $\mathcal{L}$ be a d-dimensional lattice with $\det \mathcal{L} < 2^{d^2}$, and let $\boldsymbol{v}_1, \ldots, \boldsymbol{v}_m$ be uniformly chosen cosets from $\mathcal{L}^*/\mathbb{Z}^d$.*

Suppose that we are given a set of m vectors $\boldsymbol{w}_1, \ldots, \boldsymbol{w}_m \in [0,1)^d$ such that $\mathrm{dist}_{\mathbb{R}^d/\mathbb{Z}^d}(\boldsymbol{w}_i, \boldsymbol{v}_i) < \delta$ for all $i \in [1,m] \cap \mathbb{Z}$, where $\delta = \exp(-\Omega(d))$ is sufficiently small. Then, there is an efficient classical algorithm that, with probability at least $1/4$ (over the choice of the $\boldsymbol{v}_i$), recovers a basis for a sublattice of $\mathcal{L}$ that contains all vectors in $\mathcal{L}$ of norm at most T.

Proof. We begin by constructing the lattice $\mathcal{L}'$ in Lemma 1 with the given set of vectors $\boldsymbol{w}_1, \ldots, \boldsymbol{w}_m$ and with $S = \delta^{-1}$. We then have that any vector $\boldsymbol{u} \in \mathcal{L}$ of norm at most T corresponds to a vector $\boldsymbol{u}' \in \mathcal{L}'$ of norm $\|\boldsymbol{u}'\| \leq (m+1)^{1/2} T$.

By using Claim 1 with norm bound $(m+1)^{1/2}T$, we obtain a list of vectors $\boldsymbol{z}_1', \ldots, \boldsymbol{z}_\ell'$ in $\mathcal{L}'$ of norm at most

$$2^{(d+m)/2} \cdot (d+m)^{1/2} \cdot (m+1)^{1/2} T < \delta^{-1} (4 \det \mathcal{L})^{-1/m}/6$$

where the inequality holds for sufficiently small $\delta = \exp(-\Omega(d))$ as $\det \mathcal{L} < 2^{d^2}$.

From the second property of Lemma 1, we have that with probability at least 1/4, any vector $\boldsymbol{u}' \in \mathcal{L}'$ of norm $\|\boldsymbol{u}'\| < \delta^{-1}(4 \det \mathcal{L})^{-1/m}/6$ satisfies that its first d coordinates are a vector $\boldsymbol{u} \in \mathcal{L}$. As such, with probability at least 1/4, the first d coordinates of $\boldsymbol{z}'_i$ correspond to a vector $\boldsymbol{z}_i \in \mathcal{L}$ for all $i \in [1, \ell] \cap \mathbb{Z}$.

Furthermore, any $\boldsymbol{u} \in \mathcal{L}$ of norm $\|\boldsymbol{u}\| \leq T$ can be written as a linear combination of $\boldsymbol{z}'_1, \ldots, \boldsymbol{z}'_\ell$. Thus, $\boldsymbol{z}_1, \ldots, \boldsymbol{z}_\ell$ generate a sublattice of $\mathcal{L}$ that contains all vectors $\boldsymbol{u} \in \mathcal{L}$ of norm $\|\boldsymbol{u}\| \leq T$, and with probability at least 1/4 the ℓ produced vectors can thus be used to recover a basis for this sublattice of $\mathcal{L}$. □

Recalling Regev's Quantum Algorithm. Regev's algorithm [20] induces an approximation to the state proportional to

$$\sum_{\boldsymbol{z} \in \{-D/2, \ldots, D/2-1\}^d} \rho_R(\boldsymbol{z}) \left| z_1, \ldots, z_d, \prod_{i=1}^{d} a_i^{z_i + D/2} \bmod N \right\rangle$$

where $\boldsymbol{z} = (z_1, \ldots, z_d)$. As for R and D, Regev first picks $R = 2^{C\sqrt{n}}$ for some suitable constant $C > 0$, and then lets $D = 2^{\lceil \log_2(2\sqrt{d}\,R) \rceil}$.

Quantum Fourier transforms (QFTs) of size D are then applied to the first d control registers, after which the resulting d frequencies $w_1, \ldots, w_d$ are read out and used to form the vector $\boldsymbol{w} = (w_1, \ldots, w_d)/D \in [0, 1)^d$.

The choice of the constant C impacts the cost of the quantum circuit. Our simulations, further described in Appendix B, show that selecting $C \approx 2$ is sufficient for $n = 2048$ bit integers when $d = \lceil \sqrt{n} \rceil$. The probability of successfully factoring the integer in $m = d + 4$ runs is then close to one. For more detailed notes on the choice of the constant C, see Sect. 4.1.

The idea in Regev's factoring algorithm is to leverage that $a_1, \ldots, a_d$ are small by using binary tree-based arithmetic in combination with square–and–multiply-based exponentiation to compute the product $\prod_{i=1}^{d} a_i^{z_i} \bmod N$.[1]

More specifically, a work register is first initialized to 1. For $j = \ell - 1, \ldots, 0$ the work register is then squared mod N, the product $\prod_{i=1}^{d} a_i^{z_{i,j}} \bmod N$ computed using binary tree-based arithmetic, and the result multiplied into the work register mod N. Here, $z_i = \sum_{j=0}^{\ell-1} 2^j z_{i,j}$ where $z_{i,j} \in \{0, 1\}$ and $\ell = \log_2 D$.

An issue with the above approach, as identified by Ekerå and Gidney[2], is that the work register cannot be squared in place mod N, leading to intermediary register values having to be kept around until they can be uncomputed at the end of the computation of the product. This results in an increased space usage.

To circumvent this reversibility issue in Regev's original proposal, Ragavan and Vaikuntanathan [18] propose to use Fibonacci-based exponentiation in place of Regev's square–and–multiply-based exponentiation. This optimization reduces the space requirements—but it comes at the expense of increasing the circuit size and depth by constant factors.

---

1 The constant offset by $D/2$ is easy to account for by e.g. instead initializing the work register to a constant. In practice this offset does not matter, and so we do not account for it in this explanation.

2 See Craig Gidney's comment on Scott Aaronson's blog.

Even if one accounts for the above optimization, it is currently not clear whether Regev's variation of Shor's algorithm [23,24] is more efficient in practice than the various other variations that are in the literature [2–6,8,12,21] in actual physical implementations, and for concrete problem instances of limited size. It depends on what assumptions one makes on the quantum computer, which cost metrics one considers, which problem instances one considers, and so forth.

The same holds true for the extended algorithms that we introduce in this work. For further discussion on this topic, see Sect. 4.1.

Extending Regev's Quantum Algorithm. To extend Regev's algorithm to compute discrete logarithms, we need to introduce at least one element that is not small into the state. To see why this is, note that the problem instance is defined by a generator g and an element $x = g^e$, for e the discrete logarithm. The generator g may be small, but the element x is typically not small.

Throughout this work, we therefore consider a slightly extended quantum algorithm that induces an approximation to the state proportional to

$$\sum_{\boldsymbol{z} \in \{-D/2, \dots, D/2-1\}^d} \rho_R(\boldsymbol{z}) \left| z_1, \, \dots, \, z_d, \, \prod_{i=1}^{d-k} g_i^{z_i + D/2} \cdot \prod_{i=1}^{k} u_i^{z_{d-k+i} + D/2} \right\rangle$$

where $g_1, \, \dots, \, g_{d-k}$ are $d-k$ small group elements in some finite Abelian group $\mathbb{G}$, and $u_1, \, \dots, \, u_k$ are k arbitrary elements in $\mathbb{G}$, for k a small constant.

We focus primarily on the group $\mathbb{Z}_N^*$, for N a prime or composite, although the extended algorithm is generic in that it can also work in other groups.

For $\mathbb{G} = \mathbb{Z}_N^*$, we let n be the bit length of N, where n serves as an upper bound on both the bit length of the order of $\mathbb{Z}_N^*$ and on the bit length of elements in $\mathbb{Z}_N^*$. For other groups, it may be necessary or advantageous to make a distinction between these two bounds. For the cryptographically relevant cases in $\mathbb{Z}_N^*$ this is however not the case, see Sect. 3.1 for further details.

Furthermore, for simplicity, we let $d = \lceil \sqrt{n} \, \rceil$, and we let $g_1, \dots, g_{d-k}$ be the first $d - k$ primes that when perceived as elements of $\mathbb{Z}_N^*$ are distinct from $u_1, \dots, u_k$. We require N to be coprime to the first d primes for this reason.

Note however that other choices of d and $g_1, \dots, g_{d-k}$ are possible: In particular, it is possible to let $g_1, \dots, g_{d-k}$ be any choice of small distinct primes coprime to N, see Sect. 2.2 for further details.

The idea in our extended algorithms is to use special arithmetic for the first product over the $d - k$ small group elements—i.e. arithmetic that leverages that these elements are small, in analogy with Regev's original algorithm—and to use standard arithmetic for the product over the remaining k elements.

Let us now summarize our analysis in the following lemma:

Lemma 3 (Extended quantum algorithm based on [18,20]**).** *Let $k \geq 0$ be an integer constant, let $N > 0$ be an n-bit integer that is coprime to the first $d = \lceil \sqrt{n} \, \rceil$ primes where $d > k$, and let $C > 0$ be a constant.*

Furthermore, let $u_1, \dots, u_k \in \mathbb{Z}_N^*$, and let $g_1, \dots, g_{d-k} \in \mathbb{Z}_N^*$ be the first $d-k$ primes that when perceived as elements of $\mathbb{Z}_N^*$ are distinct from $u_1, \dots, u_k$.

Finally, as in [18, Theorem 1], let G be the gate cost of a quantum circuit that takes $|\, a, b, t, 0^S \,\rangle \to |\, a, b, (t + ab) \bmod N, 0^S \,\rangle$ for $a, b, t \in [0, N) \cap \mathbb{Z}$ and S the number of ancilla qubits required by the circuit, and let

$$\mathcal{L} = \left\{ (z_1, \ldots, z_d) \in \mathbb{Z}^d \;\middle|\; \prod_{i=1}^{d-k} g_i^{z_i} \cdot \prod_{i=1}^{k} u_i^{z_{d-k+i}} = 1 \right\}.$$

Then, there is a quantum algorithm that outputs a vector $\boldsymbol{w} \in [0,1)^d$ that, except for with probability $1/\text{poly}(d)$, is within distance $\sqrt{d/2} \cdot 2^{-C\sqrt{n}}$ of a uniformly chosen coset $\boldsymbol{v} \in \mathcal{L}^* / \mathbb{Z}^d$. The quantum circuit for this algorithm has gate cost $O(n^{1/2} G + n^{3/2})$ and it requires

$$Q = S + \left(\frac{C}{\log \phi} + 8 + o(1) \right) n$$

qubits of space, for ϕ the golden ratio.

Proof. In analogy with Regev [20], the quantum algorithm first induces an approximation to the state proportional to

$$\begin{aligned} &\sum_{\boldsymbol{z} \in \{-D/2, \ldots, D/2-1\}^d} \rho_R(\boldsymbol{z}) \left|\, z_1, \,\ldots,\, z_d, \prod_{i=1}^{d-k} g_i^{z_i + D/2} \cdot \prod_{i=1}^{k} u_i^{z_{d-k+i} + D/2} \right\rangle \\ &= \sum_{\boldsymbol{z} \in \{0, \ldots, D-1\}^d} \rho_R(\boldsymbol{z} - \mathbf{c}) \left|\, z_1 - D/2, \,\ldots,\, z_d - D/2, \prod_{i=1}^{d-k} g_i^{z_i} \cdot \prod_{i=1}^{k} u_i^{z_{d-k+i}} \right\rangle \quad (1) \end{aligned}$$

where $\boldsymbol{z} = (z_1, \ldots, z_d)$ and $\mathbf{c} = (D/2, \ldots, D/2)$.

As for the parameters R and D, in analogy with Regev [20], we pick $R = 2^{C\sqrt{n}}$ for some suitable constant $C > 0$, and let $D = 2^{\lceil \log_2(2\sqrt{d}\, R) \rceil}$. QFTs of size D are then applied to the first d control registers $z_1, \ldots, z_d$ and the resulting frequencies $w_1, \ldots, w_d$ read out, yielding $\boldsymbol{w} = (w_1, \ldots, w_d)/D \in [0,1)^d$. Based on the analysis in [20], except for with probability $1/\text{poly}(d)$, the vector $\boldsymbol{w}$ is then within distance $\sqrt{d}/(\sqrt{2}R) = \sqrt{d/2} \cdot 2^{-C\sqrt{n}}$ of a uniformly chosen coset $\boldsymbol{v} \in \mathcal{L}^* / \mathbb{Z}^d$.

To simplify the notation in what follows, we shift the first d control registers by $D/2$ since this does not affect the results measured after the QFTs have been applied. That is to say, instead of inducing an approximation to the state proportional to (1), we induce an approximation to the state proportional to

$$\sum_{\boldsymbol{z} \in \{0, \ldots, D-1\}^d} \rho_R(\boldsymbol{z} - \mathbf{c}) \left|\, z_1, \,\ldots,\, z_d, \prod_{i=1}^{d-k} g_i^{z_i} \cdot \prod_{i=1}^{k} u_i^{z_{d-k+i}} \right\rangle$$

in a series of computational steps.

The first step is to approximate the state proportional to

$$\sum_{\boldsymbol{z} \in \{0, \ldots, D-1\}^d} \rho_R(\boldsymbol{z} - \mathbf{c}) \,|\, z_1, \ldots, z_d \,\rangle$$

to within $1/\text{poly}(d)$ via a quantum circuit of size $d(\log D + \text{poly}(\log d))$ as explained in [18,20]. Note that $O(d(\log D + \text{poly}(\log d))) = O(n)$.

To compute the first product, i.e. to take

$$\sum_{\boldsymbol{z} \in \{0,\ldots,D-1\}^d} \rho_R(\boldsymbol{z} - \mathbf{c}) \left| z_1, \ldots, z_d, 0^A \right\rangle$$

$$\to \sum_{\boldsymbol{z} \in \{0,\ldots,D-1\}^d} \rho_R(\boldsymbol{z} - \mathbf{c}) \left| z_1, \ldots, z_d, \prod_{i=1}^{d-k} g_i^{z_i}, 0^{A-n} \right\rangle$$

a special quantum circuit from [18] is used, that for efficiency reasons leverages that the group elements $g_1, \ldots, g_{d-k}$ are small.

By [18, Lemma 2.2], this circuit uses $O(n^{1/2}\, G + n^{3/2})$ gates and Q qubits of space[3] in total when accounting both for the d control registers and the A initial ancilla qubits, n qubits of which are used to store the product.

Note that the circuit in [18, Lemma 2.2] is for the product of the squares of the first d primes raised to short exponents. We compute the product of a subset of $d - k$ of the first d primes raised to short exponents, but these differences only serve to reduce the cost of the circuit.

To compute the second product, i.e. to take

$$\sum_{\boldsymbol{z} \in \{0,\ldots,D-1\}^d} \rho_R(\boldsymbol{z} - \mathbf{c}) \left| z_1, \ldots, z_d, \prod_{i=1}^{d-k} g_i^{z_i}, 0^{A-n} \right\rangle$$

$$\to \sum_{\boldsymbol{z} \in \{0,\ldots,D-1\}^d} \rho_R(\boldsymbol{z} - \mathbf{c}) \left| z_1, \ldots, z_d, \prod_{i=1}^{d-k} g_i^{z_i} \cdot \prod_{i=1}^{k} u_i^{z_{d-k+i}}, 0^{A-n} \right\rangle$$

a standard quantum circuit is used since $u_1, \ldots, u_k$ are not necessarily small.

More specifically, $2k \log D$ elements are classically pre-computed, and then multiplied and added into the work register conditioned on the control qubits:

Recall that D is a power of two, write $D = 2^\ell$, write

$$z_{d-k+i} = \sum_{j=0}^{\ell-1} 2^j z_{d-k+i,j} \text{ for } z_{d-k+i,j} \in \{0,1\} \quad \Rightarrow \quad u_i^{z_{d-k+i}} = \prod_{j=0}^{\ell-1} u_i^{2^j z_{d-k+i,j}},$$

and pre-compute $u_i^{2^j}$ and $u_i^{-2^j}$ for all $j \in [0, \ell) \cap \mathbb{Z}$ and $i \in [1, k] \cap \mathbb{Z}$.

Then multiply $u_i^{2^j}$ into the work register conditioned on $z_{d-k+i,j}$ for all $j \in [0, \ell) \cap \mathbb{Z}$ and $i \in [1, k] \cap \mathbb{Z}$. For p the product in the work register before multiplying in $u_i^{2^j}$, and

$$u = \begin{cases} u_i^{2^j} & \text{if } z_{d-k+i,j} = 1 \\ 1 & \text{if } z_{d-k+i,j} = 0 \end{cases}$$

[3] Note that the constant C in [18] is different from our constant C: Whereas we have defined C so that $R = 2^{Cd}$ as in [20], the authors of [18] have instead defined C so that $R = 2^{(C+2+o(1))d}$. This explains the difference between our expression for Q and the corresponding expression in [18].

the procedure, when perceived to work in $\mathbb{Z}_N$, takes

$$\begin{aligned}
& \left| z_1, \ldots, z_d, p, 0^n, 0^n, 0^{A-3n} \right\rangle \\
\text{load u} \rightarrow & \left| z_1, \ldots, z_d, p, u, 0^n, 0^{A-3n} \right\rangle \\
\text{multiply and add} \rightarrow & \left| z_1, \ldots, z_d, p, u, pu, 0^{A-3n} \right\rangle \\
\text{swap} \rightarrow & \left| z_1, \ldots, z_d, pu, u, p, 0^{A-3n} \right\rangle \\
\text{unload } u \text{ and load } -u^{-1} \rightarrow & \left| z_1, \ldots, z_d, pu, -u^{-1}, p, 0^{A-3n} \right\rangle \\
\text{multiply and add} \rightarrow & \left| z_1, \ldots, z_d, pu, -u^{-1}, 0^n = p + pu \cdot -u^{-1}, 0^{A-3n} \right\rangle \\
\text{unload } -u^{-1} \rightarrow & \left| z_1, \ldots, z_d, pu, 0^n, 0^n, 0^{A-3n} \right\rangle
\end{aligned}$$

where the load and unload operations are conditioned on $z_{d-k+i,j}$.

The S qubits required to perform the multiplications and additions fit into the $A-3n$ ancilla qubits. The circuit size is dominated by the $2k \log D$ multiplications and additions, with a cost of $O(2kG \log D) = O(n^{1/2} G)$ gates. The loading, unloading and swap operations may be modelled as requiring $O(n)$ gates. Hence the second product is on par with or less expensive than the first asymptotically.

Finally, as explained in [18, 20], the QFTs of the first d control registers may be approximated in-place by a circuit of size $O(d \log D(\log \log D + \log d)) = O(n \log n)$ to within $1/\text{poly}(d)$ with the algorithm of Coppersmith [1]. □

By plugging concrete expression for G and S into Lemma 3 above for various circuits that implement the required arithmetic, we can obtain corollaries that give concrete circuit costs, in analogy with [18, Corollary 1.1–1.3 to Theorem 1].

An analogy to Lemma 3 may be formulated for other groups for which the group operation may be implemented efficiently quantumly. Note however that it is of course not possible to give asymptotic costs in terms of circuit size and space usage unless the group is explicitly specified. Furthermore, for the algorithm to be more efficient than the other variations of Shor's algorithm that are already in the literature, the implementation needs to leverage that all but k of the d elements in the product are small.

2.2 Our Heuristic Assumption

In analogy with Regev's original analysis, we make a heuristic assumption in the analysis of our extended algorithms. More specifically, the below heuristic assumption—that is slightly stronger than Regev's original assumption—is sufficient for our analysis.

Assumption 1. *Let K be a constant, N be an n-bit integer coprime to the first $d = O(\sqrt{n})$ primes, and $g_1, \ldots, g_d$ be the first d primes perceived as elements in $\mathbb{Z}_N^*$. Then, $g_1, \ldots, g_d$ generate $\mathbb{Z}_N^*$, and the lattice*

$$\left\{ (z_1, \ldots, z_d) \in \mathbb{Z}^d \;\middle|\; \prod_{i=1}^{d} g_i^{z_i} = 1 \right\}$$

has a basis where each basis vector has norm at most $T = \exp(Kn/d)$.

A component of our assumption not present in Regev's original assumption is that we require $g_1, \ldots, g_d$ to generate $\mathbb{Z}_N^*$. If N is an odd integer with t distinct prime factors, t elements of $\mathbb{Z}_N^*$ are at minimum required to generate $\mathbb{Z}_N^*$.

In the cryptographically relevant cases, d is much larger than t: RSA integers have only two factors, and when computing discrete logarithms in $\mathbb{Z}_N^*$ the modulus N is typically prime. This leads us to expect $g_1, \ldots, g_d$ to generate $\mathbb{Z}_N^*$ in the cryptographically relevant cases.[4]

On the other hand, problem instances with $t > d$ can be constructed, and for such instances Assumption 1 does not hold. For such instances, we do however expect $g_1, \ldots, g_d$ to generate a relatively large subgroup of $\mathbb{Z}_N^*$, and unless otherwise noted we expect that our analysis can be adapted to rely on this weaker requirement on $g_1, \ldots, g_d$. For simplicity, we use Assumption 1 as stated above in this work to avoid complicating the analysis.

Motivation for the Assumption. Both Regev's original factoring algorithm and our extended algorithms assume that there exist short *interesting* vectors in a lattice

$$\mathcal{L} = \left\{ (z_1, \ldots, z_d) \in \mathbb{Z}^d \;\middle|\; \prod_{i=1}^{d} g_i^{z_i} = 1 \right\}$$

for some choice of generators $g_1, \ldots, g_d \in \mathbb{G}$, most or all of which are small.

What constitutes an interesting vector differs between our algorithms and Regev's algorithm, but in both cases it is sufficient that $\mathcal{L}$ has a short basis.[5]

In turn, whether $\mathcal{L}$ has a short basis depends on the specific choice of generators. If the generators are chosen to be void of intentionally introduced relations, it is natural to assume $\mathcal{L}$ to have some properties similar to those of random lattices. In particular, it is natural to assume that there is a basis of $\mathcal{L}$ where each vector is not significantly longer than the shortest non-zero vector in $\mathcal{L}$. By Minkowski's first theorem and the fact that $\det \mathcal{L} \leq 2^n$, see Lemma 5, we thus expect $\mathcal{L}$ to have a basis where each basis vector has length at most $\exp(O(n/d))$.

Note however that we do not prove that such a basis exists for a given choice of generators. Rather, we make a heuristic number-theoretic assumption that such a basis exists, in analogy with Regev [20]. For $\mathbb{G} = \mathbb{Z}_N^*$, for N prime or composite, a natural choice to avoid intentionally introduced relations is to let most of the generators $g_1, \ldots, g_d$ be small distinct primes coprime to N.

For our algorithm to work it would be sufficient for the assumption to hold with a noticeable probability over the specific choice of such generators, as we can re-run the algorithm with different choices of generators. However, for simplicity and, in analogy with Regev, we choose $g_1, \ldots, g_d$ to be the first d primes.

Furthermore, note that the above assumption predicts that the lattice has increasingly shorter bases as d grows larger. As such, choosing a larger value for d

4 If $g_1, \ldots, g_d$ were random elements, this would follow from Pomerance [17].

5 For Regev's algorithm, a short basis for $\mathcal{L}$ ensures that there are short vectors in $\mathcal{L}$ that are not in $\mathcal{L}^0 \subsetneq \mathcal{L}$, for $\mathcal{L}^0$ as in Sect. 2.1.

may be preferable in practice, but for simplicity we consider only the specific choice of using the first $d = \lceil \sqrt{n} \rceil$ primes as generators in this paper.

Notes on the Connection to Our Algorithms. Assumption 1 is sufficient for the analysis of all of our extensions of Regev's algorithm. However, most of our extended algorithms do not directly depend on the lattice in Assumption 1, but rather on a related lattice. Under Assumption 1, this related lattice also has a short basis, as detailed in the following lemma:

Lemma 4. *Let N be an n-bit integer and $g_1, \ldots, g_d$ be the first $d = O(\sqrt{n})$ primes perceived as elements in $\mathbb{Z}_N^*$. Furthermore, let K be a constant, k be some small constant, and $u_1, \ldots, u_k$ be arbitrary elements in $\mathbb{Z}_N^*$. Then, under Assumption 1, the lattice*

$$\left\{ (z_1, \ldots, z_{d+k}) \in \mathbb{Z}^{d+k} \;\middle|\; \prod_{i=1}^{d} g_i^{z_i} \cdot \prod_{i=1}^{k} u_i^{z_{d+i}} = 1 \right\}$$

has a basis where each basis vector has norm at most $T = \sqrt{d+1} \cdot \exp(Kn/d)$.

Proof. Consider the lattice $\mathcal{L}$ given by

$$\left\{ (z_1, \ldots, z_d) \in \mathbb{Z}^d \;\middle|\; \prod_{i=1}^{d} g_i^{z_i} = 1 \right\}$$

that, under Assumption 1, has a basis $\boldsymbol{B}$ where each basis vector has norm at most $\exp(Kn/d)$. By Assumption 1 we also have that $g_1, \ldots, g_d$ generate $\mathbb{Z}_N^*$.

Therefore, for any of the u_i, there is a vector $\boldsymbol{z} = (z_1, \ldots, z_d) \in \mathbb{Z}^d$ such that $u_i = \prod_{i=1}^{d} g_i^{z_i}$. As the longest vector in $\boldsymbol{B}$ is no longer than $\exp(Kn/d)$, the covering radius of $\mathcal{L}$ is at most $\sqrt{d}\exp(Kn/d)$. As such, $\boldsymbol{z}$ can be written as a vector in $\mathcal{L}$ plus a vector $\boldsymbol{z}^{(i)}$ of length at most $\sqrt{d}\exp(Kn/d)$.

We then see that a basis for the lattice

$$\left\{ (z_1, \ldots, z_{d+k}) \in \mathbb{Z}^{d+k} \;\middle|\; \prod_{i=1}^{d} g_i^{z_i} \cdot \prod_{i=1}^{k} u_i^{z_{d+i}} = 1 \right\}$$

is given by

$$\left(\begin{array}{c|c} \boldsymbol{B} & \boldsymbol{0}_{d \times k} \\ \hline \boldsymbol{z}^{(1)} & \\ \vdots & -\boldsymbol{I}_k \\ \boldsymbol{z}^{(k)} & \end{array} \right)$$

where each basis vector has length at most $\sqrt{d+1} \cdot \exp(Kn/d)$. □

2.3 Notes on Lattice Determinants

The post-processing in Lemma 2 requires that the lattice $\mathcal{L}$ has determinant less than 2^{d^2}. In Regev's original factoring algorithm [20], the lattice considered is

$$\mathcal{L} = \left\{ (z_1, \ldots, z_d) \in \mathbb{Z}^d \;\middle|\; \prod_{i=1}^{d} a_i^{z_i} = 1 \pmod{N} \right\},$$

and Regev shows that its determinant is less than $N \leq 2^{d^2}$.

For our extensions of Regev's algorithm, we prove the below, more general, lemma to bound the determinant of lattices of this form.

Lemma 5. *Let $g_1, \ldots, g_t$ be $t > 0$ elements of a finite Abelian group $\mathbb{G}$, and let*

$$\mathcal{L} = \left\{ (z_1, \ldots, z_t) \in \mathbb{Z}^t \;\middle|\; \prod_{i=1}^{t} g_i^{z_i} = 1 \right\}.$$

Then, the determinant of $\mathcal{L}$ is equal to the size of the subgroup of $\mathbb{G}$ that is generated by the elements $g_1, \ldots, g_t$.

Proof. Let $\mathbb{G}_0$ be the subgroup of $\mathbb{G}$ that is generated by $g_1, \ldots, g_t$. For each group element $g \in \mathbb{G}_0$, we define the coset $\mathcal{S}_g$ of $\mathbb{Z}^t/\mathcal{L}$ given by

$$\mathcal{S}_g = \left\{ (z_1, \ldots, z_t) \in \mathbb{Z}^t \;\middle|\; \prod_{i=1}^{t} g_i^{z_i} = g \right\}.$$

We obviously have that these cosets are distinct, and that every $\boldsymbol{z} \in \mathbb{Z}^t$ belongs to one of these cosets. Since $\mathcal{L}$ is an integer lattice, the determinant of $\mathcal{L}$ is given by the number of such distinct cosets of $\mathbb{Z}^t/\mathcal{L}$. Since each element of $\mathbb{G}_0$ corresponds to a unique coset $\mathcal{S}_g$, the determinant of $\mathcal{L}$ therefore equals the size of the subgroup $\mathbb{G}_0$ generated by the elements $g_1, \ldots, g_t \in \mathbb{G}$. □

In particular, if the group $\mathbb{G}$ is of size less than 2^n, the above lemma guarantees that, no matter the choice of elements $g_1, \ldots, g_t$, the corresponding lattice has determinant less than $2^n \leq 2^{d^2}$ when $d = \lceil \sqrt{n} \rceil$.

3 Computing Discrete Logarithms

In what follows, let $\mathbb{G}$ be a finite Abelian group, let $g \in \mathbb{G}$ be a generator of a cyclic group $\langle g \rangle \subseteq \mathbb{G}$ of order r, and let $x = g^e$ for $e \in (0, r) \cap \mathbb{Z}$. Given g and x, our goal is then to compute the discrete logarithm $e = \log_g x$.

To this end, we first give a basic algorithm in Sect. 3.1 that computes the discrete logarithm whilst requiring pre-computation for the group. We then show in Sect. 3.2 how the pre-computation can be performed as a part of the algorithm.

Both algorithms work if Assumption 1 holds, but a weaker heuristic assumption is sufficient for the algorithm with pre-computation to work.

Since our analysis relies on heuristic assumptions, we have developed a simulator [9], further described in Appendix B, and used it to test the post-processing algorithms. Our simulations fully support the conclusion that the assumptions hold for cryptographically relevant problem instances.

3.1 A Basic Algorithm that Requires Pre-computation

Let $g_1, \ldots, g_{d-1}$ be small distinct elements in $\langle g \rangle$, such that $g_i = g^{e_i}$ where $e_i \in (0, r) \cap \mathbb{Z}$ for all $i \in [1, d) \cap \mathbb{Z}$. In particular, for $g \in \mathbb{Z}_p^*$ for p a large n-bit prime, and for $d = \lceil \sqrt{n} \rceil$, we take $g_1, \ldots, g_{d-1}$ to be the first $d-1$ primes that are in $\langle g \rangle$ and that when perceived as elements of $\langle g \rangle$ and distinct from x.

To find such elements efficiently, and to be able to directly call upon Lemma 3 below, we assume in this section that $\langle g \rangle = \mathbb{Z}_p^*$. Note that this assumption does not imply a loss of generality: Suppose that $\gamma = g^{e_\gamma}$ generates some subgroup of $\mathbb{Z}_p^*$ of order r_γ, that $x = \gamma^{e_x} = g^e$ and that we seek $e_x = \log_\gamma x \in [0, r_\gamma) \cap \mathbb{Z}$. Then, we may compute $e = \log_g x$ and $e_\gamma = \log_g \gamma$, and finally $e_x = e / e_\gamma \bmod r_\gamma$.

By Lemma 3, there exists an efficient quantum algorithm that outputs a vector $\boldsymbol{w} \in [0, 1)^d$ that, except for with probability $1/\mathrm{poly}(d)$, is within distance $\sqrt{d/2} \cdot 2^{-C\sqrt{n}}$ of a uniformly chosen $\boldsymbol{v} \in \mathcal{L}_x^* / \mathbb{Z}^d$, where

$$\mathcal{L}_x = \left\{ (z_1, \ldots, z_d) \in \mathbb{Z}^d \;\middle|\; x^{z_d} \prod_{i=1}^{d-1} g_i^{z_i} = 1 \right\}$$

for $C > 0$ some constant. By performing $m \geq d + 4$ runs of this quantum algorithm, we obtain m such vectors $\boldsymbol{w}_1, \ldots, \boldsymbol{w}_m$.

By Lemma 2, there is an efficient classical algorithm that, with probability at least $1/4$, recovers a basis for a sublattice Λ of $\mathcal{L}_x$ given the vectors $\boldsymbol{w}_1, \ldots, \boldsymbol{w}_m$. Furthermore, Λ contains all vectors in $\mathcal{L}_x$ of norm at most $T = \exp(O(\sqrt{n}))$. Let

$$\mathcal{L}_x^0 = \left\{ (z_1, \ldots, z_d) \in \mathcal{L}_x \;\middle|\; \gcd(z_d, r) \neq 1 \right\} \subset \mathcal{L}_x$$

and note that $\mathcal{L}_x^0$ is a sublattice of $\mathcal{L}_x$.

We make the heuristic assumption that there is a non-zero vector $\boldsymbol{y} \in \mathcal{L}_x \backslash \mathcal{L}_x^0$ of norm at most T. It then follows that $\boldsymbol{y} \in \Lambda$, which in turn implies that any basis for Λ must have at least one basis vector in $\mathcal{L}_x \backslash \mathcal{L}_x^0$. The recovered basis for Λ thus directly yields a vector in $\mathcal{L}_x \backslash \mathcal{L}_x^0$.

Suppose that we know e_i such that $g_i = g^{e_i}$ for $i \in [1, d) \cap \mathbb{Z}$—e.g. because we have pre-computed these using Shor's algorithm for computing discrete logarithms [7,23,24]. Then, given $\boldsymbol{z} = (z_1, \ldots, z_d) \in \mathcal{L}_x \backslash \mathcal{L}_x^0$, we have that

$$x^{z_d} \prod_{i=1}^{d-1} g_i^{z_i} = g^{e_1 z_1 + \ldots + e_{d-1} z_{d-1} + e z_d} = g^0 = 1,$$

which implies that

$$e_1 z_1 + \ldots + e_{d-1} z_{d-1} + e z_d = 0 \pmod{r}.$$

Since $\boldsymbol{z} \in \mathcal{L}_x \backslash \mathcal{L}_x^0$, we have that $\gcd(z_d, r) = 1$, so z_d is invertible mod r, and hence we can compute the discrete logarithm

$$e = \log_g x = -(e_1 z_1 + \ldots + e_{d-1} z_{d-1}) / z_d \pmod{r}.$$

We have used our simulator, further described in Appendix B, to corroborate the soundness of our heuristic assumption, and to analyze how to select parameters to achieve a high success probability. For $n = 2048$ bits, the simulations indicate that it suffices to take $C \approx 2$. Furthermore, they indicate that the success probability is close to one after $d + 4$ runs of the quantum algorithm. This is much greater than the lower bound of $1/4$ guaranteed by the analysis.

Notes on Safe-Prime Groups and Schnorr Groups. In cryptographic applications of the discrete logarithm problem in $\mathbb{Z}_p^*$, either safe-prime groups or Schnorr groups are typically used in practice:

For safe-prime groups, we have that $p - 1 = 2r_\gamma$ for r_γ a prime, where γ generates the r_γ-order subgroup. In such groups, it is easy to find small g_i in $\langle \gamma \rangle$. Hence, it would be possible to modify the quantum algorithm in the previous section to work in $\langle \gamma \rangle$ instead of working in all of $\mathbb{Z}_p^*$ for safe-prime groups.

This being said, the orders of $\langle \gamma \rangle$ and $\mathbb{Z}_p^*$ differ only by a factor of two, so the advantage of working in $\langle \gamma \rangle$ is small. Furthermore, making the aforementioned modification would require us to design a special version of Lemma 3 to e.g. use separate bounds for the bit length of group elements and of the group order, respectively. We therefore only give the basic algorithm that works in $\mathbb{Z}_p^*$.

For Schnorr groups, we have that $p - 1 = 2kr_\gamma$ for r_γ a prime and k a large integer, where γ generates the r_γ-order subgroup. In such groups, it is typically hard to find small g_i that are in $\langle \gamma \rangle$. To overcome this problem, we need to work in a larger group, again leaving us in a similar situation to that for safe-prime groups: We could for instance work in the kr_γ-order subgroup, but this would only bring a small advantage compared to working in $\mathbb{Z}_p^*$, so we only give the basic algorithm that works in $\mathbb{Z}_p^*$.

In summary, the complexity of the quantum algorithm in the previous section depends exclusively on the bit length n of p, irrespective of whether we are in a Schnorr group or a safe-prime group, and in the latter case irrespective of whether the logarithm is short or full length. For Shor's algorithm, when solving $x = \gamma^{e_x}$ for e_x, the complexity depends on n and the bit length of r_γ when the algorithm is adapted as in [4,7], or on n and the bit length of e_x when it is adapted as in [2,3,8].

Notes on Other Options for the Pre-computation. Another way to perform the pre-computation is to use an analogous procedure to compute a basis of $\mathcal{L}_g$, and to use it to compute $\boldsymbol{e} = (e_1, \ldots, e_{d-1})$, where

$$\mathcal{L}_g = \left\{ (z_1, \ldots, z_d) \in \mathbb{Z}^d \;\middle|\; g^{z_d} \prod_{i=1}^{d-1} g_i^{z_i} = 1 \right\}.$$

This requires relying on the stronger heuristic Assumption 1 which, with Lemma 4, gives that there exists a basis of $\mathcal{L}_g$ with all basis vectors having norm at most $T = \exp(O(n/d))$. In the next section we integrate this pre-computation into the algorithm.

3.2 Integrating the Pre-computation into the Algorithm

In the algorithm in Sect. 3.1, we have to pre-compute $e_i \in (0, r) \cap \mathbb{Z}$ such that $g_i = g^{e_i}$ for all $i \in [1, d) \cap \mathbb{Z}$. To avoid this pre-computation, we can define a lattice $\mathcal{L}_{x,g}$ that depends on both $g \in \mathbb{G}$ of order r and $x = g^e$ for $e \in (0, r) \cap \mathbb{Z}$, alongside $d - 2$ small elements $g_1, \ldots, g_{d-2} \in \mathbb{G}$. In particular, for $g \in \mathbb{Z}_p^* = \mathbb{G}$ for p a large n-bit prime and $d = \lceil \sqrt{n} \rceil$, we take $g_1, \ldots, g_{d-2}$ to be the first $d - 2$ primes that when perceived as elements of $\mathbb{Z}_p^*$ are distinct from g and x.

By Lemma 3, there exists an efficient quantum algorithm that outputs a vector $\boldsymbol{w} \in [0, 1)^d$ that, except for with probability $1/\text{poly}(d)$, is within distance $\sqrt{d/2} \cdot 2^{-C\sqrt{n}}$ of a uniformly chosen $\boldsymbol{v} \in \mathcal{L}_{x,g}^* / \mathbb{Z}^d$, where

$$\mathcal{L}_{x,g} = \left\{ (z_1, \ldots, z_d) \in \mathbb{Z}^d \;\middle|\; x^{z_{d-1}} g^{z_d} \prod_{i=1}^{d-2} g_i^{z_i} = 1 \right\},$$

for $C > 0$ some constant. By performing $m \geq d + 4$ runs of this quantum algorithm, we obtain m such vectors $\boldsymbol{w}_1, \ldots, \boldsymbol{w}_m$.

By Lemma 2, there is an efficient classical algorithm that, with probability at least $1/4$, recovers a basis for a sublattice Λ of $\mathcal{L}_{x,g}$ given the vectors $\boldsymbol{w}_1, \ldots, \boldsymbol{w}_m$. Furthermore, Λ contains all vectors in $\mathcal{L}_{x,g}$ of norm at most $T = \exp(O(\sqrt{n}))$.

Lemma 4 gives that, under Assumption 1, the lattice $\mathcal{L}_{x,g}$ has a basis where each basis vector has norm at most $\exp(O(n/d)) = \exp(O(\sqrt{n})) = T$. Hence Λ is the full lattice $\mathcal{L}_{x,g}$, and Lemma 2 recovers a basis $\boldsymbol{B}$ for this lattice. By the definition of $\mathcal{L}_{x,g}$, we have that $\boldsymbol{v}_e = (0, \ldots, 0, 1, -e) \in \mathcal{L}_{x,g}$ as $x^1 g^{-e} = 1$. Since we know a basis $\boldsymbol{B}$ for $\mathcal{L}_{x,g}$, we can efficiently recover $\boldsymbol{v}_e$ and by extension e.

Note furthermore that $\boldsymbol{v}_r = (0, \ldots, 0, r) \in \mathcal{L}_{x,g}$, and that we can efficiently recover $\boldsymbol{v}_r$ and hence r. Hence, if r is unknown, we can recover r along with e at no additional quantum cost. This is useful in Sect. 3.3 below where r is needed.

Finally, note that, as we have recovered a basis for $\mathcal{L}_{x,g}$, we can also similarly recover e_i such that $g_i = g^{e_i}$ for every i such that g_i is in $\langle g \rangle$. This is useful in the context of the algorithm in Sect. 3.1.

We are now ready to summarize the above analysis in a theorem:

Theorem 1. *Let p be an n-bit prime, and let $d = \lceil \sqrt{n} \rceil$. Let $g \in \mathbb{Z}_p^*$ be of order r, and let $x = g^e$ for $e \in (0, r) \cap \mathbb{Z}$. As in [18, Theorem 1], let G be the gate cost of a quantum circuit that takes*

$$\left| a, b, t, 0^S \right\rangle \to \left| a, b, (t + ab) \bmod p, 0^S \right\rangle$$

for $a, b, t \in [0, p) \cap \mathbb{Z}$ and S the number of ancilla qubits required. Then, under Assumption 1, there is an efficient classical algorithm that, by calling a quantum circuit $d + 4$ times, yields the logarithm e with probability at least $1/4$. This quantum circuit has gate cost $O(n^{1/2} G + n^{3/2})$, and it requires

$$S + \left(\frac{C}{\log \phi} + 8 + o(1) \right) n$$

qubits of space, for some constant $C > 0$ and ϕ the golden ratio.

Proof. The proof follows from the above analysis, and from Lemma 3 where the gate and space costs of the quantum circuit are analyzed. □

The above theorem is specific to $\mathbb{Z}_p^*$ for p prime since there is a notion of small group elements in such groups, and since such groups are extensively used in cryptography. As previously stated, the algorithm may be generalized to other Abelian groups, but for the algorithm to have an advantage over other algorithms in the literature there must exist a notion of small elements in the group.

We have used our simulator, further described in Appendix B, to corroborate the soundness of the heuristic assumption in Theorem 1, and to analyze how to select parameters to achieve a high success probability. For $n = 2048$ bits, the simulations indicate that it suffices to take $C \approx 2$. Furthermore, they indicate that the success probability is close to one after $d + 4$ runs of the quantum algorithm. This is much greater than the lower bound of 1/4 guaranteed by Theorem 1.

3.3 Notes on Reducing the Circuit Size by Pre-computation

In contrast to the algorithm in Sect. 3.1, the algorithm in Sect. 3.2 does not require any pre-computation, and it does not require g to generate $\mathbb{G}$.

These benefits come with the downside, however, of the quantum part of the algorithm having to exponentiate both x and g, where neither element is guaranteed to be small. In practice, these exponentiations constitute a significant fraction of the cost of each run of the quantum part of the algorithm. In turn, this makes the algorithm in Sect. 3.2 somewhat less efficient than the algorithm in Sect. 3.1 that only has to exponentiate x at the expense of pre-computing $e_1, \ldots, e_{d-1}$ with respect to g.

One way to overcome this issue is to let g' be a small element in $\mathbb{G}$ such that $g \in \langle g' \rangle \subseteq \mathbb{G}$, and to first pre-compute $e_g = \log_{g'} g$ quantumly. It then suffices to compute $e_x = \log_{g'} x$ quantumly for each x, and to return $e = e_x / e_g \bmod r$. All but one of the d elements that are exponentiated in each run of the quantum part of the algorithm are then small as desired. Both the pre-computation of e_g and the computation of e_x for different x may be performed with the quantum algorithm in Sect. 3.2, whilst leveraging that g' is small when implementing the arithmetic so as to reduce the quantum cost. This results in an algorithm with similar performance and similar pre-computation as the one given in Sect. 3.1, but with the benefit of not requiring g to generate $\mathbb{G}$.

3.4 Notes on Computing Multiple Logarithms Simultaneously

As is the case for Shor's algorithm—see e.g. [13] and [11]—we note that our extension of Regev's algorithm can be used to compute information on multiple discrete logarithms in each run by sampling vectors close to $\mathcal{L}^*_{x_1,\ldots,x_k,g}/\mathbb{Z}^d$, where

$$\mathcal{L}_{x_1,\ldots,x_k,g} = \left\{ (z_1, \ldots, z_d) \in \mathbb{Z}^d \;\middle|\; g^{z_d} \cdot \prod_{i=1}^{d-k-1} g_i^{z_i} \cdot \prod_{i=1}^{k} x_i^{z_{d-k+i-1}} = 1 \right\}$$

and $x_i = g^{e_i}$ for all $i \in [1, k] \cap \mathbb{Z}$, instead of sampling vectors close to $\mathcal{L}^*_{x,g}/\mathbb{Z}^d$.

4 Practical Considerations

In this section, we discuss various practical considerations when implementing both Regev's original algorithm and our extensions of his algorithm.

4.1 Efficiency in Implementations

As stated in the introduction, the quantum circuit for Regev's factoring algorithm, and for our extensions of it, is asymptotically smaller than the corresponding circuits for Shor's algorithms and the various variations thereof that are in the literature—hereinafter referred to as the "existing algorithms".

Even so, for concrete problem instances of limited size, the quantum circuit for Regev's algorithm, and for our extensions of it, may in practice be significantly larger than optimized circuits for the existing algorithms. This when using the space-saving arithmetic of Ragavan and Vaikuntanathan [18]. It all comes down to constants.

Furthermore, it is not clear that it is the circuit size, i.e. the gate count, that is the best metric whereby to compare quantum algorithms. Other relevant metrics include but are not limited to the circuit depth, space usage, or volume. It also matters what kind of large-scale fault-tolerant quantum computer one envisages, and what its architectural constraints are, and so forth.

The limiting factor for when a quantum algorithm can first conceivably be run on a future large-scale fault-tolerant quantum computer is arguably the cost of the circuit as it determines the cost per run. But if and when such computers become more commonly available, the overall cost across all runs required will also be important to take into account.

What Problem Instances Are of Key Interest? Arguably, the key reason for why there is a large interest in quantum algorithms for factoring integers and computing discrete logarithms is that such algorithms may be used to break currently widely deployed asymmetric cryptography.

Hence, the concrete efficiency of the aforementioned quantum algorithms with respect to cryptographically relevant problem instances is potentially much more interesting than their asymptotic efficiency. This is especially true when one considers the fact that asymmetric cryptography based on the integer factoring and discrete logarithm problems is being phased out. Hence, we are most likely not going to see much larger instances of these problems being used in the future, and so our focus should be on n in the range from say 2048 bits up to 4096 bits.

Notes on the Constant C. In order to even begin to compare Regev's algorithm and our extensions of it to the existing algorithms, the constant C needs to be fixed since it directly affects the circuit size and depth.

Our simulations, further described in Appendix B, show that selecting $C \approx 2$ is sufficient for $n = 2048$ bit moduli when $d = \lceil \sqrt{n} \rceil$. The success probability after $m = d + 4$ runs is then close to one. Ragavan and Vaikuntanathan [18, App. A] show, based on a heuristic assumption, that selecting $C = 3 + \epsilon + o(1)$

is sufficient asymptotically as $n \to \infty$. This when using the LLL [14] lattice basis reduction algorithm. The difference between the results we obtain in our simulations and the lower bound of Ragavan and Vaikuntanathan is at least partly explained by the fact that LLL performs significantly better in practice than in theory. By instead using a better reduction algorithm such as BKZ [22], by increasing d and/or by increasing the number of runs m, it is sufficient to use a somewhat smaller C, as corroborated by our simulations.

It is also worth noting that performing $m \geq d+4$ runs is not strictly necessary for our extended algorithms to work. We have only inherited this bound from Regev's analysis. With sufficiently large C, it should be sufficient to perform significantly fewer runs, but using a larger C increases the circuit size and depth. Therefore, it is probably preferable to use a smaller C, and to run the quantum algorithm $m \geq d + 4$ times.

Notes on the Choice of Arithmetic. Our extensions of Regev's algorithm can be implemented both with Regev's original arithmetic [20] and with the space-saving arithmetic of Ragavan and Vaikuntanathan [18].

In Theorem 1, and in Theorems 3–4 in Appendix A, we express the cost in terms of using the space-saving arithmetic since it is asymptotically on par with Regev's original arithmetic[6] in terms of the circuit size, but uses less space.

It is however not clear that the space-saving arithmetic is better than Regev's original arithmetic in practice for cryptographically relevant problem instances:

Regev's original arithmetic yields a smaller circuit size, and a lower circuit depth, when accounting for constants, at the expense of using more space. If space is cheap, it may be quite competitive. Note also that most of the additional space required is not computational space, but rather space where quantum information can be stored until it is eventually needed for the uncomputation.

Notes on Optimizations. There is a plethora of optimizations for the existing algorithms already in the literature, many of which can be combined.

Not all of these optimizations carry over to Regev's algorithm, and less time has been spent on seeking to optimize Regev's algorithm, further complicating the task of comparing Regev's algorithm to the existing algorithms. The same holds true for the extensions of Regev's algorithm introduced in this work.

4.2 Handling Error-Correction Failures

Quantum computers as currently envisaged are inherently noisy, necessitating the use of some form of quantum error correction to achieve a sufficient level of fault tolerance to run complex quantum algorithms.

The quantum error correction is parameterized so as to achieve a certain lower bound on the probability of all errors that arise during the run being

[6] When ignoring constant factors.

corrected[7], and hence of the run and its output being good. The higher the bound, the more costly the error correction.

For quantum algorithms that need only yield a single good output—such as Shor's algorithms [5,6,23], and Ekerå–Håstad's variations [2,3,8] thereof when not making tradeoffs—it may be advantageous on average to select a lower bound in the error correction at the expense of potentially having to re-run the algorithm if the output is bad. Indeed, this approach was used in recent cost estimates [10] for the aforementioned algorithms.

For Regev's algorithm [20], and the extensions thereof introduced in this work, the situation is different however in that the post-processing is only guaranteed to succeed with probability at least 1/4 if all of the $m \geq d + 4$ runs yield good outputs, where we recall that $d = \lceil \sqrt{n} \rceil$ so m grows fairly rapidly in n.

If the post-processing was to fail as soon as the output from a single bad run is included in the set of vectors fed to it, then—short of us being able to efficiently distinguish the vectors output by good runs from those output by bad runs—we would need to parameterize the error correction so that we have a sufficiently high probability of being able to efficiently construct a set of m vectors yielded by good runs. In turn, this would drive up the cost of the error correction. Possible options for constructing such a set include but are not limited to exhausting subsets, or somehow efficiently filtering out good runs from bad runs via a distinguisher.

This being said, it seems that Regev's original post-processing is in fact relatively robust to errors. It continues to work even if a relatively large fraction of the vectors input to it are sampled from a different distribution—provided that it is still fed a sufficiently large number of vectors that are yielded by good runs of the quantum algorithm, and that the constant C is sufficiently large.

We evidence this by means of simulations, see Appendix B.3 for further details and tabulated results, in which we test the behavior of Regev's classical post-processing when a fraction of the vectors are yielded by bad runs, as simulated by sampling these vectors from the uniform distribution.

In this section, we further corroborate these simulations by providing an analysis of the post-processing in the setting where a fraction of the vectors fed to it are yielded by bad runs of the quantum algorithm.

Analysis of the Robustness of the Post-processing. Suppose that the post-processing algorithm is fed m vectors $\boldsymbol{w}_1, \ldots, \boldsymbol{w}_m$ generated in m runs of the quantum algorithm. However, only $d + 4 \leq m_1 \leq m$ of these vectors are from good runs, and hence guaranteed to be at most a distance δ from $\mathcal{L}^* / \mathbb{Z}^d$. The remaining $m_2 = m - m_1$ vectors are from bad runs, and hence sampled from some other unknown distribution $\mathcal{F}$. Suppose furthermore that we can not directly distinguish between vectors from good and bad runs, respectively.

The goal of the post-processing algorithm is to recover a basis for $\mathcal{L}$. In what follows, we show, based on some assumptions on $\mathcal{L}$ and $\mathcal{F}$, that the post-processing succeeds in recovering a basis for $\mathcal{L}$.

[7] Under a set of assumptions, e.g. on how the errors arise and their correlation.

However, even without any such assumptions, it can be seen that at least some vectors from $\mathcal{L}$ can be recovered. We therefore begin by detailing why a single non-zero vector is recoverable, so as to provide partial motivation for why we deem the assumptions about $\mathcal{L}$ and $\mathcal{F}$ to be reasonable, and because it may be useful in the context of the algorithm in Sect. 3.1.

Recovering a Single Vector from $\mathcal{L}$. As in the analysis of the original post-processing in Lemma 1, we consider a lattice $\mathcal{L}''$ generated by the rows of

$$\left(\begin{array}{c|ccc} \boldsymbol{I}_{d\times d} & S\cdot \boldsymbol{w}_1^{\mathrm{T}} & \cdots & S\cdot \boldsymbol{w}_m^{\mathrm{T}} \\ \hline \boldsymbol{0}_{m\times d} & & S\cdot \boldsymbol{I}_{m\times m} & \end{array}\right)$$

for $S = \delta^{-1}$ a scaling parameter.

An unknown subset of m_2 of the coordinates of the vectors in this lattice are dependent on the unknown distribution $\mathcal{F}$. Meanwhile, the vectors formed by the remaining $d + m_1$ coordinates form a lattice $\mathcal{L}'$ that is of exactly the same form as the lattices considered in Lemma 1.

By Lemma 1, the first d coordinates of any non-zero vector in $\mathcal{L}'$ shorter than $S\varepsilon/2$ is a vector in $\mathcal{L}$, provided that $\varepsilon = (4 \det \mathcal{L})^{-1/m_1}/3$. Furthermore, for any vector in $\mathcal{L}''$, if the first d coordinates are zero, the remaining coordinates are either 0, or a multiple of S which is larger than $S\varepsilon/2$. Therefore, the first d coordinates of any non-zero vector in $\mathcal{L}''$ that is shorter than $S\varepsilon/2$ is guaranteed to be a non-zero vector in $\mathcal{L}$.

The lattice $\mathcal{L}''$ has determinant S^m. By Minkowski's first theorem, we are guaranteed that it contains a vector of length at most $\sqrt{m+d} \cdot S^{m/(m+d)}$.

Thus, if

$$\sqrt{m+d} \cdot S^{m/(m+d)} < S \cdot \varepsilon/2,$$

which is true if S is sufficiently large, we are guaranteed that the first d coordinates of the shortest non-zero vector in $\mathcal{L}''$ is a vector in $\mathcal{L}$.

Furthermore, for somewhat larger S, the first d coordinates of vectors that are significantly larger than the shortest non-zero vectors in $\mathcal{L}''$ are also guaranteed to be in $\mathcal{L}$. It follows that we can recover vectors in $\mathcal{L}$ simply by using an efficient lattice reduction algorithm such as LLL [14].

Hence, even without making any assumptions on $\mathcal{L}$ or $\mathcal{F}$, we can guarantee that at least some non-zero vector from $\mathcal{L}$ can be recovered efficiently.

This guarantee is almost sufficient for us to be able to solve the discrete logarithm problem with pre-processing: As in Sect. 3.1, consider the lattice

$$\mathcal{L} = \mathcal{L}_x = \left\{ (z_1, \ldots, z_d) \in \mathbb{Z}^d \;\middle|\; x^{z_d} \prod_{i=1}^{d-1} g_i^{z_i} = 1, \right\},$$

where we are given g, x and $e_1, \ldots, e_{d-1}$ such that $g_i = g^{e_i}$, and are to compute e such that $x = g^e$. For $\boldsymbol{z} = (z_1, \ldots, z_d)$ a non-zero vector recovered from this lattice $\mathcal{L}_x$, we have that

$$0 = ez_d + \sum_{i=1}^{d-1} e_i z_i \pmod{r}$$

for r the order of g. It is then sufficient that z_d does not share any large factors with r for the discrete logarithm e to be recoverable. To suppose that this is the case with noticeable probability for the recovered vector is indeed a very weak assumption, yet this assumption is sufficient to recover the discrete logarithm with pre-computation even if some runs are bad.

To show that the post-processing robustly succeeds in recovering a basis for $\mathcal{L}$ we do, however, require a stronger assumption on $\mathcal{L}$ and $\mathcal{F}$.

Recovering a Basis for $\mathcal{L}$. As previously mentioned, to show that we are able to recover a basis for $\mathcal{L}$, we need to make some assumptions on $\mathcal{L}$ and $\mathcal{F}$.

Note that even if all m runs are good, we cannot guarantee that the post-processing succeeds in recovering a basis for $\mathcal{L}$ without making some additional assumption on $\mathcal{L}$. In particular, Theorem 1 requires a specific lattice to have a short basis, and therefore needs to use Assumption 1. For the analysis in this section, we make use of a similar assumption so as to ensure that the short vectors in $\mathcal{L}''$ yield vectors that generate $\mathcal{L}$, which in turn ensures that these vectors can be used to recover a basis for $\mathcal{L}$.

To this end, we first note that if the first d coordinates of a vector $\boldsymbol{u}'' \in \mathcal{L}''$ form a vector $\boldsymbol{u} \in \mathcal{L}$, the m_1 coordinates of $\boldsymbol{u}''$ that correspond to good runs have absolute value at most $\|\boldsymbol{u}\| S\delta = \|\boldsymbol{u}\|$. The remaining m_2 coordinates are congruent to $S\boldsymbol{u} \cdot \boldsymbol{w}_i$ modulo S, where $\boldsymbol{w}_i$ is sampled from $\mathcal{F}$. We do not have much control over the values of these m_2 coordinates, but we can expect them to be small for at least some short vectors $\boldsymbol{u}$.

To analyze the vectors in $\mathcal{L}''$ that are such that all coordinates are small, and such that the first d coordinates form a vector in $\mathcal{L}$, we consider the sublattice of $\mathcal{L}''$ where the first d coordinates are exactly the vectors in $\mathcal{L}$. This sublattice is thus generated by the rows of

$$\left(\begin{array}{c|ccc} \boldsymbol{B} & S\boldsymbol{B} \cdot \boldsymbol{w}_1^{\mathrm{T}} & \cdots & S\boldsymbol{B} \cdot \boldsymbol{w}_m^{\mathrm{T}} \\ \hline \boldsymbol{0}_{m \times d} & & S \cdot \boldsymbol{I}_{m \times m} & \end{array}\right)$$

where $\boldsymbol{B}$ is a basis for $\mathcal{L}$. For a small vector $\boldsymbol{u} \in \mathcal{L}$, we have already seen that the size of the coordinates that correspond to good runs is limited. We therefore consider a related lattice Λ that do not contain the m_1 coordinates that correspond to good runs. With $\boldsymbol{F}$ a $d \times m_2$-dimensional matrix such that the columns are equal to the m_2 vectors $\boldsymbol{w}_i$ that correspond to bad runs, we can see that this lattice Λ is generated by the rows of

$$\left(\begin{array}{c|c} \boldsymbol{B} & S\boldsymbol{B} \cdot \boldsymbol{F} \\ \hline \boldsymbol{0}_{m_2 \times d} & S \cdot \boldsymbol{I}_{m_2} \end{array} \right). \tag{2}$$

The first d coordinates of a short vector $\boldsymbol{x} \in \Lambda$ is a short vector $\boldsymbol{u} \in \mathcal{L}$. As such, $\boldsymbol{x}$ directly corresponds to a short vector in $\mathcal{L}''$, where the remaining m_1 coordinates not included in Λ have absolute value at most $\|\boldsymbol{u}\| \leq \|\boldsymbol{x}\|$. Thus, the full vector in $\mathcal{L}''$ is not longer than $\|\boldsymbol{x}\|\,(1 + m_1)$. As such, the vectors in Λ of length at most T correspond to vectors in $\mathcal{L}''$ of length at most $T(1 + m_1)$.

By using Claim 1, we recover a set $\mathcal{S}$ of vectors in $\mathcal{L}''$ that generate all vectors in $\mathcal{L}''$ of length at most $T(1 + m_1)$. The relevant coordinates of these recovered vectors thus generate all vectors in Λ of length at most T.

Next, we show that the relevant coordinates of the vectors in $\mathcal{S}$ only generate vectors in Λ. Each vector in $\mathcal{S}$ has length at most $2^{(d+m)/2} \cdot \sqrt{d+m} \cdot T(1+m_1)$. Meanwhile, as previously noted, we are guaranteed that any vector in $\mathcal{L}''$ shorter than $S\varepsilon/2$ corresponds to a vector in $\mathcal{L}$, and therefore to a vector in Λ.

Thus, if

$$2^{(d+m)/2} \cdot \sqrt{d+m} \cdot T(1 + m_1) < S\varepsilon/2 \tag{3}$$

the relevant coordinates of the vectors in $\mathcal{S}$ generate a sublattice of Λ, and we can thus recover a basis for this sublattice.

In summary, if (3) holds, we can recover vectors in $\mathcal{L}''$ that are such that the relevant coordinates generate a sublattice of Λ. Any vector $\boldsymbol{x} \in \Lambda$ such that $\|\boldsymbol{x}\| \leq T$ is guaranteed to be in this sublattice. Furthermore, as the first d coordinates of any vector in Λ is a vector in $\mathcal{L}$, we can easily recover a related sublattice of $\mathcal{L}$ from the recovered vectors in $\mathcal{L}''$. Thus, in order for this process to recover a basis for $\mathcal{L}$, it is sufficient that the vectors in Λ of length at most T are guaranteed to contain sufficient information about $\mathcal{L}$.

Required Properties of Λ. Proving that the vectors in Λ shorter than T are sufficient to recover a basis for $\mathcal{L}$ seems hard, and would presumably require significant assumptions to be made regarding both $\mathcal{L}$ and $\mathcal{F}$.

We therefore instead choose to simply assume that this is the case for lattices Λ of this form with some noticeable probability over the randomness in $\mathcal{F}$. This is equivalent to assuming that Λ has a basis where all information about $\mathcal{L}$ is contained in short basis vectors.

To determine for which bound T it is reasonable to assume that such a basis exists, we note that Λ has determinant $S^{m_2} \det(\mathcal{L})$. Therefore, by Minkowski's first theorem we are guaranteed that Λ contains a vector of length at most

$$\sqrt{m_2 + d} \cdot S^{m_2/(m_2+d)} \det(\mathcal{L})^{1/(m_2+d)}.$$

A random lattice is expected to have a basis where each basis vector is only slightly longer than the shortest vector in the lattice. This leads us to make the following concrete assumption:

Assumption 2. *Let $\boldsymbol{B}$ be a basis for $\mathcal{L}$, $F > 0$ be a constant and $\boldsymbol{F}$ be a $d \times m_2$-dimensional matrix where each of the m_2 columns are sampled from $\mathcal{F}$. Then, with noticeable probability over the randomness in $\mathcal{F}$, the lattice Λ generated by the rows of*

$$\left(\begin{array}{c|c} \boldsymbol{B} & S\boldsymbol{B} \cdot \boldsymbol{F} \\ \hline \boldsymbol{0}_{m_2 \times d} & S \cdot \boldsymbol{I}_{m_2} \end{array}\right)$$

has a basis such that each basis vector with non-zero values in its first d coordinates is shorter than $T = F\sqrt{m_2 + d} \cdot S^{m_2/(m_2+d)} \det(\mathcal{L})^{1/(m_2+d)}$.

To further motivate this assumption, we note that if $\mathcal{L}$ is a nice lattice, we expect it to contain many short vectors, and we expect these short vectors to generate the full lattice $\mathcal{L}$. We furthermore expect many of these short vectors in $\mathcal{L}$ to have an inner product far from an integer with the columns of $\boldsymbol{F}$ that are sampled from $\mathcal{F}$. These short vectors in $\mathcal{L}$ therefore do not correspond to short vectors in Λ. A small fraction of the vectors may however have an inner product close to an integer with each of the columns of $\boldsymbol{F}$.

A potential risk is hence that the distribution $\mathcal{F}$ may somehow be biased so as to cause some specific part of $\mathcal{L}$ to be more likely to have an inner product far from an integer with vectors sampled from $\mathcal{F}$, and therefore to be more likely to correspond to large vectors in Λ, leading to only a part of the lattice $\mathcal{L}$ being recovered. If no such bias exists, it is, however, natural to assume that the short vectors in $\mathcal{L}$ that have an inner product close to an integer with each of the columns of $\boldsymbol{F}$ still generate the full lattice $\mathcal{L}$.

Hence, if Assumption 1 holds for $\mathcal{L}$, and $\mathcal{F}$ is a sufficiently nice distribution, then we expect Assumption 2 to hold. In this case, we expect the lattice Λ to have a sufficiently short basis with probability close to one over the randomness in $\mathcal{F}$. In particular, if $\mathcal{F}$ is the uniform distribution, we expect such a basis to exist with probability close to one over the randomness in $\mathcal{F}$, and this is also corroborated by our simulations, see Appendix B.3 for further details.

Theorem 2 below follows from this assumption and the above analysis.

Theorem 2 (Robust post-processing derived from Theorem 1.1 in [20]). *Let $\mathcal{L}$ be a d-dimensional lattice with* $\det \mathcal{L} < 2^{d^2}$, *and let m, m_1 and m_2, and the vectors $\boldsymbol{w}_1, \ldots, \boldsymbol{w}_m$, be as above. Furthermore, let $\delta = 2^{-Cd} \cdot \sqrt{d}/2$ and $S = \delta^{-1}$ for constant*

$$C > \left(\frac{5}{2} + \frac{m}{2d}\right)\left(1 + \frac{m_2}{d}\right) + o(1).$$

Then, under Assumption 2, there is an efficient classical algorithm that, with noticeable probability over the choice of the $\boldsymbol{w}_i$, recovers a basis for $\mathcal{L}$.

Proof. The theorem essentially follows from the above analysis. The bound on C is obtained by inserting the values of ε and T in (3) and taking logarithms, leading to the requirement that

$$(d+m)/2 + \frac{Cdm_2 + \log(\det \mathcal{L})}{m_2 + d} + o(d) < Cd - \frac{\log(\det \mathcal{L})}{m_1}.$$

By using that $\det(\mathcal{L}) < 2^{d^2}$ and $m_1 \geq d$, this may be simplified to

$$\frac{5}{2} + \frac{m}{2d} + \frac{Cm_2}{m_2 + d} + o(1) < C,$$

leading to the requirement

$$C > \left(\frac{5}{2} + \frac{m}{2d}\right)\left(1 + \frac{m_2}{d}\right) + o(1)$$

and so the theorem follows. □

Acknowledgments. We are grateful to Johan Håstad for his extensive comments on early versions of this manuscript, and to Oded Regev's for his valuable comments and generous support. We thank the participants of the Quantum Cryptanalysis seminar at Schloss Dagstuhl for useful comments. Martin Ekerå thanks Schloss Dagstuhl and the organizers of the seminar for creating an environment where scientific progress is facilitated. This work was supported by the KTH Centre for Cyber Defence and Information Security (CDIS), and funded and supported by the Swedish NCSA that is a part of the Swedish Armed Forces.

Disclosure of Interests. The authors have no competing interests to declare that are relevant to the content of this article.

A Order Finding and Factoring

A.1 Finding the Order of a Group Element

Let $\mathbb{G}$ be a finite Abelian group and let $g \in \mathbb{G}$. Suppose that our goal is to find the order r of g. Let $g_1, \dots, g_{d-1}$ be $d-1$ small elements in $\mathbb{G}$.

In particular, for $\mathbb{G} = \mathbb{Z}_N^*$, for N a positive n-bit integer that is coprime to the first $d = \lceil \sqrt{n} \rceil$ primes, we take $g_1, \dots, g_{d-1}$ to be the first $d-1$ primes that when perceived as elements of $\mathbb{Z}_N^*$ are distinct from g.

By Lemma 3, there exists an efficient quantum algorithm that outputs a vector $\boldsymbol{w} \in [0,1)^d$ that, except for with probability $1/\mathrm{poly}(d)$, is within distance $\sqrt{d/2} \cdot 2^{-C\sqrt{n}}$ of a uniformly chosen $\boldsymbol{v} \in \mathcal{L}_g^*/\mathbb{Z}^d$, where

$$\mathcal{L}_g = \left\{ (z_1, \dots, z_d) \in \mathbb{Z}^d \;\middle|\; g^{z_d} \prod_{i=1}^{d-1} g_i^{z_i} = 1 \right\},$$

for $C > 0$ some constant. By performing $m \geq d + 4$ runs of this quantum algorithm, we obtain m such vectors $\boldsymbol{w}_1, \ldots, \boldsymbol{w}_m$.

By Lemma 2, there is an efficient classical algorithm that, with probability at least 1/4, recovers a basis for a sublattice Λ of $\mathcal{L}_g$ given the vectors $\boldsymbol{w}_1, \ldots, \boldsymbol{w}_m$. This sublattice Λ contains all vectors in $\mathcal{L}_g$ of norm at most $T = \exp(O(\sqrt{n}))$.

Under Assumption 1, Lemma 4 gives that there exists a basis of $\mathcal{L}_g$ with all basis vector having norm at most T. It then follows that $\Lambda = \mathcal{L}_g$, and Lemma 2 thus recovers a basis $\boldsymbol{B}$ for $\mathcal{L}_g$. Furthermore, $\boldsymbol{v}_r = (0, \ldots, 0, r)$ is in $\mathcal{L}_g$, and by definition r is the least positive integer such that $g^r = 1$. Therefore, $\boldsymbol{v}_r$ is the shortest vector in $\mathcal{L}_g$ that is non-zero only in the last coordinate. Since we know a basis $\boldsymbol{B}$ for $\mathcal{L}_g$, we can efficiently recover $\boldsymbol{v}_r$ and by extension r.

We are now ready to summarize the above analysis in a theorem:

Theorem 3. *Let N be a positive n-bit integer and let $d = \lceil \sqrt{n} \rceil$. Let $g \in \mathbb{Z}_N^*$. As in [18, Theorem 1], let G be the gate cost of a quantum circuit that takes*

$$|\, a, b, t, 0^S \,\rangle \to |\, a, b, (t + ab) \bmod N, 0^S \,\rangle$$

for $a, b, t \in [0, N) \cap \mathbb{Z}$ and S the number of ancilla qubits required. Then, under Assumption 1, there is an efficient classical algorithm that, by calling a quantum circuit $d + 4$ times, yields the order r of g with probability at least 1/4. This quantum circuit has gate cost $O(n^{1/2}\, G + n^{3/2})$, and it requires

$$S + \left(\frac{C}{\log \phi} + 8 + o(1) \right) n$$

qubits of space, for some constant $C > 0$ and ϕ the golden ratio.

Proof. The proof follows from the above analysis, and from Lemma 3 where the gate and space costs of the quantum circuit are analyzed.

Note that if N is divisible by one or more of the first d primes, then these prime powers may be factored out before quantum order finding is performed.

More specifically, order finding may be performed efficiently classically with respect to these prime powers, after which the partial results may be efficiently combined classically to yield the order r of g. □

We have used our simulator, further described in Appendix B, to corroborate the soundness of the heuristic assumption in Theorem 3, and to analyze how to select parameters to achieve a high success probability. For $n = 2048$ bits, the simulations indicate that it suffices to take $C \approx 2$. Furthermore, they indicate that the success probability is close to one after $d + 4$ runs of the quantum algorithm. This is much greater than the lower bound of 1/4 guaranteed by Theorem 3.

A.2 Factoring N via Order Finding in $\mathbb{Z}_N^*$

Let N be a positive composite integer. Suppose that we pick g uniformly at random from $\mathbb{Z}_N^*$ and compute the order r of g by using the algorithm in Appendix A.1.

Then, with very high probability—that is lower-bounded and shown to tend to one asymptotically in [5,6]—we can completely factor N given r via the procedure in [5]. This provides an alternative to Regev's factoring algorithm, that yields the complete factorization of N in $d+4$ runs by factoring via order finding, at the expense of making a stronger heuristic assumption, and at the expense of including one element that is not small in the product that is computed quantumly. It furthermore provides a connection to Shor's algorithm [23,24].

Note however that factoring via order finding is possible with only small elements in the product, see Appendix A.3–A.4, and that this is preferable in practice.

A.3 Finding the Order of an Abelian Group

Let $\mathbb{G}$ be a finite Abelian group. Suppose that our goal is to find the order $\#\mathbb{G}$ of $\mathbb{G}$. Let $g_1, \ldots, g_d$ be d small elements in $\mathbb{G}$. In particular, for $\mathbb{G} = \mathbb{Z}_N^*$, for N a positive n-bit integer that is coprime to the first $d = \lceil \sqrt{n} \rceil$ primes, we take $g_1, \ldots, g_d \in \mathbb{Z}_N^*$ to be the first d primes perceived as elements of $\mathbb{Z}_N^*$.

By Lemma 3, there exists an efficient quantum algorithm that outputs a vector $\boldsymbol{w} \in [0,1)^d$ that, except for with probability $1/\text{poly}(d)$, is within distance $\sqrt{d/2} \cdot 2^{-C\sqrt{n}}$ of a uniformly chosen $\boldsymbol{v} \in \mathcal{L}^* / \mathbb{Z}^d$, where

$$\mathcal{L} = \left\{ (z_1, \ldots, z_d) \in \mathbb{Z}^d \;\middle|\; \prod_{i=1}^{d} g_i^{z_i} = 1 \right\},$$

for $C > 0$ some constant. By performing $m \geq d + 4$ runs of this quantum algorithm, we obtain m such vectors $\boldsymbol{w}_1, \ldots, \boldsymbol{w}_m$. By Lemma 2, there is an efficient classical algorithm that, with probability at least $1/4$, recovers a basis $\boldsymbol{B}$ of a sublattice Λ of $\mathcal{L}$ when given the vectors $\boldsymbol{w}_1, \ldots, \boldsymbol{w}_m$. Furthermore, the sublattice Λ of $\mathcal{L}$ contains all vectors in $\mathcal{L}$ of norm at most $T = \exp(O(\sqrt{n}))$.

Under Assumption 1 there exists a basis for $\mathcal{L}$ with all basis vectors having norm at most T. It then follows that $\Lambda = \mathcal{L}$, and $\boldsymbol{B}$ is thus a basis for $\mathcal{L}$. Given $\boldsymbol{B}$, we can efficiently compute $\det \mathcal{L} = |\det \boldsymbol{B}|$. By Lemma 5 and Assumption 1, we then have that $\#\mathbb{Z}_N^* = \varphi(N) = \det \mathcal{L}$, where φ is Euler's totient function.

We are now ready to summarize the above analysis in a theorem:

Theorem 4. *Let N be a positive n-bit integer coprime to the first $d = \lceil \sqrt{n} \rceil$ primes, and let $g_1, \ldots, g_d \in \mathbb{Z}_N^*$ be the first d primes perceived as elements of $\mathbb{Z}_N^*$. As in [18, Theorem 1], let G be the gate cost of a quantum circuit that takes*

$$|\, a, b, t, 0^S \,\rangle \rightarrow |\, a, b, (t + ab) \bmod N, 0^S \,\rangle$$

for $a, b, t \in [0, N) \cap \mathbb{Z}$ and S the number of ancilla qubits required. Then, under Assumption 1, there is an efficient classical algorithm that, by calling a quantum circuit $d+4$ times, yields $\varphi(N)$ with probability at least $1/4$. This quantum circuit has gate cost $O(n^{1/2} G + n^{3/2})$, and it requires

$$S + \left(\frac{C}{\log \phi} + 8 + o(1) \right) n$$

qubits of space, for some constant $C > 0$ and ϕ the golden ratio.

Proof. The proof follows from the above analysis, and from Lemma 3 where the gate and space costs of the quantum circuit are analyzed. □

We have used our simulator, further described in Appendix B, to corroborate the soundness of the heuristic assumption in Theorem 4, and to analyze how to select parameters to achieve a high success probability. For $n = 2048$ bits, the simulations indicate that it suffices to take $C \approx 2$. Furthermore, they indicate that the success probability is close to one after $d + 4$ runs of the quantum algorithm. This is much greater than the lower bound of $1/4$ guaranteed by Theorem 4.

Note that if N is divisible by one or more of the first d primes in Theorem 4 above, then these prime powers may be factored out before calling the quantum algorithm. The value of φ may then be efficiently computed classically with respect to these prime powers, and all partial results efficiently combined classically to yield $\varphi(N)$. The restriction imposed in Theorem 4 that N must be coprime to the first d primes does hence not imply a loss of generality.

Note furthermore that Theorem 4 relies on $g_1, \ldots, g_d$ generating $\mathbb{Z}_N^*$. This is part of Assumption 1, but as noted in Sect. 2.2, this part of the assumption does not hold if N has many factors in relation to d. While we expect a weaker assumption to hold for such N, we can not rely on this weaker assumption to prove Theorem 4 as this theorem crucially relies on $g_1, \ldots, g_d$ generating $\mathbb{Z}_N^*$.

With a weaker assumption, we do, however, expect that an analogue of Theorem 4 can recover the order of the group $\langle g_1, \ldots, g_d \rangle$. A random element in $\mathbb{Z}_N^*$ has order $\lambda(N)$ with high probability [5], where λ is the Carmichael function, that yields the least positive integer such that $g^{\lambda(N)} = 1$ for all $g \in \mathbb{Z}_N^*$. Therefore, it is natural to assume that one of the small elements $g_1, \ldots, g_d$ has order $\lambda(N)$. The order of $\langle g_1, \ldots, g_d \rangle$ is then an integer multiple of $\lambda(N)$.

A.4 Factoring N by Finding $\varphi(N) = \#\mathbb{Z}_N^*$

Given an integer multiple of $\lambda(N)$, such as $\varphi(N)$, we may use a randomized version of Miller's algorithm [15] to factor N completely as explained in [5]. This provides yet another alternative for factoring via order finding—via Theorem 4 or an analogue thereof—that yields the complete factorization of N in $d+4$ runs at the expense of making a stronger heuristic assumption.

A clear advantage of this alternative compared to that in Appendix A.2 is that all elements that are exponentiated quantumly are small, bringing the quantum cost essentially on par with that of Regev's factoring algorithm [20].

In fact, the quantum cost is slightly lower than of Regev's algorithm: Whereas Regev's algorithm exponentiates the squares of the first d primes, the above algorithm exponentiates the first d primes, so the numbers that are exponentiated are half the size.

A.5 Notes on Generalizations

The above theorems are for algorithms specific to $\mathbb{Z}_N^*$ since there is a notion of small group elements in $\mathbb{Z}_N^*$, and since $\mathbb{Z}_N^*$ is extensively used in cryptography. As previously stated, the algorithms may be generalized to other Abelian groups, but for the algorithms to have an advantage over other algorithms in the literature there must exist a notion of small elements in the group.

B Simulations

To simulate Regev's algorithm, and our extensions thereof, we use the simulator in [9] that can simulate the algorithms for problem instances of special form.

The simulator does not simulate the actual quantum circuits for the quantum algorithms. Rather, it samples directly from the distribution induced the quantum algorithms. Hence, it can only be used to test the performance and robustness of the classical post-processing for given parameter choices—not to test the quantum algorithms themselves.

B.1 Simulating the Quantum Algorithms

Recall that the lattice $\mathcal{L}$, as given in Lemma 3, is

$$\mathcal{L} = \left\{ (z_1, \ldots, z_d) \in \mathbb{Z}^d \;\middle|\; \prod_{i=1}^{d-k} g_i^{z_i} \cdot \prod_{i=1}^{k} u_i^{z_{d-k+i}} = 1 \right\}. \tag{4}$$

The simulator uses a basis for $\mathcal{L}$ to sample vectors from a distribution close to the distribution induced by the quantum algorithms as per Regev's analysis [20]. Specifically, to produce such a sample, the simulator first samples a vector $\boldsymbol{v}$ from $\mathcal{L}^*/\mathbb{Z}^d$. It then samples a vector $\boldsymbol{w} \in \mathbb{Z}^d/D$ with probability close to

$$Q_{\boldsymbol{v}}(\boldsymbol{w}) = \frac{\rho_{1/\sqrt{2}R}(\boldsymbol{v} - \boldsymbol{w})}{\rho_{1/\sqrt{2}R}(\boldsymbol{v} - \mathbb{Z}^d/D)}$$

and outputs $\boldsymbol{w}$ mod 1. With $\boldsymbol{v}$ sampled uniformly at random from $\mathcal{L}^*/\mathbb{Z}^d$, it then follows that $\boldsymbol{w}$ is sampled from the distribution induced by the quantum algorithm as per Regev's analysis.

In general, it is hard to compute a basis for $\mathcal{L}$ classically. However, if the discrete logarithm problem can be solved efficiently in $\mathbb{Z}_N^*$, then it follows that a basis for $\mathcal{L}$ can also efficiently be computed.

In all our simulations, we therefore consider special-form integers N with distinct prime factors $p_1, \ldots, p_t$ such that $p_i - 1$ is smooth for all i, allowing us to efficiently solve the discrete logarithm problem in $\mathbb{Z}_N^*$ with the Pohlig-Hellman algorithm [16]. For such special-form N, our simulator can thus construct a basis for $\mathcal{L}$. For simplicity, we also ensure that the factors of $p_i - 1$ do not occur with multiplicity, and that $\gcd(p_i - 1, p_j - 1) = 2$ for every i, j with $i \neq j$.

Even though N is of special form for all the problem instances we consider in our simulations, we still expect the performance and robustness of the classical post-processing for the problem instances we simulate to be representative of that for general problem instances.

To in part motivate this claim, we have simulated some general problem instances that are sufficiently small for the discrete logarithm problem to be classically tractable. We did not notice any difference in the behavior of the classical post-processing for simulated outputs for these general problem instances compared to for special-form problem instances of the same size.

B.2 The Classical Post-processing

The classical post-processing is implemented in the simulator as described in Sect. 4.2, except that it makes use of the definition of $\mathcal{L}$ to verify the output. It constructs the lattice $\mathcal{L}''$ generated by the rows of

$$\left(\begin{array}{c|ccc} \boldsymbol{I}_{d\times d} & S\cdot\boldsymbol{w}_1^{\mathrm{T}} & \cdots & S\cdot\boldsymbol{w}_m^{\mathrm{T}} \\ \hline \boldsymbol{0}_{m\times d} & & S\cdot\boldsymbol{I}_{m\times m} & \end{array}\right)$$

where each vector in $\boldsymbol{w}_1,\ldots,\boldsymbol{w}_m$ is sampled either from the distribution induced by the quantum algorithm, or from some other distribution with a given failure rate when simulating error-correction failures.

The analysis in Sect. 4.2 shows that after running LLL on the basis for $\mathcal{L}''$, the d first coordinates of any sufficiently short vector in the reduced basis form a vector in $\mathcal{L}$. Based on Assumption 2, there is a high probability that the vectors thus recovered form a basis for $\mathcal{L}$.

Note that the analysis in Sect. 4.2 uses a length bound to determine if vectors in $\mathcal{L}''$ correspond to vectors in $\mathcal{L}$. In the classical post-processing as implemented in the simulator, we instead determine if a vector is in $\mathcal{L}$ by directly using the definition (4) of $\mathcal{L}$. This naturally increases the probability of success.

B.3 Simulation Results

In Sect. 4.2, we analyze the robustness of the post-processing for Regev's original algorithm, and for our extensions thereof, to error-correction failures. Our robustness analysis relies on an additional heuristic assumption, that in turn partially depends on the distribution from which bad outputs are sampled, where bad outputs stem from runs for which the error-correction fails.

We have performed simulations to verify the soundness of the heuristic assumption when bad outputs are sampled from the uniform distribution. Furthermore, we have performed simulations to ascertain how large a failure rate the post-processing can handle, as a function of the constant C and of the total number of runs, for concrete, cryptographically relevant, problem instances.

The data presented in Table 1 gives the minimum C for which the post-processing successfully solves problem instances when given both good and bad vectors. The good vectors are sampled as described in Appendix B.1 whereas the bad vectors are sampled uniformly at random from $\{0, 1/D, \ldots, (D-1)/D\}^d$.

To find the minimum C for a given problem instance, we perform a search: For each value of C to test, we sample vectors given C and execute the post-processing algorithm. If the solution is thus successfully recovered, we try again with a smaller C, otherwise with a larger C. This process is repeated until a C is found such that the test is successful for C but fails for $C - 0.01$.

Out of concern that there may be a large variance between different problem instances, we have performed the above search for a set of problem instances. The variance in the minimum C thus obtained was very small, however, never differing by more than 0.1 and, in most cases, not by more than 0.01.

Since the minimum C varies so little, and due to the relatively heavy computations involved, we have performed searches for only five different problem instances for each entry in Table 1. The table gives the minimum C that was sufficient for successfully solving all five problem instances. For C as in the table or somewhat larger, the post-processing is seemingly successful with probability close to one.

Table 1. The minimum value of C for which the post-processing is successful in solving all attempted 2048-bit problem instances. The post-processing is provided with m_1 vectors sampled from the simulator for the quantum algorithm, and m_2 vectors sampled uniformly at random from $\{0, 1/D, \ldots, (D-1)/D\}^d$. The tabulated failure rate is $m_2/(m_1 + m_2)$ rounded to the nearest percentage.

		Failure	C		
m_1	m_2	rate	Logarithm finding	Factoring	Order finding
50	0	0%	1.97	1.97	1.98
55	0	0%	1.89	1.90	1.90
55	24	30%	2.37	2.36	2.37
55	55	50%	2.99	3.00	3.00
55	127	70%	4.61	4.58	4.58

We consider three types of problem instances for logarithm finding, factoring, and order finding, respectively. For all types, we let $d = \lceil \sqrt{n} \rceil$. On the first line of Table 1, the number of good vectors is $m_1 = d + 4$, whereas $m_1 = \lceil 1.2\sqrt{n} \rceil$ on the remaining lines.

For factoring, we use Regev's original algorithm [20]. For order finding, we use the algorithm described in Appendix A.1. For both factoring and order finding, we take N to be an $n = 2048$ bit integer with two prime factors of similar size. For order finding, we pick g uniformly at random from $\mathbb{Z}_N^*$.

For discrete logarithm finding, we use the algorithm in Sect. 3.2 without pre-computation. We take N to be an $n = 2048$ bit prime, let g be the smallest element in $\mathbb{Z}_N^*$ that generates a subgroup of order $r = (p-1)/2$, and let $x = g^e$ where e is selected uniformly at random from $[0, r) \cap \mathbb{Z}$.

As may be seen in Table 1, there is no large difference between the different types of problem instances considered in terms of the minimum C required. This is expected, as the lattices for the problem instances are very similar.

References

1. Coppersmith, D.: An approximate Fourier transform useful in quantum factoring. arXiv:quant-ph/0201067 (2002). (Also IBM Research Report RC 19642)
2. Ekerå, M., Håstad, J.: Quantum algorithms for computing short discrete logarithms and factoring RSA integers. In: Lange, T., Takagi, T. (eds.) PQCrypto 2017. LNCS, vol. 10346, pp. 347–363. Springer, Cham (2017). https://doi.org/10.1007/978-3-319-59879-6_20
3. Ekerå, M.: On post-processing in the quantum algorithm for computing short discrete logarithms. Des. Codes Cryptogr. **88**(11), 2313–2335 (2020)
4. Ekerå, M.: Quantum algorithms for computing general discrete logarithms and orders with tradeoffs. J. Math. Cryptol. **15**(1), 359–407 (2021)
5. Ekerå, M.: On completely factoring any integer efficiently in a single run of an order-finding algorithm. Quantum Inf. Proc. **20**(205), 1–14 (2021)
6. Ekerå, M.: On the success probability of quantum order finding. ACM Trans. Quantum Comput. **5**(2), Article no. 11, 1–40 (2024). https://doi.org/10.1145/3655026
7. Ekerå, M.: Revisiting Shor's quantum algorithm for computing general discrete logarithms. arXiv:1905.09084v3 (2019–2023)
8. Ekerå, M.: On the success probability of the quantum algorithm for the short DLP. arXiv:2309.01754v1 (2023)
9. Ekerå, M., Gärtner, J.: Simulating Regev's quantum factoring algorithm and Ekerå–Gärtner's extensions to discrete logarithm finding, order finding and factoring via order finding. GitHub repository ekera/regevnum (2023–2024)
10. Gidney, C., Ekerå, M.: How to factor 2048 bit RSA integers in 8 hours using 20 million noisy qubits. Quantum **5**, 433 (2021)
11. Hhan, M., Yamakawa, T., Yun, A.: Quantum complexity for discrete logarithms and related problems. arXiv:2307.03065 (2023)
12. Kaliski, B.S., Jr.: A Quantum "Magic Box" for the Discrete Logarithm Problem. IACR ePrint 2017/745 (2017)
13. Litinski, D.: How to compute a 256-bit elliptic curve private key with only 50 million Toffoli gates. arXiv:2306.08585v1 (2023)
14. Lenstra, A.K., Lenstra, H.W., Lovász, L.: Factoring polynomials with rational coefficients. Math. Ann. **261**, 515–534 (1982)
15. Miller, G.L.: Riemann's hypothesis and tests for primality. J. Comput. Syst. Sci. **13**(3), 300–317 (1976)
16. Pohlig, S., Hellman, M.: An improved algorithm for computing logarithms over GF(p) and its cryptographic significance. IEEE Trans. Inf. Theory **24**(1), 106–110 (1978)
17. Pomerance, C.: The expected number of random elements to generate a finite Abelian group. Period. Math. Hungar. **43**(1–2), 191–198 (2001)
18. Ragavan, S., Vaikuntanathan, V.: Optimizing space in Regev's factoring algorithm. arXiv:2310.00899v1 (2023)

19. Ragavan, S., Vaikuntanathan, V.: Space-efficient and noise-robust quantum factoring. arXiv:2310.00899v3 (2024)
20. Regev, O.: An efficient quantum factoring algorithm. arXiv:2308.06572v3 (2023)
21. Seifert, J.-P.: Using fewer qubits in Shor's factorization algorithm via simultaneous diophantine approximation. In: Naccache, D. (ed.) CT-RSA 2001. LNCS, vol. 2020, pp. 319–327. Springer, Heidelberg (2001). https://doi.org/10.1007/3-540-45353-9_24
22. Schnorr, C.-P., Euchner, M.: Lattice basis reduction: improved practical algorithms and solving subset sum problems. Math. Program. **66**(1–3), 181–199 (1994)
23. Shor, P.W.: Algorithms for quantum computation: discrete logarithms and factoring. In: Proceedings of the 35th Annual Symposium on Foundations of Computer Science, SFCS 1994, pp. 124–134 (1994)
24. Shor, P.W.: Polynomial-time algorithms for prime factorization and discrete logarithms on a quantum computer. SIAM J. Comput. **26**(5), 1484–1509 (1997)

Transforms and Proofs

A Note on *Failing Gracefully*: Completing the Picture for Explicitly Rejecting Fujisaki-Okamoto Transforms Using Worst-Case Correctness

Kathrin Hövelmanns[1(✉)] and Christian Majenz[2]

[1] Eindhoven University of Technology, Eindhoven, The Netherlands
kathrin@hoevelmanns.net

[2] Department of Applied Mathematics and Computer Science, Technical University of Denmark, Kongens Lyngby, Denmark

Abstract. The Fujisaki-Okamoto (FO) transformation is used in most proposals for post-quantum secure key encapsulation mechanisms (KEMs) like, e.g., Kyber [BDK+18]. The security analysis of FO in the presence of quantum attackers has made huge progress over the last years, however, it had a particular quirk: unless incurring (even more) unreasonable security bounds, security was only shown for FO variants that react to invalid ciphertexts by returning a pseudorandom value ('implicit' reject) rather than 'explicitly' reporting decryption failure by returning a failure symbol. This part of the design has been subject to some debate, with the main question being whether explicitly rejecting variants could indeed be less secure than their implicitly rejecting counterparts.

A recent work by Hövelmanns, Hülsing and Majenz [HHM22] gave a proof which, in contrast to previous ones, was agnostic to the choice of how invalid ciphertexts are being dealt with, thus indicating that the two variants might be similarly secure. It involved, however, a new correctness notion for the encryption scheme that is used to encapsulate the keys. While this new notion in principle might allow to improve the overall security bound, it places a new analysis burden on designers: when looking at a concrete KEM at hand, it becomes necessary to analyze this new notion for the encryption scheme on which the KEM is based.

This note offers a trade-off between [HHM22] and its predecessors: it offers a bound for both rejection variants, but uses the established correctness notion that was used in all previous work.

Keywords: Public-key encryption · post-quantum · QROM · Fujisaki-Okamoto · decryption failures · NIST

1 Introduction

The Fujisaki-Okamoto (FO) transform [FO99, FO13, Den03] has become the defacto standard to build secure KEMs. In particular, it was used in most KEM

M.-J. Saarinen and D. Smith-Tone (Eds.): PQCrypto 2024, LNCS 14772, pp. 245–265, 2024.
https://doi.org/10.1007/978-3-031-62746-0_11

submissions to the NIST PQC standardisation process [NIS17]. In the context of post-quantum security, however, two novel issues surfaced:

1. Many of the PKE schemes used to encapsulate keys occasionally fail to decrypt a ciphertext to its plaintext (they do not have perfect correctness), and decryption failures have been shown [DGJ+19, BS20, DRV20, FKK+22] to impact security.
2. To rule out quantum attacks, the security proofs have to be done in the quantum-accessible random oracle model (QROM).

Both issues were tackled in [HHK17] and follow-up work (e.g., [SXY18, JZC+18, BHH+19, HKSU20, KSS+20, HHM22]). The QROM proofs prior to [HHM22], however, had a particular quirk: To avoid extreme additional reduction losses, they required the scheme to *reject implicitly*, that is, to return pseudo-random session keys instead of simply reporting an error when presented with a malformed ciphertext.

The FO Transformation. Before discussing the goal of this note, we briefly recall the FO KEM transformation as introduced in [Den03] and revisited as $\mathsf{FO}_m^{\perp}$ by [HHK17]. $\mathsf{FO}_m^{\perp}$ constructs a KEM from a public-key encryption scheme PKE by first modifying PKE to obtain a deterministic scheme $\mathsf{PKE}^{\mathsf{G}}$, and then applying a PKE-to-KEM transformation ($\mathsf{U}_m^{\perp}$ in [HHK17]) to $\mathsf{PKE}^{\mathsf{G}}$:
DERANDOMISED SCHEME $\mathsf{PKE}^{\mathsf{G}}$. Starting from PKE and a hash function G, $\mathsf{PKE}^{\mathsf{G}}$ encrypts messages m according to the encryption algorithm Enc of PKE, using the hash value $\mathsf{G}(m)$ as the random coins for Enc:

$$\mathsf{Enc}^{\mathsf{G}}(pk, m) := \mathsf{Enc}(pk, m; \mathsf{G}(m)) \ ,$$

$\mathsf{Dec}^{\mathsf{G}}$ uses the decryption algorithm Dec of PKE to decrypt a ciphertext c to plaintext m'. $\mathsf{Dec}^{\mathsf{G}}$ rejects by returning failure symbol $\perp$ if c fails to decrypt or m' fails to encrypt back to c. (The formal definition is recalled on page 9).
PKE-TO-KEM TRANSFORMATION $\mathsf{U}_m^{\perp}$. Starting from a deterministic encryption scheme PKE' and a hash function H, key encapsulation algorithm $\mathsf{KEM}_m^{\perp} := \mathsf{U}_m^{\perp}[\mathsf{PKE}', \mathsf{H}]$ encapsulates a key K via a ciphertext c by letting

$$\mathsf{Encaps}(pk) := (c := \mathsf{Enc}'(pk, m), K := \mathsf{H}(m)),$$

where m is picked at random from the message space. Decapsulation returns $K := \mathsf{H}(\mathsf{Dec}'(c))$ unless c fails to decrypt, in which case it returns failure symbol $\perp$.

The Role of Correctness Errors. The impact of correctness errors on security is reflected in hindrances when trying to show that FO-transformed KEMs are $\mathsf{IND\text{-}CCA}$ secure: During the proofs, the decapsulation oracle ODECAPS is replaced with a simulation. This simulation, however, is "too good" – it accurately decapsulates ciphertexts for which the real ODECAPS would fail. In other words, the change from the honest to a simulated decapsulation oracle is noticeable to attackers if they manage to craft a ciphertext where the honest decapsulation fails detectably. In [HHK17], the resulting advantage in distinguishing ODECAPS from its simulation was dealt with in two steps:

1. Bound it via a 'break-correctness' game COR. COR asks the adversary, equipped with the complete key pair *including the secret key*, to produce a plaintext m such that $\mathsf{Enc}^{\mathsf{G}}(m)$ fails to decrypt.
2. Bound the maximal COR advantage in terms of a statistical 'worst-case' quantity δ_{wc} of the underlying scheme PKE. δ_{wc} is the maximal probability for plaintexts to cause decryption failure, averaged over the key pair.

This lead to a typical search bound, as the adversary can use the secret key to check if ciphertexts fail.

Correctness Treatment in [HHM22] and Open Question. A central motivation of [HHM22] was that it is hard to estimate concrete δ_{wc}-bounds for particular schemes without relying on heuristics, and that it might be easier to estimate bounds for notions in which the attacker does not obtain the secret key.

[HHM22] therefore introduced a new family of correctness games that represent the search for failing plaintexts *without* the secret key, called *Find Failing Plaintext* (FFP) games, and then related the respective advantages to properties of the underlying encryption scheme PKE (see Fig. 1):

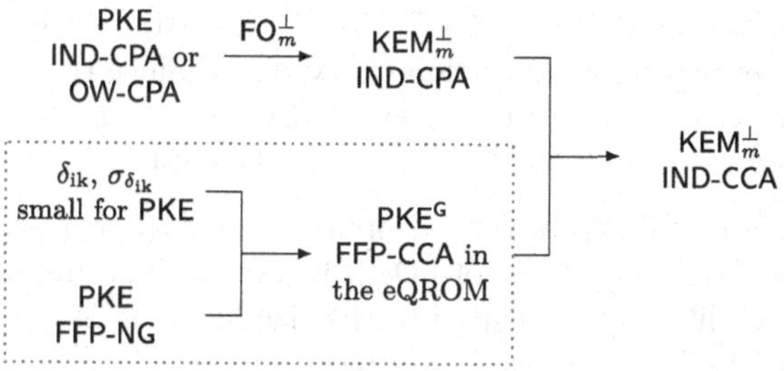

Fig. 1. Simplification of Fig. 1 in [HHM22].The red-dotted part introduces new analysis tasks for KEM designers.

The resulting correctness requirements on PKE (δ_{ik}, $\sigma_{\delta_{\mathrm{ik}}}$ and FFP-NG) are defined in a way such reasoning about their concrete estimates can safely involve computational assumptions, as they represent settings in which the attacker does not possess the secret key. On the other hand, as already mentioned in [HHM22] (and later in [MX23]), these notions nonetheless introduce new analysis tasks for designers who want to argue security of their concrete scheme. Given that δ_{wc}-correctness can be bounded heuristically by available estimator scripts, it might very well be that scheme designers are happy to resort to that heuristic. We therefore address the following open question:

> **Can we reconcile the proof for explicitly rejecting KEMs given in [HHM22] with the more established correctness notion (worst-case correctness)?**

Result of this Note. We will show that the red-dotted part of Fig. 1 can be replaced with a picture only involving the worst-case correctness parameter δ_{wc}, see Fig. 2.

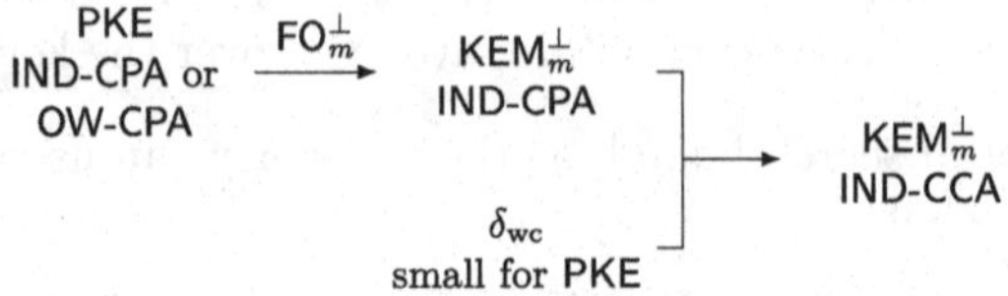

Fig. 2. Analogue of Fig. 1 with the alternative decryption failure analysis developed in this note.

To achieve this, the only part requiring a change will be how we reason that attackers cannot distinguish oDecaps from its simulation, to which end we would like to simply resort to the original COR notion.

The only hurdle is that COR, as analysed so far, isn't a seamless fit: the simulation of oDecaps in [HHM22] involves a slightly more complicated variant of the QROM, called eQROM. In the eQROM, the attacker gets an additional interface that essentially inverts certain encryptions, Since the search bound for COR was only known in the plain QROM that does not provide this additional interface, we need to reprove the bound in the eQROM.

TL;DR for Scheme Designers. Theorem 1 (on page 11) provides concrete bounds for the IND-CCA security of $\mathsf{FO}_m^{\perp}[\mathsf{PKE}, \mathsf{G}, \mathsf{H}]$. Ignoring constant factors up to 10 and an additive term related to the size of the message space (denoted "$\lesssim$"), our bound is roughly of the following form:

$$\epsilon_{\text{IND-CCA-KEM}} \lesssim \sqrt{(d + q_{\text{D}}) \cdot \epsilon_{\text{IND-CPA}}} + (q + q_{\text{D}} + 1)^2 \cdot \delta_{\text{wc}} + q_{\text{D}}(q + q_{\text{D}}) \cdot 2^{-\gamma/2} \ .$$

The bound requires to upper bound the following values:

$\epsilon_{\text{IND-CPA}}$	IND-CPA advantage against PKE
q	number of issued random oracles queries
q_{D}	number of decryption queries
d	random oracle query depth (can be bounded trivially by q)
$2^{-\gamma/2}$	maximal probability that encryption hits a specific ciphertext (see Definition 1 on page 5)
δ_{wc}	worst-case correctness of PKE as defined in [HHK17] (see Definition 4 on page 7): probability that decrypting $\mathsf{Enc}(m)$ doesn't yield m for the worst message m, averaged over KG

Assuming an attacker makes far less online queries than hash queries (so $q_{\mathsf{D}} \ll q$), trivially bounding $d < q$, and dropping constant factors up to 4, we can further simplify the bound to

$$\epsilon_{\mathsf{IND\text{-}CCA\text{-}KEM}} \lesssim \sqrt{q \cdot \epsilon_{\mathsf{IND\text{-}CPA}}} + q^2 \cdot \delta_{\mathrm{wc}} + q_{\mathsf{D}} \cdot q \cdot 2^{-\gamma/2} \ .$$

2 Preliminaries

After establishing basic notation, we recall several correctness-related notions for public-key encryption schemes that were introduced in [HHK17] and [HHM22]. (For convenience, we also recall more standard definitions for public-key encryption and key encapsulation algorithms.)

For a finite set S, we denote the sampling of a uniform random element x by $x \leftarrow_\$ S$, and we denote deterministic computation of an algorithm $\mathcal{A}$ on input x by $y := \mathcal{A}(x)$. By $[\![B]\!]$ we denote the bit that is 1 if the Boolean statement B is true, and otherwise 0.

Below, we also consider all security games in the (quantum) random oracle model, where PKE and adversary $\mathcal{A}$ are given access to (quantum) random oracles. (How we model quantum access is made explicit in Sect. 2.5 below.)

2.1 Standard Definitions for PKE

For convenience, we start by recalling the formal definition of γ-spreadness.

Definition 1 (γ-spreadness). *We say that* PKE *is γ-spread iff for all key pairs $(pk, sk) \in \mathrm{supp}(\mathsf{KG})$ and all messages $m \in \mathcal{M}$ it holds that*

$$\max_{c \in \mathcal{C}} \Pr[\mathsf{Enc}(pk, m) = c] \leq 2^{-\gamma} \ ,$$

where the probability is taken over the internal randomness Enc.

We also recall two standard security notions: One-Wayness under Chosen Plaintext Attacks (OW-CPA) and Indistinguishability under Chosen-Plaintext Attacks (IND-CPA).

Definition 2 (OW-CPA, IND-CPA). *Let* $\mathsf{PKE} = (\mathsf{KG}, \mathsf{Enc}, \mathsf{Dec})$ *be a public-key encryption scheme with message space $\mathcal{M}$. We define the* OW-CPA *game as in Fig. 3 and the* OW-CPA *advantage function of an adversary $\mathcal{A}$ against* PKE *as*

$$\mathrm{Adv}^{\mathsf{OW\text{-}CPA}}_{\mathsf{PKE}}(\mathcal{A}) := \Pr[\mathsf{OW\text{-}CPA}^{\mathcal{A}}_{\mathsf{PKE}} \Rightarrow 1] \ .$$

Furthermore, we define the 'left-or-right' version of IND-CPA *by defining games* $\mathsf{IND\text{-}CPA}_b$, *where $b \in \{0,1\}$ (also in Fig. 3), and the* IND-CPA *advantage function of an adversary $\mathcal{A} = (\mathcal{A}_1, \mathcal{A}_2)$ against* PKE *(where $\mathcal{A}_2$ has binary output) as*

$$\mathrm{Adv}^{\mathsf{IND\text{-}CPA}}_{\mathsf{PKE}}(\mathcal{A}) := |\Pr[\mathsf{IND\text{-}CPA}^{\mathcal{A}}_0 \Rightarrow 1] - \Pr[\mathsf{IND\text{-}CPA}^{\mathcal{A}}_1 \Rightarrow 1]| \ .$$

Game OW-CPA	Game IND-CPA$_b$
$(pk, sk) \leftarrow \mathsf{KG}$	$(pk, sk) \leftarrow \mathsf{KG}$
$m^* \leftarrow_\$ \mathcal{M}$	$(m_0^*, m_1^*, \mathrm{st}) \leftarrow \mathcal{A}_1(pk)$
$c^* \leftarrow \mathsf{Enc}(pk, m^*)$	$c^* \leftarrow \mathsf{Enc}(pk, m_b^*)$
$m' \leftarrow \mathcal{A}(pk, c^*)$	$b' \leftarrow \mathcal{A}_2(pk, c^*, \mathrm{st})$
return $[\![m' = m^*]\!]$	**return** b'

Fig. 3. Games OW-CPA and IND-CPA$_b$ for PKE.

Game FFP-CCA$_{\mathsf{PKE}^{\mathsf{G}}}$	Oracle oDECRYPT$(c \neq c^*)$
01 $(pk, sk) \leftarrow \mathsf{KG}$	08 $m' := \mathsf{Dec}(sk, c)$
02 $m \leftarrow \mathcal{A}^{\text{oDECRYPT},\mathsf{eCO.RO},\mathsf{eCO.Ext}}(pk)$	09 **if** $c \neq \mathsf{Enc}(pk, m'; \mathsf{G}(m'))$
03 $c := \mathsf{Enc}(pk, m; \mathsf{G}(m))$	10 **return** $\perp$
04 $m' := \mathsf{Dec}(sk, c)$	11 **else**
05 **if** $c \neq \mathsf{Enc}(pk, m'; \mathsf{G}(m'))$	12 **return** m'
06 $m' := \perp$	
07 **return** $[\![m' \neq m]\!]$	

Fig. 4. Game FFP-CCA for derandomised scheme PKE^{G}, with G modelled as an extractable compressed oracle eCO, so with oracle interface eCO.RO and additional extractor interface eCO.Ext that, intuitively, produces plaintexts for queried ciphertexts. Lines 03–05 are defined relative to the random oracle G which is modelled as an extractable QRO, we stuck with writing G for the sake of simplicity. (Formally, G represents oracle interface eCO.RO.) This game is for derandomised schemes PKE^{G} (instead of an arbitrary dPKE), the decryption oracle thus includes the respective re-encryption step.

2.2 FO-Related Correctness Notions for PKE

FINDING FAILING PLAINTEXTS (FFP). Following [HHM22], we formalise the finding of failing plaintexts as the winning condition of the FFP game below. In the FFP-CCA game, the adversary is given the public key and access to a decryption oracle, outputs a message m and wins if $\mathsf{Dec}(sk, \mathsf{Enc}(pk, m)) \neq m$. We are only concerned with the game run against PKE^{G}, i.e., a public-key encryption scheme that stems from derandomising some public-key encryption scheme PKE as sketched in the introduction and formalised in Fig. 8 on page 9).

Definition 3 (FFP-CCA of PKE^{G}). *Let* $\mathsf{PKE}^{\mathsf{G}} = (\mathsf{KG}, \mathsf{Enc}^{\mathsf{G}}, \mathsf{Dec}^{\mathsf{G}})$ *be the modified public-key encryption scheme stemming from derandomising some public-key encryption scheme* $\mathsf{PKE} = (\mathsf{KG}, \mathsf{Enc}, \mathsf{Dec})$. *We define the* FFP-CCA *game for* PKE^{G} *as in Fig. 4, and the* FFP-CCA *advantage function of an adversary* $\mathcal{A}$ *against* PKE^{G} *as*

$$\mathrm{Adv}_{\mathsf{PKE}^{\mathsf{G}}}^{\mathsf{FFP\text{-}CCA}}(\mathcal{A}) := \Pr[\mathsf{FFP\text{-}CCA}_{\mathsf{PKE}^{\mathsf{G}}}^{\mathcal{A}} \Rightarrow 1] \ .$$

We now recall the definition of worst-case-correctness introduced in [HHK17], there called δ-correctness.

Definition 4 (**δ_{wc}-worst-case-correctness**). *We say that a public-key encryption scheme* PKE *is* δ_{wc} *-worst-case-correct if*

$$\mathbf{E}[\max_{m \in \mathcal{M}} \Pr[\mathsf{Dec}(sk, c) \neq m \mid c \leftarrow \mathsf{Enc}(pk, m)]] \leq \delta_{\text{wc}} \ ,$$

where the expectation is taken over $(pk, sk) \leftarrow \mathsf{KG}$ *and the probability is over the randomness of* Enc.

In particular, δ_{wc}-worst-case correctness means that even (possibly unbounded) adversaries with access to the secret key will succeed in triggering decryption failure with probability at most δ_{wc}. This property was formalised in [HHK17] as the winning condition of a correctness game COR, in which the adversary gets the full key pair, outputs a message, and wins if the message exhibits decryption failure. The difference between FFP-CCA and COR is having the full key pair (COR) vs. having access to a decryption oracle (FFP-CCA).

Like [HHK17], we need to analyse the respective term for $\mathsf{PKE}^{\mathsf{G}}$, i.e., a public-key encryption scheme resulting from derandomising some public-key encryption scheme PKE. Since derandomisation happens via a random oracle G, [HHK17] introduced a QROM analogue of game COR, called COR-QRO, in which the attacker has quantum access to G.

Unlike in [HHK17], however, the proof structure imposed by [HHM22] makes it necessary to analyse the correctness game in an extension of the QROM, called eQROM. (For convenience, we briefly recapture the eQROM in Sect. 2.5 below.) With Definition 5 below, we hence extend the COR-QRO definition from [HHK17] to the extended QROM. In the extended QROM, G is modelled as an extractable compressed oracle eCO that provides the oracle's interface (called eCO.RO) and, additionally, an extractor interface eCO.Ext that is defined relative to some function f. We will need to refer to the unitary operator facilitating queries to eCO.RO, which we denote by O. Intuitively, the extractor interface eCO.Ext, when queried on some target value t, produces preimages x such that $f(x, \mathsf{G}(x)) = t$, assuming that such an x was already noticeable in previous oracle queries. Like [HHM22], we will work with $f := \mathsf{Enc}$. This means that eCO.Ext, when queried on a ciphertext c, will produce a plaintext m for c such that m and its random oracle value r have the property that $\mathsf{Enc}(m; r) = c$.

Definition 5. *We define correctness game* $\text{COR-eQROM}_{\mathsf{PKE}^{\mathsf{G}}}$ *for* $\mathsf{PKE}^{\mathsf{G}}$*– modelling* G *as an extended QROM – in Fig. 5, and the advantage of an adversary* $\mathcal{A}$ *against* $\mathsf{PKE}^{\mathsf{G}}$ *as*

$$\text{Adv}_{\mathsf{PKE}^{\mathsf{G}}}^{\text{COR-eQROM}_{\mathsf{Enc}}}(\mathcal{A}) := \Pr[\text{COR-eQROM}_{\mathsf{PKE}^{\mathsf{G}}}^{\mathcal{A}} \Rightarrow 1] \ .$$

2.3 Standard Notions for KEM

We now recall Indistinguishability under Chosen-Plaintext Attacks (IND-CPA) and under Chosen-Ciphertext Attacks (IND-CCA).

GAME $\mathsf{COR\text{-}eQROM}_{\mathsf{PKE^G}}$
13 $(pk, sk) \leftarrow \mathsf{KG}$
14 $m \leftarrow \mathcal{A}^{\mathsf{eCO.RO},\mathsf{eCO.Ext}}(sk, pk)$
15 $c := \mathsf{Enc}(pk, m; \mathsf{G}(m))$
16 $m' := \mathsf{Dec}^{\mathsf{G}}(sk, c)$
17 **if** $c \neq \mathsf{Enc}(pk, m'; \mathsf{G}(m'))$
18 $\quad m' := \bot$
19 **return** $[\![m' \neq m]\!]$

Fig. 5. Correctness game $\mathsf{COR\text{-}eQROM}_{\mathsf{Enc}}$ for $\mathsf{PKE^G}$ with G modelled as an extractable compressed oracle eCO, so with oracle interface eCO.RO and additional extractor interface eCO.Ext. Like in the FFP-CCA game (Fig. 4), we write G (instead of eCO.RO) in lines 03–05 for the sake of simplicity. The difference between games FFP-CCA and COR-eQROM is that in FFP-CCA, $\mathcal{A}$ has the decryption oracle oDecrypt, while in COR-eQROM, it has the full secret key.

Definition 6 (IND-CPA, IND-CCA). *Let* KEM = (KG, Encaps, Decaps) *be a key encapsulation mechanism with key space* $\mathcal{K}$. *For* ATK $\in$ {CPA, CCA}, *we define* IND-ATK-KEM *games as in Fig. 6, where*

$$\mathsf{O}_{\mathsf{ATK}} := \begin{cases} - & \mathsf{ATK} = \mathsf{CPA} \\ \text{ODECAPS} & \mathsf{ATK} = \mathsf{CCA} \end{cases} .$$

We define the IND-ATK-KEM *advantage function of an adversary* $\mathcal{A}$ *against* KEM *as*

$$\mathrm{Adv}_{\mathsf{KEM}}^{\mathsf{IND\text{-}ATK\text{-}KEM}}(\mathcal{A}) := |\Pr[\mathsf{IND\text{-}ATK\text{-}KEM}^{\mathcal{A}} \Rightarrow 1] - 1/2| .$$

Game IND-ATK-KEM
01 $(pk, sk) \leftarrow \mathsf{KG}$
02 $b \leftarrow_{\$} \{0,1\}$
03 $(K_0^*, c^*) \leftarrow \mathsf{Encaps}(pk)$
04 $K_1^* \leftarrow_{\$} \mathcal{K}$
05 $b' \leftarrow \mathcal{A}^{\mathsf{O}_{\mathsf{ATK}}}(pk, c^*, K_b^*)$
06 **return** $[\![b' = b]\!]$

oDecaps$(c \neq c^*)$
07 $K := \mathsf{Decaps}(sk, c)$
08 **return** K

Fig. 6. Game IND-ATK-KEM for KEM, where ATK $\in$ {CPA, CCA} and $\mathsf{O}_{\mathsf{ATK}}$ is defined in Definition 6.

2.4 The Fujisaki-Okamoto Transformation with Explicit Rejection

This section recalls the definition of $\mathsf{FO}_m^{\bot}$. To a public-key encryption scheme PKE = (KG, Enc, Dec) with message space $\mathcal{M}$, randomness space $\mathcal{R}$, and hash functions $\mathsf{G} : \mathcal{M} \to \mathcal{R}$ and $\mathsf{H} : \{0,1\}^* \to \{0,1\}^n$, we associate

$$\mathsf{KEM}_m^{\perp} := \mathsf{FO}_m^{\perp}[\mathsf{PKE}, \mathsf{G}, \mathsf{H}] := (\mathsf{KG}, \mathsf{Encaps}, \mathsf{Decaps}) \ .$$

Its constituting algorithms are given in Fig. 7. $\mathsf{FO}_m^{\perp}$ uses the underlying scheme PKE in a derandomized way by using $\mathsf{G}(m)$ as the encryption coins (see line 02) and checks during decapsulation whether the decrypted plaintext does re-encrypt to the ciphertext (see line 06). This building block of $\mathsf{FO}_m^{\perp}$, i.e., the derandomisation of PKE and performing a re-encryption check, is incorporated in the following transformation T:

$$\mathsf{PKE}^{\mathsf{G}} := \mathsf{T}[\mathsf{PKE}, \mathsf{G}] := (\mathsf{KG}, \mathsf{Enc}^{\mathsf{G}}, \mathsf{Dec}^{\mathsf{G}}) \ ,$$

with its constituting algorithm given in Fig. 8.

$\underline{\mathsf{Encaps}(pk)}$	$\underline{\mathsf{Decaps}(sk, c)}$
01 $m \leftarrow_\$ \mathcal{M}$	05 $m' := \mathsf{Dec}(sk, c)$
02 $c := \mathsf{Enc}(pk, m; \mathsf{G}(m))$	06 **if** $m' = \perp$ **or** $c \neq \mathsf{Enc}(pk, m'; \mathsf{G}(m'))$
03 $K := \mathsf{H}(m)$	07 **return** $\perp$
04 **return** (K, c)	08 **else**
	09 **return** $K := \mathsf{H}(m')$

Fig. 7. Key encapsulation mechanism $\mathsf{KEM}_m^{\perp} = (\mathsf{KG}, \mathsf{Encaps}, \mathsf{Decaps})$, obtained from $\mathsf{PKE} = (\mathsf{KG}, \mathsf{Enc}, \mathsf{Dec})$ by setting $\mathsf{KEM}_m^{\perp} := \mathsf{FO}_m^{\perp}[\mathsf{PKE}, \mathsf{G}, \mathsf{H}]$.

$\underline{\mathsf{Enc}^{\mathsf{G}}(pk)}$	$\underline{\mathsf{Dec}^{\mathsf{G}}(sk, c)}$
01 $m \leftarrow_\$ \mathcal{M}$	04 $m' := \mathsf{Dec}(sk, c)$
02 $c := \mathsf{Enc}(pk, m; \mathsf{G}(m))$	05 **if** $m' = \perp$ **or** $c \neq \mathsf{Enc}(pk, m'; \mathsf{G}(m'))$
03 **return** c	06 **return** $\perp$
	07 **else**
	08 **return** m'

Fig. 8. Derandomized PKE scheme $\mathsf{PKE}^{\mathsf{G}} = (\mathsf{KG}, \mathsf{Enc}^{\mathsf{G}}, \mathsf{Dec}^{\mathsf{G}})$, obtained from $\mathsf{PKE} = (\mathsf{KG}, \mathsf{Enc}, \mathsf{Dec})$ by encrypting a message m with randomness $\mathsf{G}(m)$ for a random oracle G, and incorporating a re-encryption check during $\mathsf{Dec}^{\mathsf{G}}$.

2.5 Compressed Oracles and Extraction

For convenience, we now also recapture the eQROM. It was shown in [Zha19] how a quantum-accessible random oracle $\mathsf{O} : X \to Y$ can be simulated by preparing a database D with an entry D_x for each input value x, with each D_x being initialized as a uniform superposition of all elements of Y, and omitting the "oracle-generating" measurements until after the algorithm accessing O has finished.

In [DFMS21], this oracle simulation was generalized to obtain an *extractable* oracle simulator eCO (for extractable Compressed Oracle) that has two interfaces, the random oracle interface eCO.RO and an extraction interface $\mathsf{eCO.Ext}_f$, defined relative to a function $f : X \times Y \to T$. Whenever it is clear from context which function f is used, we simply write eCO.Ext instead of $\mathsf{eCO.Ext}_f$.

In general, $\mathsf{eCO.Ext}_f$ can extract preimage entries from the "database" D during the runtime of an adversary instead of only after the adversary terminated. This allows for adaptive behaviour of a reduction, based on an adversary's queries. In [DFMS21], it was already used for the same purpose we need it for – the simulation of a decapsulation oracle, by having eCO.Ext extract a preimage plaintext from the ciphertext on which the decapsulation oracle was queried. We will denote oracles modelled as extractable quantum-accessible ROs by eQRO_f, and a proof that uses an eQRO_f will be called *a proof in the* eQROM_f.

We will now make this description more formal, closely following notation and conventions from [DFMS21]. Like in [DFMS21], we keep the formalism as simple as possible by describing an inefficient variant of the oracle that is not (yet) "compressed". Efficient simulation is possible via a standard sparse encoding, see [DFMS21, Appendix A]. The simulator eCO for a random function $\mathsf{O} : \{0,1\}^m \to \{0,1\}^n$ is a stateful oracle with a state stored in a quantum register $D = D_{0^m} \dots D_{1^m}$, where for each input value $x \in \{0,1\}^m$, register D_x has $n+1$ qubits used to store superpositions of n-bit output strings y, encoded as $0y$, and an additional symbol $\bot$, encoded as 10^n. We adopt the convention that an operator expecting n input qubits acts on the last n qubits when applied to one of the registers D_x. The compressed oracle has the following three components.

- The initial state of the oracle, $|\phi\rangle = |\bot\rangle^{2^m}$
- A quantum query with query input register X and output register Y is answered using the oracle unitary O defined by

$$O|x\rangle_X = |x\rangle_X \otimes \left(F_{D_x} \mathsf{CNOT}^{\otimes n}_{D_x:Y} F_{D_x}\right), \tag{1}$$

  where $F|\bot\rangle = |\phi_0\rangle$, $F|\phi_0\rangle = |\bot\rangle$ and $F|\psi\rangle = |\psi\rangle$ for all $|\psi\rangle$ such that $\langle\psi|\bot\rangle = \langle\psi|\phi_0\rangle = 0$, with $|\phi_0\rangle = |+\rangle^{\otimes n}$ being the uniform superposition. The CNOT operator here is responsible for XORing the function value (stored in D_x, now in superposition) into the query algorithm's output register.
- A *recovery algorithm* that recovers a standard QRO O: apply $F^{\otimes 2^m}$ to D and measure it to obtain the function table of O.

We now make our description of the extraction interface eCO.Ext formal: Given a random oracle $\mathsf{O} : \{0,1\}^m \to \{0,1\}^n$, let $f : \{0,1\}^m \times \{0,1\}^n \to \{0,1\}^\ell$ be a function. We define a family of measurements $(\mathcal{M}^t)_{t \in \{0,1\}^\ell}$. The measurement $\mathcal{M}^t$ has measurement projectors $\{\Sigma^{t,x}\}_{x \in \{0,1\}^m \cup \{\emptyset\}}$ defined as follows. For $x \in \{0,1\}^m$, the projector selects the case where D_x is the first (in lexicographical order) register that contains y such that $f(x,y) = t$, i.e.

$$\Sigma^{t,x} = \bigotimes_{x' < x} \bar{\Pi}^{t,x'}_{D'_x} \otimes \Pi^{t,x}_{D_x}, \quad \text{with} \quad \Pi^{t,x} = \sum_{\substack{y \in \{0,1\}^n : \\ f(x,y) = t}} |y\rangle\langle y| \tag{2}$$

and $\bar{\Pi} = \mathbb{1} - \Pi$. The remaining projector corresponds to the case where no register contains such a y, i.e.

$$\Sigma^{t,\emptyset} = \bigotimes_{x' \in \{0,1\}^m} \bar{\Pi}^{t,x'}_{D'_x} . \tag{3}$$

As an example, say we model a random oracle H as such an eQRO_f. Using $f(x,y) := [\![\mathsf{H}(x) = y]\!]$, $\mathcal{M}^1$ allows us to extract a preimage of y.

eCO is initialized with the initial state of the compressed oracle. eCO.RO is quantum-accessible and applies the compressed oracle query unitary O. eCO.Ext is a classical oracle interface that, on input t, applies $\mathcal{M}^t$ to eCO's internal state (i.e. the state of the compressed oracle) and returns the result. The simulator eCO has several useful properties that were characterized in [DFMS21, Theorem 3.4]. These characterisations are in terms of the quantity

$$\begin{aligned} \Gamma(f) &= \max_t \Gamma_{R_{f,t}}, \text{ with} \\ R_{f,t}(x,y) &:\Leftrightarrow f(x,y) = t \text{ and} \\ \Gamma_R &:= \max_x |\{y \mid R(x,y)\}|. \end{aligned} \tag{4}$$

For $f = \mathsf{Enc}(\cdot;\cdot)$, the encryption function of a PKE that takes as first input a message m and as second input an encryption randomness r, we have $\Gamma(f) = 2^{-\gamma}|\mathcal{R}|$ if PKE is γ-spread. In this case, $\mathsf{eCO.Ext}(c)$ outputs a plaintext m such that $\mathsf{Enc}(m, \mathsf{eCO.RO}(m)) = c$, or $\perp$ if the ciphertext c has not been computed using eCO.RO before.

3 Our Main Result

We start by stating our main result that relates IND-CCA security of $\mathsf{FO}_m^{\perp}[\mathsf{PKE},\mathsf{G},\mathsf{H}]$ to IND-CPA security, δ_{wc}-worst-case correctness and γ-spreadness of PKE.

Theorem 1 (PKE IND-CPA secure and δ_{wc}-worst-case correct $\Rightarrow$ $\mathsf{FO}_m^{\perp}[\mathsf{PKE}]$ IND-CCA). *Let PKE be a (randomized) PKE scheme that is γ-spread and δ_{wc}-worst-case-correct, with message space of size $|\mathcal{M}|$. Let $\mathcal{A}$ be an IND-CCA-KEM adversary (in the QROM) against $\mathsf{FO}_m^{\perp}[\mathsf{PKE},\mathsf{G},\mathsf{H}]$, issuing at most q_G many queries to its oracle G, q_H many queries to its oracle H, and at most q_D many queries to its decapsulation oracle* ODECAPS. *Let $q = q_\mathsf{G} + q_\mathsf{H}$, and let d be the query depth of the combined queries to G and H. Then there exists an IND-CPA adversary $\mathcal{B}$ against PKE such that*

$$\mathrm{Adv}^{\mathsf{IND\text{-}CCA\text{-}KEM}}_{\mathsf{FO}_m^{\perp}[\mathsf{PKE},\mathsf{G},\mathsf{H}]}(\mathcal{A}) \leq \mathrm{Adv}_{\mathsf{PKE},\mathcal{B}} + 10(q+1)^2\delta_{\mathrm{wc}} + \varepsilon_\gamma ,$$

with

$$\mathrm{Adv}_{\mathsf{PKE},\mathcal{B}} = 4 \cdot \sqrt{(d + q_\mathsf{D}) \cdot \mathrm{Adv}^{\mathsf{IND\text{-}CPA}}_{\mathsf{PKE}}(\mathcal{B})} + \frac{8\,(q + q_\mathsf{D})}{\sqrt{|\mathcal{M}|}} ,$$

and the additive spreadness term ε_γ *being defined by*

$$\varepsilon_\gamma = 24q_{\mathsf{D}}(q_{\mathsf{G}} + 4q_{\mathsf{D}}) \cdot 2^{-\gamma/2} .$$

The running time of $\mathcal{B}$ *is bounded by* $\mathrm{Time}(\mathcal{B}) \leq \mathrm{Time}(A) + \mathrm{Time}(\mathsf{eCO}, q+q_{\mathsf{D}}, q_{\mathsf{D}}) + O(q_{\mathsf{D}})$ *and* $\mathcal{B}$ *requires quantum memory bounded by* $\mathrm{QMem}(\mathcal{B}) \leq \mathrm{QMem}(\mathcal{A}) + \mathrm{QMem}(\mathsf{eCO}, q+q_{\mathsf{D}}, q_{\mathsf{D}})$*, where* $\mathrm{Time}(\mathsf{eCO}, q, q_E)$*, and* $\mathrm{QMem}(\mathsf{eCO}, q, q_E)$*, denote the time, and quantum memory, necessary to simulate the extractable QROM for* q *many queries to* eCO.RO *and* q_E *many queries to* eCO.Ext.

Proof. We begin by stating an implicit result of [HHM22] as Theorem 2 (below) that relates IND-CCA security of $\mathsf{FO}_m^{\perp}[\mathsf{PKE}, \mathsf{G}, \mathsf{H}]$ to IND-CPA security of PKE and FFP-CCA security of $\mathsf{PKE}^{\mathsf{G}}$ in the $\mathrm{eQROM}_{\mathsf{Enc}}$.

Theorem 1 is obtained by bounding the FFP-CCA term in Eq. (5) of Theorem 2 in terms of δ_{wc}, which we will do in Sect. 4: Theorem 3 states that the FFP-CCA term can be bounded by $10(q_{\mathsf{G}}+q_{\mathsf{H}}+q_{\mathsf{D}}+1)^2\delta_{\mathrm{wc}}$. Here, we identified $\mathcal{C}$'s number of eCO.RO queries in Theorem 3 with $q_{\mathsf{G}} + q_{\mathsf{H}} + q_{\mathsf{D}}$ as indicated by Theorem 2.

For completeness, we show that Theorem 2 indeed follows straightforwardly from the results in [HHM22] in Sect. 5. □

Theorem 2. *[*$\mathsf{PKE}^{\mathsf{G}}$ FFP-CCA *and* PKE IND-CPA *secure* $\Rightarrow$ $\mathsf{FO}_m^{\perp}[\mathsf{PKE}]$ IND-CCA*] Let* PKE *be a (randomized)* PKE *scheme that is* γ*-spread, and let* $\mathcal{A}$ *be an* IND-CCA-KEM *adversary (in the QROM) against* $\mathsf{FO}_m^{\perp}[\mathsf{PKE}, \mathsf{G}, \mathsf{H}]$*, issuing at most* q_{G} *many queries to its oracle* G*,* q_{H} *many queries to its oracle* H*, and at most* q_{D} *many queries to its decapsulation oracle* ODECAPS*. Let* $q = q_{\mathsf{G}}+q_{\mathsf{H}}$*, and let* d *be the query depth of the combined queries to* G *and* H*. Then there exist an* IND-CPA *adversary* $\mathcal{B}$ *against* PKE *and an* $\mathrm{eQROM}_{\mathsf{Enc}}$ FFP-CPA *adversary* $\mathcal{C}$ *against* $\mathsf{PKE}^{\mathsf{G}}$ *such that*

$$\mathrm{Adv}^{\mathsf{IND\text{-}CCA\text{-}KEM}}_{\mathsf{FO}_m^{\perp}[\mathsf{PKE},\mathsf{G},\mathsf{H}]}(\mathcal{A}) \leq \mathrm{Adv}_{\mathsf{PKE},\mathcal{B}} + \mathrm{Adv}^{\mathsf{FFP\text{-}CCA}}_{\mathsf{PKE}^{\mathsf{G}}}(\mathcal{C}) + \varepsilon_\gamma \ , \tag{5}$$

with

$$\mathrm{Adv}_{\mathsf{PKE},\mathcal{B}} = 4 \cdot \sqrt{(d+q_{\mathsf{D}}) \cdot \mathrm{Adv}^{\mathsf{IND\text{-}CPA}}_{\mathsf{PKE}}(\mathcal{B})} + \frac{8\,(q+q_{\mathsf{D}})}{\sqrt{|\mathcal{M}|}} \ ,$$

and the additive spreadness term ε_γ *being defined by*

$$\varepsilon_\gamma = 12q_{\mathsf{D}}(q_{\mathsf{G}} + 4q_{\mathsf{D}})2^{-\gamma/2} .$$

The running time of $\mathcal{B}$ *is bounded by* $\mathrm{Time}(\mathcal{B}) \leq \mathrm{Time}(A) + \mathrm{Time}(\mathsf{eCO}, q + q_{\mathsf{D}}, q_{\mathsf{D}}) + O(q_{\mathsf{D}})$ *and* $\mathcal{B}$ *requires quantum memory bounded by* $\mathrm{QMem}(\mathcal{B}) \leq \mathrm{QMem}(\mathcal{A}) + \mathrm{QMem}(\mathsf{eCO}, q + q_{\mathsf{D}}, q_{\mathsf{D}})$*, where* $\mathrm{Time}/\mathrm{QMem}(\mathsf{eCO}, q, q_E)$ *denotes the time/quantum memory necessary to simulate the extractable QROM for* q *many queries to* eCO.RO *and* q_E *many queries to* eCO.Ext. $\mathcal{C}$ *makes* $q_{\mathsf{G}}+q_{\mathsf{H}}+q_{\mathsf{D}}$ *queries to* eCO.RO.

4 Bounding FFP-CCA in the eQROM via worst-case correctness

We now give the alternative analysis of FFP-CCA in the $\mathrm{eQROM}_{\mathsf{Enc}}$ that allows us to replace the FFP-CCA term in Theorem 2 by $10(q+1)^2\delta_{\mathrm{wc}}$.

Theorem 3 (PKE **δ_{wc}-worst-case-correct** $\Rightarrow$ $\mathsf{PKE}^{\mathsf{G}}$ FFP-CCA)**.** *Let* PKE *be a (randomized)* PKE *scheme that is δ_{wc}-worst-case-correct, and let $\mathcal{C}$ be an* FFP-CCA *adversary $\mathcal{C}$ against* $\mathsf{PKE}^{\mathsf{G}}$ *in the* $\mathrm{eQROM}_{\mathsf{Enc}}$*, issuing at most q_D decryption queries and q many queries to its extQROM oracle interface* eCO.RO. *Then*

$$\mathrm{Adv}^{\mathsf{FFP\text{-}CCA}}_{\mathsf{PKE}^{\mathsf{G}}}(\mathcal{C}) \leq 10(q+q_D+1)^2\delta_{\mathrm{wc}} \ . \tag{6}$$

Proof. The proof proceeds in two steps.

1. Use FFP-CCA adversary $\mathcal{C}$ to construct a COR-eQROM adversary $\hat{\mathcal{C}}$ against $\mathsf{PKE}^{\mathsf{G}}$ in the $\mathrm{eQROM}_{\mathsf{Enc}}$ that has the same advantage as $\mathcal{C}$ and makes $\hat{q} := q + q_D$ many queries to eCO.RO.
2. Prove that any such $\mathsf{COR\text{-}eQROM}_{\mathsf{PKE}^{\mathsf{G}},\mathsf{Enc}}$ adversary $\mathcal{D}$, making $\hat{q}$ many queries to the oracle interface eCO.RO that models G, has advantage at most $10(\hat{q}+1)^2\delta_{\mathrm{wc}}$.

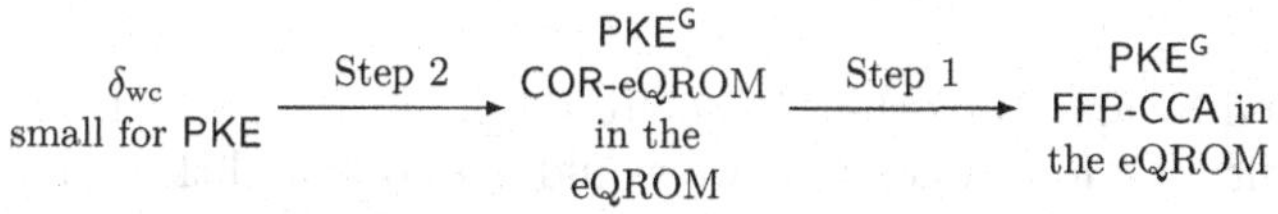

For step 1, we note that COR-eQROM adversaries get the full key pair (sk, pk) (as specified by game COR-eQROM, see Fig. 5) and can hence simulate the decryption oracle on their own. In more detail, we construct COR-eQROM adversary $\hat{\mathcal{C}}$ against $\mathsf{PKE}^{\mathsf{G}}$ as follows: $\hat{\mathcal{C}}$ runs $\mathcal{C}$, forwards all eCO.RO/eCO.Ext queries to its own extractable oracle interfaces, and simulates $\mathcal{C}$'s Dec oracle using the secret key. To perform the re-encryption check during the simulation of Dec, $\hat{\mathcal{C}}$ has to make one additional query to eCO.RO per Dec call. Once $\mathcal{C}$ finishes, $\hat{\mathcal{C}}$ simply forwards $\mathcal{C}$'s output m. $\hat{\mathcal{C}}$ perfectly simulates the FFP-CCA game for $\mathcal{C}$ and wins iff $\mathcal{C}$ wins, hence

$$\mathrm{Adv}^{\mathsf{FFP\text{-}CCA}}_{\mathsf{PKE}^{\mathsf{G}}}(\mathcal{C}) \leq \mathrm{Adv}^{\mathsf{COR\text{-}eQROM}_{\mathsf{Enc}}}_{\mathsf{PKE}^{\mathsf{G}}}(\hat{\mathcal{C}}) \ .$$

To begin with step 2 (analysing the $\mathsf{COR\text{-}eQROM}_{\mathsf{Enc}}$ advantage), we first slightly simplify the winning condition of the $\mathsf{COR\text{-}eQROM}_{\mathsf{Enc}}$ game for $\mathsf{PKE}^{\mathsf{G}}$: We introduce game 1 that only differs from game 0, the original $\mathsf{COR\text{-}eQROM}_{\mathsf{Enc}}$ game for $\mathsf{PKE}^{\mathsf{G}}$, by dropping the re-encryption check from the winning condition. It is easy to verify that the $\mathsf{COR\text{-}eQROM}_{\mathsf{Enc}}$ advantage is exactly the advantage against game 1:

- The winning condition in game 1 implies the winning condition in game 0.
- To show the other direction, we notice that $\mathcal{A}$ wins game 0 by producing a message m such that either its encryption fails to decrypt (which is the winning condition in game 1) or such that the re-encryption check fails. But if the the re-encryption check fails, then $\mathsf{Dec}(sk, c)$ cannot yield m (and $\mathcal{A}$ again wins in game 1) (Fig. 9).

$$\mathrm{Adv}_{\mathsf{PKE}^{\mathsf{G}}}^{\mathsf{COR\text{-}eQROM}_{\mathsf{Enc}}}(\hat{\mathcal{C}}) = \Pr[\hat{\mathcal{C}} \text{ wins in } G_1] \ .$$

```
GAMES 0 - 1
(pk, sk) ← KG
m ← A^{eCO.RO,eCO.Ext}(sk, pk)
c := Enc(pk, m; G(m))
m' := Dec^G(sk, c)
if c ≠ Enc(pk, m'; G(m'))      //Game G0
   m' := ⊥                     //Game G0
return [[m' ≠ m]]
```

Fig. 9. Game G_0, the correctness game $\mathsf{COR\text{-}eQROM}_{\mathsf{Enc}}$ for $\mathsf{PKE}^{\mathsf{G}}$, and Game G_1 with slightly simplified winning condition.

We proceed by analysing the $\mathsf{COR\text{-}eQROM}_{\mathsf{Enc}}$ advantage with this simplified winning condition. More concretely, we would like to bound the maximal advantage in game 1 of any adversary that makes at most $\hat{q}$ many queries. To that end, we fix the key pair and define a predicate $P_{\text{fail},\mathsf{PKE}^{\mathsf{G}}}$ by

$$P_{\text{fail},\mathsf{PKE}^{\mathsf{G}}}(m) \Leftrightarrow \mathsf{Dec}_{sk}(\mathsf{Enc}^{\mathsf{G}}_{pk}(m)) \neq m.$$

We use the predicate to rewrite the winning condition in game 1:

$$\Pr[\hat{\mathcal{C}} \text{ wins in } G_1] = \mathbf{E}_{\mathsf{KG}} \Pr_{m \leftarrow \hat{\mathcal{C}}^{\mathsf{eCO.RO},\mathsf{eCO.Ext}}(sk,pk)} [P_{\text{fail},\mathsf{PKE}^{\mathsf{G}}}(m)] \ .$$

We will now bound the right-hand side, i.e., the probability that $\hat{\mathcal{C}}$ returns a message satisfying the predicate, for any fixed key pair. To that end, we give a helper Lemma 1 below which relates $\hat{\mathcal{C}}$'s success probability to a sum of square roots of probabilities ("amplitudes"). The sum is taken over all random oracle queries (including an implicit one to check the predicate). In the sum, the k–th summand intuitively represents the following: Consider the oracle query database D for eCO to contain up to k many entries, meaning up to k many queries to eCO.RO were made so far, without satisfying the predicate. We consider the maximal probability that picking a random output value u for some oracle input value m leads to (m, u) satisfying the predicate. (In the lemma's notation, $\mathrm{Found}(D[m \mapsto u])$, where we define Found like in Lemma 1, using our predicate $P_{\text{fail},\mathsf{PKE}^\mathsf{G}}$ on the message space.) The maximum is taken over all possible oracle input values m and all query databases D such that the predicate was not yet satisfied ($\neg\text{Found}(D)$).

We continue by giving a formal argument. Note that the predicate $P_{\text{fail},\mathsf{PKE}^\mathsf{G}}$ can be computed using a single query to G, we can therefore identify variable $q_\mathcal{P}$ in Lemma 1 with 1. Applying Lemma 1, we thus obtain

$$\sqrt{\Pr_{m\leftarrow\hat{\mathcal{C}}^{\mathsf{eCO.RO},\mathsf{eCO.Ext}}(sk,pk)}[P_{\text{fail},\mathsf{PKE}^\mathsf{G}}(m)]} \leq \sum_{k=1}^{\hat{q}+1} \max_{\substack{m,D:\\|D|\leq k\\ \neg\text{Found}(D)}} \sqrt{10 \Pr_{u\leftarrow\mathcal{Y}}[\text{Found}(D[m\mapsto u])]}$$
$$\leq (\hat{q}+1) \max_{\substack{m,D:\\|D|\leq q+1\\ \neg\text{Found}(D)}} \sqrt{10 \Pr_{u\leftarrow\mathcal{Y}}[\text{Found}(D[m\mapsto u])]}$$

where the second inequality holds because any database with $\ell < q+1$ entries fulfilling the predicate can be completed to a database with $q+1$ entries still fulfilling the predicate.

To translate the summands back into terms concerning decryption failure, we note the following: If $\neg\text{Found}(D)$, but $\text{Found}(D[x\mapsto u])$, then it must be specifically the entry (x,u) that satisfies the predicate. Thus, assuming the database D before was in a state such that $\neg\text{Found}(D)$, we find

$$\text{Found}(D[x\mapsto u]) \Leftrightarrow \mathsf{Dec}_{sk}(\mathsf{Enc}_{pk}(x;u)) \neq x \ .$$

Using this fact and squaring both sides of the above inequality yields

$$\Pr_{m\leftarrow\hat{\mathcal{C}}^{\mathsf{eCO.RO},\mathsf{eCO.Ext}}(sk,pk)}[P_{\text{fail},\mathsf{PKE}^\mathsf{G}}(m)] \leq 10(\hat{q}+1)^2 \max_m \Pr_{u\leftarrow\mathcal{Y}}[\mathsf{Dec}_{sk}(\mathsf{Enc}_{pk}(m;u)) \neq x]$$

for any fixed key pair (sk,pk). Taking the expectation over KG hence yields

$$\Pr[\hat{\mathcal{C}} \text{ wins in } G_1] \leq \mathbf{E}_{\mathsf{KG}} 10(\hat{q}+1)^2 \max_m \Pr_{u\leftarrow\mathcal{Y}}[\mathsf{Dec}_{sk}(\mathsf{Enc}_{pk}(m;u)) \neq x]$$
$$= 10(\hat{q}+1)^2\delta_{\text{wc}}.$$

□

In the above proof, we used the following

Lemma 1 (Variant of Lemma 1 in [AMHJ+23]). *Let $\mathsf{G}:\mathcal{X}\to\mathcal{Y}$ be a random oracle and let $\mathcal{P}^\mathsf{G}$ be a predicate on some set $\mathcal{Z}$ that can be computed using at most $q_\mathcal{P}$ classical queries to G. Let further $\mathcal{A}^\mathsf{G}$ be an algorithm in the* eQRO$_f$ *(for an arbitrary f), making at most q quantum queries to* eCO.RO *and outputting $z\in\mathcal{Z}$. Then*

$$\sqrt{\Pr_{z\leftarrow\mathcal{A}^\mathsf{G}}[P(z)]} \leq \sum_{k=1}^{q+q_\mathcal{P}} \max_{\substack{x,D:\\|D|\leq k\\ \neg\text{Found}(D)}} \sqrt{10 \Pr_{u\leftarrow\mathcal{Y}}[\text{Found}_\mathcal{P}(D[x\mapsto u])]} \tag{7}$$

where $\mathrm{Found}_{\mathcal{P}}$ *is the database property*

$$\mathrm{Found}_{\mathcal{P}} = (\exists z \in \mathcal{Z} : \mathcal{P}^D(z)) \tag{8}$$

and $\mathcal{P}^D$ *is the algorithm that computes* $\mathcal{P}$ *but makes queries to* D *instead of* G*, and if any query returns* $\perp$*,* $\mathcal{P}^D$ *outputs 'false'.*

Before we give a proof of Lemma 1, we need to prepare some ingredients. In particular, the proof uses the concept of *transition capacities* from [CFHL21], we now recall the required notation from that paper.

A *database property* P is a predicate on the set of partial functions with the same input and output space as G. Overloading notation, we also denote by P the projector acting on a compressed oracle database register with support spanned by the computational basis states corresponding to partial functions fulfilling P. For any database property P we define the database property P_i such that f fulfils P_i iff it fulfils P and is defined on at most i inputs.

We now define the quantum transition capacity, following [CFHL21]. The quantum transition capacity $[\![P \to P']\!]$ is the quantum analogue of the maximum probability that a query transcript has a property P' after an input together with a freshly lazy-sampled output has been added to the transcript, given that the transcript has property P before. In addition, we define a q-query variant that considers q adaptively chosen inputs.

Definition 7 (Quantum transition capacity). *Let* P, P' *be two database properties. Then, the* quantum transition capacity *is defined as*

$$[\![P \xrightarrow{q} P']\!] := \sup_{U_1,\ldots,U_{q-1}} \|P' O\, U_{q-1}\, O \cdots O\, U_1\, O\, P\| \,.$$

where the supremum is over all adversary register sizes and all unitaries $U_1, \ldots, U_{q-1}$ *acting on the adversary's registers. We write*

$$[\![P \to P']\!] := [\![P \xrightarrow{1} P']\!] = \|P' O P\|$$

To bound the power of the eQROM_f for search tasks, we strengthen the model slightly by having the interface $\mathsf{eCO.Ext}$ apply the purified version (the *Stinespring dilation*) of $\mathcal{M}_t$ on input t, and return the (quantum) output register. This generalization is not strictly necessary for our proof, but is convenient as it allows us to model an algorithm with query access to eQROM_f as unitary. Concretely, the purified measurement is the isometry

$$V_{TD \to TDO} = \sum_t |t\rangle\langle t|_T \otimes V^{(t)}_{D \to DO}, \text{ with}$$
$$V^{(t)}_{D \to DO} = \sum_{x \in \{0,1\}^m} \Sigma^{t,x}_D \otimes |x\rangle_O.$$

Let us call this model the eQROM^*_f and the strengthened extraction interface $\mathsf{eCO.Ext}^*$. Any algorithm in the eQROM_f can be simulated in the eQROM^*_f by submitting any $\mathsf{eCO.Ext}$ queries to $\mathsf{eCO.Ext}^*$, measuring the output and returning the result.

In the following we prove that for query bounds for oracle search problems (like, e.g., preimage search, collision search) proven using the compressed oracle framework, the same bound holds for algorithms with eQROM$_f^*$-access, irrespective of the number of queries made to the interface $\mathsf{eCO.Ext}^*$. On a high level, this is due to the fact that the operator that facilitates a query to $\mathsf{eCO.Ext}^*$ and the projector checking the database property commute. The argument is similar to the one made in Appendix B of [AMHJ+23]. We define the *decorated* transition capacity as

$$[\![P \to P']\!]_V = \|P'VOP\|.$$

We have the following

Lemma 2. *Let V_{DE} be a controlled unitary with control register the database register D, and acting on an arbitrary additional register E. Then*

$$[\![P \to P']\!]_V = [\![P \to P']\!].$$

Proof. As V is a controlled unitary with control register D, and P' is an operator that is diagonal in the computational basis, we have $V_{DE}P'_D = P'_D V_{DE}$. We thus get

$$[\![P \to P']\!]_V = \|P'VOP\| = \|VP'OP\| = \|P'OP\| = [\![P \to P']\!].$$

Here, the second equality follows because V and P' commute, and the third equality is due to the unitary invariance of the operator norm. □

This lemma can be used to show that the framework for query bounds developed in [CFHL21] works essentially unchanged for the decorated transition capacity $[\![P \to P']\!]_V$ with a controlled unitary V as in Lemma 2 as well.[1]

Now, any algorithm $\mathcal{A}$ in the eQROM$_f^*$ proceeds without loss of generality by applying the unitary

$$U_{\mathcal{A}} = U_q O U_{q-1} O \dots O U_0$$

to a quantum register initialized in the all-0 state, where the U_i have the form

$$U_i = U_{i,\ell} V U_{i,\ell-1} V \dots V U_{i,0},$$

where the unitaries $U_{i,j}$ do not act on the compressed oracle database.

Using the prepared ingredients, we can conclude that Lemma 1 from [AMHJ+23] holds in the eQROM$_f^*$, with a bound depending on the number of $\mathsf{eCO.RO}$ queries only:

[1] Here we have only defined and characterized the decorated transition capacity as needed for analyses that don't distinguish sequential and parallel queries, which suffices for our purposes.

Proof (of Lemma 1). The proof is identical to the proof of Lemma 1 in [AMHJ+23], with one difference: If we denote the adversary's unitary (we can purify/Stinespring-dilate any adversary for this mathematical argument) between the ith and the $(i+1)$-st query to eCO.RO by U_i, we obtain the decorated transition capacity $[\![\neg\text{Found} \wedge (|D| \leq k-1) \rightarrow \text{Found}]\!]_{U_i}$ instead of the 'non-decorated' capacity $[\![\neg\text{Found} \wedge (|D| \leq k-1) \rightarrow \text{Found}]\!]$. (Note that U_i includes any eCO.Ext queries made by the adversary between the ith and the $(i+1)$st query to eCO.RO, which are controlled unitaries with control register D.) Due to Lemma 2, however, this does not make any difference and the proof proceeds as in [AMHJ+23]. □

5 Obtaining the Passive-to-Active KEM Result (Theorem 2) from [HHM22]

For the reader's convenience, we begin by restating Theorem 2.

Theorem 2. *[*$\mathsf{PKE}^{\mathsf{G}}$ FFP-CCA *and* PKE IND-CPA *secure* $\Rightarrow$ $\mathsf{FO}_m^{\perp}[\mathsf{PKE}]$ IND-CCA*] Let* PKE *be a (randomized)* PKE *scheme that is* γ*-spread, and let* $\mathcal{A}$ *be an* IND-CCA-KEM *adversary (in the QROM) against* $\mathsf{FO}_m^{\perp}[\mathsf{PKE},\mathsf{G},\mathsf{H}]$*, issuing at most* q_{G} *many queries to its oracle* G*,* q_{H} *many queries to its oracle* H*, and at most* q_{D} *many queries to its decapsulation oracle* ODECAPS*. Let* $q = q_{\mathsf{G}} + q_{\mathsf{H}}$*, and let* d *be the query depth of the combined queries to* G *and* H*. Then there exist an* IND-CPA *adversary* $\mathcal{B}$ *against* PKE *and an* $\text{eQROM}_{\mathsf{Enc}}$ FFP-CPA *adversary* $\mathcal{C}$ *against* $\mathsf{PKE}^{\mathsf{G}}$ *such that*

$$\text{Adv}^{\mathsf{IND\text{-}CCA\text{-}KEM}}_{\mathsf{FO}_m^{\perp}[\mathsf{PKE},\mathsf{G},\mathsf{H}]}(\mathcal{A}) \leq \text{Adv}_{\mathsf{PKE},\mathcal{B}} + \text{Adv}^{\mathsf{FFP\text{-}CCA}}_{\mathsf{PKE}^{\mathsf{G}}}(\mathcal{C}) + \varepsilon_\gamma \ , \tag{5}$$

with

$$\text{Adv}_{\mathsf{PKE},\mathcal{B}} = 4 \cdot \sqrt{(d+q_{\mathsf{D}}) \cdot \text{Adv}^{\mathsf{IND\text{-}CPA}}_{\mathsf{PKE}}(\mathcal{B})} + \frac{8\,(q+q_{\mathsf{D}})}{\sqrt{|\mathcal{M}|}} \ ,$$

and the additive spreadness term ε_γ *being defined by*

$$\varepsilon_\gamma = 12 q_{\mathsf{D}}(q_{\mathsf{G}} + 4q_{\mathsf{D}})2^{-\gamma/2} \ .$$

The running time of $\mathcal{B}$ *is bounded by* $\text{Time}(\mathcal{B}) \leq \text{Time}(\mathcal{A}) + \text{Time}(\mathsf{eCO}, q + q_{\mathsf{D}}, q_{\mathsf{D}}) + O(q_{\mathsf{D}})$ *and* $\mathcal{B}$ *requires quantum memory bounded by* $\text{QMem}(\mathcal{B}) \leq \text{QMem}(\mathcal{A}) + \text{QMem}(\mathsf{eCO}, q + q_{\mathsf{D}}, q_{\mathsf{D}})$*, where* $\text{Time}/\text{QMem}(\mathsf{eCO}, q, q_E)$ *denotes the time/quantum memory necessary to simulate the extractable QROM for* q *many queries to* eCO.RO *and* q_E *many queries to* eCO.Ext*.* $\mathcal{C}$ *makes* $q_{\mathsf{G}} + q_{\mathsf{H}} + q_{\mathsf{D}}$ *queries to* eCO.RO*.*

The corollary is obtained in a straightforward manner by combining Theorems 4 and 7 from [HHM22] as indicated in the figure below:

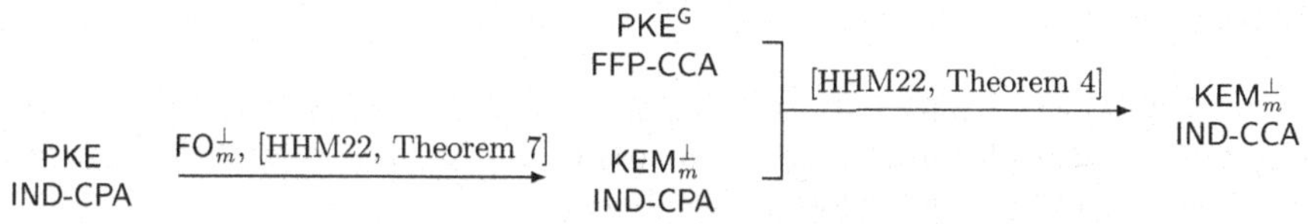

We begin by repeating [HHM22, Theorem 3].

Theorem 4 ($\mathsf{FO}_m^\perp[\mathsf{PKE}]$ IND-CPA **and** $\mathsf{PKE}^{\mathsf{G}}$ FFP-CCA $\overset{\mathrm{eQROM}_{\mathsf{Enc}}}{\Rightarrow}$ $\mathsf{FO}_m^\perp[\mathsf{PKE}]$ IND-CCA). *Let* PKE *be a (randomized)* PKE *that is* γ*-spread, and* $\mathsf{KEM}_m^\perp := \mathsf{FO}_m^\perp[\mathsf{PKE}, \mathsf{G}, \mathsf{H}]$. *Let* $\mathcal{A}$ *be an* IND-CCA-KEM*-adversary (in the QROM) against* $\mathsf{KEM}_m^\perp$*, making at most* q_{D} *many queries to its decapsulation oracle* ODECAPS*, and making* q_{G}*,* q_{H} *queries to its respective random oracles. Let furthermore* d *and* w *be the combined query depth and query width of* $\mathcal{A}$*'s random oracle queries. Then there exist an* IND-CPA-KEM *adversary* $\tilde{\mathcal{A}}$ *and an* FFP-CCA *adversary* $\mathcal{B}$ *against* $\mathsf{PKE}^{\mathsf{G}}$*, both in the* $\mathrm{eQROM}_{\mathsf{Enc}}$*, such that*

$$\mathrm{Adv}_{\mathsf{KEM}_m^\perp}^{\mathsf{IND\text{-}CCA\text{-}KEM}}(\mathcal{A}) \leq \mathrm{Adv}_{\mathsf{KEM}_m^\perp}^{\mathsf{IND\text{-}CPA\text{-}KEM}}(\tilde{\mathcal{A}}) + \mathrm{Adv}_{\mathsf{PKE}^{\mathsf{G}}}^{\mathsf{FFP\text{-}CCA}}(\mathcal{C}) + 12 q_{\mathsf{D}}(q_{\mathsf{G}} + 4q_{\mathsf{D}}) \cdot 2^{-\gamma/2} \ .$$

The adversary $\tilde{\mathcal{A}}$ *makes* $q_{\mathsf{G}} + q_{\mathsf{H}} + q_{\mathsf{D}}$ *queries to* eCO.RO *with a combined depth of* $d + q_{\mathsf{D}}$*, and* q_{D} *queries to* eCO.Ext*. Here,* eCO.RO *simulates* $\mathsf{G} \times \mathsf{H}$*. Adversary* $\mathcal{C}$ *makes* q_{D} *many queries to* ODECRYPT *and* eCO.Ext *and* q_{G} *queries to* eCO.RO*. Neither* $\tilde{\mathcal{A}}$ *nor* $\mathcal{C}$ *query* eCO.Ext *on the challenge ciphertext. The running times of the adversaries* $\tilde{\mathcal{A}}$ *and* $\mathcal{C}$ *are bounded by* $\mathrm{Time}(\tilde{\mathcal{A}}), \mathrm{Time}(\mathcal{C}) \leq \mathrm{Time}(\mathcal{A}) + O(q_{\mathsf{D}})$.

We proceed by repeating [HHM22, Theorem 7]. The bound in Theorem 2 is obtained by plugging [HHM22, Theorem 7] into [HHM22, Theorem 3] above, identifying $\tilde{q}$ with $q_{\mathsf{G}} + q_{\mathsf{H}} + q_{\mathsf{D}}$, $\tilde{d}$ with $d + q_{\mathsf{D}}$, and $\tilde{q_E}$ with q_{D}.

Theorem 5. *Let* $\tilde{\mathcal{A}}$ *be an* IND-CPA-KEM *adversary against* $\mathsf{KEM}_m^\perp := \mathsf{FO}_m^\perp[\mathsf{PKE}, \mathsf{G}, \mathsf{H}]$ *in the* $\mathrm{eQROM}_{\mathsf{Enc}}$*, issuing* $\tilde{q}$ *many queries to* eCO.RO *in total, with a query depth of* $\tilde{d}$*, and* $\tilde{q_E}$ *many queries to* eCO.Ext*, where none of them is with its challenge ciphertext. Then there exists an* IND-CPA *adversary* $\mathcal{B}$ *against* PKE *such that*

$$\mathrm{Adv}_{\mathsf{KEM}_m^\perp}^{\mathsf{IND\text{-}CPA\text{-}KEM}}(\tilde{\mathcal{A}}) \leq 4 \cdot \sqrt{\tilde{d} \cdot \mathrm{Adv}_{\mathsf{PKE}}^{\mathsf{IND\text{-}CPA}}(\mathcal{B})} + \frac{8\tilde{q}}{\sqrt{|\mathcal{M}|}} \ .$$

The running time and quantum memory footprint of $\mathcal{B}$ *satisfy* $\mathrm{Time}(\mathcal{B}) = \mathrm{Time}(\tilde{\mathcal{A}}) + \mathrm{Time}(\mathsf{eCO}, \tilde{q}, \tilde{q_E})$ *and* $\mathrm{QMem}(\mathcal{B}) = \mathrm{QMem}(\tilde{\mathcal{A}}) + \mathrm{QMem}(\mathsf{eCO}, \tilde{q}, \tilde{q_E})$.

References

[AMHJ+23] Aguilar-Melchor, C., Hülsing, A., Joseph, D., Majenz, C., Ronen, E., Yue, D.: Sdith in the qrom. Cryptology ePrint Archive, Paper 2023/756 (2023). https://eprint.iacr.org/2023/756

[BDK+18] Bos, J., et al.: CRYSTALS - Kyber: a CCA-secure module-lattice-based KEM. In: IEEE (EuroS&P) 2018, pp. 353–367 (2018)

[BHH+19] Bindel, N., Hamburg, M., Hövelmanns, K., Hülsing, A., Persichetti, E.: Tighter proofs of CCA security in the quantum random oracle model. In: Hofheinz, D., Rosen, A. (eds.) TCC 2019 Part II. LNCS, vol. 11892, pp. 61–90. Springer, Cham (2019). https://doi.org/10.1007/978-3-030-36033-7_3

[BS20] Bindel, N., Schanck, J.M.: Decryption failure is more likely after success. In: Ding, J., Tillich, J.-P. (eds.) PQCrypto 2020. LNCS, vol. 12100, pp. 206–225. Springer, Cham (2020). https://doi.org/10.1007/978-3-030-44223-1_12

[CFHL21] Chung, K.-M., Fehr, S., Huang, Y.-H., Liao, T.-N.: On the compressed-oracle technique, and post-quantum security of proofs of sequential work. In: Canteaut, A., Standaert, F.-X. (eds.) EUROCRYPT 2021 Part II. LNCS, vol. 12697, pp. 598–629. Springer, Cham (2021). https://doi.org/10.1007/978-3-030-77886-6_21

[Den03] Dent, A.W.: A designer's guide to KEMs. In: Paterson, K.G. (ed.) Cryptography and Coding 2003. LNCS, vol. 2898, pp. 133–151. Springer, Heidelberg (2003). https://doi.org/10.1007/978-3-540-40974-8_12

[DFMS21] Don, J., Fehr, S., Majenz, C., Schaffner, C.: Online-extractability in the quantum random-oracle model. Cryptology ePrint Archive, Report 2021/280 (2021). https://eprint.iacr.org/2021/280. accepted for publication at Eurocrypt 2022

[DGJ+19] D'Anvers, J.-P., Guo, Q., Johansson, T., Nilsson, A., Vercauteren, F., Verbauwhede, I.: Decryption failure attacks on IND-CCA secure lattice-based schemes. In: Lin, D., Sako, K. (eds.) PKC 2019. LNCS, vol. 11443, pp. 565–598. Springer, Cham (2019). https://doi.org/10.1007/978-3-030-17259-6_19

[DRV20] D'Anvers, J.-P., Rossi, M., Virdia, F.: *(One) failure is not an option*: bootstrapping the search for failures in lattice-based encryption schemes. In: Canteaut, A., Ishai, Y. (eds.) EUROCRYPT 2020 Part III. LNCS, vol. 12107, pp. 3–33. Springer, Cham (2020). https://doi.org/10.1007/978-3-030-45727-3_1

[FKK+22] Fahr, M., et al.: When frodo flips: End-to-end key recovery on frodokem via rowhammer. In: Proceedings of the 2022 ACM SIGSAC Conference on Computer and Communications Security, CCS 2022, pp. 979–993, Association for Computing Machinery, New York, NY, USA (2022)

[FO99] Fujisaki, E., Okamoto, T.: Secure integration of asymmetric and symmetric encryption schemes. In: Wiener, M. (ed.) CRYPTO 1999. LNCS, vol. 1666, pp. 537–554. Springer, Heidelberg (1999). https://doi.org/10.1007/3-540-48405-1_34

[FO13] Fujisaki, E., Okamoto, T.: Secure integration of asymmetric and symmetric encryption schemes. J. Cryptol. **26**(1), 80–101 (2013)

[HHK17] Hofheinz, D., Hövelmanns, K., Kiltz, E.: A modular analysis of the Fujisaki-Okamoto transformation. In: Kalai, Y., Reyzin, L. (eds.) TCC

2017 Part I. LNCS, vol. 10677, pp. 341–371. Springer, Cham (2017). https://doi.org/10.1007/978-3-319-70500-2_12

[HHM22] Hövelmanns, K., Hülsing, A., Majenz, C.: Failing gracefully: decryption failures and the Fujisaki-Okamoto transform. In: Agrawal, S., Lin, D. (eds.) ASIACRYPT 2022 Part IV. LNCS, vol. 13794, pp. 414–443. Springer, Heidelberg (2022). https://doi.org/10.1007/978-3-031-22972-5_15

[HKSU20] Hövelmanns, K., Kiltz, E., Schäge, S., Unruh, D.: Generic authenticated key exchange in the quantum random oracle model. In: Kiayias, A., Kohlweiss, M., Wallden, P., Zikas, V. (eds.) PKC 2020 Part II. LNCS, vol. 12111, pp. 389–422. Springer, Cham (2020). https://doi.org/10.1007/978-3-030-45388-6_14

[JZC+18] Jiang, H., Zhang, Z., Chen, L., Wang, H., Ma, Z.: IND-CCA-secure key encapsulation mechanism in the quantum random oracle model, revisited. In: Shacham, H., Boldyreva, A. (eds.) CRYPTO 2018 Part III. LNCS, vol. 10993, pp. 96–125. Springer, Cham (2018). https://doi.org/10.1007/978-3-319-96878-0_4

[KSS+20] Kuchta, V., Sakzad, A., Stehlé, D., Steinfeld, R., Sun, S.-F.: Measure-rewind-measure: tighter quantum random oracle model proofs for one-way to hiding and CCA security. In: Canteaut, A., Ishai, Y. (eds.) EUROCRYPT 2020 Part III. LNCS, vol. 12107, pp. 703–728. Springer, Cham (2020). https://doi.org/10.1007/978-3-030-45727-3_24

[MX23] Maram, V., Xagawa, K.: Post-quantum anonymity of Kyber. In: Boldyreva, A., Kolesnikov, V. (eds.) PKC 2023 Part I. Lecture Notes in Computer Science, vol. 13940, pp. 3–35. Springer, Cham (2023). https://doi.org/10.1007/978-3-031-31368-4_1

[NIS17] NIST. National institute for standards and technology. postquantum crypto project (2017). http://csrc.nist.gov/groups/ST/post-quantum-crypto/

[SXY18] Saito, T., Xagawa, K., Yamakawa, T.: Tightly-secure key-encapsulation mechanism in the quantum random oracle model. In: Nielsen, J.B., Rijmen, V. (eds.) EUROCRYPT 2018 Part III. LNCS, vol. 10822, pp. 520–551. Springer, Cham (2018). https://doi.org/10.1007/978-3-319-78372-7_17

[Zha19] Zhandry, M.: How to record quantum queries, and applications to quantum indifferentiability. In: Boldyreva, A., Micciancio, D. (eds.) CRYPTO 2019 Part II. LNCS, vol. 11693, pp. 239–268. Springer, Cham (2019). https://doi.org/10.1007/978-3-030-26951-7_9

Two-Round Threshold Lattice-Based Signatures from Threshold Homomorphic Encryption

Kamil Doruk Gur[1(✉)], Jonathan Katz[2], and Tjerand Silde[3]

[1] University of Maryland, College Park, USA
dgur1@cs.umd.edu
[2] Google, Menlo Park, USA
[3] Norwegian University of Science and Technology, Trondheim, Norway
tjerand.silde@ntnu.no

Abstract. Much recent work has developed efficient protocols for *threshold signatures*, where n parties share a signing key and some threshold t of those parties must interact to produce a signature. Yet efficient threshold signatures with post-quantum security have been elusive, with the state-of-the-art being a two-round scheme by Damgård et al. (PKC'21) based on lattices that supports only the full threshold case (i.e., $t = n$).

We show here a two-round threshold signature scheme based on standard lattice assumptions that supports arbitrary thresholds $t \leq n$. Estimates of our scheme's performance at the 128-bit security level show that in the 3-out-of-5 case, we obtain signatures of size 46.6 KB and public keys of size 13.6 KB. We achieve $\approx 5\times$ improved parameters if only a small number of signatures are ever issued with the same key.

As an essential building block and independent contribution, we construct an actively secure threshold (linearly) homomorphic encryption scheme that supports arbitrary thresholds $t \leq n$.

Keywords: Lattices · Threshold Signatures · Threshold Encryption

1 Introduction

In a *t-out-of-n threshold signature scheme*, a signing key is shared among n parties such that any t of those parties can jointly issue a signature. In contrast, an adversary corrupting strictly fewer than t of those parties cannot forge a signature. The past few years have witnessed remarkable progress in developing efficient protocols for threshold signatures. These efforts have been motivated largely by applications to cryptocurrency, with most attention being

The full version of this paper is available at ia.cr/2023/1318.
J. Katz—Work done in part at the University of Maryland and Dfns.
T. Silde—Work done in part while visiting the University of Maryland.

M.-J. Saarinen and D. Smith-Tone (Eds.): PQCrypto 2024, LNCS 14772, pp. 266–300, 2024.
https://doi.org/10.1007/978-3-031-62746-0_12

focused on threshold versions of ECDSA [13,14,21,25,31,40] and Schnorr-like schemes [18,36,39]. Based in part on this level of interest, NIST has announced their intention [12] to standardize threshold cryptosystems.

Efficient threshold signatures based on *post-quantum* hardness assumptions—and specifically lattice assumptions—have been elusive. While generic constructions are possible, they have drawbacks and/or are not particularly efficient. We survey other existing constructions in Sect. 1.3. The state-of-the-art is a recent construction by Damgård et al. [22] based on standard lattice assumptions that has a two-round signing protocol. Unfortunately, their solution only works for the full-threshold (i.e., $t = n$) setting and does not extend to the case of general thresholds $t \leq n$. (We discuss the challenges in adapting their technique to the case of general thresholds in Sect. 1.2).

1.1 Our Contributions

We show a t-out-of-n threshold signature scheme based on standard lattice assumptions (Ring-LWE/SIS) that supports arbitrary thresholds $t \leq n$. Our scheme features a two-round signing protocol and allows for efficient distributed key generation. Estimates of our scheme's performance at the 128-bit security level show that in the 3-out-of-5 case, we obtain signatures of size 46.6 KB and public keys of size 13.6 KB. We can also reduce the signature size by up to a factor of $5\times$ in settings where the number of signatures generated using a single key is bounded in advance; we refer to Sect. 7 for further details.

Our scheme is based on a general framework for constructing threshold signatures from a (linearly) homomorphic encryption scheme with threshold decryption. Although the particular instantiation we propose is based on a variant of the Dilithium signature scheme, our framework is general enough to be instantiated using other schemes in the future.

As an essential building block of independent interest, we show a new and actively secure t-out-of-n threshold (linearly) homomorphic encryption scheme. Our construction is based on the BGV encryption scheme [11] combined with (verifiable) Shamir secret sharing and lattice-based zero-knowledge proofs. In contrast to prior work of Boneh et al. [7], we make the standard assumption that the set of users involved in decryption is known in advance; this allows us to achieve better parameters than in their case.

1.2 Technical Overview

We begin with a high-level overview of the approach used by Damgård et al. [22] to construct n-out-of-n lattice-based threshold signatures, and explain why their scheme does not generalize easily to the t-out-of-n case. We then describe the key ideas underlying our scheme. Several technical details are omitted since this is intended only to provide intuition.

We first describe a three-message identification scheme based on lattices inspired by the Schnorr identification scheme in the discrete-logarithm setting. Fix a ring R_q. The prover's private key is a short vector $\mathbf{s} \in R_q^{\ell+k}$, and its public key consists of a matrix $\bar{\mathbf{A}} := [\mathbf{A} \,|\, \mathbf{I}] \in R_q^{k\times(\ell+k)}$ (where $\mathbf{A}$ is uniform) and the vector $\boldsymbol{y} := \bar{\mathbf{A}}\mathbf{s}$. Execution of the protocol proceeds as follows:

1. The prover samples a short vector $\boldsymbol{r} \in R_q^{\ell+k}$ and sends $\boldsymbol{w} := \bar{\mathbf{A}}\boldsymbol{r}$.
2. The verifier responds with a short challenge $c \in R_q$.
3. The prover responds with short vector $\boldsymbol{z} := c \cdot \mathbf{s} + \boldsymbol{r}$.
4. The verifier accepts iff $\boldsymbol{z}$ is short and $\bar{\mathbf{A}}\boldsymbol{z} = c \cdot \boldsymbol{y} + \boldsymbol{w}$.

Although this protocol can be shown to be *sound*, in general it is not *honest-verifier zero knowledge* (HVZK). One way to address this is by allowing the prover to *abort* [41]. Specifically, step 3 is modified so the prover only responds if a certain condition holds, but aborts (and returns to step 1) otherwise. It can be shown that an execution of such a modified protocol is HVZK *conditioned on the event that an abort does not occur.* While this is insufficient to prove security of the above as an interactive protocol (since information may be leaked in executions where the prover aborts), it suffices when the Fiat-Shamir transform is applied to the above protocol[1] to derive a signature scheme (since the prover/signer will then never release transcripts from aborted executions). We refer to the latter approach as *Fiat-Shamir with aborts* (FSwA).

Another way to make the protocol HVZK, without introducing aborts, is to use *noise drowning* [33]. We use Rényi divergence [1] to analyze the extra noise needed for security based on the number of allowed signing queries. When coupled with the Fiat-Shamir transform, this results in larger signatures than the FSwA approach but can lead to better computational efficiency. It can also benefit the threshold setting, where interaction is inherent.

Damgård et al. propose a way to distribute the FSwA version of the above scheme among n signers based on the following idea: the ith signer holds short vector $\mathbf{s}_i$ and $\mathbf{s} = \sum_{i\in[n]} \mathbf{s}_i$ is the private key. Then, the n signers can run a distributed, two-round signing protocol as follows:

1. The ith signer chooses a short vector $\boldsymbol{r}_i \in R_q^{\ell+k}$ and sends $\boldsymbol{w}_i := \bar{\mathbf{A}}\boldsymbol{r}_i$.
2. Each signer computes $\boldsymbol{w} := \sum_{i\in[n]} \boldsymbol{w}_i$ followed by $c := H(\boldsymbol{w})$. The ith signer then sends $\boldsymbol{z}_i := c \cdot \mathbf{s}_i + \boldsymbol{r}_i$.
3. Each signer then computes $\boldsymbol{z} := \sum_{i\in[n]} \boldsymbol{z}_i$ and outputs the signature $(c, \boldsymbol{z})$.

We stress that the above does *not* work directly since it does not consider the possibility that one or more of the honest signers will need to abort. Moreover, incorporating aborts in the trivial way (namely, by restarting the protocol if any of the signers abort) may not be secure since the initial message $\boldsymbol{w}_i$ of the ith signer is revealed even if that signer later aborts and, as we have noted above, aborted executions of the underlying identification protocol are not HVZK. To address this, Damgård et al. modify the above so that each signer sends a (trapdoor) homomorphic *commitment* to $\boldsymbol{w}_i$ in the first round; thus, $\boldsymbol{w}_i$ is not revealed if the ith signer aborts. We omit further details, as they are not necessary to understand the difficulties in extending this approach to the t-out-of-n case.

[1] Applying the Fiat-Shamir transform means that the challenge c is computed as a hash of the initial message $\boldsymbol{w}$ and possibly other information.

A natural way to try to extend the approach of Damgård et al. to the case of general thresholds is to share the master secret $\mathbf{s}$ among the n parties in a t-out-of-n fashion using, e.g., Shamir secret sharing. The problem with this idea, however, is that we need both the master secret $\mathbf{s}$ and each party's share $\mathbf{s}_i$ to be short, and it is not clear whether this can be achieved when using t-out-of-n secret sharing. (In contrast, this is easy to achieve in the n-out-of-n case since the sum of n short vectors is still short.) Note that the $\{\mathbf{s}_i\}$ need to be short regardless of whether one uses the FSwA approach or noise flooding (without aborts): in the former case, if any $\mathbf{s}_i$ is too large, the corresponding signer will abort too often; in the latter case, achieving HVZK with a large $\mathbf{s}_i$ would require parameters that are too large to be secure.

Here, we adopt an approach that relies on a threshold (linearly) homomorphic encryption scheme with non-interactive decryption. We describe the idea based on a generic scheme and show in Sect. 3 an instantiation based on standard lattice assumptions. We build on a version of the identification protocol described above that uses larger parameters and does not require aborts. The signing key $\mathbf{s}$ and verification key $(\bar{\mathbf{A}}, \boldsymbol{y} := \bar{\mathbf{A}}\mathbf{s})$ of the signature scheme will be as before. Now, however, instead of sharing $\mathbf{s}$ itself, the signers each hold an encryption $\mathsf{ctx}_{\mathbf{s}} = \mathsf{Enc}(\mathbf{s})$ of $\mathbf{s}$ with respect to a known public encryption key pk, and share the corresponding decryption key sk in a t-out-of-n fashion. Any set $\mathcal{U} \subseteq [n]$ of t parties can generate a signature (in the semi-honest setting) as follows:

1. For $i \in \mathcal{U}$, the ith signer chooses a bounded vector $\boldsymbol{r}_i \in R_q^{\ell+k}$ and sends $\boldsymbol{w}_i := \bar{\mathbf{A}}\boldsymbol{r}_i$. It also sends $\mathsf{ctx}_{\boldsymbol{r}_i}$, an encryption of $\boldsymbol{r}_i$.
2. Each signer in $\mathcal{U}$ locally computes $\boldsymbol{w} := \sum_{i\in\mathcal{U}} \boldsymbol{w}_i$, $c := H(\boldsymbol{w})$, and an "encrypted (partial) signature" $\mathsf{ctx}_{\boldsymbol{z}} := c \cdot \mathsf{ctx}_{\mathbf{s}} + \sum_{i\in\mathcal{U}} \mathsf{ctx}_{\boldsymbol{r}_i}$. The ith signer then sends its threshold decryption share of $\mathsf{ctx}_{\boldsymbol{z}}$.
3. Given decryption shares from all parties in $\mathcal{U}$, each signer can decrypt $\mathsf{ctx}_{\boldsymbol{z}}$ to obtain $\boldsymbol{z}$, and output the signature $(c, \boldsymbol{z})$.

The key insight is that while we cannot use t-out-of-n secret sharing for the signing key due to the required size bounds, we *can* use it for the threshold decryption key since decryption shares can be large.

While the above is secure for semi-honest adversaries, additional work is needed to handle malicious adversaries while achieving a two-round signing protocol. We refer to Sect. 5 for further details.

1.3 Related Work

Lattice-Based Threshold Signature Schemes. Bendlin et al. [6] show a threshold version of the (hash-and-sign based) GPV scheme [32]. Their protocol uses generic secure multiparty computation to distributively compute the most expensive part of the scheme (namely, Gaussian sampling [48]), and seems unlikely to yield a practical solution; moreover, their scheme requires and honest majority. Cozzo and Smart [19] and Tang et al. [54] explored the use of generic secure multiparty computation to construct threshold versions of several signature schemes submitted to the NIST post-quantum standardization process but concluded that this approach is unlikely to yield practical protocols.

Boneh et al. [7] show a "universal thresholdizer" that can be used to create a threshold version of any signature scheme. The basic idea behind their framework is to encrypt the master private key of the underlying signature scheme using a threshold fully homomorphic encryption (FHE) scheme, evaluate the underlying scheme homomorphically, and then use threshold decryption to recover the signature. Agrawal et al. [1] adapted this approach to the specific signature scheme Dilithium-G [26] and showed how to tolerate adaptive corruptions. Our approach is similar in spirit to these approaches, but by moving as many signature steps as possible outside the homomorphic evaluation we can base our protocol on threshold *linearly* homomorphic—rather than *fully* homomorphic—encryption; besides the efficiency advantages this confers, this also allows us to distribute key generation (something not achieved in [1,7]).

We have already mentioned the work of Damgård et al. [22] showing an efficient n-out-of-n threshold scheme based on lattices, and explained why it does not readily extend to give a t-out-of-n scheme. For completeness, we remark that there has recently been extensive work on lattice-based multisignatures [9,16,22,29,30] which are related to—but distinct from—n-out-of-n threshold signatures. The schemes of Boschini et al. [9] and Chen [16] can be turned into n-out-of-n threshold schemes. Unfortunately, as with the scheme by Damgård et al., it seems difficult to adapt their schemes to support arbitrary thresholds.

Threshold Homomorphic Encryption. Bendlin and Damgård [5] show a threshold homomorphic encryption scheme with semi-honest security. The scheme we construct is based on the work of Aranha et al. [3] and Hough et al. [34], which achieve malicious security for the Bendlin-Damgård scheme. Although the Bendlin-Damgård scheme supports arbitrary thresholds, the subsequent works only support the full threshold case.

The threshold FHE scheme of Boneh et al. [7] lacks an efficient mechanism for proving correctness of partial decryptions, which is needed for handling malicious behavior. Recent work by Boudgoust and Scholl [10] is similar to our threshold encryption scheme but has the same drawback; moreover, their scheme only achieves one-way security.

Chowdhury et al. [17] show a threshold fully homomorphic encryption scheme with trusted setup and semi-honest security; the size of their key shares is exponential in the number of parties n. Devevey et al. [24] also construct a lattice-based threshold encryption scheme, but this scheme also relies on a trusted dealer. Rotaru et al. [51] give an actively secure distributed key-generation protocol for lattice-based threshold encryption, but only for the full threshold case. Dahl et al. [20] present an actively secure threshold FHE scheme in the honest-majority setting. They rely on generic MPC in an offline phase.

Concurrent Work. Concurrent with or subsequent to our own work, several other lattice-based threshold signature schemes supporting general thresholds have been proposed [15,27,50]. In contrast to our work, none of these support distributed key generation.

2 Background

Let N be a power of 2, and let $q = 1 \bmod 2N$ be prime. Define the rings $R = \mathbb{Z}[X]/\langle X^N + 1\rangle$ and $R_q = \mathbb{Z}_q[X]/\langle X^N + 1\rangle$. For $f(X) = \sum_{i=0}^{N-1} \alpha_i X^i \in R_q$, we compute norms of f by viewing each $\alpha_i \in \mathbb{Z}_q$ as an integer in the range $\{-\frac{q-1}{2}, \ldots, \frac{q-1}{2}\}$ and then viewing f as a vector over $\mathbb{Z}$; thus,

$$\|f\|_1 = \sum_{i=0}^{N-1} |\alpha_i|, \quad \|f\|_2 = \left(\sum_{i=0}^{N-1} \alpha_i^2\right)^{1/2}, \quad \|f\|_\infty = \max_{i\in\{0,\ldots,N-1\}} \{|\alpha_i|\},$$

with $\alpha_i \in \{-\frac{q-1}{2}, \ldots, \frac{q-1}{2}\}$. We define the norm of a vector $\boldsymbol{f} \in R_q^k$ to be the largest norm of any of its elements, e.g., $\|\boldsymbol{f}\|_1 = \max_{i\in\{1,\ldots,k\}} \{\|f_i\|_1\}$. All vectors are column vectors by default; thus, a row vector is written as the transpose of a column vector. We use the standard definition of the discrete Gaussian distribution $D_{\boldsymbol{v},\bar{\sigma}}$ over the integer lattice $\Lambda = \mathbb{Z}^k$, with center $\boldsymbol{v} \in \mathbb{R}^k$ and standard deviation $\bar{\sigma}$. If $\boldsymbol{v} = \boldsymbol{0}$, we omit the first subscript.

Shamir secret sharing [53] of elements in R_q^ℓ can be done by independently applying standard Shamir secret sharing (over the field $\mathbb{Z}_q$) to each of the $\ell \cdot q$ coefficients of the polynomials. We use $\{x_i\}_{i\in[n]} \leftarrow \mathsf{Share}_{t,n}(x)$ to denote t-out-of-n Shamir secret sharing of coefficients of an element x, and write $x := \mathsf{Rec}_{t,n}(\{x_i\}_{i\in\mathcal{U}})$ for reconstruction (where $\mathcal{U} \subseteq [n]$ has size t).

2.1 Cryptographic Assumptions

We define the *Ring Short Integer Solution* [46] and *Ring Learning With Errors* [44] problems as follows:

Definition 1 (R-SIS). *The Ring Short Integer Solution problem* $\mathsf{R\text{-}SIS}_{k,N,q,\beta}$ *is* (t, ϵ)-hard *if for any adversary* $\mathcal{A}$ *running in time at most* t*:*

$$\Pr\left[\begin{array}{c}\{a_i\}_{i\in[k]} \leftarrow R_q;\\ \{y_i\}_{i\in[k]} \leftarrow \mathcal{A}(\{a_i\})\end{array} : \begin{array}{c}0 < \|\boldsymbol{y}\|_2 \le \beta \wedge\\ \sum_{i\in[k]} a_i y_i = 0 \bmod q\end{array}\right] \le \epsilon.$$

Definition 2 (R-LWE). *Let* χ *be a bounded distribution over* R_q *outputting element of maximum absolute norm* β*. The Ring Learning with Errors problem* $\mathsf{R\text{-}LWE}_{k,N,q,\beta}$ *is* (t, ϵ)-hard *if for any adversary* $\mathcal{A}$ *running in time at most* t*:*

$$\begin{aligned}&\big|\Pr[\{a_i\}_{i\in[k]} \leftarrow R_q; s, \{e_i\}_{i\in[k]} \leftarrow \chi : \mathcal{A}(\{a_i\}, \{a_i s + e_i\}) = 1]\\ &\quad - \Pr[\{a_i\}_{i\in[k]}, \{u_i\}_{i\in[k]} \leftarrow R_q : \mathcal{A}(\{a_i\}, \{u_i\}) = 1]\big| \le \epsilon.\end{aligned}$$

The above assumption also implies that distinguishing uniform u from $a_i s + p e_i$ is also (t, ϵ)-hard if public $p \in \mathbb{Z}_q$ is relatively prime to q [11].

2.2 Zero-Knowledge Proofs and Trapdoor Commitments

We use standard notions of non-interactive zero-knowledge proofs of knowledge (NIZKPoKs) [23] defined by algorithms $(\mathsf{Setup}, \mathsf{SetupTD}, \mathsf{Prove}, \mathsf{Vrfy}, \mathsf{Extract}, \mathsf{Sim})$, and zero-knowledge (a proof output by Sim should be indistinguishable from one by Prove except for with probability ϵ_{ZK}) and knowledge extractability (using a trapdoor and $\mathsf{Extract}$ it is possible to extract a witness from a proof by a malicious prover except for with probability $\epsilon_{\mathsf{extract}}$) properties.

Similarly, we define homomorphic trapdoor commitments as in [22] with algorithms $(\mathsf{CGen}, \mathsf{Com}, \mathsf{Open}, \mathsf{TCGen}, \mathsf{TCom}, \mathsf{Eqv})$, and hiding (commitments to two different messages should be indistinguishable), binding (a single commitment cannot be correctly opened to two separate messages) and equivocality (a commitment made with a trapdoor can extract the corresponding randomness running Eqv) properties.

We will make use of the lattice-based zero-knowledge profs of linear relations and shortness by Lyubashevsky et al. [4,8,43] in this paper, and, for concurrent security, we need zero-knowledge proofs with straight-line extractability; this can be achieved using, e.g., the transform by Katsumata [35].

2.3 Threshold Signatures

A threshold signature scheme $\mathcal{TS}$ (adapting [38, Section 4] and [22, Definition 5]) consists of the following algorithms:

- $\mathsf{KGen}_{\mathcal{TS}}$ is an interactive protocol run by n users that takes as input n and a threshold t. Each user either aborts or outputs a (common) public key pk, (common) auxiliary data aux, and a secret key share sk_i.
- $\mathsf{Sign}_{\mathcal{TS}}$ is an interactive protocol run by a set $\mathcal{U}$ of t users. Each party begins holding their secret key share, auxiliary data aux, and a message μ. Each user either aborts or outputs a signature σ.
- $\mathsf{Vrfy}_{\mathcal{TS}}$ takes as input the public key pk, a message μ, and a signature σ, and outputs 1 iff the signature is valid.

Correctness is defined in the natural way. We can consider unforgeability against either a passive (aka semi-honest) or an active (aka malicious) adversary. In either case, we consider a static corruption model in which the adversary $\mathcal{A}$ starts by corrupting a set $\mathcal{C} \subset [n]$ of up to $t-1$ users. Let $\mathcal{H} = [n] \backslash \mathcal{C}$ denote the honest users. In the *passive* setting, the attacker is given the view of the corrupted parties from the execution of the key-generation protocol; in the *malicious* setting, the attacker runs an execution of the key-generation protocol with the honest parties in which the corrupted parties can behave arbitrarily. (Here and below, we assume a *rushing* adversary who can wait to receive honest parties' messages in any given round before sending any of the corrupted parties' messages.) Following key generation, $\mathcal{A}$ can repeatedly make *signing queries* in which it specifies a message μ and a set of t users $\mathcal{U}$, and thereby initiate an execution of the signing protocol with those users holding message μ. Let

$\mathcal{C}_{\mathcal{U}} = \mathcal{U} \cap \mathcal{C}$, and $\mathcal{H}_{\mathcal{U}} = \mathcal{U} \cap \mathcal{H}$. In the passive case, $\mathcal{A}$ is given the view of the parties in $\mathcal{C}_{\mathcal{U}}$; in the malicious case, $\mathcal{A}$ runs an execution of the signing protocol with the parties in $\mathcal{H}_{\mathcal{U}}$ in which parties in $\mathcal{C}_{\mathcal{U}}$ can behave arbitrarily.

At the end of the experiment, $\mathcal{A}$ outputs a message/signature pair (μ^*, σ^*). The adversary succeeds if μ^* was never used in one of $\mathcal{A}$'s signing queries, and σ^* is a valid signature on μ^* with respect to the common public key output by[2] the honest parties in the key-generation protocol. We let $\mathsf{Adv}^{\mathsf{ts\text{-}uf\text{-}cma}}_{\mathcal{TS}}(\mathcal{A})$ denote the probability with which adversary $\mathcal{A}$ succeeds when attacking $\mathcal{TS}$.

3 Threshold Homomorphic Encryption

Our threshold signature scheme relies on an underlying threshold linearly homomorphic encryption scheme. We define the required security properties formally and show how to instantiate a scheme based on BGV [11]. We specialize our definition for schemes with non-interactive decryption.

3.1 Definitions

A homomorphic encryption scheme $\mathcal{E}$, given a set of possible circuits $\mathcal{F}$, consists of the following algorithms:

- $\mathsf{KGen}_{\mathcal{E}}$ is a probabilistic algorithm that outputs a public encryption key $\mathsf{pk}_{\mathcal{E}}$ and a decryption key $\mathsf{sk}_{\mathcal{E}}$.
- Enc is a probabilistic algorithm that takes as input a public key $\mathsf{pk}_{\mathcal{E}}$ and a plaintext ptx, and outputs a ciphertext ctx.
- Eval is a deterministic algorithm that takes as input a circuit $F \in \mathcal{F}$ and a list of ciphertexts $\mathsf{ctx}_1, \ldots, \mathsf{ctx}_k$, and outputs a ciphertext ctx^*.
- Dec is a deterministic algorithm that takes as input a decryption key $\mathsf{sk}_{\mathcal{E}}$ and a ciphertext ctx^*, and outputs a plaintext ptx.

Notationally, we allow algorithms to take as inputs a list of plaintexts, ciphertexts, or keys to denote that they are applied on each input individually. Correctness and ciphertext indistinguishability (i.e., IND-CPA security) are standard, and thus we omit the definitions here.

We now extend the above to accommodate $\mathcal{E}$ with distributed key generation and (non-interactive) threshold decryption:

- DKGen is an interactive protocol run by n users, on common input a threshold t. Either all honest users output $\perp$, or they each output a decryption key share sk_i and a (common) public key $\mathsf{pk}_{\mathcal{E}}$.
- TDec is a probabilistic algorithm that takes as input a set $\mathcal{U}$ consisting of t users, a decryption key share sk_i, and a ciphertext ctx^*, and outputs a partial decryption share ds_i.

[2] In particular, if all honest parties abort the key-generation protocol (in the malicious setting) then there is no public key and, by definition, $\mathcal{A}$ cannot succeed.

- Comb is a deterministic algorithm that takes as input a set $\mathcal{U}$ consisting of t users, a ciphertext ctx^*, and a set of decryption shares $\{\mathsf{ds}_i\}_{i \in \mathcal{U}}$, and outputs a plaintext ptx.

We define security in the threshold setting as follows:

Indistinguishability. $\mathcal{E}$ is (t, ϵ)-threshold indistinguishable if the probability of any adversary $\mathcal{A}$ running in time t succeeding in experiment $\mathsf{Exp}_{\mathcal{E}}^{\text{IND-CPA}}(\mathcal{A})$ as depicted in Fig. 1 is at most $1/2 + \epsilon$.

$\mathsf{Exp}_{\mathcal{E}}^{\text{IND-CPA}}(\mathcal{A})$

1. $\mathcal{A}$ outputs a set of corrupted users $\mathcal{C}$ of size at most $t-1$. Let $\mathcal{H} := [n] \backslash \mathcal{C}$.
2. $\mathcal{A}$ (controlling parties in $\mathcal{C}$) runs DKGen with the parties in $\mathcal{H}$. The view of the honest parties defines a public key $\mathsf{pk}_{\mathcal{E}}$ as well as keys $\{\mathsf{sk}_i\}_{i \in \mathcal{H}}$.
3. At any time during the experiment, $\mathcal{A}$ may make a "threshold decryption query" of the form $(\mathcal{U}, \{\mathsf{ptx}_j, \rho_j\}, F \in \mathcal{F})$, answered as follows:
   - Compute ciphertexts $\mathsf{ctx}_j := \mathsf{Enc}(\mathsf{pk}_{\mathcal{E}}, \mathsf{ptx}_j; \rho_j)$ for all j.
   - Evaluate the function F on $\{\mathsf{ctx}_j\}$ to get ciphertext ctx^*.
   - Let $\mathcal{H}_{\mathcal{U}} := \mathcal{H} \cap \mathcal{U}$. For $i \in \mathcal{H}_{\mathcal{U}}$, compute $\mathsf{ds}_i \leftarrow \mathsf{TDec}(\mathcal{U}, \mathsf{sk}_i, \mathsf{ctx}^*)$.
   - Return decryption shares $\{\mathsf{ds}_i\}_{i \in \mathcal{H}_{\mathcal{U}}}$ to $\mathcal{A}$.
4. At some point, $\mathcal{A}$ outputs plaintexts ptx_0 and ptx_1. Sample $b \leftarrow \{0, 1\}$, compute $\mathsf{ctx}_b := \mathsf{Enc}(\mathsf{pk}_{\mathcal{E}}, \mathsf{ptx}_b)$, and give ctx_b to $\mathcal{A}$.
5. $\mathcal{A}$ outputs a bit b' and succeeds if $b = b'$.

Fig. 1. Experiment $\mathsf{Exp}_{\mathcal{E}}^{\text{IND-CPA}}(\mathcal{A})$ implicitly parameterized by t and n.

3.2 The BGV Encryption Scheme

Our threshold scheme is based on the BGV encryption scheme [11], which we review now. Let $p \ll q$ be prime, let R_q and R_p be as in Sect. 2 (for the same dimension N), and let D_{KGen} and D_{Enc} be distributions over R_q such that elements in their support have ℓ_∞-norm bounded by B_{KGen} and B_{Enc}, respectively. The BGV encryption scheme consists of the following algorithms:

- $\mathsf{KGen}_{\mathsf{BGV}}$: Sample a uniform element $a_{\mathcal{E}} \in R_q$ along with $s, e \leftarrow D_{\mathsf{KGen}}$, and output public key $\mathsf{pk}_{\mathcal{E}} := (a_{\mathcal{E}}, b_{\mathcal{E}}) = (a_{\mathcal{E}}, a_{\mathcal{E}} s + pe)$ and secret key $\mathsf{sk}_{\mathcal{E}} := s$.
- $\mathsf{Enc}_{\mathsf{BGV}}$: On input $\mathsf{pk}_{\mathcal{E}}$ and message $\mathsf{ptx} := m \in R_p$, sample $r, e', e'' \leftarrow D_{\mathsf{Enc}}$ and output ciphertext $\mathsf{ctx} := (u, v) = (a_{\mathcal{E}} r + pe', b_{\mathcal{E}} r + pe'' + m)$.
- $\mathsf{Dec}_{\mathsf{BGV}}$: On input the secret key $\mathsf{sk}_{\mathcal{E}}$ and ciphertext ctx, output the plaintext message $\mathsf{ptx} := m = (v - su \bmod q) \bmod p$.

Correctness and IND-CPA security follows from [11,45]:

Lemma 1 (Security). *Let $B_{\mathsf{Dec}} = 2pB_{\mathsf{KGen}} B_{\mathsf{Enc}} + pB_{\mathsf{Enc}}$ be such that $B_{\mathsf{Dec}} < \lfloor q/2 \rfloor$. Let $(\mathsf{pk}_{\mathcal{E}}, \mathsf{sk}_{\mathcal{E}})$ be any key pair output from $\mathsf{KGen}_{\mathsf{BGV}}$ and let (u, v) be any ciphertext output from $\mathsf{Enc}_{\mathsf{BGV}}$ on input $\mathsf{pk}_{\mathcal{E}}$ and any message m. Then the BGV encryption scheme is perfectly correct, that is, $m = \mathsf{Dec}_{\mathsf{BGV}}(\mathsf{sk}_{\mathcal{E}}, (u, v))$. Furthermore, it is* IND-CPA *secure if* $\mathsf{R\text{-}LWE}_{N,q,B_{\mathsf{KGen}}}$ *and* $\mathsf{R\text{-}LWE}_{N,q,B_{\mathsf{Dec}}}$ *are hard.*

3.3 Distributed Key Generation for BGV

We propose a t-out-of-n distributed key-generation protocol for the BGV encryption scheme. For simplicity, we first describe a semi-honest version of the protocol, and then discuss how to add appropriate zero-knowledge proofs to ensure security against active adversaries.

In what follows, let χ_{tern} be the distribution over R_q where each coefficient a is sampled independently from $\{-1, 0, 1\}$ with $\Pr[a = 0] = 1/2$ and $\Pr[a = 1] = \Pr[a = -1] = 1/4$. We assume all parties $\mathcal{P}_i$ agree on a uniform ring element $a_{\mathcal{E}}$ which could be taken to be the output of a random oracle on some session ID or nonce. The semi-honest key-generation protocol proceeds as follows:

1. $\mathcal{P}_i$ samples $s_i, e_i \leftarrow \chi_{\mathsf{tern}}$, and computes $b_i := a_{\mathcal{E}} s_i + p e_i$. It then broadcasts b_i to all other parties.
2. $\mathcal{P}_i$ generates t-out-of-n Shamir secret shares $\{s_{i,j}\}_{j \in [n]}$ of s_i, and sends $s_{i,j}$ to $\mathcal{P}_j$ over a private channel as $[s_{i,j}]$.
3. $\mathcal{P}_i$ computes $b_{\mathcal{E}} := \sum b_j$ and outputs $\mathsf{pk} = (a_{\mathcal{E}}, b_{\mathcal{E}})$ and $\mathsf{sk}_i = \sum_j s_{j,i}$.

If we let D_{KGen} be the distribution over R_q obtained by summing n independent samples from χ_{tern}, it is clear that the above generates BGV encryption keys according to the distribution D_{KGen}.

For security against a malicious adversary, we use a commit-and-open approach so corrupted parties cannot choose their contributions based on honest parties' contributions, and add ZK proofs of correctness. Let $H : \{0,1\}^* \rightarrow \{0,1\}^\ell$ be a hash function. The modified protocol proceeds as follows:

1. $\mathcal{P}_i$ samples $s_i, e_i \leftarrow \chi_{\mathsf{tern}}$, computes $b_i := a_{\mathcal{E}} s_i + p e_i$, and then computes $h_i := H(i, b_i)$. It broadcasts h_i.
2. $\mathcal{P}_i$ broadcasts b_i, generates t-out-of-n Shamir secret shares $\{s_{i,j}\}_{j \in [n]}$ (resp., $\{e_{i,j}\}_{j \in [n]}$) of s_i (resp., e_i), and sets $b_{i,j} := a_{\mathcal{E}} s_{i,j} + p e_{i,j}$ for $j \in [n]$.
3. $\mathcal{P}_i$ samples a commitment randomness $\rho_{i,j} \in S_\rho$ and commits to $s_{i,j}$ as $\mathsf{com}_{i,j} := \mathsf{Com}(s_{i,j}; \rho_{i,j})$. It broadcasts $\{b_{i,j}, \mathsf{com}_{i,j}\}_{j \in [n]}$ and sends to $\mathcal{P}_j$ (over a private channel) the values $[s_{i,j}, e_{i,j}, \rho_{i,j}]$. $\mathcal{P}_i$ also gives an NIZK proof of knowledge of values $s_i, e_i, \{s_{i,j}, e_{i,j}\}_{j \in [n]}$ such that (1) s_i, e_i are in the support of χ_{tern}, (2) the $\{s_{i,j}\}_{j \in [n]}$ (resp., $\{e_{i,j}\}_{j \in [n]}$) are a correct t-out-of-n secret sharing of s_i (resp., e_i), and (3) the broadcasted values are consistent with a correct execution using $s_i, e_i, \{s_{i,j}, e_{i,j}\}_{j \in [n]}$ (see Sect. 6 details on the proofs).
4. $\mathcal{P}_i$ checks that the following hold for all $j \neq i$ (and aborts if not): (1) $h_j = H(j, b_j)$; (2) $\mathsf{com}_{j,i}$ has a correct opening with respect to $s_{j,i}$ and $\rho_{i,j}$ (3) the NIZK proof given by $\mathcal{P}_j$ verifies; and (4) the $\{b_{j,k}\}_{k \in [n]}$ are a correct secret sharing of a value b_j, and locally check the same for the sharings of s_j and e_j. If not, $\mathcal{P}_i$ broadcasts abort and aborts. (All parties abort if any party broadcasts abort.) Assuming that no party aborted, then $\mathcal{P}_i$ computes $b_{\mathcal{E}} := \sum_j b_j$, $\mathsf{sk}_i := \sum_j s_{j,i}$, and $\rho_i = \sum_j \rho_{j,i}$. $\mathcal{P}_i$ then computes the public commitments $\mathsf{com}_j := \sum_{k \in [n]} \mathsf{com}_{j,k}$.[3] The final public key is $\mathsf{pk}_{\mathcal{E}} := (a_{\mathcal{E}}, b_{\mathcal{E}}, \{\mathsf{com}_j\}_{j \in n})$ and secret key is then $\mathsf{sk}'_i = (\mathsf{sk}_i, \rho_i)$.

[3] By the homomorphic properties of the underlying commitment scheme these are indeed commitments to sum of $s_{j,k}$ under the randomness of sum of $\rho_{j,k}$.

$\underline{\mathsf{DKGen}(a_{\mathcal{E}}, t, n)}$

$s_i, e_i \leftarrow \chi_{\text{tern}}, \quad b_i := a_{\mathcal{E}} s_i + p e_i, \quad h_i := H(i, b_i)$

$\xrightarrow{\quad h_i \quad}$

$\xleftarrow{\quad \{h_j\}_{j \neq i} \quad}$

$\{s_{i,j}\}_{j\in[n]} \leftarrow \mathsf{Share}_{t,n}(s_i), \ \{e_{i,j}\}_{j\in[n]} \leftarrow \mathsf{Share}_{t,n}(e_i)$

$\forall j \in [n] : b_{i,j} := a_{\mathcal{E}} s_{i,j} + p e_{i,j}$

$\forall j \in [n] : \rho_{i,j} \leftarrow S_\rho, \ \mathsf{com}_{i,j} := \mathsf{Com}(s_{i,j}; \rho_{i,j})$

Compute NIZK π_i of shortness and linear relations

$\xrightarrow{\quad b_i, \{b_{i,j}, \mathsf{com}_{i,j}\}_{j\in[n]}, \pi_i, \ [s_{i,j}, e_{i,j}, \rho_{i,j}]_{j\in[n]} \quad}$

$\xleftarrow{\quad \left\{b_j, \{b_{j,k}, \mathsf{com}_{j,k}\}_{k\in[n]}, \pi_j, \ [s_{j,i}, e_{j,i}, \rho_{j,i}]\right\}_{j\neq i} \quad}$

if any $h_j \neq H(j, b_j)$: **abort** (j)

if any π_j **is invalid**: **abort** (j)

if any $0 = \mathsf{Open}(\mathsf{com}_{j,i}, s_{j,i}, \rho_{j,i})$: **abort** (j)

$b_{\mathcal{E}} := \sum_j b_j, \quad \mathsf{sk}_i := \sum_j s_{j,i}, \quad \rho_i = \sum_j \rho_{j,i}$

$\forall j \in [n] : \mathsf{com}_j := \sum_{k\in[n]} \mathsf{com}_{j,k}$

return $\mathsf{pk}_{\mathcal{E}} := (a_{\mathcal{E}}, b_{\mathcal{E}}, \{\mathsf{com}_j\}_{j\in[n]}), \quad \mathsf{sk}'_i := (\mathsf{sk}_i, \rho_i)$

Fig. 2. Actively secure key-generation protocol, from the point of view of $\mathcal{P}_i$. The elements in square brackets with subscript j are sent to $\mathcal{P}_j$ over a private channel.

We remark that this protocol leads to the following equation for the distributed secret key: $\sum_{j\in\mathcal{U}} \lambda_j \mathsf{sk}_j = \mathsf{sk}$, for Lagrange coefficients λ_j.

Remark 1. We note that while the adversary can bias the distribution of the final key, the zero-knowledge proofs ensures that the noise values are properly bounded, and the honest parties ensures that the final key pair has appropriately entropy for a secure scheme.

3.4 Threshold Decryption for BGV

We now describe how threshold decryption is done. We begin by considering the semi-honest setting, and then define appropriate zero-knowledge proofs to defend against malicious behavior. For statistical security parameter sec and noise bound B_{Dec} described in Sect. 3.2, we have:

TDec: On input a set of users $\mathcal{U}$ of size t, decryption key share sk_i, and ciphertext $\mathsf{ctx} = (u, v)$, let λ_i be the Lagrange coefficient for party i with respect to $\mathcal{U}$. Sample noise $E_i \leftarrow D_{\mathsf{TDec}}$ such that $\|E_i\|_\infty \leq B_{\mathsf{TDec}} = 2^{\mathsf{sec}} B_{\mathsf{Dec}}/tp$ and output decryption share $\mathsf{ds}_i := \lambda_i \mathsf{sk}_i u + pE_i$.

Comb: On input a ciphertext $\mathsf{ctx} = (u, v)$ and partial decryption shares $\{\mathsf{ds}_j\}_{j\in\mathcal{U}}$, output plaintext message $\mathsf{ptx} := (v - \sum_{j\in\mathcal{U}} d_j) \bmod q \bmod p$.

Let $B_{\mathsf{Dec}} + tpB_{\mathsf{TDec}} < \lfloor q/2 \rfloor$. To show correctness, we note that

$$v - \sum_{j \in \mathcal{U}} d_j = v - \sum_{j \in \mathcal{U}} (\lambda_j \mathsf{sk}_j u + pE_j) = v - \mathsf{sk}\, u - p \sum_{j \in \mathcal{U}} E_j.$$

Then, from the definition of the encryption algorithm and Lemma 1 we know that $\|v - \mathsf{sk} u\|_\infty \leq B_{\mathsf{Dec}}$, and from the definition of the threshold decryption algorithm we have that $\|E_i\|_\infty \leq B_{\mathsf{TDec}}$. It follows that the total amount of noise is bounded by $\lfloor q/2 \rfloor$, and the scheme is perfectly correct.

The threshold decryption includes the following and is depicted in Fig. 3:

1. TDec produces a proof $\pi_{\mathsf{ds},i}$ to show that partial decryption d_i is computed correctly (see Sect. 6). ds_i now also includes $\pi_{\mathsf{ds},i}$.
2. During Comb upon receiving ds_j, it first verifies each proof $\pi_{\mathsf{ds},j}$ and aborts with output j if any of them fails. Otherwise, it outputs ptx as above.

$\underline{\mathsf{TDec}(\mathsf{ctx}^* = (u, v), \mathsf{sk}_i = (\mathsf{sk}_i, \rho_i), \mathcal{U})}$

if $\mathsf{ctx}^* = \perp$: **return** $\perp$

$m_i := \lambda_i \mathsf{sk}_i u, \quad E_i \leftarrow D_{\mathsf{TDec}}, \quad d_i := m_i + pE_i$

Compute NIZK $\pi_{\mathsf{ds},i}$ of boundedness and linear relations

return $\mathsf{ds}_i := (d_i, \pi_{\mathsf{ds},i})$

$\underline{\mathsf{Comb}(\mathsf{ctx}^*, \{\mathsf{ds}_j = (d_j, \pi_{\mathsf{ds},j})\}_{j \in \mathcal{U}})}$

if any $\pi_{\mathsf{ds},j}$ **is invalid**: **abort** (j)

$\mathsf{ptx} := v - \sum_{j \in \mathcal{U}} d_j \mod p$

return ptx

Fig. 3. Threshold decryption and share combination algorithms.

3.5 Proof of Security

We now prove that the protocol is secure against an active adversary $\mathcal{A}$ corrupting at most $t - 1$ parties. We remark that we do not detail the running time of the adversary here and the rest of the paper, but it is straightforward to see that is tight with respect to the underlying assumptions.

Theorem 1 (Indistinguishability). *Let the* $\mathsf{R\text{-}LWE}_{N,q,B_{\mathsf{tern}}}$ *and* $\mathsf{R\text{-}LWE}_{N,q,B_{\mathsf{TDec}}}$ *be* $\epsilon_{\mathsf{R\text{-}LWE}}$*- and* $\epsilon'_{\mathsf{R\text{-}LWE}}$*-hard. We model the hash function* H *as a random oracle and let* Q_H *be the number of queries made to* H*. Let the proof system* Π_x *for the relation* $\mathcal{R}_x$ *be* $(\epsilon_{\mathsf{ZK},x}, \epsilon_{\mathsf{extract},x})$*-secure and* Com *be* $\epsilon_{\mathsf{hiding}}$ *secure. Let* Q_{TDec} *be number of threshold decryption queries made. Finally, let the BGV scheme be perfectly correct and* ϵ_{BGV}*-IND-CPA secure with respect to* $(N, q, B_{\mathsf{KGen}}, B_{\mathsf{Dec}})$*. Then, for any adversary* $\mathcal{A}$ *corrupting up to* $t-1$ *parties:*

$$\epsilon_{\text{IND-CPA}} := \mathsf{Adv}_{\mathcal{E}}^{\text{IND-CPA}}(\mathcal{A}) \leq |\mathcal{H}| \cdot (\epsilon_{\mathsf{ZK,sk}} + |\mathcal{H}| \cdot \epsilon_{\mathsf{hiding}}) + |\mathcal{C}| \cdot \epsilon_{\mathsf{extract}} + \epsilon_{\mathsf{R\text{-}LWE}} + \frac{Q_H}{2^\ell} + Q_{\mathsf{TDec}} \cdot (|\mathcal{H}_{\mathcal{U}}| \cdot (\epsilon'_{\mathsf{R\text{-}LWE}} + \epsilon_{\mathsf{ZK,ds}})) + \epsilon_{\mathsf{BGV}}.$$

Proof. We prove security through a series of experiments:

Experiment G_0**.** The first experiment corresponds to the threshold ciphertext indistinguishability experiment shown in Fig. 1.

Experiment G_1**.** We change how proofs during partial decryption are computed for honest parties $j \in \mathcal{H}_{\mathcal{U}}$. The proofs $\pi_{\mathsf{ds},j}$ are now computed by the simulator $\mathsf{Sim}_{\mathsf{ds}}$ of Π_{ds}. The rest of the experiment remains the same. G_1 is indistinguishable from G_0 by the zero-knowledge property of Π_{ds} and the distinguishing advantage of $\mathcal{A}$ per partial decryption query is $|\mathcal{H}_{\mathcal{U}}| \cdot \epsilon_{\mathsf{ZK,ds}} \leq t \cdot \epsilon_{\mathsf{ZK,ds}}$ by a hybrid argument.

Experiment G_2**.** During DKGen, we use the knowledge extractor to obtain $\{s_{k,j}\}_{j \in [n]}$ for each corrupted party $\mathcal{P}_k$. (We abort the experiment if such extraction fails.) Then derive sk_k for $k \in \mathcal{C}$. The rest of the experiment remains the same. G_2 is then indistinguishable from G_1 by the knowledge extraction property of Π_{sk}. The distinguishing advantage of $\mathcal{A}$ is the cumulative bound on independent extraction failure properties, which is $|\mathcal{C}| \cdot \epsilon_{\mathsf{extract,sk}}$.

Experiment G_3**.** We replace how partial decryptions are computed for one of the honest parties. Let $m = \mathsf{ptx}$ be the message in a decryption query, and let (u, v) be the (honestly generated) encryption of m. Fix an index $i \in \mathcal{H}_{\mathcal{U}}$ and compute d_j for $j \neq i \in \mathcal{H}_{\mathcal{U}}$ as in the previous experiment. Then set the ith partial decryption share equal to $d'_i := v - m - \sum_{j \in \mathcal{U}, j \neq i} \lambda_j \mathsf{usk}_j + pE'_i \mod q$. The rest of the experiment is the same.

In G_2 the partial decryption share d_i is computed as $d_i := \lambda_i \mathsf{usk}_i + pE_i$, whereas here

$$\begin{aligned} d'_i &= v - m - \sum_{j \in \mathcal{U}, j \neq i} \lambda_j \mathsf{usk}_j + pE'_i = v - m - (\mathsf{usk} - \lambda_i \mathsf{usk}_i) + pE'_i \\ &= v - \mathsf{usk} - m + \lambda_i \mathsf{usk}_i + pE'_i. \end{aligned}$$

The statistical distance between d_i and d'_i is thus the distance between pE_i and $v - \mathsf{usk} - m + pE'_i$. First note that, E_i and E'_i are bounded uniforms from the same distribution, and $\|v - \mathsf{usk}\|_\infty \leq B_{\mathsf{Dec}}$ and $\|m\|_\infty \leq p$. We also can rewrite $v-\mathsf{usk}-m+pE'_i$ as $p((v-\mathsf{usk}-m)/p+E'_i)$. The distinguishing probability between two distributions using a statistical argument is then how well the distribution of E_i and E'_i "smudges" the difference term $(v - \mathsf{usk} - m)/p$:

$$\frac{\|(v - \mathsf{usk} - m)/p\|_\infty}{\|E'_i\|_\infty} \leq \frac{(B_{\mathsf{Dec}} + p)/p}{(2^{\mathsf{sec}} B_{\mathsf{Dec}}/tp)} \approx t \cdot 2^{-\mathsf{sec}}.$$

G_2 and G_3 are thus statistically indistinguishable.

Experiment G_4**.** We replace the rest of the honest shares, i.e., all but the special party i. Instead of honestly computing d_j for $j \in \mathcal{H}_\mathcal{U}, j \neq i$, the simulator samples a uniform $d_j \in R_q$. In addition, d'_i is now replaced with as $d''_i := v - m - \sum_{j\in\mathcal{C}_\mathcal{U}} \lambda_j \mathsf{usk}_j - \sum_{j\in\mathcal{H}_\mathcal{U}, j\neq i} d_j \mod p + pE'_i \mod q$. The rest is the same as G_3. We need to show both d''_i and $\{d_j\}_{j\in\mathcal{H}_\mathcal{U}, j\neq i}$ are indistinguishable from their counterparts in G_3. We first show the former assuming the latter. In G_3, d'_i is computed as $v - m - \sum_{j\in\mathcal{U}, j\neq i} \lambda_j \mathsf{usk}_j + pE'_i$ whereas $d''_i = v - m - \sum_{j\in\mathcal{C}_\mathcal{U}} \lambda_j \mathsf{usk}_j - \sum_{j\in\mathcal{H}_\mathcal{U}, j\neq i} d_j \mod p + pE'_i \mod q$. If $\{d_j\}_{j\in\mathcal{H}_\mathcal{U}, j\neq i}$ sampled uniformly is indistinguishable from $\{d_j\}_{j\in\mathcal{H}_\mathcal{U}, j\neq i}$ computed as $d_j = \lambda_j \mathsf{usk}_j + pE_j$, then the distributions of $\sum_{j\in\mathcal{H}_\mathcal{U}, j\neq i} d_j \mod p$ are indistinguishable from $\sum_{j\in\mathcal{H}_\mathcal{U}, j\neq i} \lambda_j \mathsf{usk}_j \mod p$ since $d_j \mod p = \lambda_j \mathsf{usk}_j + pE_j \mod p = \lambda_j \mathsf{usk}_j \mod p$. Then if $\sum_{j\in\mathcal{H}_\mathcal{U}, j\neq i} d_j \mod p$ and $\sum_{j\in\mathcal{H}_\mathcal{U}, j\neq i} \mathsf{usk}_j$ are indistinguishable, so are d'_i and d''_i.

All it remains to show that $\lambda_j \mathsf{usk}_j + pE_j$ is indistinguishable from uniform. Since λ_j are invertible in $\mathbb{Z}_q$, if we can argue $\lambda as + pe \approx as + \lambda^{-1}pe = as + p'e \approx as + e$ for uniform a and s, invertible p', and relatively short e then we can argue $\lambda as + pe$ is indistinguishable from uniform.

We first argue that $\mathcal{A}$ distinguishing $\mathsf{usk}_j + \lambda_j^{-1} pE_j$ from uniform d_j can be used to break R-LWE: The R-LWE distinguisher interacts with $\mathcal{A}$ and uses its replies in G_4 to answer R-LWE challenges. The distinguisher obtains an R-LWE challenge (a_i, u_i), for each partial decryption query and sets partial ciphertext $u = a_i$ and partial decryption share $d_j = u_i$. During each query, if $\mathcal{A}$ behaves noticeably different than G_3, the R-LWE distinguisher replies that u_i is uniform.

Since λ_j is invertible and p is a prime, λ_j^{-1} exists and $\lambda^{-1}p$ is relatively prime with q. Hence, if u is an R-LWE instance, then there is no reason for the adversary to behave different than G_3 since $a_i \mathsf{sk}_j + e_i$ is indistinguishable from $a_i \mathsf{sk}_j + \lambda_j^{-1} pe_i$ for $\lambda_j^{-1} p$ relatively prime with q [11]. If u_i is uniform, any significant advantage $\mathcal{A}$ has is R-LWE distinguisher advantage. Hence we conclude $\mathsf{usk}_j + \lambda_j^{-1} pE_j$ is indistinguishable from uniform d_j.

If $\mathsf{usk}_j + \lambda_j^{-1} pE_j$ is indistinguishable from uniform d_j then $\lambda_j(\mathsf{usk}_j + \lambda_j^{-1} pE_j) = \lambda_j \mathsf{usk}_j + pE_j$ is indistinguishable from $\lambda_j d_j$. Since d_j is uniform in R_q, so is $\lambda_j d_j$. Thus we conclude that $\lambda_j \mathsf{usk}_j + pE_j$ is indistinguishable from uniform d_j by $\mathsf{R\text{-}LWE}_{N,q,B_{\mathsf{TDec}}}$ assumption.

Experiment G_5**.** Now that partial decryption does not rely on $\mathsf{sk}_\mathcal{E}$, we start to modify DKGen. Here we modify G_4 by simulating π_i sent during key generation for all honest parties. It follows immediately from the zero-knowledge property of the proof system that G_4 and G_5 are indistinguishable.

Experiment G_6. For all honest parties, we now replace the unopened commitments to $\{s_{i,j}\}$. After deriving $\boldsymbol{b}_{\mathcal{E}}$, each honest party commits to a random ring element instead. Since the commitments for the shares between honest parties are not opened, G_6 is indistinguishable from G_5 as long as the hiding property of the underlying commitment holds.

Experiment G_7. For i we now replace the public key share b_i. Sample a random b_i and t-out-of-n secret share it into $\{b_{i,j}\}_{j\in[n]}$. Then derive $s_{i,j}$,$e_{i.j}$ from $b_{i,j}$. The rest of the experiment remains the same.

We again show that $\mathcal{A}$ distinguishing between G_6 and G_7 can be used to break R-LWE assumption. We initiate the challenger for $\text{R-LWE}_{N,q,B_{\text{tern}}}$ with $a_{\mathcal{E}}$ being the uniform element. We then forward the answer of the challenger as b_i. If the $\mathcal{A}$ behaves significantly differently than G_5 we reply the challenger as the sample being uniform.

We have that $b_i = a_{\mathcal{E}}s_i + pe_i$ is an R-LWE sample, hence if the challenger returns an R-LWE sample, $\mathcal{A}$ has no reason to behave differently. If the challenger returns a uniform sample, however, any non-negligible advantage $\mathcal{A}$ has is non-negligible advantage in answering challenger's queries since any behavioral difference is forwarded directly. Since b_i is t-out-of-n secret shared, each $b_{i,j}$ is uniform in R_q. This is statistically indistinguishable from the real execution where s_i and e_i are t-out-of-n shared therefore $s_{i,j}$, $e_{i,j}$ and consequently $b_i = a_{\mathcal{E}}s_i + pe_i$ is uniform in R_q. G_6 is then indistinguishable from G_5 by R-LWE assumption and $\mathcal{A}$'s distinguishing advantage can be bounded by $\epsilon_{\text{R-LWE}}$.

Experiment G_8. We now derive b_i a posteriori. Before step 1 of DKGen, $\mathcal{B}$ receives a BGV key pair $(a_{\mathcal{E}}, b_{\mathcal{E}})$. In step 1 samples a random $h_i \leftarrow \{0,1\}^{\ell}$. After receiving h_k for $k \in \mathcal{C}$ from $\mathcal{A}$ finds b_k such that $h_k = H(k, b_k)$. Then derive $b_i := b_{\mathcal{E}} - \sum_{j\neq i\in[n]} b_j$ and program H such that $H(i, b_i) = h_{b_i}$. If programming fails, abort. The rest of the experiment is the same as before.

The distribution of h_i is statistically indistinguishable from the output of H by the random oracle model. By the R-LWE assumption, $b_{\mathcal{E}}$ is indistinguishable from uniform. Then, G_6 and G_7 are indistinguishable as long as the programming does not fail. The advantage of $\mathcal{A}$ is the probability of programming failing, which by a standard argument can be bounded by $\frac{Q_{\text{DKGen}}}{2^{\ell}}$.

We now show that if $\mathcal{A}$ wins G_8, then $\mathcal{A}$ can be used to break the IND-CPA security of BGV scheme. $\mathcal{B}$ interacts with the challenger to IND-CPA security of BGV and obtains $a_{\mathcal{E}}, b_{\mathcal{E}}$ which then are used during DKGen. Whenever $\mathcal{A}$ sends the challenge plaintexts ptx_0 and ptx_1 $\mathcal{B}$ forwards them to the BGV challenger and obtains the ciphertext ctx*. $\mathcal{B}$ sends ctx* along with its simulated proof to $\mathcal{A}$. When $\mathcal{A}$ replies with 0 or 1, $\mathcal{B}$ forwards the response to BGV challenger.

The public key $\mathcal{A}$ generates as part of DKGen contains the same $(a_{\mathcal{E}}, b_{\mathcal{E}})$ as $\mathcal{B}$ received from the BGV oracle as a challenge. Hence ctx* received by $\mathcal{B}$ and consequently $\mathcal{A}$ is a BGV ciphertext encrypted under $a_{\mathcal{E}}, b_{\mathcal{E}}$ which indistinguishable from ctx derived as part of the protocol execution. Then, a correct answer given by $\mathcal{A}$ is also a correct answer for $\mathcal{B}$ for the encryption oracle.

This concludes the proof. □

4 Passively Secure t-out-of-n Threshold Signatures

We give a passively secure version of our t-out-of-n threshold signature protocol $\mathcal{TS}$. For brevity, we omit the exact bounds and parameters as this section serves mainly as a warm-up. Let $\mathcal{E} = (\mathsf{DKGen}, \mathsf{Enc}, \mathsf{Eval}, \mathsf{Dec}, \mathsf{TDec}, \mathsf{Comb})$ be a threshold (linearly) homomorphic encryption scheme.

4.1 Dilithium Without Aborts

We use a ring version of Dilithium without rejection sampling as the underlying signature scheme, extending [1]. The underlying signature scheme is also similar to Raccoon [49] (which was developed in concurrent work). We define the challenge set $\mathcal{C}_\nu = \{c \in R_q : \|c\|_\infty = 1, \|c\|_1 = \nu\} \subset R_q$ to be the set of polynomials with coefficients in $\{-1, 0, 1\}$ and exactly ν non-zero coefficients. We also let $\bar{\mathcal{C}}_\nu = \{c - c' : c, c' \in \mathcal{C}_\nu, c \neq c'\}$.

KGen_L Samples a uniform $a \in R_q$, then set $\boldsymbol{a} := [a\ 1]$. Samples bounded uniform short secret key s_1, s_2 with $\|s_1\|_\infty = \|s_2\|_\infty \leq \eta$ then set $\mathbf{s} := [s_1\ s_2]$. Finally, computes $y := \langle \boldsymbol{a}, \mathbf{s} \rangle$ and outputs $\mathsf{sk} = \mathbf{s}$ and $\mathsf{pk} = (\boldsymbol{a}, y)$.

Sign_L Takes as input $(\mathsf{sk}, \mathsf{pk}, \mu)$, samples $r_1, r_2 \leftarrow D_\sigma$ from a Gaussian distribution with standard deviation σ, and set $\boldsymbol{r} := [r_1\ r_2]$. Computes $w := \langle \boldsymbol{a}, \boldsymbol{r} \rangle$, derive challenge $c := H(w, \mathsf{pk}, \mu) \in \mathcal{C}_\nu$, and outputs signature $(c, \boldsymbol{z} := c\mathbf{s} + \boldsymbol{r})$.

Vrfy_L Takes as input $(\mathsf{pk}, (\boldsymbol{z}, c), \mu)$ and checks that $\|\boldsymbol{z}\|_2 \leq B$ and $c = H_0(\langle \boldsymbol{a}, \boldsymbol{z} \rangle - cy, \mathsf{pk}, \mu)$ and then outputs 1, otherwise outputs 0.

Agrawal et al. [1, Section 4] prove the correctness and security of this scheme:

Lemma 2. *Let $\gamma = \lambda + (N \log_2 q)/(\log_2(2\eta + 1))$, and furthermore set $\beta = 2B + 2 \cdot \eta \cdot \nu \cdot \sqrt{\gamma}$ and $\sigma \geq \nu \cdot \eta \cdot \sqrt{\gamma \cdot Q}$, where Q is the maximum number of signing queries an adversary can make, and let H be modeled as a random oracle. If the $\mathsf{R\text{-}SIS}_{N,q,\beta}$ problem is hard, then the signature scheme above is* uf-cma-*secure.*

4.2 Threshold Key Generation and Signing Protocols

We describe the underlying protocols of $\mathcal{TS}$ from the viewpoint of a single signer $\mathcal{S}_i$ with $i \in [n]$ (for DKGen) and $i \in \mathcal{U} \subset [n]$, $|\mathcal{U}| = t$ (for Sign). We once again assume access to a crs consisting of a uniform ring element $a_{\mathcal{TS}} \in R_q$. The key generation protocol is depicted in Fig. 4.

$\mathsf{KGen}_{\mathcal{TS}}(\mathsf{crs} = (\boldsymbol{a}_{\mathcal{TS}}, a_{\mathcal{E}}), t, n)$

$\mathsf{DKGen}(\mathsf{crs} = a_{\mathcal{E}}, t, n)$

return $\mathsf{pk}_{\mathcal{E}}, \mathsf{sk}_i$

$s_{i,1}, s_{i,2} \leftarrow D, \quad \mathbf{s}_i := [s_{i,1}\ s_{i,2}]$

$y_i := \langle \boldsymbol{a}_{\mathcal{TS}}, \mathbf{s}_i \rangle, \quad \mathsf{ctx}_{\mathbf{s},i} \leftarrow \mathsf{Enc}(\mathsf{pk}_{\mathcal{E}}, \mathbf{s}_i)$

$\xrightarrow{y_i, \mathsf{ctx}_{\mathbf{s},i}}$

$\xleftarrow{\{(y_j, \mathsf{ctx}_{\mathbf{s},j})\}_{j \neq i}}$

$y := \sum_{j \in [n]} y_j, \quad \mathsf{ctx}_{\mathbf{s}} := \sum_{j \in [n]} \mathsf{ctx}_{\mathbf{s},j}$

return $\mathsf{pk}_{\mathcal{TS}} := (\boldsymbol{a}_{\mathcal{TS}}, y), \quad \mathsf{sk}_i, \quad \mathsf{aux}_{\mathcal{TS}} := (\mathsf{pk}_{\mathcal{E}}, \mathsf{ctx}_{\mathbf{s}})$

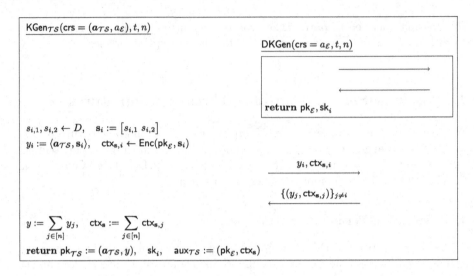

Fig. 4. Passively secure key-generation protocol for signer $\mathcal{S}_i$.

The key generation $\mathsf{KGen}_{\mathcal{TS}}$ goes as follows:

1. The parties begin by invoking the passively secure distributed key generation protocol DKGen of the underlying threshold homomorphic encryption scheme with inputs t,n for all circuits consisting of one multiplication with an element from C_ν and t additions and all circuits consisting of n additions. $\mathcal{S}_i$ learns the public encryption key $\mathsf{pk}_{\mathcal{E}}$ and its decryption key share sk_i.
2. The parties are given $\boldsymbol{a}_{\mathcal{TS}} = [a_{\mathcal{TS}}\ 1]$ as the common reference string. Then $\mathcal{S}_i$ samples short $s_{i,1}, s_{i,2}$ and sets $\mathbf{s}_i = [s_{i,1}\ s_{i,2}]$ and $y_i := \langle \boldsymbol{a}_{\mathcal{TS}}, \mathbf{s}_i \rangle$. It computes the ciphertext $\mathsf{ctx}_{\mathbf{s},i} := \mathsf{Enc}(\mathsf{pk}_{\mathcal{E}}, \mathbf{s}_i)$ and broadcasts it with y_i.
3. The parties compute $\mathsf{ctx} := \sum \mathsf{ctx}_{\mathbf{s},j} = \mathsf{Enc}(\mathsf{pk}_{\mathcal{E}}, \mathbf{s})$ and $y := \sum y_j = \langle \boldsymbol{a}_{\mathcal{TS}}, \mathbf{s} \rangle$, where $\mathbf{s} = \sum \mathbf{s}_j$, and define the public verification key to be $\mathsf{pk}_{\mathcal{TS}} := (\boldsymbol{a}_{\mathcal{TS}}, y)$. The secret key of $\mathcal{S}_i$ consists of its decryption key share sk_i, and the auxiliary information $\mathsf{aux} := (\mathsf{pk}_{\mathcal{E}}, \mathsf{ctx}_{\mathbf{s}})$. The signing share $\mathbf{s}_i$ is deleted.

The signing protocol depicted in Fig. 5 $\mathsf{Sign}_{\mathcal{TS}}$ goes as follows:

1. To sign a message μ, party $\mathcal{S}_i$ first samples short ring elements $r_{i,1}$,$r_{i,2}$ and defines vector $\boldsymbol{r}_i := [r_{i,1}\ r_{i,2}]$. Signer $\mathcal{S}_i$ then computes $w_i := \langle \boldsymbol{a}_{\mathcal{TS}}, \boldsymbol{r}_i \rangle$ and generates the ciphertext $\mathsf{ctx}_{\boldsymbol{r},i} := \mathsf{Enc}(\mathsf{pk}_{\mathcal{E}}, \boldsymbol{r}_i)$ and broadcasts that ciphertext and w_i to the other signers in $\mathcal{U}$.
2. The signers compute $w := \sum_{j \in \mathcal{U}} w_j$ and $c := H(w, \mathsf{pk}_{\mathcal{TS}}, \mu) \in \mathcal{C}_\nu$, followed by the ciphertext $\mathsf{ctx}_{\boldsymbol{z}} := c \cdot \mathsf{ctx}_{\mathbf{s}} + \sum_{j \in \mathcal{U}} \mathsf{ctx}_{\boldsymbol{r},j}$. Party $\mathcal{S}_i$ then computes a decryption share $\mathsf{ds}_i := \mathsf{TDec}(\mathsf{sk}_i, \mathsf{ctx}_{\boldsymbol{z}}, \mathcal{U})$ and sends it to the other signers. The signers decrypt $\mathsf{ctx}_{\boldsymbol{z}}$ to obtain $\boldsymbol{z}$, and output the signature $(c, \boldsymbol{z})$.

$\mathsf{Vrfy}_{\mathcal{TS}}$: A signature $(c, \boldsymbol{z})$ on a message μ is valid with respect to the public key $\mathsf{pk}_{\mathcal{TS}} = (\boldsymbol{a}_{\mathcal{TS}}, y)$ if (1) $\boldsymbol{z}$ is short and (2) $H(\langle \boldsymbol{a}_{\mathcal{TS}}, \boldsymbol{z} \rangle - cy, \mathsf{pk}_{\mathcal{TS}}, \mu) = c$.

For a signature $(c, \boldsymbol{z})$ output by the signing protocol on a message μ and a set of users $|\mathcal{U}| \geq t$, we have $\boldsymbol{z} = c \cdot \mathbf{s} + \sum_{j \in \mathcal{U}} \boldsymbol{r}_j$ by the linearity of the encryption

$\underline{\mathsf{Sign}_{\mathcal{TS}}(\mathsf{sk}_i, \mathsf{aux}_{\mathcal{TS}}, \mathcal{U}, \mu)}$

$r_{i,1}\ r_{i,2} \leftarrow D_r, \quad \boldsymbol{r}_i := \left[r_{i,1}\ r_{i,2}\right]$

$w_i := \langle \boldsymbol{a}_{\mathcal{TS}}, \boldsymbol{r}_i \rangle, \quad \mathsf{ctx}_{\boldsymbol{r},i} := \mathsf{Enc}(\mathsf{pk}_{\mathcal{E}}, \boldsymbol{r}_i)$

$\xrightarrow{w_i,\ \mathsf{ctx}_{\boldsymbol{r},i}}$

$\xleftarrow{\{(w_j, \mathsf{ctx}_{\boldsymbol{r},j})\}_{j \in \mathcal{U} \setminus \{i\}}}$

$w := \sum_{j \in \mathcal{U}} w_j, \quad c := H(w, \mathsf{pk}_{\mathcal{TS}}, \mu)$

$\mathsf{ctx}_{\boldsymbol{z}} := c \cdot \mathsf{ctx}_{\mathbf{s}} + \sum_{j \in \mathcal{U}} \mathsf{ctx}_{\boldsymbol{r},j}$

$\mathsf{ds}_i := \mathsf{TDec}(\mathsf{ctx}_{\boldsymbol{z}}, \mathsf{sk}_i, \mathcal{U})$

$\xrightarrow{\mathsf{ds}_i}$

$\xleftarrow{\{\mathsf{ds}_j\}_{j \in \mathcal{U} \setminus \{i\}}}$

$\boldsymbol{z} := \mathsf{Comb}(\mathsf{ctx}_{\boldsymbol{z}}, \{\mathsf{ds}_j\}_{j \in \mathcal{U}})$

return $\sigma := (c, \boldsymbol{z})$

Fig. 5. Passively secure t-out-of-n threshold signing protocol for signer $\mathcal{S}_i$.

scheme (assuming parameters are set so that decryption errors never occurs). Since $c \in \mathcal{C}_\nu$ and $\mathbf{s}, \{\boldsymbol{r}_j\}$ are short, then $\boldsymbol{z}$ is short as well. Moreover, we have

$$\langle \boldsymbol{a}_{\mathcal{TS}}, \boldsymbol{z} \rangle - cy = c\langle \boldsymbol{a}_{\mathcal{TS}}, \mathbf{s} \rangle + \langle \boldsymbol{a}_{\mathcal{TS}}, \sum_{j \in \mathcal{U}} \boldsymbol{r}_j \rangle - c\langle \boldsymbol{a}_{\mathcal{TS}}, \mathbf{s} \rangle \;=\; w;$$

thus, $H(\langle \boldsymbol{a}_{\mathcal{TS}}, \boldsymbol{z} \rangle - cy, \mathsf{pk}_{\mathcal{TS}}, \mu) = H(w, \mathsf{pk}_{\mathcal{TS}}, \mu) = c$ and verification succeeds.

4.3 Proof of Security

Theorem 2 (Informal). *The threshold signature scheme $\mathcal{TS}$ is threshold existentially unforgeable under chosen message attacks (*ts-uf-cma*) in the random oracle model (ROM) if the underlying signature scheme is existentially unforgeable under chosen message attacks in the ROM, the threshold homomorphic encryption scheme $\mathcal{E}$ is indistinguishable, and the LWE assumption is secure.*

Proof. We sketch the argument here by summarizing each game in a sequence of hybrids and refer the reader to the full version for the full proof:

$\mathbf{G}_0$: The first experiment corresponds to the real life where a passive adversary $\mathcal{A}$ corrupts $\mathcal{C} \subset [n]$ such that $|\mathcal{C}| < t$ and attacks the threshold signature scheme $\mathcal{TS}$ in the real world. This is the same as the unforgeability experiment defined in Sect. 2.3.

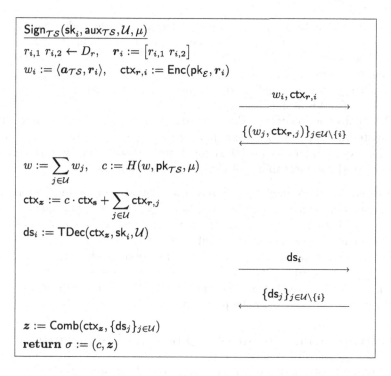

$\mathbf{G}_1$-$\mathbf{G}_0$: The first hybrid replaces ciphertexts from $\mathcal{B}$ with random encryptions. The security in this experiment reduces to indistinguishability of $\mathcal{E}$.

$\mathbf{G}_2$-$\mathbf{G}_1$: The second hybrid removes the dependence on the signing key $\mathbf{s}$ by simulating the responses based on the public key and the signature received by the challenger for the single party signature. The security in this experiment reduces to R-LWE problem.

$\mathbf{G}_2$: The final experiment has the same distribution for signature and public key material as it is in the single party case. Any forgery to the scheme can also be used as a forgery for the single party signature therefore the security reduces to the unforgeability of the single party scheme.

Since we remove the reliance on aborts, each signature may leak information about the secret key as discussed by Lyubashevsky [41]. Exact parameters rely on either limiting the number of signatures issued or on noise drowning. Parameters for active security are analyzed in detail in Sect. 7.

The actively secure version of our protocol is more involved since we assume a rushing and active adversary, and hence, we need parties to commit to specific values, provide zero-knowledge proofs, and conduct consistency checks to ensure the privacy and correctness of the protocol.

5 Actively Secure t-out-of-n Threshold Signatures

We now describe our main contribution: an actively secure threshold signature scheme, constructed by bootstrapping the passively secure protocol described in Sect. 4. The key generation and signing protocols are depicted in Fig. 6 and Fig. 7, respectively. We extend the previous section by giving concrete bounds and dimensions for the protocol, discussing the communication efficiency in each round, and giving a detailed security proof.

We start by modifying the underlying signature protocol. Instead of using w directly as part of the oracle input for challenge derivation, we use a commitment com to w instead. This is the same approach taken by Damgård et al. [22] on Dilithium-G [26] and does not have any important security implications on the signatures as long as the underlying commitment scheme is secure.

5.1 Key Generation and Signing Protocols

We retain our notation and viewpoint from the passive protocol and introduce homomorphic commitments and non-interactive zero-knowledge proofs. Note that we change the signatures so that the challenge is computed as the hash of the sum of commitments to the values w_j instead of the values themselves, and openings are published afterward as a part of the signature.

$\mathsf{KGen}_{\mathcal{TS}}$ works as follows:

1. $\mathcal{S}_i$ starts by invoking the distributed key generation DKGen of the underlying encryption scheme $\mathcal{E}$ with inputs t and n as in the passive case and obtains the public encryption key $\mathsf{pk}_{\mathcal{E}}$, its threshold decryption key share sk_i and any auxiliary information $\mathsf{aux}_{\mathcal{E}}$ associated with $\mathcal{E}$.

$\underline{\mathsf{KGen}_{\mathcal{TS}}(\mathsf{crs} = (\boldsymbol{a}_{\mathcal{TS}}, a_{\mathcal{E}}), t, n)}$

$\mathsf{DKGen}(\mathsf{crs} = a_{\mathcal{E}}, t, n)$

$\longrightarrow$

$\longleftarrow$

return $\mathsf{sk}_i = \mathsf{sk}_{\mathcal{E},i}, \mathsf{pk}_{\mathcal{E}}, \mathsf{aux}_{\mathcal{E}}$

$s_{i,1}, s_{i,2} \leftarrow D_s, \quad \mathbf{s}_i := [s_{i,1}\ s_{i,2}]$

$y_i = \langle \boldsymbol{a}_{\mathcal{TS}}, \mathbf{s}_i \rangle, \quad h_{y,i} := H_0(i, y_i)$

$\xrightarrow{h_{y,i}}$

$\xleftarrow{\{h_{y,j}\}_{j \neq i}}$

$\mathsf{ctx}_{\mathbf{s},i} := \mathsf{Enc}(\mathsf{pk}_{\mathcal{E}}, \mathbf{s}_i)$

Compute NIZK $\pi_{\mathbf{s},i}$ of $\mathsf{ctx}_{\mathbf{s},i}$ $\quad \xrightarrow{(y_i, \mathsf{ctx}_{\mathbf{s},i}, \pi_{\mathbf{s},i})}$

$\xleftarrow{\{(y_j, \mathsf{ctx}_{\mathbf{s},j}, \pi_{\mathbf{s},j})\}_{j \neq i}}$

if any $h_{y,j} \neq H_0(j, y_j)$: **abort** (j)

if any $\pi_{\mathbf{s},j}$ **is invalid**: **abort** (j)

$y := \sum_{j \in [n]} y_j, \quad \mathsf{ctx}_{\mathbf{s}} := \sum_{j \in [n]} \mathsf{ctx}_{\mathbf{s},j}$

return $\mathsf{pk}_{\mathcal{TS}} := (\boldsymbol{a}_{\mathcal{TS}}, y)$, sk_i,

and $\mathsf{aux}_{\mathcal{TS}} := (\mathsf{aux}_{\mathcal{E}}, \mathsf{pk}_{\mathcal{E}}, \mathsf{ctx}_{\mathbf{s}})$

Fig. 6. Actively secure key generation protocol for signer $\mathcal{S}_i$.

2. $\mathcal{S}_i$ then samples short signing key $s_{i,1}, s_{i,2}$ sets $\mathbf{s}_i := [s_{i,1}\ s_{i,2}]$, $y_i := \langle \boldsymbol{a}_{\mathcal{TS}}, \mathbf{s}_i \rangle$, hash $h_{y,i} := H_0(i, y_i)$ as a commitment to y_i, and broadcasts $h_{y,i}$. Upon receiving $h_{y,j}$ for all $j \neq i$, $\mathcal{S}_i$ encrypts $\mathbf{s}_i$ as $\mathsf{ctx}_{\mathbf{s},i} := \mathsf{Enc}(\mathsf{pk}_{\mathcal{E}}, \mathbf{s}_i)$ and computes a NIZK proof $\pi_{\mathbf{s},i}$ to prove that the correct $\mathbf{s}_i$ was used for y_i and $\mathsf{ctx}_{\mathbf{s},i}$ (see Sect. 6), then broadcasts $(y_i, \mathsf{ctx}_{\mathbf{s},i}, \pi_{\mathbf{s},i})$.
3. Finally, upon receiving $\mathsf{ctx}_{\mathbf{s},j}$, $\pi_{\mathbf{s},j}$ and y_j from each $j \neq i$, $\mathcal{S}_i$ verifies that $h_{y,j} = H_0(j, y_j)$ and that $\pi_{\mathbf{s},j}$ is valid with respect to $\mathsf{ctx}_{\mathbf{s},j}$ and y_j, and aborts with output j if any of them fails. If all checks succeed, it defines the public key $\mathsf{pk}_{\mathcal{TS}} = (\boldsymbol{a}_{\mathcal{TS}}, y)$, secret key sk_i, and auxiliary information $\mathsf{aux}_{\mathcal{TS}} = (\mathsf{aux}_{\mathcal{E}}, \mathsf{pk}_{\mathcal{E}}, \mathsf{ctx}_{\mathbf{s}})$ where $y := \sum y_j = \langle \boldsymbol{a}_{\mathcal{TS}}, \mathbf{s} \rangle$, $\mathsf{ctx}_{\mathbf{s}} := \sum \mathsf{ctx}_{\mathbf{s},j}$.

$\mathsf{Sign}_{\mathcal{TS}}$ works as follows:

1. Let $\mathcal{S}_i$ be one out of t signers in the set $\mathcal{U}$. Upon receiving the message μ to be signed, $\mathcal{S}_i$ samples per signatures randomness $r_{i,1}, r_{i,2} \leftarrow D_\sigma$ and commitment randomness $\rho_i \leftarrow \chi$, derives per message commitment key $\mathsf{ck} = H_1(\mathsf{pk}_{\mathcal{TS}}, \mu)$, set $\boldsymbol{r}_i := [r_{i,1}\ r_{i,2}]$, and computes $w_i := \langle \boldsymbol{a}_{\mathcal{TS}}, \boldsymbol{r}_i \rangle$ and commitment $\mathsf{com}_i := \mathsf{Com}_{\mathsf{ck}}(w_i, \rho_i)$. $\mathcal{S}_i$ then encrypts the randomness $\boldsymbol{r}_i$ with the encryption key $\mathsf{pk}_{\mathcal{E}}$ as $\mathsf{ctx}_{r,i} := \mathsf{Enc}(\mathsf{pk}_{\mathcal{E}}, \boldsymbol{r}_i)$, and computes a

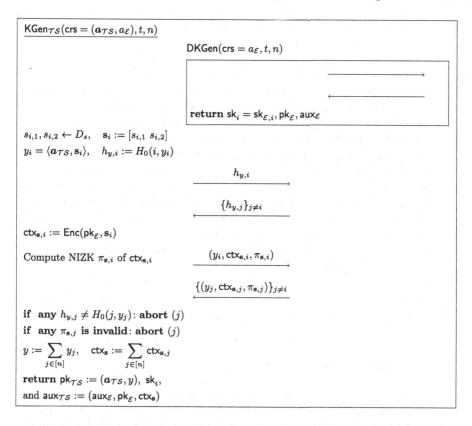

NIZK proof $\pi_{r,i}$ to prove that $\boldsymbol{r}_i$ was used for both com_i and $\mathsf{ctx}_{r,i}$ (see Sect. 6). $\mathcal{S}_i$ then sends $\mathsf{ctx}_{r,i}$, com_i and $\pi_{r,i}$ to all $j \in \mathcal{U}\backslash\{i\}$.
2. Upon receiving $\mathsf{ctx}_{r,j}$, com_j and $\pi_{r,j}$ for each $j \in \mathcal{U}\backslash\{i\}$, $\mathcal{S}_i$ aborts with output j if $\pi_{r,j}$ does not verify with respect to $\mathsf{ctx}_{r,j}$ and com_j. Otherwise it computes $\mathsf{com} := \sum \mathsf{com}_j$ for all $j \in \mathcal{U}$ and derives the challenge $c := H_2(\mathsf{com}, \mathsf{pk}_{\mathcal{TS}}, \mu)$. It then computes the encryption of the signature as $\mathsf{ctx}_{\boldsymbol{z}} := c \cdot \mathsf{ctx}_{\boldsymbol{s}} + \sum_{j \in \mathcal{U}} \mathsf{ctx}_{r,j}$ (that is, computing Eval on the ciphertexts where F is the function taking an element from $\mathcal{C}_\nu$, multiplying it with $\mathsf{ctx}_{\boldsymbol{s}}$, and adding t ciphertexts $\mathsf{ctx}_{r,j}$ to the result) and decrypts its share as $\mathsf{ds}_i := \mathsf{TDec}(\mathsf{ctx}_{\boldsymbol{z}}, \mathsf{sk}_i, \mathcal{U})$ and sends the partial decryption ds_i along with opening w_i and commitment randomness ρ_i to the signers in $\mathcal{U}$.
3. Upon receiving ds_j, w_j, and ρ_j for all $j \in \mathcal{U}\backslash\{i\}$, $\mathcal{S}_i$ aborts with output j if $\mathsf{Open}(\mathsf{com}_j, w_j, \rho_j) = 0$ for any j. Then tries to combine the decryptions as $\boldsymbol{z} := \mathsf{Comb}(\mathsf{ctx}_{\boldsymbol{z}}, \{\mathsf{ds}_j\}_{j \in \mathcal{U}})$ and aborts with output j if $\boldsymbol{z} = \perp$ and Comb aborts with output j. $\mathcal{S}_i$ finally outputs the signature $\sigma := (c, \boldsymbol{z}, \rho)$ where $\rho := \sum \rho_j$ for all $j \in \mathcal{U}$.

$\mathsf{Vrfy}_{\mathcal{TS}}$: Upon receiving $\sigma := (c, \boldsymbol{z}, \rho)$ and μ, checks that $\|\boldsymbol{z}\| \leq B_z$ and $\|\rho\| \leq B_\rho$, computes $w^* := \langle \boldsymbol{a}_{\mathcal{TS}}, \boldsymbol{z} \rangle - cy$, derives $c^* := H_2(\mathsf{Com}(w^*; \rho), \mathsf{pk}_{\mathcal{TS}}, \mu)$, then finally outputs 1 if and only if checks hold and $c = c^*$, and 0 otherwise.

5.2 Correctness, Bounds, and Sizes

We proved the correctness of the passively secure signature scheme in Sect. 4.2, and as the commitment scheme and the zero-knowledge schemes are complete, then it follows that the actively secure signature scheme is correct. Furthermore, the bounds in the protocol depend on the distributions we sample from. If we sum t samples from a uniform distribution over the values $[-B, B]$, the sum will be in the interval $[-tB, tB]$. However, suppose we sample from a discrete Gaussian distribution of standard deviation σ. In that case, each sample is with a high probability of 2-norm less than $2\sigma\sqrt{2N}$ for an integer vector of length $2N$, and the sum is bounded by $2\sigma\sqrt{2tN}$. Hence, the bounds $B_{\boldsymbol{z}}$ and B_ρ must be decided based on the distribution of choice, and the concrete choice of parameters and distribution impacts the security and efficiency overall.

When rejection sampling is removed, the signatures might leak information about the secret key, but this can be prevented by increasing the per-signature randomness $\boldsymbol{r}$ or limiting the number of signatures performed by the same key. We get optimal parameters if the key is used only once, as the key has high entropy and only leaks a few bits of information per signature. A recent analysis by Agrawal et al. [1] using Rényi divergence shows that leakage scales with $\sqrt{Q}$ where Q is the number of signatures, and hence, we can keep the bounds on $\boldsymbol{r}$ small when limiting the number of signatures.

Looking at the key generation, each signer first executes the interactive key generation for the underlying encryption scheme, which has communication size $|\mathsf{DKGen}|$. Each signer sends a ring element of size $N \log_2 q$ bits. Each partial

$\underline{\mathsf{Sign}_{\mathcal{TS}}(\mathsf{pk}_{\mathcal{TS}}, \mathsf{sk}_i, \mathsf{aux}_{\mathcal{TS}}, \mathcal{U}, \mu)}$

$\mathsf{ck} := H_1(\mathsf{pk}_{\mathcal{TS}}, \mu), \quad r_{i,1}, r_{i,2} \leftarrow D_\sigma$

$\boldsymbol{r}_i := [r_{i,1}\ r_{i,2}], \quad \rho_i \leftarrow \chi, w_i := \langle \boldsymbol{a}_{\mathcal{TS}}, \boldsymbol{r}_i \rangle$

$\mathsf{com}_i := \mathsf{Com}_{\mathsf{ck}}(w_i, \rho_i), \mathsf{ctx}_{\boldsymbol{r},i} \leftarrow \mathsf{Enc}(\mathsf{pk}_{\mathcal{E}}, \boldsymbol{r}_i)$

Compute NIZK proof $\pi_{\boldsymbol{r},i}$ of correct encryption $\xrightarrow{(\mathsf{ctx}_{\boldsymbol{r},i}, \mathsf{com}_i, \pi_{\boldsymbol{r},i})}$

$\xleftarrow{\{(\mathsf{ctx}_{\boldsymbol{r},j}, \mathsf{com}_j, \pi_{\boldsymbol{r},j})\}_{j \in \mathcal{U} \setminus \{i\}}}$

if any $\pi_{\boldsymbol{r},j}$ **is invalid**: **abort** (j)

$\mathsf{com} := \sum_{j \in \mathcal{U}} \mathsf{com}_j, \quad c := H_2(\mathsf{com}, \mathsf{pk}_{\mathcal{TS}}, \mu)$

$\mathsf{ctx}_{\boldsymbol{z}} := c \cdot \mathsf{ctx}_{\boldsymbol{s}} + \sum_{j \in \mathcal{U}} \mathsf{ctx}_{\boldsymbol{r},j}$

$\mathsf{ds}_i := \mathsf{TDec}(\mathsf{ctx}_{\boldsymbol{z}}, \mathsf{sk}_i, \mathcal{U})$

$\xrightarrow{(w_i, \rho_i, \mathsf{ds}_i)}$

$\xleftarrow{\{(w_j, \rho_j, \mathsf{ds}_j)\}_{j \in \mathcal{U} \setminus \{i\}}}$

if any $\mathsf{Open}(\mathsf{com}_j, w_j, \rho_j) = 0$: **abort** (j)

$\boldsymbol{z} := \mathsf{Comb}(\mathsf{ctx}_{\boldsymbol{z}}, \{\mathsf{ds}_j\}_{j \in \mathcal{U}}), \quad \rho := \sum_{j \in \mathcal{U}} \rho_j$

if $\boldsymbol{z} = \perp$ with **abort** (j): **abort** (j)

return $\sigma := (c, \boldsymbol{z}, \rho)$

Fig. 7. Actively secure 2-round t-out-of-n threshold signature protocol for signer $\mathcal{S}_i$.

signing public key is of size $N \log_2 q$ bits. It also sends the ciphertext and a zero-knowledge proof, which we denote the sizes by $|\mathsf{ctx}|$ and $|\pi_{\boldsymbol{s}}|$ bits, respectively.

In the signature protocol, each party sends a ciphertext and a commitment of size $|\mathsf{ctx}|$ and $|\mathsf{com}|$, respectively, in addition to a zero-knowledge proof of size $|\pi_{\boldsymbol{r}}|$. They furthermore send values w_i of size $N \log_2 q$, opening randomness ρ_i of size $|\rho|$ and partial decryptions ds_i of size $N \log_2 q$.

5.3 Proof of Security

We prove security of our protocol by constructing an algorithm $\mathcal{B}$ interacting with an active adversary $\mathcal{A}$. Note we assume a rushing adversary, so honest users always send their messages first.

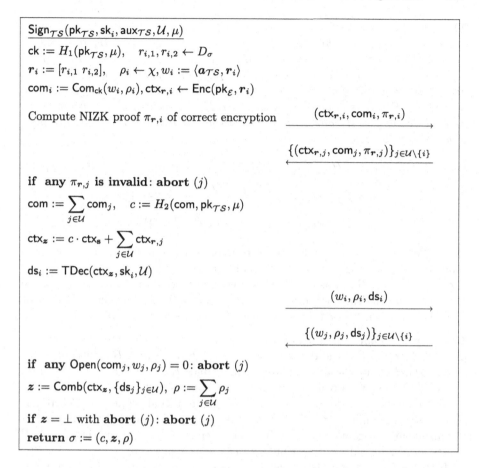

Theorem 3. *Let* $\mathsf{R\text{-}LWE}_{N,q,B_r}$ *be* $\epsilon_{\mathsf{R\text{-}LWE}}$*-hard. Let* Q_S*,* Q_H *denote the number of signing queries and the total queries made to* H_0*,* H_1*, and* H_2 *respectively. Let* ℓ *be the bit-length of the output of* H_0*. Let* $\mathcal{E}$ *be* $\epsilon_{\text{IND-CPA}}$ *secure. Finally, let proof systems* Π_x *for the relations* $\mathcal{R}_x$ *be* $\epsilon_{\mathsf{ZK},x}$*, and* $\epsilon_{\mathsf{extract},x}$*-secure. Then, the actively secure* t*-out-of-*n *threshold signature scheme* $\mathcal{TS}$*, described in Sect. 5 and depicted in Fig. 7, is* ts-uf-cma *secure when* H_0 *is modeled as a programmable random oracle and* H_1 *and* H_2 *are modeled as random oracles. The advantage of adversary* $\mathcal{A}$ *is:*

$$\begin{aligned}\mathsf{Adv}_{\mathcal{TS}}^{\mathsf{ts\text{-}uf\text{-}cma}}(\mathcal{A}) \leq\ & e(Q_H+Q_S+1)\big(|\mathcal{H}|\cdot\epsilon_{\mathsf{ZK,s}}+|\mathcal{H}_{\mathcal{U}}|\cdot\epsilon_{\mathsf{ZK},r}+|\mathcal{C}|\cdot\epsilon_{\mathsf{extract,s}}\\ &+|\mathcal{C}_{\mathcal{U}}|\cdot\epsilon_{\mathsf{ZK},r}+\frac{|\mathcal{C}|(Q_H+Q_S)}{2^{\ell}}+(Q_H+Q_S)\cdot\epsilon_{\mathsf{td}}\\ &+2\cdot\epsilon_{\text{IND-CPA}}+\epsilon_{\mathsf{R\text{-}LWE}}+\mathsf{Adv}^{\mathsf{uf\text{-}cma}}(\mathcal{A})\big).\end{aligned}$$

Proof. We prove this through a series of hybrids written out in full detail. The simulator $\mathcal{B}$ is communicating with a challenger $\mathcal{D}$, and we show that a forgery by $\mathcal{A}$ can be used by $\mathcal{B}$ to answer $\mathcal{D}$. This time, however, $\mathcal{D}$ targets a variant of the signature scheme described in Sect. 4.1 where c is derived using the commitment to $\boldsymbol{w}$. Hence when queried for a message, $\mathcal{D}$ outputs $\sigma=(c,\boldsymbol{z},\rho)$.

$\mathbf{G}_0$*:* The first game corresponds to the real world. Specifically, $\mathcal{B}$ follows the protocol according to the description, and $\mathcal{A}$ interacts with $\mathcal{B}$ arbitrarily. The oracles H_0,H_1, and H_2 are simulated using tables $\mathcal{HT}_0$, $\mathcal{HT}_1$, and $\mathcal{HT}_2$. Since we assume a rushing adversary, $\mathcal{B}$ sends its messages first.

When $\mathcal{A}$ outputs a forgery $(\sigma^*=(c^*,\boldsymbol{z}^*,\rho^*),\mu^*)$, $\mathcal{B}$ aborts if $\mu^*\in\mathcal{M}$. If not, $\mathcal{B}$ derives the commitment key $\mathsf{ck}^*:=H_1(\mathsf{pk}_{\mathcal{TS}},\mu^*)$, computes $w^*:=\langle\boldsymbol{a}_{\mathcal{TS}},\boldsymbol{z}^*\rangle-c^*y$ and $\mathsf{com}^*:=\mathsf{com}_{\mathsf{ck}^*}(w^*;\rho^*)$. If the challenge $c^*\neq H_2(\mathsf{com}^*,\mathsf{pk}_{\mathcal{TS}},\mu^*)$, $\mathcal{B}$ aborts, otherwise halts with output (σ^*,μ^*) and $\mathcal{A}$ succeeds.

If the real world is indistinguishable from the programmable random oracle model, then the random oracle simulation is perfect, $\mathcal{B}$'s behavior is exactly the same as in the unforgeability experiment, and we get that

$$\Pr[\mathbf{G}_0]=\mathsf{Adv}_{\mathcal{TS}}^{\mathsf{ts\text{-}uf\text{-}cma}}(\mathcal{A}).$$

$\mathbf{G}_1$*:* In this game $\mathcal{B}$ changes how non-interactive zero-knowledge proofs are answered for honest parties. $\mathcal{B}$ executes the protocol the same as $\mathbf{G}_0$, but instead of honestly generating $\pi_{\mathsf{s},i}$ for $i\in\mathcal{H}$, $\pi_{r,i}$ for $i\in\mathcal{H}_{\mathcal{U}}$, $\mathcal{B}$ uses the corresponding honest-verifier zero-knowledge simulators, $\mathsf{Sim}_{\mathsf{s}}$ and Sim_r for relations $\mathcal{R}_{\mathsf{s}}$ and $\mathcal{R}_r$ respectively where $\pi_{\mathsf{s},i}:=\mathsf{Sim}(\boldsymbol{a}_{\mathcal{TS}},y_i,\mathsf{pk}_{\mathcal{E}},\mathsf{ctx}_{\mathsf{s},i},B_{\mathsf{s}})$ and $\pi_{r,i}:=\mathsf{Sim}(\boldsymbol{a}_{\mathcal{TS}},\mathsf{com}_i,\mathsf{pk}_{\mathcal{E}},\mathsf{ctx}_{r,i},B_r)$. $\mathcal{B}$ follows the remaining parts of the protocol honestly. $\mathbf{G}_0$ and $\mathbf{G}_1$ is indistinguishable by HVZK of the NIZKs:

$$\Pr[\mathbf{G}_1]-\Pr[\mathbf{G}_0]\leq|\mathcal{H}|\cdot\epsilon_{\mathsf{ZK,s}}+|\mathcal{H}_{\mathcal{U}}|\cdot\epsilon_{\mathsf{ZK},r}.$$

$\mathbf{G}_2$*:* $\mathbf{G}_2$ is the same as $\mathbf{G}_1$ except $\mathcal{B}$ uses the extractability properties of the NIZKs to learn the signing key shares and the signature randomness encrypted by parties in $\mathcal{C}$. During key generation, after receiving $\pi_{\mathsf{s},j}$ for $j\in\mathcal{C}$, $\mathcal{B}$ calls the extractor $\mathbf{s}_j := \mathsf{Extract}_{\mathbf{s}}(\pi_{\mathbf{s},j}; \boldsymbol{a}, y_j, \mathsf{pk}_{\mathcal{E}}, \mathsf{ctx}_{\mathbf{s},j}, B_{\mathbf{s}})$. Similarly, during signing after receiving $\pi_{r,i}$, $\mathcal{B}$ computes $\boldsymbol{r}_i := \mathsf{Extract}_{\boldsymbol{r}}(\pi_{r,i}; \boldsymbol{a}_{\mathcal{TS}}, \mathsf{com}_i, \mathsf{pk}_{\mathcal{E}}, \mathsf{ctx}_{\boldsymbol{r},i}, B_{\boldsymbol{r}})$. If any of the extractions fails, $\mathcal{B}$ aborts.

By assumption, the extractor $\mathsf{Extract}_x$ for $\mathcal{R}_x$ is efficiently computable. If $\mathcal{B}$ does not abort due to a failed extraction, $\mathbf{G}_2$ and $\mathbf{G}_3$ is indistinguishable for $\mathcal{A}$. $\mathcal{A}$'s advantage in $\mathbf{G}_3$ is bounded by the sum of independent extraction failures:

$$\Pr[\mathbf{G}_2] - \Pr[\mathbf{G}_1] \leq |\mathcal{C}| \cdot \epsilon_{\mathsf{extract,s}} + |\mathcal{C}_{\mathcal{U}}| \cdot \epsilon_{\mathsf{extract},\boldsymbol{r}}.$$

$\mathbf{G}_3$*:* $\mathbf{G}_3$ is exactly the same as $\mathbf{G}_2$ except $\mathcal{B}$ embeds a trapdoor to the commitment key ck with high probability. Then the forgery by $\mathcal{A}$ must be for an honestly generated commitment key ck.

$\mathcal{B}$ initially generates only a single commitment key $\mathsf{ck} \leftarrow S_{\mathsf{ck}}$. $\mathcal{B}$ keeps a trapdoor table $\mathcal{TDT}$ similarly to other random oracles throughout the protocol. When there is a query for H_1 for a new message-public key pair, with probability ϕ, $\mathcal{B}$ samples a trapdoor $(\mathsf{ck}, \mathsf{td})$ by invoking TCGen, updates the corresponding entry in $\mathcal{TDT}$ to td and updates the corresponding entry in $\mathcal{HT}_2$ to ck. Otherwise $\mathcal{B}$ uses a freshly sampled $\mathsf{ck} \leftarrow S_{\mathsf{ck}}$.

When $\mathcal{A}$ queries H_1, $\mathcal{B}$ sets the flag *bad* and aborts if $\mathcal{TDT}[\mathsf{pk}_{\mathcal{TS}}, \mu] = \perp$. Otherwise, $\mathcal{B}$ obtains the trapdoor td. Then, for $j \in \mathcal{H}_{\mathcal{U}}$, $\mathcal{B}$ samples $r_{j,1}, r_{j,2}$ and computes $\boldsymbol{r}_j, w_j$ according to $\mathsf{Sign}_{\mathcal{TS}}$. Furthermore, $\mathcal{B}$ samples commitments com_j by invoking TCom on input td. The rest of the first round continues as in $\mathbf{G}_2$. When $\mathcal{B}$ has received messages from all users, it checks if the proofs for $\boldsymbol{r}_j$ verify and computes the challenge and derives randomness $\rho_j \leftarrow \mathsf{Eqv}_{\mathsf{ck}}(\mathsf{td}, \mathsf{com}_j, w_j)$ for each $j \in \mathcal{H}_{\mathcal{U}}$. It then continues with the rest as before. When $\mathcal{A}$ sends a forgery $(\sigma^* := (c^*, \boldsymbol{z}^*, \rho^*), \mu^*)$, then $\mathcal{B}$ repeats the steps of $\mathbf{G}_2$. At the final step, if $\mathcal{TDT}[\mathsf{pk}_{\mathcal{TS}}, \mu^*] \neq \perp$, $\mathcal{B}$ aborts.

If $\mathcal{B}$ does not abort, then $\mathsf{ck}^* = H_1(\mathsf{pk}_{\mathcal{TS}}, \mu^*)$ and the simulated $\pi_{r,j}$ must verify for each honest part $j \in \mathcal{H}_{\mathcal{U}}$. This follows from the fact that the simulation is only successful if the oracle uses the trapdoor commitment for all but one query to H_1 and uses the predefined ck for the one associated with forgery, i.e., *bad* is not set. The trapdoor commitment scheme ensures that:

$$\Pr[\mathbf{G}_3] \geq \phi^{Q_H+Q_S} \cdot (1-\phi) \cdot \Pr[\mathbf{G}_2] - (Q_H + Q_S) \cdot \epsilon_{\mathsf{td}}.$$

By setting $\phi = (Q_H + Q_S)/(Q_H + Q_S + 1)$ we get

$$\Pr[\mathbf{G}_3] \geq \frac{\Pr[\mathbf{G}_2]}{e(Q_H + Q_S + 1)} - (Q_H + Q_S) \cdot \epsilon_{\mathsf{td}},$$

where $(1/(1 + 1/(Q_H + Q_S)))^{Q_H+Q_S} \geq 1/e$ when $Q_H + Q_S \geq 0$.

$\mathbf{G}_4$*:* In this hybrid $\mathcal{B}$ changes how ciphertexts are computed similar to $\mathbf{G}_1$ in the passive case. $\mathcal{B}$ fixes some index $i' \in \mathcal{H}$ which is also in $\mathcal{H}_{\mathcal{U}}$. $\mathcal{B}$ computes $\mathsf{ctx}_{\mathbf{s},i'} := \mathsf{Enc}(\mathsf{pk}_{\mathcal{E}}, 0)$ during key generation and $\mathsf{ctx}_{\boldsymbol{r},i'} := \mathsf{Enc}(\mathsf{pk}_{\mathcal{E}}, 0)$ during signing. The rest of the game is as it is in $\mathbf{G}_4$. Since $\boldsymbol{r}_j$ and $\mathbf{s}_j$ for $j \in \mathcal{C}_{\mathcal{U}}$ are extracted in $\mathbf{G}_2$, $\mathcal{B}$ can compute $\boldsymbol{z} = c\sum_{i\in\mathcal{U}} \mathbf{s}_i + \sum_{i\in\mathcal{U}} \boldsymbol{r}_i$, which is the combined signature hence the threshold decryption can be simulated. Similar to the $\mathbf{G}_1$ in the passive case, we can now reduce to the indistinguishability of $\mathcal{E}$:

$$|\Pr[\mathbf{G}_4] - \Pr[\mathbf{G}_3]| \leq 2 \cdot \epsilon_{\text{IND-CPA}}.$$

$\mathbf{G}_5$*:* In this hybrid $\mathcal{B}$ changes how $h_{y,i'}$ is computed. $\mathcal{B}$ sends a random $h_{y,i'} \in \{0,1\}^{\ell_1}$ as the commitment $y_{i'}$ then programs H_0 such that $H_0(i', y_{i'}) = h_{y,i'}$. If programming fails, $\mathcal{B}$ aborts. Then the only difference in $\mathcal{A}'s$ view is how $h_{y,i'}$ is computed. By the oracle assumption, the distributions are indistinguishable between these two games hence from the view of the adversary $\mathcal{A}$, $\mathbf{G}_4$ and $\mathbf{G}_5$ are indistinguishable as long as $\mathcal{B}$ does not abort during programming. Thus we can bound the advantage of $\mathcal{A}$ in distinguishing $\mathbf{G}_4$ and $\mathbf{G}_5$ by the failure probability of programming of H_0:

$$|\Pr[\mathbf{G}_5] - \Pr[\mathbf{G}_4]| \leq \frac{|\mathcal{C}|(Q_H + Q_S)}{2^{\ell_1}}.$$

$\mathbf{G}_6$*:* Now, $\mathcal{B}$ removes its reliance on the secret key $\mathbf{s}$ for signing similar to $\mathbf{G}_3$ in the passive case. During key generation, $\mathcal{B}$ initializes the signing challenger $\mathcal{D}$ with the parameters of the combined signature and queries the oracle to obtain public keys, then sets $\mathsf{crs} = \boldsymbol{a}_{\mathcal{TS}}$. Instead of honestly computing $y_{i'}$, $\mathcal{B}$ derives $y_{i'} = y - \sum\limits_{j \in [n] \setminus \{i'\}} y_j$ where y is received from $\mathcal{D}$ and continues the rest of key generation as in $\mathbf{G}_5$.

For $i \in \mathcal{H}_{\mathcal{U}} \setminus \{i'\}$, signing starts as $\mathbf{G}_5$. When a signing query for μ comes, $\mathcal{B}$ commits to a random $w_{i'}$ as part of the first message then forwards μ to $\mathcal{D}$ to obtain $(c, \boldsymbol{z}, \rho)$. $\mathcal{B}$ then computes $w := \langle \boldsymbol{a}_{\mathcal{TS}}, \boldsymbol{z} \rangle - cy$ and uses $\boldsymbol{z}$ for simulation to obtain ds_i. For $j \in \mathcal{U} \setminus \{i'\}$, w_j is computed the same. $\mathcal{B}$ then derives $w_{i'} = w - \sum_{j \in \mathcal{U} \setminus \{i'\}} w_j$ and equivocates the commitment to get the randomness $\rho_{i'} := \mathsf{Eqv}(\mathsf{td}, \mathsf{com}_{i'}, w_{i'})$ using trapdoor td. Otherwise, signing proceeds as $\mathbf{G}_5$.

Since $\boldsymbol{a}_{\mathcal{TS}}, y$ received from $\mathcal{D}$ is a valid R-LWE instance, the distribution of $a_{\mathcal{TS}}$ therefore $y_{i'}$ in $\mathbf{G}_6$ is same as $\mathbf{G}_5$ by linearity of operations the derived $y_{i'} = \langle \boldsymbol{a}_{\mathcal{TS}}, \mathbf{s}'_{i'} \rangle$ for an unknown $\mathbf{s}'_{i'}$.

$\mathcal{B}$ now has to fix the signature and its shares in a way consistent with the first round of communication in signing. Since $\mathcal{D}$ uses the variant that derives c based on a commitment to w, it is possible to obtain consistent $(c, \boldsymbol{z})$ such that $w := \langle \boldsymbol{a}_{\mathcal{TS}}, \boldsymbol{z} \rangle - cy$. The remaining difference in $\mathcal{A}$'s view is the $w_{i'}$, which is indistinguishable from uniform the way it is computed. Using the same argument in $\mathbf{G}_3$ of passive, an adversary distinguishing between $w_{i'}$ in $\mathbf{G}_5$ and $\mathbf{G}_6$ can be used as a distinguisher for R-LWE. We then have:

$$|\Pr[\mathbf{G}_6] - \Pr[\mathbf{G}_5]| \leq \epsilon_{\text{R-LWE}}.$$

The signatures in $\mathbf{G}_7$ are independent of secret key material defined as part of the protocol and solely depend on the signature received from the challenger $\mathcal{D}$. A forgery against the $\mathcal{TS}$ scheme is then a forgery against the underlying signature scheme. If $\mathcal{A}$ outputs a forgery $(c^*, \boldsymbol{z}^*, \rho^*), \mu^*$, $\mathcal{B}$ can submit the same forgery to $\mathcal{D}$ as a valid forgery for the underlying signature. Hence if $\mathcal{A}$ can output a forgery at the end of $\mathbf{G}_7$, it can be used to break the uf-cma security of the underlying scheme, the advantage if $\mathcal{A}$ can then be bounded as:

$$|\Pr[\mathbf{G}_6]| \leq \mathsf{Adv}^{\mathsf{uf\text{-}cma}}(\mathcal{A}).$$

This conclude the proof. □

6 Instantiating the NIZKPoKs

There are four main relations of the signature protocol (including the homomorphic encryption subprotocols) to be proven in zero-knowledge. Here we define the exact relations that have to be proven and show how we can instantiate corresponding zero-knowledge proofs using proofs of shortness and linear relations.

- The relation $\mathcal{R}_{\mathsf{sk}}$ during $\mathsf{KGen}_{\mathcal{E}}$ defines the correctness of partial key shares as part of the key generation. For fixed public parameters B_{tern} and p, the common reference string $\mathsf{crs} = a_{\mathcal{E}}$, public b_i, $\{b_{i,j}\}_{i\in[n]}$, and public commitments to secret *short* s_i, e_i and secret $s_{i,j}$, $e_{i,j}$ the relation shows (1) $b_i = a_{\mathcal{E}} s_i + pe_i$; (2) $\mathsf{com}_i, \mathsf{com}'_i$ are commitments to s_i, e_i; and (3) $\{\mathsf{com}_{i,j}\}_{i\in[n]}, \{\mathsf{com}'_{i,j}\}_{i\in[n]}$ are commitments to $\{s_{i,j}\}_{i\in[n]}, \{e_{i,j}\}_{i\in[n]}$ such that $\{s_{i,j}\}_{i\in[n]}, \{e_{i,j}\}_{i\in[n]}$ are valid t-of-n secret sharings of s_i and e_i; (4) $\{s_{i,j}\}_{j\in[n]}$ are correct t-out-of-n shares of s_i; (5) $\{e_{i,j}\}_{j\in[n]}$ are correct t-out-of-n shares of e_i; (6) $\{b_{i,j}\}_{j\in[n]}$ is correctly computed from $s_{i.j}$ and $e_{i,j}$. More formally:

$$\mathcal{R}_{\mathsf{sk}} := \left\{ (x,w) \left| \begin{array}{c} x := (b_i, \{b_{i,j}\}, \mathsf{com}_i, \mathsf{com}'_i, \{\mathsf{com}_{i,j}\}_{i\in[n]}, \{\mathsf{com}'_{i,j}\}_{i\in[n]}) \wedge \\ w := (s_i, \rho_i, e_i, \rho'_i, \{s_{i,j}\}_{j\in[n]}, \{\rho_{i,j}\}_{j\in[n]}, \{e_{i,j}\}_{j\in[n]}, \{\rho_{i,j}\}_{j\in[n]}): \\ \\ \|s_i\|, \|e_i\| \leq B_{\mathsf{tern}} \ \wedge \ b_i = a_{\mathcal{E}} s_i + pe_i \ \wedge \ \forall j \ b_{i,j} = a_{\mathcal{E}} s_{i,j} + pe_{i,j} \\ \wedge \ b_j = \mathsf{Rec}_{t,n}(\{b_{i,j}\}) \ \wedge \ s_i = \mathsf{Rec}_{t,n}(\{s_{i,j}\}) \ \wedge \ e_i = \mathsf{Rec}_{t,n}(\{e_{i,j}\}) \\ \wedge \ \mathsf{Open}(\mathsf{com}_i, s_i, \rho_i) \ \wedge \ \mathsf{Open}(\mathsf{com}'_i, e_i, \rho'_i) \ \wedge \\ \forall i \ \mathsf{Open}(\mathsf{com}_{i,j}, s_{i,j}, \rho_{i,j}) \ \wedge \ \forall j \ \mathsf{Open}(\mathsf{com}'_{i,j}, e_{i,j}, \rho'_{i,j}) \end{array} \right. \right\}.$$

  The knowledge of s_i and e_i, and consequently $s_{i,j}$ and $e_{i,j}$ can be proven based on b_i and $b_{i,j}$ using proofs of linearity and shortness once commitments to s_i, e_i, and $e_{i,j}$ are available. For which we modify the distributed key generation algorithm given in Fig. 2 as follows: Party $\mathcal{P}_i$ as part of π_i commits to these secret values and broadcasts them as part of the proof. For partial shares that are sent through private channels, $\mathcal{P}_i$ also sends opening i.e. randomness $\rho'_{i,j}$ corresponding to the commitment to $e_{i,j}$ as well.
  It is also possible to show s_i and e_i are correctly secret shared. Once knowledge of s_i, e_i, $s_{i,j}$ and $\boldsymbol{e}_{i,j}$ is proven, since b_i and $b_{i,j}$ is public, it is possible to check if every subset of size t of $b_{i,j}$ can be used to reconstruct b_i.
- The relation $\mathcal{R}_{\mathsf{ds}}$ during TDec defines the correctness of the partial decryptions where the correct secret key share sk_i was used to generate the public decryption share $\boldsymbol{d}_i$ for a given ciphertext $\mathsf{ctx} = (u, v)$. For fixed parameters $\lambda_i, p, B_{\mathsf{TDec}}$, common reference string $\mathsf{crs} = (a_{\mathcal{E}}, b_{\mathcal{E}})$ and public commitments

to secret sk_i, E_i the relation shows: (1) The secret error E_i has norm smaller than B_{TDec}, (2) $\boldsymbol{d}_i$ is correctly computed with respect to $\lambda_i, \mathsf{sk}_i, u, p, E_i$:

$$\mathcal{R}_{\mathsf{ds}} := \left\{ (x, w) \middle| \begin{array}{c} x := (\boldsymbol{d}_i, \mathsf{ctx}, \mathsf{com}_{\mathsf{sk},i}, \mathsf{com}_{E,i}) \wedge w := (\mathsf{sk}_i, \rho_{\mathsf{sk},i}, E_i, \rho_{E,i}): \\ \|E_i\|_\infty \leq B_{\mathsf{TDec}} \wedge \boldsymbol{d}_i = \lambda_i \mathsf{sk}_i u + pE_i \wedge \\ \mathsf{Open}(\mathsf{com}_{\mathsf{sk},i}, \mathsf{sk}_i, \rho_{\mathsf{sk},i}) \wedge \mathsf{Open}(\mathsf{com}_{E,i}, E_i, \rho_{E,i}) \end{array} \right\}.$$

Since the commitment to the secret key shares are also included as part of the distributed key generation, it is trivial to prove the above statements using the proof of linear relations as before, once the commitments to E_i are available. For which we instantiate the proof $\pi_{\mathsf{ds},i}$ as a proof of linear relation to show d is correctly computed alongside a commitment to E_i.

- The relation $\mathcal{R}_{\mathbf{s}}$ for $\mathsf{KGen}_{\mathcal{TS}}$ proves that the short $\mathbf{s}_i$ was both used to compute the public key share y_i and was encrypted in $\mathsf{ctx}_{\mathbf{s},i}$. For a publicly fixed parameter $B_{\mathbf{s}}$, the common reference string $\mathsf{crs} = (\boldsymbol{a}_{\mathcal{TS}}, \mathsf{pk}_{\mathcal{E}})$ and public y_i and the commitment to the secret $\mathbf{s}_i$, the relation $\mathcal{R}_{\mathbf{s}}$ shows:(1) secret $\mathbf{s}_i$ has norm smaller than $B_{\mathbf{s}}$ (2) $\mathbf{s}_i$ is the same $\mathbf{s}_i$ used for the calculation of y_i (3) $\mathsf{ctx}_{\mathbf{s},i}$ is the encryption of the $\mathbf{s}_i$ using $\mathsf{pk}_{\mathcal{E}}$.

$$\mathcal{R}_{\mathbf{s}} := \left\{ (x, w) \middle| \begin{array}{c} x := (\boldsymbol{a}_{\mathcal{TS}}, y_i, \mathsf{pk}_{\mathcal{E}}, \mathsf{ctx}_{\mathbf{s},i}, B_{\mathbf{s}}) \wedge w := \mathbf{s}_i \wedge \\ \|\mathbf{s}_i\| \leq B_{\mathbf{s}} \wedge y_i = \langle \boldsymbol{a}_{\mathcal{TS}}, \mathbf{s}_i \rangle \wedge \mathsf{ctx}_{\mathbf{s},i} = \mathsf{Enc}(\mathsf{pk}_{\mathcal{E}}, \mathbf{s}_i) \end{array} \right\}.$$

Since $\mathbf{s}_i$ is boundend, the relation above is once again a linear relation with respect to $\boldsymbol{a}$. y_i and $\mathbf{s}_i$. Only non-trivial part is to show the knowledge of $\mathbf{s}_i$ as plaintext, which we discuss at the end of this section. So $\pi_{\mathbf{s},i}$ includes commitment to $\mathbf{s}_i$ and proof linear relation and plaintext knowledge for $\mathbf{s}_i$.

- The relation $\mathcal{R}_{\boldsymbol{r}}$ for $\mathsf{Sign}_{\mathcal{TS}}$ proves that a bounded signature randomness $\boldsymbol{r}_i$ was both committed to in com_i and encrypted in $\mathsf{ctx}_{\boldsymbol{r},i}$. For a publicly fixed parameter $B_{\boldsymbol{r}}$, the common reference string $\mathsf{crs} = (\boldsymbol{a}_{\mathcal{TS}}, \mathsf{pk}_{\mathcal{E}})$, public com_i,$\mathsf{ctx}_{\boldsymbol{r},i}$ for secret w_i,$\boldsymbol{r}_i$, ρ_i the relation $\mathcal{R}_{\boldsymbol{r}}$ shows: (1) randomness $\boldsymbol{r}_i$ has a norm smaller than $B_{\boldsymbol{r}}$ (2) $\boldsymbol{r}_i$ is the same $\boldsymbol{r}_i$ used for w_i and therefore the commitment com_i using randomness ρ_i (3) $\mathsf{ctx}_{\boldsymbol{r},i}$ is the encryption of the $\boldsymbol{r}_i$.

$$\mathcal{R}_{\boldsymbol{r}} := \left\{ (x, w) \middle| \begin{array}{c} x = (\boldsymbol{a}_{\mathcal{TS}}, \mathsf{com}_i, \mathsf{pk}_{\mathcal{E}}, \mathsf{ctx}_{\boldsymbol{r},i}, B_{\boldsymbol{r}}) \wedge w = (w_i, \boldsymbol{r}_i, \rho_i) \\ \wedge \|\boldsymbol{r}_i\| \leq B_{\boldsymbol{r}} \wedge \mathsf{ctx}_{\boldsymbol{r},i} = \mathsf{Enc}(\mathsf{pk}_{\mathcal{E}}, \boldsymbol{r}_i) \\ \wedge w_i = \langle \boldsymbol{a}_{\mathcal{TS}}, \boldsymbol{r}_i \rangle \wedge \mathsf{com}_i = \mathsf{Com}_{\mathsf{ck}}(w_i, \rho_i) \end{array} \right\}.$$

$\mathcal{R}_{\boldsymbol{r}}$ is almost exactly the same as $\mathcal{R}_{\mathbf{s}}$ with the exception of knowledge of openings to trapdoor commitments. For which, we do the same treatment to the protocol where $\pi_{\boldsymbol{r},i}$ includes a proof of linear relation with respect to $\boldsymbol{r}_i$ alongside a proof of plaintext knowledge which we will show next. Both $\mathcal{R}_{\mathbf{s}}$ and $\mathcal{R}_{\boldsymbol{r}}$ rely on the availability of a proof of plaintext knowledge where a given ciphertext corresponds to, for which, we introduce a final relation $\mathcal{R}_{\mathsf{Enc}}$ which also can be instantiated through proofs of linear relations since we use BGV as our underlying encryption scheme.

- The $\mathcal{R}_{\mathsf{Enc}}$ shows that, for fixed public parameters B_{Enc}, p, and a common reference string $\mathsf{crs} = (a_{\mathcal{E}}, b_{\mathcal{E}})$ and a statement consisting of ciphertext $\mathsf{ctx} =$

(u, v) and public commitments com_r, $\mathsf{com}_{e'}$, $\mathsf{com}_{e''}$, com_m to short secrets r, e', e'', m. Then the proof shows that (1) commitments open to suitably short values r, e', e'', m, respectively, such that (2) $u = a_{\mathcal{E}}r + pe'$ and (3) $v = b_{\mathcal{E}}r + pe'' + m$:

$$\mathcal{R}_{\mathsf{Enc}} := \left\{ (x, w) \left| \begin{array}{c} x := (\mathsf{ctx}, \mathsf{com}_r, \mathsf{com}_{e'}, \mathsf{com}_{e''}, \mathsf{com}_m) \ \wedge\ w := (r, e', e'', m, \rho_r, \rho_{e'}, \rho_{e''}, \rho_m): \\ \|r\|_\infty, \|e'\|_\infty, \|e''\|_\infty \le B_{\mathsf{Enc}} \ \wedge u = a_{\mathcal{E}}r + pe' \ \wedge\ v = b_{\mathcal{E}}r + pe'' + m \ \wedge \\ \mathsf{Open}(\mathsf{com}_r, r, \rho_r) \ \wedge\ \mathsf{Open}(\mathsf{com}_{e'}, e', \rho_{e'}) \ \wedge \\ \mathsf{Open}(\mathsf{com}_{e''}, e'', \rho_{e''}) \ \wedge\ \mathsf{Open}(\mathsf{com}_m, m, \rho_m) \ \wedge\ \|m\| \le p \end{array} \right. \right\}.$$

The proof of plaintext knowledge proofs in both $\mathcal{R}_{\mathbf{s}}$ and $\mathcal{R}_{\boldsymbol{r}}$ then can be instantiated as a proof of linear relation where $\mathbf{s} = m$ and $\boldsymbol{r} = m$ with different B_{Enc} respectively. $\pi_{\mathbf{s}}$ already includes a commitment to $\mathbf{s}_i$, so we can add commitments to remaining encryption randomnesses as well as a linear relation proof for $\mathsf{ctx}_{\mathbf{s},i}$ to complete. $\pi_{\boldsymbol{r},i}$ however is a bit non trivial as commitments sent as part of the message are trapdoor commitments.

Trapdoor commitments and normal commitments can be instantiated using the commitment scheme by Damgård et al. [4,22], and the proofs of linearity and exact proof of shortness can be instantiated using the zero-knowledge protocols by Lyubashevsky et al. [4,8,43] combined with the Katsumata-transform [35].

7 Example Uses Cases and Performance

To estimate the practicality of our actively secure scheme we give example parameters for $(3, 5)$-threshold signatures in three different settings: (1) where a signature is only produced once (1-SIG), (2) where at most β signatures are produced (β-SIG), for some moderate β, and (3) where up to 2^{64} signatures is issued (∞-SIG), as per NIST recommendations. Schemes secure for issuing one signature may be of interest for cryptocurrency applications, and there has been ongoing discussion in the context of the NIST post-quantum cryptography standardization effort[4], especially with regard to SPHINCS+ [37], about applications where the assumption of a bounded number of signatures might be reasonable.

For simplicity, we let the distribution χ_{tern} be the uniform ternary distribution in each of the three cases. We use the threshold scheme described in Sect. 3 as the underlying additive homomorphic encryption scheme and the homomorphic trapdoor commitment scheme by Damgård et al. [22].

We emphasize that these are rough estimates, and a more careful analysis is needed before this scheme is ready for real-world use. The main point of this exercise is to showcase that we can achieve practical signatures and verification keys using our techniques. We acknowledge that the total amount of communication in the protocol is quite large, and we will provide more details on communication in the full version of the paper. Furthermore, this section assumes trusted setup and only focuses on the signing protocol, not distributed key generation. We summarize the results in Table 1.

[4] See https://groups.google.com/a/list.nist.gov/g/pqc-forum/c/LUczQNCw7HA.

Table 1. Estimated sizes of (3, 5)-threshold signatures SIG and public keys PK for settings: 1) where the signature is only produced once, 2) where a signature is produced at most $\beta = 365$ times, and 3) where a signature can be produced $\infty = 2^{64}$ times. These parameters achieve 128 bits R-SIS / R-LWE security using the lattice estimator [2].

Comm.	1-SIG	1-PK	β-SIG	β-PK	∞-SIG	∞-PK
Size	8.5 KB	2.6 KB	10.4 KB	3.1 KB	46.6 KB	13.6 KB

7.1 One-Time Signatures

The simplest case is when each key is only used to create a single signature before it is discarded and never used again. One such setting is Bitcoin transactions, where some funds are tied to a specific public key. When a new transaction is performed, the remaining funds are sent to a new address tied to a different public key owned by the same user(s). The setup can be done in advance, independent of the blockchain and future transactions, and one key is used for each transaction. This leads to smaller keys and signatures to minimize on-chain data.

With no rejection sampling, publishing a single signature leaks minimal information about the secret key. Agrawal et al. [1] show that the leakage in each signature grows linearly in the square root of the number of signatures produced, but since we only output a single signature, we can keep the parameters identical to when rejection sampling is performed.

All signing key shares are ternary, which means that even secrets of absolute norm 1 should ensure that the R-SIS and R-LWE problems are hard. The R-SIS problem is hard when the logarithm of the ℓ_2 norm of the secret is less than $2\sqrt{N \log_2 q \log_2 \delta}$, see [47], and we get more roughly 128 bits of security when $\delta \approx 1.005$, and better when it is smaller. The ring dimension N must be a power of two, so we set $N = 1024$. Then we let elements of $\boldsymbol{r}$ be sampled from a Gaussian distribution D_σ with standard deviation $\sigma = \nu \cdot \sqrt{\gamma}$, where $\gamma = 128 + (N \log_2 q)/(\log_2(2\eta + 1))$.

Each signer must prove in zero-knowledge that these bounds are satisfied to ensure protocol correctness. The most efficient exact zero-knowledge proofs used today are the proof systems by Lyubashevsky et al. [8,43], allowing us to prove the exact maximum norm of the secret values $\boldsymbol{r}$. The latter proof system is improved by Aranha et al. [3] and extended by Hough et al. [34] to large values using bit decomposition.

We let the ℓ_2 norm of $\boldsymbol{z}$ be $B = 2 \cdot \sigma \cdot \sqrt{2 \cdot t \cdot N}$ in our signature scheme. We finally set $\nu = 16$ (so that $|\bar{\mathcal{C}}| > 2^{128}$) to get $\sigma \approx 2^{10.9}$, $B_z \approx 2^{18.1}$ and $q \approx 2^{20}$. This leads to more than 128 bits of R-SIS security when inserting the parameters into the equation above and more than 128 bits of R-LWE security according to the LWE-estimator [2] when revealing only one signature per key.

The absolute norm of each coefficient in $\boldsymbol{z}$ is with high probability bounded by $4 \cdot \sqrt{t} \cdot \sigma$, and this leads to $\boldsymbol{z}$ being approximately $2N \log_2(4 \cdot \sqrt{t} \cdot \sigma)$ bits. Following [28], the standard deviation to sample ρ should be roughly $1.17 \cdot \sqrt{q}$ when using NTRU trapdoors, which means that ρ is of size $3 \cdot N \log_2(4.68 \cdot \sqrt{t \cdot q})$

bits. This leads to a signature 1-SIG of size 8.5 KB with the given parameters. The verification key 1-PK is of size $N \log_2 q$ bits ($\boldsymbol{a}_{TS}$ can be generated by a random oracle as in Dilithium [26]), resulting in a verification key of 2.6 KB.

The communication consists of commitments, ciphertexts, and NIZKs being sent in the signing protocol. Similar to Damgård et al. [22] we use the commitment scheme by Baum et al. [4] but with NTRU trapdoors [28], and instantiate this with module dimension one to match our security assumptions. We then need to increase the dimension and the moduli of the encryption scheme to be able to encrypt partial signatures, and use noise drowning to achieve secure threshold decryption. This leads to communication of ≈ 750 KB per party.

7.2 Bounded Number of Signatures

Another interesting setting is where a service is used at most once a day each year, and a signature is required to use the service. An example is FIDO authentication[5] where the signing key is secret shared over several devices to ensure both that the user can log in despite lost devices and at the same time that no one can impersonate the user even two devices are stolen. Hence, we must make sure that the signing key does not leak when up to 365 signatures are produced.

Following a similar analysis as above, where we extend the standard deviation to $\sigma = \nu \cdot \sqrt{\gamma \cdot 365}$ (see [1, Theorem 4.1]) to ensure that the signature does not leak too much information when producing at most 365 signatures. We keep $N = 1024$, and get $\sigma \approx 2^{15.2}$, $B \approx 2^{22.5}$ and $q \approx 2^{24}$ to ensure at least 128 bits of security with respect to the hardness of $\mathsf{R\text{-}SIS}$ and $\mathsf{R\text{-}LWE}$. The signatures are of size 10.4 KB and the verification key is of size 3.1 KB.

Since q is similar in this setting as in the previous, the size of intermediate communication within the signing protocol is essentially the same as above.

7.3 Unbounded Number of Signatures

In general, it is undesirable to upper-bound the number of signatures that can be produced with a signing key before it is not secure to use it anymore. One reason for this is that it is hard to keep a state over a longer time, and if the signing is running in a virtual environment it might be re-booted from a backup with an older state and a fresh counter, and hence, end up producing more signatures than initially recommended. In practice, we often upper limit the number of signatures by 2^{64}, or some other number that is close to the capacity of what modern computers can compute when choosing concrete parameters for certain security levels. Hence, we expand the number of signatures and use the square-root bound as above to compute the parameters for general-use signatures.

This leads to $\sigma = \nu \cdot \sqrt{\gamma \cdot 2^{64}} \approx 2^{44}$ for $\nu = 14$ when $N = 2048$ and get $B \approx 2^{51.9}$. Hence, we need to set $q \approx 2^{53}$ to get correctness and 128 bits of security. We get signatures of size 46.7 KB, and verification keys of 13.6 KB.

[5] See https://fidoalliance.org for more details.

Since q is approximately twice the number of bits, the dimension of the lattice needs to be doubled, and we estimate the intermediate communication to be approximately four times larger compared to the previous settings, leading to communication of ≈ 3 MB per party.

8 Extensions

There are several possible considerations for increased efficiency and security:

Compression. The most efficient lattice-based schemes in the literature use compression techniques to reduce the size of communication. The compression rate is chosen based on the hardness of the underlying assumptions so that one gives an approximate relation instead with a fine-tuned reduction to a problem of the appropriate hardness level, see for example Kyber [52] or Dilithium [42] for details. These techniques can potentially reduce the size of public keys and signatures in our case as well, in addition to reducing the communication on our protocol where the security is much higher to ensure the correctness of the distributed decryption protocol.

Reducing Communication via an Optimistic Approach. Assuming non-malicious behavior we can omit sending w_j and $\pi_{\mathsf{ds},j}$ for $j \in \mathcal{U}$, and send only ds_j and ρ_j for the second round of signing. If signature verification fails then each signer sends w_j and $\pi_{\mathsf{ds},j}$ in a third round as proof of correct computation. In an honest execution, this saves $t \cdot (|w_j| + |\pi_{\mathsf{ds},j}|)$ bits per party, significantly reducing the overall communication. For one-time signatures, roughly 400 KB of 750 KB per party communication is due to π_{ds}, which then can be removed.

Removing Trapdoor Commitments for Pre-processing. The pre-processing in Boschini et al. [9] to remove the trapdoor commitments is an immediate extension to our protocol, as the committed values in both protocols are similar to the ones in [22]. However, the application is a bit trickier and results in an increase in communication. Unlike their work, the commitments in our protocol are to the encryptions of per-signature randomness. This would require each commitment to have an associated NIZK of correct encryption, increasing the communication size for a set of commitments. This also raises the non-trivial question of computing NIZKs for random linear combinations of bounded values, which gives an extensive overhead to the protocol.

Acknowledgments. The work of Kamil Doruk Gur and Jonathan Katz was supported in part by NSF award CNS-2154705. We thank Shuichi Katsumata, Mary Maller, and Thomas Prest for pointing out a mistake in our parameter estimates in an earlier version of this work and for helping us correct them.

References

1. Agrawal, S., Stehlé, D., Yadav, A.: Round-optimal lattice-based threshold signatures, revisited. In: Bojańczyk, M., Merelli, E., Woodruff, D.P. (eds.) 49th International Colloquium on Automata, Languages, and Programming (ICALP 2022). Leibniz International Proceedings in Informatics (LIPIcs), vol. 229, pp. 8:1–8:20. Schloss Dagstuhl – Leibniz-Zentrum für Informatik, Dagstuhl, Germany (2022). https://doi.org/10.4230/LIPIcs.ICALP.2022.8
2. Albrecht, M.R., Player, R., Scott, S.: On the concrete hardness of learning with errors. J. Math. Cryptol. **9**(3), 169–203 (2015). https://doi.org/10.1515/jmc-2015-0016
3. Aranha, D.F., Baum, C., Gjøsteen, K., Silde, T.: Verifiable mix-nets and distributed decryption for voting from lattice-based assumptions. In: ACM CCS 2023, pp. 1467–1481. ACM (2023). https://doi.org/10.1145/3576915.3616683
4. Baum, C., Damgård, I., Lyubashevsky, V., Oechsner, S., Peikert, C.: More efficient commitments from structured lattice assumptions. In: Catalano, D., De Prisco, R. (eds.) SCN 2018. LNCS, vol. 11035, pp. 368–385. Springer, Cham (2018). https://doi.org/10.1007/978-3-319-98113-0_20
5. Bendlin, R., Damgård, I.: Threshold decryption and zero-knowledge proofs for lattice-based cryptosystems. In: Micciancio, D. (ed.) TCC 2010. LNCS, vol. 5978, pp. 201–218. Springer, Heidelberg (2010). https://doi.org/10.1007/978-3-642-11799-2_13
6. Bendlin, R., Krehbiel, S., Peikert, C.: How to share a lattice trapdoor: threshold protocols for signatures and (H)IBE. In: Jacobson, M., Locasto, M., Mohassel, P., Safavi-Naini, R. (eds.) ACNS 2013. LNCS, vol. 7954, pp. 218–236. Springer, Heidelberg (2013). https://doi.org/10.1007/978-3-642-38980-1_14
7. Boneh, D., et al.: Threshold cryptosystems from threshold fully homomorphic encryption. In: Shacham, H., Boldyreva, A. (eds.) CRYPTO 2018. LNCS, vol. 10991, pp. 565–596. Springer, Cham (2018). https://doi.org/10.1007/978-3-319-96884-1_19
8. Bootle, J., Lyubashevsky, V., Nguyen, N.K., Seiler, G.: More efficient amortization of exact zero-knowledge proofs for LWE. In: Bertino, E., Shulman, H., Waidner, M. (eds.) ESORICS 2021. LNCS, vol. 12973, pp. 608–627. Springer, Cham (2021). https://doi.org/10.1007/978-3-030-88428-4_30
9. Boschini, C., Takahashi, A., Tibouchi, M.: MuSig-L: lattice-based multi-signature with single-round online phase. In: Dodis, Y., Shrimpton, T. (eds.) CRYPTO 2022, Part II. LNCS, vol. 13508, pp. 276–305. Springer, Cham (2022). https://doi.org/10.1007/978-3-031-15979-4_10
10. Boudgoust, K., Scholl, P.: Simple threshold (fully homomorphic) encryption from LWE with polynomial modulus. In: Guo, J., Steinfeld, R. (eds.) ASIACRYPT 2023, Part I. LNCS, vol. 14438, pp. 371–404. Springer, Cham (2023). https://doi.org/10.1007/978-981-99-8721-4_12
11. Brakerski, Z., Gentry, C., Vaikuntanathan, V.: (Leveled) fully homomorphic encryption without bootstrapping. In: Goldwasser, S. (ed.) ITCS 2012, pp. 309–325. ACM (2012). https://doi.org/10.1145/2090236.2090262
12. Brandão, L.T.A.N., Peralta, R.: NIST first call for multi-party threshold schemes (2023). https://doi.org/10.6028/NIST.IR.8214C.ipd
13. Canetti, R., Gennaro, R., Goldfeder, S., Makriyannis, N., Peled, U.: UC non-interactive, proactive, threshold ECDSA with identifiable aborts. In: Ligatti, J., Ou, X., Katz, J., Vigna, G. (eds.) ACM CCS 2020, pp. 1769–1787. ACM Press (2020). https://doi.org/10.1145/3372297.3423367

14. Castagnos, G., Catalano, D., Laguillaumie, F., Savasta, F., Tucker, I.: Bandwidth-efficient threshold EC-DSA. In: Kiayias, A., Kohlweiss, M., Wallden, P., Zikas, V. (eds.) PKC 2020. LNCS, vol. 12111, pp. 266–296. Springer, Cham (2020). https://doi.org/10.1007/978-3-030-45388-6_10
15. Chairattana-Apirom, R., Tessaro, S., Zhu, C.: Partially non-interactive two-round lattice-based threshold signatures (2024). https://eprint.iacr.org/2024/467
16. Chen, Y.: DualMS: efficient lattice-based two-round multi-signature with trapdoor-free simulation. In: Handschuh, H., Lysyanskaya, A. (eds.) CRYPTO 2023, Part V. LNCS, vol. 14085, pp. 716–747. Springer, Cham (2023). https://doi.org/10.1007/978-3-031-38554-4_23
17. Chowdhury, S., et al.: Efficient threshold FHE with application to real-time systems (2022). https://eprint.iacr.org/2022/1625
18. Chu, H., Gerhart, P., Ruffing, T., Schröder, D.: Practical Schnorr threshold signatures without the algebraic group model. In: Handschuh, H., Lysyanskaya, A. (eds.) CRYPTO 2023, Part I. LNCS, vol. 14081, pp. 743–773. Springer, Cham (2023). https://doi.org/10.1007/978-3-031-38557-5_24
19. Cozzo, D., Smart, N.P.: Sharing the LUOV: threshold post-quantum signatures. In: Albrecht, M. (ed.) IMACC 2019. LNCS, vol. 11929, pp. 128–153. Springer, Cham (2019). https://doi.org/10.1007/978-3-030-35199-1_7
20. Dahl, M., et al.: Noah's ark: Efficient threshold-FHE using noise flooding. In: Proceedings of the 11th Workshop on Encrypted Computing & Applied Homomorphic Cryptography, pp. 35–46. WAHC 2023, Association for Computing Machinery, New York, NY, USA (2023). https://doi.org/10.1145/3605759.3625259
21. Damgård, I., Jakobsen, T.P., Nielsen, J.B., Pagter, J.I., Østergaard, M.B.: Fast threshold ECDSA with honest majority. In: Galdi, C., Kolesnikov, V. (eds.) SCN 2020. LNCS, vol. 12238, pp. 382–400. Springer, Cham (2020). https://doi.org/10.1007/978-3-030-57990-6_19
22. Damgård, I., Orlandi, C., Takahashi, A., Tibouchi, M.: Two-round n-out-of-n and multi-signatures and trapdoor commitment from lattices. In: Garay, J.A. (ed.) PKC 2021. LNCS, vol. 12710, pp. 99–130. Springer, Cham (2021). https://doi.org/10.1007/978-3-030-75245-3_5
23. De Santis, A., Di Crescenzo, G., Ostrovsky, R., Persiano, G., Sahai, A.: Robust non-interactive zero knowledge. In: Kilian, J. (ed.) CRYPTO 2001. LNCS, vol. 2139, pp. 566–598. Springer, Heidelberg (2001). https://doi.org/10.1007/3-540-44647-8_33
24. Devevey, J., Libert, B., Nguyen, K., Peters, T., Yung, M.: Non-interactive CCA2-secure threshold cryptosystems: achieving adaptive security in the standard model without pairings. In: Garay, J.A. (ed.) PKC 2021. LNCS, vol. 12710, pp. 659–690. Springer, Cham (2021). https://doi.org/10.1007/978-3-030-75245-3_24
25. Doerner, J., Kondi, Y., Lee, E., shelat, A.: Threshold ECDSA from ECDSA assumptions: the multiparty case. In: 2019 IEEE Symposium on Security and Privacy, pp. 1051–1066. IEEE Computer Society Press (2019). https://doi.org/10.1109/SP.2019.00024
26. Ducas, L., et al.: CRYSTALS-Dilithium: a lattice-based digital signature scheme. IACR TCHES **2018**(1), 238–268 (2018). https://doi.org/10.13154/tches.v2018.i1.238-268, https://tches.iacr.org/index.php/TCHES/article/view/839
27. Espitau, T., Katsumata, S., Takemure, K.: Two-round threshold signature from algebraic one-more learning with errors (2024). https://eprint.iacr.org/2024/496
28. Espitau, T., Nguyen, T.T.Q., Sun, C., Tibouchi, M., Wallet, A.: Antrag: annular NTRU trapdoor generation - making mitaka as secure as falcon. In: Guo, J., Steinfeld, R. (eds.) ASIACRYPT 2023, Part VII. LNCS, vol. 14444, pp. 3–36. Springer, Cham (2023). https://doi.org/10.1007/978-981-99-8739-9_1

29. Fleischhacker, N., Simkin, M., Zhang, Z.: Squirrel: efficient synchronized multi-signatures from lattices. In: Yin, H., Stavrou, A., Cremers, C., Shi, E. (eds.) ACM CCS 2022, pp. 1109–1123. ACM Press (2022). https://doi.org/10.1145/3548606.3560655
30. Fukumitsu, M., Hasegawa, S.: a lattice-based provably secure multisignature scheme in quantum random oracle model. In: Nguyen, K., Wu, W., Lam, K.Y., Wang, H. (eds.) ProvSec 2020. LNCS, vol. 12505, pp. 45–64. Springer, Cham (2020). https://doi.org/10.1007/978-3-030-62576-4_3
31. Gennaro, R., Goldfeder, S.: Fast multiparty threshold ECDSA with fast trustless setup. In: Lie, D., Mannan, M., Backes, M., Wang, X. (eds.) ACM CCS 2018, pp. 1179–1194. ACM Press (2018). https://doi.org/10.1145/3243734.3243859
32. Gentry, C., Peikert, C., Vaikuntanathan, V.: Trapdoors for hard lattices and new cryptographic constructions. In: Ladner, R.E., Dwork, C. (eds.) 40th ACM STOC, pp. 197–206. ACM Press (2008). https://doi.org/10.1145/1374376.1374407
33. Goldwasser, S., Kalai, Y.T., Peikert, C., Vaikuntanathan, V.: Robustness of the learning with errors assumption. In: Yao, A.C.C. (ed.) ICS 2010, pp. 230–240. Tsinghua University Press (2010)
34. Hough, P., Sandsbråten, C., Silde, T.: Concrete NTRU security and advances in practical lattice-based electronic voting (2023). https://eprint.iacr.org/2023/933
35. Katsumata, S.: A new simple technique to bootstrap various lattice zero-knowledge proofs to QROM Secure NIZKs. In: Malkin, T., Peikert, C. (eds.) CRYPTO 2021. LNCS, vol. 12826, pp. 580–610. Springer, Cham (2021). https://doi.org/10.1007/978-3-030-84245-1_20
36. Komlo, C., Goldberg, I.: FROST: flexible round-optimized Schnorr threshold signatures. In: Dunkelman, O., Jacobson, Jr., M.J., O'Flynn, C. (eds.) SAC 2020. LNCS, vol. 12804, pp. 34–65. Springer, Cham (2021). https://doi.org/10.1007/978-3-030-81652-0_2
37. Kölbl, S.: A note on SPHINCS$^+$ parameter sets (2022). https://eprint.iacr.org/2022/1725
38. Lindell, Y.: Fast secure two-party ECDSA signing. In: Katz, J., Shacham, H. (eds.) CRYPTO 2017 Part II. LNCS, vol. 10402, pp. 613–644. Springer, Cham (2017). https://doi.org/10.1007/978-3-319-63715-0_21
39. Lindell, Y.: Simple three-round multiparty schnorr signing with full simulatability. IACR Commun. Cryptol. **1**(1) (2024). https://doi.org/10.62056/a36c0l5vt
40. Lindell, Y., Nof, A.: Fast secure multiparty ECDSA with practical distributed key generation and applications to cryptocurrency custody. In: Lie, D., Mannan, M., Backes, M., Wang, X. (eds.) ACM CCS 2018, pp. 1837–1854. ACM Press (2018). https://doi.org/10.1145/3243734.3243788
41. Lyubashevsky, V.: Lattice signatures without trapdoors. In: Pointcheval, D., Johansson, T. (eds.) EUROCRYPT 2012. LNCS, vol. 7237, pp. 738–755. Springer, Heidelberg (2012). https://doi.org/10.1007/978-3-642-29011-4_43
42. Lyubashevsky, V., et al.: CRYSTALS-DILITHIUM. Technical report, National Institute of Standards and Technology (2020). https://csrc.nist.gov/projects/post-quantum-cryptography/post-quantum-cryptography-standardization/round-3-submissions
43. Lyubashevsky, V., Nguyen, N.K., Planccon, M.: Lattice-based zero-knowledge proofs and applications: shorter, simpler, and more general. In: Dodis, Y., Shrimpton, T. (eds.) CRYPTO 2022, Part II. LNCS, vol. 13508, pp. 71–101. Springer, Cham (2022). https://doi.org/10.1007/978-3-031-15979-4_3

44. Lyubashevsky, V., Peikert, C., Regev, O.: On ideal lattices and learning with errors over rings. In: Gilbert, H. (ed.) EUROCRYPT 2010. LNCS, vol. 6110, pp. 1–23. Springer, Heidelberg (2010). https://doi.org/10.1007/978-3-642-13190-5_1
45. Lyubashevsky, V., Peikert, C., Regev, O.: A toolkit for ring-LWE cryptography. In: Johansson, T., Nguyen, P.Q. (eds.) EUROCRYPT 2013. LNCS, vol. 7881, pp. 35–54. Springer, Heidelberg (2013). https://doi.org/10.1007/978-3-642-38348-9_3
46. Micciancio, D.: Generalized compact knapsacks, cyclic lattices, and efficient one-way functions from worst-case complexity assumptions. In: 43rd FOCS, pp. 356–365. IEEE Computer Society Press (2002). https://doi.org/10.1109/SFCS.2002.1181960
47. Micciancio, D., Regev, O.: Lattice-based cryptography. In: Bernstein, D.J., Buchmann, J., Dahmen, E. (eds.) Post-Quantum Cryptography, pp. 147–191. Springer, Heidelberg (2009). https://doi.org/10.1007/978-3-540-88702-7_5
48. Peikert, C.: An efficient and parallel gaussian sampler for lattices. In: Rabin, T. (ed.) CRYPTO 2010. LNCS, vol. 6223, pp. 80–97. Springer, Heidelberg (2010). https://doi.org/10.1007/978-3-642-14623-7_5
49. del Pino, R., et al.: Raccoon: a side-channel secure signature scheme (2023). https://csrc.nist.gov/csrc/media/Projects/pqc-dig-sig/documents/round-1/spec-files/raccoon-spec-web.pdf
50. del Pino, R., Katsumata, S., Maller, M., Mouhartem, F., Prest, T., Saarinen, M.J.: Threshold raccoon: practical threshold signatures from standard lattice assumptions (2024). https://eprint.iacr.org/2024/184. Eurocrypt 2024, to appear
51. Rotaru, D., Smart, N.P., Tanguy, T., Vercauteren, F., Wood, T.: Actively secure setup for SPDZ. J. Cryptol. **35**(1), 5 (2022). https://doi.org/10.1007/s00145-021-09416-w
52. Schwabe, P., et al.: CRYSTALS-KYBER. Technical report, National Institute of Standards and Technology (2020). https://csrc.nist.gov/projects/post-quantum-cryptography/post-quantum-cryptography-standardization/round-3-submissions
53. Shamir, A.: How to share a secret. Commun. Assoc. Comput. Mach. **22**(11), 612–613 (1979). https://doi.org/10.1145/359168.359176
54. Tang, G., Pang, B., Chen, L., Zhang, Z.: Efficient lattice-based threshold signatures with functional interchangeability. IEEE Trans. Inf. Forensics Secur. **18**, 4173–4187 (2023). https://doi.org/10.1109/TIFS.2023.3293408

Hash Your Keys Before Signing

BUFF Security of the Additional NIST PQC Signatures

Thomas Aulbach[1], Samed Düzlü[1(✉)], Michael Meyer[1], Patrick Struck[2], and Maximiliane Weishäupl[1]

[1] Universität Regensburg, Regensburg, Germany
{thomas.aulbach,samed.duzlu,maximiliane.weishaeupl}@ur.de, michael@random-oracles.org

[2] Universität Konstanz, Konstanz, Germany
patrick.struck@uni-konstanz.de

Abstract. In this work, we analyze the so-called Beyond UnForgeability Features (BUFF) security of the submissions to the current standardization process of additional signatures by NIST. The BUFF notions formalize security against maliciously generated keys and have various real-world use cases, where security can be guaranteed despite misuse potential on a protocol level. Consequently, NIST declared the security against the BUFF notions as *desirable features*. Despite NIST's interest, only 6 out of 40 schemes consider BUFF security at all, but none give a detailed analysis. We close this gap by analyzing the schemes based on codes, isogenies, lattices, and multivariate equations. The results vary from schemes that achieve neither notion (e.g., WAVE) to schemes that achieve all notions (e.g., PROV). In particular, we dispute certain claims by SQUIRRELS and VOX regarding their BUFF security. Resulting from our analysis, we observe that three schemes (CROSS, HAWK and PROV) achieve BUFF security without having the hash of public key and message as part of the signature, as BUFF transformed schemes would have. HAWK and PROV essentially use the lighter PS-3 transform by Pornin and Stern (ACNS'05). We further point out whether this transform suffices for the other schemes to achieve the BUFF notions, with both positive and negative results.

Keywords: Signature Schemes · BUFF · Additional Security Properties

1 Introduction

Nowadays, digital signature schemes are fundamental cryptographic primitives. They allow a signer Alice to generate a signature `sig` of a message `msg`, using her private key `sk`, such that anybody, using Alice's public key `pk`, can verify the validity of the signature. *Existential unforgeability under chosen message attacks* (EUF-CMA) has become the standard security notion for digital signature schemes. EUF-CMA secure schemes come with the guarantee that an adversary, seeing several message-signature pairs generated by Alice, cannot generate a new message-signature pair that is accepted as a signature by Alice.

M.-J. Saarinen and D. Smith-Tone (Eds.): PQCrypto 2024, LNCS 14772, pp. 301–335, 2024.
https://doi.org/10.1007/978-3-031-62746-0_13

Unforgeability is essential for digital signature schemes and in most use cases also sufficient. However, the EUF-CMA security notion only covers scenarios where Alice's key pair is honestly generated. Depending on the use case of a digital signature scheme, other attacks are possible which are not ruled out by using a signature scheme that is unforgeable. This led to the development of additional security notions: *exclusive ownership*, *message-bound signatures*, and *non-resignability*. In the following, we give high-level descriptions of these notions, covering the gist of each.

The first security notion, *exclusive ownership*, provides the adversary with a valid message-signature pair $(\mathtt{msg}, \mathtt{sig})$ under a public key $\mathtt{pk}$ and asks it to find a different public key $\overline{\mathtt{pk}}$ under which $(\mathtt{msg}, \mathtt{sig})$ remains a valid message-signature pair. The lack of exclusive ownership allows an adversary to "claim" signatures as its own by providing $\overline{\mathtt{pk}}$. The relevance can be seen by the real-world attack against the Let's Encrypt protocol, where an adversary can exploit such claimed signatures to obtain certificates for domains despite not owning them [1]. The notion comes in two flavors: the one just described, which is called *conservative exclusive ownership* (S-CEO), and *destructive exclusive ownership* (S-DEO), where the adversary needs to find a different message.

The second security notion, *message-bound signatures* (MBS), asks the adversary to come up with two messages $\mathtt{msg} \neq \overline{\mathtt{msg}}$, a signature $\mathtt{sig}$, and a public key $\mathtt{pk}$, such that both $(\mathtt{msg}, \mathtt{sig})$ and $(\overline{\mathtt{msg}}, \mathtt{sig})$ are valid message-signature pairs under $\mathtt{pk}$. Absence of this property allows adversaries to bypass non-repudiation: when the adversary is accused of having signed $\mathtt{msg}$, it can claim to have signed $\overline{\mathtt{msg}}$ instead. At the first glance, it seems that this should already be covered by standard EUF-CMA—finding $\overline{\mathtt{msg}}$ immediately yields a forged signature. The difference is that EUF-CMA is limited to honestly generated keys whereas the notion we describe here is more permissive by letting the adversary output an arbitrary public key, in particular, not constrained to be the outcome of the key generation algorithm.

The third security notion, *non-resignability* (NR), provides the adversary with a signature $\mathtt{sig}$ of an unknown message $\mathtt{msg}$ under some public key $\mathtt{pk}$ and asks the adversary for a different public key $\overline{\mathtt{pk}}$ and signature $\overline{\mathtt{sig}}$, such that $\overline{\mathtt{sig}}$ verifies correctly under $\overline{\mathtt{pk}}$ for the unknown[1] message $\mathtt{msg}$. Jackson et al. [24] showed that a resignable signature scheme, i.e., one for which the adversary can find $\overline{\mathtt{pk}}$ and $\overline{\mathtt{sig}}$ as described above, allows for attacks against the "Dynamically Recreatable Key" (DRKey) protocol [25]. Here, the adversary has to re-sign a message which contains a—to the adversary unknown—symmetric key.

The additional security properties exclusive ownership, message-bound signatures, and non-resignability were formalized in [14], which also provides a generic transformation—called the BUFF transform—to achieve them. Furthermore, the authors of [14] analyzed the signature schemes selected to be standardized by NIST: Dilithium [27], Falcon [33], and Sphincs$^+$ [23]. Dilithium was shown to achieve the notions and while Falcon does not, the authors of Falcon

[1] This part is crucial. If the adversary was to know the message $\mathtt{msg}$, it could generate a new key pair $(\overline{\mathtt{sk}}, \overline{\mathtt{pk}})$ and sign $\mathtt{msg}$ using $\overline{\mathtt{sk}}$ to obtain $\overline{\mathtt{sig}}$ and output $(\overline{\mathtt{pk}}, \overline{\mathtt{sig}})$.

announced to deploy the BUFF transform in the next update. For SPHINCS$^+$ it is informally argued that it achieves the additional security properties. While the notions are not a requirement in the ongoing NIST standardization process for digital signature schemes [29], the call-for-algorithms mentions them as "additional desirable security properties beyond standard unforgeability". Despite this, only six out of 40 submissions mention these security properties at all, but none give a detailed analysis. Thus, there is a gap with respect to the security achieved by the signature schemes submitted to the NIST standardization process. A gap that we (partially) close in this work.

A Note on Non-resignability. Note that the initial definition of non-resignability in [14] was identified to be flawed in [17]. The problem lies in the auxiliary information which allowed for an (arguably artificial) attack. New proposals for the definition of non-resignability are given in [17] and an updated version of [14]. However, it is unclear which definition will ultimately define non-resignability, and if the BUFF transform achieves either notion. Given these problems, we opt for a weaker form of non-resignability (wNR) in which there is no auxiliary information—thus considering a weaker notion than the one introduced in [17]. Nevertheless, we provide concrete attacks against most schemes. Thus, they are also vulnerable to any stronger form of non-resignability, in particular, to the existing ones [14,17].

1.1 Our Contribution

We analyze the submissions to the NIST standardization process for post-quantum signatures [29]. We focus on the submissions that are based on either codes, isogenies, lattices, or multivariate equations—excluding those for which attacks against EUF-CMA have been identified. More precisely, we analyze four code-based schemes (CROSS [3], LESS [2], MEDS [12], WAVE [4]), the sole isogeny-based scheme (SQISIGN [10]), five lattice-based schemes (HAETAE [11], HAWK [9], HUFU [35], RACCOON [15], SQUIRRELS [19]), and seven multivariate schemes (MAYO [6], PROV [22], QR-UOV [20], SNOVA [34], TUOV [16], UOV [7], VOX [31]). The results are summarized in Table 1.

In the following, we describe the main results. First, we remark that MBS is almost always satisfied and the security can be traced back to the security of the hash function. In the two cases of SQUIRRELS and WAVE, where MBS is not satisfied, the reason is the scheme-dependent construction of a public key that allows multiple messages to verify under the same signature. Note that the specification of SQUIRRELS claims MBS security, which our analysis refutes.

Secondly, we note that all schemes—except for SQISIGN, MEDS and LESS—satisfy either both S-CEO and S-DEO, or neither. Despite the general separation by [14], our results indicate that in practice, these two notions often behave similarly. In fact, both proofs and attacks usually use the same idea for S-CEO and S-DEO, where for S-DEO, one needs to be slightly more careful in the choices. One group among the schemes that satisfy these exclusive ownership notions achieves them by hashing the public key, together with the message, to generate a target (resp. challenge), which the signature of the message corresponding to the given public key solves. In this way, any modification of the public key uncontrollably changes the target in a random manner. Then, the signature, which is required to be the same as the given one, cannot solve the new target, hence rendering the scheme secure. All schemes that do not satisfy exclusive ownership security are attacked by explicitly constructing new public keys which are compatible with the target generated independently of the public key, and the given signature. Differences between S-CEO and S-DEO can arise, when the message, but not the public key, is used to derive the target. Then it depends on the inherent properties of the scheme if different public keys can be constructed for the same (S-CEO) or a new (S-DEO) target value. An exception to the above rule is CROSS, where the security reduces to solving an underdetermined system of linear equations.

Finally, we consider non-resignability. All schemes that satisfy wNR are also secure with respect to both exclusive ownership and MBS. However, there are schemes (SQISIGN, MEDS and LESS), that satify S-DEO but not wNR. Indeed, we see a relationship to their exclusive ownership security: While fixing a signature fixes the public key in a certain sense, one can attack non-resignability by modifying both in a compatible manner, which does not require any knowledge about the message being signed. For the schemes that satisfy wNR, we see a similar argument as for exclusive ownership, namely that producing the target using a hash of the public key and the message, makes the target untraceable, even if one can control the signature. The exception, again, is CROSS, where the security results from the Merkle tree structure and an underdetermined system of linear equations. The other schemes that do not satisfy wNR are attacked, as in the case of exclusive ownership, by explicit constructions. Neither of those attacks rely on any auxiliary information about the unknown message, which an adversary is provided in stronger versions of non-resignability.

From our results, we can deduce the following interesting conjecture. Even though [14] shows that in general the BUFF transform is necessary to achieve full BUFF security, it turns out that in practice, it is most often sufficient to use the PS-3 transform as suggested in [32]. That means, instead of using a mere hash-and-sign paradigm, one needs to hash the message *and* the public key, and then sign the hash value. The PS-3 transform is more lightweight than the BUFF transform as the latter requires to also append the hash value to the signature. One important caveat in this regard is that it is often *not* sufficient to hash only a part of the public key. Important examples where such an approach does not help to satisfy BUFF security are given by various multivariate schemes, e.g., VOX, where this approach is used explicitly to gain BUFF security, but is not sufficient.

Structure of the Analyses. The analyses presented in this work follow a common structure, which we explain briefly. To analyze the BUFF security, the relevant information is the structure of the public key and signature, and the verification algorithm. Those are introduced at the beginning of each section, followed by the analysis of S-CEO, S-DEO, MBS, and wNR. In Sect. 6 on multivariate schemes, we give a more detailed general outline and give a generic proof of MBS and a generic attack on wNR, as the schemes allow such an all-encompassing formulation. The remaining analyses in the section follow the same structure.

Table 1. Overview of our results. A ✓ indicates that a signature scheme achieves a security notion, while a ✗ indicates that there is an attack. A ✦ indicates that we identified an attack that seems not to be relevant in practice. A superscript † indicates that the result disproves a claim made for the scheme. For LESS and MEDS, the results for S-CEO depend on the parameter sets.

Scheme	S-CEO	S-DEO	MBS	wNR	Type
CROSS [3]	✓	✓	✓	✓	Code (Sect. 3)
LESS [2]	✓ | ✗	✓	✓	✗	
MEDS [12]	✓ | ✗	✓	✓	✗	
WAVE [4]	✗	✗	✗	✗	
SQISIGN [10]	✦	✓	✓	✗	Isogeny (Sect. 4)
HAETAE [11]	✓	✓	✓	✓	Lattice (Sect. 5)
HAWK [9]	✓	✓	✓	✓	
HUFU [35]	✗	✗	✓	✗	
RACCOON [15]	✓	✓	✓	✓	
SQUIRRELS [19]	✗	✗	✗†	✗	
MAYO [6]	✗	✗	✓	✗	Multivariate (Sect. 6)
PROV [22]	✓	✓	✓	✓	
QR-UOV [20]	✗	✗	✓	✗	
SNOVA [34]	✗	✗	✓	✗	
TUOV [16]	✗	✗	✓	✗	
UOV [7]	✗	✗	✓	✗	
VOX [31]	✗†	✗†	✓	✗†	

1.2 Related Work

Unforgeability notions can be traced back to [21]. Exclusive ownership originates from [8,28], which introduces a specialized version under the name *Duplicate-Signature Key Selection.* A generalized version was developed in [32] which also coins the term exclusive ownership. Non-resignability was first mentioned in [24] though without a formal definition. Eventually, formal definitions of all beyond unforgeability properties (exclusive ownership, message-bound signatures, and non-resignability) were developed in [14], which also gives two generic transformations to achieve them.

2 Preliminaries

2.1 Notation

For integers m, n with $m < n$, we write $[m]$ and $[m, n]$ for the sets $\{1, 2, \dots, m\}$ and $\{m, m+1, \dots, n\}$, respectively. Throughout this work, $\mathtt{H}$ will denote a hash function (optionally with a subscript if multiple hash functions are used) which is often modeled as a random oracle [5]. For a matrix M, we denote the entries by m_{ij}. Similarly, for a vector x_i, its entries are denoted by $x_{i,j}$. We use ϑ to denote a generic bound (used for the lattice-based schemes).

2.2 Signature Schemes and Security Notions

A signature scheme Σ consists of three efficient algorithms:

KGen: the key generation gets a security parameter 1^λ as input and outputs a secret key sk along with a public key pk.

Sign: the signing algorithm gets a secret key sk and a message msg as input and outputs a signature sig.

Verify: the verification algorithm takes as input a public key pk, a message msg, and a signature sig, and it outputs a bit v.

A signature scheme is correct if, for any key pair $(\mathtt{sk}, \mathtt{pk}) = \mathtt{KGen}(1^\lambda)$, we have $\mathtt{Verify}(\mathtt{pk}, \mathtt{msg}, \mathtt{Sign}(\mathtt{sk}, \mathtt{msg})) = 1$ with overwhelming probability in the security parameter 1^λ.

In this work, we are using the security notions conservative/destructive exclusive ownership and message-bound signatures as formalized in [14], as well as a weaker form of non-resignability. Below we give the definitions. The corresponding security games S-CEO, S-DEO, MBS, and wNR, are shown in Fig. 1.

For conservative exclusive ownership, the adversary can obtain signatures for arbitrary messages and is then challenged to find a different public key that verifies one of the received message-signature pairs. Destructive exclusive ownership is similar to conservative exclusive ownership. The difference is that the adversary needs to find not just a different public key but also a different message that verify using one of the received signatures. The message-bound signature property guarantees that it is hard to find a signature that verifies two different messages under the same public key.

Definition 1. A signature scheme $\Sigma = (\mathtt{KGen}, \mathtt{Sign}, \mathtt{Verify})$ is said to have *conservative exclusive ownership*, *destructive exclusive ownership*, and *message-bound signatures* if for any efficient adversary $\mathcal{A}$, its probability in winning game S-CEO, S-DEO, and MBS, respectively, is negligible.

Non-resignability provides the adversary with a signature of an unknown message and asks to find a different public key and (not necessarily different) signature that verify the unknown message. We consider a slightly weaker form of non-resignability, which we call weak NR (wNR), which does not grant the adversary auxiliary information about the message. Note that for the majority

$$\begin{array}{l}\underline{\text{Game S-CEO/S-DEO}}\\ \mathcal{Q} \leftarrow \emptyset\\ (\mathtt{sk}, \mathtt{pk}) \leftarrow \mathtt{KGen}()\\ (\overline{\mathtt{pk}}, \overline{\mathtt{msg}}, \overline{\mathtt{sig}}) \leftarrow \mathcal{A}^{\mathsf{Sign}(\mathtt{sk},\cdot)}(\mathtt{pk})\\ \mathtt{v}_1 \leftarrow \mathtt{Verify}(\overline{\mathtt{pk}}, \overline{\mathtt{msg}}, \overline{\mathtt{sig}})\\ \mathtt{v}_2 \leftarrow \mathsf{Valid}(\overline{\mathtt{msg}}, \overline{\mathtt{sig}})\\ \textbf{return } (\mathtt{v}_1 = 1 \wedge \mathtt{v}_2 = 1 \wedge \overline{\mathtt{pk}} \neq \mathtt{pk})\end{array}$$

$$\begin{array}{l}\underline{\text{Game wNR}}\\ (\mathtt{sk}, \mathtt{pk}) \leftarrow \mathtt{KGen}()\\ \mathtt{msg} \leftarrow \mathcal{A}_0(\mathtt{pk})\\ \mathtt{sig} \leftarrow \mathtt{Sign}(\mathtt{sk}, \mathtt{msg})\\ (\overline{\mathtt{sig}}, \overline{\mathtt{pk}}) \leftarrow \mathcal{A}_1(\mathtt{pk}, \mathtt{sig})\\ \mathtt{v} \leftarrow \mathtt{Verify}(\overline{\mathtt{pk}}, \mathtt{msg}, \overline{\mathtt{sig}})\\ \textbf{return } (\overline{\mathtt{pk}} \neq \mathtt{pk} \wedge \mathtt{v} = 1)\end{array}$$

$$\begin{array}{l}\underline{\text{Game MBS}}\\ (\mathtt{msg}, \overline{\mathtt{msg}}, \mathtt{sig}, \mathtt{pk}) \leftarrow \mathcal{A}()\\ \mathtt{v}_1 \leftarrow \mathtt{Verify}(\mathtt{pk}, \mathtt{msg}, \mathtt{sig})\\ \mathtt{v}_2 \leftarrow \mathtt{Verify}(\mathtt{pk}, \overline{\mathtt{msg}}, \mathtt{sig})\\ \textbf{return } (\mathtt{msg} \neq \overline{\mathtt{msg}} \wedge \mathtt{v}_1 = 1 \wedge \mathtt{v}_2 = 1)\end{array}$$

$$\begin{array}{l}\underline{\text{Oracle } \mathsf{Sign}(\mathtt{sk}, \mathtt{msg})}\\ \mathtt{sig} \leftarrow \mathtt{Sign}(\mathtt{sk}, \mathtt{msg})\\ \mathcal{Q} \leftarrow \mathcal{Q} \cup \{(\mathtt{msg}, \mathtt{sig})\}\\ \textbf{return sig}\end{array}$$

$$\begin{array}{l}\underline{\mathsf{Valid}(\overline{\mathtt{msg}}, \overline{\mathtt{sig}}) \text{ in S-CEO}}\\ \textbf{if } (\overline{\mathtt{msg}}, \overline{\mathtt{sig}}) \in \mathcal{Q}\\ \quad \textbf{return } 1\\ \textbf{return } 0\end{array}$$

$$\begin{array}{l}\underline{\mathsf{Valid}(\overline{\mathtt{msg}}, \overline{\mathtt{sig}}) \text{ in S-DEO}}\\ \textbf{if } \exists \mathtt{msg} \neq \overline{\mathtt{msg}} \text{ s.t. } (\mathtt{msg}, \overline{\mathtt{sig}}) \in \mathcal{Q}\\ \quad \textbf{return } 1\\ \textbf{return } 0\end{array}$$

Fig. 1. Security games S-CEO, S-DEO, MBS, and wNR, for signature schemes.

of signature schemes we give attacks against wNR which are also valid attacks against any stronger form of non-resignability, in particular, those including auxiliary information for the adversary.

Definition 2. A signature scheme $\Sigma = (\mathtt{KGen}, \mathtt{Sign}, \mathtt{Verify})$ is said to have *non-resignability* if for any efficient adversary $(\mathcal{A}_0, \mathcal{A}_1)$, where $\mathcal{A}_0$ outputs uniformly random message, its probability in winning game wNR is negligible.

We say that a signature scheme Σ has full BUFF security, if it satisfies S-CEO, S-DEO, MBS, and wNR.

2.3 Transformations

There are several generic transformations that turn a signature scheme and a hash function into a signature scheme that achieves the aforementioned BUFF notions. For this work, we mainly need two: The BUFF transform [14] (cf. Fig. 3) and the PS-3 transform [32] (cf. Fig. 2). The former was shown to achieve all the BUFF notions—based on the assumptions on the used hash function. The latter was shown to not achieve all notions, due to a property that [14] calls *weak keys*, i.e., public keys that verify multiple messages. Both transformations work by first computing the hash of the public key and message. This hash value is then

$\texttt{KGen}^*()$	$\texttt{Sign}^*(\texttt{sk}, \texttt{msg})$	$\texttt{Verify}^*(\texttt{pk}, \texttt{msg}, \texttt{sig})$
$(\texttt{sk}, \texttt{pk}) \leftarrow \texttt{KGen}()$	$\texttt{h} \leftarrow \texttt{H}(\texttt{msg}, \texttt{pk})$	$\bar{\texttt{h}} \leftarrow \texttt{H}(\texttt{msg}, \texttt{pk})$
return $(\texttt{sk}, \texttt{pk})$	$\texttt{sig} \leftarrow \texttt{Sign}(\texttt{sk}, \texttt{h})$	$\texttt{v} \leftarrow \texttt{Verify}(\texttt{pk}, \bar{\texttt{h}}, \texttt{sig})$
	return $\texttt{sig}$	**return** $\texttt{v} = 1$

Fig. 2. The signature scheme PS-3$[\texttt{H}, \Sigma] = (\texttt{KGen}^*, \texttt{Sign}^*, \texttt{Verify}^*)$ constructed from a hash function $\texttt{H}$ and a signature scheme $\Sigma = (\texttt{KGen}, \texttt{Sign}, \texttt{Verify})$.

$\texttt{KGen}^*()$	$\texttt{Sign}^*(\texttt{sk}, \texttt{msg})$	$\texttt{Verify}^*(\texttt{pk}, \texttt{msg}, (\texttt{sig}, \texttt{h}))$
$(\texttt{sk}, \texttt{pk}) \leftarrow \texttt{KGen}()$	$\texttt{h} \leftarrow \texttt{H}(\texttt{msg}, \texttt{pk})$	$\bar{\texttt{h}} \leftarrow \texttt{H}(\texttt{msg}, \texttt{pk})$
return $(\texttt{sk}, \texttt{pk})$	$\texttt{sig} \leftarrow \texttt{Sign}(\texttt{sk}, \texttt{h})$	$\texttt{v} \leftarrow \texttt{Verify}(\texttt{pk}, \bar{\texttt{h}}, \texttt{sig})$
	return $(\texttt{sig}, \texttt{h})$	**return** $(\texttt{v} = 1 \wedge \texttt{h} = \bar{\texttt{h}})$

Fig. 3. The signature scheme BUFF$[\texttt{H}, \Sigma] = (\texttt{KGen}^*, \texttt{Sign}^*, \texttt{Verify}^*)$ constructed from a hash function $\texttt{H}$ and a signature scheme $\Sigma = (\texttt{KGen}, \texttt{Sign}, \texttt{Verify})$.

signed[2] by the signature scheme. The difference is that the BUFF transform additionally appends this hash value to the signature (which PS-3 does not).

3 Code-Based Schemes

In this section, we analyze the code-based signature schemes. They rely on two distinct code-related problems: the more classical syndrome decoding problem (CROSS and WAVE), and the fairly new code equivalence problem (MEDS and LESS). Although they are based on the same underlying problem, CROSS and WAVE are still very different, and while CROSS satisfies all BUFF properties, we show that WAVE is vulnerable with respect to each of the notions. WAVE fails to satisfy full BUFF security even after the PS-3 transform. We analyze CROSS in Sect. 3.1 and WAVE in Sect. 3.4. The two schemes based on code equivalences (MEDS and LESS) are very similar. We therefore only present MEDS in full detail (in Sect. 3.2), as the analysis of LESS (in Sect. 3.3) is almost verbatim the same. A surprising result of this analysis is that exclusive ownership notions are satisfied due to the inherent structure of the code equivalence problem. Indeed, for a given signature, there can essentially only be a single public key that verifies the message correctly. As this does not suffice to satisfy wNR, we show that using the PS-3 transform ensures full BUFF security for MEDS and LESS. Moreover, we note that PS-3-transformed MEDS and LESS can be considered to implement the full BUFF transform.

[2] Typically, the signature scheme itself first hashes the message. It is understood that in this case, the transformed scheme would in fact replace this hash operation, i.e., it signs $\texttt{H}(\texttt{msg}, \texttt{pk})$ instead of $\texttt{H}(\texttt{H}(\texttt{msg}, \texttt{pk}))$.

3.1 CROSS

CROSS is a code-based signature scheme based on a zero-knowledge identification protocol, the security of which relies on the NP-complete *restricted syndrome decoding problem*. To increase the soundness of the Fiat-Shamir transform, CROSS incorporates Merkle trees into its signature definition. There are two variants of CROSS, R-SDP and R-SDP(G), where the latter restricts the problem to a subgroup G, to achieve shorter signature sizes. As the analysis regarding BUFF security is the same for both versions, we will only consider CROSS-R-SDP(G).

The protocol uses integers k, m, n, t, w, λ, prime numbers p and z, and an element $g \in \mathbb{F}_p^*$ of order z. The cyclic subgroup generated by g is denoted by $\mathbb{E} \subseteq \mathbb{F}_p^*$ and G denotes a subgroup of $\mathbb{E}^n$. Further, a pseudorandom number generator PRNG is used, which we assume to be ideal throughout our analysis, i.e., the outputs are random.

Key Pair. The public key consists of a tuple $(\mathtt{seed}_{\mathtt{pk}}, s)$ for $\mathtt{seed}_{\mathtt{pk}} \in \{0,1\}^\lambda$ and $s \in \mathbb{F}_p^{n-k}$. The *secret key* is given by $\mathtt{seed}_{\mathtt{sk}} \in \{0,1\}^\lambda$.

Signature. The signature of a message `msg` consists of

$$\mathtt{salt}||d_{01}||d_b||\mathtt{MerkleProofs}||\mathtt{SeedPath}||\mathtt{rsp}_0||\mathtt{rsp}_1$$

for $d_{01}, d_b \in \{0,1\}^\lambda$, $\mathtt{MerkleProofs} \in \{0,1\}^{l_m}$, $\mathtt{SeedPath} \in \{0,1\}^{l_s}$ with

$$l_m = 2\lambda\left(1 + (t-w)\log_2\left(\frac{t}{t-w}\right)\right), \quad l_s = \lambda(t-w)\log_2\left(\frac{t}{t-w}\right),$$

$\mathtt{rsp}_0 \in (\mathbb{F}_p^n \times \mathbb{F}_z^m)^{t-w}$, and $\mathtt{rsp}_1 \in (\{0,1\}^\lambda)^{t-w}$.

Verify. Given a public key $\mathtt{pk} = (\mathtt{seed}_{\mathtt{pk}}, s)$, a message `msg`, and a signature $\mathtt{sig} = (\mathtt{salt}||d_{01}||d_b||\mathtt{MerkleProofs}||\mathtt{SeedPath}||\mathtt{rsp}_0||\mathtt{rsp}_1)$, the verification algorithm is shown in Fig. 4.

S-CEO. Given a public key $\mathtt{pk} = (\mathtt{seed}_{\mathtt{pk}}, s)$, a message `msg`, and a signature `sig` such that $\mathtt{Verify}(\mathtt{pk}, \mathtt{msg}, \mathtt{sig}) = 1$, we need to find a different public key $\overline{\mathtt{pk}} = (\mathtt{seed}_{\overline{\mathtt{pk}}}, \overline{s})$ such that $\mathtt{Verify}(\overline{\mathtt{pk}}, \mathtt{msg}, \mathtt{sig}) = 1$. Note that for $b[i] = 0$, the values t_i are computed as $x_i H^\top - \beta[i]s$, then hashed to $\mathtt{cmt}_0[i]$.

First, one sees that a change in the t_i leads to a change of $\mathtt{cmt}_0[i]$, consequently a change in d_0' and d_{01}', hence finally an invalid signature. Here, we use that changing the values in the Merkle tree results in another root, as long as the hash function is collision-resistant. Thus, any change of the public key that results in a change in any of the t_i will not be accepted in the verification.

Verify(pk, msg, sig)

$(\texttt{seed}_{\text{pk}}, s) \leftarrow \texttt{pk}$
$(\texttt{salt}, d_{01}, d_b, \texttt{MerkleProofs}, \texttt{SeedPath}, \texttt{rsp}_0, \texttt{rsp}_1) \leftarrow \texttt{sig}$
$H, M_G \leftarrow \text{PRNG}(\texttt{seed}_{\text{pk}})$ // $H \in \mathbb{F}_p^{(n-k)\times k},\ M_G \in \mathbb{F}_z^{m\times n}$
$\beta \leftarrow \text{PRNG}(\texttt{H}(\texttt{H}(\texttt{msg})||d_{01}||\texttt{salt}))$ // $\beta \in (\mathbb{F}_p^*)^t$
$b \leftarrow \text{PRNG}(d_b)$ // $b \in \{0,1\}^t$ with hamming weight w
$(\texttt{seed}_0, \ldots, \texttt{seed}_{t-1}) \leftarrow \texttt{RebuildSeedTreeLeaves}(\texttt{SeedPath}, b, \texttt{salt})$
$j \leftarrow 0$
for $i = 0, \ldots, t-1$ **do**
  if $b[i] = 1$
    $(\texttt{cmt}_1[i], y_i) \leftarrow F_{b1}(\texttt{seed}_i, \texttt{salt}, M_G, \beta[i], i)$
  else
    $(\texttt{cmt}_0[i], \texttt{cmt}_1[i], y_i) \leftarrow F_{b0}(\texttt{rsp}_0[j], \texttt{rsp}_1[j], M_G, H, \beta[i], s, \texttt{salt}, i, j)$
    $j \leftarrow j + 1$
$d_0' \leftarrow \texttt{RecomputeMerkleRoot}(\texttt{cmt}_0, \texttt{MerkleProofs}, b)$
$d_1' \leftarrow \texttt{H}(\texttt{cmt}_1[i], \ldots, \texttt{cmt}_1[t-1]),\ d_{01}' = \texttt{H}(d_0'||d_1'),\ d_b' = \texttt{H}(y_0||\ldots||y_{t-1})$
if $(d_{01} = d_{01}' \wedge d_b = d_b')$
  return 1
return 0

$F_{b1}(\texttt{seed}_i, \texttt{salt}, M_G, \beta[i], i)$

$\texttt{cmt}_1[i] \leftarrow \texttt{H}(\texttt{seed}_i||\texttt{salt}||i)$
$(u_i, \xi_i) \leftarrow \text{PRNG}(\texttt{seed}_i)$
// $u_i \in \mathbb{F}_p^n, \xi_i \in \mathbb{F}_z^m$
$\eta_i \leftarrow \xi_i M_G$
$e_i \leftarrow (g^{\eta_i[1]}, \ldots, g^{\eta_i[n]})$
return $(\texttt{cmt}_1[i], y_i = u_i + \beta[i]e_i)$

$F_{b0}(\texttt{rsp}_0[j], \texttt{rsp}_1[j], M_G, H, \beta[i], s, \texttt{salt}, i, j)$

$(y_i, \delta_i) \leftarrow \texttt{rsp}_0[j]$ // $(y_i, \delta_i) \in \mathbb{F}_p^n \times \mathbb{F}_z^m$
verify $\delta_i \in G$
$\sigma_i \leftarrow \delta_i M_G$
$v_i \leftarrow (g^{\sigma_i[1]}, \ldots, g^{\sigma_i[n]})$
$x_i \leftarrow v_i \star y_i$ // component-wise multiplication
$t_i = x_i H^\top - \beta[i]s$
$\texttt{cmt}_0[i] = \texttt{H}(t_i||\delta_i||\texttt{salt}||i)$
$\texttt{cmt}_1[i] = \texttt{rsp}_1[j]$
return $(\texttt{cmt}_0[i], \texttt{cmt}_1[i], y_i)$

Fig. 4. The verification algorithm of CROSS. Note that the PRNG generation of H, M_G, u_i and ξ_i is depicted in a simplified fashion; further observe that `RecomputeMerkleRoot` only needs the subset $\{\texttt{cmt}_0[i] \mid i \text{ s.t. } b[i] = 0\}$ of commitments. We do not provide definitions for functions that are not relevant for the BUFF analysis.

Hence, we have to find $\texttt{pk} = (\texttt{seed}_{\text{pk}}, s) \neq (\overline{\texttt{seed}_{\text{pk}}}, \overline{s}) = \overline{\texttt{pk}}$ such that $\overline{t}_i = t_i$ holds for all i with $b[i] = 0$. Note that we can assume that b has roughly $t/2$ bits equal to 0 as it is generated with the PRNG. Then the problem corresponds to solving the system $t_i = \overline{x}_i\overline{H}^\top - \beta[i]\overline{s}$ of $t/2$ random equations in the single indeterminate $\overline{s}$. If we choose $\texttt{seed}_{\overline{\texttt{pk}}} = \texttt{seed}_{\texttt{pk}}$, we have $\overline{H} = H$ and $\overline{x}_i = x_i$, thus there is no other solution than s. If we choose $\texttt{seed}_{\overline{\texttt{pk}}} \neq \texttt{seed}_{\texttt{pk}}$, we obtain a different pseudorandom matrix $\overline{H} \neq H$ and vector $\overline{x}_i \neq x_i$ and the probability that the resulting system is solvable is $\left(1/p^{n-k}\right)^{t/2}$. For all parameter sets of CROSS, this is less than $2^{-20\,000}$. Therefore, CROSS fulfills S-CEO security.

S-DEO. Given a public key pk, a message msg, and a signature sig such that Verify(pk, msg, sig) = 1, we need to find a second public key $\overline{\texttt{pk}} \neq \texttt{pk}$ and a second message $\overline{\texttt{msg}} \neq \texttt{msg}$ such that $\texttt{Verify}(\overline{\texttt{pk}}, \overline{\texttt{msg}}, \texttt{sig}) = 1$. Here, the same argument as in the S-CEO analysis is applicable. Even though the message can be changed, this brings no advantage to an adversary as it is directly hashed, so that the value of $\overline{\beta}$ cannot be controlled. Thus, the situation is again that $\overline{s}$ needs to be chosen such that $\overline{s} = (\overline{x}_i \overline{H}^{\top} - t_i) \cdot \overline{\beta}[i]^{-1}$ holds for all i with $b[i] = 0$. With the same argument as above, this implies that CROSS is S-DEO-secure.

MBS. One needs to find a public key pk, two distinct messages $\overline{\texttt{msg}} \neq \texttt{msg}$, and a signature sig, such that Verify(pk, msg, sig) = 1 and $\texttt{Verify}(\texttt{pk}, \overline{\texttt{msg}}, \texttt{sig}) = 1$. For different messages, but the same signature and public key, only the values for β differ in the computation of t_i for i such that $b[i] = 0$. This implies $\overline{t_i} \neq t_i$ and hence the verification fails, as long as the hash function is collision-resistant. Therefore, MBS security is given.

wNR. Given a public key pk and a signature sig to an unknown message msg, one has to find another public key $\overline{\texttt{pk}} \neq \texttt{pk}$, and a signature $\overline{\texttt{sig}}$ such that $\texttt{Verify}(\overline{\texttt{pk}}, \texttt{msg}, \overline{\texttt{sig}}) = 1$. For unknown messages, the values of β are also unknown. Thus, even though the public key and signature can be chosen freely, an attacker cannot know what to set them to, making this problem as hard as a random search of two hash values, each of size at least 256 bits, depending on the security level. Hence, the success probability is at most 2^{-512}. We conclude that CROSS is wNR-secure.

3.2 MEDS

MEDS is a signature scheme based on the difficulty of finding equivalences of matrix codes in the rank metric. It is constructed from a zero-knowledge identification protocol and involves a technique to increase the soundness and thereby reduce the signature size. The protocol uses integers m, n, s, t, a prime power q, and the field $\mathbb{F}_q$ with q elements. The hash function H maps to $\{0, \ldots, s\}^t$, its entries are denoted h_i. The standard form of a code is the unique generator matrix in row-reduced echelon form.

Key Pair. The public key consists of matrices $G_0, \ldots, G_s \in \mathbb{F}_q^{k \times nm}$, all in standard form. For $i = 0, \ldots, s$, let C_i denote the code generated by G_i. The secret key consists of code equivalence maps $\pi_{A_i,B_i} : C_0 \to C_i$ for $i = 1, \ldots, s$, where A_i and B_i are square matrices of the appropriate sizes. It holds that G_i is the standard form of $A_i G_0 B_i$.

Signature. The signature of a message $\mathtt{msg}$ to a public key $(G_0, \ldots, G_s)$ consists of (h, π_{i,h_i}), where $h = \mathtt{H}(\tilde{G}_0, \ldots, \tilde{G}_t, \mathtt{msg}) \in \{0,1\}^t$, and $\pi_{i,h_i} : G_{h_i} \to \tilde{G}_i$ are code equivalences, for $i = 1, \ldots, t$. The matrices $\tilde{G}_i$ are constructed as $\tilde{A}_i G_0 \tilde{B}_i$ using random matrices $\tilde{A}_i$ and $\tilde{B}_i$, for $i = 1, \ldots, t$.

Verify. The verification algorithm computes $\tilde{G}_i$ using $\pi_{i,h_i} G_{h_i}$ and checks if $h = \mathtt{H}(\tilde{G}_1, \ldots, \tilde{G}_t, \mathtt{msg})$ holds.

S-CEO. Let $(G_j)_j$ be a public key and $\mathtt{msg}$ be a message with signature $\mathtt{sig} = (h, \pi_{i,h_i})$. Fix an index i and set $j = h_i$. Then, $\pi_{i,h_i} G_j$ and $\tilde{G}_i$ define the same code. Thus, if $(G'_j)_j$ would be another public key accepting the same signature for the message $\mathtt{msg}$, we find that $\pi_{i,h_i}^{-1} \tilde{G}_i$ and G'_j both define the same code as G_j. Hence, $G_j = G'_j$ by normalization. Thus, a message-signature pair cannot be attacked if the following assumption holds: For each j there is an index i such that $h_i = j$. Conversely, suppose j^* is an index such that $h_i \neq j^*$ for all i. Then we may pick an arbitrary G'_{j^*} different from G_{j^*}, while setting $G'_j = G_j$ for all $j \neq j^*$. As G_{j^*} or G'_{j^*} are not used, the verification succeeds. If an index j^* exists, the new public key is constructed in constant time.

We conclude that a message-signature pair is vulnerable to an S-CEO attack, if and only if for the corresponding h there is such an index j which is not one of the components of h. Assuming that h is uniformly random, this translates to picking uniformly maps $\{1, \ldots, t\} \to \{0, \ldots, s-1\}$ which are non-surjective.

As any such choice depends on a query to a signature oracle, we bound the number of queries by 2^{64}, cf. [29, Section 4.B.2]. We say a parameter set is vulnerable against an S-CEO attacker if, with less than 2^{64} queries, the probability of finding a non-surjective mapping exceeds 50%. Conversely, we declare a parameter set to be secure if, after 2^{64} queries, the probability of finding a non-surjective map is still negligible.

To compute these probabilities, we define A_ℓ as the event that after ℓ queries, no non-surjective map has been found. It is easy to see that

$$1 - \left(1 - \left(\frac{s-1}{s}\right)^t\right)^\ell \leq \mathbb{P}(A_\ell) \leq 1 - \left(1 - s\left(\frac{s-1}{s}\right)^t\right)^\ell .$$

Using standard formulas and approximations for logarithm, we find that for

$$q \approx \frac{\log(2)}{\left(\frac{s-1}{s}\right)^t},$$

the probability of finding non-surjective maps exceeds $\frac{1}{2}$. As can be seen in Table 2, this shows that all but two parameter sets of MEDS are vulnerable to attacks. For the remaining two parameter sets, we can use the upper bound

$$\mathbb{P}(A_{2^\lambda}) \leq 2^\lambda s \left(\frac{s-1}{s}\right)^t,$$

which is valid if $s\left(\frac{s-1}{s}\right)^t$ is sufficiently small. The bounds are given in the final row of Table 2.

Table 2. The third row denotes the number of queries q such that the attack probability is above 50%. The probability in the final row denotes the chance of finding a message-signature pair that is vulnerable after 2^{64} queries.

Security Level	I	I	III	III	V	V
s	4	5	4	5	5	6
t	1152	192	608	160	192	112
Lower bound $\log_2(q)$	477	61	251	50	61	28
Success probability after 2^{64} queries	2^{-412}	≈ 1	2^{-186}	≈ 1	≈ 1	≈ 1

S-DEO. MEDS satisfies S-DEO as any change in the message yields a change in the hash h that is part of the signature, unless a collision of the hash is found.

MBS. MEDS satisfies MBS security trivially, if the hash function is collision-resistant, as distinct messages yield distinct hashes, contained in the signature.

wNR. MEDS does not satisfy wNR security. Indeed, given a public key $(G_i)_i$ and a signature $(h, (\pi_{i,h_i}))$ that verify an unknown message $\texttt{msg}$, we can adapt the public key and the signature as follows. Pick arbitrary matrices $\overline{A}, \overline{B}$ of the correct size, apply to G_1 the transformation $\pi_{\overline{A},\overline{B}}$, and update this new generator matrix $\overline{G}_1$ as the first component in the public key. For each i such that $h_i = 1$, modify the function $\pi_{i,1}$ to $\pi_{i,1} \circ \pi^{-1}_{\overline{A},\overline{B}}$. The verification will succeed, as by construction, $\pi_{i,1} \circ \pi^{-1}_{\overline{A},\overline{B}} \overline{G}_1 = \pi_{i,1} G_1 = \tilde{G}_i$. Note that h in the signature is unchanged.

Remark 3. The signature scheme MEDS would additionally satisfy wNR, if in the signing process, h would be redefined as $h := \texttt{H}(\tilde{G}_1, \ldots, \tilde{G}_t, \texttt{msg}, \texttt{pk})$, which corresponds to an application of PS-3. Indeed, as h itself is part of the signature, this change can be viewed as applying the BUFF transform to MEDS, making it secure against all BUFF notions.

3.3 LESS

LESS is, like MEDS, a signature scheme that relies on the code-equivalence problem and is based on a zero-knowledge identification protocol. Due to the strong similarity with MEDS, we do not provide all details. In short, LESS does not satisfy wNR, but satisfies S-DEO and MBS. Like in the analysis of MEDS, S-CEO security depends on the parameter set. The detailed results can be found in Table 3. Note that the second parameter set requires fewer queries than the security parameter and after 2^{64} queries, the success probability of an attack is 2^{-35}. While 2^{100} signature queries are too many, this parameter set seems to be an edge case which we cannot safely declare to be secure. Adding the public key in the hash computation makes LESS BUFF secure, as this is essentially the BUFF transform.

Table 3. The third row denotes the number of queries q such that the attack probability is above 50%. The probability in the final row denotes the chance of finding a message-signature pair that is vulnerable after 2^{64} queries.

Security Level	I	I	I	III	III	V	V
s	2	4	8	2	3	2	3
t	247	244	198	759	895	1352	907
Lower bound $\log_2(q)$	246	100	37	758	523	inf	530
Success probability after 2^{64} queries	2^{-182}	2^{-35}	≈ 1	2^{-694}	2^{-457}	≈ 0	2^{-464}

3.4 WAVE

WAVE is a code-based signature scheme using the Hamming weight over the field $\mathbb{F}_3$. The security of WAVE relies on the syndrome decoding problem and a scheme-specific problem regarding the indistinguishability of the public key.

The Hamming weight of a vector over $\mathbb{F}_3$ is denoted $|\_|$. WAVE uses integer parameters n and k, which are the length and dimension of the codes, and ω, a target Hamming weight.

Key Pair. The public key is a matrix $M = M(R) \in \mathbb{F}_3^{k\times(n-k)}$, where $R \in \mathbb{F}_3^{(n-k)\times k}$ is a matrix and $M(R)$ is defined row-wise by

$$\begin{aligned} \mathsf{row}(M, 2i) &= \mathsf{col}(R, 2i) + \mathsf{col}(R, 2i+1) \\ \mathsf{row}(M, 2i+1) &= \mathsf{col}(R, 2i) - \mathsf{col}(R, 2i+1), \end{aligned}$$

for $0 \le i < \frac{k-1}{2}$, and if k is odd, then $\mathsf{row}(M, k-1) = -\mathsf{col}(R, k-1)$.

Signature. A signature $\mathtt{sig} = (\mathtt{salt}, s)$ consists of an element $s \in \mathbb{F}_3^k$ and a random value $\mathtt{salt}$. It defines a valid signature for a message $\mathtt{msg}$ and the public key $M = M(R)$, if and only if

$$|s| + |\mathtt{H}(\mathtt{msg}||\mathtt{salt}) + Rs| = \omega, \tag{1}$$

where $\mathtt{H}$ is a hash function that maps to $\mathbb{F}_3^{n-k}$.

Verify. The verification algorithm checks whether Eq. (1) holds.

S-CEO. Given a public key $M = M(R)$, any message $\mathtt{msg}$, and a signature $\mathtt{sig} = (\mathtt{salt}, s)$, we pick a matrix $\overline{R}$ such that $\overline{R}s = Rs$ but $\overline{R} \neq R$, for instance by extending s to a basis and defining $\overline{R}$ on the other basis vectors randomly. Then, Eq. (1) holds trivially with $\overline{R}$. Setting $\overline{M} = M(\overline{R})$ yields the new public key.

S-DEO. Given a public key $M = M(R)$, any message $\texttt{msg}$, and a signature $\texttt{sig} = (\texttt{salt}, s)$, we randomly pick a new message $\overline{\texttt{msg}} \neq \texttt{msg}$ and compute $\overline{\texttt{h}} := \texttt{H}(\overline{\texttt{msg}}||\texttt{salt})$. We pick a vector $t \in \mathbb{F}_3^{n-k}$ such that $|\overline{\texttt{h}} - t| = \omega - |s| =: \omega_s$, which can be done by choosing a random t' with hamming weight ω_s and setting $t = \overline{\texttt{h}} - t'$. Then we choose $\overline{R}$ such that $\overline{R}s = t$ and set $\overline{M} = M(\overline{R})$. We find that Eq. (1) is satisfied, indeed, $|s| + |\overline{\texttt{h}} - \overline{R}s| = |s| + |t'| = \omega$.

MBS. The MBS security of WAVE can be attacked as follows. First, we pick random messages $\texttt{msg} \neq \overline{\texttt{msg}}$, and a random $\texttt{salt}$. We compute $h = \texttt{H}(\texttt{msg}||\texttt{salt})$ and $\overline{h} = \texttt{H}(\overline{\texttt{msg}}||\texttt{salt})$. Then we need to find $t \in \mathbb{F}_3^{n-k}$, such that

$$\omega' := |h - t| = |\overline{h} - t| < \omega.$$

Indeed, if we have found such a t, we define s such that $|s| = \omega - \omega'$ and R such that $Rs = t$. Then, both messages are verified with the signature $\texttt{sig} = (\texttt{salt}, s)$ under the public key $M = M(R)$, as Eq. (1) is satisfied for both.

A simple but tedious combinatorial construction shows that such a t can be found in almost all cases.[3]

wNR. The attack against the S-CEO security of WAVE applies to wNR, as no information about the message is required.

Remark 4. For WAVE, we can show that applying the PS-3 transform *does not suffice* to achieve full BUFF security. Let us suppose that the value h in the signature is set to $\texttt{H}(\texttt{msg}||\texttt{pk}||\texttt{salt})$, and a signature $(\texttt{salt}, s)$ is valid, if Eq. (1) holds with this h. Then, the resulting signature scheme is not MBS secure. Indeed, we begin by picking a matrix R from which pk is deduced and for which we know an efficient decoding algorithm $\mathcal{G}$. We set $\texttt{salt}$ randomly. We pick random messages $\texttt{msg}$ and $\overline{\texttt{msg}}$ and compute $\texttt{h} = \texttt{H}(\texttt{msg}||\texttt{pk}||\texttt{salt})$ and $\overline{\texttt{h}}(\overline{\texttt{msg}}||\texttt{pk}||\texttt{salt})$. As in the attack against MBS security for the original WAVE scheme, we can find t such that $\omega' := |\texttt{h} - t| = |\overline{\texttt{h}} - t|$. We set $d = \omega - \omega'$ and run $\mathcal{G}$ with target vector t and Hamming weight d to obtain s. Then, $\texttt{sig} = (\texttt{salt}, s)$ is a valid signature for both $\texttt{msg}$ and $\overline{\texttt{msg}}$ under the public key pk.

Despite this, the PS-3-transformed version of WAVE does satisfy S-CEO, S-DEO, and wNR.

4 Isogeny-Based Schemes

In this section, we analyze the BUFF security of SQISIGN [10], the sole isogeny-based signature scheme submitted to the NIST standardization process. We first give some background and notation that we require for the analysis.

[3] A Python script is provided online.

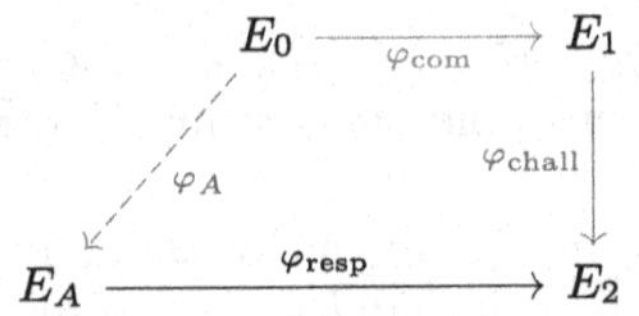

Fig. 5. The SQISIGN protocol with three phases: commitment φ_{com}, challenge φ_{chall}, and response φ_{resp}.

Background and Notation. For elliptic curves E, E' over a finite field $\mathbb{F}_q$, an isogeny is a non-constant morphism $\varphi : E \to E'$ such that $\varphi(\infty_E) = \infty_{E'}$ for the respective points at infinity on E resp. E'. A subgroup G of order m uniquely (up to composition with isomorphisms) determines an isogeny $\varphi : E \to E/G$, where the kernel $\ker(\varphi) = G$ and the degree of φ is m. Such a subgroup can be described by a single point $K \in E$ of order m, i.e., $G = \langle K \rangle$. SQISIGN uses a compressed representation of subgroups: Given a deterministic basis (P, Q) of the m-torsion subgroup $E[m]$, we can represent a suitable point as $K = P + [s]Q$ or $K = [s]P + Q$ for an $s \in \mathbb{Z}/m\mathbb{Z}$. Hence, given s and a decision bit $b \in \{0, 1\}$, we can compute $K = P + [s]Q$, where b indicates whether P and Q need to swapped prior to computing K. All occurring values s and b (with indices) will be of this form, and we refer to this computation as $\texttt{Decompress}_{P,Q}(s, b)$, where b can be omitted if no point swap is necessary. Each isogeny $\varphi : E \to E'$ has a unique dual isogeny $\widehat{\varphi} : E' \to E$ such that the composition $\widehat{\varphi} \circ \varphi$ resp. $\varphi \circ \widehat{\varphi}$ is the multiplication-by-m map on E resp. E'. We will only use supersingular curves E over $\mathbb{F}_{p^2}$ for a large prime p.

4.1 SQIsign

SQISIGN applies the Fiat-Shamir transform to an identification protocol based on isogenies. Following Fig. 5, we define a public starting curve E_0, and the prover computes a secret isogeny $\varphi_A : E_0 \to E_A$, where E_A is published. The prover commits to the codomain E_1 of the commitment isogeny $\varphi_{com} : E_0 \to E_1$, followed by the challenger providing a challenge isogeny $\varphi_{chall} : E_1 \to E_2$. The prover answers with an isogeny $\varphi_{resp} : E_A \to E_2$. For the computation and the zero-knowledge property of φ_{resp} we refer to the SQISIGN specification [10]. The standard Fiat-Shamir transform turns this protocol into a non-interactive signature scheme. We note that, due to the exponentially large challenge space, a single round of the protocol suffices.

Key Pair. For a fixed supersingular curve E_0 over $\mathbb{F}_{p^2}$ of known endomorphism ring, a secret key is an isogeny $\varphi_A : E_0 \to E_A$. The public key is given by E_A.

Signature. A signature consists of compressed descriptions of the isogenies φ_{resp} and φ_{chall}. For fixed positive integers e, f, g, n with $e = nf$ it is of the form

$$\texttt{sig} = (b, s^{(1)}, \ldots, s^{(n)}, r, b_2, s_2, b_3, s_3),$$

Verify(pk, msg, sig)

$(b, s^{(1)}, \ldots, s^{(n)}, r, b_2, s_2, b_3, s_3) \leftarrow \texttt{sig}$
$E^{(1)} \leftarrow \texttt{pk}$
$(P^{(1)}, Q^{(1)}) \leftarrow \texttt{FindBasis}_{2^f}(E^{(1)})$
$K^{(1)} \leftarrow \texttt{Decompress}_{P^{(1)},Q^{(1)}}(s^{(1)}, b)$
for $j = 1, \ldots, n-1$ **do**
  $\varphi^{(j)} : E^{(j)} \rightarrow E^{(j+1)} = E/\langle K^{(j)} \rangle$
  $Q^{(j+1)} \leftarrow \varphi^{(j)}(Q^{(j)})$
  $P^{(j+1)} \leftarrow \texttt{CompleteBasis}_{2^f}(E^{(j+1)}, Q^{(j+1)})$
  $K^{(j+1)} \leftarrow \texttt{Decompress}_{P^{(j+1)},Q^{(j+1)}}(s^{(j+1)})$
$\varphi^{(n)} : E^{(n)} \rightarrow E^{(n+1)} = E/\langle K^{(n)} \rangle$
$Q', E_1 = \texttt{Decompress-}$
  $\texttt{Challenge}(E^{(n+1)}, b_2, s_2, b_3, s_3)$
if $[r]Q' = \mathcal{H}(\texttt{msg}, E_1)$
  return 1
return 0

Fig. 6. Verification algorithm of SQISIGN.

where $b, b_2, b_3 \in \{0,1\}$, $s^{(j)}, s_2 \in \mathbb{Z}/2^f\mathbb{Z}$, $s_3 \in \mathbb{Z}/3^g\mathbb{Z}$, and $r \in \mathbb{Z}/2^f3^g\mathbb{Z}$, following the notation from [13].

Verify. The verification algorithm, described in Fig. 6, consists of three parts. The most relevant part for the following discussion is the recomputation of $\varphi_{\text{resp}} : E_A \rightarrow E_2$ through a chain of n isogenies $\varphi^{(j)}$ of degree 2^f. Each isogeny $\varphi^{(j)}$ is determined by a kernel generator $K^{(j)}$. We compute these $K^{(j)}$ by deterministically sampling a basis $(P^{(j)}, Q^{(j)})$ of $E^{(j)}[2^f]$ through `FindBasis` if no point is given resp. `CompleteBasis` if $Q^{(j)}$ is given, and running `Decompress` with input $s^{(j)}$ (and b for $j = 1$). In particular, for $j > 1$, only $P^{(j)}$ is sampled, while we get $Q^{(j)} = \varphi^{(j-1)}(Q^{(j-1)})$, such that $Q^{(j)}$ generates the kernel of the dual isogenies $\widehat{\varphi^{(j-1)}}$. Therefore, we compute φ_{resp} through the following chain:

$$E_A = E^{(1)} \xrightarrow{\varphi^{(1)}} E^{(2)} \xrightarrow{\varphi^{(2)}} E^{(3)} \xrightarrow{\varphi^{(3)}} \cdots \xrightarrow{\varphi^{(n)}} E^{(n+1)} = E_2$$

In the second step, summarized in `DecompressChallenge`, we recompute the dual $\widehat{\varphi_{\text{chall}}} : E_2 \rightarrow E_1$ of order $D_{\text{chall}} = 2^f 3^g$ using `FindBasis` and `Decompress` with input (b_2, s_2, b_3, s_3). For a deterministically sampled point $Q'' \in E_2$ of order D_{chall} that is linearly independent of $\ker(\widehat{\varphi_{\text{chall}}})$, it computes $Q' \leftarrow \widehat{\varphi_{\text{chall}}}(Q'')$. Furthermore, this function verifies that the composition $\widehat{\varphi_{\text{chall}}} \circ \varphi_{\text{resp}}$ is cyclic.

The final step verifies that $[r]Q'$ corresponds to the kernel generator of the challenge isogeny, i.e. $[r]Q' = \mathcal{H}(\texttt{msg}, E_1)$. The function $\mathcal{H}$ is defined to first compute $a = \texttt{H}(\texttt{msg}, j(E_1)) \in \mathbb{Z}/D_{\text{chall}}\mathbb{Z}$ for a hash function H and the j-invariant $j(E_1)$, and output $R_1 + [a]S_1$ with a deterministic basis (R_1, S_1) of $E_1[D_{\text{chall}}]$.

S-CEO. Let sig be a valid signature for $\texttt{pk} = E_A$ and msg, i.e., Verify(pk, msg, sig) $= 1$. Our aim is to construct a public key $\overline{\texttt{pk}} = E_{A'} \neq E_A$ such that $\texttt{Verify}(\overline{\texttt{pk}}, \texttt{msg}, \texttt{sig}) = 1$. This amounts to finding $E_{A'}$ for which the compression in sig describes an isogeny $\psi_{\text{resp}} : E_{A'} \rightarrow E_2$ that has the same codomain E_2.

In this case, the second and third step of the verification are the same as when running `Verify(pk, msg, sig)`.

A naive way to find such a $E_{A'}$ is to compute random 2^e-isogenies $\psi' : E_2 \to E_{A'}$ and check if $(b, s^{(1)}, \ldots, s^{(n)})$ generates an isogeny $\psi_{\text{resp}} : E_{A'} \to E_2$ mapping to the correct E_2. However, the fact that we know several curves on the path between E_A and E_2 from `sig` allows for an easier S-CEO attack as follows:

1. Find $\widetilde{\psi}^{(1)} : E^{(2)} \to E_{A'}$ of degree 2^f with `FindBasis` and `Decompress`$(s^{(1)}, b)$ generating the 2^f-isogeny $\psi^{(1)} : E_{A'} \to E^{(2)}$ with the desired codomain.
2. Ensure that the following 2^f-isogenies satisfy $\psi^{(j)} = \varphi^{(j)}$ for $j > 1$, and hence ψ_{resp} maps to E_2.

Explicitly generating $E_{A'}$ in the first step seems infeasible, hence we resort to a search approach, going through all 2^f suitable isogenies $\widetilde{\psi}$. We require that the deterministic basis $(\widetilde{P}, \widetilde{Q})$ of $E_{A'}[2^f]$ and $b, s^{(1)} \in$ `sig` construct a suitable kernel generator $\widetilde{K}$ such that $\psi^{(1)} : E_{A'} \to E_{A'}/\langle \widetilde{K} \rangle = E^{(2)}$. Since there are $3 \cdot 2^{f-1}$ isogenies of degree 2^f starting from $E_{A'}$ and `sig` determines exactly one of these, the success probability for this step, given `sig`, is $1/(3 \cdot 2^{f-1})$. Thus, we can expect to find a suitable curve $E_{A'}$ with a probability of roughly 50%.

Assuming we found a suitable $E_{A'}$, we obtain a basis $(P^{(2)}, \widetilde{Q}^{(2)})$ of $E^{(2)}[2^f]$, where $\widetilde{Q}^{(2)} = \psi^{(1)}(\widetilde{Q})$. In contrast, a verification starting from E_A obtains the basis $(P^{(2)}, Q^{(2)})$ with the same sampled point $P^{(2)}$, but $Q^{(2)} = \varphi^{(1)}(Q^{(1)})$. Since the dual isogenies of $\varphi^{(1)}$ and $\psi^{(1)}$ are not equal, we have $\widetilde{Q}^{(2)} \notin \langle Q^{(2)} \rangle$. For the second attack step, we require for $j > 1$ that

$$\langle P^{(j)} + [s^{(j)}]Q^{(j)} \rangle = \langle P^{(j)} + [s^{(j)}]\widetilde{Q}^{(j)} \rangle.$$

All following steps trivially succeed if $s^{(j)} = 0$ for all $j > 1$. Furthermore, if $[2^k]Q^{(2)} = [2^k]\widetilde{Q}^{(2)}$ for $0 < k < f$, we succeed if $s^{(j)} \equiv 0 \mod 2^k$ for all $j > 1$. Even though the attack can only succeed if the signature values $s^{(j)}$ for $j > 1$ have a very special shape, it appears infeasible to enumerate all such possibilities, and compute an explicit success probability.

Instead, we implemented this attack using the AprèsSQI software [13], which closely follows the NIST submission of SQIsign.[4] For reduced parameters that allow feasible running times, i.e., a 36-bit prime p and $f \in \{7, 8, 9, 10\}$, our implementation suggests that the probability of a given $(s^{(1)}, \ldots, s^{(n)})$ to be vulnerable to this attack is below 2^{-f}. If we conjecture that this behavior scales to the SQIsign parameter sizes featuring $f = 75, 97, 145$ for NIST-I/III/V, this means that for each given `sig`, the S-CEO attack has a search complexity of $O(2^f)$ and success probability of 2^{-f}. Although we can conjecture that this attack does not break S-CEO security, we emphasize that better attack avenues might exist, and our probability estimations can only be viewed as a lower bound.

Remark 5. The probability and effort for a possible attack depend on the size of f. E.g., the SQIsign variant AprèsSQI [13] proposes much larger values of f, which push the success probability below the probability of breaking EUF-CMA.

[4] The implementation is available online.

S-DEO. In contrast to S-CEO, we additionally need to find a message $\overline{\texttt{msg}} \neq \texttt{msg}$ such that $\texttt{Verify}(\overline{\texttt{pk}}, \overline{\texttt{msg}}, \texttt{sig}) = 1$. Thus, we can only repeat the S-CEO attack above if the challenge curves E_2 resp. E_2' when signing msg with pk resp. $\overline{\texttt{msg}}$ with $\overline{\texttt{pk}}$ are equal, requiring $\mathcal{H}(\texttt{msg}, E_1) = \mathcal{H}(\overline{\texttt{msg}}, E_1)$, and therefore a hash collision of H modulo D_{chall}.

If $\mathcal{H}(\texttt{msg}, E_1) \neq \mathcal{H}(\overline{\texttt{msg}}, E_1)$, i.e. $E_2' \neq E_2$, this attack is not available, hence we can only pick a random public key $\overline{\texttt{pk}}$. During verification, after recomputing ψ_{resp} and running DecompressChallenge, we end up at $E_1' \neq E_1$, such that the check $[r]Q' = \mathcal{H}(\overline{\texttt{msg}}, E_1')$ only succeeds with negligible probability $1/D_{\text{chall}}$. Therefore SQIsign is S-DEO-secure.

MBS. Assume that we have a valid signature sig for pk and msg, i.e., $\texttt{Verify}(\texttt{pk}, \texttt{msg}, \texttt{sig}) = 1$, and a message $\overline{\texttt{msg}} \neq \texttt{msg}$ such that $\texttt{Verify}(\texttt{pk}, \overline{\texttt{msg}}, \texttt{sig}) = 1$. In both verification runs, the first and second step that recompute φ_{resp} and $\widehat{\varphi_{\text{chall}}}$ are equal. In the last step, both runs compute $Q' \leftarrow \widehat{\varphi_{\text{chall}}}(Q'')$ and verify that $[r]Q' = \mathcal{H}(\texttt{msg}, E_1)$ resp. $[r]Q' = \mathcal{H}(\overline{\texttt{msg}}, E_1)$. However, if verification for msg and $\overline{\texttt{msg}}$ succeeds, we have $\texttt{H}(\texttt{msg}, j(E_1)) = \texttt{H}(\overline{\texttt{msg}}, j(E_1))$, yielding a hash collision of H modulo D_{chall}. Since this probability is negligible, SQIsign is MBS-secure.

wNR. Given a public key pk and a signature sig for an unknown message msg, an attacker has to find a public key $\overline{\texttt{pk}} \neq \texttt{pk}$ and a signature $\overline{\texttt{sig}}$ such that $\texttt{Verify}(\overline{\texttt{pk}}, \texttt{msg}, \overline{\texttt{sig}}) = 1$. To construct $\overline{\texttt{pk}}$ and $\overline{\texttt{sig}}$, we run the first step of $\texttt{Verify}(\texttt{pk}, \texttt{msg}, \texttt{sig})$ to obtain the curve E_2. We choose a random 2^f-isogeny $\widehat{\psi}^{(n)} : E_2 \to \widetilde{E}^{(n)}$ such that the composition $\varphi_{\text{chall}} \circ \widehat{\psi}^{(n)}$ is cyclic. Starting from $j = n-1$ in decreasing order, we then construct random 2^f-isogenies $\widehat{\psi}^{(j)} : \widetilde{E}^{(j+1)} \to \widetilde{E}^{(j)}$ such that the composition $\widehat{\psi} = \widehat{\psi}^{(1)} \circ \cdots \circ \widehat{\psi}^{(n)}$ is cyclic. For each of the $\widehat{\psi}^{(j)}$, we pick a point $R \in \widetilde{E}^{(j+1)}$ of order 2^f such that R is linearly independent of $\ker(\widehat{\psi}^{(j)})$. Therefore, $K^{(j)} = \widehat{\psi}^{(j)}(R)$ generates the kernel of the dual isogeny $\psi^{(j)}$ of $\widehat{\psi}^{(j)}$.

For the signature $\overline{\texttt{sig}}$ we use $\psi_{\text{resp}} = \psi^{(n)} \circ \cdots \circ \psi^{(1)}$ and the public key $\overline{\texttt{pk}} = E_{A'} = \widetilde{E}^{(1)}$. For a valid signature the kernel generator points $K^{(j)}$ have to be represented in a compressed form. To compute this representation, we follow the approach of SQIsign. For the deterministic basis $(\widetilde{P}^{(1)}, \widetilde{Q}^{(1)})$ this allows us to find $\widetilde{s}^{(1)}$ to get a suitable kernel generator $\widetilde{P}^{(1)} + [\widetilde{s}^{(1)}]\widetilde{Q}^{(1)})$ for $\psi^{(1)}$, potentially swapping $\widetilde{P}^{(1)}$ and $\widetilde{Q}^{(1)}$ by setting $\widetilde{b} = 1$, and $\widetilde{b} = 0$ otherwise. The following steps proceed analogously, computing $\widetilde{s}^{(j)}$ through discrete logarithms without requiring to swap points.

Since E_2 is the codomain of ψ and $\widehat{\varphi_{\text{chall}}} \circ \psi$ is cyclic by construction, we can reuse the values r, b_2, s_2, b_3, s_3 for the second and third step of the verification of $\overline{\texttt{sig}}$. Hence, we have constructed a public key $\overline{\texttt{pk}} \neq \texttt{pk}$ and signature $\overline{\texttt{sig}} \neq \texttt{sig}$ of the form $\overline{\texttt{sig}} = (\widetilde{b}, \widetilde{s}^{(1)}, \ldots, \widetilde{s}^{(n)}, r, b_2, s_2, b_3, s_3)$ such that $\texttt{Verify}(\overline{\texttt{pk}}, \texttt{msg}, \overline{\texttt{sig}}) = 1$ without requiring knowledge of msg.

Remark 6. For SQIsign, the PS-3 transform suffices to achieve full BUFF security. In this case, the signer computes the challenge generator through

$\mathcal{H}(\texttt{msg}, \texttt{pk}, E_1)$, which uses the hash value $a = \texttt{H}(\texttt{msg}, \texttt{pk}, j(E_1)) \in \mathbb{Z}/D_{\text{chall}}\mathbb{Z}$ as described above. This means that $r \in \texttt{sig}$, which satisfies $[r]Q' = \mathcal{H}(\texttt{msg}, \texttt{pk}, E_1)$ for a deterministic point Q', can be viewed as an encoding of the hash value $\texttt{H}(\texttt{msg}, \texttt{pk}, j(E_1))$, resembling the BUFF transform.

In this case, the problem to solve S-CEO is equivalent to the description of C-DEO above. For wNR, the PS-3 transform implies that the curve E_2 in $\texttt{Verify}(\texttt{pk}, \texttt{msg}, \texttt{sig})$ is not a valid challenge curve in $\texttt{Verify}(\overline{\texttt{pk}}, \texttt{msg}, \overline{\texttt{sig}})$. Attacking wNR thus requires to pick $\overline{\texttt{pk}}, \overline{\texttt{sig}}$ and hope for $[r]Q' = \mathcal{H}(\overline{\texttt{msg}}, E_1')$ to hold for the chosen r, which has negligible success probability.

5 Lattice-Based Schemes

The lattice-based schemes we deal with in this section can be divided into two groups: Raccoon and Haetae, which are closely related to Dilithium; Hawk, HuFu, and Squirrels, which follow a GPV-like approach. For Raccoon and Haetae, we give an outline of the analysis from [14] in Sect. 5.4. The cases of Hawk (Sect. 5.1), HuFu (Sect. 5.2), and Squirrels (Sect. 5.3) are quite different, and we do a hands-on analysis. The results turn out to differ case by case. While Hawk achieves full BUFF security and HuFu only lacks wNR security, Squirrels is insecure with respect to all notions. We remark that a PS-3-transformed HuFu would satisfy all BUFF security notions. Finally, Squirrels is vulnerable even after the PS-3 transform and only the full BUFF transform could achieve all notions.

5.1 HAWK

Hawk applies a GPV-like approach. It uses module lattices and its security is based on the *One More Approximate Shortest Vector* problem [18].

Key Pair. Consider the number field $K_n = \mathbb{Q}[X]/(X^n+1)$ and its ring of integers $R_n = \mathbb{Z}[X]/(X^n + 1)$ for $m \in \mathbb{N}$ and $n = 2^m$. The secret key $\texttt{sk}$ is a matrix

$$B = \begin{pmatrix} f & F \\ g & G \end{pmatrix} \in \mathrm{GL}_2(R_n),$$

and the public key $\texttt{pk} = (q_{00}, q_{01}) \in R_n^2$ is computed from

$$Q = B^*B = \begin{pmatrix} q_{00} & q_{01} \\ q_{10} & q_{11} \end{pmatrix}.$$

The matrix Q induces the norm $\|\cdot\|_Q : K_n^2 \to \mathbb{Q},\ f \mapsto \sqrt{\frac{1}{n}\mathrm{Tr}(f^*Qf)}$. Since $Q = B^*B$, this norm fulfills $\|f\|_Q = \|Bf\|$ for all $f \in K_n^2$.

Signature. Hawk signatures consist of $\texttt{sig} = (\texttt{salt}, s_1)$ for $s_1 \in R_n$.

Verify(pk, msg, sig)

$(\mathtt{salt}, s_1) \leftarrow \mathtt{sig}$
$(q_{00}, q_{01}) \leftarrow \mathtt{pk}$
$M \leftarrow \mathtt{H}(\mathtt{msg} \| \mathtt{H}(\mathtt{pk}))$
$(h_0, h_1) \leftarrow \mathtt{H}(M \| \mathtt{salt})$
$s_0 \leftarrow \left\lfloor \frac{h_0}{2} - \frac{q_{01}}{q_{00}} \left(\frac{h_1}{2} - s_1 \right) \right\rceil$
$h \leftarrow (h_0, h_1), \ s \leftarrow (s_0, s_1)$
$w \leftarrow h - 2s$
if $\|w\|_Q \leq \vartheta$
  return 1
return 0

Fig. 7. Verification algorithm of HAWK.

Verify. Given a public key $\mathtt{pk} = (q_{00}, q_{01})$, a message $\mathtt{msg}$, and a signature $\mathtt{sig} = (\mathtt{salt}, s_1)$, the verification algorithm is shown in Fig. 7.

S-CEO. Given a public key $\mathtt{pk} = (q_{00}, q_{01})$, a message $\mathtt{msg}$, and a signature $\mathtt{sig} = (\mathtt{salt}, s_1)$ such that $\mathtt{Verify}(\mathtt{pk}, \mathtt{msg}, \mathtt{sig}) = 1$, we need to find a public key $\overline{\mathtt{pk}} \neq \mathtt{pk}$ with $\mathtt{Verify}(\overline{\mathtt{pk}}, \mathtt{msg}, \mathtt{sig}) = 1$. Assuming $\mathtt{H}$ to be a random oracle, choosing $\overline{\mathtt{pk}} \neq \mathtt{pk}$ implies $\overline{h}_1 \neq h_1$ and hence $\overline{w}_1 \neq w_1$. In order for an S-CEO attacker to be successful, $\|(0, \overline{w}_1)\|_{\overline{Q}} \leq \|(\overline{w}_0, \overline{w}_1)\|_{\overline{Q}} \leq \vartheta$ must hold. However, as $\overline{w}_1$ is random in R_n, the probability for this is negligible. Indeed, for the parameters in HAWK, a θ-ball is of size $2^{31 \cdot 3}$, while the space of possible values is (much larger than) $2^{31 \cdot 256}$. So a random value will be in a θ-ball with probability about $2^{-31 \cdot 253}$.

S-DEO. Given a public key $\mathtt{pk}$, a message $\mathtt{msg}$, and a signature $\mathtt{sig} = (\mathtt{salt}, s_1)$ such that $\mathtt{Verify}(\mathtt{pk}, \mathtt{msg}, \mathtt{sig}) = 1$, we need to find $\overline{\mathtt{pk}} \neq \mathtt{pk}$ and $\overline{\mathtt{msg}} \neq \mathtt{msg}$ with $\mathtt{Verify}(\overline{\mathtt{pk}}, \overline{\mathtt{msg}}, \mathtt{sig}) = 1$. As the message is only used in the computation of h, the analysis works completely analogously as for S-CEO.

MBS. One needs to find a public key $\mathtt{pk}$, distinct messages $\overline{\mathtt{msg}} \neq \mathtt{msg}$, and a signature $\mathtt{sig} = (\mathtt{salt}, s_1)$, s.t. $\mathtt{Verify}(\mathtt{pk}, \mathtt{m}, \mathtt{sig}) = 1$ for $\mathtt{m} \in \{\mathtt{msg}, \overline{\mathtt{msg}}\}$. Assume one can find such $\mathtt{pk}$, $\overline{\mathtt{msg}}$, $\mathtt{msg}$, and $\mathtt{sig}$. Then, by definition of the verification, $\|w\|_Q, \|\overline{w}\|_Q \leq \vartheta$ and hence $\|w - \overline{w}\|_Q \leq 2\vartheta$ hold. Using the definition of B and $s_0 = \frac{h_0}{2} - \frac{q_{01}}{q_{00}} \left(\frac{h_1}{2} - s_1 \right) + \varepsilon$ for $\varepsilon \in [-\frac{1}{2}, \frac{1}{2})$ (and the analogue for $\overline{s}_0$), we obtain

$$\|w - \overline{w}\|_Q = \|B(w - \overline{w})\| = \left\| \begin{pmatrix} f(h_0 - \overline{h}_0 - 2s_0 + 2\overline{s}_0) + F(h_1 - \overline{h}_1) \\ g(h_0 - \overline{h}_0 - 2s_0 + 2\overline{s}_0) + G(h_1 - \overline{h}_1) \end{pmatrix} \right\|$$
$$= \left\| \begin{pmatrix} (h_1 - \overline{h}_1) \left(\frac{q_{01}}{q_{00}} f - F \right) + f(\varepsilon + \overline{\varepsilon}) \\ (h_1 - \overline{h}_1) \left(\frac{q_{01}}{q_{00}} g - G \right) + g(\varepsilon + \overline{\varepsilon}) \end{pmatrix} \right\|.$$

The probability for this to be smaller than 2ϑ is negligible as $\frac{q_{01}}{q_{00}} f - F$ and $\frac{q_{01}}{q_{00}} g - G$ are fixed values, while $h_1 - \overline{h}_1$ and $\varepsilon + \overline{\varepsilon}$ are random. Hence, the advantage of any attacker against MBS-security of HAWK is similar to the S-CEO advantage.

wNR. Given a public key $\mathtt{pk}$ and a signature $\mathtt{sig} = (\mathtt{salt}, s_1)$ to an unknown message $\mathtt{msg}$, one has to find $\overline{\mathtt{pk}} \neq \mathtt{pk}$ and a signature $\overline{\mathtt{sig}} = (\overline{\text{salt}}, \overline{s}_1)$ (which may be the same as the given signature) such that $\mathtt{Verify}(\overline{\mathtt{pk}}, \mathtt{msg}, \overline{\mathtt{sig}}) = 1$. Independent of the choice of the public key $\overline{\mathtt{pk}} \neq \mathtt{pk}$, the value of $\overline{h}$ is unknown (as $\mathtt{msg}$ is) and as in the S-CEO analysis $\overline{w}_1 \neq w_1$ holds. Hence, it is infeasible to choose $\overline{s}_1$ in a way such that $\overline{w} = \overline{h} - 2\overline{s}$ is small in the $\overline{Q}$-norm. Indeed, $\overline{s}_1$ must be chosen so that $2\overline{s}$ is in the $\overline{Q}$-norm ball about $\overline{h}$, which amounts to the same probability as computed in the proof of S-CEO.

Remark 7. The HAWK specification [9] states that the design facilitates an application of the full BUFF transform. This is the case as the HAWK signature generation already computes $M = \mathtt{H}(\mathtt{msg}||\mathtt{H}(\mathtt{pk}))$, which—in the full BUFF transform—needs to be appended to the signature. In the given form, HAWK can be seen to apply the PS-3 transform, which does not in general guarantee the BUFF properties. However, our analysis shows that in the concrete case of HAWK, BUFF security is fulfilled for this weaker transform, i.e., an application of the full BUFF transform is not necessary, which avoids appending the hash value to a signature. This is especially interesting given the fact that HAWK is based on FALCON. FALCON does not use the public key to construct the target value and was proven to be S-CEO, S-DEO and wNR-insecure.

5.2 HuFu

HUFU applies the GPV approach. It uses unstructured lattices and is based on the short integer solution and learning with errors problems.

Key Pair. Consider a distribution χ over $\mathbb{Z}$, $m, n \in \mathbb{N}$, and $Q = pq$ for p, q some powers of 2. The secret key is a tuple of matrices $\mathtt{sk} = (S, E, L_{22}, L_{32}, L_{33})$ for $(S, E) \leftarrow \chi^{n\times m} \times \chi^{m\times m}$ and $L_{22} \in \mathbb{R}^{n\times n}$, $L_{32} \in \mathbb{R}^{m\times n}$, and $L_{33} \in \mathbb{R}^{m\times m}$. The public key is a pair $\mathtt{pk} = (\text{seed}_{\hat{A}}, B = p \cdot I - (\hat{A}S + E))$ for $\hat{A} \in \mathbb{Z}_Q^{m\times n}$ generated using $\text{seed}_{\hat{A}}$.

Signature. The signature $\mathtt{sig}$ of a message $\mathtt{msg}$ consists of a tuple $(\mathtt{salt}, s)$ for $s = \mathtt{Compress}(x_1, x_2)$, where $x_1 \in \mathbb{Z}^n$ and $x_2 \in \mathbb{Z}^m$.

Verify. Given a public key $\mathtt{pk} = (\text{seed}_{\hat{A}}, B)$, a message $\mathtt{msg}$, and a signature $\mathtt{sig} = (\mathtt{salt}, s)$, the verification algorithm is shown in Fig. 8.

S-CEO. Given a public key $\mathtt{pk} = (\mathtt{seed}_{\hat{A}}, B)$, a message $\mathtt{msg}$ and a signature $\mathtt{sig} = (\mathtt{salt}, s)$ such that $\mathtt{Verify}(\mathtt{pk}, \mathtt{msg}, \mathtt{sig}) = 1$, we need to find a second public key $\overline{\mathtt{pk}} = (\overline{\mathtt{seed}}_{\hat{A}}, \overline{B})$ such that $\mathtt{Verify}(\overline{\mathtt{pk}}, \mathtt{msg}, \mathtt{sig}) = 1$. We choose $\overline{\mathtt{seed}}_{\hat{A}} = \mathtt{seed}_{\hat{A}}$, which expand to the same matrix $\hat{A}$. As $(\mathtt{salt}, s)$ is a valid signature, we know that $||(x_0, x_1, x_2)|| \leq \vartheta$, where $x_0 = (u - \hat{A}x_1 - Bx_2) \mod Q$. Thus, if we find $\overline{B}$ s.t. $\overline{x_0} = x_0$, we obtain $||(\overline{x_0}, x_1, x_2)|| = ||(x_0, x_1, x_2)|| \leq \vartheta$, which shows that S-CEO security is not given. In order to construct such a $\overline{B}$, first note that we can assume that there is at least one i such that $x_{2,i} \neq 0$, as

Verify(pk, msg, sig)

$(\mathtt{salt}, s) \leftarrow \mathtt{sig}$
$(x_1, x_2) \leftarrow \mathtt{Decompress}(s)$
$(\mathtt{seed}_{\hat{A}}, B) \leftarrow \mathtt{pk}$
$u \leftarrow \mathtt{H}(\mathtt{msg}, \mathtt{salt})$
$\hat{A} \leftarrow \mathtt{XOF}(\mathtt{seed}_{\hat{A}})$
$x_0 \leftarrow (u - \hat{A}x_1 - Bx_2) \mod Q$
if $||(x_0, x_1, x_2)|| \leq \vartheta$
  return 1
return 0

Fig. 8. Verification algorithm of HuFu. Note that (x_0, x_1, x_2) denotes the vector obtained from concatenating x_0, x_1, and x_2 and $||\cdot||$ is the l_2-norm.

otherwise one can trivially choose $\overline{B} \neq B$ with the desired properties. Without loss of generality, we assume $x_{2,1} \neq 0$. Then we define $\overline{B} \neq B$ as follows: $\overline{b}_{11} = (b_{11} + x_{2,2})$, $\overline{b}_{12} = (b_{12} - x_{2,1})$, and $\overline{b}_{ij} = b_{ij}$ for all other i, j. It holds that $(\overline{B}x_2)_1 = (Bx_2)_1$. Thus $\overline{B}x_2 = Bx_2$ as only the first row differs for $\overline{B}$ and B. This implies $\overline{x_0} = x_0$.

S-DEO. Given a public key $\mathtt{pk} = (\mathtt{seed}_{\hat{A}}, B)$, a message $\mathtt{msg}$, and a signature $\mathtt{sig} = (\mathtt{salt}, s)$ s.t. $\mathtt{Verify}(\mathtt{pk}, \mathtt{msg}, \mathtt{sig}) = 1$, we need to find a second public key $\overline{\mathtt{pk}} \neq \mathtt{pk}$ and a second message $\overline{\mathtt{msg}} \neq \mathtt{msg}$ s.t. $\mathtt{Verify}(\overline{\mathtt{pk}}, \overline{\mathtt{msg}}, \mathtt{sig}) = 1$. We choose again $\overline{\mathtt{seed}}_{\hat{A}} = \mathtt{seed}_{\hat{A}}$, which yield the same matrix $\hat{A}$. Further we choose $\overline{\mathtt{msg}} \neq \mathtt{msg}$ randomly and compute u and $\overline{u}$. If we find $\overline{B}$ such that $\overline{x_0} = \overline{u} - \hat{A}x_1 - \overline{B}x_2 = 0 \mod Q$, we obtain $||(\overline{x_0}, x_1, x_2)|| \leq ||(x_0, x_1, x_2)|| \leq \vartheta$. Then, we have $\mathtt{Verify}(\overline{\mathtt{pk}}, \overline{\mathtt{msg}}, \mathtt{sig}) = 1$ for $\overline{\mathtt{pk}} = (\mathtt{seed}_{\hat{A}}, \overline{B})$, which gives an attack against S-DEO security. A matrix $\overline{B}$ such that $\overline{B}x_2 = \overline{u} - \hat{A}x_1$ can be constructed if $\gcd(x_{2,i}) = 1$.[5] As $m \geq 768$, the coefficients of $x_2 \in \mathbb{Z}^m$ are coprime with overwhelming probability given by $\zeta(m)^{-1} \approx 1$.

MBS. One needs to find a public key $\mathtt{pk} = (\mathtt{seed}_{\hat{A}}, B)$, two distinct messages $\mathtt{msg} \neq \overline{\mathtt{msg}}$, and a signature $\mathtt{sig} = (\mathtt{salt}, s)$ such that $\mathtt{Verify}(\mathtt{pk}, \mathtt{msg}, \mathtt{sig}) = 1$ and $\mathtt{Verify}(\mathtt{pk}, \overline{\mathtt{msg}}, \mathtt{sig}) = 1$. Assume, we have found $\mathtt{pk}, \mathtt{msg}, \overline{\mathtt{msg}}$, and $\mathtt{sig} = (\mathtt{salt}, s)$ with these properties. Then $||(x_0, x_1, x_2)||, ||(\overline{x_0}, x_1, x_2)|| \leq \vartheta$ and hence in particular $||x_0||, ||\overline{x_0}|| \leq \vartheta$. Observe that this implies $||u - \overline{u}|| = ||u - (\hat{A}x_1 - Bx_2) + (\hat{A}x_1 - Bx_2) - \overline{u}|| = ||x_0 - \overline{x_0}|| \leq ||x_0|| + ||\overline{x_0}|| \leq 2\vartheta$. As $u = \mathtt{H}(\mathtt{msg}, r)$ and $\overline{u} = \mathtt{H}(\overline{\mathtt{msg}}, r)$, the probability to find messages that yield u and $\overline{u}$ which are close to each other is negligible (near-collision resistance of the hash function).[6]

wNR. Given a public key $\mathtt{pk} = (\mathtt{seed}_{\hat{A}}, B)$ and a signature $\mathtt{sig} = (\mathtt{salt}, s)$ to an unknown message $\mathtt{msg}$, one has to find another public key $\overline{\mathtt{pk}} \neq \mathtt{pk}$, and a signature $\overline{\mathtt{sig}} = (\overline{\mathtt{salt}}, \overline{s})$ such that $\mathtt{Verify}(\overline{\mathtt{pk}}, \mathtt{msg}, \overline{\mathtt{sig}}) = 1$. To do this, we can

[5] If $\gcd(x_{2,i}) = 1$, then $\langle x_2 \rangle$ is saturated. Equivalently, $\mathbb{Z}^m/\langle x_2 \rangle$ is free, hence x_2 is part of a basis, on which $\overline{B}$ can be defined according to the requirement.

[6] Near-collision resistance is a stronger form of collision resistance, where it is even hard to find inputs whose hash values are close (with respect to some norm).

Verify(pk, msg, sig)

1 : (salt, s) ← sig	5 : **if** $c_n = \sum_{i=1}^{n-1} v_i \cdot c_i \mod p \quad \forall p \in P_\Delta$
2 : $h \leftarrow$ H(msg‖salt)	6 : **if** $\|s'\|^2 \leq \lfloor \vartheta^2 \rfloor$
3 : $s' \leftarrow$ Decompress(s)	7 : **return** 1
4 : $c \leftarrow s' + h$	8 : **return** 0

Fig. 9. Verification algorithm of SQUIRRELS.

proceed exactly as we did for S-CEO. Note that for the attack it is not necessary to know the message and we can choose $\overline{\texttt{sig}} = (\overline{\texttt{salt}}, \bar{s}) = (\texttt{salt}, s) = \texttt{sig}$.

Remark 8. We showed that HUFU only achieves MBS security. We observe, however, that by applying the PS-3 transform, i.e., changing the computation of $u = \texttt{H(msg, salt)}$ to $u = \texttt{H(msg, pk, salt)}$, full BUFF security can be achieved. This is the case, as the above change prevents an attacker to control x_0 by their choice of pk—any change to pk also changes the value of u and hence h in an uncontrollable way. Using this, S-DEO, S-CEO, and wNR security can be proven, while the proof for MBS security given for unmodified HUFU still applies.

5.3 Squirrels

SQUIRRELS incorporates a GPV-like approach. It is based on unstructured lattices and uses lattices modulo various distinct primes simultaneously. The public key is composed of a single vector which is used to check if a target is contained in the lattice modulo each of the primes. r,s Let n and q be positive integers. The target determinant is denoted by $\Delta = \prod_{p \in P_\Delta} p$, for P_Δ a set of primes in $[2^{30}, 2^{31}]$. The hash function H maps to $[0, \ldots, q-1]^{n-1} \times \{0\}$ viewed as an element in $\mathbb{Z}^n$ with last component being 0.

Key Pair. The SQUIRRELS secret key consists of a matrix $B \in \mathbb{Z}^{n \times n}$, which, by design, has a Hermite normal form

$$\mathrm{HNF}(B) = \begin{pmatrix} I_{n-1} & v_i^\mathsf{T} \\ 0 & \Delta \end{pmatrix}.$$

The resulting vector $v := (v_i)_{i=1,\ldots,n-1}$ is the public key.

Signature. The signature of a message msg for a public key v consists of (salt, s) where salt is a random string and $s = \texttt{Compress}(s')$ with $s' \in \mathbb{Z}^n$.

Verify. Given a public key pk $= v$, a message msg, and a signature sig $=$ (salt, s), the verification algorithm is described in Fig. 9.

In the analysis below, we write $c' := (c_1, \ldots, c_{n-1})^\mathsf{T}$ for $c = (c_1, \ldots, c_n)^\mathsf{T}$ and $\langle \cdot, \cdot \rangle$ for the standard inner product. Note that in the search for elements $v \in \mathbb{Z}^{n-1}$ that satisfy a certain algebraic condition modulo Δ, it suffices to give $v \mod p$ for each $p \in P_\Delta$, by making use of the Chinese Remainder Theorem. We make use of this argument, without explicitly stating it again.

S-CEO. Given a public key $\mathtt{pk} = v$, a message $\mathtt{msg}$ and a signature $\mathtt{sig} = (\mathtt{salt}, s)$ such that $\mathtt{Verify}(\mathtt{pk}, \mathtt{msg}, \mathtt{sig}) = 1$, we need to find a distinct public key $\overline{\mathtt{pk}} = \overline{v}$ such that $\mathtt{Verify}(\overline{\mathtt{pk}}, \mathtt{msg}, \mathtt{sig}) = 1$. This translates to finding $\overline{v}$, which is in the kernel of $\langle c', \cdot \rangle - c_n : \mathbb{F}_p^{n-1} \to \mathbb{F}_p$ for all $p \in P_\Delta$. Note that $\dim_{\mathbb{F}_p}(\ker(\langle c', \cdot \rangle) - c_n) = n - 2$. Hence, for each p one can find an element $\overline{v}_p$ such that $\langle c', \overline{v}_p \rangle - c_n = 0 \mod p$. Then, $\overline{\mathtt{pk}} = \overline{v}$ is given by the $\overline{v}_p$.

S-DEO. Given a public key $\mathtt{pk} = v$, a message $\mathtt{msg}$, and a signature $\mathtt{sig} = (\mathtt{salt}, s)$ such that $\mathtt{Verify}(\mathtt{pk}, \mathtt{msg}, \mathtt{sig}) = 1$, we need to find a second public key $\overline{\mathtt{pk}} = \overline{v} \neq v$ and a second message $\overline{\mathtt{msg}} \neq \mathtt{msg}$ such that $\mathtt{Verify}(\overline{\mathtt{pk}}, \overline{\mathtt{msg}}, \mathtt{sig}) = 1$. For this, we choose a random $\overline{\mathtt{msg}} \neq \mathtt{msg}$ and compute $\overline{c} = s' + \mathtt{H}(\overline{\mathtt{msg}}||\mathtt{salt})$. Hence it is left to find $\overline{v}$ such that $\langle \overline{v}, \overline{c}' \rangle - \overline{c}_n = 0 \mod p$ holds for all $p \in P_\Delta$. For this, the same argument as for the S-CEO attack applies.

MBS. One needs to find a public key $\mathtt{pk} = v$, two distinct messages $\mathtt{msg} \neq \overline{\mathtt{msg}}$, and a signature $\mathtt{sig} = (\mathtt{salt}, s)$ such that $\mathtt{Verify}(\mathtt{pk}, \mathtt{msg}, \mathtt{sig}) = 1$ and $\mathtt{Verify}(\mathtt{pk}, \overline{\mathtt{msg}}, \mathtt{sig}) = 1$. For this, we choose s' such that $||s'||^2 < \lfloor \vartheta^2 \rfloor$ holds and compute $s = \mathtt{Compress}(s')$. We then set $\mathtt{sig} = (\mathtt{salt}, s)$ for some randomly chosen $\mathtt{salt}$. Further we consider two random messages $\overline{\mathtt{msg}} \neq \mathtt{msg}$ and compute $c = s' + \mathtt{H}(\mathtt{msg}||\mathtt{salt})$ and $\overline{c} = s' + \mathtt{H}(\overline{\mathtt{msg}}||\mathtt{salt})$. Hence it is left to find v such that $\langle v, c' \rangle - c_n = 0 \mod p$ and $\langle v, \overline{c}' \rangle - \overline{c}_n = 0 \mod p$ holds for all $p \in P_\Delta$. Consider for $p \in P_\Delta$ the map

$$f : \mathbb{F}_p^{n-1} \to \mathbb{F}_p^2, \; x \mapsto (\langle x, c' \rangle, \langle x, \overline{c}' \rangle)$$

and observe that $\dim_{\mathbb{F}_p}(\ker(f)) = n - 3$. Hence, we can find v_p with the desired properties, which constitutes v.

Remark 9. In the SQUIRRELS specification it is claimed that MBS security is fulfilled, which the above disproves. While their claim is based on the similarity to FALCON, the MBS security of FALCON still holds. The subtle differences between SQUIRRELS and FALCON are thus important, when it comes to BUFF security.

wNR. Given $\mathtt{pk} = v$, and a signature $(\mathtt{salt}, s)$ which verifies an unknown message $\mathtt{msg}$, we can find a new public key $\overline{\mathtt{pk}} = \overline{v}$ and a new signature $(\mathtt{salt}, \overline{s})$ that verifies $\mathtt{msg}$ as follows. Let $s' = \mathtt{Decompress}(s)$. We can assume that with large probability, s'_n is divisible by a prime ϖ which is not in P_Δ. E.g., if s'_n is close to uniform, it will be even with about 0.5 probability. In this case, we set $\overline{s}'_n := \varpi^{-1} s'_n$. Further, we set $\overline{v}_p := \varpi^{-1} v_p$ for each p and let $\overline{v} \in \mathbb{Z}^{n-1}$ be the corresponding vector over $\mathbb{Z}$. Choosing $\overline{s}'_i = s'_i$ for $i = 1, \ldots, n-1$, and $\overline{\mathtt{salt}} = \mathtt{salt}$ yields a new public key $\overline{v}$ and signature $(\overline{\mathtt{salt}}, \overline{s})$, with $\overline{s} = \mathtt{Compress}(\overline{s}')$ that verifies the unknown message. Indeed, the hash h did not change by the procedure and for each $p \in P_\Delta$, we have $\sum_{i=1}^{n-1} \overline{v}_{i,p} c_{i,p} = \varpi^{-1} \sum_{i=1}^{n-1} v_{i,p} c_{i,p} = \varpi^{-1} c_{n,p} = \overline{s}'_n = c_{n,p}$ using that $h_n = 0$. Thereby the verification succeeds.

Remark 10. Modifying SQUIRRELS to incorporate the PS-3 transform (i.e., replacing $h \leftarrow \mathtt{H}(\mathtt{msg}||\mathtt{salt})$ by $h \leftarrow \mathtt{H}(\mathtt{msg}||\mathtt{salt}, \mathtt{pk})$) does not suffice to achieve full BUFF security. This is the case, as we can still find S-CEO/S-DEO attacks that are successful with probability greater than $\frac{1}{2^{31}}$: As above we can reduce to the case of a single $p \in P_{\Delta}$. While the above change to the scheme prevents an attacker to choose v in the kernel of $\langle c', \cdot \rangle - c_n : \mathbb{F}_p^{n-1} \rightarrow \mathbb{F}_p$, the probability that this holds for a random v is equal to $\frac{1}{p} \geq \frac{1}{2^{31}}$ (finding v by randomly hitting an element from a subset of size p^{n-2} contained in a set of size p^{n-1}).

5.4 Further Lattice Candidates

The remaining NIST candidates based on lattices are HAETAE and RACCOON. Both use the Fiat-Shamir with aborts framework and are based on the module versions of the learning with errors and short integer solution problems. Both schemes are similar to DILITHIUM and their BUFF analyses are analogous to the DILITHIUM analysis in [14]. In short, HAETAE signs the hash of public key and message and appends a hash value generated (among other inputs) from public key and message to the signature. Thus, HAETAE can be considered to use the BUFF transform, and if we assume the used hash function to be collision-resistant and ϕ-non-malleable (as defined in [14]), we obtain BUFF security by [14, Theorem 5.5]. This is also true for RACCOON, which is structurally very similar to DILITHIUM and hence can be viewed to implement the BUFF transform.

6 Multivariate Schemes

In this section we analyze the signatures that belong to the family of multivariate (MV) schemes. After introducing the foundations and basic properties, we will give a short generic BUFF analysis, i.e., present results that hold for (nearly) all MV schemes under consideration. After this, we turn to the scheme-specific analyses: UOV, which is the basis of all remaining candidates, is treated in Sect. 6.1. This is followed by the analysis of MAYO in Sect. 6.2. While MAYO is based on UOV, its polynomials are constructed in a way that makes the analysis more involved. We present the details to show that despite the complex structure of the public key, MAYO dose not achieve full BUFF security. Both UOV and MAYO—and all MV schemes considered in this paper, except PROV—fulfill MBS as the only BUFF notion. The analysis of PROV, which achieves full BUFF security, follows in Sect. 6.3. For the remaining schemes QR-UOV, SNOVA, TUOV, and VOX, the BUFF analyses are similar to the one given for UOV. We provide a short outline for each scheme in Sect. 6.4.

Background and Notation of MV Schemes. The main object in multivariate cryptography is a multivariate quadratic map $\mathcal{P} \colon \mathbb{F}_q^n \rightarrow \mathbb{F}_q^m$, which consists of m homogeneous quadratic polynomials $(p^{(1)}(x), \ldots, p^{(m)}(x))$ in n variables $x = (x_1, \ldots, x_n)$. The coefficients of each of these quadratic polynomials $p^{(k)}(x)$

can be stored in a matrix $P^{(k)}$, where the (i, j)-th entry $(p^{(k)})_{i,j}$ represents the coefficient of the monomial $x_i x_j$. Thus, $p^{(k)}(x)$ can be evaluated as $x^\top P^{(k)} x$.

The task of finding a preimage $s \in \mathbb{F}_q^n$ for a given target vector $t \in \mathbb{F}_q^m$ under a given multivariate quadratic map $\mathcal{P}$ is hard in general, as it amounts to solving a system of multivariate quadratic equations, known as the $\mathcal{MQ}$-Problem. Consequently, a trapdoor needs to be included in the map $\mathcal{P}$, that allows to find such $s \in \mathbb{F}_q^m$ with $\mathcal{P}(s) = t$, which constitutes the signature `sig`. The precise realization of this trapdoor varies from scheme to scheme.

Generic BUFF Analysis of MV Schemes. In the following, we provide the parts of the BUFF analysis that are the same for (nearly) all multivariate schemes under consideration—namely the MBS proof and wNR attack. The arguments for these two notions will hence not be repeated in the scheme-specific sections. Furthermore, we provide a generic result on the BUFF security of the considered MV schemes using the PS-3 transform.

MBS Security for MV Schemes. Since the target vector $t \in \mathbb{F}_q^n$ is computed as the hash of (at least) the message `msg`, multivariate schemes naturally satisfy MBS. It is not possible that a single signature $\texttt{sig} = s$ verifies different messages $\texttt{msg} \neq \overline{\texttt{msg}}$, because $\texttt{H}(\texttt{msg}||\cdot) = \mathcal{P}(s) = \texttt{H}(\overline{\texttt{msg}}||\cdot)$ would imply a collision of H.

wNR Attack Against MV Schemes. For an wNR attack, one is given a public key `pk`, from which we derive the public map $\mathcal{P}$, and a signature $\texttt{sig} = s$ to an unknown message `msg`, and has to find $\overline{\texttt{pk}} \neq \texttt{pk}$ and $\overline{\texttt{sig}} = \overline{s}$ such that $\mathcal{P}(s) = \texttt{H}(\texttt{msg}||\cdot) = \overline{\mathcal{P}}(\overline{s})$. Firstly, note that $\mathcal{P}(s) = t = \texttt{H}(\texttt{msg}||\cdot)$ can be computed without knowing `msg`, as s is a valid signature. Next, we generate a key pair $(\overline{\texttt{sk}}, \overline{\texttt{pk}})$ with $\overline{\texttt{pk}} \neq \texttt{pk}$ and use it to sign the target vector t. This results in a signature $\overline{s}$ that fulfills $\overline{\mathcal{P}}(\overline{s}) = t = \texttt{H}(\texttt{msg}||\cdot) = \mathcal{P}(s)$.

Note that this attack is not applicable for Prov, as it hashes the whole public key alongside the message, which prevents us from being able to compute the target *before* choosing the second public key $\overline{\texttt{pk}}$. We give a proof for wNR security of Prov in Sect. 6.3. For all other schemes under consideration the above attack works, however, for Vox and Snova some extra care is necessary, as both schemes hash parts of the public key alongside the message. In Vox the public key consists of a seed SeedPub and the quadratic map Pub, which is generated using SeedPub. By modifying the seed for the secret key while keeping SeedPub the same, we get a new quadratic map $\overline{\text{Pub}} \neq \text{Pub}$. The new secret key is known to the adversary and can be used to sign to the same target. In Snova the public key is of the form $(s_{\text{public}}, (P_i^{22})_{i \in [m]})$. Here, s_{public} is a seed used to generate the remaining components of the public map $\mathcal{P}$, which is done in the signing and verification algorithm. Choosing $\overline{s}_{\text{public}} = s_{\text{public}}$ and $\overline{\texttt{sk}} \neq \texttt{sk}$ guarantees $(\overline{P}_i^{22})_{i \in [m]} \neq (P_i^{22})_{i \in [m]}$ and yields a key pair $(\overline{\texttt{sk}}, \overline{\texttt{pk}})$ for which we can apply the above attack.

BUFF Security Using PS-3 *Transform.* Our analysis reveals that from the family of multivariate schemes only Prov satisfies full BUFF security. The main design feature that contributes to this is the hashing of the public key alongside the message. As all multivariate schemes considered in this paper verify signatures by comparing $\mathtt{H}(\mathtt{msg}, \cdot)$ to $\mathcal{P}(s)$, we can achieve BUFF security for all of them, by adding the *complete*[7] public key alongside the message into the hash function. To prove this, the same arguments as for PROV apply—note that in the analysis of PROV, we use little scheme-specific details except for the size of the domain of $\mathcal{P}$. This approach is very similar to applying the PS-3 transform, except for the fact that an application of PS-3 would result in an additional hash computation (see Fig. 2) that can be avoided by modifying the existing computation of $\mathtt{H}(\mathtt{msg}||\cdot)$ instead. In the following we write PS-3, but it is understood that the simpler modification described above is applied if possible.

Proposition 11. *For* $\Sigma \in \{$MAYO, QR-UOV, SNOVA, TUOV, UOV, VOX$\}$ *and* $\mathtt{H}$ *a random oracle, the transformed scheme* PS-3$[\mathtt{H}, \Sigma]$ *fulfills BUFF security.*

6.1 UOV

The unbalanced oil and vinegar (UOV) signature scheme is the oldest candidate and the foundation of the remaining multivariate schemes, [26,30]. The trapdoor information in UOV is a secret linear m-dimensional subspace, the so-called oil space O, which is annihilated by the public key map $\mathcal{P}$, i.e., $\mathcal{P}(o) = 0$ for all $o \in O$. The dimension of the oil space m needs to equal the number of quadratic equations and the number of variables n usually satisfies $n \approx 2.5m$. We introduce the algorithms of classic UOV here, instead of the compressed versions. The analysis holds for all variants similarly, as we argue below.

Key Pair. The public key $\mathtt{pk} = \{P_i\}_{i\in[m]}$ consists of m matrices

$$P_i = \begin{pmatrix} P_i^{(1)} & P_i^{(2)} \\ 0 & P_i^{(3)} \end{pmatrix},$$

where $P_i^{(1)} \in \mathbb{F}_q^{v\times v}$, $P_i^{(2)} \in \mathbb{F}_q^{v\times m}$ and $P_i^{(3)} \in \mathbb{F}_q^{m\times m}$. Here, the matrices $P_i^{(1)}$ and $P_i^{(2)}$ are generated randomly from a seed and $P_i^{(3)}$ is computed via

$$P_i^{(3)} = -O^\top P_i^{(1)} O - O^\top P_i^{(2)},$$

with a randomly generated oil space $O \in \mathbb{F}_q^{v\times m}$.

The secret key $\mathtt{sk} = (\mathtt{seed_{sk}}, O, \{P_i^{(1)}, S_i\}_{i\in[m]})$ consists of a seed $\mathtt{seed_{sk}}$, the oil space O, a part of the public key matrices $\{P_i^{(1)}\}_{i\in[m]}$, and some auxiliary matrices $\{S_i\}_{i\in[m]}$ needed for signing, given by $S_i = (P_i^{(1)} + P_i^{(1)\top})O + P_i^{(2)}$.

Signature. The signature is given by $\mathtt{sig} = (s, \mathtt{salt})$, containing a vector $s \in \mathbb{F}_q^n$ and a random $\mathtt{salt}$.

Verify. Given a public key $\mathtt{pk} = (P_i^{(1)}, P_i^{(2)}, P_i^{(3)})$, a message $\mathtt{msg}$, and a signature $\mathtt{sig} = (s, \mathtt{salt})$, the verification algorithm is shown in Fig. 10.

[7] VOX and SNOVA hash parts of the public key, which is insufficient for BUFF security.

$\texttt{Verify}(\texttt{pk}, \texttt{msg}, \texttt{sig})$	$\mathsf{Target}(\texttt{pk}, \texttt{msg}, \texttt{sig})$	
$\mathcal{P} \leftarrow \mathsf{Map}(\texttt{pk})$	$(\cdot, \texttt{salt}) \leftarrow \texttt{sig}$	
$t \leftarrow \mathsf{Target}(\texttt{pk}, \texttt{msg}, \texttt{sig})$	$t \leftarrow \texttt{H}(\texttt{msg}\Vert\texttt{salt})$	// Uov
if $\mathcal{P}(\texttt{sig}) = t$	$t \leftarrow \texttt{H}(\texttt{H}(\texttt{msg})\Vert\texttt{salt})$	// Mayo
return 1	$t \leftarrow \texttt{H}_2(\texttt{H}_1(\texttt{pk})\Vert\texttt{msg}\Vert\texttt{salt})$	// Prov
return 0	**return** t	

$\mathsf{Map}(\texttt{pk})$ in Uov	$\mathsf{Map}(\texttt{pk})$ in Prov	$\mathsf{Map}(\texttt{pk})$ in Mayo
$(P_i^{(1)}, P_i^{(2)}, P_i^{(3)}) \leftarrow \texttt{pk}$	$(\texttt{seed}_{\texttt{pk}}, (P_i^{(3)})) \leftarrow \texttt{pk}$	$(\texttt{seed}_{\texttt{pk}}, \{P_i^{(3)}\}) \leftarrow \texttt{pk}$
$P_i \leftarrow \begin{pmatrix} P_i^{(1)} & P_i^{(2)} \\ 0 & P_i^{(3)} \end{pmatrix}$	$(P_i^{(1)}, P_i^{(2)}) \leftarrow \texttt{E}(\texttt{seed}_{\texttt{pk}})$	$\{P_i^{(1)}, P_i^{(2)}\} \leftarrow \texttt{E}(\texttt{seed}_{\texttt{pk}})$
return $\mathcal{P}$	$P_i = \begin{pmatrix} P_i^{(1)} & P_i^{(2)} \\ 0 & P_i^{(3)} \end{pmatrix}$	**return** $\mathcal{P}^*$
	return $\mathcal{P}$	

Fig. 10. Verification algorithm of Uov, Mayo, and Prov. Recall that the public map $\mathcal{P}$ consists of m homogeneous quadratic polynomials $(p^{(1)}(x), \ldots, p^{(m)}(x))$, and can be computed from $P_1, \ldots, P_k$ using the relation $p^i(x) = x^\top P_i x$. For Mayo the larger map $\mathcal{P}^*$ is used, which can be computed from $\mathcal{P}$ as described in Eq. (2). Lastly, note that $\texttt{E}(\cdot)$ is used as an abbreviation for $\texttt{Expand}(\cdot)$.

S-CEO. Given a public key $\texttt{pk}$, a message $\texttt{msg}$, and a signature $\texttt{sig} = (s, \texttt{salt})$ such that $\texttt{Verify}(\texttt{pk}, \texttt{msg}, \texttt{sig}) = 1$, we need to find a second public key $\overline{\texttt{pk}} \neq \texttt{pk}$ such that for the corresponding public key map $\overline{\mathcal{P}}$ it holds that $\overline{\mathcal{P}}(s) = \texttt{H}(\texttt{msg}\Vert\texttt{salt})$. Let $p_{i,j}^{(k)}$ be the (i,j)-th entry of the public key matrix P_k coming from $\texttt{pk}$. We define $\overline{p}_{i,j}^{(k)}$, the coefficients of $\overline{P}_k$ from $\overline{\texttt{pk}}$ as $p_{i,j}^{(k)}$, except for the following adjustment. We pick an arbitrary $i \in [v+1, n-1]$ and change $\overline{p}_{i,i}^{(k)}$ and $\overline{p}_{i+1,i+1}^{(k)}$ s.t. $p_{i,i}^{(k)} s_i^2 + p_{i+1,i+1}^{(k)} s_{i+1}^2 = \overline{p}_{i,i}^{(k)} s_i^2 + \overline{p}_{i+1,i+1}^{(k)} s_{i+1}^2$. Keeping all other coefficients, we get $\overline{P}_k(s) = P_k(s)$ for all k, hence verification succeeds for $\overline{\texttt{pk}}$.

S-DEO. Given a public key $\texttt{pk}$, a message $\texttt{msg}$, and a signature $\texttt{sig} = (s, \texttt{salt})$ such that $\texttt{Verify}(\texttt{pk}, \texttt{msg}, \texttt{sig}) = 1$, we need to find a second public key $\overline{\texttt{pk}} \neq \texttt{pk}$ and a second message $\overline{\texttt{msg}} \neq \texttt{msg}$ such that $\overline{\mathcal{P}}(s) = \overline{h} = (\overline{h}_k) = \texttt{H}(\overline{\texttt{msg}}\Vert\texttt{salt})$. We take some index $l \in [v+1, n]$, with $s_l \neq 0$. For each $k \in [m]$, set $\overline{p}_{i,i}^k = (\overline{h}_k - \sum_{i<j,(i,j)\neq(l,l)} p_{i,j}^k s_i s_j)/(s_l^2)$. Then we found $\overline{\mathcal{P}}$ with $\overline{\mathcal{P}}(s) = \overline{h}$.

Variants. The statements also hold for the compressed variants pkc and pkc+skc. For these, the public key does not consist of the matrices $\{P_i\}_{i\in[m]}$, but only of the submatrices $\{P_i^{(3)}\}_{i\in[m]}$ and a seed that is used to generate $\{P_i^{(1)}\}_{i\in[m]}$ and $\{P_i^{(2)}\}_{i\in[m]}$. The results of our analysis only require a change of the $P_i^{(3)}$, so that the attacks work for the compressed versions as well.

6.2 MAYO

In MAYO, the public key map $\mathcal{P}$ has the same structure as in UOV, but it is publicly whipped up to a k-fold larger map $\mathcal{P}^* : \mathbb{F}_q^{kn} \to \mathbb{F}_q^m$ via

$$\mathcal{P}^*(s_1, \ldots, s_k) = \sum_{i=1}^{k} E_{ii}\mathcal{P}(s_i) + \sum_{i=1}^{k} \sum_{j=i+1}^{k} E_{ij}\mathcal{P}'(s_i, s_j), \tag{2}$$

where $E_{ij} \in \mathbb{F}_q^{m\times m}$ are system parameters and $\mathcal{P}'$ is the bilinear map associated to $\mathcal{P}$, i.e., component-wise $P_l'(s_i, s_j) = s_i^\top(P_l + P_l^\top)s_j$, for each l. The benefit of this approach is a smaller public key size at the expense of a slightly larger signature and an additional security assumption: the *Multi-Target Whipped MQ* problem [6, Section 5.1].

Key Pair. The secret key is given by a private seed $\texttt{sk} = \texttt{seed}_{\texttt{sk}}$. It is used to derive a public seed $\texttt{seed}_{\texttt{pk}}$ and the secret linear oil space $O \in \mathbb{F}_q^{(n-o)\times o}$. The public key is given by $\texttt{pk} = (\texttt{seed}_{\texttt{pk}}, \{P_i^{(3)}\}_{i\in[m]})$, where

$$P_i^{(3)} = -O^\top P_i^{(1)} O - O^\top P_i^{(2)} \in \mathbb{F}_q^{o\times o}.$$

Hereby, $P_i^{(1)} \in \mathbb{F}_q^{(n-o)\times(n-o)}$ and $P_i^{(2)} \in \mathbb{F}_q^{(n-o)\times o}$ are expanded from $\texttt{seed}_{\texttt{pk}}$.

Signature. The signature is given by $\texttt{sig} = (s_1, \ldots, s_k, \texttt{salt})$, with $s_i \in \mathbb{F}_q^n$.

Verify. Given a public key $\texttt{pk} = (\texttt{seed}_{\texttt{pk}}, \{P_i^{(3)}\}_{i\in[m]})$, a message $\texttt{msg}$, and a signature $\texttt{sig} = (s_1, \ldots, s_k, \texttt{salt})$, the verification is shown in Fig. 10.

S-CEO. Given a public key $\texttt{pk} = (\texttt{seed}_{\texttt{pk}}, \{P_i^{(3)}\}_{i\in[m]})$, a message $\texttt{msg}$, and a signature $\texttt{sig} = (s_1, \ldots, s_k, \texttt{salt})$, such that $\texttt{Verify}(\texttt{pk}, \texttt{msg}, \texttt{sig}) = 1$, we need to find a second public key $\overline{\texttt{pk}} \neq \texttt{pk}$ such that $\overline{\mathcal{P}}^*(s_1, \ldots, s_k) = t = \texttt{H}(\texttt{H}(\texttt{msg})||\texttt{salt})$ holds, where $\overline{\mathcal{P}}^*$ is derived from $\overline{\texttt{pk}}$. The main observation to tackle this task, is that the map $\mathcal{P}^*$ is linear with respect to the entries of its corresponding public key matrices P_i.

The strategy is now to generate various $\tilde{\texttt{pk}}_a$, where we always use the same $\texttt{seed}_{\texttt{pk}}$, but randomly generated $(\{P_{i,a}^{(3)}\}_{i\in[m]})_a$ for $a \in \{1, 2, \ldots\}$. Denote by $\tilde{\mathcal{P}}_a$ the quadratic map associated to this public key. Then, we consecutively compute $\tilde{\mathcal{P}}_a^*(s_1, \ldots, s_k) = x_a$ until we gathered m linearly independent vectors x_a. Thus, we find $\lambda_a \in \mathbb{F}_q$, such that $t = \sum_{a=1}^m \lambda_a \cdot x_a$. Now we add up the randomly generated matrices accordingly and define $\overline{pk} = (\texttt{seed}_{pk}, \{\overline{P}_i^{(3)}\}_{i\in[m]})$, where $\overline{P}_i^{(3)} := \sum_{a=1}^m \lambda_a (P_i^{(3)})_a$ for all $i \in [m]$. Due to the linearity we have

$$\overline{\mathcal{P}}^*(s_1, \ldots, s_k) = \sum_{a=1}^{m} \lambda_a \tilde{\mathcal{P}}_a^*(s_1, \ldots, s_k) = \sum_{a=1}^{m} \lambda_a x_a = t.$$

Thus, an attacker is able to find a different public key $\overline{\texttt{pk}} \neq \texttt{pk}$, such that $\texttt{Verify}(\overline{\texttt{pk}}, \texttt{msg}, \texttt{sig}) = 1$ and MAYO is not S-CEO-secure.

S-DEO. Given a public key $\texttt{pk} = (\texttt{seed}_{\texttt{pk}}, \{P_i^{(3)}\}_{i\in[m]})$, a message $\texttt{msg}$, and a signature $\texttt{sig} = (s_1, \ldots, s_k, \texttt{salt})$ such that $\texttt{Verify}(\texttt{pk}, \texttt{msg}, \texttt{sig}) = 1$, we need to find a second public key $\overline{\texttt{pk}} \neq \texttt{pk}$ and message $\overline{\texttt{msg}} \neq \texttt{msg}$ such that $\overline{\mathcal{P}}^*(s_1, \ldots, s_k) = t = \texttt{H}(\texttt{H}(\overline{\texttt{msg}})||\texttt{salt})$. Since the vectors x_a we generated in the S-CEO analysis give a basis for the complete vector space $\mathbb{F}_q^m$, an attacker can compute $\bar{t} = \texttt{H}(\texttt{H}(\overline{\texttt{msg}})||\texttt{salt})$ and find $\overline{\lambda}_a$ such that $\bar{t} = \sum \overline{\lambda}_a x_a$ for some randomly chosen message $\overline{\texttt{msg}} \neq \texttt{msg}$. Thus, the same attack that was developed to analyze S-CEO, works here and MAYO is not S-DEO-secure.

6.3 PROV

Key Pair. Let $\mathbb{F}$ denote the finite field $\mathbb{F}_{2^8}$ and $\delta := o - m$. The public key $\texttt{pk}$ is a pair $(\texttt{seed}_{\texttt{pk}}, (P_i^{(3)})_{i\in[m]})$ where $P_i^{(3)} \in \mathbb{F}^{(m+\delta)\times(m+\delta)}$ for all i. From $\texttt{seed}_{\texttt{pk}}$ the matrices $(P_i^{(1)}, P_i^{(2)})_{i\in[m]}$ with $P_i^{(1)} \in \mathbb{F}^{(n-m-\delta)\times(n-m-\delta)}$ and $P_i^{(2)} \in \mathbb{F}^{(n-m-\delta)\times(m+\delta)}$ for all i, are generated. We denote by P_i the matrix

$$\begin{pmatrix} P_i^{(1)} & P_i^{(2)} \\ 0 & P_i^{(3)} \end{pmatrix}.$$

The secret key is the triple $(\texttt{seed}_{\texttt{pk}}, \texttt{seed}_{\texttt{sk}}, \texttt{H}(\texttt{pk}))$. From $\texttt{seed}_{\texttt{sk}}$ the matrix $O \in \mathbb{F}^{(n-m-\delta)\times(m+\delta)}$ is generated.

Signature. A signature is given by $\texttt{sig} = (\texttt{salt}, s)$ for $s \in \mathbb{F}^n$.

Verify. Given a public key $\texttt{pk} = (\texttt{seed}_{\texttt{pk}}, (P_i^{(3)})_{i\in[m]})$, a message $\texttt{msg}$, and a signature $\texttt{sig} = (\texttt{salt}, s)$, the verification is shown in Fig. 10.

S-CEO. Given a public key $\texttt{pk}$, a message $\texttt{msg}$, and a signature $\texttt{sig} = (\texttt{salt}, s)$ such that $\texttt{Verify}(\texttt{pk}, \texttt{msg}, \texttt{sig}) = 1$, we need to find a different public key $\overline{\texttt{pk}} = (\overline{\texttt{seed}}_{\texttt{pk}}, (\overline{P}_i^3)_{i\in[m]})$ such that $(\bar{t}_i)_{i\in[m]} = \bar{h}$ and hence $(s^\top \overline{P}_i s)_{i\in[m]} = \texttt{H}_2(\texttt{H}_1(\overline{\texttt{pk}})||\texttt{msg}||\texttt{salt})$. As both sides of the latter equation depend on $\overline{\texttt{pk}}$ and the value on the right is random (assuming $\texttt{H}_1$ and $\texttt{H}_2$ to be random oracles), the probability to find a suitable $\overline{\texttt{pk}}$ is $\frac{1}{|\mathbb{F}^m|} = \frac{1}{2^{8m}} \leq 2^{-368}$, for all proposed variants.

S-DEO. Given a public key $\texttt{pk}$, a message $\texttt{msg}$, and a signature $\texttt{sig} = (\texttt{salt}, s)$ such that $\texttt{Verify}(\texttt{pk}, \texttt{msg}, \texttt{sig}) = 1$, we need to find a second public key $\overline{\texttt{pk}} \neq \texttt{pk}$ and a second message $\overline{\texttt{msg}} \neq \texttt{msg}$ such that $\texttt{Verify}(\overline{\texttt{pk}}, \overline{\texttt{msg}}, \texttt{sig}) = 1$. This is not feasible by the same argument that was used for S-CEO security, as changing the message only influences the hash value $\bar{h} = \texttt{H}_2(\texttt{H}_1(\overline{\texttt{pk}})||\texttt{msg}||\texttt{salt})$.

wNR. Given a public key $\texttt{pk}$ and a signature $\texttt{sig}$ to an unknown message $\texttt{msg}$, one has to find another public key $\overline{\texttt{pk}} \neq \texttt{pk}$, and a signature $\overline{\texttt{sig}}$ such that $\texttt{Verify}(\overline{\texttt{pk}}, \texttt{msg}, \overline{\texttt{sig}}) = 1$. This is not feasible as one would have to find $\overline{\texttt{pk}}$ such that $(\bar{t}_i)_{i\in[m]} = \bar{h}$, where $\bar{h} = \texttt{H}_2(\texttt{H}_1(\overline{\texttt{pk}})||\texttt{msg}||\overline{\texttt{salt}})$ is unknown as $\texttt{msg}$ is. Note that we can compute $h = (s^\top P_i s)_i$ but not $\texttt{msg}$ and hence not $\bar{h}$. Thus, the probability for the equality $(\bar{t}_i)_{i\in[m]} = \bar{h}$ to hold is $\frac{1}{2^{8m}}$ and therefore less than 2^{-368} for all variants.

6.4 Further Multivariate Candidates

The remaining NIST signature candidates based on multivariate polynomials are QR-UOV, SNOVA, TUOV and VOX. For all of them, the BUFF analysis follows the same idea as the one given for UOV in Sect. 6.1. We provide a short overview over the main arguments in the following.

The main difference between QR-UOV and UOV is that the public key matrices $P_1^{(i)}, P_2^{(i)}$, and $P_3^{(i)}$ of QR-UOV are block matrices, where each component $\Phi_g^f \in \mathbb{F}_q^{l\times l}$ corresponds to an element g of the quotient ring $\mathbb{F}_q[x]/(f)$, with an irreducible polynomial $f \in \mathbb{F}_q[x]$ of degree l. The polynomial matrices of the subalgebra $\mathcal{A}_f := \{\Phi_g^f \in \mathbb{F}_q^{l\times l} \mid g \in \mathbb{F}_q[x]/(f)\}$ are defined entry-wise such that $(\Phi_g^f)_{ij}$ is the coefficient of x^{i-1} in $x^{j-1} \cdot g$. In the S-CEO/S-DEO analysis for QR-UOV we cannot modify single entries $p_{i,j}^{(k)}$ of the matrices $P_k^{(3)}$ that were used to control the values $y_k = s^\top P_k s$ in the analysis of UOV. Instead, we can only alter one coefficient (or more) of the polynomials $g = \sum_{i=0}^{l-1} a_i x^i \in \mathcal{A}_f$ that are stored in the $P_k^{(3)}$ part of the public key $\mathtt{pk}$. This will change l values in the corresponding block $\Phi_g^f \in \mathbb{F}_q^{l\times l}$ of $P_i^{(3)}$. However, we can still dictate the result $r_k = s_l^\top \Phi_g^f s_l$ by choosing the coefficients of g accordingly. Here s_l denote the l entries of the vector $s \in \mathbb{F}^n$ that are multiplied with this block.

SNOVA differs from UOV in the fact that it works over the non-commutative ring $R = \mathbb{F}_q^{l\times l}$ instead of $\mathbb{F}_q$. Further, SNOVA computes the target vector as $t = \mathtt{H}(\mathrm{seed}_p || \mathtt{H}(\mathtt{msg}) || \mathtt{salt})$ for $\mathtt{pk} = (\mathrm{seed}_p, \{P_i^{22}\}_{i\in[m]})$ with $P_i^{22} \in R^{o\times o}$, while for UOV we have $t = \mathtt{H}(\mathtt{msg}||\mathtt{salt})$. However, for neither of the BUFF security notions, the adversary has to provide honestly generated keys, hence it can choose two different public keys $\overline{\mathtt{pk}} \neq \mathtt{pk}$ that have the same seed, which then result in the same target t. Then, S-CEO and S-DEO insecurity follows by using the concrete parameters provided in SNOVA to prove systems of equations solvable.

The TUOV analysis is completely analogous to the UOV analysis, as the additional affine transformation $S\colon \mathbb{F}_q^m \to \mathbb{F}_q^m$ has no impact on the analysis.

VOX is a UOV-based scheme that incorporates the quotient ring technique. Despite their claim to achieve BUFF security, VOX only satisfies MBS. S-CEO and S-DEO can be attacked as in UOV. In short the attack proceeds as follows: One keeps the part SeedPub of the public key $\mathtt{pk} = (\mathrm{SeedPub}, \mathrm{Pub})$ unchanged. The Pub part can be changed independently and is chosen as in the attack against UOV. Note that VOX uses the quotient ring technique, however, the problem of defining Pub is still the same as in UOV, just over the extension field. The wNR security can be attacked as described at the beginning of this section.

7 Conclusion

In this work, we analyzed the signature schemes based on codes, isogenies, lattices, and multivariate polynomials submitted to the additional NIST PQC standardization effort for signatures regarding their BUFF security. Besides the analysis of the original schemes, we included comments on the BUFF security after a light transform, the so-called PS-3 transform. In fact, we see that often, the PS-3 transform suffices to ensure BUFF security, despite the fact that the PS-3 transform is not sufficient for generic schemes. This gap between the general statement and the empirical evidence on practical schemes can be analyzed further.

In the NIST competition, there are even more signature schemes, which we have not analyzed in this work. An interesting future work is to analyze those. In particular, this would give a chance to assess the empirical evidence regarding the relation of BUFF security and the PS-3 transform.

We considered a weaker form of non-resignability (wNR) as the initial definition turned out to be unachievable—the problem being the auxiliary information. The majority of our results regarding wNR—attacks against 12 out of 17 signature schemes—remain relevant regardless of how the auxiliary information issue gets resolved eventually. The reason is that neither attack relies on any auxiliary information. On the other hand, our positive results only guarantee security against non-resignability in this restricted form. Once the matter of defining non-resignability is completely resolved, our positive results given here should be re-evaluated. Note, however, that for the 5 positive results, the schemes implicitly use either the PS-3 or the BUFF transform. Hence, if either the PS-3 or BUFF transform can be shown to generally satisfy a new definition of NR, the results would apply to the 5 positive results presented here.

Acknowledgements. This work has been funded by the Deutsche Forschungsgemeinschaft (DFG – German Research Foundation) – 505500359 and SFB 1119 – 236615297, by the German Federal Ministry of Education and Research (BMBF) under the projects 6G-RIC (16KISK033) and Quant-ID (16KISQ111), and by the Hector Foundation II.

References

1. Ayer, A.: Duplicate signature key selection attack in let's encrypt (2015). https://www.agwa.name/blog/post/duplicate_signature_key_selection_attack_in_lets_encrypt
2. Baldi, M., et al.: LESS. Technical report, National Institute of Standards and Technology (2023)
3. Baldi, M., et al.: CROSS. Technical report, National Institute of Standards and Technology (2023)
4. Banegas, G., et al.: Wave. Technical report, National Institute of Standards and Technology (2023)
5. Bellare, M., Rogaway, P.: Random oracles are practical: a paradigm for designing efficient protocols. In: Denning, D.E., Pyle, R., Ganesan, R., Sandhu, R.S., Ashby, V. (eds.) ACM CCS 1993, pp. 62–73. ACM Press (1993)
6. Beullens, W., Campos, F., Celi, S., Hess, B., Kannwischer, M.J.: MAYO. Technical report, National Institute of Standards and Technology (2023)
7. Beullens, W., et al.: UOV. Technical report, National Institute of Standards and Technology (2023)

8. Blake-Wilson, S., Menezes, A.: Unknown key-share attacks on the station-to-station (STS) protocol. In: Imai, H., Zheng, Y. (eds.) PKC 1999. LNCS, vol. 1560, pp. 154–170. Springer, Heidelberg (1999). https://doi.org/10.1007/3-540-49162-7_12
9. Bos, J., et al.: HAWK. Technical report, National Institute of Standards and Technology (2023)
10. Chavez-Saab, J., et al.: SQIsign. Technical report, National Institute of Standards and Technology (2023)
11. Cheon, J.H., et al.: HAETAE. Technical report, National Institute of Standards and Technology (2023)
12. Chou, T., et al.: MEDS. Technical report, National Institute of Standards and Technology (2023)
13. Corte-Real Santos, M., Eriksen, J.K., Meyer, M., Reijnders, K.: AprèsSQI: Extra Fast Verification for SQIsign Using Extension-Field Signing. Cryptology ePrint Archive, Paper 2023/1559 (2023)
14. Cremers, C., Düzlü, S., Fiedler, R., Fischlin, M., Janson, C.: BUFFing signature schemes beyond unforgeability and the case of post-quantum signatures. In: 2021 IEEE Symposium on Security and Privacy, pp. 1696–1714. IEEE Computer Society Press (2021)
15. del Pino, R., et al.: Raccoon. Technical report, National Institute of Standards and Technology (2023)
16. Ding, J., et al.: TUOV. Technical report, National Institute of Standards and Technology (2023)
17. Don, J., Fehr, S., Huang, Y.-H., Struck, P.: On the (in)security of the BUFF transform. IACR Cryptology ePrint Archive 2023:1634 (2023)
18. Ducas, L., Postlethwaite, E.W., Pulles, L.N., van Woerden, W.: Hawk: module LIP makes lattice signatures fast, compact and simple. In: Agrawal, S., Lin, D. (eds.) ASIACRYPT 2022. LNCS, vol. 13794, pp. 65–94. Springer, Cham (2022). https://doi.org/10.1007/978-3-031-22972-5_3
19. Espitau, T., Niot, G., Sun, C., Tibouchi, M.: SQUIRRELS. Technical report, National Institute of Standards and Technology (2023)
20. Furue, H., et al.: QR-UOV. Technical report, National Institute of Standards and Technology (2023)
21. Goldwasser, S., Micali, S., Rivest, R.: A digital signature scheme secure against adaptive chosen-message attacks. SIAM J. Comput. (1988)
22. Goubin, L., et al.: PROV. Technical report, National Institute of Standards and Technology (2023)
23. Hülsing, A., et al.: SPHINCS$^+$. Technical report, National Institute of Standards and Technology (2020)
24. Jackson, D., Cremers, C., Cohn-Gordon, K., Sasse, R.: Seems legit: automated analysis of subtle attacks on protocols that use signatures. In: Cavallaro, L., Kinder, J., Wang, X., Katz, J. (eds.) ACM CCS 2019, pp. 2165–2180. ACM Press (2019)
25. Kim, T.H.-J., Basescu, C., Jia, L., Lee, S.B., Hu, Y.-C., Perrig, A.: Lightweight source authentication and path validation. In: Proceedings of the 2014 ACM Conference on SIGCOMM (2015)
26. Kipnis, A., Patarin, J., Goubin, L.: Unbalanced oil and vinegar signature schemes. In: Stern, J. (ed.) EUROCRYPT 1999. LNCS, vol. 1592, pp. 206–222. Springer, Heidelberg (1999). https://doi.org/10.1007/3-540-48910-X_15
27. Lyubashevsky, V., et al.: CRYSTALS-DILITHIUM. Technical report, National Institute of Standards and Technology (2020)

28. Menezes, A., Smart, N.: Security of signature schemes in a multi-user setting. Des. Codes Cryptography **33**, 261–274 (2004). https://doi.org/10.1023/B:DESI.0000036250.18062.3f
29. National Institute of Standards and Technology. Call for additional digital signature schemes for the post-quantum cryptography standardization process (2022). https://csrc.nist.gov/csrc/media/Projects/pqc-dig-sig/documents/call-for-proposals-dig-sig-sept-2022.pdf
30. Patarin, J.: The oil and vinegar signature scheme (1997)
31. Patarin, J., et al.: VOX. Technical report, National Institute of Standards and Technology (2023)
32. Pornin, T., Stern, J.P.: Digital signatures do not guarantee exclusive ownership. In: Ioannidis, J., Keromytis, A., Yung, M. (eds.) ACNS 2005. LNCS, vol. 3531, pp. 138–150. Springer, Heidelberg (2005). https://doi.org/10.1007/11496137_10
33. Prest, T., et al.: FALCON. Technical report, National Institute of Standards and Technology (2020)
34. Wang, L.-C., et al.: SNOVA. Technical report, National Institute of Standards and Technology (2023)
35. Yu, Y., et al.: HuFu. Technical report, National Institute of Standards and Technology (2023)

Revisiting Anonymity in Post-quantum Public Key Encryption

Yao Cheng, Xianhui Lu(✉), Ziyi Li, and Bao Li

Key Laboratory of Cyberspace Security Defense, Institute of Information Engineering, Chinese Academy of Science, Beijing, China
{chengyao,luxianhui,liziyi,libao}@iie.ac.cn

Abstract. This paper revisits the anonymity of post-quantum public key encryption in the presence of CCA attacks (ANO-CCA). Specifically, we demonstrate the anonymity of key encapsulation mechanisms (KEMs) obtained from Fujisaki-Okamoto (FO) transformations in the quantum random oracle model (QROM) and the anonymity of hybrid encryption via the KEM-DEM paradigm in both implicit and explicit cases. Our results are presented as follows:

- Implicit Case. We establish the ANO-CCA secure KEM with implicit rejection through FO, followed by achieving ANO-CCA secure hybrid encryption via the KEM-DEM paradigm. Specifically, the security of the FO-KEM relies on weaker assumptions, eliminating the need for collision-freeness security in derandomized public-key encryption (DPKE), as mandated by Grubbs et al. (EUROCRYPT 2022). In contrast to Xagawa's result (EUROCRYPT 2022), our approach relies on weak anonymity (wANO-CPA) instead of strong disjoint-simulatability-a stronger security notion implying wANO-CPA. Subsequently, we demonstrate that an ANO-CCA KEM with implicit rejection, where the decapsulation algorithm generates a random key for an invalid ciphertext, can be used to obtain ANO-CCA hybrid encryption. This property is inherent in KEMs obtained from FO, resulting in the establishment of anonymity of hybrid encryption using FO.
- Explicit Case. We prove the anonymity of the textbook FO, a consideration not addressed in prior literature that only focused on the variant with an additional hash. Similarly, we demonstrate that an ANO-CCA KEM with explicit rejection, where the decapsulation algorithm returns "$\perp$" for an invalid ciphertext, can be employed to achieve ANO-CCA hybrid encryption, thereby establishing the anonymity of hybrid encryption using FO.

Keywords: Anonymity · Fujisaki-Okamoto Transformations · KEM-DEM Paradigm · Quantum Random Oracle

1 Introduction

Indistinguishability under chosen-ciphertext attack (IND-CCA) security [14], as the standard security for public-key encryption (PKE) schemes, primarily

M.-J. Saarinen and D. Smith-Tone (Eds.): PQCrypto 2024, LNCS 14772, pp. 336–370, 2024.
https://doi.org/10.1007/978-3-031-62746-0_14

captures the confidentiality of the encrypted messages. However, in various PKE applications, such as anonymous cryptocurrencies like Zcash [5], anonymous credential systems [7], auction protocols [23], anonymous authenticated key exchange [24], and etc., the demand for security properties beyond IND-CCA arises, specifically anonymity [4]. A PKE scheme is considered anonymous (ANO-CPA) if a ciphertext conceals information about the public key used in its creation. Stronger forms of anonymity (ANO-CCA) involve providing the adversary with decryption oracles.

Similar to the constructions of IND-CCA PKEs, an ANO-CCA secure PKE can be derived from a weakly anonymous (ANO-CPA) PKE. Specifically, a KEM is obtained from a weakly-secure PKE using the REACT [21], GEM [8], or FO [11,12] transformations. Subsequently, a hybrid encryption is created through the KEM-DEM paradigm [16] (DEM denotes the Data Encapsulation Mechanism). Among the transformations mentioned earlier, it's noteworthy that FO transformations are widely adopted by most post-quantum KEM schemes listed by the US National Institute of Standards and Technology (NIST)[1]. This paper investigates the anonymity of the FO transformations and the KEM-DEM paradigm.

Anonymous Post-quantum KEMs. KEMs obtained from FO (FO-KEMs) can be categorized into two cases: KEMs with implicit rejection, where the decapsulation algorithm returns a random string for an invalid ciphertext, and KEMs with explicit rejection, where the decapsulation algorithm returns a rejection symbol "$\perp$" for an invalid ciphertext. In the context of this paper, anonymous post-quantum KEMs refer to the anonymity of FO in QROM [6], allowing the quantum adversary to access it with a superposition state.

The implicit and explicit cases have their own more appropriate scenarios. The finalist of NIST PQC KEMs adopts the implicit one, which releases less information to adversaries. Whereas security notions such as robustness [1] need the explicit one. This paper investigates both implicit and explicit cases.

KEMs with Implicit Rejection. The shared key in the KEM obtained from FO contains the information of the ciphertext c and the plaintext m, i.e., $K = H(m, c)$. The customary trick to simulate the decapsulation oracle in QROM is using an internal random oracle mapping from c to K, named "Remapping Technique". Two independent internal random oracles are required to simulate two decapsulation oracles in the proof of ANO-CCA security. Imperfect simulation occurs if two decapsulation oracles need to respond with the same K. Grubbs et al. [15] addressed this issue by introducing a collision-freeness (SCFR-CPA) property, where the probability of generating the same shared key under two different secret keys is considered negligible. Later, Xagawa [26] proposed a stronger property, strong pseudorandomness (SPR), which implies anonymity and proved the SPR security if the underlying PKE satisfies strong disjoint-simulatability (SDS-IND) [22], a security property implying weak anonymity (wANO-CPA).

[1] NIST is an institution that is committed to selecting the standard KEM/PKE used for decades to resist the increasing threat of quantum computers.

KEMs with Explicit Rejection. To the best of our knowledge, no prior work exists on the anonymity of KEM obtained from the textbook FO in QROM. Xagawa [26] considered variants of FO, namely HFO and HFO_m, where "H" denotes the additional key-confirmation hash, and "m" implies that the computation of key K involves only a plaintext m instead of both m and ciphertext c.

Anonymous Hybrid Encryption. Mohassel [20] initially studied the anonymity of hybrid encryption via the KEM-DEM paradigm. He stated that more property than ANO-CCA security of KEM is necessary to guarantee the ANO-CCA security of the hybrid encryption, even if the DEM part has achieved ideal security. Besides, he proposed that such additional property can be robustness. Informally speaking, robustness requires the probability that $m \neq \perp \wedge m' \neq \perp$ is negligible, where m, m' are plaintexts decrypted under distinct secret keys by one ciphertext. Such a property can never be achieved for KEMs with implicit rejection. Subsequently, Xagawa [26] discussed the hybrid encryption's anonymity from the point of SPR security in the implicit case and explicit case, respectively.

1.1 Our Contribution

This paper revisits the anonymity of KEMs obtained from FO in QROM and the anonymity of hybrid encryption via the KEM-DEM paradigm in both implicit and explicit cases. As opposed to the existing results of FO, this paper weakens the security assumption for the implicit case and requires no additional hash for the explicit case. As opposed to the existing results of KEM-DEM, this paper refines the paradigm into the implicit and explicit cases to discuss respectively, making the conclusions clearer.

Anonymity of FO. This paper focuses on the anonymity of FO in QROM. We exhibit the comparison of the current results in Fig. 1. For the implicit case, we establish the ANO-CCA security of FO-KEM based on a wANO-CPA and OW-CPA secure PKE with γ-spread property, where γ-spread is quite a common characteristic. In comparison, we eliminate the requirement for SCFR-CPA secure derandomized PKE (the result of Grubbs et al. [15]). Additionally, wANO-CPA security is weaker than SDS-IND security[2] (the result of Xagawa [26]). For the explicit case, we initially prove the anonymity of the KEM obtained from the textbook FO in QROM without the additional hash part in the ciphertext.

Anonymity of KEM-DEM Paradigm. We aim to investigate the additional properties that a KEM needs to satisfy, beyond anonymity, to ensure anonymity

[2] Roughly, an SDS-IND PKE scheme means that the ciphertext obtained by $\text{Enc}(pk, m)$ for a randomly chosen pk is indistinguishable from a ciphertext generated without pk, i.e. the ciphertext contains no information of the public key (wANO-CPA). However, a wANO-CPA secure PKE may not have an invalid ciphertext in the ciphertext space, leading to the non-existence of a simulator that is required to generate an invalid ciphertext in SDS-IND security.

FO	Works	Underlying Security					Additional Hash
		wANO-CPA	OW-CPA	SDS-IND	γ-spread	SCFR-CPA	
Implicit	[15]	✓	✓	×	×	✓	×
	[26]	✓	✓	✓	×	×	×
	Our work	✓	✓	×	✓	×	×
Explicit	[26]	✓	✓	✓	×	×	✓
	Our work	✓	✓	×	✓	×	×

Fig. 1. Comparison of different results for anonymous FO.

for hybrid encryption. This objective is based on Mohassel's conclusion [20] that the anonymity of a KEM alone cannot guarantee the anonymity of hybrid encryption. This paper explores the anonymity of hybrid encryption concerning KEMs with implicit and explicit rejection. For the explicit case, the anonymity of hybrid encryption is derived directly from the anonymity of the KEM. For the implicit case, the additional requirement is that the decapsulation algorithm returns a random key for an invalid ciphertext. This property is inherently present in KEMs obtained from the FO transformation, thereby establishing the anonymity of hybrid encryption using FO.

1.2 Technical Overview

Hofheinz et al. [17] proposed a modular analysis of FO transformations. Specifically, we consider two variants of FO: $\mathsf{FO}^{\perp} = \mathsf{U}^{\perp} \circ \mathsf{T}$ and $\mathsf{FO}^{\not\perp} = \mathsf{U}^{\not\perp} \circ \mathsf{T}$, where superscripts $^{\not\perp}$ and $^{\perp}$ represent implicit rejection and explicit rejection, respectively. We adopted their modular analysis approach, decomposing FO transformations into U transformations and T transformations, to establish the anonymity.

U : *from wANO-CCOA/wANO-CCOVA to ANO-CCA.* A KEM with implicit rejection $\mathsf{KEM}^{\not\perp} = \mathsf{U}^{\not\perp}[\mathsf{PKE}_1, H]$, is obtained from an DPKE PKE_1 and a random oracle H by defining $\mathsf{Encaps}(pk) := (c := \mathsf{Enc}_1(pk, m), K := H(m, c))$, for a randomly chosen m, and $\mathsf{Decaps}(sk, c) := H(m, c)$ for $m \neq \perp$ and $\mathsf{Decaps}(sk, c) := H(s, c)$ for $m = \perp$, where $m := \mathsf{Dec}_1(sk, c)$. Similarly, a KEM with explicit rejection $\mathsf{KEM}^{\perp} = \mathsf{U}^{\perp}[\mathsf{PKE}_1, H]$ is obtained with only difference from $\mathsf{KEM}^{\not\perp}$ in decapsulation that $\mathsf{Decaps}(sk, c) := \perp$ for $m = \perp$, where $m := \mathsf{Dec}_1(sk, c)$.

"Remapping Technique" in combination with "Domain Separation Technique" is commonly employed to address the simulation of decapsulation oracles in QROM [15,17]. In the case of a single public-key/secret-key pair, the decapsulation service provides information from the ciphertext c to the encapsulated key K, which is also supplied by the random oracle H for (m, c) pairs, where $\mathsf{Dec}_1(sk, c) = m$. To simulate the decapsulation oracle without the secret key, an internal oracle from c to K is utilized to maintain consistency between the decapsulation oracle and the random oracle. This mapping, known as "remapping", avoids obtaining the plaintext m first. For the remaining input pairs (m, c) of H, where c contains no information about m, we cannot represent it using the internal oracle from c to K as just mentioned. To simulate H, we need to separate the inputs first, i.e., "domain separation", where the criterion here is "$m \stackrel{?}{=} \mathsf{Dec}_1(sk, c)$".

In the explicit case, the only additional requirement is the provision of a ciphertext validity oracle (CVO) by the underlying PKE. The CVO is utilized to ascertain the validity of the ciphertext, determining whether the decapsulation oracle outputs the rejection symbol for explicit cases.

For anonymity, two public-key/secret-key pairs need to be considered. When simulating two decapsulation oracles by "Remapping Technique" with two independent internal randomized oracles, such an issue will occur that the simulation is incorrect if $\mathsf{Dec}_1(sk_0, c) = \mathsf{Dec}_1(sk_1, c) = m \neq \perp$. Different from Grubbs et al. [15]'s method of increasing the requirement of collision-freeness, we mandate the underlying DPKE to provide a collision confirmation oracle (CCO) to detect this scenario. Consequently, the simulator responds with another identical independent internal oracle for such ciphertexts. This requirement naturally results in a finer domain separation for H: "$m \stackrel{?}{=} m' \wedge m \neq \perp \wedge m' \neq \perp$", where $m := \mathsf{Dec}_1(sk_0, c)$ and $m' := \mathsf{Dec}_1(sk_1, c)$.

T: *from wANO-CPA to wANO-CCA.* A DPKE $\mathsf{PKE}_1 = \mathsf{T}[\mathsf{PKE}_0, G]$ is obtained from a probabilistic PKE and a random oracle G by defining $\mathsf{Enc}_1(pk, m) := \mathsf{Enc}_0(pk, m; G(m))$, where $G(m)$ is used as the random coins for Enc_0.

In the previous part, we emphasized the necessity for the underlying DPKE of the transformation U to be anonymous, providing a CCO (wANO-CCOA/wANO-CCOVA for the implicit case and the explicit case, respectively). Here, we demonstrate that the transformation T can achieve stronger security (wANO-CCA, implying wANO-CCOA/wANO-CCOVA) when the underlying PKE is γ-spread. Informally, γ-spreadness guarantees that an adversary is hard to generate a valid ciphertext c without querying the corresponding plaintext m to the random oracle G. We can then simulate the random oracle G using the compressed oracle technique, as proposed by Zhandry [27]. Subsequently, we extract the correct plaintext for a valid ciphertext using the online extractability technique [10].

KEM-DEM Paradigm: Intuitively, adversaries may gain more information about c_0^* by querying two decryption oracles of hybrid encryption with $(c_0^*, c_1 \neq c_1^*)$, where (c_0^*, c_1^*) is the challenge, whereas adversaries cannot obtain information about c_0^* through the decapsulation oracles of KEM. The additional information acquired by the adversary could potentially compromise the anonymity of hybrid encryption. Mohassel [20] proposed an additional robustness requirement for the KEM to achieve anonymity in hybrid encryption. It's important to note that Mohassel considers the KEM in a general sense, focusing on decapsulation correctness requirements without specific considerations for handling invalid ciphertexts. We aim to demonstrate that the anonymity of this paradigm can be better understood when considering KEM with implicit rejection and explicit rejection, respectively.

As mentioned earlier, our objective is to ensure that the adversary gains no information about c_0^* through two decryption oracles. Specifically, we aim to maintain consistency in the behavior of $(c_0^*, c_1 \neq c_1^*)$ under two decapsulation oracles. In this context, we consider the DEM to be an authenticated encryption satisfying INT-CTXT security, wherein the adversary cannot produce a valid ciphertext for an unknown key K.

Let's discuss the case of the decapsulation oracle $\mathsf{Dec}_b(c_0^*, c_1 \neq c_1^*)$. Since c_0^* is a valid ciphertext under sk_b, the corresponding shared key K is treated as random, guaranteed by the IND-CCA security of KEM. Therefore, we can respond with "$\perp$" for $\mathsf{Dec}_b(c_0^*, c_1 \neq c_1^*)$, as the adversary cannot query with a valid c_1 due to their lack of knowledge about K.

Moving to the decapsulation oracle $\mathsf{Dec}_{1-b}(c_0^*, c_1 \neq c_1^*)$, we aim to establish a property that allows us to also respond with "$\perp$". In the implicit case, two scenarios exist: when c_0^* is a valid ciphertext and when c_0^* is an invalid ciphertext under sk_{1-b}. The IND-CCA security of KEM addresses the first scenario, enabling us to reply with "$\perp$", consistent with the analysis of $\mathsf{Dec}_b(c_0^*, c_1 \neq c_1^*)$. For the second scenario, the decapsulation algorithm yields a random key K, resulting in a "$\perp$" response for $\mathsf{Dec}_{1-b}(c_0^*, c_1 \neq c_1^*)$. The explicit case is similar, except that for the invalid case, we reply with "$\perp$" directly.

2 Preliminaries

2.1 Cryptographic Primitives

This part provides the formal definitions of PKE, KEM, DEM and their security notions.

Definition 1 (PKE). *A PKE scheme* $\mathsf{PKE} = (\mathsf{Gen}, \mathsf{Enc}, \mathsf{Dec})$ *consists of a triple of polynomial time algorithms with the security parameter* λ. Gen *is the key generation algorithm, which is probabilistic and outputs a public/secret key-pair* (pk, sk) *on the input* 1^λ. Enc *is the encryption algorithm, which is probabilistic and outputs a ciphertext* c *on the input* pk *and a message* m. Dec *is the decryption algorithm, which is deterministic and outputs a message* m *on the input* sk *and a ciphertext* c.

δ-Correctness [17]. A PKE scheme PKE *is δ-correct if* $\Pr[\mathrm{COR}_{\mathsf{PKE}}^{\mathcal{A}} \Rightarrow 1] \leq \delta$, *where the correctness game* COR *is defined as in Fig. 2.*

Definition 2 (γ-spread [17]). *We say* $\mathsf{PKE} = (\mathsf{Gen}, \mathsf{Enc}, \mathsf{Dec})$ *is γ-spread if*

$$\max_{m \in \mathcal{M}, c \in C, pk} \Pr[c = \mathsf{Enc}(pk, m)] \leq 2^{-\gamma},$$

where the probability is over the randomness of the encryption. For a (pk, sk) *pair sampled by* Gen, *we also define parameter*

$$\gamma(pk, sk) := \max_{m \in \mathcal{M}, c \in C} \Pr[c = \mathsf{Enc}(pk, m)].$$

Definition 3 (Security notions for PKE). *Let* $\mathsf{PKE} = (\mathsf{Gen}, \mathsf{Enc}, \mathsf{Dec})$ *be a PKE scheme. We define the* Goal-ATK $\in$ {OW-ATK, SCFR-CPA} *advantage function of an adversary* $\mathcal{A}$ *against* PKE *as*

$$\mathrm{Adv}_{\mathsf{PKE}}^{\text{Goal-ATK}}(\mathcal{A}) := \Pr[\text{Goal-ATK}_{\mathsf{PKE}}^{\mathcal{A}} \Rightarrow 1]$$

GAME COR:	**GAME OW-ATK:**	**GAME IND-ATK:**
1: $(pk, sk) \stackrel{\$}{\leftarrow}$ Gen	1: $(pk, sk) \stackrel{\$}{\leftarrow}$ Gen	1: $(pk, sk) \leftarrow$ Gen
2: $m \stackrel{\$}{\leftarrow} \mathcal{A}(pk, sk)$	2: $m^* \stackrel{\$}{\leftarrow} \mathcal{M}$	2: $m_0, m_1, st \leftarrow \mathcal{A}^{O_{\text{ATK}}}(pk)$
3: $c \stackrel{\$}{\leftarrow}$ Enc(pk, m)	3: $c^* \stackrel{\$}{\leftarrow}$ Enc(pk, m^*)	3: $b \stackrel{\$}{\leftarrow} \{0,1\}, c^* \leftarrow$ Enc(pk, m_b)
4: **return** $[\text{Dec}(sk, c) \neq m]$	4: $m' \leftarrow \mathcal{A}^{O_{\text{ATK}}}(pk, c^*)$	4: $b' \leftarrow \mathcal{A}^{O_{\text{ATK}}}(pk, c^*, st)$
	5: **return** $[m = m']$	5: **return** $[b' = b]$

GAME wANO-ATK:	**GAME ANO-ATK:**	**GAME SCFR-CPA:**
1: $(pk_0, sk_0) \leftarrow$ Gen	1: $(pk_0, sk_0) \leftarrow$ Gen	1: $(pk_0, sk_0) \leftarrow$ Gen
2: $(pk_1, sk_1) \leftarrow$ Gen	2: $(pk_1, sk_1) \leftarrow$ Gen	2: $(pk_1, sk_1) \leftarrow$ Gen
3: $b \stackrel{\$}{\leftarrow} \{0,1\}, m^* \stackrel{\$}{\leftarrow} \mathcal{M}$	3: $m^*, st \leftarrow \mathcal{A}^{O_{\text{ATK}}}(pk_0, pk_1)$	3: $c \leftarrow \mathcal{A}(pk_0, pk_1)$
4: $c^* \leftarrow$ Enc(pk_b, m^*)	4: $b \stackrel{\$}{\leftarrow} \{0,1\}, c^* \leftarrow$ Enc(pk_b, m^*)	4: $m_0 := \text{Dec}(sk_0, c)$
5: $b' \leftarrow \mathcal{A}^{O_{0\text{ATK}}, O_{1\text{ATK}}}(pk_0, pk_1, c^*)$	5: $b' \leftarrow \mathcal{A}^{O_{0\text{ATK}}, O_{1\text{ATK}}}(pk_0, pk_1, c^*, st)$	5: $m_1 := \text{Dec}(sk_1, c)$
6: **return** $[b' = b]$	6: **return** $[b' = b]$	6: **return** $[m_0 = m_1 \neq \perp]$

Dec$(c \neq c^*)$	CVO$(c \neq c^*)$	CCO$(c \neq c^*)$
1: **return** Dec(sk, c)	1: $m := \text{Dec}(sk, c)$	1: **return** $[\text{Dec}(sk_0, c) = \text{Dec}(sk_1, c) \neq \perp]$
	2: **return** $[m \in \mathcal{M}]$	

Fig. 2. Security notions for PKE.

where Goal-ATK games are defined in Fig. 2. We define the Goal-ATK \in {IND-ATK, wANO-ATK, ANO-ATK} advantage of an adversary \mathcal{A} against PKE as

$$\text{Adv}_{\text{PKE}}^{\text{Goal-ATK}}(\mathcal{A}) := \Pr[\text{Goal-ATK}_{\text{PKE}}^{\mathcal{A}} \Rightarrow 1] - \frac{1}{2}$$

where Goal-ATK games are defined in Fig. 2. Specifically, the correspondence between O_{ATK} and ATK is shown in the table below. For wANO-ATK, ANO-ATK games, the adversary can can access $O_{0\text{ATK}}$ and $O_{1\text{ATK}}$, where subscripts 0,1 mean that the oracle is associated with sk_0 and sk_1.

O_{ATK}	-	Dec	CVO	CCO	CCO, CVO
ATK	CPA	CCA	VA	CCOA	CCOVA

where Dec is the decryption oracle, CVO is the ciphertext validity oracle, and CCO is the collision confirmation oracle, defined in Fig. 2. Similarly, we define Goal-qATK security for PKE with the only difference that the adversary \mathcal{A} can query the O_{ATK} with quantum superposition states.

Definition 4 (KEM). *A KEM scheme* KEM = (Gen, Encaps, Decaps) *consists of a triple of polynomial time algorithms with the security parameter* λ. Gen *is the key generation algorithm, which is probabilistic and outputs a public/secret key-pair* (pk, sk) *on the input* 1^λ. Decaps *is the encapsulation algorithm, which is probabilistic and outputs a ciphertext* c *and a key* K *on the input* pk. Decaps *is the decryption algorithm, which is deterministic and outputs a key* K *or a rejection symbol* $\perp$ *on the input* sk *and a ciphertext* c.

Correctness. The correctness requirement of KEM is $\Pr[\mathsf{Decaps}(sk, c) = K : (pk, sk) \leftarrow \mathsf{Gen}, (c, K) \leftarrow \mathsf{Encaps}(pk)] = 1$.

Definition 5 (Security notions for KEM). *Let* $\mathsf{KEM} = (\mathsf{Gen}, \mathsf{Encaps}, \mathsf{Decaps})$ *be a KEM scheme. We define the* Goal-ATK $\in$ {IND-CCA, ANO-CCA} *advantage function of an adversary* $\mathcal{A}$ *against* KEM *as*

$$\mathrm{Adv}^{\text{Goal-ATK}}_{\mathsf{KEM}}(\mathcal{A}) := \Pr[\text{Goal-ATK}^{\mathcal{A}}_{\mathsf{KEM}} \Rightarrow 1] - \frac{1}{2}$$

where Goal-ATK *games are defined in Fig. 3.*

GAME IND-CCA:	**GAME** ANO-CCA:	$\mathrm{Dec}(c \neq c^*)$:
$b \xleftarrow{\$} \{0,1\}$	$b \xleftarrow{\$} \{0,1\}$	**return** $\mathrm{Dec}(sk, c)$
$(pk, sk) \xleftarrow{\$} \mathsf{Gen}$	$(pk_0, sk_0) \xleftarrow{\$} \mathsf{Gen}$	$\mathrm{Dec}_0(c \neq c^*)$:
$c^*, K_0^* \xleftarrow{\$} \mathsf{Enc}(pk)$	$(pk_1, sk_1) \xleftarrow{\$} \mathsf{Gen}$	**return** $\mathrm{Dec}(sk_0, c)$
$K_1^* \xleftarrow{\$} \mathcal{K}$	$c^*, K^* \xleftarrow{\$} \mathsf{Enc}(pk_b)$	
$b' \leftarrow \mathcal{A}^{\mathrm{Dec}}(pk, c^*, K_b^*)$	$b' \leftarrow \mathcal{A}^{\mathrm{Dec}_0, \mathrm{Dec}_1}(pk_0, pk_1, c^*, K^*)$	$\mathrm{Dec}_1(c \neq c^*)$:
return $[\![b' = b]\!]$	**return** $[\![b' = b]\!]$	**return** $\mathrm{Dec}(sk_1, c)$

Fig. 3. Security notions for KEM.

Definition 6 (DEM). *A DEM scheme* $\mathsf{DEM}(\mathsf{E}, \mathsf{D})$ *consists a pair of polynomial time algorithms.* E *is the encapsulation algorithm, which outputs ciphertext* c *on input key* K *and data* m. D *is the decapsulation algorithm, which outputs data* m *or a rejection symbol* $\perp$ *on input key* K *and ciphertext* c.

Correctness. The correctness requirement of DEM is $\Pr[\mathsf{D}(K, \mathsf{E}(K, m)) = m] = 1$ *for any* K *and* m.

Definition 7 (Security notions for DEM). *Let* $\mathsf{DEM} = (\mathsf{E}, \mathsf{D})$ *be a DEM scheme. We define the* Goal-ATK $\in$ {INT-CTXT} *advantage function of an adversary* $\mathcal{A}$ *against* DEM *as* $\mathrm{Adv}^{\text{Goal-ATK}}_{\mathsf{DEM}}(\mathcal{A}) := \Pr[\text{Goal-ATK}^{\mathcal{A}}_{\mathsf{DEM}} \Rightarrow 1]$, *where* Goal-ATK *games are defined in Fig. 4.*

2.2 Quantum Random Oracle Model

This part provides lemmas commonly used in proofs in QRO.

GAME INT-CTXT:	Enc(m):	Dec(c):
1 : $K \xleftarrow{\$} \mathcal{K}$	1 : $c \leftarrow \mathsf{E}(K, m)$	1 : $m \leftarrow \mathsf{D}(K, c)$
2 : $flag \leftarrow 0, L \leftarrow \emptyset$	2 : $L \leftarrow L \cup \{c\}$	2 : **if** $m \neq \perp \wedge c \notin L$ **then** $flag := 1$
3 : $\mathcal{A}^{\text{Enc,Dec}}(\cdot)$	3 : **return** c	3 : **return** m
4 : **return** $flag$		

Fig. 4. Security notions for DEM.

Lemma 1 ([22]). *Let $h : \mathcal{M} \times \mathcal{X} \to \mathcal{Y}$ and $h' : \mathcal{X} \to \mathcal{Y}$ be two independent random oracles. If an unbounded time quantum adversary $\mathcal{A}$ that queries H at most q_H times, then we have*

$$|\Pr[1 \leftarrow \mathcal{A}^{|h\rangle, |h(k,\cdot)\rangle} | k \leftarrow \mathcal{M}] - \Pr[1 \leftarrow \mathcal{A}^{|h\rangle, |h'\rangle}| \leq \frac{2q_H}{\sqrt{|\mathcal{M}|}}$$

Lemma 2 (One-Way to Hiding (OW2H)[3]). *Let Ω_H be the set of all functions $H : \mathcal{X} \to \mathcal{Y}$ and let $H \xleftarrow{\$} \Omega_H$ be a random oracle. Consider an oracle algorithm $\mathcal{A}^H$ that makes at most q queries to H. Let $\mathcal{B}^H$ be an oracle algorithm that on input x does the following: picks $i \leftarrow \{1, ..., q\}$ and $y \leftarrow \mathcal{Y}$, runs $\mathcal{A}^H(x, y)$ until (just before) the i-th query, measures the argument of the query in the computational basis and outputs the measurement outcome (if A makes less than i queries, $\mathcal{B}$ outputs $\perp \notin \mathcal{X}$. Let,*

$$P_{\mathcal{A}}^1 = \Pr[b' = 1 : H \xleftarrow{\$} \Omega_H, x \xleftarrow{\$} \mathcal{X}, b' \leftarrow \mathcal{A}^{|H\rangle}(x, H(x))]$$

$$P_{\mathcal{A}}^2 = \Pr[b' = 1 : H \xleftarrow{\$} \Omega_H, x \xleftarrow{\$} \mathcal{X}, y \xleftarrow{\$} \mathcal{Y}, b' \leftarrow \mathcal{A}^{|H\rangle}(x, y)]$$

$$P_{\mathcal{B}} = \Pr[x' = x : H \xleftarrow{\$} \Omega_H, x \xleftarrow{\$} \mathcal{X}, x' \leftarrow \mathcal{B}^{|H\rangle}(x, y)]$$

Then, we have $|P_{\mathcal{A}}^1 - P_{\mathcal{A}}^2| \leq 2q\sqrt{P_{\mathcal{B}}}$.

2.3 The Extractable RO-Simulator

In [10], Don et al. introduced the extractable RO-simulator. Which simulates the quantum random oracle H by using the compressed standard oracle [27], and has an extraction interface that can extract a x satisfies $f(x, H(x)) = t$ for an input t from the database. In this section, we recall some definitions, lemmas and introduce the efficient version of the extractable RO-simulator given in [13].

Definition 8 (Database). *A database D is a collection of pairs as:*

$$D = ((x_1, y_1), (x_2, y_2), \ldots, (x_i, y_i), (\perp, 0^n), \ldots, (\perp, 0^n)),$$

where $\perp \notin \{0,1\}^m$, $\perp \notin \{0,1\}^n$[3], $(x_j, y_j) \in \{0,1\}^m \times \{0,1\}^n$ $(j = 1, \ldots, i)$, $x_1 < \cdots < x_i$, and all $(\perp, 0^n)$ are at the end of the collection. Let $\mathbf{D}_q$ be the

[3] $\perp$ is an extra symbol indicating the empty state.

set of all database with q pairs. For a x, we say $D(x) = y$ if y exists such that $(x, y) \in D$, and $D(x) = \perp$ otherwise.

Definition 9 (Compressed standard oracle). *Let X (resp. Y) be the quantum register defined over $\{0,1\}^m$ (resp. $\{0,1\}^n$), let D_q be the database register defined over the database set $\mathbf{D}_q$. Let $|D^\perp\rangle$ be the initial state on the database register D_q, where $D^\perp \in \mathbf{D}_q$ is the database containing q pairs $(\perp, 0^n)$. A query to the compressed standard oracle with input/output register X/Y is implemented by performing the following unitary operation CStO on registers XYD_q.*

$$\mathsf{CStO} := \sum_{x \in \{0,1\}^m} |x\rangle\langle x|_{\mathsf{X}} \otimes \mathsf{StdDecomp}_x \circ \mathsf{CNOT}^x_{\mathsf{YD}_q} \circ \mathsf{StdDecomp}_x.$$

Here $\mathsf{StdDecomp}_x$ is the local decompression procedure [27] acts on the database register D_q. For state $|y, D\rangle$ ($y \in \{0,1\}^n$, $D \in \mathbf{D}_q$), $\mathsf{CNOT}^x_{\mathsf{YD}_q}|y, D\rangle = |y \oplus D(x), D\rangle$ if $D(x) \neq \perp$, and $\mathsf{CNOT}^x_{\mathsf{YD}_q}|y, D\rangle = |y, D\rangle$ otherwise.

Lemma 3 ([27]). *For any adversary making at most q queries, the compressed standard oracle defined in Definition 9 and quantum random oracle $H : \{0,1\}^m \to \{0,1\}^n$ are perfectly indistinguishable.*

Definition 10. *Let $f : \{0,1\}^m \times \{0,1\}^n \to T$ be a fixed function. For a fixed $t \in T$, we define relation $R^f_t := \{(x, y) | f(x, y) = t\}$ and parameter*

$$\Gamma_{R^f_t} := \max_{x \in \mathcal{X}} |\{y \in \mathcal{Y} | f(x, y) = t\}|.$$

Definition 11 (Purified measurement related to relation R^f_t [10]). *For the relation R^f_t, define the following projectors act on database register D_q:*

$$\Sigma^x := \sum_{\substack{D \text{ s.t. } (x, D(x)) \in R^f_t \\ x' < x, (x', D(x')) \notin R^f_t}} |D\rangle\langle D|, \quad \Sigma^\perp := \mathrm{I} - \sum_{x \in \{0,1\}^m} \Sigma^x.$$

Define measurement $\mathbb{M}^{R^f_t}$ on database register D_q to be the set of projectors $\{\Sigma^x\}_{x \in \{0,1\}^m \cup \perp}$, its measurement result is the smallest x such that $(x, D(x)) \in R^f_t$. If such x does not exist, $\mathbb{M}^{R^f_t}$ will return $\perp$. The purified measurement $\mathbb{M}^{R^f_t}_{\mathsf{D}_q\mathsf{P}}$ of $\mathbb{M}^{R^f_t}$ is defined as a unitary operation such that

$$\mathbb{M}^{R^f_t}_{\mathsf{D}_q\mathsf{P}} |D, p\rangle_{\mathsf{D}_q\mathsf{P}} := \sum_{x \in \{0,1\}^m \cup \perp} \Sigma^x |D\rangle_{\mathsf{D}_q} |p \oplus x\rangle_{\mathsf{P}}.$$

Definition 12 (The extractable RO-simulator (efficient version)). *The extractable RO-simulator $\mathcal{S}(f)$ with an internal database register D_q is a blackbox oracle with two interfaces: the RO-interface $\mathsf{eCO.RO}$ and the extraction-interface $\mathsf{eCO.E}_f$. $\mathcal{S}(f)$ prepares its database register D_q to be in state $|D^\perp\rangle$ at the beginning, where $D^\perp \in \mathbf{D}_q$ is the database containing q pairs $(\perp, 0^n)$. Then, the RO-interface $\mathsf{eCO.RO}$ and the extraction-interface $\mathsf{eCO.E}_f$ act as follows:*

- $\mathsf{eCO.RO}$: *For any quantum RO-query on query registers* XY, $\mathcal{S}(f)$ *implements a compressed standard oracle query on registers* XYD_q *by the* CStO *defined in Definition 9.*
- $\mathsf{eCO.E}_f$: *For any quantum extraction-query on query registers* TP, $\mathcal{S}(f)$ *applies*

$$\mathsf{Ext}_f := \sum_{t \in T} |t\rangle\langle t|_{\mathsf{T}} \otimes \mathrm{M}^{R_t^f}_{\mathsf{D}_q\mathsf{P}}$$

to registers $\mathsf{TD}_q\mathsf{P}$. *Here* T *is the quantum register defined over the set* T.

Furthermore, the total runtime of $\mathcal{S}(f)$ *is bounded as*

$$T_{\mathcal{S}} = O(q_{RO} \cdot q_E \cdot \mathrm{Time}[f] + q_{RO}^2),$$

where $q_{RO} (\leq q)$ *(resp.* q_E*) is the number of queries to* $\mathsf{eCO.RO}$ *(resp.* $\mathsf{eCO.E}_f$*).*

2.4 Fujisaki-Okamoto Transformation

This part gives transformation $\mathsf{U}^{\not\perp}(\mathsf{U}^{\perp})$ and transformation T. Then $\mathsf{FO}^{\perp} = \mathsf{U}^{\perp} \circ \mathsf{T}$ and $\mathsf{FO}^{\not\perp} = \mathsf{U}^{\not\perp} \circ \mathsf{T}$.

The Constructions. Let $\mathsf{PKE}_0 = (\mathsf{Gen}_0, \mathsf{Enc}_0, \mathsf{Dec}_0)$ be a PKE scheme with nonce space $\mathcal{R}$ and a random oracle $G : \{0,1\}^* \to \mathcal{R}$, the algorithms of the DPKE $\mathsf{PKE}_1 = \mathrm{T}[\mathsf{PKE}_0, G] = (\mathsf{Gen}_1, \mathsf{Enc}_1, \mathsf{Dec}_1)$ are defined in Fig. 5.

Let $\mathsf{PKE}_1 = (\mathsf{Gen}_1, \mathsf{Enc}_1, \mathsf{Dec}_1)$ be a PKE scheme with message space $\mathcal{M}$, and $H : \{0,1\}^* \to \mathcal{M}$ be a random oracle, the algorithms of the KEM with implicit rejection scheme $\mathsf{KEM}^{\not\perp} = \mathsf{U}^{\not\perp}[\mathsf{PKE}_1, H] = (\mathsf{Gen}^{\not\perp}, \mathsf{Encaps}^{\not\perp}, \mathsf{Decaps}^{\not\perp})$ are defined in Fig. 5, and the algorithms of the KEM with explicit rejection scheme $\mathsf{KEM}^{\perp} = \mathsf{U}^{\perp}[\mathsf{PKE}_1, H] = (\mathsf{Gen}^{\perp}, \mathsf{Encaps}^{\perp}, \mathsf{Decaps}^{\perp})$ are defined in Fig. 5.

2.5 KEM-DEM Paradigm

The Constructions. The hybrid PKE $\mathsf{PKE}_{\mathsf{hy}} = (\mathsf{Gen}_{\mathsf{hy}}, \mathsf{Enc}_{\mathsf{hy}}, \mathsf{Dec}_{\mathsf{hy}})$ using KEM-DEM paradigm constructed from $\mathsf{KEM} = (\mathsf{Gen}, \mathsf{Encaps}, \mathsf{Decaps})$ and $\mathsf{DEM} = (\mathsf{E}, \mathsf{D})$ is defined in Fig. 5.

3 Anonymity of FO Transformations

In this section, we follow the modular analysis approach of Hofheinz et al. [17] and discuss the anonymity of transformation U and transformation T separately.

3.1 Transformation U

Theorem 1 (PKE_1 $\mathsf{wANO\text{-}CCOA}$ $\overset{\mathrm{QROM}}{\Rightarrow}$ $\mathsf{U}^{\not\perp}[\mathsf{PKE}_1, G]$ $\mathsf{ANO\text{-}CCA}$)**.** *Let* PKE_1 *be a DPKE scheme that is* δ_1*-correct with message space* $\mathcal{M}$. *Let* $\mathcal{A}$ *be an* $\mathsf{ANO\text{-}CCA}$ *adversary against* $\mathsf{KEM}^{\not\perp} = \mathsf{U}^{\not\perp}[\mathsf{PKE}_1, H]$ *making* q_H *quantum queries to the random oracle* H *and* q_D *classical queries in total to the decapsulation oracles*

$\mathsf{Gen_1}$:	$\mathsf{Enc_1}(pk, m)$:	$\mathsf{Dec_1}(sk, c)$:
1 : $(pk, sk) \xleftarrow{\$} \mathsf{Gen_0}$	1 : $r := G(m)$	1 : $m' := \mathsf{Dec_0}(sk, c)$
2 : **return** (pk, sk)	2 : $c \leftarrow \mathsf{Enc_0}(pk, m, r)$	2 : **if** $\mathsf{Enc_0}(pk, m', G(m')) = c$
	3 : **return** c	3 : **return** m'
		4 : **else return** \perp

$\mathsf{Gen}^{\not{\perp}}$:	$\mathsf{Encaps}^{\not{\perp}}(pk)$:	$\mathsf{Decaps}^{\not{\perp}}(sk, c)$:
1 : $(pk, sk') \xleftarrow{\$} \mathsf{Gen_1}$	1 : $m \xleftarrow{\$} \mathcal{M}, c \leftarrow \mathsf{Enc_1}(pk, m)$	1 : Parse $sk = (sk', s)$
2 : $s \xleftarrow{\$} \mathcal{M}, sk := (sk', s)$	2 : $K := H(m, c)$	2 : $m' := \mathsf{Dec_1}(sk', c)$
3 : **return** (pk, sk)	3 : **return** (c, K)	3 : **if** $m' \neq \perp$
		4 : **return** $K := H(m, c)$
		5 : **else return** $K := H(s, c)$

Gen^{\perp}:	$\mathsf{Encaps}^{\perp}(pk)$:	$\mathsf{Decaps}^{\perp}(sk, c)$:
1 : $(pk, sk) \xleftarrow{\$} \mathsf{Gen_1}$	1 : $m \xleftarrow{\$} \mathcal{M}, c \leftarrow \mathsf{Enc_1}(pk, m)$	1 : $m' := \mathsf{Dec_1}(sk, c)$
2 : **return** (pk, sk)	2 : $K := H(m, c)$	2 : **if** $m' \neq \perp$
	3 : **return** (c, K)	3 : **return** $K := H(m, c)$
		4 : **else return** \perp

$\mathsf{Gen_{hy}}$:	$\mathsf{Enc_{hy}}(pk, m)$:	$\mathsf{Dec_{hy}}(sk, c)$:
1 : $(pk, sk) \xleftarrow{\$} \mathsf{Gen}$	1 : $c_0, K \leftarrow \mathsf{Enc}(pk)$	1 : $K \leftarrow \mathsf{Dec}(sk, c_0)$
2 : **return** (pk, sk)	2 : $c_1 \leftarrow \mathsf{E}(K, m)$	2 : **if** $K = \perp$ **then return** \perp
	3 : **return** $c := (c_0, c_1)$	3 : $m \leftarrow \mathsf{D}(K, c_1)$
		4 : **if** $m = \perp$ **then return** \perp
		5 : **return** m

Fig. 5. Constructions of FO transformations and the KEM-DEM Paradigm.

$\mathsf{Dec_0}$ and $\mathsf{Dec_1}$. *Then we can construct a* wANO-CCOA *adversary* \mathcal{B} *and* OW-CPA *adversary* \mathcal{C} *against* $\mathsf{PKE_1}$, *such that:*

$$\mathrm{Adv}_{\mathsf{KEM}^{\not{\perp}}}^{\mathsf{ANO\text{-}CCA}}(\mathcal{A}) \leq \mathrm{Adv}_{\mathsf{PKE_1}}^{\mathsf{wANO\text{-}CCOA}}(\mathcal{B}) + 2q_H \sqrt{\mathrm{Adv}_{\mathsf{PKE_1}}^{\mathsf{OW\text{-}CPA}}(\mathcal{C})} + \frac{4q_H}{\sqrt{|\mathcal{M}|}} + 2\delta_1.$$

Sketch. The key is simulating two different decapsulation oracles correctly without secret keys. The basic simulation trick in the Quantum Random Oracle Model (QROM), namely remapping [15,19], is followed. The decapsulation algorithm utilizes a common Key-Derivation Function (KDF) "$K = H(m, c)$" for two different public keys pk_0, pk_1. Consequently, two internal random oracles are associated, where given an input (m, c), if $c = \mathsf{Enc}(pk_i, m)$, then $K = H_i(c)$.

As highlighted by Grubbs et al. [15], it's crucial to account for pairs (m, c) where $\mathsf{Enc}(pk_0, m) = \mathsf{Enc}(pk_1, m) = c$, as the reduction cannot determine which public key was used to generate c during key encapsulation. Rather than requiring collision-freeness, we demand that the anonymity of the underlying PKE_1 provides an additional CCO oracle to identify a ciphertext c if its plaintexts under two keys are equivalent. This allows us to establish a finer domain separation for H. In the case of pairs (m, c) in this scenario, we simulate with an independent internal random oracle, i.e., $K = H_2(m, c)$. Full details of the proof can be found in Appendix A in the full version. □

Theorem 2 (PKE_1 $\mathsf{wANO\text{-}CCOVA} \overset{\mathrm{QROM}}{\Rightarrow} \mathsf{U}^{\perp}[\mathsf{PKE}_1, G]$ $\mathsf{ANO\text{-}CCA}$). *Let PKE_1 be a DPKE scheme that is δ_1-correct with message space $\mathcal{M}$. Let $\mathcal{A}$ be an $\mathsf{ANO\text{-}CCA}$ adversary against $\mathsf{KEM}^{\perp} = \mathsf{U}^{\perp}[\mathsf{PKE}_1, H]$ making q_H quantum queries to the random oracle H and q_D classical queries in total to the decapsulation oracles* Dec_0 *and* Dec_1. *Then we can construct a $\mathsf{wANO\text{-}CCOVA}$ adversary $\mathcal{B}$ and $\mathsf{OW\text{-}VA}$ adversary $\mathcal{C}$ against PKE_1, such that:*

$$\mathrm{Adv}_{\mathsf{KEM}^{\perp}}^{\mathsf{ANO\text{-}CCA}}(\mathcal{A}) \le \mathrm{Adv}_{\mathsf{PKE}_1}^{\mathsf{wANO\text{-}CCOVA}}(\mathcal{B}) + 2q_H\sqrt{\mathrm{Adv}_{\mathsf{PKE}_1}^{\mathsf{OW\text{-}VA}}(\mathcal{C})} + \frac{4q_H}{\sqrt{|\mathcal{M}|}} + 2\delta_1.$$

Sketch. The proof follows the same structure as the proof of Theorem 1, with the modification that the decapsulation oracles Decaps incorporate queries to ciphertext validity oracles CVO to determine whether to output "$\perp$". □

3.2 Transformation T

Lemma 4 ([17, Lemma 4.3]). *Let PKE_0 be δ-correct. Then PKE_1 is δ_1-correct in QROM, where $\delta_1 = \delta_1(q_G) \le 8 \cdot (q_G + 1)^2 \cdot \delta$.*

We will present the proof of the $\mathsf{wANO\text{-}CCOVA}$ security and the $\mathsf{OW\text{-}VA}$ security of PKE_1 to conclude the demonstration of the $\mathsf{ANO\text{-}CCA}$ security of the FO transformation ($\mathsf{FO}^{\not\perp}/\mathsf{FO}^{\perp}$). Importantly, it's worth emphasizing that the transformation T can achieve stronger security in the form of $\mathsf{wANO\text{-}CCA}$, a proof of which is provided here.

Lemma 5 ($\mathsf{wANO\text{-}CCA} \Rightarrow \mathsf{wANO\text{-}CCOVA}$). *Let $\mathcal{A}$ be a $\mathsf{wANO\text{-}CCOVA}$ adversary against $\mathsf{DPKE} = (\mathsf{Gen}, \mathsf{Enc}, \mathsf{Dec})$, making at most q_C classical queries to the ciphertext confirmation oracle* CCO, *q_V classical queries to the ciphertext validity oracle* CVO. *Then we can construct a $\mathsf{wANO\text{-}CCA}$ adversary $\mathcal{B}$ against DPKE, making at most $q \le q_C + q_V$, classical queries to the decryption oracle Dec such that:*

$$\mathrm{Adv}_{\mathsf{DPKE}}^{\mathsf{wANO\text{-}CCOVA}}(\mathcal{A}) \le \mathrm{Adv}_{\mathsf{DPKE}}^{\mathsf{wANO\text{-}CCA}}(\mathcal{B}).$$

Proof. The proof is obvious. $\mathcal{B}$ forwards the challenge to $\mathcal{A}$ and returns $\mathcal{A}$'s response. As for CCO, CVO oracles, $\mathcal{A}$ simulates by accessing the decryption oracles. □

Theorem 3 (PKE_0 $\mathsf{OW\text{-}CPA} \overset{\mathrm{QROM}}{\Rightarrow} \mathsf{T}[\mathsf{PKE}_0, G]$ $\mathsf{OW\text{-}VA}$). *Let* PKE_0 *be a PKE scheme that is* δ*-correct and* γ*-spread. Let* $\mathcal{A}$ *be an* $\mathsf{OW\text{-}VA}$ *adversary against* $\mathsf{PKE}_1 = \mathsf{T}[\mathsf{PKE}_0, G]$*, making* q_G *quantum queries to the random oracle* G *and* q_C *classical queries to the ciphertext validity oracle* CVO*. Then we can construct an* $\mathsf{OW\text{-}CPA}$ *adversary* $\mathcal{B}$ *against* PKE_0*, running in about the same time and resources as* $\mathcal{A}$*, such that*

$$\mathrm{Adv}_{\mathsf{PKE}_1}^{\mathsf{OW\text{-}VA}}(\mathcal{A}) \leq O(q_G)\sqrt{\mathrm{Adv}_{\mathsf{PKE}_0}^{\mathsf{OW\text{-}CPA}}(\mathcal{B})} + O(q_C) \cdot 2^{-\gamma/2} + O(q_G)\sqrt{\delta}.$$

Sketch. The key challenge lies in simulating the ciphertext validity oracle CVO without access to the secret key. Intuitively, leveraging γ-spreadness makes it challenging for an adversary to generate a valid ciphertext c without querying m to G. Therefore, the simulator can verify the validity of a ciphertext queried by the adversary through re-encryption. In other words, the simulator searches its Random Oracle (RO) query-list to check if there exists m such that $\mathsf{Enc}(pk, m; G(m)) = c$.

Handling a list of queries in the quantum setting presented a technical challenge until Zhandry introduced the compressed oracle technique [27], which allows adversary to access with quantum superposition states. Subsequently, Don et al. proposed the online extraction technique [10], providing a practical way to extract the adversary's queries.

To implement the CVO, we design a unitary operation, storing the plaintext m in a register for the input c, naturally determining the validity of c. Full details of the proof can be found in Appendix B for the complete version. □

Theorem 4 (PKE_0 $\mathsf{wANO\text{-}CPA} \overset{\mathrm{QROM}}{\Rightarrow} \mathsf{T}[\mathsf{PKE}_0, G]$ $\mathsf{wANO\text{-}CCA}$). *Let* PKE_0 *be a PKE scheme that is* δ*-correct and* γ*-spread. Let* $\mathcal{A}$ *be a* $\mathsf{wANO\text{-}CCA}$ *adversary against* $\mathsf{T}[\mathsf{PKE}_0, G]$*, making* q_G *quantum queries to the random oracle* G *and* q_D *classical queries in total to the decryption oracle* Dec_0 *and* Dec_1*. Then we can construct an* $\mathsf{wANO\text{-}CPA}$ *adversary* $\mathcal{B}$ *against* PKE_0 *and an* $\mathsf{OW\text{-}CPA}$ *adversary* $\mathcal{C}$ *against* PKE_0*, running in about the same time and resources as* $\mathcal{A}$*, such that*

$$\mathrm{Adv}_{\mathsf{T}[\mathsf{PKE}_0, G]}^{\mathsf{wANO\text{-}CCA}}(\mathcal{A}) \leq \mathrm{Adv}_{\mathsf{PKE}_0}^{\mathsf{wANO\text{-}CPA}}(\mathcal{B}) + O(q_G)\sqrt{\mathrm{Adv}_{\mathsf{PKE}_0}^{\mathsf{OW\text{-}CPA}}(\mathcal{C})} \\ + O(q_D) \cdot 2^{-\gamma/2} + O(q_G)\sqrt{\delta}.$$

Sketch. We tackle the simulation of two decryption oracles without access to the secret keys. Drawing inspiration from the idea presented in the previous proof, we accomplish the simulation by employing an extractable Random Oracle (RO) simulator. The distinction lies in defining two related unitary operations to implement Dec_0 and Dec_1, followed by storing the plaintexts m_0 and m_1 in two separate registers. It's important to clarify that in this scenario, the simulator searches from the same G query list and checks for the existence of m such that $\mathsf{Enc}(pk_0, m; G(m)) = c$ and $\mathsf{Enc}(pk_1, m; G(m)) = c$, respectively, making these two operations feasible. Full details of the proof are available in Appendix C in the complete version. □

4 Anonymity of KEM-DEM Paradigm

This paper explores the anonymity of hybrid encryption concerning KEMs with implicit and explicit rejection, respectively.

For the implicit case, we require that the invalid key is random and define η-randomness for invalid keys as a relaxation.

Definition 13 (η-Randomness for Invalid Keys). *We say* KEM *is* η-*random for invalid keys if for* $(pk, sk) \leftarrow \mathsf{Gen}$ *and* $c \in C_{Inv}$*, where* $C_{Inv} := \{c, \mathsf{Encaps}(pk) \neq c\}$.

$$\Pr[b' = b | b' \leftarrow \mathcal{A}(pk, c, K_b^*), K_0^* = \mathsf{Dec}(sk, c), K_1^* \leftarrow \mathcal{K}, b \leftarrow \{0,1\}] \leq \frac{1}{2} + \eta.$$

Theorem 5. *Let* $\mathsf{KEM}^{\not\perp}$ *be a* δ*-correct KEM with* η*-randomness for invalid keys and* DEM *be a DEM. Let* $\mathcal{A}$ *be an* ANO-CCA *adversary against the hybrid encryption scheme* $\mathsf{PKE_{hy}}$ *using KEM-DEM paradigm obtained by* $\mathsf{KEM}^{\not\perp}$ *and* DEM*. Then we construct a* wANO-CCA *adversary* $\mathcal{B}$*,* IND-CCA *adversary* $\mathcal{C}$*, and* INT-CTXT *adversary* $\mathcal{D}$ *against* DEM *and such that:*

$$\mathrm{Adv}_{\mathsf{PKE_{hy}}}^{\mathsf{ANO\text{-}CCA}}(\mathcal{A}) \leq 3\mathrm{Adv}_{\mathsf{KEM}^{\not\perp}}^{\mathsf{IND\text{-}CCA}}(\mathcal{B}) + 2\mathrm{Adv}_{\mathsf{DEM}}^{\mathsf{INT\text{-}CTXT}}(\mathcal{C}) + \mathrm{Adv}_{\mathsf{KEM}^{\not\perp}}^{\mathsf{wANO\text{-}CCA}}(\mathcal{D}) + \delta + \eta$$

Proof. Consider the sequence of games $\mathbf{G}_0$- $\mathbf{G}_5$ described in Fig. 6.

Game $\mathbf{G}_0$: This game is exactly the ANO-CCA game for $\mathsf{PKE_{hy}}$.

$$\mathrm{Adv}_{\mathsf{PKE_{hy}}}^{\mathsf{ANO\text{-}CCA}}(\mathcal{A}) = \left| \Pr[1 \leftarrow \mathbf{G}_0] - \frac{1}{2} \right| \tag{1}$$

Game $\mathbf{G}_1$: We start with some "cosmetic" adjustments in this game. Specifically, the pair (c_0^*, K^*) is formed by running $\mathsf{Encaps}(pk_b)$ for a uniformly random bit b before the adversary $\mathcal{A}$ selecting a message m^*. This modification has no effect on $\mathcal{A}$'s point of view. Then we modify the decryption oracle $\mathrm{Dec}(sk_b, c_0^*, c_1)$ that responds with $\mathsf{D}(K^*, c_1)$ instead of $\mathsf{D}(\mathsf{Decaps}(sk_b, c_0), c_1)$. Obviously, such a modification can be bounded by the decapsulation error. Hence,

GAMES G_0-G_5		$\text{Dec}_b(c \neq c^*)$	$//G_0$-G_5
1: $(pk_0, sk_0), (pk_1, sk_1) \leftarrow \text{Gen}$ $//G_0$-G_5		1: Parse $c = (c_0, c_1)$	$//G_0$-G_5
2: $inp' \leftarrow (pk_0, pk_1)$ $//G_0$-G_5		2: if $c_0 = c_0^*$	$//G_1$-G_5
3: $b \xleftarrow{\$} \{0,1\}, c_0^*, K^* \leftarrow \text{Encaps}(pk_b)$ $//G_1$-G_5		3: $\quad K' := K^*$	$//G_1$
4: $m^*, st \leftarrow \mathcal{A}^{\text{Dec}_0, \text{Dec}_1}(inp')$ $//G_0$-G_5		4: $\quad K' := K_1^*, K_1^* \leftarrow \mathcal{K}$	$//G_2$
5: $b \xleftarrow{\$} \{0,1\}, c_0^*, K^* \leftarrow \text{Encaps}(pk_b)$ $//G_0$		5: \quad return \perp	$//G_3$-G_5
6: $c_1^* \leftarrow \text{E}(K^*, m^*)$ $//G_0$-G_1		6: else $\quad K' := \text{Decaps}(sk_b, c_0)$	$//G_1$-G_5
7: $K_1^* \leftarrow \mathcal{K}, c_1^* \leftarrow \text{E}(K_1^*, m^*)$ $//G_2$-G_5		7: $K' := \text{Decaps}(sk_b, c_0)$	$//G_0$
8: $c^* := (c_0^*, c_1^*), int := int', c^*$ $//G_0$-G_5		8: $m' := \text{D}(K', c_1)$	$//G_0$-G_5
9: $b' \leftarrow \mathcal{A}^{\text{Dec}_0, \text{Dec}_1}(inp, st)$ $//G_0$-G_5		9: return m'	$//G_0$-G_5
10: return $[\![b' = b]\!]$ $//G_0$-G_5		$\text{Dec}_{1-b}(c \neq c^*)$	$//G_0$-G_5
		1: Parse $c = (c_0, c_1)$	$//G_0$-G_5
		2: if $c_0 = c_0^*$	$//G_4$-G_5
		3: $\quad K' := K_2^*, K_2^* \leftarrow \mathcal{K}$	$//G_4$
		4: \quad return \perp	$//G_5$
		5: else $K' := \text{Decaps}(sk_{1-b}, c_0)$	$//G_1$-G_5
		6: $K' := \text{Decaps}(sk_{1-b}, c_0)$	$//G_0$
		7: $m' := \text{D}(K', c_1)$	$//G_0$-G_5
		8: return m'	$//G_0$-G_5

Fig. 6. Games G_0 to G_5 in the proof of Theorem 5.

$$|\Pr[1 \leftarrow G_0] - \Pr[1 \leftarrow G_1]| \leq \delta \qquad (2)$$

Game G_2: In this game, we modify the way of generating c_1^* that is computed by $\text{E}(K_1^*, m^*)$, $K_1^* \xleftarrow{\$} \mathcal{K}$ instead of $\text{E}(K^*, m^*)$. Correspondingly, $\text{Dec}(sk_b, c_0^*, c_1)$ returns $\text{D}(K_1^*, c_1)$. Such a modification can be bounded by the advantage of the adversary \mathcal{B} against IND-CCA security of KEM. Then,

$$|\Pr[1 \leftarrow G_1] - \Pr[1 \leftarrow G_2]| \leq 2\text{Adv}_{\text{KEM}^{\perp}}^{\text{IND-CCA}}(\mathcal{B}) \qquad (3)$$

We construct the adversary \mathcal{B} in Fig. 7. \mathcal{B} simulates the decryption oracles $\text{Dec}_0, \text{Dec}_1$ in the same way as in G_2.

Challenger		Adv \mathcal{B}		Adv \mathcal{A}
$(pk, sk) \leftarrow \text{Gen}$		$b, \hat{b} \xleftarrow{\$} \{0,1\}, pk_b = pk$		
$b^* \xleftarrow{\$} \{0,1\}, K_1^* \xleftarrow{\$} \mathcal{K}$	$pk, c^*, K_{b^*}^*$	$(pk_{1-b}, sk_{1-b}) \leftarrow \text{Gen}$	pk_0, pk_1	$m \leftarrow \mathcal{A}^{\text{Dec}_0, \text{Dec}_1}$
$c^*, K_0^* \leftarrow \text{Encaps}(pk)$	\longrightarrow	$c_0^* := c^*, c_1^* := \text{D}(K_{b^*}^*, m)$	\longrightarrow	
		if $b' = b, b'' := b$	c_0^*, c_1^*	
Return $[\![b'' = b^*]\!]$	b''	else $b'' := \hat{b}$	b'	$b' \leftarrow \mathcal{A}^{\text{Dec}_0, \text{Dec}_1}$
	\longleftarrow		\longleftarrow	

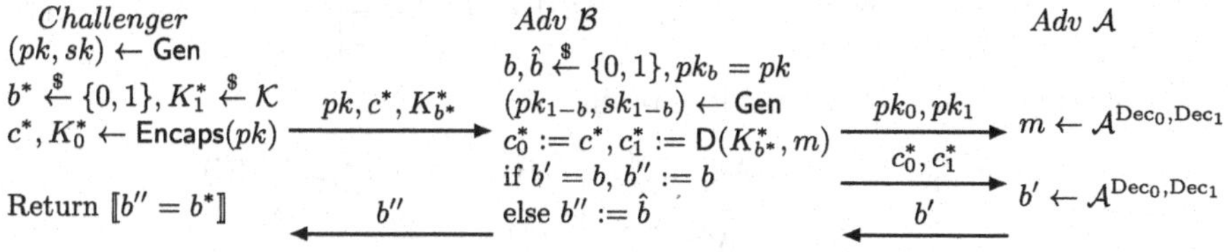

Fig. 7. The adversary \mathcal{B} in the proof of Theorem 5.

Game $\mathbf{G_3}$: In this game, we modify the decryption oracle $\mathrm{Dec}(sk_b, c_0^*, c_1)$ that responds with "$\perp$" instead of $\mathsf{D}(K_1^*, c_1)$. There is no difference between $\mathbf{G_3}$ and $\mathbf{G_2}$ unless $\mathcal{A}$ queries $\mathrm{Dec}(sk_b, \cdot)$ with (c_0^*, c_1) such that $\mathsf{D}(K_1^*, c_1) \neq \perp$, for a uniformly random key. This event can be bounded by the advantage of an adverdary $\mathcal{C}$ in the $\mathsf{INT\text{-}CTXT}$ game of DEM. Then,

$$|\Pr[1 \leftarrow \mathbf{G_2}] - \Pr[1 \leftarrow \mathbf{G_3}]| \leq \mathrm{Adv}_{\mathsf{DEM}}^{\mathsf{INT\text{-}CTXT}}(\mathcal{C}) \tag{4}$$

Game $\mathbf{G_4}$: In this game, we modify the decryption oracle $\mathrm{Dec}(sk_{1-b}, c_0^*, c_1)$ to return $\mathsf{D}(K_2^*, c_1)$, $K_2^* \leftarrow \mathcal{K}$. Specifically, the are two disjoint cases as follows:

- $\mathsf{Decaps}(sk_{1-b_0}, c_0^*)$ results in an "implicit rejection".
- $\mathsf{Decaps}(sk_{1-b_0}, c_0^*)$ results in a "valid key".

For the first case, the change from $\mathsf{Decaps}(sk_{1-b_0}, c_0^*)$ to a random key is bounded by η-randomness for invalid key of KEM. For the second case, we construct the adverdary $\mathcal{B}$ against $\mathsf{IND\text{-}CCA}$ security of KEM in Fig. 8. $\mathcal{B}$ simulates the decryption oracles $\mathrm{Dec}_0, \mathrm{Dec}_1$ in the same way as in $\mathbf{G_4}$. Thus,

$$|\Pr[1 \leftarrow \mathbf{G_3}] - \Pr[1 \leftarrow \mathbf{G_4}]| \leq \mathrm{Adv}_{\mathsf{KEM}^{\not\perp}}^{\mathsf{IND\text{-}CCA}}(\mathcal{B}) + \eta \tag{5}$$

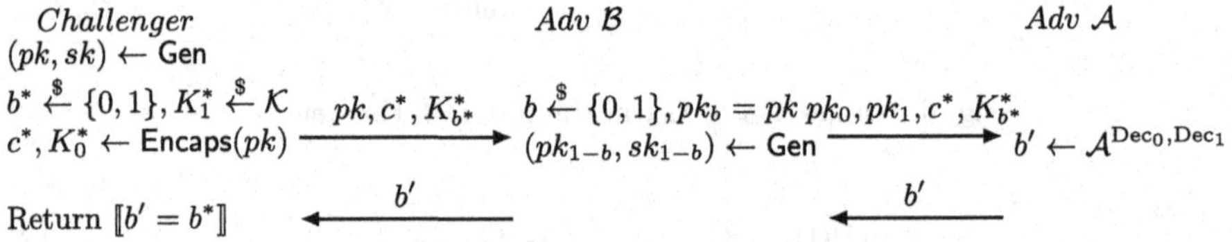
Challenger
Adv B
Adv A
(pk, sk) ← Gen
b* ←$ {0,1}, K1* ←$ K
c*, K0* ← Encaps(pk)
pk, c*, Kb**
b ←$ {0,1}, pkb = pk pk0, pk1, c*, Kb**
(pk1−b, sk1−b) ← Gen
b′ ← A^{Dec0,Dec1}
b′
b′
Return ⟦b′ = b*⟧

Fig. 8. The adversary $\mathcal{B}$ in the proof of Theorem 5.

Game $\mathbf{G_5}$: In this game, we modify $\mathsf{Dec}(sk_{1-b}, c_0^*, c_1)$ to return "$\perp$" instead of $\mathsf{D}(K_2^*, c_1)$. The analysis is the same as the "game-hop" between $\mathbf{G_3}$ and $\mathbf{G_2}$. Then,

$$|\Pr[1 \leftarrow \mathbf{G_5}] - \Pr[1 \leftarrow \mathbf{G_4}]| \leq \mathrm{Adv}_{\mathsf{DEM}}^{\mathsf{INT\text{-}CTXT}}(\mathcal{C}) \tag{6}$$

Finally, we show that $\mathcal{A}$'s success probability in $\mathbf{G_5}$ can be bounded by the advantage of the adversary $\mathcal{D}$ against $\mathsf{wANO\text{-}CCA}$ security of $\mathsf{KEM}^{\not\perp}$ in Fig. 9. $\mathcal{D}$ simulates the decryption oracles $\mathrm{Dec}_0, \mathrm{Dec}_1$ in the same way as in $\mathbf{G_5}$. Then,

$$\mathrm{Adv}_{\mathsf{KEM}^{\not\perp}}^{\mathsf{wANO\text{-}CCA}}(\mathcal{A}) = \left|\Pr[1 \leftarrow \mathbf{G_5}] - \frac{1}{2}\right| \tag{7}$$

Combining (1) to (7), we finally obtain

$$\begin{aligned}\mathrm{Adv}_{\mathsf{PKE_{hy}}}^{\mathsf{ANO\text{-}CCA}}(\mathcal{A}) \leq \mathrm{Adv}_{\mathsf{KEM}^{\not\perp}}^{\mathsf{wANO\text{-}CCA}}(\mathcal{B}) + 3\mathrm{Adv}_{\mathsf{KEM}^{\not\perp}}^{\mathrm{IND\text{-}CCA}}(\mathcal{C}) \\ + 2\mathrm{Adv}_{\mathsf{DEM}}^{\mathsf{INT\text{-}CTXT}}(\mathcal{D}) + \delta + \eta\end{aligned}$$

□

□

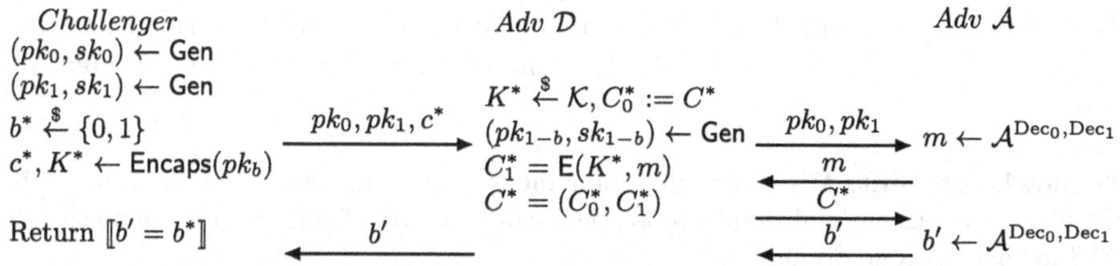

Fig. 9. The adversary \mathcal{D} in the proof of Theorem 5.

Theorem 6. *Let* KEM^{\perp} *be a* δ*-correct KEM and* DEM *be a DEM. Let* \mathcal{A} *be an* ANO-CCA *adversary against the hybrid encryption scheme* $\mathsf{PKE_{hy}}$ *using KEM-DEM paradigm abtained by* $\mathsf{KEM}^{\not\perp}$ *and* DEM*. Then we construct a* wANO-CCA *adversary* \mathcal{B}*,* IND-CCA *adversary* \mathcal{C}*, and* INT-CTXT *adversary* \mathcal{D} *against* DEM *and such that:*

$$\mathrm{Adv}^{\mathsf{ANO\text{-}CCA}}_{\mathsf{PKE_{hy}}}(\mathcal{A}) \leq 3\mathrm{Adv}^{\mathsf{IND\text{-}CCA}}_{\mathsf{KEM}^{\not\perp}}(\mathcal{B}) + 2\mathrm{Adv}^{\mathsf{INT\text{-}CTXT}}_{\mathsf{DEM}}(\mathcal{C})$$
$$+ \mathrm{Adv}^{\mathsf{wANO\text{-}CCA}}_{\mathsf{KEM}^{\not\perp}}(\mathcal{D}) + \delta$$

Schetch. This proof is the same as the proof of Theorem 5, except that in the rejection case of Game $\mathbf{G_4}$, $\mathsf{Decaps}(sk_{1-b_0}, c_0^*)$ return "\perp" directly. □

Theorem 7. *Let* $\mathsf{KEM}^{\not\perp} = \mathsf{U}^{\not\perp}[\mathsf{T}[\mathsf{PKE_0}, G], H]$ *be a KEM scheme. Then* $\mathsf{KEM}^{\not\perp}$ *is* η*-random for invalid keys, where* $\eta = \frac{2q_H}{\sqrt{|M|}}$*.*

Proof. We modify $K_0^* = H(s_{1-b}, c^*)$, to $H'(c^*)$, where H' is an internal random oracle. Such a modification can be bounded by $\frac{2q_H}{\sqrt{|M|}}$ according to Lemma 1. Then K_0^* and K_1^* are both uniformly random. Thus $\eta = \frac{2q_H}{\sqrt{|M|}}$. □

5 Conclusions

The demand for anonymous PKEs in practical applications, coupled with the threat of quantum computers, highlights the need for a more focused exploration of constructing anonymous post-quantum PKEs. This paper revisits the anonymity of FO and the KEM-DEM paradigm in both implicit and explicit cases. Specifically, for FO, in the implicit case, we base on the existing results by refining the underlying assumptions. In the explicit case, we provide an initial demonstration of the anonymity of the textbook FO in QROM. Concerning the KEM-DEM paradigm, we establish that anonymity is clear when considering the implicit and explicit cases, respectively. Furthermore, we demonstrate the anonymity of KEM-DEM using FO.

Future Work: The exploration of the anonymity of other transformations, such as REACT and GEM in QROM, is a future direction of interest for our research. Similarly, within the scope of constructing multiple KEM-DEM combinations for

IND-CCA hybrid encryption [2,9,18], our goal is to investigate various security combination approaches specifically for constructing ANO-CCA hybrid encryption.

Acknowledgement. We thank the anonymous PQCrypto 2024 reviewers for their helpful comments. Special thanks to Jiaxia Ge of Institute of Information Engineering, CAS for his valuable discussion.

A Proof of Theorem 1

Theorem 1 (PKE_1 wANO-CCOA $\overset{\text{QROM}}{\Rightarrow}$ $\mathsf{U}^{\not\perp}[\mathsf{PKE}_1, G]$ ANO-CCA). *Let* PKE_1 *be a DPKE scheme that is* δ_1*-correct with message space* $\mathcal{M}$. *Let* $\mathcal{A}$ *be an* ANO-CCA *adversary against* $\mathsf{KEM}^{\not\perp} = \mathsf{U}^{\not\perp}[\mathsf{PKE}_1, H]$ *making* q_H *quantum queries to the random oracle* H *and* q_D *classical queries in total to the decapsulation oracles* Dec_0 *and* Dec_1. *Then we can construct a* wANO-CCOA *adversary* $\mathcal{B}$ *and* OW-CPA *adversary* $\mathcal{C}$ *against* PKE_1, *such that:*

$$\mathrm{Adv}^{\mathsf{ANO\text{-}CCA}}_{\mathsf{KEM}^{\not\perp}}(\mathcal{A}) \le \mathrm{Adv}^{\mathsf{wANO\text{-}CCOA}}_{\mathsf{PKE}_1}(\mathcal{B}) + 2q_H\sqrt{\mathrm{Adv}^{\mathsf{OW\text{-}CPA}}_{\mathsf{PKE}_1}(\mathcal{C})} + \frac{4q_H}{\sqrt{|\mathcal{M}|}} + 2\delta_1.$$

```
GAMES G_0-G_7
(pk_0, sk_0), (pk_1, sk_1) <- Gen^⊥̸                 //G_0-G_7
H_0, H'_0, H_1, H'_1, H_2 <-$ Ω_H                   //G_0-G_7
H_3 <-$ Ω_{H'}, H_4 <-$ Ω_{H''}                     //G_0-G_7
b <-$ {0,1}, m* <-$ M                               //G_0-G_7
c* <- Enc_1(pk_b, m*, r*)                           //G_0-G_7
K* <- H(m*, c*)                                     //G_0-G_5
K* <-$ K                                            //G_6-G_7
inp <- (pk_0, pk_1, (c*, K*))                       //G_0-G_7
b' <- A^{H,Decaps_0(·),Decaps_1(·)}(inp)            //G_0-G_6
return [[b' = b]]                                   //G_0-G_6
run A^{H,Decaps_0(·),Decaps_1(·)}(inp)
until i-th query to H                               //G_7
measure the i-th query
and get the output m'                               //G_7
return [[m' = m*]]                                  //G_7
```

```
H(m, c)                                                      //G_0-G_7
return H_3(m, c)                                             //G_0-G_1
if c = c*      return H_4(c)                                 //G_5-G_7
elseif Dec_1(sk_0, c) = m ∧ Dec_1(sk_1, c) = m               //G_2-G_3
elseif Enc_1(pk_0, m) = c ∧ Dec_1(sk_1, c) = m               //G_3.5
elseif Enc_1(pk_0, m) = c ∧ Enc_1(pk_1, m) = c               //G_4-G_7
        return H_0(c)                                        //G_2-G_7
elseif Dec_1(sk_0, c) ≠ m ∧ Dec_1(sk_1, c) = m               //G_2-G_3
elseif Enc_1(pk_0, m) ≠ c ∧ Dec_1(sk_1, c) = m               //G_3.5
elseif Enc_1(pk_0, m) ≠ c ∧ Enc_1(pk_1, m) = c               //G_4-G_7
        return H_1(c)                                        //G_2-G_7
elseif Dec_1(sk_0, c) = m ∧ Dec_1(sk_1, c) ≠ m               //G_2-G_3
elseif Enc_1(pk_0, m) = c ∧ Dec_1(sk_1, c) ≠ m               //G_3.5
elseif Enc_1(pk_0, m) = c ∧ Enc_1(pk_1, m) ≠ c               //G_4-G_7
        return H_2(c)                                        //G_2-G_7
else   return H_3(m, c)                                      //G_2-G_7
```

```
Decaps_0(c ≠ c*)                                    //G_0-G_7
Parse  sk_0 = (sk'_0, s_0)                          //G_0-G_2
m' := Dec_1(sk'_0, c)                               //G_0-G_2
if m' ≠ ⊥ return K := H(m', c)                      //G_0-G_2
else   return K := H(s_0, c)                        //G_0
else   return K := H'_0(c)                          //G_0.5-G_2
if CCO(c) = 1                                       //G_2.5-G_7
return K := H_2(c)                                  //G_2.5-G_7
else   return K := H_0(c)                           //G_2.5-G_7
```

```
Decaps_1(c ≠ c*)                                    //G_0-G_7
Parse  sk_1 = (sk'_1, s_0)                          //G_0-G_2.5
m' := Dec_1(sk'_1, c)                               //G_0-G_2.5
if m' ≠ ⊥      return K := H(m', c)                 //G_0-G_2.5
else   return K := H(s_1, c)                        //G_0-G_0.5
else   return K := H'_1(c)                          //G_1-G_2.5
if CCO(c) = 1                                       //G_3-G_7
return K := H_2(c)                                  //G_3-G_7
else   return K := H_1(c)                           //G_3-G_7
```

Fig. 10. Games $\mathbf{G}_0$ to $\mathbf{G}_7$ in the proof of Theorem 1.

Full. Denote Ω_H, $\Omega_{H'}$, and $\Omega_{H''}$, to be the set of all functions $H : \mathcal{C} \to \mathcal{K}$, $H' : \mathcal{M} \times \mathcal{C} \to \mathcal{K}$ and $H'' : \mathcal{M} \to \mathcal{K}$ respectively, where $\mathcal{K}$ is the encapsulated keyspace of $\mathrm{KEM}^{\not\perp}$ and $\mathcal{C}$ is the ciphertext space of $\mathrm{PKE}/\mathrm{KEM}^{\not\perp}$.

Let $\mathcal{A}$ be an adversary in the ANO-CCA game for $\mathrm{KEM}^{\not\perp}$ making at most q_D (random) queries to the oracles $\mathrm{Decaps}_0(\cdot)$ and $\mathrm{Decaps}_1(\cdot)$ and q_H quantum queries to the random oracles H. Consider the sequence of games G_0-G_7 described in Fig. 10.

Game $\mathbf{G_0}$: This game is exactly the ANO-CCA game for $\mathsf{KEM}^{\not\perp}$.

$$\mathrm{Adv}^{\mathsf{ANO\text{-}CCA}}_{\mathsf{KEM}^{\not\perp}}(\mathcal{A}) = \left|\Pr[1 \leftarrow \mathbf{G_0}] - \frac{1}{2}\right| \tag{8}$$

Game $\mathbf{G_{0.5}}$: In this game, we modify the decapsulation oracle $\mathrm{Decaps}_0(c)$ for an invalid ciphertext c from $H(s_0, c)$ to $H_0'(c)$. Such a modification can be bounded by Lemma 1, for $\mathcal{A}$'s view is independent from (the uniform secret) s_0. Then,

$$|\Pr[1 \leftarrow \mathbf{G_0}] - \Pr[1 \leftarrow \mathbf{G_{0.5}}]| \leq \frac{2q_H}{\sqrt{|\mathcal{M}|}}. \tag{9}$$

Game $\mathbf{G_1}$: In this game, we modify the decapsulation oracle $\mathrm{Decaps}_1(c)$ similarly as in $\mathbf{G_{0.5}}$, that for an invalid ciphertext c from $H(s_0, c)$ to $H_1'(c)$. The modification can be analyzed in a similar manner as the previous "game-hop".

$$|\Pr[1 \leftarrow \mathbf{G_{0.5}}] - \Pr[1 \leftarrow \mathbf{G_1}]| \leq \frac{2q_H}{\sqrt{|\mathcal{M}|}}. \tag{10}$$

Game $\mathbf{G_2}$: In this game, we separate the domain of H and simulate with internal random functions. Specifically, (m, c) pairs are divided into four disjoint categories. For (m, c) that

- $\mathsf{Dec}_1(sk_0, c) = m \wedge \mathsf{Dec}_1(sk_1, c) = m$, responds with $H_0(c)$;
- $\mathsf{Dec}_1(sk_0, c) \neq m \wedge \mathsf{Dec}_1(sk_1, c) = m$, responds with $H_1(c)$;
- $\mathsf{Dec}_1(sk_0, c) = m \wedge \mathsf{Dec}_1(sk_1, c) \neq m$, responds with $H_2(c)$;
- $\mathsf{Dec}_1(sk_0, c) \neq m \wedge \mathsf{Dec}_1(sk_1, c) \neq m$, responds with $H_3(m, c)$.

H_0, H_1 and H_2 are internal random functions not directly accessible to the adversary $\mathcal{A}$. Therefore,

$$\Pr[1 \leftarrow \mathbf{G_1}] = \Pr[1 \leftarrow \mathbf{G_2}]. \tag{11}$$

Game $\mathbf{G_{2.5}}$: In this game, we modify the decapsulation oracle $\mathrm{Decaps}_0(\cdot)$ to make no use of the secret key sk_0'. Namely, $H_2(c)$ is returned when $\mathrm{CCO}(c) = 1$ and $H_0(c)$ is returned otherwise. Then,

$$\Pr[1 \leftarrow \mathbf{G_2}] = \Pr[1 \leftarrow \mathbf{G_{2.5}}]. \tag{12}$$

We explain the equivalence in more details. For a fixed ciphertext c, let $m_0 = \mathsf{Dec}_1(sk_0, c)$, $m_1 = \mathsf{Dec}_1(sk_1, c)$. Consider the following disjoint cases:

- $m_0 \neq \perp \wedge m_0 = m_1 = m$. The $\text{Decaps}_0(c)$ returns $H(m_0, c) = H_0(c)$ in $\mathbf{G_2}$ for $\mathsf{Dec}_1(sk_0, c) = m \wedge \mathsf{Dec}_1(sk_1, c) = m$, and it returns $H_0(c)$ in $\mathbf{G_{2.5}}$, which is the same.
- $m_0 \neq \perp \wedge m_0 \neq m_1$. The $\text{Decaps}_0(c)$ returns $H(m, c) = H_2(c)$ in $\mathbf{G_2}$ for $\mathsf{Dec}_1(sk_0, c) = m \wedge \mathsf{Dec}_1(sk_1, c) \neq m$, and it returns $H_2(c)$ in $\mathbf{G_{2.5}}$, which is the same.
- $m_0 = \perp$. The $\text{Decaps}_0(c)$ returns $H_0'(c)$ and $H_0(c)$ are returned $\mathbf{G_2}$ and $\mathbf{G_{2.5}}$, respectively. In $\mathbf{G_2}$, H_0' is a random function independent of H. In $\mathbf{G_{2.5}}$, the value of $H_0(c)$ can never be known through H, for the case that $\mathsf{Dec}_1(sk_0, c) = m$ never happens for an invalid c. Hence, in $\mathcal{A}$'s view, $H_0(c)$ is totally uniform at random like $H_0'(c)$.

Game $\mathbf{G_3}$: In this game, we modify the decapsulation oracle $\text{Decaps}_1(\cdot)$ to make no use of the secret key sk_1' similarly as the previous game. Namely, $H_2(c)$ is returned when $\text{CCO}(c) = 1$ and $H_1(c)$ is returned otherwise. The analysis is the same as the previous "game-hop". Then,

$$\Pr[1 \leftarrow \mathbf{G_{2.5}}] = \Pr[1 \leftarrow \mathbf{G_3}]. \tag{13}$$

Game $\mathbf{G_{3.5}}$: In this game, we modify the conditions for domain separation of H from $\mathsf{Dec}_1(sk_0, c) = m$ to $\mathsf{Enc}_1(pk_0, m) = c$, and from $\mathsf{Dec}_1(sk_0, c) \neq m$ to $\mathsf{Enc}_1(pk_0, m) \neq c$. Such a modification can be bounded by the decapsulation error. Then,

$$|\Pr[1 \leftarrow \mathbf{G_3}] - \Pr[1 \leftarrow \mathbf{G_{3.5}}]| \leq \delta. \tag{14}$$

Game $\mathbf{G_4}$: In this game, we modify the conditions for domain separation of H from $\mathsf{Dec}_1(sk_1, c) = m$ to $\mathsf{Enc}_1(pk_1, m) = c$, and from $\mathsf{Dec}_1(sk_1, c) \neq m$ to $\mathsf{Enc}_1(pk_1, m) \neq c$. The analysis is the same as the previous "game-hop". Then,

$$|\Pr[1 \leftarrow \mathbf{G_{3.5}}] - \Pr[1 \leftarrow \mathbf{G_4}]| \leq \delta. \tag{15}$$

Game $\mathbf{G_5}$: In this game, we answer H-queries of the form (m, c^*) with $H_4(m)$, where H_4 is an independent random function. The adversary knows nothing about $H_4(m)$ through the Decaps oracles since c^* is a forbidden decapsulation query. Then,

$$\Pr[1 \leftarrow \mathbf{G_4}] = \Pr[1 \leftarrow \mathbf{G_5}]. \tag{16}$$

Game $\mathbf{G_6}$: In this game, $K^* = H(m^*, c^*)(= H_4(m^*))$ is replaced by $K^* \xleftarrow{\$} \mathcal{K}$. Such a modification can be bounded by Lemma 2. Then,

$$|\Pr[1 \leftarrow \mathbf{G_5}] - \Pr[1 \leftarrow \mathbf{G_6}]| \leq 2q_H \sqrt{\Pr[1 \leftarrow \mathcal{E}^{H_4}]}. \tag{17}$$

We give details here to explain more clearly. Let $\mathcal{D}^{H_4}$ be an oracle algorithm on input (m^*, K^*) that has quantum access to H_4 as in Fig. 11, where $H, \text{Decaps}_0(\cdot), \text{Decaps}_1(\cdot)$ respond the same as in $\mathbf{G_5}$.

$\mathcal{D}^{H_4}(m^*, K^*)$:

1 : $(pk_0, sk_0'), (pk_1, sk_1') \leftarrow \mathsf{Gen}^{\not\perp}; H_0, H_1, H_2 \xleftarrow{\$} \Omega_H, H_3 \xleftarrow{\$} \Omega_{H'}$

2 : $b \xleftarrow{\$} \{0,1\}, c^* \leftarrow \mathsf{Enc}_1(pk_b, m^*), inp \leftarrow (pk_0, pk_1, (c^*, K^*))$

3 : $b' \leftarrow \mathcal{A}^{H,\mathrm{Decaps}_0(\cdot),\mathrm{Decaps}_1(\cdot)}(inp)$

4 : **return** $[\![b' = b]\!]$

Fig. 11. The oracle algorithm $\mathcal{D}^{H_4}$ in the proof of Theorem 1.

$$\Pr[b' = 1 : H_4 \xleftarrow{\$} \Omega_{H''}, m^* \xleftarrow{\$} \mathcal{M}, b' \leftarrow \mathcal{D}^{H_4}(m^*, H_4(m^*))] = \Pr[1 \leftarrow \mathrm{G}_5]$$
$$\Pr[b' = 1 : H_4 \xleftarrow{\$} \Omega_{H''}, m^* \xleftarrow{\$} \mathcal{M}, K^* \xleftarrow{\$} \mathcal{K}, b' \leftarrow \mathcal{D}^{H_4}(m^*, K^*))] = \Pr[1 \leftarrow \mathrm{G}_6]$$

Let $\mathcal{E}^{H_4}$ be an oracle algorithm that on input m^* does the following: pick $i \xleftarrow{\$} \{1, ..., q_H\}$ and $K_0^* \xleftarrow{\$} \mathcal{K}$, run $\mathcal{D}^{H_4}(m^*, K_0^*)$ until the i-th query to H_4, measure the argument of the query in the computational basis, output the measurement outcome. Then the bound is obtained applying Lemma 2.

Game $\mathbf{G_7}$: In this game, run $\mathcal{A}^{H,\mathrm{Decaps}_0(,\cdot),\mathrm{Decaps}_1(,\cdot)}(inp)$ until i-th query to H, measure the i-th query and get the output m'. The game returns $[\![m' = m^*]\!]$.

$$\Pr[1 \leftarrow \mathbf{G_7}] = \Pr[1 \leftarrow \mathcal{E}^{H_4}]. \quad (18)$$

In the following part, we construct the adversary $\mathcal{B}$ and $\mathcal{C}$ against the wANO-CCOA and OW-CPA security of PKE_1 to bound $\Pr[1 \leftarrow \mathbf{G_6}]$ and $\Pr[1 \leftarrow \mathbf{G_7}]$, respectively.

The adversary $\mathcal{B}$ simulates H_0, H_1, H_2, H_3, H_4 by quantum-accessible pseudorandom functions, answer H queries and decapsulation queries in the same way as in $\mathbf{G_6}$ (Fig. 12).

$$\mathrm{Adv}_{\mathsf{PKE}_1}^{\mathsf{wANO\text{-}CCOA}}(\mathcal{B}) \geq \left|\Pr[1 \leftarrow \mathbf{G_6}] - \frac{1}{2}\right| \quad (19)$$

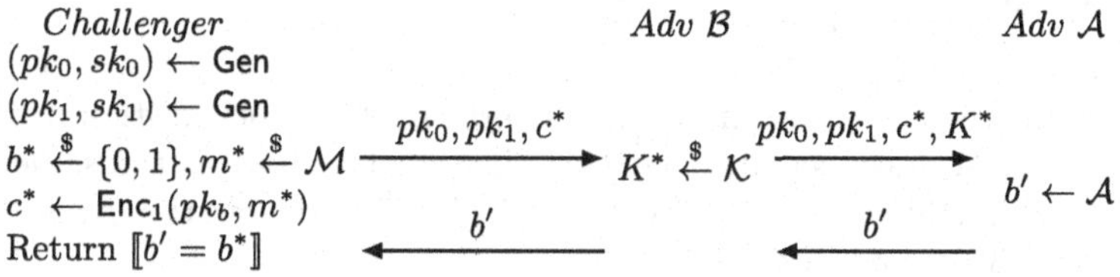

Fig. 12. The adversary $\mathcal{B}$ in the proof of Theorem 1.

The adversary $\mathcal{C}$ simulates H_0, H_1, H_2, H_3, H_4 by quantum-accessible pseudorandom functions, answer H queries and decapsulation queries in the same way as in $\mathbf{G_6}$. When the decapsulation oracle calls $\mathrm{CCO}(c)$, $\mathcal{C}$ computes $m := \mathsf{Dec}_1(sk_{1-b}, c)$, and returns $[\![\mathsf{Enc}_1(pk_b, m) = c]\!]$ (Fig. 13).

$$\mathrm{Adv}^{\mathsf{OW\text{-}CPA}}_{\mathsf{PKE}_1}(\mathcal{C}) \geq \Pr[1 \leftarrow \mathbf{G_7}] \tag{20}$$

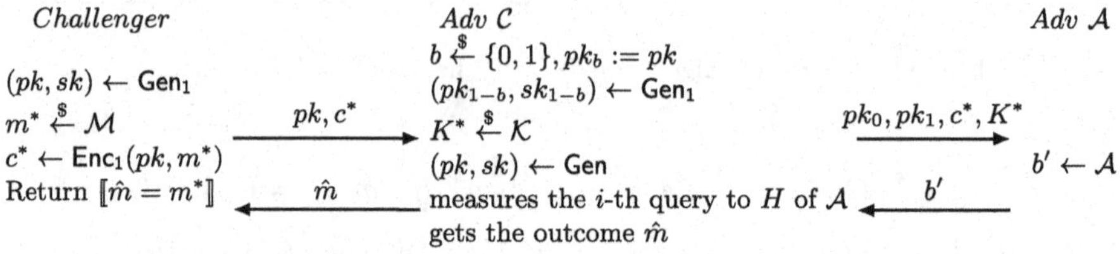

Fig. 13. The adversary $\mathcal{C}$ in the proof of Theorem 1.

Hence by collecting (8) to (20), we arrive at

$$\mathrm{Adv}^{\mathsf{ANO\text{-}CCA}}_{\mathsf{KEM}^{\not\perp}}(\mathcal{A}) \leq \mathrm{Adv}^{\mathsf{wANO\text{-}CCOA}}_{\mathsf{PKE}_1}(\mathcal{B}) + 2q_H\sqrt{\mathrm{Adv}^{\mathsf{OW\text{-}CPA}}_{\mathsf{PKE}_1}(\mathcal{C}) + \frac{4q_H}{\sqrt{|\mathcal{M}|}}} + 2\delta_1.$$

□

□

B Proof of Theorem 3

To prove the OW-VA security of $\mathsf{T}[\mathsf{PKE}_0, G]$, we first design a unitary operation to implement the ciphertext validity oracle CVO. Denote I/O as the input/output register of CVO. The reply of CVO needs to query G to perform the re-encryption check (i.e., check whether $\mathsf{Enc}(pk, m'; G(m'))$ equals c), and then outputs $[\![m' \in \mathcal{M}]\!]$ if m' passes the re-encryption check. Following it, let M be a quantum register defined over $\{0,1\}^m$, we design a unitary operation U_m acting on registers IM as:

$$\mathrm{U}_m|c\rangle_{\mathsf{I}}|0^m\rangle_{\mathsf{M}} = \begin{cases} |c\rangle_{\mathsf{I}}|m'\rangle_{\mathsf{M}} \text{ if } m' = \mathsf{Dec}(sk, c) \neq \perp \wedge \mathsf{Enc}(pk, m'; G(m')) = c \\ |c\rangle_{\mathsf{I}}|\perp\rangle_{\mathsf{M}} \text{ otherwise.} \end{cases} \tag{21}$$

Obviously, the re-encryption check can be performed in superposition by unitary operation U_m. We also remark that this U_m defined above is the same as the "U_m" defined in [13], except that we use capital "G" to denote the random oracle and "H" in [13] is used instead.

Define $\mathrm{P}_{c^*} := |c^*\rangle\langle c^*|$ as a projector on the input register I of CVO, where c^* is the challenge ciphertext. Let $\mathrm{U}_\perp$ be a unitary operation that acts on the output register O of CVO and maps $|b\rangle$ to $|b \oplus \perp\rangle$. Now, for an input state $|c\rangle_{\mathsf{I}}|b\rangle_{\mathsf{O}}$, we act the following unitary operation on state $|c\rangle_{\mathsf{I}}|b\rangle_{\mathsf{O}}|0^m\rangle_{\mathsf{M}}$ to implement CVO:

$$\mathrm{U}_{\mathrm{CVO}} := \mathrm{U}_{\perp} \circ \mathrm{P}_{c^*} + (\mathrm{U}_m)^{\dagger} \circ O_{\mathcal{M}} \circ \mathrm{U}_m \circ (\mathbf{I} - \mathrm{P}_{c^*}). \tag{22}$$

Here unitary operation $O_{\mathcal{M}}$ maps $|b\rangle_{\mathsf{O}}|m'\rangle_{\mathsf{M}}$ to $|b \oplus 1\rangle_{\mathsf{O}}|m'\rangle_{\mathsf{M}}$ if $m' \in \mathcal{M}$, and $|b\rangle_{\mathsf{O}}|m'\rangle_{\mathsf{M}}$ otherwise. $\mathbf{I}$ is the identity operator on register I. The register M used by U_m can be viewed as the internal register of $\mathrm{U}_{\mathrm{CVO}}$, it stores the plaintext m'. Note that this register is always in state $|0^m\rangle_{\mathsf{M}}$ before and after once application of $\mathrm{U}_{\mathrm{CVO}}$, since we perform $(\mathrm{U}_m)^{\dagger}$ just after $O_{\mathcal{M}}$.

Theorem 3 (PKE$_0$ OW-CPA $\overset{\text{QROM}}{\Rightarrow}$ T[PKE$_0$, G] OW-VA). *Let* PKE$_0$ *be a PKE scheme that is δ-correct and γ-spread. Let $\mathcal{A}$ be an* OW-VA *adversary against* T[PKE$_0$, G], *making q_G quantum queries to the random oracle G and q_C classical queries to the ciphertext validity oracle* CVO.

Then we can construct an OW-CPA *adversary $\mathcal{B}$ against* PKE$_0$, *running in about the same time and resources as $\mathcal{A}$, such that*

$$\mathrm{Adv}^{\mathsf{OW\text{-}VA}}_{\mathsf{PKE}_1}(\mathcal{A}) \leq O(q_G) \cdot \mathrm{Adv}^{\mathsf{OW\text{-}CPA}}_{\mathsf{PKE}_0}(\mathcal{B}) + O(q_C) \cdot 2^{-\gamma/2} + O(q_G)\sqrt{\delta}.$$

Proof. Denote Ω_G to be the set of all functions $G : \{0,1\}^m \to \{0,1\}^n$. Consider the sequences of games as shown in Fig. 14.

GAMES $\mathbf{G_0}$-$\mathbf{G_6}$			$G(m)$	$//\mathbf{G_1}$-$\mathbf{G_5}$
1 :	$(pk, sk) \leftarrow \mathsf{Gen}_0$	$//\mathbf{G_0}$-$\mathbf{G_6}$	1 : Simulated by eCO.RO	
2 :	$G \overset{\$}{\leftarrow} \Omega_G$	$//\mathbf{G_0}$	$\mathrm{CVO}(c \neq c^*)$	$//\mathbf{G_0}$-$\mathbf{G_5}$
3 :	$m^* \overset{\$}{\leftarrow} \mathcal{M}$	$//\mathbf{G_0}$-$\mathbf{G_6}$	1 : Simulated by $\mathrm{U}_{\mathrm{CVO}}$	$//\mathbf{G_0}$-$\mathbf{G_1}$
4 :	$c^* \leftarrow \mathsf{Enc}_0(pk, m^*, G(m^*))$	$//\mathbf{G_0}$-$\mathbf{G_4}$	2 : Simulated by $\mathrm{U}'_{\mathrm{CVO}}$	$//\mathbf{G_2}$
5 :	$r^* \overset{\$}{\leftarrow} \mathcal{R}, c^* \leftarrow \mathsf{Enc}_0(pk, m^*, r^*)$	$//\mathbf{G_5}$-$\mathbf{G_6}$	3 : Simulated by $\mathrm{U}^*_{\mathrm{CVO}}$	$//\mathbf{G_3}, \mathbf{G_5}$
6 :	$m' \leftarrow \mathcal{A}^{G,\mathrm{CVO}}(pk, c^*)$	$//\mathbf{G_0}$-$\mathbf{G_5}$	4 : Simulated by $\mathrm{U}^{**}_{\mathrm{CVO}}$	$//\mathbf{G_4}$
7 :	$m' \leftarrow \mathcal{B}(pk, c^*)$	$//\mathbf{G_0}$-$\mathbf{G_6}$		
8 :	**return** $[\![m' = m^*]\!]$	$//\mathbf{G_0}$-$\mathbf{G_6}$		

Fig. 14. Games $\mathbf{G_0}$ to $\mathbf{G_6}$ in the proof of Theorem 3.

Game $\mathbf{G_0}$: This game is exactly the OW-VA game of T[PKE$_0$, G] with the adversary $\mathcal{A}$. The ciphertext validity oracle CVO in this game is simulated by the unitary operation $\mathrm{U}_{\mathrm{CVO}}$ defined in (22)[4].

$$\mathrm{Adv}^{\mathsf{OW\text{-}VA}}_{\mathsf{T}[\mathsf{PKE}_0,G]}(\mathcal{A}) = \left|\Pr[\mathbf{G_0} \to 1] - \frac{1}{2}\right|. \tag{23}$$

[4] Note that the oracle CVO can only be classical accessed in the OW-VA game of T[PKE$_0$, G]. Here, we actually use a unitary operation to reply the classical queries to CVO. We stress that this is acceptable, because any classical queries can be implemented by quantum queries in conjunction with quantum measurement.

Based on the Definition 8, we consider the database set $\mathbf{D}_{q_G}$, the database $D \in \mathbf{D}_{q_G}$ satisfies that it contains q_G pairs. Let D_G be the database register defined over the database set $\mathbf{D}_{q_G}$. Now we introduce the extractable RO-simulator $\mathcal{S}(f_1) := \{\mathsf{eCO.RO}, \mathsf{eCO.E}_{f_1}\}$ (Definition 12), where the internal database register is D_G and function $f_1 : \mathcal{M} \times (\{0,1\}^n \cup \bot) \to \mathcal{C} \cup \bot$ is

$$f_1(x,y) = \begin{cases} c \text{ if } y \neq \bot \wedge \mathsf{Enc}(pk, x; y) = c \wedge x = \mathsf{Dec}(sk, c) \\ \bot \text{ otherwise.} \end{cases}$$

Here $\mathcal{C}$ is the ciphertext space of PKE_0, the query registers of the RO-interface $\mathsf{eCO.RO}$ is XY, where X is defined over $\{0,1\}^m$ and Y is defined over $\{0,1\}^n$. Hence, $\mathsf{eCO.RO}$ can be used to answer the quantum queries to random oracle G.

Game $\mathbf{G_1}$: This game is the same as game $\mathbf{G_0}$, except that the extractable RO-simulator $\mathcal{S}(f_1) := \{\mathsf{eCO.RO}, \mathsf{eCO.E}_{f_1}\}$ is introduced and the quantum queries to random oracle G are answered by querying the RO-interface $\mathsf{eCO.RO}$.

Note that the $\mathsf{eCO.RO}$ is implemented by the compressed standard oracle and the extraction-interface $\mathsf{eCO.E}_{f_1}$ is never queried in game $\mathbf{G_1}$. Thus, by using Lemma 3, we have

$$\Pr[1 \leftarrow \mathbf{G_0}] = \Pr[1 \leftarrow \mathbf{G_1}]. \tag{24}$$

Game $\mathbf{G_2}$: This game is the same as game $\mathbf{G_1}$, except that the unitary operation $\mathrm{U}_{\mathsf{CVO}}$ used to simulate oracle CVO is changed into $\mathrm{U}'_{\mathsf{CVO}}$, which is defined as:

$$\mathrm{U}'_{\mathsf{CVO}} := \mathrm{U}_\bot \circ \mathrm{P}_{c^*} + \mathsf{eCO.E}_{f_1} \circ O_{\mathcal{M}} \circ \mathsf{eCO.E}_{f_1} \circ (\mathbf{I} - \mathrm{P}_{c^*}).$$

Compared with the $\mathrm{U}_{\mathsf{CVO}}$ defined in (22), the unitary operation $\mathrm{U}'_{\mathsf{CVO}}$ does not use U_m to perform the re-encryption check, it directly queries the extraction-interface $\mathsf{eCO.E}_{f_1}$ to extract the plaintext that passes the re-encryption check[5].

By the Definition 12, we know $\mathsf{eCO.E}_{f_1}$ is implemented by the unitary operation $\mathsf{Ext}_{f_1} := \sum_{c \in \mathcal{C}} |c\rangle\langle c|_{\mathsf{I}} \otimes \mathrm{M}^{R_c^{f_1}}_{\mathsf{D}_{q_G}\mathsf{M}}$. Indeed, we can rewrite Ext_{f_1} as:

$$\mathsf{Ext}_{f_1} |c, D, m\rangle_{\mathsf{ID}_{q_G}\mathsf{M}} = |c, D, m \oplus x\rangle_{\mathsf{ID}_{q_G}\mathsf{M}}.$$

Here x is the smallest value satisfies $f_1(x, D(x)) = c$. If such x does not exist, Ext_{f_1} returns $\bot$ in register M.

Lemma 6. $|\Pr[1 \leftarrow \mathbf{G_1}] - \Pr[1 \leftarrow \mathbf{G_2}]| \leq 8q_C \cdot 2^{-\gamma/2}$.

Proof. In the proof of Theorem 2 in [13], they introduce two unitary operations $\mathrm{U}^1_{\mathsf{qD}}$ and $\mathrm{U}^2_{\mathsf{qD}}$, and for a fixed (pk, sk) pair, they also prove the following inequality in their Appendix D.2:

$$\left\| \mathrm{U}^1_{\mathsf{qD}} |\Phi\rangle |0^m\rangle_{\mathsf{M}} - \mathrm{U}^2_{\mathsf{qD}} |\Phi\rangle |0^m\rangle_{\mathsf{M}} \right\| \leq 8\sqrt{\gamma_{pk,sk}}.$$

[5] Here we make a notation abuse, we say $\mathrm{U}'_{\mathsf{CVO}}$ is a unitary operation, which actually means that we view the extraction-interface $\mathsf{eCO.E}_{f_1}$ ($\mathsf{eCO.E}_{f_1}$ is an interface, or an oracle in other words) also a unitary operation. We stress that this is tolerable since $\mathsf{eCO.E}_{f_1}$ is implemented by the unitary operation Ext_{f_1} as defined in Definition 12.

Here $|\Phi\rangle$ is a unit joint state on registers IOD_{q_G}, $\gamma_{pk,sk}$ is a parameter defined in Definition 2, it satisfies $\mathbb{E}_{(pk,sk)\leftarrow \mathsf{Gen}}[\gamma_{pk,sk}] \leq 2^{-\gamma}$ since the underlying PKE scheme is γ-spread.

Compared $\mathrm{U}^1_{\mathsf{qD}}$ (resp. $\mathrm{U}^2_{\mathsf{qD}}$) with the unitary operation $\mathrm{U}_{\mathrm{CVO}}$ (resp. $\mathrm{U}'_{\mathrm{CVO}}$) used in this proof, we find that they are identical except that the internal unitary operation "O_G" used by $\mathrm{U}^1_{\mathsf{qD}}$ (resp. $\mathrm{U}^2_{\mathsf{qD}}$) is replaced into $O_{\mathcal{M}}$ in $\mathrm{U}_{\mathrm{CVO}}$ (resp. $\mathrm{U}'_{\mathrm{CVO}}$). In fact, this replacement does not change the operator norm, thus, we also have

$$\|\mathrm{U}_{\mathrm{CVO}}|\Phi\rangle|0^m\rangle_{\mathsf{M}} - \mathrm{U}'_{\mathrm{CVO}}|\Phi\rangle|0^m\rangle_{\mathsf{M}}\| \leq 8\sqrt{\gamma_{pk,sk}}.$$

Note that CVO is queried with times q_C, then for a fixed (pk, sk) pair, we have

$$|\Pr[1 \leftarrow \mathbf{G_1} : (pk, sk)] - \Pr[1 \leftarrow \mathbf{G_2} : (pk, sk)]| \leq 8q_C \cdot \sqrt{\gamma_{pk,sk}}.$$

By averaging the (pk, sk), we get $|\Pr[1 \leftarrow \mathbf{G_1}] - \Pr[1 \leftarrow \mathbf{G_2}]| \leq 8q_C 2^{-\gamma/2}$. □
□

Game $\mathbf{G_3}$: This game is the same as game $\mathbf{G_2}$, except that the unitary operation $\mathrm{U}'_{\mathrm{CVO}}$ used to simulate CVO is changed into $\mathrm{U}^*_{\mathrm{CVO}}$, which is defined as

$$\mathrm{U}^*_{\mathrm{CVO}} := \mathrm{U}_\perp \circ \mathrm{P}_{c^*} + \mathsf{eCO.E}_{f_2} \circ O_{\mathcal{M}} \circ \mathsf{eCO.E}_{f_2} \circ (\mathbf{I} - \mathrm{P}_{c^*}).$$

Here $\mathsf{eCO.E}_{f_2}$ is a new extraction-interface based on the function $f_2(x, y) = \mathsf{Enc}(pk, x; y)$.

Similar with $\mathsf{eCO.E}_{f_1}$, we know $\mathsf{eCO.E}_{f_2}$ is implemented by the unitary operation $\mathsf{Ext}_{f_2} := \sum_{c\in\mathcal{C}} |c\rangle\langle c|_{\mathsf{I}} \otimes \mathrm{M}^{R^{f_2}_c}_{\mathsf{D}_{q_G}\mathsf{M}}$. We can also rewrite Ext_{f_2} as:

$$\mathsf{Ext}_{f_2}|c, D, m\rangle_{\mathsf{ID}_{q_G}\mathsf{M}} = |c, D, m \oplus x\rangle_{\mathsf{ID}_{q_G}\mathsf{M}}.$$

Here x is the smallest value satisfies $f_2(x, D(x)) = c$. If such x does not exist, Ext_{f_2} returns $\perp$ in register M. We note that the implementation of Ext_{f_2} does not require sk since the computation of function f_2 only uses pk. Therefore, the implementation of $\mathrm{U}^*_{\mathrm{CVO}}$ also does not require sk.

Lemma 7. $|\Pr[1 \leftarrow \mathbf{G_2}] - \Pr[1 \leftarrow \mathbf{G_3}]| \leq 8\sqrt{q_G(q_G+1)\cdot\delta} + 64q_G \cdot \delta$.

Proof. The proof of this lemma follows the proof of Lemma 6 in [13], the reason is that the unitary operation $\mathrm{U}^2_{\mathsf{qD}}$ (resp. $\mathrm{U}^3_{\mathsf{qD}}$) consider in [13] is identical with the unitary operation $\mathrm{U}'_{\mathrm{CVO}}$ (resp. $\mathrm{U}^*_{\mathrm{CVO}}$) considered here, except that the internal unitary operation used by our $\mathrm{U}'_{\mathrm{CVO}}$ (resp. $\mathrm{U}^*_{\mathrm{CVO}}$) is $O_{\mathcal{M}}$. □ □

Game $\mathbf{G_4}$: This game is the same as game $\mathbf{G_3}$, except that the unitary operation $\mathrm{U}^*_{\mathrm{CVO}}$ used to simulate CVO is changed into $\mathrm{U}^{**}_{\mathrm{CVO}}$, which is defined as

$$\mathrm{U}^{**}_{\mathrm{CVO}} := \mathrm{U}_\perp \circ \mathrm{P}_{c^*} + \underline{\mathsf{S}_{m^*} \circ \mathsf{eCO.E}_{f_2} \circ \mathsf{S}_{m^*}} \circ O_{\mathcal{M}} \circ \underline{\mathsf{S}_{m^*} \circ \mathsf{eCO.E}_{f_2} \circ \mathsf{S}_{m^*}} \circ (\mathbf{I} - \mathrm{P}_{c^*}).$$

Here S_{m^*} is an abbreviation of the local decompression procedure $\mathsf{StdDecomp}_{m^*}$.

For a fixed (pk, sk) pair, with the same analysis between "game $\mathbf{G_3}$" and "game $\mathbf{G_4}$" of [13], we can obtain the following inequality since the underlying PKE scheme is γ-spread:

$$\|[\mathsf{eCO.E}_{f_2}, \mathsf{S}_{m^*}]\| \leq 16\sqrt{\gamma(pk, sk)}.$$

Notice that $\mathsf{S}_{m^*} \circ \mathsf{S}_{m^*} = \mathbf{I}$, thus we can conclude that $\mathsf{S}_{m^*} \circ \mathsf{eCO.E}_{f_2} \circ \mathsf{S}_{m^*}$ is indistinguishable from $\mathsf{eCO.E}_{f_2}$ except for an error of $16\sqrt{\gamma(pk, sk)}$.

In game $\mathbf{G_4}$, the query times of CVO is q_C, this means that the unitary operation $\mathrm{U}_{\mathrm{CVO}}^{**}$ is implemented at most q_C times. Hence, for a fixed (pk, sk) pair, we can obtain

$$|\Pr[1 \leftarrow \mathbf{G_3} : (pk, sk)] - \Pr[1 \leftarrow \mathbf{G_4} : (pk, sk)]| \leq 32q_C\sqrt{\gamma(pk, sk)}.$$

By averaging the (pk, sk), we get

$$|\Pr[1 \leftarrow \mathbf{G_3}] - \Pr[1 \leftarrow \mathbf{G_4}]| \leq 32q_C \cdot 2^{-\gamma/2}. \tag{25}$$

Game $\mathbf{G_5}$: In this game, we pick $r^* \xleftarrow{\$} \mathcal{R}$ and generate the challenge ciphertext as $c^* = \mathsf{Enc}(pk, m^*; r^*)$. And we use unitary operation $\mathrm{U}_{\mathrm{CVO}}^{*}$ to simulate CVO.

Lemma 8. *We can construct an* OW-CPA *adversary* $\mathcal{B}_1$ *against* PKE_0, *running in about the same time and resourse as* $\mathcal{A}$, *such that*

$$|\Pr[1 \leftarrow \mathbf{G_4}] - \Pr[1 \leftarrow \mathbf{G_5}]| \leq O(q_G)\sqrt{\mathrm{Adv}_{\mathsf{PKE}_0}^{\mathsf{OW\text{-}CPA}}(\mathcal{B}_1)}.$$

Sketch. The proof of this lemma is similar to the proof of Theorem 6 in [25]. Here we explain the main idea.

First, since the $\mathsf{eCO.E}_{f_2}$ performs a purified measurement on the database register D_G, it can disturb the simulation of (quantum accessible) random oracle G performed by the RO-interface $\mathsf{eCO.RO}$. Note that the generation of challenge ciphertext c^* also needs to query G by m^*. Hence the $\mathsf{eCO.E}_{f_2}$ can cause disturbances to the simulation of $G(m^*)$ performed by the $\mathsf{eCO.RO}$. In our game $\mathbf{G_4}$, we use the operation $\mathsf{S}_{m^*} \circ \mathsf{eCO.E}_{f_2} \circ \mathsf{S}_{m^*}$ to avoid this disturbance, which is actually the main idea of "**Game 2**" in the proof of Theorem 6 in [25]. It is important for $\mathsf{eCO.E}_{f_2}$ not to disturb the simulation of $G(m^*)$. In this case, we can conclude that the simulation of $\mathsf{eCO.RO}$ is perfect at least for the value $G(m^*)$. In other words, the $G(m^*)$ simulated by $\mathsf{eCO.RO}$ is uniformly random in the adversary $\mathcal{A}$'s views if $\mathcal{A}$ does not query G by input m^*.

Second, we need to perform reprogramming, which means instead of simulating $G(m^*)$ by the RO-interface $\mathsf{eCO.RO}$, we directly set $G(m^*)$ as a random string $r^* \xleftarrow{\$} \mathcal{R}$. As mentioned above, it is sufficient to ensure that the adversary $\mathcal{A}$ does not query the random oracle G simulated by $\mathsf{eCO.RO}$ by input m^*. However, G is quantum accessible, it is unreasonable to directly state that $\mathcal{A}$ does not query G by input m^*. Here, we need to use the semi-classical O2H theorem [3,

Theorem 1], similar to the "**Game 3**" and "**Game 4**" in the proof of Theorem 6 in [25], to prove that the advantage of distinguishing $G(m^*)$ from the random string $r^* \xleftarrow{\$} \mathcal{R}$ can be upper bounded by the advantage of an adversary $\mathcal{B}_1$ against the OW-CPA security of PKE_0. Here the running time and resourse of $\mathcal{B}_1$ is about that of $\mathcal{A}$. Since $\mathcal{A}$ makes q_G queries to G, according to the semi-classical oracle O2H theorem, the upper bound will be $O(q_G)\sqrt{\mathrm{Adv}^{\mathsf{OW\text{-}CPA}}_{\mathsf{PKE}_0}(\mathcal{B}_1)}$.

Furthermore, although we have completed the reprogramming, the oracle CVO at this point is still simulated using $\mathsf{S}_{m^*} \circ \mathsf{eCO.E}_{f_2} \circ \mathsf{S}_{m^*}$. However, we cannot perform S_{m^*} if we do not know the challenge plaintext m^*. Fortunately, just like the "**Game 5**" in the proof of Theorem 6 in [25], $\mathsf{S}_{m^*} \circ \mathsf{eCO.E}_{f_2} \circ \mathsf{S}_{m^*}$ is actually equivalent to $\mathsf{eCO.E}_{f_2}$ after we completed the reprogramming. Hence we can simulate CVO by using $\mathrm{U}^*_{\mathrm{CVO}}$, which is what we did in our game $\mathbf{G_5}$. □
□

Game $\mathbf{G_6}$: This game is the same as game $\mathbf{G_5}$, except that we replace the adversary $\mathcal{A}$ by a new adversary $\mathcal{B}_2$ defined as:

1. The input of $\mathcal{B}_2$ is (pk, c^*), where $c^* = \mathsf{Enc}(pk, m^*; r^*)$.
2. $\mathcal{B}_2$ initializes register M with state $|0^m\rangle$, prepares database register D_{q_G}, and implements the extractable RO-simulator $\mathcal{S}(f_2) = \{\mathsf{eCO.RO}, \mathsf{eCO.E}_{f_2}\}$. Then $\mathcal{B}_2$ runs adversary $\mathcal{A}$, simulates game $\mathbf{G_5}$ for it, and outputs $\mathcal{A}$'s output.
   (a) When $\mathcal{A}$ queries random oracle G, $\mathcal{B}_2$ answers it by applying the RO-interface $\mathsf{eCO.RO}$.
   (b) When $\mathcal{A}$ queries CVO, $\mathcal{B}_2$ answers it by implementing unitary operation
   $$\mathrm{U}^*_{\mathrm{CVO}} = \mathrm{U}_\perp \circ \mathrm{P}_{c^*} + \mathsf{eCO.E}_{f_2} \circ O_{\mathcal{M}} \circ \mathsf{eCO.E}_{f_2} \circ (\mathbf{I} - \mathrm{P}_{c^*})$$
   on registers $\mathsf{IOD}_{q_G}\mathsf{M}$.

Obviously, the running time and resourse of $\mathcal{B}_2$ is about that of $\mathcal{A}$.

One can note that the change in game $\mathbf{G_6}$ is only conceptual and $\mathcal{B}_2$ can be viewed as an OW-CPA adversary against PKE_0. Thus, we have

$$\Pr[1 \leftarrow \mathbf{G_5}] = \Pr[1 \leftarrow \mathbf{G_6}] \text{ and } \Pr[1 \leftarrow \mathbf{G_6}] = \mathrm{Adv}^{\mathsf{OW\text{-}CPA}}_{\mathsf{PKE}_0}(\mathcal{B}_2). \quad (26)$$

Combining (23) to (26) and Lemma 6 to Lemma 8, we finally obtain

$$\begin{aligned}\mathrm{Adv}^{\mathsf{OW\text{-}VA}}_{\mathsf{PKE}_1}(\mathcal{A}) \leq O(q_G)\sqrt{\mathrm{Adv}^{\mathsf{OW\text{-}CPA}}_{\mathsf{PKE}_0}(\mathcal{B}_1)} + \mathrm{Adv}^{\mathsf{OW\text{-}CPA}}_{\mathsf{PKE}_0}(\mathcal{B}_2)\\ + O(q_C) \cdot 2^{-\gamma/2} + O(q_G)\sqrt{\delta}.\end{aligned}$$

Without loss of generality, we can fold $\mathcal{B}_1$ and $\mathcal{B}_2$ into one single adversary $\mathcal{B}$, that is,

$$\mathrm{Adv}^{\mathsf{OW\text{-}VA}}_{\mathsf{PKE}_1}(\mathcal{A}) \leq O(q_G)\sqrt{\mathrm{Adv}^{\mathsf{OW\text{-}CPA}}_{\mathsf{PKE}_0}(\mathcal{B})} + O(q_C) \cdot 2^{-\gamma/2} + O(q_G)\sqrt{\delta}.$$

□ □

C Proof of Theorem 4

To prove the wANO-CCA security of $\mathsf{T}[\mathsf{PKE}_0, G]$, we first show that how to implement the two decryption oracles Dec_0 and Dec_1 by two unitary operations. These two unitary operations will be used in the next proof. We noticed that the only difference between Dec_0 and Dec_1 is the public and private keys used. Hence, here we first design the unitary operation to implement Dec_0, the unitary operation to implement Dec_1 can be designed in a similar way.

Denote I/O as the input/output register of Dec_0. Compared with the ciphertext validity oracle CVO, Dec_0 also computes a plaintext m' by using the private key sk_0 and then perform the re-encryption check. The difference is that Dec_0 finally outputs m' if m' passes the re-encryption check, while oracle CVO outputs $[\![m' \in \mathcal{M}]\!]$ instead. That is to say, based on the unitary operation $\mathrm{U}_{\mathrm{CVO}}$ defined in (22), Dec_0 can be implemented by the following unitary operation:

$$\mathrm{U}_{\mathrm{Dec}_0} := \mathrm{U}_\perp \circ \mathrm{P}_{c^*} + (\mathrm{U}_m^0)^\dagger \circ U_\oplus \circ \mathrm{U}_m^0 \circ (\mathbf{I} - \mathrm{P}_{c^*}).$$

Here $\mathrm{U}_\perp, \mathrm{P}_{c^*}$ are the same as (22), U_m^0 is the same as the U_m defined in (21), which acts on registers IM, except that we replace the public and private keys into (pk_0, sk_0). $U_\oplus$ here maps $|y\rangle_{\mathsf{O}}|m\rangle_{\mathsf{M}}$ into $|y \oplus m\rangle_{\mathsf{O}}|m\rangle_{\mathsf{M}}$. Similarly, Dec_1 can be implemented by the following unitary operation:

$$\mathrm{U}_{\mathrm{Dec}_1} := \mathrm{U}_\perp \circ \mathrm{P}_{c^*} + (\mathrm{U}_m^1)^\dagger \circ U_\oplus \circ \mathrm{U}_m^1 \circ (\mathbf{I} - \mathrm{P}_{c^*}).$$

Here U_m^1 is the same as the U_m defined in (21), which acts on registers IM, except that we replace the public and private keys into (pk_1, sk_1).

Theorem 4 (PKE$_0$ wANO-CPA $\overset{\text{QROM}}{\Rightarrow}$ $\mathsf{T}[\mathsf{PKE}_0, G]$ wANO-CCA). *Let* PKE$_0$ *be a PKE scheme that is δ-correct and γ-spread. Let $\mathcal{A}$ be an* wANO-CCA *adversary against* $\mathsf{T}[\mathsf{PKE}_0, G]$, *making q_G quantum queries to the random oracle G and q_D classical queries in total to the decryption oracle* Dec_0 *and* Dec_1.

Then we can construct an wANO-CPA *adversary $\mathcal{B}$ against* PKE$_0$ *and an* OW-CPA *adversary $\mathcal{C}$ against* PKE$_0$, *running in about the same time and resources as $\mathcal{A}$, such that*

$$\mathrm{Adv}^{\mathsf{wANO\text{-}CCA}}_{\mathsf{T}[\mathsf{PKE}_0,G]}(\mathcal{A}) \le \mathrm{Adv}^{\mathsf{wANO\text{-}CPA}}_{\mathsf{PKE}_0}(\mathcal{B}) + O(q_G)\sqrt{\mathrm{Adv}^{\mathsf{OW\text{-}CPA}}_{\mathsf{PKE}_0}(\mathcal{C})} + O(q_D)\cdot 2^{-\gamma/2} + O(q_G)\sqrt{\delta}.$$

Proof. Denote Ω_G to be the set of all functions $G : \{0,1\}^m \to \{0,1\}^n$. Consider the sequences of games as shown in Fig. 15.

GAMES $\mathbf{G}_0$-$\mathbf{G}_5$	
$(pk_0, sk_0) \leftarrow \mathsf{Gen}_0, (pk_1, sk_1) \leftarrow \mathsf{Gen}_0$	$//\mathbf{G}_0$-$\mathbf{G}_5$
$G \xleftarrow{\$} \Omega_G$	$//\mathbf{G}_0$
$b \xleftarrow{\$} \{0,1\}, m^* \xleftarrow{\$} \mathcal{M}$	$//\mathbf{G}_0$-$\mathbf{G}_5$
$c^* \leftarrow \mathsf{Enc}_0(pk, m^*, G(m^*))$	$//\mathbf{G}_0$-$\mathbf{G}_3$
$r^* \xleftarrow{\$} \mathcal{R}, c^* \leftarrow \mathsf{Enc}_0(pk, m^*, r^*)$	$//\mathbf{G}_4$-$\mathbf{G}_5$
$b' \leftarrow \mathcal{A}^{G, \mathrm{Dec}_0, \mathrm{Dec}_1}(pk_0, pk_1, c^*)$	$//\mathbf{G}_0$-$\mathbf{G}_3$
$b' \leftarrow \mathcal{B}(pk_0, pk_1, c^*)$	$//\mathbf{G}_4$-$\mathbf{G}_5$
return $[\![b' = b]\!]$	$//\mathbf{G}_0$-$\mathbf{G}_5$

$G(m)$	$//\mathbf{G}_1$-$\mathbf{G}_4$
Simulated by eCO.RO	

$\mathrm{Dec}_0(c \neq c^*)$	$//\mathbf{G}_0$-$\mathbf{G}_4$
Simulated by $\mathrm{U}_{\mathrm{Dec}_0}$	$//\mathbf{G}_0$-$\mathbf{G}_1$
Simulated by $\mathrm{U}^*_{\mathrm{Dec}_0}$	$//\mathbf{G}_2$-$\mathbf{G}_3$
Simulated by $\mathrm{U}^{**}_{\mathrm{Dec}_0}$	$//\mathbf{G}_4$

$\mathrm{Dec}_1(c \neq c^*)$	$//\mathbf{G}_0$-$\mathbf{G}_4$
Simulated by $\mathrm{U}_{\mathrm{Dec}_1}$	$//\mathbf{G}_0$-$\mathbf{G}_2$
Simulated by $\mathrm{U}^*_{\mathrm{Dec}_1}$	$//\mathbf{G}_3$
Simulated by $\mathrm{U}^{**}_{\mathrm{Dec}_1}$	$//\mathbf{G}_4$

Fig. 15. Games $\mathbf{G}_0$ to $\mathbf{G}_5$ in the proof of Theorem 4.

Game $\mathbf{G}_0$: This game is exactly the wANO-CCA game of $\mathsf{T}[\mathsf{PKE}_0, G]$ with the adversary $\mathcal{A}$. The decryption oracle Dec_0 (resp. Dec_1) in this game is simulated by the unitary operation $\mathrm{U}_{\mathrm{Dec}_0}$ (resp. $\mathrm{U}_{\mathrm{Dec}_1}$) as defined above[6].

$$\mathrm{Adv}^{\mathsf{wANO\text{-}CCA}}_{\mathsf{T}[\mathsf{PKE}_0, G]}(\mathcal{A}) = \left| \Pr[\mathbf{G}_0 \to 1] - \frac{1}{2} \right|. \quad (27)$$

Based on the Definition 8, we consider the database set $\mathbf{D}_{q_G}$, the database $D \in \mathbf{D}_{q_G}$ satisfies that it contains q_G pairs. Let D_G be the database register defined over the database set $\mathbf{D}_{q_G}$. Now we introduce the extractable RO-simulator

$$\mathcal{S}(f_{1,pk_0}, f_{1,pk_1}) := \{\mathsf{eCO.RO}, \mathsf{eCO.E}_{f_{1,pk_0}}, \mathsf{eCO.E}_{f_{1,pk_1}}\},$$

where the internal database register is D_G and functions $f_{1,pk_0}, f_{1,pk_1} : \mathcal{M} \times (\{0,1\}^n \cup \perp) \to \mathcal{C} \cup \perp$ are

$$f_{1,pk_0}(x, y) = \begin{cases} c \text{ if } y \neq \perp \wedge \mathsf{Enc}(pk_0, x; y) = c \wedge x = \mathsf{Dec}(sk_0, c) \\ \perp \text{ otherwise.} \end{cases}$$

$$f_{1,pk_1}(x, y) = \begin{cases} c \text{ if } y \neq \perp \wedge \mathsf{Enc}(pk_1, x; y) = c \wedge x = \mathsf{Dec}(sk_1, c) \\ \perp \text{ otherwise.} \end{cases}$$

Here $\mathcal{C}$ is the ciphertext space of PKE_0, the query registers of the RO-interface eCO.RO is XY, where X is defined over $\{0,1\}^m$ and Y is defined over $\{0,1\}^n$. Hence, eCO.RO can be used to answer the quantum queries to random oracle G.

[6] Note that oracles Dec_0 and Dec_1 can only be classical accessed in the wANO-CCA game of $\mathsf{T}[\mathsf{PKE}_0, G]$. Here, we actually use unitary operations to reply the classical queries to Dec_0 and Dec_1. We stress that this is acceptable, because any classical queries can be implemented by quantum queries in conjunction with quantum measurement.

In the definition of the extractable RO-simulator (Definition 12), there is only one extraction-interface. However, a extractable RO-simulator can have multiple extraction-interfaces, this does not lead to ambiguity in Definition 12. Since each extraction-interface is implemented by a purified measurement, a extractable RO-simulator with multiple extraction-interfaces will perform multiple different purified measurements.

Game $\mathbf{G_1}$: This game is the same as game $\mathbf{G_0}$, except that the extractable RO-simulator $\mathcal{S}(f_{1,pk_0}, f_{1,pk_1})$ is introduced and the quantum queries to random oracle G are answered by querying the RO-interface $\mathsf{eCO.RO}$.

Note that the $\mathsf{eCO.RO}$ is implemented by the compressed standard oracle and the extraction-interfaces $\mathsf{eCO.E}_{f_{1,pk_0}}$ and $\mathsf{eCO.E}_{f_{1,pk_1}}$ are never queried in game $\mathbf{G_1}$. Thus, by using Lemma 3, we have

$$\Pr[1 \leftarrow \mathbf{G_0}] = \Pr[1 \leftarrow \mathbf{G_1}]. \tag{28}$$

Game $\mathbf{G_2}$: This game is the same as game $\mathbf{G_1}$, except that the unitary operation $\mathrm{U}_{\mathrm{Dec}_0}$ used to simulate oracle Dec_0 is changed into $\mathrm{U}^*_{\mathrm{Dec}_0}$, which is defined as

$$\mathrm{U}^*_{\mathrm{Dec}_0} := \mathrm{U}_\perp \circ \mathrm{P}_{c^*} + \underline{\mathsf{S}_{m^*} \circ \mathsf{eCO.E}_{f_{2,pk_0}} \circ \mathsf{S}_{m^*}} \circ U_\oplus \circ \underline{\mathsf{S}_{m^*} \circ \mathsf{eCO.E}_{f_{2,pk_0}} \circ \mathsf{S}_{m^*}} \circ (\mathbf{I} - \mathrm{P}_{c^*}).$$

Here S_{m^*} is an abbreviation of the local decompression procedure $\mathsf{StdDecomp}_{m^*}$, $\mathsf{eCO.E}_{f_{2,pk_0}}$ is a new extraction-interface based on the function $f_{2,pk_0}(x, y) = \mathsf{Enc}(pk_0, x; y)$.

Indeed, with the same analysis between game "$\mathbf{G_1}$" and game "$\mathbf{G_4}$" in the proof of Theorem 3, we can obtain the following inequality since the underlying PKE scheme PKE_0 is δ-correct and γ-spread.

$$|\Pr[1 \leftarrow \mathbf{G_1}] - \Pr[1 \leftarrow \mathbf{G_2}]| \leq O(q_D) \cdot 2^{-\gamma/2} + O(q_G)\sqrt{\delta}. \tag{29}$$

Game $\mathbf{G_3}$: This game is the same as game $\mathbf{G_1}$, except that the unitary operation $\mathrm{U}_{\mathrm{Dec}_1}$ used to simulate oracle Dec_1 is changed into $\mathrm{U}^*_{\mathrm{Dec}_1}$, which is defined as

$$\mathrm{U}^*_{\mathrm{Dec}_1} := \mathrm{U}_\perp \circ \mathrm{P}_{c^*} + \underline{\mathsf{S}_{m^*} \circ \mathsf{eCO.E}_{f_{2,pk_1}} \circ \mathsf{S}_{m^*}} \circ U_\oplus \circ \underline{\mathsf{S}_{m^*} \circ \mathsf{eCO.E}_{f_{2,pk_1}} \circ \mathsf{S}_{m^*}} \circ (\mathbf{I} - \mathrm{P}_{c^*}).$$

Here $\mathsf{eCO.E}_{f_{2,pk_1}}$ is a new extraction-interface based on the function $f_{2,pk_1}(x, y) = \mathsf{Enc}(pk_1, x; y)$.

Similarly, with the same analysis between game "$\mathbf{G_1}$" and game "$\mathbf{G_4}$" in the proof of Theorem 3, we can obtain the following inequality since the underlying PKE scheme PKE_0 is δ-correct and γ-spread.

$$|\Pr[1 \leftarrow \mathbf{G_2}] - \Pr[1 \leftarrow \mathbf{G_3}]| \leq O(q_D) \cdot 2^{-\gamma/2} + O(q_G)\sqrt{\delta}. \tag{30}$$

Game $\mathbf{G_4}$: In this game, we pick $r^* \xleftarrow{\$} \mathcal{R}$ and generate the challenge ciphertext as $c^* = \mathsf{Enc}(pk_b, m^*; r^*)$. And we use the following unitary operation $\mathrm{U}^{**}_{\mathrm{Dec}_0}$ (resp. $\mathrm{U}^{**}_{\mathrm{Dec}_1}$) to simulate the oracle Dec_0 (resp. Dec_1).

$$\mathrm{U}^{**}_{\mathrm{Dec}_0} := \mathrm{U}_\perp \circ \mathrm{P}_{c^*} + \mathsf{eCO.E}_{f_{2,pk_0}} \circ U_\oplus \circ \mathsf{eCO.E}_{f_{2,pk_0}} \circ (\mathbf{I} - \mathrm{P}_{c^*}),$$
$$\mathrm{U}^{**}_{\mathrm{Dec}_1} := \mathrm{U}_\perp \circ \mathrm{P}_{c^*} + \mathsf{eCO.E}_{f_{2,pk_1}} \circ U_\oplus \circ \mathsf{eCO.E}_{f_{2,pk_1}} \circ (\mathbf{I} - \mathrm{P}_{c^*}).$$

Lemma 9. *We can construct an* OW-CPA *adversary* $\mathcal{C}$ *against* $\mathsf{PKE_0}$*, running in about the same time and resourse as* $\mathcal{A}$*, such that*

$$|\Pr[1 \leftarrow \mathbf{G_3}] - \Pr[1 \leftarrow \mathbf{G_4}]| \le O(q_G)\sqrt{\mathrm{Adv}^{\mathsf{OW\text{-}CPA}}_{\mathsf{PKE_0}}(\mathcal{C})} + O(q_D) \cdot 2^{-\gamma}.$$

Sketch. The proof of this lemma is almost the same as the proof of Lemma 8, the only difference is that we need to process two extraction-interfaces in this lemma, and this is why the upper bound of this lemma has an additional term $q_D \cdot \sqrt{2^{-\gamma}}$. In the following, we explain why the term $q_D \cdot 2^{-\gamma}$ is needed when we process two extraction-interfaces.

We stress that the aim of the above game $\mathbf{G_4}$ is to achieve the reprogramming of random oracle G, which means that instead of simulating $G(m^*)$ using the RO-interface $\mathsf{eCO.RO}$, we directly set $G(m^*)$ as a random string $r^* \xleftarrow{\$} \mathcal{R}$. Intuitively, as long as the adversary $\mathcal{A}$ does not query G by input m^*, $G(m^*)$ is uniformly random in $\mathcal{A}$'s view. Hence, similar to the proof of Lemma 8, by using the semi-classical O2H theorem [3, Theorem 1], we can achieve the reprogramming of G with the error term $O(q_G)\sqrt{\mathrm{Adv}^{\mathsf{OW\text{-}CPA}}_{\mathsf{PKE_0}}(\mathcal{C})}$.

However, since the generation of challenge ciphertext c^* also needs to query G by m^* in game $\mathbf{G_3}$, the database register will contain the information about $G(m^*)$ and $\mathsf{eCO.E}_{f_{2,pk_0}}$, $\mathsf{eCO.E}_{f_{2,pk_1}}$ may extract this information. That is to say, $G(m^*)$ in game $\mathbf{G_3}$ is not independent of the decryption oracle responses. Therefore, even if $\mathcal{A}$ does not query G by m^*, we cannot say that $G(m^*)$ is uniformly random in $\mathcal{A}$'s view.

For example, suppose $c^* = \mathsf{Enc}(pk_0, m^*; G(m^*))$. At this point the database D will record $G(m^*)$ as $D(m^*)$, that is, $D(m^*) = G(m^*)$. The operation of $\mathsf{eCO.E}_{f_{2,pk_0}}$ is to take the input $c (\neq c^*)$ and search the database D to see if there exists m such that $\mathsf{Enc}(pk_0, m; D(m)) = c$. Since c is not equal to c^*, $\mathsf{eCO.E}_{f_{2,pk_0}}$ will not use the stored $G(m^*)$ in the database. However, $\mathsf{eCO.E}_{f_{2,pk_1}}$ may use the stored $G(m^*)$ because the operation of $\mathsf{eCO.E}_{f_{2,pk_1}}$ is based on a different public key pk_1. It takes the input $c (\neq c^*)$ and searches the database to see if there exists m such that $\mathsf{Enc}(pk_1, m; D(m)) = c$. More specifically, it is possible that there exists a value c such that $\mathsf{Enc}(pk_1, m^*; G(m^*)) = c$ and $c \neq c^*$.

Note that our underlying PKE scheme $\mathsf{PKE_0}$ is γ-spread. Hence, there are at least 2^{n-r} possible ciphertexts for m^*, we denote the set of these possible ciphertexts as C_{m^*}. Indeed, due to the γ-spread property of $\mathsf{PKE_0}$, when r^* is uniformly chosen from $\mathcal{R}$, we can conclude that $\Pr[\mathsf{Enc}(pk, m^*; r^*) = c] \le 2^{-r}$ for any pk sampled by Gen and any ciphertext $c \in C_{m^*}$. This means that, the adversary $\mathcal{A}$ generates a value c such that $\mathsf{Enc}(pk_1, m^*; G(m^*)) = c$ and $c \neq c^*$ with probability at most 2^{-r}. Since $\mathcal{A}$ makes q_D classical queries to the oracles Dec_0 and Dec_1, the upper bound on the probability that $\mathcal{A}$ does not query the oracles Dec_0 and Dec_1 by a such that c is $O(q_D) \cdot 2^{-r}$. □ □

Game $\mathbf{G_5}$: This game is the same as game $\mathbf{G_4}$, except that we replace the adversary $\mathcal{A}$ by a new adversary $\mathcal{B}$ defined as:

1. The input of $\mathcal{B}$ is (pk_0, pk_1, c^*), where $c^* = \mathsf{Enc}(pk, m^*; r^*)$.

2. $\mathcal{B}$ initializes register M with state $|0^m\rangle$, prepares database register D_{q_G}, and implements the extractable RO-simulator

$$\mathcal{S}(f_{1,pk_0}, f_{1,pk_1}) := \{\mathsf{eCO.RO}, \mathsf{eCO.E}_{f_{1,pk_0}}, \mathsf{eCO.E}_{f_{1,pk_1}}\}.$$

Then $\mathcal{B}$ runs adversary $\mathcal{A}$, simulates game $\mathbf{G_4}$ for it, and outputs $\mathcal{A}$'s output.

(a) When $\mathcal{A}$ queries random oracle G, $\mathcal{B}$ answers it by applying the RO-interface $\mathsf{eCO.RO}$.

(b) When $\mathcal{A}$ queries Dec_0, $\mathcal{B}$ answers it by implementing unitary operation

$$\mathrm{U}^{**}_{\mathrm{Dec}_0} = \mathrm{U}_\perp \circ \mathrm{P}_{c^*} + \mathsf{eCO.E}_{f_{2,pk_0}} \circ O_{\mathcal{M}} \circ \mathsf{eCO.E}_{f_{2,pk_0}} \circ (\mathbf{I} - \mathrm{P}_{c^*})$$

on registers $\mathsf{IOD}_{q_G}\mathsf{M}$.

(c) When $\mathcal{A}$ queries Dec_1, $\mathcal{B}$ answers it by implementing unitary operation

$$\mathrm{U}^{**}_{\mathrm{Dec}_1} = \mathrm{U}_\perp \circ \mathrm{P}_{c^*} + \mathsf{eCO.E}_{f_{2,pk_1}} \circ O_{\mathcal{M}} \circ \mathsf{eCO.E}_{f_{2,pk_1}} \circ (\mathbf{I} - \mathrm{P}_{c^*})$$

on registers $\mathsf{IOD}_{q_G}\mathsf{M}$.

Obviously, the running time and resourse of $\mathcal{B}$ is about that of $\mathcal{A}$.

One can note that the change in game $\mathbf{G_5}$ is only conceptual and $\mathcal{B}$ can be viewed as an $\mathsf{wANO\text{-}CPA}$ adversary against $\mathsf{PKE_0}$. Thus, we have

$$\Pr[1 \leftarrow \mathbf{G_4}] = \Pr[1 \leftarrow \mathbf{G_5}] \text{ and } \Pr[1 \leftarrow \mathbf{G_5}] = \mathrm{Adv}^{\mathsf{wANO\text{-}CPA}}_{\mathsf{PKE_0}}(\mathcal{B}). \tag{31}$$

Combining (27) to (31) and Lemma 9, we finally obtain

$$\mathrm{Adv}^{\mathsf{wANO\text{-}CCA}}_{\mathsf{T[PKE_0},G]}(\mathcal{A}) \leq \mathrm{Adv}^{\mathsf{wANO\text{-}CPA}}_{\mathsf{PKE_0}}(\mathcal{B}) + O(q_G)\sqrt{\mathrm{Adv}^{\mathsf{OW\text{-}CPA}}_{\mathsf{PKE_0}}(\mathcal{C})} + O(q_D) \cdot 2^{-\gamma/2} + O(q_G)\sqrt{\delta}.$$

□

□

References

1. Abdalla, M., Bellare, M., Neven, G.: Robust encryption. In: Micciancio, D. (ed.) TCC 2010. LNCS, vol. 5978, pp. 480–497. Springer, Heidelberg (2010). https://doi.org/10.1007/978-3-642-11799-2_28
2. Abe, M., Gennaro, R., Kurosawa, K.: Tag-KEM/DEM: a new framework for hybrid encryption. J. Cryptol. **21**(1), 97–130 (2008)
3. Ambainis, A., Hamburg, M., Unruh, D.: Quantum security proofs using semi-classical oracles. In: Boldyreva, A., Micciancio, D. (eds.) CRYPTO 2019. LNCS, vol. 11693, pp. 269–295. Springer, Cham (2019). https://doi.org/10.1007/978-3-030-26951-7_10
4. Bellare, M., Boldyreva, A., Desai, A., Pointcheval, D.: Key-privacy in public-key encryption. In: Boyd, C. (ed.) ASIACRYPT 2001. LNCS, vol. 2248, pp. 566–582. Springer, Heidelberg (2001). https://doi.org/10.1007/3-540-45682-1_33

5. Ben-Sasson, E., et al.: Zerocash: decentralized anonymous payments from bitcoin. In: IEEE Symposium on Security and Privacy, pp. 459–474. IEEE Computer Society (2014)
6. Boneh, D., Dagdelen, Ö., Fischlin, M., Lehmann, A., Schaffner, C., Zhandry, M.: Random oracles in a quantum world. In: Lee, D.H., Wang, X. (eds.) ASIACRYPT 2011. LNCS, vol. 7073, pp. 41–69. Springer, Heidelberg (2011). https://doi.org/10.1007/978-3-642-25385-0_3
7. Camenisch, J., Lysyanskaya, A.: An efficient system for non-transferable anonymous credentials with optional anonymity revocation. In: Pfitzmann, B. (ed.) EUROCRYPT 2001. LNCS, vol. 2045, pp. 93–118. Springer, Heidelberg (2001). https://doi.org/10.1007/3-540-44987-6_7
8. Jean-Sébastien, C., Handschuh, H., Joye, M., Paillier, P., Pointcheval, D., Tymen, C.: GEM: a generic chosen-ciphertext secure encryption method. In: Preneel, B. (ed.) CT-RSA 2002. LNCS, vol. 2271, pp. 263–276. Springer, Heidelberg (2002). https://doi.org/10.1007/3-540-45760-7_18
9. Desmedt, Y., Gennaro, R., Kurosawa, K., Shoup, V.: A new and improved paradigm for hybrid encryption secure against chosen-ciphertext attack. J. Cryptol. **23**(1), 91–120 (2010)
10. Don, J., Fehr, S., Majenz, C., Schaffner, C.: Online-extractability in the quantum random-oracle model. In: Dunkelman, O., Dziembowski, S. (eds.) EUROCRYPT 2022. LNCS, vol. 13277, pp. 677–706. Springer, Cham (2022). https://doi.org/10.1007/978-3-031-07082-2_24
11. Fujisaki, E., Okamoto, T.: Secure integration of asymmetric and symmetric encryption schemes. In: Wiener, M. (ed.) CRYPTO 1999. LNCS, vol. 1666, pp. 537–554. Springer, Heidelberg (1999). https://doi.org/10.1007/3-540-48405-1_34
12. Fujisaki, E., Okamoto, T.: Secure integration of asymmetric and symmetric encryption schemes. J. Cryptol. **26**(1), 80–101 (2013)
13. Ge, J., Shan, T., Xue, R.: Tighter QCCA-secure key encapsulation mechanism with explicit rejection in the quantum random oracle model. In: Handschuh, H., Lysyanskaya, A. (eds.) CRYPTO 2023. LNCS, vol. 14085, pp. 292–324. Springer, Cham (2023). https://doi.org/10.1007/978-3-031-38554-4_10
14. Goldwasser, S., Micali, S.: Probabilistic encryption. J. Comput. Syst. Sci. **28**(2), 270–299 (1984)
15. Grubbs, P., Maram, V., Paterson, K.G.: Anonymous, robust post-quantum public key encryption. In: Dunkelman, O., Dziembowski, S. (eds.) EUROCRYPT 2022. LNCS, vol. 13277, pp. 402–432. Springer, Cham (2022). https://doi.org/10.1007/978-3-031-07082-2_15
16. Herranz, J., Hofheinz, D., Kiltz, E.: KEM/DEM: necessary and sufficient conditions for secure hybrid encryption. IACR Cryptology ePrint Archive (2006). https://api.semanticscholar.org/CorpusID:1600207
17. Hofheinz, D., Hövelmanns, K., Kiltz, E.: A modular analysis of the Fujisaki-Okamoto transformation. In: Kalai, Y., Reyzin, L. (eds.) TCC 2017. LNCS, vol. 10677, pp. 341–371. Springer, Cham (2017). https://doi.org/10.1007/978-3-319-70500-2_12
18. Hofheinz, D., Kiltz, E.: Secure hybrid encryption from weakened key encapsulation. In: Menezes, A. (ed.) CRYPTO 2007. LNCS, vol. 4622, pp. 553–571. Springer, Heidelberg (2007). https://doi.org/10.1007/978-3-540-74143-5_31
19. Jiang, H., Zhang, Z., Chen, L., Wang, H., Ma, Z.: IND-CCA-secure key encapsulation mechanism in the quantum random oracle model, revisited. In: Shacham, H., Boldyreva, A. (eds.) CRYPTO 2018. LNCS, vol. 10993, pp. 96–125. Springer, Cham (2018). https://doi.org/10.1007/978-3-319-96878-0_4

20. Mohassel, P.: A closer look at anonymity and robustness in encryption schemes. In: Abe, M. (ed.) ASIACRYPT 2010. LNCS, vol. 6477, pp. 501–518. Springer, Heidelberg (2010). https://doi.org/10.1007/978-3-642-17373-8_29
21. Okamoto, T., Pointcheval, D.: REACT: rapid enhanced-security asymmetric cryptosystem transform. In: Naccache, D. (ed.) CT-RSA 2001. LNCS, vol. 2020, pp. 159–174. Springer, Heidelberg (2000). https://doi.org/10.1007/3-540-45353-9_13
22. Saito, T., Xagawa, K., Yamakawa, T.: Tightly-secure key-encapsulation mechanism in the quantum random oracle model. In: Nielsen, J.B., Rijmen, V. (eds.) EUROCRYPT 2018. LNCS, vol. 10822, pp. 520–551. Springer, Cham (2018). https://doi.org/10.1007/978-3-319-78372-7_17
23. Sako, K.: An auction protocol which hides bids of losers. In: Imai, H., Zheng, Y. (eds.) PKC 2000. LNCS, vol. 1751, pp. 422–432. Springer, Heidelberg (2000). https://doi.org/10.1007/978-3-540-46588-1_28
24. Schwabe, P., Stebila, D., Wiggers, T.: Post-quantum TLS without handshake signatures. In: CCS, pp. 1461–1480. ACM (2020)
25. Shan, T., Ge, J., Xue, R.: QCCA-secure generic transformations in the quantum random oracle model. In: Boldyreva, A., Kolesnikov, V. (eds.) PKC 2023. LNCS, vol. 13940, pp. 36–64. Springer, Cham (2023). https://doi.org/10.1007/978-3-031-31368-4_2
26. Xagawa, K.: Anonymity of NIST PQC round 3 KEMS. In: Dunkelman, O., Dziembowski, S. (eds.) EUROCRYPT 2022. LNCS, vol. 13277, pp. 551–581. Springer, Cham (2022). https://doi.org/10.1007/978-3-031-07082-2_20
27. Zhandry, M.: How to record quantum queries, and applications to quantum indifferentiability. In: Boldyreva, A., Micciancio, D. (eds.) CRYPTO 2019. LNCS, vol. 11693, pp. 239–268. Springer, Cham (2019). https://doi.org/10.1007/978-3-030-26951-7_9

Author Index

M.-J. Saarinen and D. Smith-Tone (Eds.): PQCrypto 2024, LNCS 14772, pp. 371–372, 2024.
https://doi.org/10.1007/978-3-031-62746-0

' in the United States
& Taylor Publisher Services